تفسير العياشي

MUḤAMMAD B. MASʿŪD
AL-ʿAYYĀSHĪ

Tafsīr al-ʿAyyāshī

A Fourth/Tenth Century
Shīʿī Commentary on the Qurʾan

تفسير العياشي

Translated by
Nazmina Dhanji

Edited by
Wahid M. Amin

Introduction by
Meir M. Bar-Asher

VOLUME I

AMI PRESS

AMI Press
60 Weoley Park Road, Selly Oak
Birmingham, B29 6RB
United Kingdom

First published 2020

A catalogue record for this book is available from the British Library

Vol. 1 ISBN 978-1-8380320-7-4
Vol. 2 ISBN 978-1-8380320-8-1
Vol. 3 ISBN 978-1-8380320-9-8
Set ISBN 978-1-8380320-6-7

Designed and typeset by Titus Nemeth, assisted by Doris Lang

Contents

Volume 1

Preface

Introduction *i*

1. Al-ʿAyyāshī's Life and Work *i*
    1.1 Work *v*
        1.1.1 Al-ʿAyyāshī's Commentary on the Qur'an *vi*
        1.1.2 Manuscripts and Printed Editions of Tafsīr al-ʿAyyāshī *viii*
        1.1.3 Tafsīr al-ʿAyyāshī as a prominent representation of the pre-Buwayhid Imāmī Shīʿī school of Exegesis *viii*
2. The question of the integrity of the Qur'an *xi*
3. The Qur'an as a multilayered and polyvalent text *xvii*
4. The Imam as the primary authority for Qur'an interpretation *xix*
5. Concluding Remarks *xxvi*

Prelude *2*

On the Virtues of the Qur'an *2*

Casting aside reports (*riwāyāt*) that contradict the Qur'an *22*

The Content of what has been revealed in the Qur'an *26*

The meaning of the terms 'abrogating' (*al-nāsikh*), 'abrogated' (*al-mansūkh*), 'the apparent' (*al-ẓāhir*), 'the hidden' (*al-bāṭin*), 'the ambiguous' (*al-muḥkam*) and 'the unambiguous' (*al-mutashābih*) *30*

The Interpretation of the Seven Revealed Recitations of the Qur'an having various aspects *36*

References to the Imams in the Qur'an *36*

The Imams and their Knowledge of the Qur'an's Interpretation (*ta'wīl*) *40*
On Those Who Interpret The Qur'an According To Their Own Opinion *50*
On the Reprehensibility of Using the Qur'an for the Purpose of Disputation *54*

1. The Opening *58*
2. The Cow *74*
3. The Family of 'Imrān *406*
4. Women *536*

VOLUME 2

5. The Feast *2*
6. Livestock *154*
7. The Heights *236*
8. The Battle Gains *320*
9. The Impunity *378*
10. Yūnus *492*
11. Hūd *542*
12. Yūsuf *604*

VOLUME 3

13. The Thunder *2*
14. Ibrāhīm *52*
15. Ḥijr *94*
16. The Bee *124*
17. The Children of Israel *174*
18. The Cave *278*
19. Mary *352*
20. Ṭā-hā *356*
21. The Prophets *360*
22. The Pilgrimage *366*
23. The Believers *374*
24. Light *380*
25. The Criterion *384*
26. The Poets *388*
27. The Ants *392*
28. The Story *398*
29. The Spider *404*
31. Luqmān *408*
35. The Creator *412*
36. Yā-Sīn *416*
37. Ranged in Rows *424*
38. Ṣād *434*
39. The Throngs *440*
42. Consultation *446*
43. Ornaments of Gold *450*
48. Triumph *456*
52. The Mountain *462*
54. The Moon *466*
55. The All-Compassionate Lord *470*

56. The Imminent Event *476*
57. Iron *480*
58. The Dispute *486*
61. Solid Lines *490*
65. Divorce *494*
66. The Prohibition *500*
67. Sovereignty *504*
68. The Pen *508*
74. Wrapped in his Cloak *512*
75. The Resurrection *516*
76. Man *520*
78. The Announcement *530*
80. He Frowned *534*
81. Shrouded in Darkness *538*
83. Those Who Give Short Measure *542*
84. The Ripping Apart *546*
85. The Towering Constellations *550*
87. The Most High *554*
90. The City *558*
92. The Night *562*
93. The Morning Brightness *566*
94. Relief *570*
97. The Night of Ordainment *574*
102. Rivalry for More *578*
104. The Slanderer *582*
105. The Elephants *586*
106. Quraysh *590*
107. Common Kindness *594*
114. People *598*

Bibliography *601*
Index of Groups, Sects and Tribes *607*
Index of Names *611*
Index of Places *627*
Index of Subjects *629*

Preface

The work presented here is the first complete translation into English of a classical Shīʿī commentary on the Qurʾan. The *tafsīr* of Abū al-Naḍr Muḥammad b. Masʿūd al-ʿAyyāshī (d. 320/932) belongs to a relatively small number of Shīʿī commentaries dating from the early fourth-century of Islam and is the only surviving work to have reached us from the corpus of writings known to have been authored by al-ʿAyyāshī. Its style and form are typical of the era in which al-ʿAyyāshī was alive, and like the other main formative disciplines of the time—namely, *fiqh* and *kalām*—prioritises the sayings and traditions of the Prophet Muḥammad and the Imams of the *ahl al-bayt* as the main sources of our knowledge of the Qurʾan's meanings. The emphasis that is placed on the Imams as the true interpreters of the Qurʾan's inner (*bāṭin*) and outer (*ẓāhir*) meanings is significant for the reason that it aims to supercede two other popular forms of exegesis during this period; namely, (1) personal speculation (*raʾy*) and (2) commentary by way of traditions sourced from authorities deemed unacceptable to the religious worldview of the Shīʿī community. The *tafsīr* of al-ʿAyyāshī is therefore a quintessentially 'Shīʿī *tafsīr*' belonging to the wider genre of Qurʾanic exegesis known as *tafsīr bi-l-maʾthūr*, exegesis by means of traditions from the Prophet Muḥammad and the Imams of the *ahl al-bayt*, and is thus illustrative of the attempts made by late third- and early fourth-century Imāmī scholars to assert a strong Shīʿī identity and counter-narrative to prevailing assumptions about, and methods to, the interpretation of the Qurʾan by the proto-Sunnī community. Despite the occasional criticism the work has generally been received through the centuries with notable acclaim from Shīʿī scholars and remains until this day perhaps the most important source of Imāmī traditions on the Qurʾan alongside the *tafsīr* of ʿAlī b. Ibrāhīm al-Qummī (d. *ca.* 307/919). Al-ʿAyyāshī's traditions are copiously copied in major *ḥadīth* compilations of subsequent periods such as, for instance, in Muḥammad

Bāqir al-Majlisī's (d. 1110/1699) *Biḥār al-anwār*, and later Shīʿī commentaries on the Qur'an such as Sayyid Hāshim al-Baḥrānī's (d. *ca.* 1107/1696) *al-Burhān fī tafsīr al-Qur'ān* and Sayyid Muḥammad Hussayn Ṭabāṭabā'ī's (d. 1402/1981) *al-Mīzān fī tafsīr al-Qur'ān*.

Al-ʿAyyāshī's *tafsīr* survives in a number of extant manuscripts, but none of these preserves the work that was originally composed by the author himself. Firstly, the chains of transmission connecting al-ʿAyyāshī to the Imams in the extant copies are truncated forms of the author's original manuscript, and hence what was once originally a work comprising complete chains of transmission is now, due to the copyist's redaction, a considerably shortened work. Secondly, the part of al-ʿAyyāshī's *tafsīr* belonging to its so-called 'second part' (*al-juz' al-thānī*) can no longer be found in the surviving manuscripts: what does remain only goes so far as the end of Sūra 18 (*al-kahf*) of the Qur'an. A more complete version of al-ʿAyyāshī's *tafsīr*, one that is said to have included fuller versions of the *isnād*s as well as his selection of *ḥadīth*s commenting on chapters beyond Sūra 18, was apparently accessible to previous scholars of earlier centuries. Most notable among these are al-Ḥāfiẓ ʿUbayd Allāh b. ʿAbd Allāh al-Naysābūrī, better known as al-Ḥākim al-Ḥaskānī (d. 490/1097), a Ḥanafī judge who narrates sections from the latter part of al-ʿAyyāshī's *tafsīr* in his work *Shawāhid al-tanzīl*, and the Shīʿī exegete al-Faḍl b. al-Ḥasan al-Ṭabrisī (d. 548/1154), who likewise has traditions from the non-extant part of al-ʿAyyāshī's *tafsīr* in his Qur'anic commentary *Majmaʿ al-bayān*. There is some evidence to suggest that Sayyid Raḍī al-Dīn ʿAlī b. Mūsā Ibn Ṭāwūs (d. 664/1266) may have also had access to a more complete version, but this, as pointed out by Professor Meir M. Bar-Asher in his Introduction, remains inconclusive.

In preparing this translation we have relied on the Arabic edition of al-ʿAyyāshī's *tafsīr* that was published by the Islamic Studies department of the Biʿtha Foundation in Qom, Iran. This edition is a much better one than a previous edition that was published in Beirut in 1991 and edited by Sayyid Hāshim al-Rasūlī al-Maḥallātī. It relies not only on a greater number of manuscript witnesses than the earlier Beirut edition, but also collates in the form of an added appendix (*mustadrak*) the traditions that relate to the second part of al-ʿAyyāshī's *tafsīr* that have been compiled from other sources. (As for the manuscripts on which the Biʿtha edition is based, these are listed in the Introduction of the published edition as follows: MS. Dastaghīb Library, Shiraz, copied 1091 AH [no other details provided]; MS. Āstān-i Quds-i Raḍawī 180, Mashhad, copied in 1301 AH by ʿAbd al-Razzāq al-Rahābādī al-Ardakānī al-Yazdī; MS. Āstān-i Quds-i Raḍawī 7513, copied in Najaf in the year 1353 AH by Muḥammad Ḥusayn b. Zayn al-ʿĀbidīn al-Urmawī al-Riḍāʾī; MS. Āstān-i Quds-i Raḍāwī 1490, copied in 1348 AH by Ḥusayn b. Muḥammad ʿArabshāh al-ʿAlawī al-Ḥusaynī.) We include the Arabic edition prepared by the Biʿtha Foundation without emendations, thereby allowing the reader to have parallel access to the Arabic text on which our translation is based.

Concerning the translation itself, this was initially prepared in its entirety by Nazmina Dhanji, Head of Arabic Studies at the Al-Mahdi Institute, and then edited by myself. The translation aims to provide an accurate rendition of the Arabic text in readable English. Though we have tried to keep the translation as close as possible to the literal Arabic, we have made a conscious attempt to strike a balance between literal accuracy, on the one hand, and user-friendliness, on the other. The translation, which spans three volumes, is designed to be read easily and naturally in English, which has therefore at times necessitated a certain liberty given the syntactical idiosyncrasies of the Arabic language. For Qurʾanic verses, we have relied on the translations of Muhammad Abdel Haleem, *The Qurʾan* (Oxford: OUP, 2004) and Ali Quli Qarai, *The Qurʾan: With a Phrase-by-Phrase English Translation* (London: ICAS Press, 2005) in the order just mentioned, but where each of these has been deemed inadequate for the context in question we have translated the Qurʾanic verses ourselves. I have also edited the translation to ensure consistency across all volumes, provided intra-Qurʾanic references to other verses of the Qurʾan using a superscripted method of numbering, and added accompanying footnotes to provide some contextual background to the narrators, places, events, and key personalities that are mentioned in al-ʿAyyāshī's *tafsīr*. Occasionally, I have also provided some references to secondary literature. Indeed there is much that can be said and commented on in al-ʿAyyāshī's *tafsīr*, but given the fact that the three volumes at present already exceed 2000 pages I have decided to keep the footnotes to a minimum, only sparingly mentioning other scholarship wherever I have felt the need to do so. Where I have taken some liberty is with respect to the narrators within the *isnād*s of the *ḥadīth*s included by al-ʿAyyāshī. The biographical tradition—by which I mean not just the *tarājim*-literature but the more developed science of *ʿilm al-rijāl*—provides key insights on the personalities from whom these traditions have been received and contains interesting assessments and adjudications of later scholars as to their reliability and trustworthiness as narrators of the Imams' traditions. For this undertaking I have relied principally on al-ʿAllāma al-Ḥillī's *Khulāṣat al-aqwāl* which, though not without its own complications, nonetheless serves as a useful compendium of the views of earlier *rijāl* scholars such as Aḥmad b. ʿAlī al-Najāshī (d. 450/1058), Abū Jaʿfar Muḥammad b. al-Ḥasan al-Ṭūsī (d. 460/1067), Abū ʿAmr Muḥammad b. ʿUmar al-Kishshī (d. fourth/tenth century), and Ibn al-Ghaḍā'irī (d. 411/1020). Wherever possible I have provided cross-references to Hossein Modarressi's indispensable *Tradition and Survival: A Biographical Survey of Early Shi'ite Literature* which undertakes many of the same aims as the *Khulāṣat al-aqwāl* of al-ʿAllāma al-Ḥillī.

The entire project was commissioned under the auspices of the Al-Mahdi Institute and would not have been possible without the generous financial support of its patrons. We are extremely grateful to these individuals for the commitment they have shown throughout the process. I am also very grateful to Professor Meir M. Bar-Asher for accepting my invitation to write an Introduction to our translation with great enthusiasm. There are few in the field of Qur'anic/Shīʿī studies who can boast to have a better understanding of early Imāmī exegesis and knowledge of al-ʿAyyāshī's *tafsīr* than Professor Bar-Asher. I would also like to thank Titus Nemeth for designing and typesetting the publication and Mahmood Dhalla for sharing his thoughts on style and formatting at different stages of the project. Finally, both Nazmina and I are extremely grateful to our respective families for their love and support, as well as to our colleagues and friends at the Al-Mahdi Institute for encouraging and supporting us to persevere with such a gruelling endeavour. What results from all this is the book you now hold in your hands: the first complete translation into English of a classical Shīʿī commentary on the Qur'an with accompanying Arabic text. As such, the translation provides an invaluable resource to anybody interested in the history of Qur'anic exegesis, for whom there continues to be a dearth of primary sources in translation for classical Shīʿī thought. It is our hope that this translation goes some way in redressing this situation in contemporary Islamic Studies in the western academe.

Wahid M. Amin

Introduction*

Meir M. Bar-Asher
(The Hebrew University of Jerusalem)

1. Al-ʿAyyāshī's Life and Work

1.1 Life

Abū al-Naḍr Muḥammad b. Masʿūd al-ʿAyyāshī al-Sulamī al-Samarqandī, better known as al-ʿAyyāshī, was one of the eminent Imāmī Shīʿī scholars who flourished in the last decades of the 3rd/9th century and the beginning of the 4th/10th century, that is, prior to the Great Occultation (*al-ghayba al-kubrā*) which occurred in the year 329/941. He was one of a few representatives of Imāmī Shīʿī Qur'an exegesis of this period. The other leading exegetes of this period known to us were Furāt b. Ibrāhīm al-Kūfī (d. *ca.* at the beginning of the 4th/10th century), ʿAlī b. Ibrāhīm al-Qummī (d. *ca.* 307/919), and somewhat later Muḥammad b. Ibrāhīm b. Jaʿfar al-Nuʿmānī (d. *ca.* 360/971), to whom a treatise constituting a sort of introduction to the Qur'an is ascribed.[1] To these authors one may add al-Ḥusayn b. al-Ḥakam al-Ḥibarī (d. 286/899), presumably representing the early phase of

* I would like to thank Prof. Etan Kohlberg for his instructive comments on earlier drafts of this introduction.

1 See M. M. Bar-Asher, *Scripture and Exegesis in Early Imāmī Shiism* (Jerusalem and Leiden 1999), pp. 63–70. All references to *Tafsīr al-ʿAyyāshī* below are to the al-Biʿtha edition. This edition, used by Al-Mahdi Institute in preparing the English translation of *Tafsīr al-ʿAyyāshī* is the best to have been published to date (for the details see below §1.2.2). I am much indebted to Dr. Wahid Amin of the Al-Mahdi Institute for drawing my attention to this edition of *Tafsīr al-ʿAyyāshī*.

Zaydī exegesis.[2] Apparently these are the only authors of this period whose writings have survived in the form of exegetical compositions. However, the only commentator among them who received some attention in late nineteenth and early twentieth century Western scholarship is ʿAlī b. Ibrāhīm al-Qummī. Theodor Nöldeke, in his seminal study on the Qur'an, discussed some aspects of al-Qummī's *tafsīr*.[3] The work then became the basis for Ignaz Goldziher's description of Shīʿī exegesis in his groundbreaking book *Die Richtungen der islamischen Koranauslegung*.[4]

While al-Qummī became familiar to Western scholarship, the other Imāmī Shīʿī commentators of this period have remained largely unknown. The aim of this introduction is twofold: (a) to outline a picture of the author of *Tafsir al-ʿAyyāshī*, undoubtedly the most prominent of this group of commentators; (b) to attempt to place his work in the broad context in which it was created and developed. The contextualization will be exemplified by three major issues, all of which occupy a very important role in *Tafsir al-ʿAyyāshī* and early Imāmī Shīʿī Qur'an exegesis in general: (1) The question of the integrity of the Qur'an; (2) the Qur'an as a multilayered and polyvalent text; and (3) the Imam as the primary authority for Qur'an interpretation.

Biographical sources, both early and late, provide little information about al-ʿAyyāshī's life. Instead, they heap praise on him and emphasize his prolific scholarly output. Ibn al-Nadīm describes him as 'unique in his generation in the abundance of his knowledge *(awḥad zamānihi wa-dahrihi fi ghazārat al-ʿilm)*'[5] and states that 'his books are of major importance in the district of Khurasan *(wa-li-kutubihi bi-nawāḥī Khurāsān sha'n min*

2 See M. A. Amir-Moezzi, 'The *Tafsīr* of al-Ḥibarī (d. 286/899): Qur'anic Exegesis and Early Shiʿi Esotericism', in F. Daftary and G. Miskinzoda eds., *The Study of Shiʿi Islam: History, Theology and Law* (London 2014), pp. 113–134.

3 T. Nöldeke and F. Schwally, *Geschichte des Qorans* (Leipizig 1909–1938), vol. 2, pp. 93–112 (English translation: idem, *The History of the Qur'ān*, ed. and trans. W. H. Behn [Leiden and Boston 2013], pp. 288–303).

4 The book was first published in Leiden in 1920. See chap. 5 (Sektiererische Koranauslegung), pp. 263–309 (English translation: idem, *Schools of Koranic Commentaries*, ed. and trans. W. H. Behn [Wiesbaden 2006], pp. 167–196).

5 Muḥammad b. Isḥāq Ibn al-Nadīm, *Kitāb al-Fihrist*, ed. G. Flügel (Leipzig 1872), p. 194 (=*The Fihrist of al-Nadīm: A Tenth-Century Survey of Muslim Culture*, ed. and trans. B. Dodge [New York 1970], p. 483).

al-sha'n)'.[6] In a similar vein, al-Najāshī describes him as 'trustworthy, truthful, a pillar of the [Shī'ī] community] *(thiqa, ṣādiq, 'ayn min a'yān al-ṭā'ifa).'*[7] Al-Ṭūsī outdoes them both in his praise, declaring: 'There are those who say that [al-'Ayyāshī] was the greatest scholar in the East *(afḍal ahl al-mashriq 'ilman).'*[8] His love of learning is exemplified in al-Najāshī's account of the enormous wealth he inherited from his father, which he spent on the study of religion and the support of his pupils.[9] His house became a workshop for the Shī'īs and for those seeking knowledge, and a centre for students, scribes and commentators.[10] The titles *min ghilmān al-'Ayyāshī* (one of al-'Ayyāshī's apprentices) and *min aṣḥāb al-'Ayyāshī* (one of the companions or disciples of al-'Ayyāshī) which appear often in al-Ṭūsī's *Kitāb al-rijāl*, seem to substantiate al-Najāshī's description.[11] These titles probably refer to a group of disciples, of whom some were most likely al-'Ayyāshī's apprentices, and who studied religion and copied manuscripts in the study centre he maintained in his home.

According to al-Najāshī and later sources dependent on him, al-'Ayyāshī began his career as a Sunnī, he 'received Sunnī traditions and often engaged in them, but later, when still young, his eyes were opened and he joined the Shī'a.'[12] Ibn al-Nadīm does not mention this detail explicitly but suggests it when relating that several of al-'Ayyāshī's writings (biographies of the first

6 Ibid.; cf. W. Madelung, 'al-Kashshī,' *EI²*, vol. 4, p. 711, who states that al-'Ayyāshī was responsible for spreading Imāmī Shī'ism in this region. See also I. Poonawalla, "Ayyāšī, Abu'l-Nażr Moḥammad b. Mas'ūd b. Moḥammad b. al-'Ayyāš al-Solamī al-Samraqandī', in *Encyclopaedia Iranica*, vol. 3, pp. 163–164.

7 Abū al-'Abbās Aḥmad b. 'Alī al-Najāshī, *Rijāl* (Qom 1407[1986]), p. 350.

8 Abū Ja'far al-Ṭūsī, *Kitāb al-rijāl* (Najaf 1381/1961), p. 497. An extended version of al-Ṭūsī's words is found in Muḥammad al-Khwānsārī, *Rawḍāt al-jannāt fī aḥwāl al-'ulamā' wa-l-sādāt* (Tehran and Qom 1390–1392), vol. 4, p. 130: 'Al-'Ayyāshī was the greatest man in the East in his time in knowledge, nobility, behaviour, understanding and greatness of spirit *(akbar ahl al-mashriq 'ilman wa-faḍlan wa-adaban wa-fahman wa-nublan fi zamānihi)*'.

9 Al-Najāshī, p. 372 (in his brief account on Abū 'Amr Muḥammad b. 'Umar al-Kishshī) states, undoubtedly in gross exaggeration, that the size of the inheritance was 300,000 dinars.

10 Ibid. This account is cited also by other sources, e.g. in al-Khwānsārī, *Rawḍāt al-jannāt,* vol. 4, p. 130; 'Abd Allāh al-Māmaqānī, *Tanqīḥ al-maqāl* (Najaf, 1349–1352/1930–1933), biography 11367.

11 On the first title see e.g. al-Ṭūsī, *Kitāb al-rijāl* (Najaf 1381/1961), p. 409, no. 10; p. 489, nos. 40 and 41. For the second title see ibid., p. 409, no. 13; p. 472, nos. 2 and 9; p. 478, no, 9; p. 479, nos. 10–12.

12 Literally: 'he returned to us' ; see al-Najāshī, *Rijāl*, p. 350.

three caliphs and of Muʿāwiya) were based on Sunnī traditions (*mimmā ṣannafahu min riwāyat al-ʿāmma).*[13] However, apart from these two early Shīʿī sources — and later Shīʿī sources dependent on them — I have not come across other references to al-ʿAyyāshī or his 'conversion'.

According to al-Najāshī, al-ʿAyyāshī received his education from scholars in Kūfa, Baghdad and Qom, all important Shīʿī centres in those days.[14] Al-Najāshī mentions specifically his first circle of teachers, who were disciples of the scholars ʿAlī b. al-Ḥasan b. Faḍḍāl, a Shīʿī *ḥadith* scholar of Kūfa[15] and ʿAbd Allāh b. Muḥammad b. Khālid al-Ṭayālisī, who also was a *ḥadith* scholar.[16] As for al-ʿAyyāshī's disciples, al-Najāshī mentions Abū ʿAmr al-Kishshī (d. 340/951), author of the famous book of *Rijāl,* who often quotes *ḥadiths* in his name.[17] Another prominent disciple was Abū al-Naṣr Aḥmad b. Yaḥyā, like his teacher a native of Samarqand, who was one of the outstanding *ḥadith* and *fiqh* scholars of his day.[18] Other disciples men-

13 Ibn al-Nadīm, *Kitāb al-Fihrist* (ed. Flügel), p. 194 (= *The Fihrist of al-Nadīm,* trans. Dodge, p. 483). It is noteworthy that Dodge mistakenly translated the word *ʿāmma* as 'common people' instead of 'Sunnīs'. See also Muḥammad b. ʿAlī ibn Shahrāshūb, *Maʿālim al-ʿulamā'* (Najaf 1380/1961), p. 100.

14 Al-Najāshī, *Rijāl,* p. 350.

15 He apparently lived in the third/ninth century and is said to have transmitted *ḥadiths* (through his father) from Imam al-Riḍā. See Abū ʿAmr al-Kishshī, *Kitāb al-rijāl* (Najaf, n.d.), pp. 433–435 and 437; al-Najāshī, *Rijāl,* pp. 257–259. It should be noted that according to Āghā Buzurg al-Ṭihrānī (*Ṭabaqāt aʿlām al-shīʿa* [Najaf 1373/1954], p. 306), the version in al-Najāshī is wrong and should read: *samiʿa aṣḥāb al-Ḥasan b. ʿAlī b. Faḍḍāl.* This refers to the son of al-Ḥasan, whose name is ʿAlī.

16 He probably flourished in the third/ninth century (al-Najāshī, *Rijāl,* p. 219).

17 See e.g. al-Najāshī, *Rijāl,* p. 372; al-Ṭihrānī, *al-Dharīʿa ilā taṣānīf al-shīʿa,* vol. 4, p. 295. Al-ʿAyyāshī is referred to many times throughout al-Kishshī's work as Muḥammad b. Masʿūd, but is seldom designated Abū al-Naḍr (p. 148 and 330). He is mentioned twice by name and designation: Abū al-Naḍr Muḥammad b. Masʿūd (p. 76 and 287) and three times in a combination of name and *nisba:* Muḥammad b. Masʿūd al-ʿAyyāshī (p. 11, 227 and 237). These examples suffice to prove that the man is indeed our al-ʿAyyāshī and that there is no truth to the opinion cited by al-Māmaqānī (*Tanqīḥ al-maqāl,* biography 11367), which he rejects, that instead of the Muḥammad b. Masʿūd common in al-Kishshī one should read Muḥammad b. Manshūd.

18 On him see W. Madelung, *Religious Trends in Early Islamic Iran,* Columbia Lectures on Iranian Studies, 4 (New york 1988), p. 85.

tioned are al-ʿAyyāshī's son, Jaʿfar,[19] and a certain Ḥaydar b. Muḥammad al-Samarqandī.[20]

Al-ʿAyyāshī's dates of birth and death are not mentioned in any of the earlier sources. From the fact that he was al-Kishshī's teacher, however, one can deduce that he probably lived toward the end of the third/ninth and beginning of fourth/tenth centuries.[21]

1.2 WORK

Al-ʿAyyāshī was a prolific author. The early Shīʿī biographical sources credit him with over two hundred works covering various branches of religious literature,[22] particularly jurisprudence. It appears however that most of the writings in this area that are listed as separate works (approximately one hundred in number) were in fact fascicles of one larger composition.[23]

The titles of most of the legal compositions mentioned in the biographical and bibliographical sources do not suggest a specifically Shīʿī content. Nevertheless, two works presumably dealt with issues which were in dispute between the Sunna and the Shīʿa. These are *Kitāb al-mutʿa* (Book on Temporary Marriage) which apparently discussed the permissibility of such a marriage, and *Kitāb al-masḥ ʿalā al-qadamayn* (Book of Wiping of the Feet [during purification before prayer]), which probably dealt with the question of whether a believer must wash (*ghasl*) his feet during the purification process before prayer or whether it is sufficient for him to wipe them (*masḥ*). Both opinions are based on Qur'an 5:8, yet the two camps have read

19 Al-Ṭūsī, *Rijāl*, p. 409 (biography no. 10).

20 See Ibn al-Nadīm, *al-Fihrist* (Flügel), p. 136 (=*The Fihrist of al-Nadīm*, trans. Dodge, p. 487, which mentions him by his personal name only).

21 ʿUmar Riḍā Kaḥḥāla in his *Muʿjam al-muʾallifīn* (Damascus 1380/1960), vol. 12, p. 20 is the only one of the later biographers whom I have found mentioning an exact date (310/932) for al-ʿAyyāshī's death, although this statement is apparently not based on an early source; see also F. Sezgin, *Geschichte des arabischen Schrifttums* (Leiden 1967–1984), vol. 1, p. 42, who also mentions this year, but adds the word 'gegen' (approximately).

22 See Ibn al-Nadīm, *al-Fihrist* (Flügel), p. 136 (=*The Fihrist of al-Nadīm*, trans. Dodge, p. 487); al-Najāshī, *Rijāl*, p. 372

23 This fact can be gleaned from some of the names of these compositions: *Kitāb al-ṣawm, Kitāb al-ṣalāt, Kitāb al-zakāt, Kitāb al-jizya wa-l-kharāj, Kitāb al-ḥayḍ*, which are the sort of names reserved for volumes or sections within collections of *ḥadīth* and *fiqh*, in both Sunnī and Shīʿī compilations.

diametrically opposite meanings into it. The Sunna holds that the believer must wash his feet before each prayer, while the Shīʿa claim that he can absolve himself by wiping them.[24] In addition, several other works deal with fundamental Shīʿī doctrines: *Kitāb al-taqiyya* (Book on the [doctrine] of Disimmulation); *Kitāb al-ghayba* (Book on the Occultation [of the Imam]); *Kitāb al-badāʾ* (Book on the [doctrine] of God Changing His Will), an issue that was of great significance for early Imāmī theology; *Kitāb al-anbiyāʾ wa-l-aʾimma* (Book of Prophets and Imams); *Kitāb al-awṣiyāʾ* (Book of the Prophet's Heirs i.e. the Imams); *Ithbāt imāmat ʿAlī b. Abī Ṭālib* (Proving the Imamate of ʿAlī b. Abī Ṭālib); and *Dalāʾil al-aʾimma* (Proofs of the Imams).

Of special interest are the four *sīra* compositions that al-ʿAyyāshī is reported to have devoted to the first three caliphs and to Muʿāwiya, which he presumably composed before becoming a Shīʿī. One can assume that these books consisted of traditions that contradict other traditions found in his commentary on the Qurʾan portraying these figures in a thoroughly negative light (see below).

1.2.1 *Al-ʿAyyāshī's Commentary on the Qurʾan*

Of all these works, only al-Ayyāshī's commentary on the Qurʾan has been preserved, and even this work has not come down to us in its entirety.[25] The composition in its present form includes only a commentary on the first eighteen *sūras* of the Qur'an (up to the end of the 18th *sūra* [*al- kahf*]); yet there is no doubt that *Tafsīr al-ʿAyyāshī* originally included more material which has not survived. This can be gleaned from the many references to *Tafsīr al-ʿAyyāshī* found in writings of early Imāmī Shīʿī scholars, who mention both the sections of this work that are available to us and the sections that come after *sūrat al-kahf*. Of these, the most prominent is

24 For a discussion of this issue in the Shīʿī exegetical literature, see M.M. Bar-Asher, 'Variant Readings and Additions of the Imāmī-Šīʿa to the Quran,' *Israel Oriental Studies*, vol. 13 (1993), pp. 39–74 at pp. 56–57 and notes 58–59 (reprinted in G. Giorgione, ed. *Which Koran? Variants, Manuscripts, Linguistics* (New-York 2011), pp. 575–612 (at pp. 595–596 and 607). References are given to this last edition.

25 One should also mention the quotations from his work *Kitāb al-libās* (they appear, e.g. in al-Najāshī's *Rijāl*, p. 352, and in al-Ṭihrānī's *Dharīʿa*, vol. 18, p. 293), which are often cited by Abū ʿAlī al-Faḍl al-Ṭabrisī in his *Makārim al-akhlāq*, edited by ʿA. Ṭāleqānī (Karbala, n.d.) e.g. p. 49, 54, 60, *62*, 64, 69, 70, 75.

Majmaʿ al-bayān fī tafsīr al-Qurʾān by Abū ʿAlī al-Faḍl b. al-Ḥasan al-Ṭabrisī (d. 548/1153) – which frequently mentions *Tafsīr al-ʿAyyāshī*;[26] but it is also referred to by Muḥammad b. ʿAlī Ibn Shahrāshūb (d. 588/1192)[27] and ʿAlī Ibn Ṭāwūs (d. 664/1266).[28] An examination of these references reveals that they are not interpretations of verses from the latter part of the Qurʾan *(sūra* 19 [Maryam] onward) incorporated into a commentary on *sūras* 1–18), but rather material that is totally missing from *Tafsīr al-ʿAyyāshī* as we now know it.[29] It is not easy to decide when exactly the last part of *Tafsīr al-ʿAyyāshī* was lost, but it appears that even the most learned Imāmī Shīʿī scholars of the eighteenth century – such as Muḥammad Bāqir al-Majlisī (d. 1111/1699) and al-Ḥurr al-ʿĀmilī (d. 1104/1693) famous for their erudition in Imāmī Shīʿī literature of all generations – were not familiar with the entire Qurʾan commentary of al-ʿAyyāshī. When mentioning *Tafsīr al-ʿAyyāshī* in his *Wasāʾil al-shīʿa,* al-Ḥurr al-ʿĀmilī notes explicitly that ʻits second half has not come down to us (*kitāb tafsīr al-ʿAyyāshī fa-inna al-niṣfa al-thāniya minhu lam yaṣil ilaynā).*ʼ[30] A more detailed description is that by Muḥammad Ḥusayn al-Ṭabāṭabāʾī: ʻThe second half [of *Tafsīr al-ʿAyyāshī*] is still lost, so that even the leading scholars of traditional exegesis (*arbāb al-tafāsīr al-riwāʾiyya)* and *ḥadith* experts, such as al-Baḥrānī in his *Tafsīr al-burhān,* al-Ḥuwayzī in his *Nūr al-thaqalayn,* al-Kāshānī in his *al-Ṣāfī* and al-Majlisī in his *Biḥār,*

26 Here are some examples from his *Majmaʿ al-bayān* (all from *sūra* 19 onward): vol. 16, p. 129 (on verse 19:83); vol. 18, p. 68 (on verse 24:55); vol. 28, p. 120 (on the first verses in *sūra* 66); vol. 29, p. 141 (on verse 76:1); vol. 30, p. 239, line 3 from bottom (on *sūra* 114).

27 See e.g. the following four citations occurring in his *Manāqib āl Abī Ṭālib:* (a) vol. 2, p. 166 (on verse 18:6 not found in *Tafsīr al-ʿAyyāshī*); (b) vol. 2, p. 226 (on verse 5:3 = *Tafsīr al-ʿAyyāshī,* vol. 2, pp. 9–10, traditions 1180/21 and 1181/22); (c) vol. 2, p. 299 (on the word *salam* in 39:29, not found in *Tafsīr al-ʿAyyāshī*); (d) vol. 3, p. 314, (on verse 6:19 = *Tafsīr al-ʿAyyāshī,* vol. 2, pp. 92–93, tradition 1407/1212).

28 The only example noted is in his *Saʿd al-suʿūd* (Najaf 1369/1950), p. 79, where Ibn Ṭāwūs quotes al-ʿAyyāshī for verse 35:32. This verse is mentioned in *Tafsīr al-ʿAyyāshī* in reference to another verse (16:70), though it is not interpreted there. It is likely that the quotation in Ibn Ṭāwūs refers to a broader commentary on this verse in *Tafsīr al-ʿAyyāshī* – i.e. in his lost commentary on *sūra* 35. See E. Kohlberg, *A Medieval Muslim Scholar at Work: Ibn Ṭāwūs and his Library* (Leiden 1992), pp. 347–348, no. 573.

29 In addition to the references to the lost part of *Tafsīr al-ʿAyyāshī* cited above, see now the numerous traditions assembled in the supplement (*mustadrak*) to the al-Biʿtha edition of the *Tafsīr*, vol. 3, pp. 129–176 and in this edition/translation by the Al-Mahdi Institute.

30 Muḥammad b. al-Ḥasan al-Ḥurr al-ʿĀmilī, *Wasāʾil al-shīʿa* (Tehran 1378–1389), vol. 9, p. 3.

have not quoted traditions in his [al-Ayyāshī's] name beyond those found in its first part.'[31]

1.2.2 *Manuscripts and Printed Editions of Tafsīr al-ʿAyyāshī*

Manuscripts of *Tafsīr al-ʿAyyāshī* have been found mostly in Iran and Iraq.[32] One such manuscript – no. 4153 of the India Office in London, dating from the 17th century – was consulted for this introduction. This manuscript consists of 233 folios. According to the colophon on the last folio, the copying was completed in the month of Rajab 1085 (October 1674) by Qāsim ʿAlī ibn al-Muʿizz al-Shushtarī.[33]

To the best of my knowledge, there are three editions of this work: (1) the first was edited by Hāshim al-Rasūlī al-Maḥallātī (Qom, 1380/ [1960–1]); (2) the second was published by Mu'assasat al-Aʿlamī in Beirut (1411/1991); and (3) the third was prepared by Mu'assasat al-Biʿtha (Qom 1421H [=2000]). The pagination of the three editions is different, while the enumeration of the traditions is identical in the first two editions but occasionally different in the third.

The important contribution of all three editions is the list of references provided by the editors for citations of *Tafsīr al-ʿAyyāshī* in various Imāmī Shīʿī sources. The most important of these are the three exegetical works of Abū ʿAlī al-Faḍl b. al-Ḥasan al-Ṭabrisī, al-Kāshānī and al-Baḥrānī, all of whom are cited in this introduction as well as the *Wasā'il al-shīʿa* and *Ithbāt al-hudāt* by al-Ḥurr al-ʿĀmilī and the *Biḥār al-anwār* of al-Majlisī.

1.2.3 *Tafsīr al-ʿAyyāshī as a prominent representation of the pre-Buwayhid Imāmī Shīʿī school of Exegesis*

Tafsīr al-ʿAyyāshī begins with a short introduction, which includes traditions in praise of the Qur'an, the prohibition against interpreting it rationally, the exclusivity of the Imams in their understanding and

31 See his preface to *Tafsīr al-ʿAyyāshī*, Qom edition, p. iii (=reprinted in Beirut edition, p. 7)

32 See Sezgin, *Geschichte des arabischen Schrifttums*, vol. 1, p. 42.

33 For a detailed description of this manuscript, see *Catalogue of the Arabic Manuscripts in the India Office Library*, vol. 2, pp. 10–11. For other manuscripts of *Tafsīr al-ʿAyyāshī*, see al-Biʿtha edition of the *Tafsīr*, vol. 1, p. 50.

interpretation, and other related issues. The exegetical views of the author are given indirectly. Loyal to the *ḥadīth* statement that 'whosoever interprets [rationally] a verse from the Qur'an is an infidel (*man fassara bi-ra'yihi āya min kitāb Allāh fa-qad kafara*)'[34] al-'Ayyāshī and other early (pre-Occultation) Imāmī Shī'ī commentators drastically reduced their participation in the process of interpretation, limiting themselves to citing traditions in the name of the Imams and only very rarely stating their own opinions on the material they present. This should not, however, lead us to the simplistic conclusion that al-'Ayyāshī or the Imāmī Shī'ī commentators operating in this period did not have an overall exegetical viewpoint, since their opinion – although not explicitly pronounced – may be implicitly discerned from their choice and selection of material cited and omitted. If we take as an example the attitude to the first three caliphs and to the Prophet's Companions in general, we are able to see that al-'Ayyāshī consistently incorporated every tradition that denigrated them, and in this he outdid the other commentators of his age.[35] In an utterance attributed to the Imam Muḥammad al-Bāqir, cited by al-'Ayyāshī, he goes so far as to state that 'every occurrence in the Qur'an of the words 'Satan says' is [to be understood as referring to] "the second" [namely the caliph 'Umar b. al-Khaṭṭāb] *(laysa fī al-Qur'ān [shay'] wa-qāla al-shayṭān illā wa-huwa al-thānī)*.'[36]

In other aspects, *Tafsīr al-'Ayyāshī* is close to the other major exegetical works of his period mentioned above. In attempting to characterize the major exegetical features of this group of commentators operating in the third part of the 3rd/9th and first decades of 4th/10th century, I coined the term 'pre-Buwayhid school of exegesis' and suggested four criteria by which this school can be defined, as opposed both to later Shī'ī exegesis and to its Sunnī counterpart. It seems to me that these features faithfully describe not only pre-Buwayhid exegesis but partially – i.e. features (b) and (d) below – also Ismā'īlī exegesis of the equivalent period. These features are: (a) interpretation by means of *ḥadīth*; (b) selective concern with the text of the Qur'an – that is, putting an emphasis mainly on verses with

34 *Tafsīr al-'Ayyāshī*, vol. 1, pp. 96–97, traditions 65/2, 67/4 and 68/5.

35 See e.g. *Tafsīr al-'Ayyāshī*, vol. 2, p. 53, tradition 1290/131; vol. 2, pp. 421–422, tradition 1852/85; vol. 3, pp. 68–70, tradition 2576/132.

36 See ibid., vol. 2, p. 404, tradition 2265/7.

potential Shīʿī relevance; (c) scant interest in theological issues (among Shīʿī doctrinal issues, mainly *walāya* and *barāʾa* draw significant attention); and (d) an anti-Sunnī stance and a hostile attitude to the Companions of the Prophet and to other persons or groups who are conceived as hostile to the Shīʿa (e.g. the Umayyad and Abbasid dynasties).[37]

One may rightly claim that the first two characteristics are also present in early Sunnī exegesis: Qurʾan commentaries such as those of Mujāhid (d. 104/723) or ʿAbd al-Razzāq (d. 211/826) are based almost entirely on *ḥadīths*. The second characteristic is also not exclusive to early Imāmī Shīʿī exegesis. However, the presence of all four characteristics in the same composition, as is the case of *Tafsīr al-ʿAyyāshī*, imparts a unique character that indisputably qualifies pre-Buwayhid Imāmī Shīʿī Qurʾan exegesis as a school in its own right. Later, beginning with Abū Jaʿfar al-Ṭūsī (d. 460/1067), a shift in the attitude of Imāmī Shīʿī exegetes becomes evident.[38] The exegesis of this period can be characterized as being more independent and more ambivalent about the use of *ḥadīth*. This can be clearly seen both in the marginal position of *ḥadīths* in commentaries of this period and in the omission or abbreviation of the chains of transmitters (*isnāds*). The commentators who represent the new trend of Imāmī Shīʿī exegesis are ambivalent in their approach to Sunnī Islam in general and to the generation of the Companions of the Prophet in particular. Theirs is a middle road. They have reservations about blatant criticism of the Companions of the Prophet and are careful not to detract from the images of the first three caliphs in the manner of their pre-Buwayhid predecessors.[39]

All the features used here as criteria for distinguishing between two major periods in the history of Shīʿism place the emphasis mainly on points of content. Amir-Moezzi in his chapter on al-Ḥibarī, in line with his previous studies on early Shīʿism, stresses other dimensions that distinguish the pre-Buwayhid from the Buwayhid and post-Buwayhid periods.[40] The earliest phase, that is the pre-Buwayhid phase, is marked, according to

37 See Bar-Asher, *Scripture and Exegesis,* pp. 71–86. For the attitude toward the Umayyads and Abbasids see ibid., pp. 204–223.

38 Other explanations for this shift are offered by Amir-Moezzi, 'The *Tafsīr* of al-Ḥibarī', pp. 113–134 at pp. 118–121.

39 For the details, see Bar-Asher, *Scripture and Exegesis,* pp. 84–86

40 See his 'The *Tafsīr* of al-Ḥibarī', pp. 125–134.

him, by its esoteric, mystical and magic dimensions. These dimensions are abundantly present in both exegetical and non-exegetical works of this period, but they gradually disappear from writings post-dating the Buwayhid period. It is noteworthy that later in the history of Imāmī Shīʿism the ancient phase, with its markedly sectarian, isolationist and anti-Sunnī elements that characterizes the pre-Buwayhid period re-emerges in the writings of leading authorities of the Ṣafavid period. Among these should be mentioned here prominent scholars such as Sharaf al-Dīn ʿAlī al-Ḥusaynī al-Astarābādī (fl. 10th/16th century), the author of *Taʾwīl al-āyāt al-ẓāhira fī faḍāʾil al-ʿitra al-ṭāhira* (Qom, 1407/1986); Muḥammad b. Murtaḍā al-Kāshānī (d. 1091/1680), the author of *Kitāb al-ṣāfī fī tafsīr al-Qurʾān* (Beirut, 1389/1979) and Hāshim b. Sulaymān al-Baḥrānī (d. 1107/1693 or 1109/1697), the writer of *al-Burhān fī tafsīr al-Qurʾān* (Tehran, n.d.). Their comprehensive Imāmī Shīʿī *tafsīr* works are mainly compilations of early sources.[41]

2. The question of the integrity of the Qur'an

A major bone of contention between Sunnī and Shīʿī Islam, which occupies a principal place in *Tafsīr al-ʿAyyāshī*, concerns the integrity of the Qur'an. The Shīʿa disputed the canonical validity of the ʿUthmānic codex, the *textus receptus*, of the Qur'an and cast doubt on the quality of its editing, alleging political tendentiousness on the part of the editors – namely, the three first caliphs, particularly ʿUthmān b. ʿAffān (r. 23–35/644–656). Shīʿī (mainly Imāmī) criticism of the Qur'anic text was most severe in the first centuries of Islam. The editors were accused of falsification (*taḥrīf*) of the Qur'anic text both by the omission of some phrases and by the addition of others. Moreover, the claim that the Qur'an has been falsified is one of the principal arguments to which early Shīʿī – that is, mainly pre-Buwayhid – tradition resorted to explain the absence of any explicit reference to the Shīʿa in the Qur'an. In Shīʿī Qur'an commentaries, many traditions are found accusing the Companions of the Prophet of violating the integrity of the Qur'anic text. A treasure trove of such traditions is *Kitāb al-qirāʾāt* (also known as *Kitāb al-tanzīl*

41 For the names of the major exegetes of this period, see M. M. Bar-Asher, 'The Qur'an and its Shiʿi Interpretations: Introduction', in F. Daftary and G. Miskinzoda, *The Study of Shiʿi Islam,* pp. 91–93.

wa-l-taḥrīf) by Aḥmad b. Muḥammad al-Sayyārī (fl. late third/ninth century), an annotated edition of which by E. Kohlberg and M. A. Amir-Moezzi is now available.[42]

It is noteworthy that the commentators do not attempt to validate their general claim with examples of texts that, in their opinion, have been altered. Just how unspecific these traditions are can be demonstrated by a number of traditions in *Tafsīr al-ʿAyyāshī*. In an account ascribed to Jaʿfar al-Ṣādiq, cited in relation to verse Q2:279, it is reported that on leaving the house of the caliph ʿUthmān, ʿAbd Allāh b. ʿAmr b. al-ʿĀṣ met the Commander of the Faithful [ʿAlī] and said to him, "O ʿAlī, we have spent the whole night discussing a matter which we hope God will use to fortify this community (*umma*)." ʿAlī answered: "What you have spent the night doing I am well aware of. You distorted and twisted and changed nine hundred letters [of the Qur'an]; three hundred of which you distorted, three hundred of which you twisted, and three hundred of which you changed around: 'So woe to those who write something down with their hands and then claim, 'This is from God'" [Q. 2:79][43]

It is obvious that the numbers are not to be taken at face value, just as the three different verbs used to describe the editorial activity (*ḥarrafa*, *ghayyara* and *baddala*) do not indicate discrete falsification techniques.

Numerous Shīʿī utterances refer to the nature of the original text of the Qurʾan prior to its alleged corruption by the Sunnīs. In a well-known tradition, which appears in *Tafsīr al-ʿAyyāshī* as well as in the writings of most early Shīʿī commentators, Imam Muḥammad al-Bāqir declares: 'The Qurʾan was revealed [consisting of] four parts: One part concerning us [the Shīʿa], one part concerning our enemies, one part commandments and regulations (*farāʾiḍ wa-aḥkām*) and one part customs and parables (*sunan wa-amthāl*). And the exalted parts of the Qur'an refer to us (*wa-lanā karāʾim al-Qurʾān*)'.[44]

42 E. Kohlberg and M. A. Amir-Moezzi (eds.), *Revelation and Falsification – The* Kitāb al-qirāʾāt *of Aḥmad b. Muḥammad al-Sayyārī: Critical Edition with an Introduction and Notes* (Leiden: Brill, 2009).

43 *Tafsīr al-ʿAyyāshī*, vol. 1, p. 139, tradition 166/65. The translations of this and other passages from *Tafsīr al-ʿAyyāshī* are taken from the present English translation.

44 *Tafsīr al-ʿAyyāshī*, vol. 1, p. 84, tradition 27/3, where a tripartite division is suggested. Cf. also Kohlberg and Amir-Moezzi, *Revelation and Falsification*, p. 8, tradition 11 (the Arabic text) and p. 59 (the English section).

Other accounts refer to the length of the original Qur'an. It is believed to have contained seventeen thousand verses.[45] Sūra 33 (*al-aḥzāb*) is often given as an example of a text that in the original Qur'an was two and two-thirds longer than Sūra 2 (*al-baqara*),[46] which in turn was longer than the version now present in the 'Uthmānic codex.[47]

A major concern of Shī'ī hermeneutical tradition was the identification of those parts of the Qur'an which were allegedly revealed concerning the family of the Prophet (*ahl al-bayt*). Of extraordinary significance is the decipherment of names of persons referring to the Shī'a or to its enemies that are believed to be alluded to in the Qur'an, for 'knowing the names of [these] persons is the religion of God (*ma'rifat al-rijāl dīn allāh*)', as we are told in a number of utterances attributed to the Imams.[48] The caliph 'Uthmān and his associates, as claimed by the Shī'a, were bent on eliminating from the canonical text as revealed to the Prophet all traces of Shī'ī legitimacy, that is, all references to the family of the Prophet (*ahl al-bayt*) and his heirs, the Shī'ī Imams; to the Shī'ī supremacy over the Muslim community; and to certain Shī'ī doctrines. Revealing the 'original' text is, in the eyes of the pre-Buwayhid Shī'a, a vital step in the direction of correcting the falsification thus created.

A key method which al-'Ayyāshī, as well as other early Imāmī Shī'ī exegetes, employed in order to demonstrate the claim of falsification is to point to variant readings (*qirā'āt*) in the Qur'an and additions to it, which the Shī'a uphold and which are believed to be part and parcel of the original Qur'an. It is not my aim in this introduction to go into detail about the different types of these variants and additions. I shall illustrate them by two types recurrent in *Tafsīr al-'Ayyāshī*: (a) exchanging one word for another; and (b) additions of words.

The best illustration for the first sort of alteration is the insertion of the word *a'imma* (Imams) in place of the word *umma* (nation/community) found in the 'Uthmānic codex. For example: '*Kuntum khayra* ummatin *ukhrijat li-l-nās* (You are the best nation ever brought forth to men)' in

45 Ibid., p. 9, tradition 16 (the Arabic text) and pp. 61–62 (the English section).

46 Ibid. p. 109, tradition 418 (the Arabic text) and pp. 198–199 (the English section).

47 Ibid. p. 110, tradition 421 (the Arabic text) and p. 200 (the English section).

48 See al-Ṣaffār al-Qummī, *Baṣā'ir al-darajāt* (Tabriz, 1380H), p. 526; Amir-Moezzi, 'The *Tafsīr* of al-Ḥibarī,' p. 113.

Q3:110. The tradition reported by al-ʿAyyāshī and other Imāmī Shīʿī commentators on the authority of Imam Jaʿfar al-Ṣādiq reads: *'Kuntum khayra* aʾimmatin (you are the best Imams).'[49] The implication of this kind of variant is that the doctrine of the Imamate and other principles associated with it originate in the Qurʾan.

As for the other type of alteration – the addition of words which the Imāmī Shīʿa believes to have been omitted from the "original" Qurʾan – prominent among them are the words (a) *fī ʿAlī* (concerning ʿAlī) in various Qurʾanic verses such as Q2:91 'Believe in what God has revealed to you concerning ʿAlī (*āminū bi-mā anzala Allāh* fī ʿAlī)'[50] ; or Q4:166 'But God bears witness to what He has revealed to you concerning ʿAlī] (*lākinna Allāha yashhadu bi-mā anzala ilayka* fi ʿAlī);'[51] (b) the words *āl Muḥammad* (the family of Muḥammad) or occasionally *āl Muḥammad ḥaqqahum*, '(deprived) the family of Muḥammad of their right' as the first and second direct objects of a verb from the root *ẓlm* (to do injustice/to usurp) which appear often in the Qurʾan. Imāmī Shīʿī tradition stresses that the injustice referred to by words and verbs derived from the root *ẓlm* alludes specifically to the injustice perpetrated against the family of the Prophet and his offspring, i.e. the Shīʿa.[52]

The same method is applied in *Tafsīr al-ʿAyyāshī* with regard to other Imāmī Shīʿī doctrines deduced from the Qurʾan. The insertion of the words *fī walāyat ʿAlī* (concerning the [duty of] loyalty to ʿAlī) in several verses in the Qurʾan is intended to provide scriptural authority to the doctrine of *walāya*,[53] as the addition of the word *ilā ajalin musamman* (for a given time) to the *mutʿa* verse (Q4:24) is meant to emphasize the temporary nature of *mutʿa* marriage, an issue on which Shīʿīs and Sunnīs have disagreed throughout history.[54]

49 *Tafsīr al-ʿAyyāshī*, vol. 1, p. 335, traditions 767/128–768/129. For other sources, see Bar-Asher, 'Variant Readings,' p. 588; Kohlberg and Amir-Moezzi, *Revelation and Falsification*, p. 32, tradition 114 (the Arabic text) and p. 98 (the English section).

50 *Tafsīr al-ʿAyyāshī*, vol. 1, p. 143, tradition 176/75.

51 Ibid., vol. 1, p. 456, tradition 1152/310.

52 See e.g. ibid., vol. 1, p. 135, tradition 153/52; and p. 456, tradition 1152/310.

53 See e.g. ibid., vol. 1, p. 456, tradition 1152/310; and vol. 3, p. 82, tradition 2610/166.

54 See e.g. ibid., vol. 1, p. 386, traditions 929/87–930/88.

In many places where al-ʿAyyāshī and other commentators suggest a Shīʿī variant reading to a Qurʾanic verse, they do so by using typical formulas. The Shīʿī version is followed by statements such as *nazala bihā Jibrāʾīl/Jibrīl hā-kadhā* (thus [the verse] was revealed by the [archangel] Gabriel)[55] or *kadhā* (or *hā-kadhā*) *nazalat* (thus [the verse] was revealed),[56] or by stating explicitly that the version suggested was the reading of one of the Imams.[57] Sometimes even stronger expressions are used to stress that particular passages of the Qurʾan as preserved by the Sunna are incorrect. These include statements formulated in the negative, such as *ʿalā khilāf mā anzala Allāh* ([The verse in the *textus receptus* version] contradicts the form in which God repeated it),[58] or *fīmā ḥurrifa min kitāb Allāh* ([The verse] is one of those falsified/altered in the Book of God).[59]

The discrepancy between the Qurʾanic text and the Shīʿī viewpoint is not necessarily one that a 'correct' interpretation can remedy. This discrepancy results from a textual gap between the incomplete Qurʾanic text found in the possession of the Sunnīs and the ideal text that, according to Shīʿī belief, is no longer in anyone's possession but will be revealed by the Mahdī in the eschatological era.

Beginning in the Buwayhid period, here again in the wake of political and social changes that Imāmī Shīʿism underwent, a tendency to moderation became apparent, and some of the criticism as reflected in *Tafsīr al-ʿAyyāshī* became muted. Leading Imāmī Shīʿī scholars such as Muḥammad b. Muḥammad b. al-Nuʿmān, better known as al-Shaykh al-Mufīd (d. 413/1022), al-Sharīf al-Murtaḍā (d. 436/1044), Abū Jaʿfar al-Ṭūsī and – a century later – Abū ʿAlī al-Ṭabrisī (d. 548/1153), held the view that although the text of the Qurʾan as we have it is incomplete, it does not contain any falsification. In other words, what is found in the ʿUthmānic codex is the truth but not the whole truth since it does not include all the revelations made to Muḥammad. As demonstrated by Etan Kohlberg, recurring changes took

55 See e.g. ibid., vol. 3, pp. 93–94, tradition 2652/28. For similar versions, see ibid., vol. 1, p. 135, tradition 153/52, and also *Tafsīr al-Qummī,* vol. 2, p. 111.

56 See e.g. *Tafsīr al-Qummī,* vol. 1, p. 142 and 197; vol. 2, p. 21.

57 See e.g. *Tafsīr al-ʿAyyāshī,* vol. 1, p. 333, tradition 758/119; and p. 335, tradition 767/28.

58 See e.g. *Tafsīr al-Qummī,* vol. 1, p. 10 which cites as examples for such verses 3:110 and 25:74. See also the note of the editor (al-Ṭayyib al-Mūsawī al-Jazāʾirī), ibid., p. 5.

59 See ibid., vol. 2, p. 295.

place throughout the history of Imāmī Shīʿism in its attitude regarding the question of the integrity of the Qur'an.[60] This process of change can be likened to the swing of a pendulum: in early Shīʿism, up to the mid-fourth/tenth century, Imāmī Shīʿīs maintained a very radical view; later – that is, in the Buwayhid period – a much more moderate view became prevalent; then, 'with the re-emergence during the Ṣafavid period of the *akhbāriyyūn*, who set great store by individual traditions, the question of the attitude to the ʿUthmānic codex was revived.'[61] The dominant view in this period was a rejection of the *taḥrīf* theory. Yet some leading scholars of the late Ṣafavid period – such as Muḥammad Ṣālih al-Māzandarānī in his commentary on al-Kulīnī's *Uṣūl min al-Kāfī*, Hāshim al-Baḥrānī in his *al-Burhān fī tafsīr al-Qur'ān* and Niʿmat Allāh al-Jazā'irī in his *al-Anwār al-nuʿmāniyya* – reverted to the views of pre-Buwayhid Imāmī scholars, accusing the Companions of the Prophet of falsifying the Qur'anic text.[62] The most radical representative of the falsification theory in modern times is al-Ḥusayn b. Muḥammad Taqī al-Nūrī al-Ṭabrisī (d. 1320/1905). A recurrent tradition, on which Nūrī bases his argument in favour of *taḥrīf* draws an analogy between the Shīʿīs and the Jews. 'Just as the Jews and the Christians altered and falsified the Book of their prophet [sic] after him, this community [i.e. the Muslims] shall alter and falsify the Qur'an after our Prophet – may God bless him and his family – for everything that happened to the Children of Israel is bound to happen to this community.'[63] It should be stressed, however, that Nūrī's extreme anti-Sunnī tone was criticized even by the Shīʿī scholars of his day. Nonetheless, the question of *taḥrīf* never ceased to be a burning issue in Shīʿī-Sunnī discourse, to the point that 'there is hardly a new book on the general

60 On the various positions taken by Imāmī Shīʿīs on this question, see Kohlberg, 'Some Notes on the Imāmite Attitude to the Qur'an,' in *Islamic Philosophy and the Classical Tradition: Essays Presented to Richard Walzer*, ed. S. M. Stern et al. (Oxford 1972), pp. 209–224.

61 Ibid., p. 217. See also Amir-Moezzi, 'The *Tafsīr* al-Ḥibarī,' pp. 119–120.

62 Kohlberg and Amir-Moezzi, *Revelation and Falsification*, p. 28.

63 Al-Ḥusayn b. Muḥammad Taqī al-Nūrī al-Ṭabrisī, *Faṣl al-khiṭāb fī taḥrīf kitāb rabb al-arbāb* ([Tehran] 1298/1881 [lith.]), p. 35, whence R. Brunner, 'The Dispute about the Falsification of the Qur'an between Sunnīs and Shīʿīs in the twentieth century,' Leder et al. eds., *Studies in Arabic and Islam: Proceedings of the 19th Congress, Union Europeénne des Arabisants et Islamisants [Halle 1998]* (Leuven and Paris 2002), pp. 437–446, at p. 439.

subject of the Qur'anic sciences whose author can afford not to include a chapter dealing with *taḥrīf*.'[64]

3. The Qur'an as a multilayered and polyvalent text

All Shīʿī groups sought to discover reference points in the Qur'an to which they could anchor their beliefs. Various beliefs and doctrines that crystallized during the early phases of Shīʿism, and that later changed form and substance as a result *inter alia* of polemics with rival tendencies, are presented as though they were directly formulated in the Qur'an. In this, Shīʿī exegetes are no different from their Sunnī counterparts. Both Sunnīs and Shīʿīs believe that the Qur'an is multi-layered and that any concept or outlook can, with the help of various methods of interpretation, be discovered within the Qur'anic text. The Qur'an is believed to contain verses that convey an obvious or at least apparent (*ẓāhir*) message as opposed to others implying an esoteric, inner (*bāṭin*) sense. This principle is believed to be expressed in the Qur'an itself, e.g. 'and He has lavished on you His blessings, outward and inward' (*wa-asbagha ʿalaykum niʿamahu ẓāhiratan wa-bāṭinatan* [Q. 31:20]), and 'Forsake the outward sin, and the inward' (*wa-dharū ẓāhira al-ithmi wa-bāṭinahu* [Q. 6:120]). The occurrence of the opposing pair of terms *ẓāhir* versus *bāṭin* in the very text of the Qur'an is used by the exegete as an anchoring point for a fundamental exegetical principle, namely: the requirement to read the text thoroughly, making a continuous attempt to discover these two dimensions, as well as others, hidden in it.

Similar to the Ismāʿīlīs, the Imāmī Shīʿa allot a central role to esoteric writing. This style of writing is characterised by a reliance on allegorical and typological interpretation, as well as by the use of encoding techniques. In the words of Henry Corbin, Shīʿism is 'the shrine of esotericism in Islam' (le sanctuaire de l'ésoterisme de l'Islam).[65] Another accurate and eloquent

---

64 See Brunner, 'The Dispute,' p. 445. The *taḥrīf* problem in modern times, with special emphasis on al-Nūrī al-Ṭabrisī's views, is extensively analysed by R. Brunner in his *Die Schia und die Koranfälschung* (Würzburg 2001), especially pp. 39–69.

65 H. Corbin, *En Islam iranien: Aspects spirituels et philosophiques* (Paris 1971–1972), vol. 1, p. xiv, whence D. de Smet, '*Zāhir* et *bāṭin*', in J. Servier, ed., *Dictionnaire de l'ésotérisme* (Paris 1998), p. 1387–1392.

definition of the nature of Shīʿī exegesis is Amir-Moezzi's assertion that since its earliest days Shīʿism has defined itself as a 'hermeneutical doctrine'.[66]

In Shīʿism (as well as in various religious groups outside of Islam), the penchant for esoteric writing stems from two major factors. The first is the notion of the group's supremacy and religious exclusivity. The group believes itself to be the holder of supreme religious truths – truths that should not be shared with everyone. Sometimes the use of esoteric techniques derives from an existential necessity. Religious and ideological minorities may find themselves in danger as a consequence of the overt and careless expression of ideas unpalatable to the ruling majority. And indeed many Shīʿī factions throughout history which flourished under Sunnī rule required the use of survival techniques both in everyday life and when committing their religious doctrines to writing. Shīʿī scholars of all factions had to walk a fine line: on the one hand, they wished whenever possible to give expression to their views; on the other hand, they had to ascertain that the expression of such ideas did not arouse the wrath of their Sunni opponents. These two factors combined constitute the essence of the doctrine of *taqiyya* (caution and dissimulation) and *kitmān* (secrecy).

Esoteric language in Imāmī Shīʿī exegesis is evident on two levels as is strongly reflected in *Tafsīr al-ʿAyyāshī*. The first level, the exegetes believe, is found in the Qur'an itself; it underlines obscure or general Qur'anic expressions such as *al-jibt wa-l-ṭāghūt* (demon and idols), *al-faḥshāʾ wa-l-munkar* (indecency and dishonour), *al-maghḍūb ʿalayhim* (those who earn [God's] anger) and *al-ẓālimūn* (evildoers), which refer to various enemies of the Shīʿa. The second level is that of the exegetical tradition itself and is also recurrently attested in *Tafsīr al-ʿAyyāshī*. The commentator never claims explicitly that pair-expressions, such as those in the first two examples just mentioned, refer to Abū Bakr and ʿUmar, as well as to other enemies of the Shīʿa. Rather he resorts to such code words as *al-awwal* (the first) and *al-thānī* (the second); *ḥabtar* (fox) is usually applied to Abū Bakr, while *zurayq* ('the blue-eyed' or 'shiny-eyed') refers to ʿUmar.[67] In other words, the tran-

66 Amir-Moezzi, 'The *Tafsīr* of al-Ḥibarī,' p. 117.

67 For these and a plethora of derogatory appellations, see I. Goldziher, 'Spottnamen der ersten Chalifen bei den Schiʿiten', in I. Goldziher, *Gesammelte Schriften*, ed. J. Desomogyi (Hildesheim 1967–1976), vol. 4, pp. 295–308; E. Kohlberg, 'Some Imāmī Shīʿī Views on the *ṣaḥāba*', *Jerusalem Studies in Arabic Islam* 5 (1984), pp. 143–175, repr. in Etan Kohlberg,

sition from the covert stratum in the Qur'an to the overt stratum of the interpretation is not direct but undergoes a further process of encoding. The underlying assumption is that Shī'īs are familiar with these code words which are an integral part of their religious-cultural upbringing.

4. The Imam as the primary authority for Qur'an interpretation

The dilemma of the authority of reason versus that of tradition has preoccupied Sunnī and Shī'ī commentators alike. There is, however, an essential difference between the two. The prevalent view in Shī'ī exegetical tradition, unlike that of Sunnism, is that the authority to interpret the Qur'an does not lie with ordinary believers but is rather a privilege exclusive to 'Alī and his descendants, the Imams. This privilege accompanies their status as recipients of divine knowledge – one of several superhuman features with which they are believed to be endowed.

I will now offer a brief survey of the principal verses and *ḥadīths* employed by al-'Ayyāshī and other Imāmī Shī'ī commentators as proof texts for this claim. Perhaps the most widely known of the verses invoked to endorse this concept is Q. 3:7:

> It is He who revealed the Book to you, in which appear clear signs [or verses], which are the Essence of the Book, and other ambiguous [signs/verses] [...] and none knows its interpretation, save only God. And those firmly rooted in knowledge (*wa-l-rāsikhūn fī-l-'ilm*) say, 'We believe in it'. All is from our Lord; yet none remember, but men possessed of minds.[68]

Belief and Law in Imāmī Shī'ism (Aldershot 1991), pp. 143–175, at pp. 160–167; Bar-Asher, *Scripture and Exegesis*, pp. 113–120. See also the numerous examples in the texts cited by Amir-Moezzi, 'The *Tafsīr* of al-Ḥibarī', pp. 128–131.

68 See, for example, Abū Zakariyā Yaḥyā b. Muḥammad al-Farrā', *Ma'ānī al-qur'ān* (Cairo 1980), vol. 1, p. 191; al-Ṭabarī, *Jāmi' al-bayān 'an ta'wīl āy al-qur'ān* (Cairo 1388/1968), vol. 3, pp. 182–184 who surveys many traditions supporting both interpretations but clearly prefers the second possibility (p. 184), as do al-Farrā' and other Sunnī commentators. See also John Wansbrough, *Quranic Studies: Sources and Methods of Scriptural Interpretation* (Oxford 1977), p. 152.

The commentary on this verse raises the syntactic question of how to read the phrase '*al-rāsikhūn fī-l-ʿilm*' (those firmly rooted in knowledge): is it the second subject, next to Allāh in the previous sentence (i.e., only God and those firmly rooted in knowledge know its meaning), or is it the subject of the next sentence (those firmly rooted in knowledge say)? The Sunnī exegetical tradition leans towards the second interpretation. The prevalent attitude in Shīʿī exegesis, both Imāmī Shīʿī and Ismāʿīlī – in which the verse was employed as a proof text for the Imams' authority in Qurʾanic exegesis, preferred the first interpretation.[69] The words *al-rāsikhūn fī-l-ʿilm* became one of the most common phrases to denote the Imams in their role as exclusive interpreters of the Qurʾan.

Another verse employed in this manner is Q. 4:83: 'When there comes to them a matter, be it of security or fear, they broadcast it; if they had referred it to the Messenger and to those in authority among them, those of them whose task is to investigate would have known the matter.' There is an instructive tradition regarding this verse related in the name of the Imam ʿAlī al-Riḍā and reported by al-ʿAyyāshī. The historical context of the tradition is a written exchange between al-Riḍā and his disciple ʿAbd Allāh b. Jundab.[70] Ibn Jundab mentioned a group of Shīʿī believers who had become enemies of the Shīʿa, to which the Imam responded: 'The Devil [*al-shayṭān*] had insinuated ideas into these people, beguiled them with controversy and obscured matters of their religion.' Al-Riḍā went on to refer to the Shīʿī view on the authority of the Imams as interpreters of the Qurʾan. He stated that the believers in question had erred because they wished to seek the truth independently, inquiring why, who and how (*arādū al-hudā min tilqāʾi nafsihim wa-saʾalū li-mā wa-man wa-kayfa*). These issues were not within their authority and contradicted their obligation to obey the Imams, since 'rather the duty incumbent and mandatory upon them was to halt in the face of

69 *Tafsīr al-ʿAyyāshī*, vol. 1, p. 292, tradition 644/5; al-Nuʿmān b. Ḥayyūn al-Tamīmī al-Maghribī (=al-Qāḍī al-Nuʿmān), *Asās al-taʾwīl*, ed. ʿA. Tamir (Beirut 1960), p. 29.

70 Ibn Jundab was also a disciple of al-Riḍā's grandfather and father, i.e. the Imams Jaʿfar al-Ṣādiq and Mūsā al-Kāẓim. On Ibn Jundab see al-Ṭūsī, *Rijāl*, p. 229, 355, 379; Māmaqānī, *Tanqīḥ al-maqāl*, biography 6791, who adds in al-Ṭūsī's name that Ibn Jundab was a *wakīl* (i.e. spokesman and appointee) of the Imam Abū Ibrāhīm (i.e. al-Kāẓim) and al-Riḍā and was highly regarded by them (*rafīʿ al-manzila ladayhim*); al-Kishshī, *Kitāb al-rijāl*, pp. 489–490. See also Kohlberg and Amir-Moezzi, *Revelation and Falsification*, pp. 131–132 (the Arabic text), pp. 220–221 (the English section).

confusion and to refer all that they were ignorant of back to their teacher and the one who could seek out its meaning, because God says in the decisive verses of His Book: 'If they referred it to the Messenger and those in authority among them, those seeking its meaning would have found it from them'.[71]

As stated earlier, the authority of the Imams as interpreters of the Qur'an is reiterated in a number of traditions, some of which will be mentioned here. Among these, perhaps the most recurrent in both exegetical and non-exegetical works is *ḥadīth al-thaqalayn* (the tradition of the two weighty things). According to both Shīʿī and Sunnī sources, Muḥammad related this *ḥadīth* to the believers during the sermon he delivered on the last pilgrimage to Mecca after its conquest (in the ninth year of the Hijra), an event referred to in Muslim historiography as *khuṭbat ḥajjat al-wadāʿ*. There are, however, significant differences between the Sunnī and Shīʿī interpretations of this tradition. Furthermore, both Sunnī and Shīʿī texts comprise more than one version of this tradition. According to one version, cited in the Sunnī text *Sīrat rasūl Allāh* by Muḥammad Ibn Isḥāq (d. 151/768) as transmitted and edited by ʿAbd al-Malik b. Hishām (d. 218/834), Muḥammad said to his disciples:

> I have left with you something clear; if you hold fast to it, you will never fall into error – the Book of God and the practice of His Prophet (*qad taraktu fīkum mā in iʿtaṣamtum bihi lan taḍillū abadan amran bayyinan – kitāb Allāh wa-sunnat nabiyyihi*).[72]

The two things Muḥammad left in the hands of his community (which, in parallel traditions, are referred to as *thaqalān*) later became the first two

71 *Tafsīr al-ʿAyyāshī*, vol. 1, p. 422, tradition 1050/208. The tradition is cited in a number of works of the Ṣafavid period. See the editor's comment, ibid., note 4. A similar version is cited by al-Shaykh al-Mufīd (d. 413/1022) in his *al-Ikhtiṣāṣ*, ed. ʿAlī Akbar al-Ghaffārī (Tehran 1379), p. 258. See also Muḥammad b. al-Ḥusayn Ṭabāṭabāʾī's observation in his *al-Mīzān fī tafsīr al-qurʾān* (Beirut 1403–1405/1983–1985), vol. 5, p. 24.

72 Muḥammad Ibn Isḥāq, *Kitāb sīrat rasūl Allāh*, ed. F. Wüstenfeld (Leipzig 1858–1859), vol. 2, p. 969. The English translation cited here is that of A. Guillaume, *The Life of the Prophet Muhammad* (Oxford 1955), p. 651, with slight modifications.

principles of Muslim jurisprudence (*uṣūl al-fiqh*) – namely, the Qur'an and the Sunna (the prophetic practice).

Two other versions of this tradition are also recorded in Sunnī texts: a widely known version, in which the *thaqalān* are the Qur'an, which is designated in many traditions *al-thaqal al-akbar* (the more weighty object), and the Family of the Prophet (*ahl al-bayt*), designated *al-thaqal al-aṣghar* (the less weighty object). The second version is a tradition in which only the first of the pair of *thaqalān* is mentioned – the Qur'an.

An example of the first of these two types of tradition is the following, cited, for example, in Muslim's *Ṣaḥīḥ*:

> I leave among you the two weighty things (*thaqalān*): the first is the book of God (*kitāb Allāh*), which contains correct guidance and light (*al-hudā wa-l-nūr*). Cling therefore to the book of God and hold fast to it. And he [Muḥammad] encouraged his disciples [to follow] the book of God (*fa-ḥaththa 'alā kitāb Allāh wa-raghghaba fīhi*); then he said: 'and my family' (*ahl baytī*).[73]

The existence of a version mentioning *ahl al-bayt* (the Family of the Prophet) instead of *sunnat nabiyyihi* (the practice of His Prophet) provided the Shī'ī exegetical tradition with room for sectarian interpretation. An investigation of how Shī'ī tradition made use of *ḥadīth al-thaqalayn* brings to light two main features: first, a restrictive interpretation of *ahl al-bayt*, so that the term denotes only 'Alī and the Imams, descendants of Fāṭima, and thus excludes others such as the wives of the Prophet or other branches of the Hāshimī House;[74] and secondly, an application of the *ḥadīth* as proof text for the authority of the Imams as the exclusive interpreters of the Qur'an. The analogy between one tradition, according to which the second

73 See, for example, Abū al-Ḥusayn Muslim b. al-Ḥajjāj al-Qushayrī al-Naysābūrī, *Ṣaḥīḥ Muslim* (Cairo 1374–1375/1981), vol. 4, p. 1873 (tradition 36); p. 1384 (tradition 37). See also A. J. Wensinck, *Concordance et indices de la tradition musulmane* (Leiden 1936–1969), s.v. *thaqal*.

74 For an indication that this tradition was indeed interpreted inclusively, see Muslim, *Ṣaḥīḥ Muslim*, vol. 4, p. 1873 (tradition 36) where the question is explicitly raised: 'And who are his family? ... are not the Prophet's wives [included] in his family'? The answer given there is that the Prophet's wives are indeed included in the term *ahl baytihi*, although in general it signifies the various households of Hāshim's family (p. 1384, tradition 37).

thaqal refers to the practice of the Prophet (*sunnat nabiyyihi*), and the other tradition, according to which it is his family (*ahl baytī* or *ʿitratī ahl baytī*), indicates the position of Shīʿī scholars on the exclusive exegetical role of the Family of the Prophet in the interpretation of the Qur'an.[75] In other words, while in the Sunnī exegetical tradition the *practice* of the Prophet is invoked for the interpretation of the Qur'an (and is therefore mentioned in conjunction with the Book itself), in Shīʿī tradition the Family of the Prophet plays the equivalent role – that is, only through the mediation of the Imams, the descendants of the Prophet, is the true meaning of the Qur'anic text revealed to believers. An example of the Shīʿī version of this tradition is cited by al-ʿAyyāshī:

> I [Muḥammad] am going ahead of you, and you will arrive at fountain [in the Garden]... I will ask you about the two weighty things that I had left behind for you when you come to me, to see how you treated them. They asked: 'What are these two weighty things, O Messenger of God?' He replied: 'The greater one is the Book of God, one end of it is in the hands of God, while the other is in yours hands. Hold fast to it and you will never be led astray nor be disgraced. The lesser one is my family, the People of my Household. Indeed, the most Gentle and Omniscient Lord has informed me that the two will never separate from each other until they meet me. I have requested them from God, so He granted them both to me. So do not race ahead of them lest you deviate, nor lag behind them lest you perish, nor seek to teach them for they are more knowledgeable than you.[76]

The *thaqalān* are thus intertwined with each other forever. The first one, the Qur'an, remains meaningless without the other, namely the Imams, who invest it with life. From here to the creation of a well-known metaphor describing the Imams as 'the speaking Qur'an' (*kitāb Allāh al-nāṭiq*),

75 For more on the term *ahl al-bayt* and its political and factional connotations (from the pre-Islamic period to the Qur'an and its commentators), see M. Sharon, '*Ahl al-Bayt* – People of the House', *Jerusalem Studies in Arabic and Islam* 8 (1986), pp. 169–184. See also W. Madelung, 'The Hāshimiyyāt of al-Kumayt and Hāshimī Shiʿism', *Studia Islamica* 70 (1989), pp. 5–26.

76 *Tafsīr al-ʿAyyāshī*, vol. 1, p. 76, tradition 3/3.

the path is short indeed. This recurrent expression is employed *inter alia* by the Imāmī Shīʿī scholar Abū Rajab al-Bursī (d. 813/1411) with regard to Q. 23:62: 'With us is a Book speaking the truth (*wa-ladaynā kitāb yanṭiqu bi-l-ḥaqq*).' Al-Bursī comments: 'The Speaking Book is the friend [of God, i.e., the Imam]' (*al-kitāb al-nāṭiq huwa al-walī*).[77]

The version of this tradition as it appears in *Tafsīr al-ʿAyyāshī*, as well as in other Imāmī Shiʿi and Ismāʿīlī sources,[78] differs in various details from the one cited above in Muslim's *Ṣaḥīḥ*. However, it is unique particularly in its ending, which underscores the duty to subject oneself to and obey the *thaqalān*: it is forbidden to compete with them or to presume a greater knowledge or authority than theirs.

Another well-known tradition relates that the Prophet defined ʿAlī's role as a fighter for the interpretation of the Qurʾan, just as the Prophet himself fought for its revelation (*inna fīkum man yuqātilu ʿalā taʾwīl al-Qurʾān kamā qātaltu ʿalā tanzīlihi wa-huwa ʿAlī b. Abī Ṭālib*). This tradition, which a few years ago was subjected to a meticulous analysis by Mohammad Ali Amir-Moezzi,[79] is recurrent in Sunnī,[80] Imāmī Shīʿī[81] and Ismaili works.[82]

77 Abū Rajab al-Bursī, *Mashāriq anwār al-yaqīn fī asrār amīr al-muʾminīn* (Beirut, n.d.), p. 135. On al-Bursī and on another tradition he cites in a similar spirit, see P. Lory, 'Souffrir pour la vérité selon l'ésotérisme chiite de Rajab al-Borsī', in M. A. Amir-Moezzi, M. M. Bar-Asher and S. Hopkins, eds., *Le shiʿisme imāmite quarante ans après: Hommage à Etan Kohlberg* (Paris 2009), pp. 315–323, at p. 319. See also M. Ayoub, 'The Speaking Qurʾan and the Silent Qurʾan: A Study of the Principles and Development of Imāmī Tafsīr', in A. Rippin, ed., *Approaches to the History of the Interpretation of the Qurʾān* (Oxford 1988), pp. 177–198, at p. 183, note 17; and see now M. A. Amir-Moezzi, *The Silent Qurʾan and the Speaking Qurʾan: Scriptural Sources of Islam Between history and Fervor* (New York 2016).

78 For Ismāʿīlī works in which the *ḥadīth al-thaqalayn* is cited, see for example the Ṭayyibī *dāʿī* ʿAlī Ibn al-Walīd, *Tāj al-ʿaqāʾid wa-maʿdin al-fawāʾid* (Beirut 1967), p. 90. See also al-Qāḍī al-Nuʿmān, *Asās al-taʾwīl.*

79 M. A. Amir-Moezzi, 'The Warrior of *Taʾwīl*': A Poem about ʿAlī by Mollā Ṣadrā', in idem., *The Spirituality of Shiʿi Islam* (London 2011), pp. 307–337, where the expression taken from the *ḥadīth* – 'the warrior of *taʾwīl*' – forms part of the title.

80 See, for example, al-Muḥibb al-Ṭabarī, *al-Riyāḍ al-naḍira* (Tanta 1372/1953), vol. 2, pp. 52–53.

81 See, for example, *Tafsīr al-ʿAyyāshī*, vol. 1, p. 93, tradition 56/6.

82 See 'Fragments of *the Kitāb al-rushd wa-l-hidāya*, the Arabic text edited by M. Kamil Hussein', in W. Ivanow, ed., *Collectanea*, 1 (1948), pp. 185–213, at p. 211. It is noteworthy that the text in question reflects Ismaili doctrine at the beginning of the 4th/10th century. See also Abū al-Fatḥ ʿAlī b. ʿAbd al-Karīm al-Shahrastānī, *Kitāb al-milal wa-l-niḥal* (Beirut, n.d.), p. 189; Shahrastānī, *Livre des religions et des sectes*, trans. and ed. D. Gimaret, J. Jolivet and

Needless to say, the above texts represent only a few among many examples. Shīʿī exegesis, in all the currents, is rich in interpretations of Qurʾanic verses and in traditions that aim to reinforce the status and exclusive authority of the Imams as the exclusively authoritative Qurʾan interpreters.[83]

Reviewing the exegetical literature of early Imāmī Shīʿism with regard to the question of authority, one discovers two distinct tendencies that can be defined in both chronological and doctrinal terms. Chronology and doctrine, it should be stressed, are in this case intertwined. By chronology, I mean the distinction between literature written up to the major Occultation (329/941), or according to another time-definition, before the rise to power of the Buwayhid dynasty (334/945–447/1055), and the literature written after the Occultation (or after the Buwayhid period had begun). Doctrinally, I mean the distinction between the traditional and the rational attitude; to put it differently, if I may use an anachronistic terminology, the distinction between the *akhbārī* and *uṣūlī* attitude in dealing with the authority issue. The pre-Occultation period is characterised by a traditional (*akhbārī* or more precisely proto-*akhbārī*) attitude, while the post-Occultation is characterised by a more rationalist (proto-*uṣūlī*) attitude.

In the pre-Occultation period, there clearly emerges from Imāmī Shīʿī writings a rejection of rational interpretation of the Qurʾan and an emphasis on the exclusivity of the Imams as possessors of divine knowledge, including the knowledge of interpreting the Qurʾan. As stated above, at this stage the exegetical views of the authors are given indirectly. Beginning with Abū Jaʿfar al-Ṭūsī, the leading Imāmī Shīʿī theologian and commentator of the Buwayhid period, there is evidence of a remarkable shift in the attitude of the Imāmī Shīʿī exegetes. Al-Ṭūsī – representing a new tendency which may be designated 'independent exegesis' – is ambivalent about the use of *ḥadīth* in his commentary. On the one hand, he does not deny his indebtedness to tradition and explicitly states that 'the Qurʾan should only be interpreted according to sound traditions (*illā bi-l-athar al-ṣaḥīḥ*) transmitted by the Prophet, [the people] of his household and the Imams, peace be upon

G. Monnot (Paris and Louvain 1986), vol. 1, p. 543 and note 231, where other sources are cited. See also M. M. Bar-Asher, 'Outlines of Early Ismāʿīlī-Faṭimid Qurʾan Exegesis', *Journal Asiatique*, 296 (2008), pp. 257–296, at p. 267; *Tāj al-ʿaqāʾid* (op. cit., note 74), p. 90.

83 For further details regarding Imāmī Shīʿī views on the authority of the Imams as Qurʾan interpreters, see Bar-Asher, *Scripture and Exegesis*, pp. 93–101.

them, whose words are as exemplary (*ḥujja*) as those of the Prophet [himself]; it should not be interpreted rationally (*wa-inna al-qawla fīhi bi-l-raʾy lā yajūzu*)'.[84] Yet even a cursory review of his work – and that of his great follower, who lived nearly a century after him, Abū ʿAlī al-Faḍl b. al-Ḥasan al-Ṭabrisī (d. 548/1153) – reveals that (as with al-Ṭabarī, perhaps even under his inspiration) a new path had been paved. While their comprehensive Qurʾan commentaries are replete with early Imāmī Shīʿī traditions, these are presented in a radically different manner from the way similar traditions are cited in the pre-Buwayhid exegetical (and non-exegetical) works. This can be seen both in the marginal positioning of these traditions in the works of al-Ṭūsī and al-Ṭabrisī and in the omission or abbreviation of the chains of transmitters (*isnāds*). These commentaries primarily take the form of a continuous discourse in which the authors often voice their own opinions and preferences.

5. Concluding Remarks

Al-ʿAyyāshī was undoubtedly one of the leading Imāmī Shīʿī scholars at the end of the 3rd/9th and the beginning of the 4th/10th century, that is, before the Great Occultation in the year 329/941. He was not only a prolific author who is reported to have written on a wide range of topics, but also a leader of the Imāmī Shīʿī community in his homeland Samarqand and a disseminator of Shīʿism in the district of Khurasan. Unfortunately, of the numerous works which he is known to have composed, only the first part of his Qurʾan commentary – covering the first eighteen suras of the Qurʾan – has come down to us. Despite the incomplete form in which it has survived it can be regarded as one of the most important compositions in the field of early Imāmī Shīʿī exegesis. Although – like most writings of its time – it comprises a collection of hadiths, the views of the author can often be gleaned through the material he chose to include.

84 Abū Jaʿfar al-Ṭūsī, *al-Tibyān fī tafsīr al-Qurʾān*, vol. 1, p. 4. In the lines following this quotation al-Ṭūsī mentions several Companions of the Prophet and sages of Medina who were renowned for their strong opposition to rational interpretation.

It is noteworthy that although the Shīʿī dimension holds a predominant place in *Tafsīr al-ʿAyyāshī*, the work includes many traditions on topics which are not specifically Shīʿī: the life of the Prophet, the early Islamic raids (*sīra* and *maghāzī*), *Isrāʾīliyyāt*, legal questions and dogma, and *asbāb al-nuzūl* literature. The use of Sunnī subject matter, which might be construed as a deviation from the straight and narrow path of Shīʿī dogma, was probably seen by al-ʿAyyāshī as a means of stressing explicitly or implicitly certain Shīʿī concepts. Nevertheless, on many occasions al-ʿAyyāshī interprets non-Shīʿī aspects of the Qurʾanic text for their own, inherent content.

The importance of *Tafsīr al-ʿAyyāshī* can be further demonstrated by the place it holds in Shīʿī writings throughout the ages. It is frequently cited by authors of different periods and is held up as a shining example of the Shīʿī exegetical tradition.

Tafsīr al-ʿAyyāshī

Prelude

In the Name of God, the Most Compassionate, the Most Merciful

Praise be to God for His abundant favours and may His choicest blessings be upon Muḥammad and his Household. This feeble servant, utterly impoverished and in dire need of God's mercy says: I examined the interpretation *(tafsīr)* [of the Qur'an] composed by Abū al-Naḍr Muḥammad b. Mas'ūd b. Muḥammad b. 'Ayyāsh al-Sulamī together with his chains of transmission (*isnād*), and wishing to transcribe it I began searching for someone who may have heard it directly from the author. But alas, I have not found anyone in the towns surrounding us who claims to have heard it [directly or indirectly] from the author or to have received permission to transmit it on his behalf. Therefore, in light of these circumstances, I have chosen not to include the chains of transmission, but as for the rest I have written it exactly as I have found it so as to make it easy for the one who investigates it to read it, and the one who copies it to write it. If afterwards I am fortunate to encounter someone who has heard it or received permission to convey it directly from the author, I will hastily append the chains of transmission and include them exactly in the manner in which the author mentions. I ask God, the Sublime, for His help in enabling me to complete it, and my success lies only with God, upon whom alone I rely and unto Him I turn.

On the Virtues of the Qur'an:

1. Ja'far b. Muḥammad b. Mas'ūd from his father [Muḥammad b. Mas'ūd al-'Ayyāshī] from Abū 'Abd Allāh Ja'far b. Muḥammad عليه السلام who reports on his father's authority, who likewise reports on his forefathers' authority, peace be upon them all, saying, 'The Prophet ﷺ said, "O people, you are currently living at a time which is illusory in the midst of a rapidly moving journey.

مقدّمة

بسم الله الرحمن الرحيم

الحمدُ للهِ على افْضَاله، والصّلاة على محمّد وآله:

قال العبدُ الفقير إلى رحمة الله: إنّي أَمْعَنْتُ النَّظر في التفسير الذي صنّفه أبو النَّضر محمّد بن مسعود بن محمّد بن عيّاش السّلمي رحمه الله بإسناده، ورَغِبت بانتساخه، وطلبتُ مَنْ عنده سَماعًا من المصنّف أو غيره، فلم أجد في ديارنا مَن كان عنده سَماع أو إجازة منه، فحينئذٍ حَذَفتُ منه الإسناد، وكتبت الباقي على وجهه، ليكون أسهل على الكاتب والناظر فيه، فإن وَجَدتُ بعد ذلك مَن عنده سَماعٌ أو إجازةٌ من المُصنّف أتبعت الأسانيد وكَتَبْتُها على ما ذكره المصنّف، أسأل الله تعالى التوفيق لإتمامه، وما توفيقي إلاّ بالله، عليه توكّلت وإليه أُنيب.

[في فضل القرآن]

١. روى جعفر بن محمّد بن مسعود بأسانيد عن أبيه، عن أبي عبدالله جعفر بن محمّد عليهما السلام، عن أبيه، عن آبائه عليهم السلام، قال: قال رسول الله صلّى الله عليه وآله: أيّها الناس، إنّكم في زمان هُدْنَةٍ، وأنتم على ظهر السَّفر، والسيرُ بكم سريعٌ، فقد رأيتهم اللّيل والنّهار والشّمس

Surely you have seen how the night and the day, and the sun and the moon, cause all that is new to be gradually worn away – they make whatever is far away seem yet even closer, and bring nearer to fulfilment everything that has been promised. So gather your provisions and make suitable preparations for the long crossing." Thereupon Miqdād stood up and asked, "O Messenger of God, what is this abode you are calling illusory?" He replied, "It is an abode in which time causes everything to wither away and in which [you] are [temporarily] cut off [from the world that is truly everlasting]. When trials overcome you like the darkness of the night sky then hold tightly to the Qur'an, for it is a cure whose intercession is accepted and an advocate whose testimony is honest. Whosoever places it at the forefront, it will lead him to Paradise; and when someone forsakes it, it will drive him to the Fire. It is a signpost that points to the best way; a book wherein details, clear exposition and means of attaining [true felicity] are contained. It is the criterion and should not be taken lightly. It has both an exterior and a hidden interior. Its outer is decisive, whilst its inner is knowledge. Its outer is wonderfully elegant, whilst its inner is deep. It has underlying depths within which are yet farther depths. Neither can its wonders be enumerated nor its marvels fathomed. It contains the lamp of guidance and the lighthouse of wisdom. It is a guide to the commendable course of action for those who recognise it."'

2. From Yūsuf b. 'Abd al-Raḥmān[1] who, without mentioning his source, cited al-Ḥārith al-A'war[2] as having said, 'I went to the Commander of the Faithful 'Alī b. Abī Ṭālib عليه السلام and asked him, "O Commander of the Faithful! Whenever we are with you we hear things that strengthen our faith, but no sooner

1 Yūsuf b. 'Abd al-Raḥmān al-Kināsī, on whom there is scant information, was a companion of the sixth Imam Ja'far b. Muḥammad al-Ṣādiq. See Khū'ī, *Mu'jam rijāl al-ḥadith* (Qom: Manshūrāt Madīnat al-'Ilm, 1403/1982), vol. 21, p. 181 (*ḥadīth* nr. 13825) [henceforth *Mu'jam*].

2 Abū Zuhayr al-Ḥārith b. 'Abd Allāh al-A'war (65/684), a companion of the first Imam 'Alī b. Abī Ṭālib and prominent *tābi'ī*. He was a staunch supporter of 'Alī b. Abī Ṭālib and the 'Alid cause, and was part of the group of ten Kūfan dissidents who revolted against 'Uthmān b. 'Affān's govener in Kufa thereby capturing the city. See Ḥillī, *Khulāṣat al-aqwāl fī ma'rifat al-rijāl*, ed. Jawād al-Qayyūmī (Qom: Nashr al-Faqāha, 1431/2010), 122–123 (nr. 316) [henceforth *Khulāṣat al-aqwāl*]; Modarressi, H. *Tradition and Survival: A Bibliographical Survey of Early Shī'ite Literature* (Oxford: Oneworld Publications, 2003), 45–59 (nr. 2).

والقمر، يُبليان كلّ جديد، ويُقرّبان كلّ بعيد، ويأتيان بكلّ موعود، فأعدُّو الجَهَاز لبعد المَجَاز.

فقامَ المِقداد فقال: يا رَسُوْل الله، ما دار الهُدْنة؟

قالَ ﷺ: دار بلاءٍ وانقطاعٍ، فإذا التبست عليكم الفِتَن كقِطَع اللّيل المظلم، فعليكم بالقرآن، فإنّه شافِعٌ مُشفَّع، وماحِلٌ مُصدَّقٌ، من جعله أمامه قاده إلى الجنّة، ومن جعله خلفه ساقه إلى النار.

وهو الدليل يَدُلُّ على خير سبيلٍ، وهو كتابٌ فيه تفصيلٌ وبيانٌ وتحصيلٌ، وهو الفصل ليس بالهَزل، وله ظهرٌ وبطنٌ، فظاهره حِكمةٌ، وباطنه علمٌ، ظاهره أنيقٌ، وباطنه عميقٌ، له نُجُومٌ وعلى نُجُومه نُجُومٌ، لا تُحصى عجائبُه، ولا تبلى غرائبه، فيه مصابيح الهُدى ومنازل الحكمة، ودليلٌ على المعروف لمن عرفه.

٢. عن يوسف بن عبد الرّحمن، رفعه إلى الحارث الأعور، قال: دخلتُ على أمير المؤمنين عليّ بن أبي طالب عليه السلام فقلت: يا أمير المؤمنين، إنّا إذا كنّا عندك سَمِعنا الّذي نَسدّ به ديننا، وإذا خرجنا من عندك سَمِعنا أشياء مختلفةً مغموسةً، لا ندري ما هي؟

قال: أو قد فعلوها؟ قال: قلت: نعم. قال: سَمِعتُ رسول الله ﷺ يقول: أتاني جَبْرَئيل فقال: يا محمّد، سيكون في أُمّتك فِتنة، قلت: فما المخرج منها؟ فقال: كتاب الله، فيه بيان ما قبلكم من خبرٍ، وخبر ما بعدكم، وحُكم ما بينكم، وهو الفَصل ليس بالهَزل، مَن وليه مِن جبّار فعَمِل بغيره قَصَمه الله، ومن التمس الهُدى في غيره أضلّه الله.

have we departed your company than we hear of things strange and divergent, about which we have no familiar acquaintance."

He replied, "And do you act upon them?"

I replied, "Yes."

He said, "I heard the Messenger of God ﷺ say, 'Jibrā'īl came to me saying, "O Muḥammad, there will come a time when your community is afflicted by internal strife and discord."

Thereupon I asked, "What is it that will take them out of it?"

He replied, "The Book of God – it contains the account of what has preceded you and all that shall transpire after you, as well as the arbitration of everything that is between you. It is the criterion, not to be taken lightly. A tyrant who adopts it yet acts contrary to it will be destroyed by God, and whoever seeks guidance from other than what is contained within it, God shall cause him to go astray; for it is the firm handle of God and the wise narrative. It is the straight path that whims can never cause to deviate. Whatever tongues say about it, it shall never be covered up [by their falsehoods]. The frequency of recitation can never wear it out. Its wonders never cease and never shall it satiate the yearning of those seeking knowledge from it. It is the book about which the Jinn, when they heard it being recited, exclaimed: ﴾ *We have heard a wondrous Recitation, which gives guidance to righteousness* ﴿(72:1). Whoever speaks according to it, tells the truth; whoever acts by it is rewarded, and whoever holds fast to it is guided to a path which is straight. It is the mighty book to which falsehood shall never come near, neither from in front of it nor from behind – a revelation sent down from the all-Praiseworthy, the all-Wise."'"'

3. From Abū Jamīla al-Mufaḍḍal b. Ṣāliḥ[3] from one of his associates, who said, 'The Messenger of God ﷺ gave a sermon on Friday after the noon prayer. He addressed the people saying, "O people, the most Gentle and Omniscient One has informed me that no prophet lives to more than half the age of the Prophet preceding him. I believe I am about to be called back [i.e. to

3 Abū Jamīla Mufaḍḍal b. Ṣāliḥ al-Asadī al-Nakhkhās, a weak (*ḍaʿīf*) and unreliable narrator of the Imams' traditions who is accused of being a liar (*kadhdhāb*) and a fabricator of *ḥadīth*; see Ḥillī, *Khulāṣat al-aqwāl*, 407 (nr. 1648); Khūʾī, *Muʿjam*, 19:311–4 (nr. 12607); Modarressi, *Tradition and Survival*, 333 (nr. 145).

وهو حبل الله المتين، وهو الذكر الحكيم، وهو الصراط المستقيم، لا تُزيغه الأهواء، ولا تُلبِسه الألسنة، ولا يَخْلَق على الردّ، ولا تنقضي عجائبه، ولا يشبَع منه العلماء. هو الذي لم تَكِنّه الجنّ إذا سَمِعته أن قالوا: ﴿إِنَّا سَمِعْنَا قُرْآنًا عَجَبًا ۝ يَهْدِي إِلَى الرُّشْدِ﴾.

من قال به صَدَق، ومن عَمِل به أُجِر، ومن اعتصم به هُدي إلى صراطٍ مستقيمٍ، هو الكتاب العزيز الذي لا يأتيه الباطل من بين يديه ولا من خلفه، تنزيلٌ من حكيمٍ حميدٍ.

٠٣ عن أبي جميلة المفضّل بن صالح، عن بعض أصحابه، قال: «لمّا» خَطَب رسول الله ﷺ يوم الجُحْفَة بعد صلاة الظُهر، انصرف على النّاس، فقال: يا أيّها النّاس، إنّي قد نبّأني اللطيف الخبير أنّه لن يُعمَّر من نبيّ إلاّ نصف عُمر الذي يليه من قبله، وإنّي لأظُنّني أُوشِك أن أُدعى فأُجيب، وإنّي مسؤول وإنّكم مسؤولون، فهل بلّغتُكُم؟ فما ذا أنتم قائلون؟ قالوا: نَشْهَد بأنّك قد بَلّغتَ ونَصَحْتَ وجاهدت، فجزاك الله عنّا خيرًا. قال: اللّهم اشْهَد.

ثمّ قال: يا أيّها النّاس، ألم تَشهَدوا أن لا إله إلا الله، وأنّ محمّدًا عبده ورسوله، وأنّ الجنّة حقٌّ، وأنّ النار حقٌّ، وأنّ البعث حقٌّ من بعد الموت؟ قالوا: نعم. قال اللّهم اشْهَد.

ثمّ قال: يا أيّها النّاس، إنّ الله مولاي، وأنا أولى بالمؤمنين من أنفسهم، ألا مَن كنتُ مَوْلاهُ فعليٌّ مولاه، اللّهمّ والِ من والاه، وعادِ من عاداه.

ثم قال: أيّها النّاس، إنّي فَرَطكم، وأنتم واردون عليّ الحوض، وحوضي أعرض ما بين بُصرى وصَنعاء، فيه عدد النجوم قِدحان من فِضّة، ألا وإنّي سائلكم –حين تَرِدُون عليّ– عن الثّقَلين، فانظُروا كيف تَخْلُفوني فيهما حتّى تَلْقَوني. قالوا: وما الثّقلان، يا رسول الله؟

die] and I shall accept this invitation. Know that just as I am held to account [for my deeds] so too shall you be held to account [for your actions]. Have I not discharged my duty towards you and informed you [of your responsibilities]?"

Thereupon those who were present in the company of the Messenger of God replied, "We bear witness that you have conveyed the message, advised [us in the best possible manner] and strived [to accomplish the duties that were incumbent upon you], so may God reward you well on our behalf."

He exclaimed, "O God, bear witness to this!"

Then the Messenger of God صلى الله عليه وآله وسلم, asked them, "Do you bear witness that there is no god but God and that Muhammad is His servant and His Messenger? And do you bear witness that the Garden is real, that the Fire is real, that death is real, and that the Resurrection after death is real too?"

They all responded by saying, "Yes."

The Messenger of God then exclaimed, "O God, witness this!"

Then he said, "O people, God is my Master, and I have greater authority over the believers than their own selves, so of whomsoever I have been Master, ʿAlī here is to be his Master. O God, be a supporter of whoever supports him, and be an enemy to whoever opposes him."'

Then he continued, "O people, I am going ahead of you, and you will arrive at my Fountain [in the Garden] which is wider in expanse than the distance between Basra and Sanʿa. It has receptacles as numerous as the stars and cups of gold and silver. I will ask you about the two weighty things that I had left behind for you when you come to me, to see how you treated them."

They asked, "And what are these two weighty things, O Messenger of God?"

He replied, "The greater one is the Book of God – one end of it is in the hands of God, while the other is in your hands. Hold fast to it and you will never be led astray nor shall you ever be disgraced. The lesser one is my family, the People of my Household. Indeed, the most Gentle and Omniscient Lord has informed me that these two will never separate from each other until they meet me. I have requested them from God, so He granted them both to me. So do not race ahead of them lest you deviate, nor lag behind them lest you perish, nor seek to teach them for they are more knowledgeable than you."

قال: الثّقَل الأكبر: كتاب الله، سبب طَرَفه بيدي الله، وطَرف في أيديكم فاسْتَمْسِكوا به ولا تَضِلّوا ولا تذِلّوا، ألا وعترتي أهل بيتي، فإنّه قد نبّأني اللطيف الخبير أن لا يفترقا حتّى يَلقَياني، وسألت الله لهما ذلك فأعطانيه، فلا تَسْبِقوهم فتضِلّوا، ولا تُقَصّروا عنهم فتَهْلِكوا، ولا تُعلِّموهم فهم أعلم منكم.

4. From Abū 'Abd Allāh, a client of the tribe of Banū Hāshim, from Abū Sukhayla[4] who reported, 'Salmān al-Fārisī[5] and I departed for the Hajj pilgrimage from Kufa and met Abū Dharr[6] on the way, who said, "If, on your travels after passing me by there is internal strife and discord, then be careful and take heed. You must hold on to two things: the Book of God and 'Alī, the son of Abū Ṭālib, for I have heard the Messenger of God speak about 'Alī, saying of him that 'He is the first one to believe in me, and will be the first to shake my hand on the Day of Reckoning. He is the most veracious person and the criterion which demarcates between that which is truth and that which is falsehood. He is the captain of the believers, whereas wealth is captain of the hypocrites.'"'

5. From Zurāra[7] from Abū Ja'far [al-Bāqir] ﵇ who said, 'The Messenger of God delivered a sermon in Medina, and among the things he said to those gathered with him was the above-mentioned narration.'

---

4 Abū Sukhayla 'Āṣim b. Ṭarīf, on whom there is scant information, was reportedly a companion of 'Alī b. Abī Ṭālib; see Ḥillī, *Khulāṣat al-aqwāl*, 310 (nr. 1225).

5 Abū 'Abd Allāh Salmān al-Fārisī (d. *ca.* 35/656), one of the highest ranking companions of the Prophet and the first Persian convert to Islam who is lauded by both Shī'a and Sunnī Muslims alike. He was a supporter of 'Alī b. Abī Ṭālib and one of the great figures of the early Islamic community renowned for his piety, asceticism and knowledge. He is unanimously considered an authority and reliable narrator of the traditions of the Prophet and the first Imam 'Alī b. Abī Ṭālib as well as a member of the Prophet's household (*ahl al-bayt*). See Ḥillī, *Khulāṣat al-aqwāl*, 164 (nr. 477); s.v. "Salmān al-Fārisī," *Encyclopaedia of Islam*, Second Edition, vii, 701b (G. Levi Della Vida).

6 Abu Dharr Jundab b. Junāda al-Ghifārī al-Kinānī (d. 32/652–3), a leading companion of the Prophet noted for his truthfulness and loyalty to the Prophet and his family, the Ahl al-Bayt. He is highly venerated by Shī'ī Muslims as one of the Four Companions (*al-arkān al-arba'a*) who gave their unfledging support to 'Alī b. Abī Ṭālib along with Salmān al-Fārisī, 'Ammār b. Yāsir (d. 37/657) and Miqdād b. 'Amr [al-Aswad] al-Kindī. He is noted among Islamic historians for his staunch opposition to the third Islamic Caliph 'Uthmān b. 'Affān (r. 23–35/644–55) and Mu'āwiya b. Abī Ṣufiyān (r. 41–60/661–80). See Ḥillī, *Khulāṣat al-aqwāl*, 96 (nr. 215); s.v. "Abū Dharr," *Encyclopaedia of Islam*, Second Edition, i, 114b (J. Robson).

7 Abū al-Ḥasan Zurāra b. A'yan b. Sunsun al-Shaybānī (d. *ca.* 150/767), a leading companion of the fifth, sixth and seventh Imams and a reliable transmitter of their traditions. He was the most learned companion of his generation, renowned for his knowledge of the Qur'an and Imāmī traditions, as well as a *faqīh* and *mutakallim* of the Imāmī school of thought. He is counted among the so-called People of Consensus (*aṣḥāb al-ijmā'*) whose narrations Imāmī scholars consider to be correct (*ṣaḥīḥ*). Despite numerous reports which question

٤. عن أبي عبدالله مولى بني هاشم، عن أبي سُخَيْلة. قال: حججتُ أنا وسلمان الفارسي من الكوفة، فمررتُ بأبي ذرّ، فقال: انظُروا إذا كانت بعدي فِتنةٌ -وهي كائنةٌ- فعليكم بخَصْلتين: بكتاب الله، وبعليّ بن أبي طالب، فإنّي سَمِعتُ رسول الله ﷺ يقول لعليّ عليه السلام: هذا أوّل من آمن بي، وأوّل من يُصافِحني يوم القيامة، وهو الصِّدّيق الأكبر، وهو الفاروق، يَفرُقُ بين الحقّ والباطل، وهو يَعسُوب المؤمنين، والمال يَعسُوب المنافقين.

٥. عن زُرارة، عن أبي جعفر عليه السلام، قال: خَطَب رسول الله ﷺ بالمدينة، فكان فيما قال لهم «الحديث».

6. From Dawūd b. Farqad[8] who reported, 'I heard Abū 'Abd Allāh عليه السلام say, "You must adhere to the Qur'an: any verse you find therein which mentions people who were saved before you, then act upon its dicates; and likewise you should keep away from whatever you find has ruined the people before you."'

7. From al-Ḥasan b. Mūsā al-Khashshāb[9] who, without mentioning his source, cited Abū 'Abd Allāh عليه السلام as having said, 'The prerogative to rule and succeed [the Prophet] could never have been decreed for the progeny of Abū Bakr nor for the progeny of 'Umar, nor for the descendents of Umayya, nor even the descendants of Ṭalḥa and Zubayr, for this reason and this reason alone – that they cut themselves off from the Qur'an, nullified the prophetic practices and discontinued the laws [which God and His Messenger had established].'

Said the Messenger of God, 'The Qur'an is a guidance from error, an illumination from blindness, a steadfastness from stumbling, a light in the darkness, a brightness during sorrows, an immunity from ruin, a guide away from waywardness, a clarity during trials, and a deliverer from this world to the next. It contains the perfection of your faith. This is the description which the Messenger of God gave of the Qur'an, and no sooner does anyone veer away from it than he ends up in the Fire.'

8. From Mas'ada b. Ṣadaqa[10] who reported that Abū 'Abd Allāh عليه السلام said, 'God made our authority as the Household of the Prophet pivotal to the Qur'an,

---

his allegiance to the Imams and some in which he is directly condemned by them, which for the majority of Shī'ī scholars were issued by the Imams in a state of precautionary dissimulation (*taqiyya*), he is the most important narrator of the fifth and sixth Imams during their lifetimes. See Ḥillī, *Khulāṣat al-aqwāl*, 153 (nr. 441); Modarressi, *Tradition and Survival*, 404–5 (nr. 234). See Ḥillī, *Khulāṣat al-aqwāl*, 152 (nr. 441).

8 Dāwūd b. Farqad, a trustworthy and reliable narrator of the sixth and seventh Imams' traditions. See Ḥillī, *Khulāṣat al-aqwāl*, 141 (nr. 389); Modarressi, *Tradition and Survival*, 214 (nr. 52).

9 Ḥasan b. Mūsā al-Khashshāb, a well-known authority (*mashhūr*) among Imāmī narrators known for his knowledge and piety. See Ḥillī, *Khulāṣat al-aqwāl*, 104 (nr. 240).

10 Abū Muḥammad Mas'ada b. Ṣadaqa, who appears frequently in the chains of transmission in 'Ayyāshī's *tafsīr*, was a non-Imāmī narrator of the Imams' traditions. While considered by Shaykh al-Ṭūsī as a Sunnī, he is counted as a follower of one of the subsects of the Zaydī school of thought by Kishshī. See Ḥillī, *Khulāṣat al-aqwāl*, 410 (nr. 1661); Modarressi, *Traditoin and Survival*, 319–22 (nr. 138).

٦. عن داود بن فَرْقَد، قال: سَمِعتُ أبا عبدالله عليه السلام، يقول: عليكم بالقرآن، فما وَجَدتُم آية نجا بها من كان قبلكم فاعملوا بها، وما وجدتموه ممّا هلك به من كان قبلكم فاجتنبوه.

٧. عن الحسن بن موسى الخشّاب، رفعه، قال: قال أبو عبدالله عليه السلام : لا يُرْفَع الأمر والخلافة إلى آل أبي بكر أبدًا، ولا إلى آل عُمر، ولا إلى آل بني أُميّة، ولا في ولد طلحة والزبير أبدًا، وذلك أنّهم بَتَروا القرآن، وأبطلوا السُّنن، وعطّلوا الأحكام.

وقال رسول الله صلى الله عليه وآله وسلم: القرآن هُدىً من الضلالة، وتِبيانٌ من العمى، واستقالةٌ من العَثرة، ونُورٌ من الظُّلمة، وضياءٌ من الأحزان، وعصمةٌ من الهَلَكة، ورُشدٌ من الغِواية، وبيانٌ من الفِتن، وبلاغٌ من الدُنيا إلى الآخرة، وفيه كمال دينكم. فهذه صفة رسول الله صلى الله عليه وآله وسلم للقرآن، وما عَدَل أحدٌ عن القرآن إلاّ إلى النّار.

٨. عن مَسعدة بن صَدَقة قال: قال أبو عبدالله عليه السلام : إنّ الله جعل ولايتنا أهل البيت قُطب القرآن، وقُطب جميع الكُتُب، عليها يستديرُ مُحكمُ القرآن وبها نَوَّهت الكُتُب ويستبينُ الإيمان.

وقد أمر رسول الله صلى الله عليه وآله وسلم أن يُقتدى بالقرآن وآل محمّد عليهم السلام، وذلك حيث قال في آخر خُطبةٍ خَطَبها: إنّي تارك فيكم الثّقَلين: الثّقَل الأكبر، والثّقَل الأصغر. فأمّا الأكبر فكتاب ربّي، وأمّا الأصغر فِعترتي أهل بيتي، فاحفَظُوني فيهما، فلن تَضِلّوا ما تَمسّكتُم بهما.

and pivotal to all the Divine scriptures. Around it [i.e. our authority] all of the unambiguo us verses of the Qur'an revolve; it is what the Divine scriptures have extolled and by [its acknowledgment] faith becomes manifest. The Messenger of God commanded [all of you] to follow the Qur'an and the family of Muḥammad, and this is the purport of his last sermon in which he stated, "I leave among you the two weighty things: the greater one and the lesser one. The greater one is the Book of my Lord, while the lesser one is my progeny, my Household. So maintain [your faith in] me through them both, for you shall never go astray as long as you hold fast to them both.'"'

9. From Fuḍayl b. Yasār[11] who reported, 'I asked [Imam] al-Riḍā about the Qur'an, and he replied, "It is the Word of God."'

10. From al-Ḥasan b. ʿAlī who reported, 'The Messenger of God was told that his community would be afflicted with internal discord, so he asked what the way out of it would be. He was told, "The Mighty Book of God, which falsehood cannot touch, neither from in front nor from behind. It is a revelation from the all-Praiseworthy, the all-Wise. Whoever seeks knowledge from other than it will have cause to be led astray by God, and a tyrant who adopts it yet goes against it will be thwarted by God. It is the Wise Reminder, the Manifest Light and the Straight Path. It contains accounts of those who preceded you, news of what is yet to transpire after you, and the arbitration of everything you have before you. It is the Criterion, not to be taken lightly. When the Jinn heard its recitation they excitedly exclaimed, ﴾ *We have heard a wondrous Recitation, which gives guidance to righteousness* ﴿(72:1). The frequency of its recitation can never wear it out, its lessons never expire, and its wonders never cease."'

---

11 Abū al-Qāsim al-Fuḍayl b. Yasār al-Nahdī (d. before 148/765), was a loyal companion of the fifth and sixth Imams and a reliable transmitter of their traditions. He is counted among the People of Consensus (*aṣḥāb al-ijmāʿ*) in Shīʿī works of *rijāl*. See Ḥillī, *Khulāṣat al-aqwāl*, 228 (nr. 766); Modarressi, *Tradition and Survival*, 225–26 (nr. 63). Note that in this tradition Fuḍayl reports directly from the eighth Imam ʿAlī b. Mūsā al-Riḍā, which is impossible given that he died in the lifetime of Imam Jaʿfar al-Ṣādiq.

٩. عن فُضَيل بن يَسَار، قال: سألتُ الرّضا عليه السلام عن القرآن؟ فقال لي هو كلام الله.

١٠. عن الحسن بن عليّ، قال: قيل لرسول الله صلى الله عليه وآله وسلم: إنّ أُمّتك ستفتتن، فسُئل ما المخرج من ذلك؟ فقال: كتاب الله العزيز الذي لا يأتيه الباطل من بين يديه ولا من خلفه تنزيلٌ من حكيمٍ حميد، مَن ابتغى العلم في غيره أضلّه الله، ومَن ولي هذا الأمر من جبّارٍ فعَمِل بغيره قَصَمه الله، وهو الذِكر الحكيم، والنُور المبين، والصراط المستقيم.

فيه خبر ما قبلكم، ونبأ ما بعدكم، وحُكم ما بينكم، وهو الفَصْل ليس بالهَزل، وهو الذي سَمِعته الجنّ فلم تناها أن قالوا: ﴿إِنَّا سَمِعْنَا قُرْآنًا عَجَبًا ۞ يَهْدِي إِلَى الرُّشْدِ ۞ فَآمَنَّا بِهِ﴾ لا يَخْلَق على طُول الرّد، ولا تنقضي عِبَرُه، ولا تفنى عجائبُه.

11. From Muḥammad b. Ḥumrān[12], from Abū ʿAbd Allāh عليه السلام who stated, 'When God created humankind He divided them into two groups and placed into one of these groups an individual most beloved to Him. Then He further divided them into thirds, and placed His most beloved into one of these thirds. He continued to do this until He chose ʿAbd Manāf. From [the descendents of] ʿAbd Manāf He chose Hāshim, and from [his descendents] He chose ʿAbd al-Muṭṭalib. He chose ʿAbd Allāh from [the sons of] ʿAbd al-Muṭṭalib, and from ʿAbd Allāh He chose Muḥammad عليه السلام as the Messenger of God. He was the best and purest of all people to be born, so God dispatched him thereupon with the truth as a giver of glad tidings and a warner to people, and He revealed to him the Book in which there is naught except that it has been elucidated therein.'

12. From ʿAmr b. Qays[13], from Abū Jaʿfar who said, 'I heard him say that God, Blessed and most High, has not failed to mention in His Book anything that the people may need until the Day of Reckoning except that He has revealed it therein and explained it to His Messenger. He has decreed a limit for each and every thing and has placed proofs that lead to it. God penalizes those who transgress this limit.'

13. From Zurāra who reported, 'I asked Abū Jaʿfar عليه السلام about the Qur'an, so he said to me, "It is neither the creator nor something created, but rather it is the Word of the Creator."'

14. From Zurāra who reported, 'I asked Abū Jaʿfar عليه السلام whether or not the Qur'an was eternal? He replied, "No." So I asked him, "Then is it a creation?" And he replied, "No, it is the Word of the Creator."'

15. From Masʿada b. Ṣadaqa who reported from Abū ʿAbd Allāh عليه السلام who reported on his father's authority, who reported from his grandfather who narrated, 'We asked the Commander fo the Faithful to deliver a sermon to us, to

12 Abū Jaʿfar Muḥammad b. Ḥumrān al-Nahdī, a reliable narrator of traditions from the sixth Imam Jaʿfar al-Ṣādiq. See Ḥillī, *Khulāṣat al-aqwāl*, 262 (nr. 919); Modarressi, *Tradition and Survival*, 342–3 (nr. 152).

13 ʿAmr b. Qays al-Mashriqī, an unrealiable narrator of the Imams' traditions. See Ḥillī, *Khulāṣat al-aqwāl*, 377 (nr. 1012).

١١. عن محمّد بن حُمران، عن أبي عبد الله ﷺ، قال: إنّ الله لمـّا خَلَق الخلق فجعله فرقتين، فجعل خِيرَتهُ في إحدى الفرقتين، ثمّ جعلهم أثلاثاً، فجعل خِيَرَتَهُ في إحدى الأثلاث، ثمّ لم يزل يختار حتّى اختار عبد مَنَاف، ثمّ اختار من عبد مَنَاف هاشماً، ثمّ اختار من هاشم عبد المطلب، ثمّ اختار من عبد المطلب عبد الله، واختار من عبد الله محمّداً رسول الله ﷺ، فكان أطيب النّاس ولادةً وأطهرها، فبعثه الله بالحقّ بشيرًا ونذيرًا، وأنزل عليه الكّتاب، فليس من شيءٍ إلاّ في الكّتاب تِبيانه.

١٢. عن عمر بن قيس، عن أبي جعفر ﷺ، قال: سَمِعتُه يقول: إنّ الله تبارك وتعالى لم يَدَع شيئًا تحتاج إليه الأُمّة إلى يوم القيامة إلاّ أنزله في كّتابه وبَيّنه لرسوله ﷺ، وجعل لكلّ شيء حدّاً، وجعل دليلاً يَدُلّ عليه، وجعل على من تعدّى ذلك الحدّ حدّاً.

١٣. عن زُرارة، قال سألتُ أبا جعفر ﷺ عن القرآن، فقال لي: لا خالق ولا مخلوق، ولكنّه كلام الخالق.

١٤. عن زُرارة، قال سألتُه عن القرآن، أخالق هو؟ قال: لا، قلت: أمخلوق؟ قال: لا، ولكنّه كلام الخالق، يعني أنّه كلام الخالق بالفعل.

١٥. عن مَسْعَدَة بن صَدَقة، عن أبي عبد الله، عن أبيه، عن جدّه عليهم السلام، قال: خَطبنا أمير المؤمنين ﷺ خُطْبَةً فقال فيها: نَشْهَدُ أن لا إله إلا الله، وحده لا شريك له، وأنّ محمّدًا عبده ورسوله، أرسله بكّتابٍ فَصّلهُ وأحكمه وأعزّه، وحَفِظه بعلمه، وأحكمه بنُوره،

which he obliged by saying, "We bear witness that there is no god but God alone and without a partner, and that Muḥammad is His servant and His Messenger, whom He sent with a Book that He has detailed and made decisive, distinguished and protected with His knowledge, consolidated with His light and supported by His authority. He who is neither distracted by caprice nor inclined to any desire guards it lest falsehood approach it from in front or from behind. It is a revelation from the all-Wise, the all-Praiseworthy. Reciting it frequently does not wear it out, nor do its wonders ever cease. The one who uses it to express himself is honest, and the one who acts in accordance with it is rewarded. Whoever litigates with it wins, whoever fights for it is victorious, and whoever puts it into practice is guided to the straight path. Within it are accounts of all those who preceded you as well as the judgement of what is before you now, and information about your ultimate destination. He revealed it with His knowledge and called upon the angels to testify to its veracity. God, Exalted be His Splendour, says: ﴾ *But God Himself bears witness to what He has sent down to you. He sent it down with His full knowledge, and the angels too bear witness, though God is a sufficient witness.* ﴿(4:166). So God made it a light that would guide to that which is more upright and said: ﴾ *When We have recited it, repeat the recitation* ﴿(75:18) and further, ﴾ *Follow what has been sent down to you from your Lord; do not follow other masters beside Him. How seldom you take heed!* ﴿(7:3); and yet further still, ﴾ *So keep to the right course as you have been commanded, together with those who have turned to God with you. Do not overstep the limits, for He sees everything you do.* ﴿(11:112). So, in following that which has come down to you from God lies great victory, and in abandoning it a clear error. He says: ﴾ *Whoever follows My guidance when it comes to you, he will not go astray nor fall into misery.* ﴿(20:123) Thus in following it He has placed every good that can be hoped for in the life of this world and in the Hereafter, for the Qur'an both commands as well as restrains. Limits have been outlined therein, practices prescribed, and parables set forth. He has established the religion as a responsibility from Himself as well as a proof over His creation, in exchange for which He has taken their covenant and holds their souls in security so that He may elucidate to them what they should approach and what they should be wary of. Thus let the one who perishes perish through the clear proof, and let the one who succeeds do so through it, and indeed God is the all-Hearing, the Omniscient."'

وأيَّده بسلطانه، وكلأهُ مَن لم يتنزّه هوًى أو تميل به شهوةً، لا يأتيه الباطل من بين يديه ولا من خلفه تنزيل من حكيم حميد، ولا يَخْلَقه طُول الردّ ولا تفنى عجائبُه. من قال به صدق، ومنن عمل به أُجر، ومن خاصم به فَلَح، ومن قاتل به نُصِر، ومن قام به هُدي إلى صراطٍ مستقيم، فيه نبأ من كان قبلكم، والحكم فيما بينكم، وخبر معادكم.

أنزله بِعلمه وأشهد الملائكة بتصديقه، قال الله جل وجهه: ﴿لَّكِنِ ٱللَّهُ يَشْهَدُ بِمَآ أَنزَلَ إِلَيْكَ أَنزَلَهُۥ بِعِلْمِهِۦ وَٱلْمَلَٰٓئِكَةُ يَشْهَدُونَ وَكَفَىٰ بِٱللَّهِ شَهِيدًا﴾ فجعله الله نورًا يهدي للتي هي أقوم، وقال: ﴿فَإِذَا قَرَأْنَٰهُ فَٱتَّبِعْ قُرْءَانَهُۥ﴾، وقال: ﴿ٱتَّبِعُوا۟ مَآ أُنزِلَ إِلَيْكُم مِّن رَّبِّكُمْ وَلَا تَتَّبِعُوا۟ مِن دُونِهِۦٓ أَوْلِيَآءَ قَلِيلًا مَّا تَذَكَّرُونَ﴾، وقال: ﴿فَٱسْتَقِمْ كَمَآ أُمِرْتَ وَمَن تَابَ مَعَكَ وَلَا تَطْغَوْا۟ إِنَّهُۥ بِمَا تَعْمَلُونَ بَصِيرٌ﴾، ففي اتِّباع ما جاءكم من الله الفوز العظيم، وفي تركه الخطأ المبين، قال: ﴿فَإِمَّا يَأْتِيَنَّكُم مِّنِّى هُدًى فَمَنِ ٱتَّبَعَ هُدَاىَ فَلَا يَضِلُّ وَلَا يَشْقَىٰ﴾ فجعل في اتِّباعه كلّ خير يُرجى في الدنيا والآخرة.

فالقرآن آمرٌ وزاجرٌ، حدّ فيه الحدود، وسنّ فيه السُّنن، وضرب فيه الأمثال، وشرّع فيه الدّين، إعذارًا من نفسه، وحُجّة على خَلقه، أخذ على ذلك ميثاقهم، وارتهن عليه أنفسهم، ليُبيّن لهم ما يأتون وما يتّقون، ليَهْلِك من هلك عن بيّنةٍ، ويحيا من حيي عن بيّنةٍ، وإنّ الله سميعٌ عليمٌ.

16. From Yāsir al-Khādim[14] who reported from Imam al-Riḍā عليه السلام that the Imam was once asked about the Qur'an, to which he responded saying, 'May God curse the Murji'a[15] and may He curse Abū Ḥanīfa. The Qur'an is the Word of God and not a creation, regardless of where and when it is being uttered. Wherever you recite it or utter it, it is the Divine speech, the news, and the narrative accounts.'

17. From Samā'a[16] who reported that Abū 'Abd Allāh عليه السلام said, "God has revealed His Book to you and He most surely is the Honest and Upright One. It contains your news, as well as that of the people who preceded you and those who are yet to come after you; it also contains knowledge about the sky and the earth. If anyone else were to inform you of all this, you would be astonished by it."'

---

14 Yāsir al-Khādim, a client of Ḥamza b. al-Yasa', was a servant of the eighth Imam 'Alī b. Mūsā al-Riḍā. See Khū'ī, *Mu'jam*, 21:10–12 (nr. 13439).

15 The Murji'a were an early politico-religious movement which upheld the doctrine of deferred judgment (*irjā'*). According to Murji'ī doctrine, faith (*īmān*) is entirely synonymous with the belief in the declaration of Islam, the *shahāda*, i.e. a person's delcaration of the unity of God and the messengership of the Prophet Muhammad. A person's faith is therefore unaffected by their actions, and whatever the consequences of these acts, their judgment, according to Murji'ī doctrine, is left to God to judge; s.v. "Murdji'a," *Encyclopaedia of Islam*, Second Edition, vii, 605b (W. Madelung).

16 Samā'a b. Mihrān b. 'Abd al-Raḥmān al-Ḥaḍramī, known by the agnomens Abū Nāshira and Abū Muḥammad, was an adherent of the Wāqifiyya – a subsect of the Shī'a whose followers believed that the seventh Imam Mūsā al-Kāẓim had been raised by God only to return as the Mahdī. (On the Wāqifiyya, s.v. "Al-Wāḳifa," *Encyclopaedia of Islam*, Second Edition, xi, 103a [H. Halm]; M. Ali Buyukkara, "The Schism in the Party of Mūsā al-Kāẓim and the Emergence of the *Wāqifa*," *Arabica* 42:1 (2000): 78–99.) He died in Medina and is considered by the majority of Shī'ī-Imāmī scholars to be extremely reliable in his narrations of the Imams' traditions. See Ḥillī, *Khulāṣat al-aqwāl*, 356 (nr. 1410); Modarressi, *Tradition and Survival*, 369–70 (nr. 190).

١٦. عن ياسر الخادم، عن الرضا عليه السلام أنّه سُئل عن القرآن، فقال: لعن الله المُرجِئة، ولعن الله أبا حنيفة، إنّه كلام الله غير مخلوقٍ حيثما تكلّمتَ به، وحيثما قرأتَ ونَطَقتَ، فهو كلامٌ وخبرٌ وقَصَصٌ.

١٧. عن سَماعة، قال: قال أبو عبد الله عليه السلام: إنّ الله أنزل عليكم كتابه، وهو الصّادق البرّ، فيه خبركم، وخبر مَن قبلكم؟، وخبر مَن بعدكم، وخبر السّماء والأرض، ولو أتاكم مَن يُخْبِركم عن ذلك لتعجبّكم مِن ذلك.

Casting aside reports (*riwāyāt*) that contradict the Qur'an:

1. From Hishām b. al-Ḥakam[17], from Abū ʿAbd Allāh عليه السلام who states that 'The Messenger of God said in a sermon delivered either in Mina or Mecca, "O people, whatever you hear being reported from me that agrees with the Qur'an, then know I have indeed said it. And whatever reaches you on my authority that does not agree with the Qur'an, then be sure I have not said it."'

2. From Ismāʿīl b. Abī Ziyād al-Sakūnī[18], from Abū Jaʿfar عليه السلام on his father's authority, from ʿAlī عليه السلام who said, 'To suspend judgment in the face of ambiguity is better than plunging into disaster; and your casting aside a report that you have not narrated is better for you than narrating a report that you have not comprehended. Every truth has a reality to it, and every right action a

---

17 Abū Muḥammad Hishām b. al-Ḥakam (d. *ca.* 199/815), a renowned *mutakallim* and the most distinguished apologist of the proto-Imāmiyya *madhhab* in Kufa and later toward the end of his life in Baghdad. While there are reports in which the Imams question some of Hishām's theological views, he is regarded by virtually all Shīʿa scholars of *rijāl* to have been a reliable and trustworthy narrator of the Imams' traditions and one of the earliest (if not the earliest) Imāmī scholars to participate in the *kalām* debates of the ninth century. See DeAngelis, Michele Angela Margherita, *The Collected Fragments of Hishām b. al-Ḥakam, Imamite* mutakallim *of the Second Century of the Hegira: together with a Discussion of the Sources for and an Introduction to His Teaching* (Unpublished Phd Thesis, Albany: New York University, 1974); Ḥillī, *Khulāṣat al-aqwāl*, 288–89 (nr. 1061); Modarressi, *Tradition and Survival*, 259–68 (nr. 87); s.v. "Hishām b. al-Ḥakam," *Encyclopaedia of Islam*, Second Edition, iii, 496–8 (W. Madelung).

18 Ismāʿīl b. Abī Ziyād al-Sakūnī al-Shuʿayrī, deemed realiable even though he was Sunnī. See Ḥillī, *Khulāṣat al-aqwāl*, 316 (nr. 1238); Modarressi, *Tradition and Survival*, 304–5 (nr. 116). Note that scholars of *rijāl* make an important distinction between the *ʿadāla* of the narrators in the chains of transmission of the Imams' traditions and their *wathāqa*. The term *ʿadāla*, usually translated in a somewhat misleadingly manner as 'justice', more accurately signifies the confessional identity of transmitters and whether or not an individual upheld the Shīʿī doctrine of the Imamate: a narrator (*rāwī*) who acknowledges the divine authority (*walāya*) of the Imams and thus identifies himself as a Shīʿī is described as *ʿādil*. However, the *ʿadāla* of a narrator is in no way a guarantor of his or her reliability *qua* narrator, and thus a distinction is made between the confessional identity (i.e. *ʿadāla*) of a narrator and their trustworthiness/reliability (i.e. *wathāqa*) in reporting the traditions of the Imams. Many individuals who were not upholders of the Shīʿī doctrine of *walāya* are deemed reliable (*thiqa*) in their transmission of the Imams' traditions. Ismāʿīl b. Abī Ziyād al-Sakūnī is a good example of someone who Shīʿī scholars consider to be *thiqa* even though he was not *ʿādil.*

باب ترك الرواية التي بخلاف القرآن

١. عن هِشام بن الحكم، عن أبي عبد الله ﵇، قال: قال رسول الله ﷺ في خُطبةٍ بمنىً أو بمكّة: يا أيّها النّاس، ما جاءكم عنّي يُوافق القرآن فأنا قُلتُه، وما جاءكم عنّي لا يُوافق القرآن فلم أقُله.

٢. عن إسماعيل بن أبي زياد السّكُوني، عن جعفر، عن أبيه، عن عليّ ﵃، قال: الوقوفُ عند الشُّبهة خيرٌ من الاقتحام في الهَلَكة، وتركُكَ حديثًا لم تَروِه خيرٌ من روايتك حديثًا لم تُحْصِه، إنّ على كُلّ حقٍّ حقيقةً، وعلى كلّ صواب نُورًا، فما وافق كتاب الله فخُذُوه به، وما خالف كتاب الله فدَعُوه.

light. So take whatever is in agreement with the Book of God and discard whatever contradicts it.'

3. From Muḥammad b. Muslim[19] who narrated Abū 'Abd Allāh عليه السلام as saying, 'O Muḥammad, whatever narration comes to you concerning an upright or corrupt person and it correlates with the Qur'an, accept it. And whatever narration you hear concerning an upright or corrupt person that contradicts the Qur'an, reject it.'

4. From Ayyūb b. Ḥurr[20] who narrated, 'I heard Abū 'Abd Allāh عليه السلام say, "Everything must be referred to the Book and the Sunnah [Prophetic practice]; any narration you hear that does not correspond with the Qur'an is simply prattle speech."'

5. From Kulayb al-Asadī who said, 'I heard Abū 'Abd Allāh عليه السلام say, "Any narration that reaches you on our authority that is not substantiated by the Qur'an is false."'

6. From Sadīr[21] who narrated, 'Abū Ja'far عليه السلام and Abū 'Abd Allāh عليه السلام only licensed us to narrate that which was in agreement with the Qur'an and the practice of His Prophet.'

7. From al-Ḥasan b. al-Jahm[22], from the Righteous Servant[23] عليه السلام who said, 'When two conflicting narrations come to you compare them with Book of God and our narrations, and if it resembles them both then it is true, and if it does not resemble them both then it is false.'

---

19 Abū Ja'far Muḥammad b. Muslim b. Riyāḥ al-Awqaṣ al-Ṭaḥḥān (d. 150/767–8), a prominent member of the Imāmī sect in Kufa and a trustworthy companion of Muḥammad al-Bāqīr and Ja'far al-Ṣādiq who is counted among the People of Consensus (*aṣḥāb al-ijmā'*) in Shī'ī works of *rijāl*. See Ḥillī, *Khulāṣat al-aqwāl*, 251–2 (nr. 858).

20 Ayyūb b. al-Ḥurr al-Ju'fī, reliable narrator from Imam Ja'far al-Ṣādiq. See Ḥillī, *Khulāṣat al-aqwāl*, 59 (nr. 59); Modarressi, *Tradition and Survival*, 212–3 (nr. 50).

21 Abū al-Faḍl Sadīr b. Ḥakīm, generally considered a reliable narrator of the Imams' traditions. See Ḥillī, *Khulāṣat al-aqwāl*, 165 (nr. 479).

22 Abū Muḥammad al-Ḥasan b. al-Jahm b. Bukayr b. A'yan al-Shaybānī, a realible narrator from Mūsā al-Kāẓim and 'Alī al-Riḍā. See Ḥillī, *Khulāṣat al-aqwāl*, 106 (nr. 251).

23 The Righteous Servant (*al-'abd al-ṣāliḥ*) was one of the titles of Imam Mūsā al-Kāẓim.

٣. عن محمّد بن مسلم، قال: قال أبو عبدالله عليه السلام: يا محمّد ما جاءك في روايةٍ من برٍّ أو فاجرٍ يُوافق القرآن فخُذ به، وما جاءك في رواية من برٍّ أو فاجرٍ يُخالف القرآن فلا تأخُذ به.

٤. عن أيّوب بن حُرّ، قال: سَمعتُ أبا عبدالله عليه السلام يقول: كلُّ شيءٍ مردودٌ إلى الكتاب والسُّنّة، وكلُّ حديثٍ لا يُوافق كتاب الله فهو زُخرُف.

٥. عن كُليب الأسدي، قال: سَمعتُ أبا عبدالله عليه السلام يقول: ما أتاكم عنّا من حديثٍ لا يُصدّقه كتاب الله فهو باطل.

٦. عن سَدِير قال: كان أبو جعفر وأبو عبدالله عليهما السلام يقولان: لا تُصدّق علينا إلا بما يُوافق كتاب الله وسُنّة نبيّه صلى الله عليه وآله وسلم.

٧. عن الحسن بن الجَهْم، عن العبد الصالح عليه السلام، قال: إذا كان جاءك الحديثان المختلفان، فقِسها على كتاب الله وعلى أحاديثنا، فإن أشبههما فهو حقّ، وإن لم يُشبهها فهو باطل.

The Content of what has been revealed in the Qur'an:

1. From Abū al-Jārūd[24] who said, 'I heard Abū Ja'far عليه السلام state that "The Qur'an has been revealed as four quarters: one part therein concerns us [the Family of the Prophet] and another part concerning our enermies; a third part concerns the laws and what has been made obligatory; and a final part concerning practices and parables. Of these, the most noble part is the one concerning us."'

2. From 'Abd Allāh b. Sinān[25] who said, 'I asked Abū 'Abd Allāh عليه السلام about the Qur'an and the Criterion (*furqān*). He answered by saying, "The Qur'an is the Scripture as a whole and contains a foretelling of all that shall come to pass, while the Criterion is every unambiguous verse upon which actions are based. Every verse which is unambiguous is therefore a 'criterion'."'

3. From al-Aṣbagh b. Nubāta[26] who said, 'I heard the Commander of the Faithful عليه السلام say, "The Qur'an was sent down in three parts: a part concerning us [the Family of the Prophet] and those hostile toward us; a part which deals with practices and parables; and a third part to do with obligations and regulations."'

---

24 Abū al-Jārūd Ziyād b. al-Mundhir al-Hamdānī, the eponymous founder of the Zaydī sect known as the Jārūdiyya (s.v. "Al-Djārūdiyya," *Encyclopaedia of Islam*, Second Edition, ii, 103a [M. G. S. Hodgson]), was a companion of Imam Muḥammad al-Bāqir and a regular narrator of Imam Ja'far al-Ṣādiq's traditions. He is regarded by Imāmī scholars in a negative light and considered blameworthy and unreliable. See Ḥillī, *Khulāṣat al-aqwāl*, 348 (nr. 1378); Modarressi, *Tradition and Survival*, 121–5 (nr. 13).

25 'Abd Allāh b. Sinān b. Tarīf, originally of Kufa, was a clerk employed at the court of four Abbasid Caliphs: Abū Ja'far al-Manṣūr (r. 754–775), al-Mahdī (r. 775–785), Abū Muḥammad Mūsā b. Mahdī al-Hādī (r. 785–86) and Hārūn al-Rashīd (r. 786–809). A companion of the sixth Imam Ja'far al-Ṣādiq, he is regarded to be a reliable (*thiqa*) and trustworthy narrator. See Ḥillī, *Khulāṣat al-aqwāl*, 192 (nr. 599); Modarressi, *Tradition and Survival*, 157–61 (nr. 15).

26 Abū al-Qāsim al-Aṣbagh b. Nubāta al-Tamīmī al-Ḥanẓalī al-Mujāshi'ī, a close disciple of 'Alī b. Abī Ṭālib. He fought alongside the army of 'Alī in the battles of the Camel (36/656) and Ṣiffīn (36/657). For Shī'īs he is considered a loyal and pious companion of 'Alī b. Abī Ṭālib and a reliable narrator of his traditions. See Ḥillī, *Khulāṣat al-aqwāl*, 77 (nr. 141); Modarressi, *Tradition and Survival*, 59–73 (nr. 3).

فيما أنزل القرآن

١. عن أبي الجارود قال: سَمِعتُ أبا جعفر عليه السلام يقول: نزل القرآن على أربعة أرباع: رُبع فينا، ورُبع في عدوّنا، ورُبع في فرائضٍ وأحكام، ورُبع سُنن وأمثال، ولنا كرائم القرآن.

٢. عن عبدالله بن سِنان، قال: سألتُ أبا عبدالله عليه السلام عن القرآن والفُرقان، قال: القرآن: جملة الكتاب، وأخبار ما يكون، والفرقان: المحكم الذي يُعمل به، وكُلّ محكمٍ فهو فُرقان.

٣. عن الأصبغ بن نُبَاتة، قال: سَمِعتُ أمير المؤمنين عليه السلام يقول: نزل القرآن أثلاثاً: ثُلث فينا وفي عدوّنا، وثُلث سُنن وأمثال، وثُلث فرائض وأحكام.

4. From 'Abd Allāh b. Bukayr[27], from Abū 'Abd Allāh ﷺ who said, 'The Qur'an came down as: "It is you I address [O Prophet] but let the neighbour also take heed."'

5. From Ibn Abī 'Umayr[28], from whoever narrated it to him, from Abū 'Abd Allāh ﷺ that he said, 'Whenever God admonishes His Prophet, He intends by it other people whose example has already been mentioned in the Qur'an, such as His verse: ﴿ *If we had not made you stand firm, you would almost have inclined a little towards them* ﴾(17:74) by which God intended someone other than the Prophet.'

6. From Abū Baṣīr[29] who said, 'I heard Abū 'Abd Allāh ﷺ say, "The Qur'an both restrains as well as enjoins – it enjoins towards the Garden and restrains against the Fire."'

---

27 Abū 'Alī 'Abd Allāh b. Bukayr (=Ibn Bukayr) b. A'yan, though he belonged to the Faṭḥiyya *madhhab*, is deemed a reliable and trustworthy transmitter of the Imams' narrations. See Ḥillī, *Khulāṣat al-aqwāl*, 195 (nr. 609); Modaressi, *Tradition and Survival*, 140–1 (nr. 8).

28 Muḥammad b. Ziyād (=Abū 'Umayr) b. 'Īsā (=Abū Aḥmad) al-Azdī (d. 217/832–3), a high-ranking companion of the seventh, eighth and ninth Imams and a leading figurehead of the Imāmī school in his day. He is regarded by Shī'ī tradition as one of the *aṣḥāb al-ijmā'* (i.e. those companions in whom there is consensus *vis-à-vis* their reliability) who, on account of his unwavering loyalty and fidelity (*tashayyu'*) toward the 'Alid Imams, was imprisoned by the Abbasid caliphs for a period of almost seventeen years. He is an author to whom a number of writings have been attributed in *kalām*, *fiqh* and *ḥadīth*. He died in the lifetime of Imam Muḥammad al-Jawād in Baghdad in the year 217/832–3 at an elderly age approximating 90 years. See Khū'ī, *Mu'jam*, 15: 291–306 (nr. 10043).

29 Abū Baṣīr Yaḥyā' b. al-Qāsim al-Asadī (d. 150/767) was a high-ranking companion of Imam Muḥammad al-Bāqir and Imam Ja'far al-Ṣādiq and possibly Imam Mūsā al-Kāẓim. He is said to have been the leader of the Imāmī community in Kufa and has narrated a significant number of traditions from the Imams in Shī'ī *ḥadīth* compilations. He is regarded by the majority of Imāmī scholars to be one of the six major companions of the fifth and sixth Imams who are known collectively as the People of Consensus (*aṣḥāb al-ijmā'*), indicating their reliability and acceptance as narrators of *ḥadīth* among the Imamiyya. However, as the editor of al-'Allāma al-Ḥillī's *Khulāṣat al-aqwāl* notes, the 'Allāma confused Abū Baṣīr Yaḥyā' b. al-Qāsim al-Asadī with his namesake Yaḥyā b. al-Ḥadhā' al-Wāqifī, which is why some later scholars considered him to be a Wāqifī. See Ḥillī, *Khulāṣat al-aqwāl*, 416–17 (nr. 1687); Modarressi, *Tradition and Survival*, 395 (nr. 220).

٤. عن عبدالله بن بُكير، عن أبي عبدالله ﷺ، قال: نزل القرآن بـ (إيّاك أعني واسمعي يا جارة).

٥. عن ابن أبي عمير، عمّن حدثّه، عن أبي عبدالله ﷺ، قال: ما عاتب الله نبيّه فهو يعني به من قد مضى في القرآن، مثل قوله: ﴿وَلَوْلَا أَنْ ثَبَّتْنَاكَ لَقَدْ كِدْتَ تَرْكَنُ إِلَيْهِمْ شَيْئًا قَلِيلًا﴾. عنى بذلك غيره.

٦. عن أبي بصير، قال: سَمِعتُ أبا عبدالله ﷺ يقول: إنّ القرآن زاجرٌ وآمرٌ، يأمُرُ بالجنّة، ويَزْجُرُ عن النار.

7. From Muḥammad b. Khālid b. al-Ḥajjāj al-Karkhī, from one of his associates who, without mentioning his source, reported Khaythama [b. ʿAbd al-Raḥmān al-Juʿfī][30] as having narrated that Abū Jaʿfar عليه السلام said, "Khaythama, the Qur'an was sent down in three parts: one part therein is about us and those who love us; another part concerns those who are our enemies as well as those who opposed our predecessors; and a third part dealing with practices and parables. Nothing of the Qur'an would have remained if a verse should have been sent down for a particular people who have long since passed away, since that verse would have died with their death. Nay, the Qur'an shall continue to remain from its beginning to its end so long as the heavens and the earth exist. Whichever of its verses is recited by a community of people there is something in what they have read concerning them, be it something good or something bad."'

The meaning of the terms 'abrograting' (*al-nāsikh*), 'abrogated' (*al-mansūkh*), 'the apparent' (*al-ẓāhir*), 'the hidden' (*al-bāṭin*), 'the ambiguous' (*al-muḥkam*) and 'the unambiguous' (*al-mutashābih*):

1. From Abū Muḥammad al-Hamadānī, from someone anonymous, from Abū ʿAbd Allāh عليه السلام. He [the anonymous reporter] said, 'I asked him [Imam Jaʿfar al-Ṣādiq] about those verses which are abrogating and those which are abrogated and about those which are unambiguous and those which are ambiguous. The Imam replied, "The verse which abrogates is the one [whose ruling is] fixed, whereas the abrogated is the one [whose ruling] was [but no longer is]. The unambiguous verse is that which is acted upon [due to its clarity] whereas the ambiguous is the verse in which a part of it resembles another."

2. From Jābir who said, 'Abū ʿAbd Allāh عليه السلام said, "Jābir, the Qur'an has a hidden part, and its hidden part has an apparent aspect." Then he continued, "O Jābir, nothing else is at a greater distance from man's comprehension than this, for the beginning of a verse is revealed concerning something, its

---

30 Khaythama b. ʿAbd al-Raḥmān al-Juʿfī, described as someone whose narrations are deemed preferable. See Ḥillī, *Khulāṣat al-aqwāl*, 139 (nr. 385).

٧. عن محمّد بن خالد بن الحجّاج الكَرْخي، عن بعض أصحابه رفعه إلى خَيْثَمَة، قال: قال أبو جعفر: يا خَيْثَمَة، القرآن نزل أثلاثًا: ثُلُث فينا وفي أحبّائنا، وثُلُث في أعدائنا وعدوّ من كان قبلنا، وثُلُث سُنّة ومثل، ولو أنّ الآية إذا نزلت في قومٍ ثمّ مات أُولئك القوم ماتت الآية، لما بقي من القرآن شيءٌ ولكنّ القرآن يجري أوّله على آخره ما دامت السّماوات والأرض، ولكلّ قوم آيةٌ يتلونها، وهم منها من خيرٍ أو شرّ.

تفسير الناسخ والمنسوخ والظاهر والباطن والمحكم والمتشابه

١. عن أبي محمّد الهَمداني، عن رجل، عن أبي عبد الله عليه السلام، قال: سألتُهُ عن الناسخ والمنسوخ، والمحكم والمتشابه، قال: الناسخ: الثابت، والمنسوخ: ما مضى، والمحكم: ما يُعمل به، والمتشابه: الذي يُشبِه بعضه بعضًا.

٢. عن جابر، قال: قال أبو عبد الله عليه السلام: يا جابر، إنّ للقرآن بطنًا، وللبطن ظهرًا، ثمّ قال: يا جابر، وليس شيءٌ أبعد من عقول الرجال منه، إنّ الآية لينزل أوّلها في شيءٍ، وأوسطها في شيءٍ، وآخرها في شيءٍ، وهو كلامٌ متّصلٌ مُتصرّف على وجوه.

middle may apply to another thing, and its end with regard to something else. It is but one continuous form of speech applying to all its various dimensions."'

3. From Zurāra, from Abū Jaʿfar عليه السلام who said, 'The Qur'an has been revealed in a manner that contains abrogating and abrogated verses.'

4. From Ḥumrān b. Aʿyan[31], from Abū Jaʿfar عليه السلام who said, 'The apparent sense of the Qur'an refers to those about whom the verse was revealed, and its hidden aspect to those who acted as the former ones did.'

5. From Fuḍayl b. Yasār who narrated, 'I asked Abū Jaʿfar عليه السلام about this report: "There is not a single verse in the Qur'an that does not consist of an apparent and hidden meaning, nor does it contain a single letter therein except that it has a boundary, and each boundary something further yet to be discovered." What does he mean by the statement that it has an apparent and hidden meaning?' He replied, "There is the apparent sense, and the hidden is its [esoteric] interpretation (*ta'wīl*) such as what has passed and what has not yet come to pass, but they run their course just like the sun and the moon continue to run their course. Whenever part of it applies, it happens [in actuality]. God, most High, says ﴿ *Only God and those firmly rooted in knowledge know their* [*the ambiguous verses*] *meaning.* ﴾(3:7) [And we are among those who know their meaning.]"'

6. From Abū Baṣīr who said, 'I heard Abū ʿAbd Allāh عليه السلام say, "The Qur'an contains unambiguous and ambiguous verses. As for the verses which are unambiguous, we have faith in them and act upon them, and hold ourselves accountable to them. As for the ambiguous verses we need only have faith in them, but we do not act upon them. [That is to say, we do not base our judgments upon them.]"'

---

31 Ḥumrān b. Aʿyan al-Shaybānī, a *tābiʿī* of Kufan origin who was reportedly described by Imam Muḥammad al-Bāqir as 'One of our Shīʿa in this world and the next.' He is regarded as an eminent transmitter of the Imams' traditions among Imāmī traditionists. See Ḥillī, *Khulāṣat al-aqwāl*, 134–5 (nr. 361).

٣. عن زُرارة، عن أبي جعفر ﵇، قال: نَزَل القرآن ناسخًا ومنسوخًا.

٤. عن حُمران بن أَعْين، عن أبي جعفر ﵇، قال: ظَهْر القرآن الذين نزل فيهم، وبطنه الذين عَملوا بمثل أعمالهم.

٥. عن الفُضيل بن يَسار، قال: سألتُ أبا جعفر ﵇ عن هذه الرواية: ما في القرآن آيةٌ إلاّ ولها ظَهْر وبَطْن، وما فيه حرفٌ إلاّ وله حدٌّ، ولكلّ حدٍّ مُطَّلع، ما يعين بقوله: لها ظَهْرٌ وبَطْن؟

قال: ظَهْره وبَطْنه تأويلُهُ، منه ما مضى، ومنه ما لم يَكنْ بعد، يجري كما تجري الشمس والقمر، كلمّا جاء منه شيءٌ وقع، قال الله تعالى: ﴿وَمَا يَعْلَمُ تَأْوِيلَهُ إِلَّا اللَّهُ وَالرَّاسِخُونَ فِي الْعِلْمِ﴾ نحن نعلمه.

٦. عن أبي بصير، قال: سَمعتُ أبا عبدالله ﵇ يقول: إنّ القرآن فيه محكمٌ ومتشابه، فأمّا المحكم فنُؤمن به ونعمل به ونَدين به، وأمّا المتشابه فنُؤمن به ولا نعمل به.

7. From Mas'ada b. Ṣadaqa who said, 'I asked Abū 'Abd Allāh عليه السلام about the verses that are abrogating and abrogated, unambiguous and ambiguous. He replied, "The abrogating verse is the one [whose ruling] is fixed and upon which actions [and judgments] are based, whereas the abrogated is that verse [whose ruling] used to be practiced but was then replaced by the one abrogating it. The ambiguous verse is that which equivocates the mind of the one who is ignorant of it."'

8. From Jābir who said, 'I asked Abū Ja'far عليه السلام about something to do with the interpretation of the Qur'an, so he answered me. Then I asked him a second time, and he gave me a totally different reply, so I said, "May I be your ransom – you replied today with an answer different to the one you gave yesterday regarding the same matter." So he said to me, "Jābir, the Qur'an has a hidden aspect which itself has an aspect that is apparent. O Jābir, nothing is more difficult for people to grasp than the interpretation of the Qur'an. The beginning of a verse may pertain to one thing and its end to something else. It is but one form of continuous speech albeit applicable in different senses."'

9. From Abū 'Abd al-Raḥmān al-Sulamī that 'Alī عليه السلام passed by a judge and asked him, 'Are you conversant with the verses that abrogate and those which are are abrogated?' He replied, 'No.' So he said, 'You are in trouble, and in turn you have caused others ruin; the interpretation of each and every letter of the Qur'an has several aspects.'

٧. عن مَسْعَدة بن صَدقة، قال: سألتُ أبا عبدالله عليه السلام عن الناسخ والمنسوخ والمحكم والمتشابه؟ قال: الناسخ: الثابت المعمول به، والمنسوخ ما قد كان يُعْمَل به ثمّ جاء ما نسخه، والمتشابه: ما اشتبه على جاهله.

٨. عن جابر، قال: سألتُ أبا جعفر عليه السلام عن شيءٍ في تفسير القرآن فأجابني، ثمّ سألته ثانيةً فأجابني بجوابٍ آخر، فقلت: جُعلت فداك، كنتَ أجبتَ في هذه المسألة بجواب غير هذا قبل اليوم؟

فقال عليه السلام لي: يا جابر، إنّ للقرآن بطنًا، وللبطن بطن وظهر، وللظهر ظهر. يا جابر، وليس شيءٌ أبعد من عقول الرجال من تفسير القرآن، إنّ الآية ليكون أوّلها في شيء، وآخرها في شيءٍ، وهوكلام متّصل يتصرّف على وجوه.

٩. عن أبي عبد الرّحمن السُّلمي، أنّ عليًّا عليه السلام مرّ على قاضٍ فقال: هل تعرف الناسخ من المنسوخ؟ فقال: لا. فقال: هلكت وأهلكت.

The Interpretation of the Seven Revealed Recitations of the Qur'an having various aspects:

1. From Ibrāhīm b. 'Umar[32] who said, 'Abū 'Abd Allāh ﷺ said, "In the Qur'an there is mention of what has already happened, what is happening right now, and what shall happen in the future. Because it named certain individuals by name, part of it was abandoned – yet each individual name can be interpreted in several senses the number of which cannot be enumerated. Those who are the trustees [of the Messenger of God] know them.'

2. From Ḥammād b. 'Uthmān[33] who said, 'I said to Abū 'Abd Allāh ﷺ, "The traditions attributed to you have divergent meanings." Then he said, "The Qur'an came down in seven recitations (*aḥruf*), and the least which befits the Imam is to pass a judgment according to each and every one of them. He then recited the following verse: ﴿ *This is Our gift, so grant or withhold without account* ﴾(38:39).'

References to the Imams in the Qur'an:

1. From Ibn Muskān[34] who reported that Abū 'Abd Allāh ﷺ said, "Whoever is unaware of our authority in the Qur'an will not be able to avoid tribulations."'

---

32 Abū Isḥāq Ibrāhīm b. 'Umar al-Yamānī al-Ṣan'ānī, a Yemeni Shī'ī, was a trustworthy reporter according to Najāshī, though Ibn al-Ghaḍā'irī deems him to be very weak (*ḍā'īf jiddan*). 'Allāma al-Ḥillī argues that his narrations ought to be relied on given that there are many doubts surrounding the reports in which he is criticised. See Ḥillī, *Khulāṣat al-aqwāl*, 51 (nr. 15); Modarressi, *Tradition and Survival*, 291–3 (nr. 107).

33 Ḥammād b. 'Uthmān b. 'Amr b. Khālid al-Fazarī (d. 190/805–6), originally of Kufa and the brother of 'Abd Allāh b. 'Uthmān, both of whom are considered realible narrators of the Imams' traditions. See Ḥillī, *Khulāṣat al-aqwāl*, 125 (nr. 325); Modarressi, *Tradition and Survival*, 239 (nr. 72).

34 Abū Muḥammad 'Abd Allāh b. Muskān (d. before 183/799), a trustworthy companion of Imam 'Alī b. Mūsā al-Riḍā. See Ḥillī, *Khulāṣat al-aqwāl*, 194 (nr. 607); Modarressi, *Tradition and Survival*, 150–5 (nr. 13).

تأويل كلّ حرفٍ من القرآن على وجوه

١. عن إبراهيم بن عمر، قال: قال أبو عبد الله ﷺ: إن في القرآن ما مضى وما يَحدُث وما هو كائن، كانت فيه أسماء الرّجال فأُلقيت، وإنّما الاسم الواحد منه في وجوه لا تُحصى، يَعْرِف ذلك الوُصاة.

٢. عن حمّاد بن عُثمان، قال: قلتُ لأبي عبد الله ﷺ: إن الأحاديث تختلف عنكم؟ قال: فقال: إنّ القرآن نزل على سبعة أحرف، وأدنى ما للإمام أن يُفتي على سبعة وجوه، ثمّ قال: ﴿هَـٰذَا عَطَآؤُنَا فَٱمْنُنْ أَوْ أَمْسِكْ بِغَيْرِ حِسَابٍ﴾.

ما عنى به الأئمّة عليهم السلام من القرآن

١. عن ابن مُسكان قال: قال أبو عبد الله ﷺ: من لم يَعْرِف أمرنا من القرآن لم يَتَنكَّب الفِتَن.

2. From Ḥanān b. Sadīr[35] on his father's authority, who narrated that Abū Ja'far عليه السلام said, "O Abū al-Faḍl, we have a God-given right in God's decisive book, should they erase it and deny it being from God or if they are actually unaware of it, it does not make the slightest difference."'

3. From Muḥammad b. Muslim who narrated Abū Ja'far عليه السلام as saying, "O Muḥammad, when you hear God mentioning anyone from this community in a positive light then know that we are the ones he is intending. And when you hear Him disparage a group of people from the past, then know that they are our enemies."'

4. From Dāwūd b. Farqad, from whoever narrated it to him, from Abū 'Abd Allāh عليه السلام who said, 'Were the Qur'an to be recited in the way it had been revealed, you would have found us mentioned therein by name.'

5. Sa'īd b. al-Ḥusayn al-Kindī[36] narrated the same report from Abū Ja'far عليه السلام adding: 'just as those before us have been mentioned by name' [to the end of the previous report].

6. From Muyassar [b. 'Abd al-'Azīz][37], from Abū Ja'far عليه السلام who said, 'Had it not been for the fact that some additions and some omissions have occurred to the book of God, our right would not have been unknown to intelligent people. When our Qā'im rises and speaks, the Qur'an will assent to the truth of what he says.'[38]

---

35 Ḥanān b. Sadīr al-Ṣayrafī, a close associate of Mūsā al-Kāẓim and an adherent of the Wāqifī sect. Shaykh al-Ṭūsī considers him to be a reliable narrator. 'Allāma al-Ḥillī on the other hand suspends judgment on his reliability. See Ḥillī, *Khulāṣat al-aqwāl*, 342 (nr. 1354); Modaressi, *Tradition and Survival*, 240 (nr. 74).

36 This may be a transcription error for Sa'īd b. al-Ḥasan al-Kindī.

37 Muyassar b. 'Abd al-'Azīz, a reliable narrator of the Imams' traditions and himself the subject of numerous traditions in which he is praised by Imams. See Ḥillī, *Khulāṣat al-aqwāl*, 278–9 (nr. 1022).

38 Al-Qā'im, lit. 'one who rises', refers to the Twelfth Imam in Ithnā'ashrī Shī'ism. He is considered by the Twelver Shī'as to be in a state of major occultation (*al-ghaybat al-kubrā*) and shall reappear and rise up against the enemies of the Prophet's Household toward the end of times. For more on the Twelfth Imam and Shī'ī messianism, see Abdulaziz Abdulhussein Sachedina, *Islamic Messianism: The Idea of the Mahdi in Twelver Shi'ism* (Albany, NY:

٢. عن حَنَان بن سَدير، عن أبيه، قال: قال: أبو جعفر عليه السلام: يا أبا الفضل، لنا حقٌّ في كتاب الله المحكم من الله، لو محوه فقالوا: ليس من عند الله، أولم يعلموا، لكان سواء.

٣. عن محمّد بن مسلم، قال أبو جعفر عليه السلام: يا محمّد، إذا سَمِعت الله ذكر أحدًا من هذه الأُمة بخيرٍ، فنحنُ هُم، وإذا سَمِعتَ الله ذَكرَ قومًا بسوءٍ ممّن مضى، فهم عَدُوّنا.

٤. عن داود بن فَرْقَد، عمّن أخبره، عن أبي عبدالله عليه السلام، قال: لو قد قُرِئَ القرآن كما أُنزل، لألفَيْتَنا فيه مُسَمّين.

٥. وقال سعيد بن الحسين الكِندي، عن أبي جعفر عليه السلام — بعد مُسَمّين — كما سُمّيَ مَن قَبْلنا.

٦. عن مُيَسَّر، عن أبي جعفر عليه السلام، قال: لولا أنَه زِيْد في كتاب الله ونُقص منه، ما خَفِي حقّنا على ذي حِجا، ولو قد قام قائمنا فنَطَق صَدّقه القرآن.

7. From Mas'ada b. Ṣadaqa, from Abū Ja'far ﷺ on his father's authority, on his grandfather's authority who narrated the Commander of the Faithful ﷺ as saying, "They called them, i.e. the family of the Prophet, by the most beautiful metaphors in the Qur'an: ﴾ *this one sweet and fresh* ﴿ so drink from it, ﴾ *and the other salty and bitter* ﴿(25:53) so avoid it."'

8. From 'Umar b. Ḥanẓala[39], from Abū 'Abd Allāh ﷺ: 'I asked about the verse: ﴾ *Say, 'God is sufficient witness between me and you, and he who possesses the knowledge of the Scripture.* ﴿'(13:43) [He narrated], 'When he saw me striving to follow this and other similar verses of the Qur'an, he said, "It should suffice [for you to know] that everything in the Qur'an, from its beginning to its end, refers to the Imams."'

The Imams and their Knowledge of the Qur'an's Interpretation (*ta'wīl*):

1. From al-Aṣbagh b. Nubāta who said, 'When the Commander of the Faithful ﷺ came to Kufa he led them in prayer for forty dawn prayers, in each of them reciting Sūrat al-A'lā (The Most High). Thereupon the hypocrites from among them said, "By God we swear that the son of Abū Ṭālib is incapable of reciting the Qur'an. Had he been capable of reciting it well he would have recited other chapters besides this chapter for us." When news of this reached him the Commander of the Faithful ﷺ said, "Woe to them! [Do they not know that] I know [better than them] which of the verses of the Qur'an are abrogating and which of them has been abrogated, which of them is an unambiguous verse and which are ambiguous, of its succinct parts and their corollaries, and of its [disconnected] letters and their meanings. I swear by God that there is not a single letter that was revealed to Muḥammad ﷺ except that I am familiar with the person to whom it pertains, on which day it was sent down and on which occasion. Damn them! Do they not read that ﴾ *All this is in the earlier scriptures, the scriptures of*

State University of New York Press, 1981); s.v. "Al-Mahdī," *Encyclopaedia of Islam*, Second Edition, v, 1230a (W. Madelung).

39 Abū Sakhr 'Umar b. Ḥanẓala al-'Ijlī, concerning whom Sayyid Khū'ī says there is no explicit statement establishing his reliability, was a companion of the fifth and sixth Imams. See Khū'ī, *Mu'jam*, 14:31–5 (nr. 8738).

٧. عن مَسْعَدة بن صَدقة، عن أبي جعفر، عن أبيه، عن جدّه عليهم السلام، قال: قال أمير المؤمنين عليه السلام: سَمّوهم بأحسن أمثال القرآن – يعني عِترة النبي صلى الله عليه وآله – هذا عَذْبٌ فُراتٌ فاشْرَبُوا، وهذا مِلحٌ أُجاجٌ فاجْتَنِبُوا.

٨. عن عمر بن حَنْظلة، عن أبي عبد الله عليه السلام، قال: سألتُ عن قول الله: ﴿قُلْ كَفَىٰ بِاللَّهِ شَهِيدًا بَيْنِي وَبَيْنَكُمْ وَمَنْ عِندَهُ عِلْمُ الْكِتَابِ﴾، فلمّا رآني أتتبّع هذا وأشباهه من الكتاب، قال عليه السلام: حسبُكَ كلّ شيء في الكتاب من فاتحته إلى خاتمته مثل هذا، فهو في الأئمة عنى به.

علم الأئمة عليهم السلام بالتأويل

١. عن الأصبغ بن نُباتة، قال: لمّا قَدِم أمير المؤمنين عليه السلام الكوفة صلّى بهم أربعين صباحًا يقرأ بهم: ﴿سَبِّحِ اسْمَ رَبِّكَ الْأَعْلَى﴾، قال: فقال المنافقون: لا والله، ما يُحسن ابن أبي طالب أن يقرأ القرآن، ولو أحسن أن يقرأ القرآن لقرأ بنا غير هذه السورة.

قال: فَبَلَغه ذلك، فقال: ويلٌ لهم، إنّي لأعرِف ناسخه من منسوخه، ومُحكمه من مُتشابهه، وفَصْله من فِصَاله، وحُروفه من معانيه. والله ما من حرفٍ نزل على محمد صلى الله عليه وآله إلاّ وأنا أعرِف فيمن أُنزل، وفي أيّ يوم، وفي أيّ موضع.

ويلٌ لهم، أما يقرءُون: ﴿إِنَّ هَٰذَا لَفِي الصُّحُفِ الْأُولَىٰ ۞ صُحُفِ إِبْرَاهِيمَ وَمُوسَىٰ﴾؟ والله عندي، وَرِثتها من رسول الله صلى الله عليه وآله، ووَرِثها رسول الله صلى الله عليه وآله من إبراهيم وموسى عليهما السلام.

Ibrāhīm and Mūsā ﴾?(87:18–19) I swear to God that these scriptures are in my possession, both of which I inherited from the Messenger of God who inherited them from Ibrāhīm and Mūsā. Let them be cursed for I am the one being referred to by God in the verse: ﴿ *and that attentive ears may take heed.* ﴾(69:12) We would be in the presence of the Messenger of God whenever he received the relevation; he would inform us about it so I and whoever else was present would try to retain [his explications], except no sooner had we left than they would [turn to me and] ask, 'What did he just say?"'

2. From Sulaym b. Qays al-Hilālī[40] who reported the Commander of the Faithful عليه السلام as saying, "Whenever a verse was revealed to the Messenger of God he would recite it to me and dictate it, and I would write it down with my own hand. He would teach me its interpretation (*tafsīr*) and its esoteric meaning (*ta'wīl*). He taught me which of its verses are abrogating and which of them had been abrogated. He taught me which of them are the unambiguous verses and which of them are the ambiguous. Then he would pray in order that God may be the one who teaches me to comprehend it and memorise it. Thus it was that never once did I forget a single verse from God's scripture nor the knowledge of that which he, the Messenger of God, had dictated to me. From the time he supplicated his prayer for me, I have been writing down God's book. Everything that God taught the Messenger of God, the Messenger of God taught me. He taught me everything God had taught him, such as the things which are permissible and impermissible, the commands and prohibitions, the knowledge of what was and what had yet to pass, the acts of obedience and disobedience. Everything he taught me I

40 Abū Ṣādiq Sulaym b. Qays al-Hilālī al-ʿĀmirī (d. 76/678), a prominent and highly respected companion of ʿAlī b. Abī Ṭālib and the author of one of the earliest pre-canonical works of Imāmī traditions. Notwithstanding the fact that Sulaym himself is widely acknowledged as one of the highest ranking companions of the first Imam in Shīʿī biographical literature, there is nonetheless considerable debate and disagreement among later scholars such as Ibn al-Ghadā'irī and al-ʿAllāma al-Ḥillī about whether the extant work known as *Kitāb Sulaym b. Qays* is in fact the same work as that which was supposedly authored by Sulaym, or whether it is a fabricated text falsely attributed to him. On him see s.v. "Sulaym b. Ḳays," *Encyclopaedia of Islam*, Second Edition, ix, 818b [M. Djebli]; Ḥillī, *Khulāṣat al-aqwāl*, 161–3 (nr. 473); Modarressi, *Tradition and Survival*, 82–6 (nr. 6); see also Robert Gleave, "Early Shiite hermeneutics and the dating of *Kitāb Sulaym ibn Qays*," *Bulletin of SOAS*, 78:1 (2015): 83–103.

ويل لهم، والله أنا الذي أنزل الله فيّ ﴿وَتَعِيَهَا أُذُنٌ وَاعِيَةٌ﴾، فإنّما كُنّا عند رسول الله ﷺ فيُخبرنا بالوحي فأعيه أنا ومَن يعيه، فإذا خرجنا قالوا: ماذا قال آنفًا؟

٢. عن سُليم بن قَيس الهِلالي، قال: سَمِعتُ أمير المؤمنين عليه السلام يقول: ما نزلت آية على رسول الله ﷺ إلاّ أقرأنيها، وأملاها عليَّ، فأكتُبها بخطّي، وعلّمني تأويلها وتفسيرها، وناسخها ومنسوخها، ومحكمها ومتشابهها، ودعا الله لي أن يُعلّمني فَهمها وحِفظها، فما نسيتُ آيةً من كتاب الله، ولا عِلمًا أملاه عليَّ فكتبته منذ دعا لي بما دعا، وما ترك شيئًا علمه الله من حلالٍ ولا حرامٍ، ولا أمرٍ ولا نهيٍ، كان أو لا يكون، من طاعةٍ أو معصية، إلاّ علّمنيه وحَفِظته، فلم أنس منه حرفًا واحدًا. ثم وضع يده على صدري، ودعا الله أن يملأ قلبي علمًا وفهمًا وحِكمةً ونُورًا، ولم أنسَ شيئًا، ولم يَفُتني شيءٌ لم أكتبه. فقلت: يا رسول الله، أوَ تخوّفتَ عليَّ النسيان فيما بعد؟ فقال: لستُ أتخوّفُ عليك نَسيانًا ولا جَهلاً، وقد أخبرني ربّي أنّه قد استجابَ لي فيك، وفي شُركائك الذين يكونون من بعدك.

فقلت: يا رسول الله، ومن شُركائي من بعدي؟ قال: الذين قَرَنَهم الله بنفسه وبي، فقال: الأوصياءُ منّي إلى أن يَرِدوا عليَّ الحوض، كلُّهم هادٍ مُهتدٍ، لا يَضرّهم من خَذلهم، هم مع القرآن، والقرآن معهم، لا يُفارقهم ولا يُفارقونه، بهم تُنصَر أُمّتي، وبهم يُمطَرون، وبهم يُدفَع عنهم، وبهم استَجَاب دُعاءهم.

فقلت: يا رسول الله، سمّهم لي؟ فقال: ابني هذا — ووضع يده على رأس الحسن عليه السلام — ثم ابني هذا — ووضع يده على رأس الحسين عليه السلام —، ثم ابن له يقال له: عليّ، وسَيُولد في حياتك، فأقرئه منّي السلام، [ثُم] تَكمِلَة اثني عشر من ولد محمّد ﷺ.

have preserved in my memory, and I have not forgotten a single thing even if it be [the position or meaning of] a letter. Then he placed his hand on my chest and beseeched God to fill my heart with knowledge, understanding, wisdom, and light, and I never forgot anything after that. No sooner would he utter a ruling than I would write it down.

I then inquired, 'O Messenger of God, do you still fear that I will forget something?'

He replied, 'No, I am never fearful, neither of you forgetting nor of you remaining ignorant, for my Lord has informed me that He has answered my prayer for you and for your associates who will come after you.'

So I asked, 'O Messenger of God, who are my associates after me?'

He replied, 'The individuals whom God has joined to Himself and to me. They are the vicegerents after me until they meet me at the Fountain. Each one of them is a rightly-guided adviser who can never be harmed by those who seek to disgrace them. They are one with the Qur'an and the Qur'an is one with them; never do they separate from each other. They are the ones through whom my community will prosper and have abundant good. Through them my community shall protect itself and through them their supplication will be answered.'

So I asked, 'O Messenger of God, name them for me.' He replied, 'This son of mine,' placing his hand on al-Ḥasan's head, 'then this one,' placing his hand on al-Ḥusayn's head, 'then one of his sons named ʿAlī, who will be born during your lifetime, so pass on my greetings to him. There will be twelve of them, all from the progeny of Muḥammad.'

Then I asked him, 'May my mother and father be your ransom – please name them for me.'

So he named them one by one, and by God, my brother, O son of Hilāl, the Mahdī (i.e. the Twelfth Imam) of the community of Muḥammad will be the one who shall fill the earth with equity and justice after it has been filled with corruption and oppression. I swear by God that I know the names of those who will pay allegiance to him between the *rukn* and the *maqām,*[41] as well as the names of their fathers and tribes."'

41 The area between the corner of the Kaʿba that houses the Black Stone (*rukn*) and the station of Ibrāhīm (*maqām*) is reported as being the place where people will pay allegiance to the Twelfth Imam upon his reappearance.

فقلت له: بأبي أنت، فسمِّهم لي؟ فسمّاهم رجلاً رجلاً، فيهم وَاللّٰهِ يا أخا بني هلال - مهديّ أُمّة محمّد الذي يملأ الأرض قِسطًا وعدلاً كما مُلئت جَورًا وظُلمًا، واللّٰه إنّي لأعرِف من يُبايعه بين الرُّكن والمقام، وأعرِف أسماء آبائهم وقبائلهم.

3. From Salama b. Kuhayl[42], from whoever narrated it to him, from 'Alī عليه السلام who said, 'Had the reins of authority been set up for me and rulership been placed at my disposal, I would have goverened the people of the Torah in accordance with what God has revealed in the Torah, until it [i.e. the Torah] would return to God and testify that I had governed exactly as God had revealed therein. Had the reins of authority been set up for me and rulership been placed at my disposal, I would have governed the people of the Injīl [Gospel] in accordance with that which God has revealed in the Injīl, until it [i.e. the Gospel] would return to God and testify that I had governed exactly as God had revealed therein. Had the reins of authority been set up for me and rulership been placed at my disposal, I would have governed the people of the Qur'an precisely as God has revealed in the Qur'an, until it [i.e. the Qur'an] too would return to God and testify that I had governed by what God had revealed therein.'

4. From Ayyūb b. Ḥurr, from Abū 'Abd Allāh عليه السلام. Says Ayyūb b. Ḥurr, 'I asked him [Ja'far al-Ṣādiq], "Are some of the Imams more knowledgeable than others?" He replied, "Yes, but their knowledge of the permissible and the prohibited, and of the interpretation of the Qur'an is one and the same."'

5. From Ḥafṣ b. Qurṭ al-Juhanī, from Ja'far b. Muḥammad al-Ṣādiq عليه السلام. Says Ḥafṣ b. Qurṭ al-Juhnī, 'I heard him [Ja'far al-Ṣādiq] say, "'Alī عليه السلام had complete knowledge of the permissible and the prohibited, and knew everything there was to know about the interpretation of the Qur'an, and we all follow his way."'

6. From al-Sakūnī, from Ja'far [al-Ṣādiq] on his father's authority, on his grandfather's authority, on his father's authority (peace be upon them all) who narrated, 'The Messenger of God عليه السلام stated, "There is in your midst a person who fights [to defend] the inner meaning (*ta'wīl*) of the Qur'an just as I have fought [to defend] its revelation (*tanzīl*), and this is 'Alī b. Abī Ṭālib."'

42 One of 'Alī b. Abī Ṭalib's supporters. See Ḥillī, *Khulāṣat al-aqwāl*, 307 (nr. 1179).

٣. عن سَلَمة بن كُهَيل، عمّن حدثه، عن علي عليه السلام، قال: لو استقامت لي الإمرة وكُسرت — أو ثُنيت — لي الوِسادة، لحَكَمْتُ لأهل التوراة بما أنزل الله في التوراة، حتى تذهب إلى الله أني قد حَكَمْتُ بما أنزل الله فيها، ولحَكَمْتُ لأهل الإنجيل بما أنزل الله في الإنجيل، حتى يذهب إلى الله أنّي قد حكمتُ بما أنزل الله، ولحَكَمْتُ في أهل القرآن بما أنزل الله في القرآن، حتى يذهب إلى الله أنّي قد حَكَمْتُ بما أنزل الله فيه.

٤. عن أيُّوب بن حُرّ، عن أبي عبدالله عليه السلام، قال: قلتُ له الأئمّة بعضهم أعلم من بعض؟ قال: نعم، وعلمهم بالحلال والحرام وتفسير القرآن واحد.

٥. عن حَفْص بن قُرط الجُهَنِيّ، عن جعفر بن محمّد الصادق عليه السلام قال: سَمِعتُه يقول: كان عليّ عليه السلام صاحب حلالٍ وحرامٍ وعِلمٍ بالقرآن، ونحن على مِنهاجه.

٦. عن السّكوني، عن جعفر، عن أبيه، عن جدّه، عن أبيه عليهم السلام، قال: قال رسول الله صلى الله عليه وآله: إنّ فيكم من يُقاتِل على تأويل القرآن كما قاتلتُ على تنزيله، وهو عليّ بن أبي طالب.

7. From Bashīr al-Dahhān[43] who narrated, 'I heard Abū 'Abd Allāh عليه السلام say, "God has made obedience to us obligatory in the Qur'an, so let not the people claim ignorance. For us is reserved the purest wealth, the spoils of war and the most noble verses of the Qur'an. I do not claim that we [the Imams of the *ahl al-bayt*] possess the knowledge of the unseen (*'ilm al-ghayb*), but I do say that we know the Book of God – a book which encompasses everything within it. God has taught us things which none besides us knows, things which He taught only to His angels and His prophets. Whatever is known to His angels and His messengers is also known to us."'

8. From Murāzim [b. Ḥakīm al-Azadī al-Madāyinī][44] who narrated, 'I heard Abū 'Abd Allāh عليه السلام say, "We are the people of a household, and from among this household God shall forever send an individual who is well-versed in His Book from its beginning to its end. We are the ones who possess knowledge of the things that God has made permissible and the things that He has made prohibited, and that only we have the capacity to harbour and that we cannot discuss with anyone."'

9. From al-Ḥakam b. 'Utayba[45] who narrated, 'Abū 'Abd Allāh عليه السلام said to a man from Kufa when he asked him about something, "Had I met you in Medina, I would have shown you the traces of Jibra'īl in our houses. I would have shown you [the places in which] he came down to deliver the revelation to my grandfather, [the places in which] the Qur'an [had been sent down] and knowledge [communicated to the Messenger of God]. Do people think they can extract knowledge from us so as to be guided but nonetheless accuse us of being the ones who are led astray? That is absurd!"'

---

43 Bashīr al-Dahhān, a companion of the sixth (and possibly fifth) Imam. Not much else is known about him. See Khū'ī, *Mu'jam*, 4:238–9 (nr. 1814).

44 Abū Muḥammad Murāzim b. Ḥakīm al-Azadī al-Madāyinī, a realiable narrator of traditions from Ja'far al-Ṣādiq and Mūsā al-Kāẓim. See Ḥillī, *Khulāṣat al-aqwāl*, 278 (nr. 1018).

45 Abū Muḥammad al-Ḥakam b. 'Utayba al-Kūfī al-Kindī, a blameworthy (*madhmūm*) legist originally of Sunnī persuasion (*min fuqahā' al-'āmma*) and later an adherent of the proto-Zaydī sect known as the Batriyya (s.v. "Batriyya," *Encyclopaedia of Islam*, Third Edition [N. Haider]). See Ḥillī, *Khulāṣat al-aqwāl*, 341 (nr. 1351).

٧. عن بَشير الدهّان، قال: سَمِعتُ أبا عبدالله ﵇ يقول: إنّ الله فَرَض طاعتنا في كتابه، فلا يَسَع الناس جهلاً، لنا صفو المال، ولنا الأنفال، ولنا كرائم القرآن، ولا أقول لكم إنّا أصحاب الغيب؛ ونعلم كتاب الله، وكتاب الله يحتمل كلّ شيء، إنَّ الله أعلمنا عِلمًا لا يَعْلَمُه أحدٌ غيره، وعلمًا قد أعلمه ملائكته ورُسُله، فما عَلِمته ملائكته ورُسُله فنحن نعلمه.

٨. عن مُرازِم، قال: سَمِعتُ أبا عبدالله ﵇ يقول: إنّا أهل بيت لم يَزَل الله يبعث فينا من يعلم كتابه من أوّله إلى آخره، وإنَّ عندنا من حلال الله وحرامه ما يَسَعنا كتمانه، ما نستطيع أن نُحدِّث به أحدًا.

٩. عن الحكَم بن عُتيبة، قال: قال أبو عبدالله ﵇ لرجلٍ من أهل الكوفة — وسأله عن شيء —: لو لَقِيتُك بالمدينة لأريتُك أثر جبْرَئيل في دُورنا، ونزوله على جدّي بالوحي والقرآن والعلم، أفيستقي الناس العِلم من عندنا فيُهْدَون هم، وضَلَلْنا نحن؟! هَذا مُحال.

10. From Yūsuf b. al-Sukht al-Baṣrī[46] who said, 'I saw a document signed in the handwriting of Muḥammad b. Muḥammad b. ʿAlī which read, "It is incumbent upon you to proclaim that we are God's examplars, His leaders, and His vicegerents on earth; that we are His guardians over His creation and His proofs on the land; that we know the permissible and the prohibited, and that we are conversant with the inner meaning (*ta'wīl*) of the Book and the conclusive speech."'

11. From Thuwayr b. Abī Fākhita[47], on his father's authority who narrated, "Alī عليه السلام said, "There is nothing contained in the two Tablets except that I have knowledge thereof."'

12. From Sulaymān al-Aʿmash, on his father's authority who narrated, "Alī عليه السلام said, "Not a single verse was revealed without my knowing who it was revealed about, where it descended, and concerning whom it was intended. My Lord has indeed bestowed me with a sagacious heart and an articulate tongue."'

13. From Abū al-Ṣabbāḥ[48] who narrated that 'Abū 'Abd Allāh عليه السلام said, "God taught His Prophet صلى الله عليه وآله the knowledge of the [outer] revelation (*tanzīl*) and its inner meaing (*ta'wīl*), and the Messenger of God taught it to 'Alī عليه السلام."'

On Those Who Interpret The Qur'an According To Their Own Opinion:

1. From Zurāra, from Abū Jaʿfar عليه السلام who said, 'Nothing is further from man's understanding than the interpretation of the Qur'an. The beginning of a verse may refer to one thing, its middle to another and its end to something

46 Yūsuf b. al-Sukht al-Baṣrī, a weak narrator who frequently skips names within the chain of transmitters (*isnād*). See Ḥillī, *Khulāṣat al-aqwāl*, 418–19 (nr. 1699).

47 Thuwayr b. Abī Fākhita (=Saʿīd b. ʿAlāqa), whose reliability is not known. See Ḥillī, *Khulāṣat al-aqwāl*, 87 (nr. 182).

48 Abū al-Ṣabbāḥ Ibrāhīm b. Nuʿaym al-Kinānī, regarded by al-ʿAllāma al-Ḥillī as a reliable narrator and transmitter of traditions. He was a companion of Imam Jaʿfar al-Ṣādiq and Imam Mūsā al-Kāẓim. See Ḥillī, *Khulāṣat al-aqwāl*, 47 (nr. 1); Khū'ī, *Muʿjam*, 22:208 (nr. 14408); Modarressi, *Tradition and Survival*, 289 (nr. 105).

١٠. عن يوسف بن السُّخت البصريّ، قال: رأيتُ التوقيع بخطّ محمّد بن محمّد بن عليّ فكان فيه: الذي يجب عليكم ولكم أن تقولوا: إنّا قُدوة الله وأئمّته، وخلفاء الله في أرضه، وأُمناؤه على خَلقه، وحُججه في بلاده، نعرِف الحلال والحرام، ونعرف تأويل الكتاب وفَصْل الخطاب.

١١. عن ثُوير بن أبي فاخِتَة، عن أبيه، قال: قال علي عليه السلام: ما بين اللَّوحين شيءٌ إلاّ وأنا أعلمه.

١٢. عن سُليمان الأعمش، عن أبيه، قال: قال عليّ عليه السلام: ما نزلت آيةٌ إلاّ وأنا عَلِمتُ فيمن أُنزلت، وأين أُنزلت، وعلى من نزلت، إن ربّي وهب لي قلبًا عقولاً، ولسانًا طَلِقًا.

١٣. عن أبي الصَّبّاح، قال: قال أبو عبد الله عليه السلام: إنّ الله علّم نبيّه صلى الله عليه وآله وسلم التنزيل والتأويل، فعلّمه رسول الله صلى الله عليه وآله وسلم عليًّا عليه السلام.

فيمن فسّر القرآن برأيه

١. عن زُرارة، عن أبي جعفر عليه السلام، قال: ليس شيءٌ أبعد من عُقُول الرجال من تفسير القرآن، إنّ الآية ينزل أوّلها في شيءٍ، وَأوسطها في شيءٍ، وآخرها في شيءٍ، ثمّ قال: ﴿إِنَّمَا يُرِيدُ اللَّهُ لِيُذْهِبَ عَنكُمُ الرِّجْسَ أَهْلَ الْبَيْتِ وَيُطَهِّرَكُمْ تَطْهِيرًا﴾، من ميلاد الجاهليّة.

else.' Then he recited: ﴿ *God wishes to keep uncleanness away from you, people of the [Prophet's] Household, and to purify you thoroughly* ﴾[49] from the very onset of paganism.'

2. From Hishām b. Sālim[50], from Abū 'Abd Allāh عليه السلام who said, 'Whoever interprets the Qur'an according to his own opinion and his interpretation just so happens to be correct, he will not be rewarded for it; and if his interpretation is incorrect, then he bears the sin for it.'

3. From Abū al-Jārūd who narrated, 'Abū Ja'far عليه السلام said, "Speak only about things whereof you have knowledge, and whatever you do not know, then say 'God knows best'. Indeed, a man may use a verse to prove a point but unwittingly ends up falling a distance further than the distance between the earth and the sky."'

4. From Abū Baṣīr, from Abū 'Abd Allāh عليه السلام that he said, 'Whoever interprets the Qur'an according to his opinion and happens to be right will not be rewarded for it; and if he is wrong, then he will be farther [from the truth] than the sky [from earth].'

5. From 'Abd al-Raḥmān b. al-Ḥajjāj[51] who narrated, 'I heard Abū 'Abd Allāh عليه السلام say, "There is nothing more incomprehensible to men's intellects than the Qur'an."'

---

49 The first part of this verse (Q. 33:33) is about the Prophet's wives, the middle part enjoins the prayer and alms-giving, and the end of it according to Shī'ī tradition is about the purification and immaculateness of the Ahl al-Bayt.

50 Abū Muḥammad Hishām b. Sālim al-Jawālīqī, a client of Abū al-Ḥakam Bishr b. Marwān, is deemed a very realible narrator of the Imams' traditions. See Ḥillī, *Khulāṣat al-aqwāl*, 289 (nr. 1062); Modarressi, *Tradition and Survival*, 269–71 (nr. 89).

51 Abū 'Alī [also Abū 'Abd Allāh] 'Abd al-Raḥmān b. al-Ḥajjāj al-Bajalī (d. before 203/818) was a companion and narrator of the sixth and seventh Imams and an acquaintance of the eighth Imam also. Although originally of Kufa, he spent a large part of his life in Baghdad, but was accused of having associations with the Kaysāniyya (s.v. "Kaysāniyya," *Encyclopaedia of Islam*, Second Edition, iv, 836b [W. Madelung]). He is recorded in the books of Shī'ī *rijāl* as a very prominent and reliable transmitter of the Imams' teachings and is reported to have returned to the Imāmī *madhhab* after becoming acquainted with Imam 'Alī b. Mūsā al-Riḍā. See Ḥillī, *Khulāṣat al-aqwāl*, 204 (nr. 650); and especially Modarressi, *Tradition and Survival*, 168–71 (nr. 23).

٢. عن هشام بن سالم، عن أبي عبد الله ﷺ، قال: من فَسّر القرآن برأيه فأصاب لم يُؤجَر، وإن أخطأ كان إثمه عليه.

٣. عن أبي الجارود، قال: قال أبو جعفر ﷺ: ما عَلِمتم فقولوا، وما لم تعلموا فقولوا: الله أعلم، فإنّ الرجل يَنْزِع بالآية فيَخرُّ بها أبعد ما بين السّماء والأرض.

٤. عن أبي بصير، عن أبي عبد الله ﷺ، قال: من فَسَّر القرآن برأيه، إن أصاب لم يؤجر، وإن أخطأ فهو أبعد من السَّماء.

٥. عن عبد الرّحمن بن الحجَّاج، قال: سَمِعتُ أبا عبد الله ﷺ يقول: ليس أبعد من عُقُول الرجال من القرآن.

6. From 'Ammār b. Mūsā[52], from Abū 'Abd Allāh عليه السلام that he was asked about passing judgements, to which he said, 'Whoever judges between two people using his opinion has blasphemed (*fa-qad kafar*), and whoever interprets a single verse of the Qur'an according to his opinion has also blasphemed.'

On the Reprehensibility of Using the Qur'an for the Purpose of Disputation:

1. From Zurāra, from Abū Ja'far عليه السلام who said, 'Avoid disputation for it thwarts good deeds and destroys the religion. When someone uses a verse of the Qur'an to prove a point, the extent to which he falls into error is farther than the distance of the sky [from earth].'

2. From al-Qāsim b. Sulaymān[53] from Abū 'Abd Allāh عليه السلام that he narrated, 'My father عليه السلام said, "No sooner does a man use part of the Qur'an to prove a point against another part of it than he has committed an act of infidelity (*fa-qad kafar*)."'

3. From Ya'qūb b. Yazīd[54] from Yāsir, from Abū al-Ḥasan al-Riḍā عليه السلام who said, 'Disputation using the Qur'an is an act of infidelity.'

4. From Dāwūd b. Farqad, from Abū 'Abd Allāh عليه السلام who said, 'Do not label every verse by saying "This one applies to so-and-so" and "This one applies to so-and-so," for the Qur'an contains verses about the permissible and prohibited, information about the past, news of the future, and rulings pertaining to what is concurrent between you. This was how the Messenger of God ﷺ was authorized to deal with it. If he willed he either acted upon it

---

52 Abū al-Faḍl 'Ammār b. Mūsā al-Sābāṭī, a realiable narrator. He lived in Ctesiphon and was a transmitter from Ja'far al-Ṣādiq and Mūsā al-Kāẓim. He belonged to the Faṭḥiyya sect. See Ḥillī, *Khulāṣat al-aqwāl*, 381 (nr. 1533); Modarressi, *Tradition and Survival*, 199–200 (nr. 40).

53 Qāsim b. Sulaymān, on whom there is scant information, was a transmitter of the sixth Imam's traditions. See Modarressi, *Tradition and Survival*, 359 (nr. 171).

54 Abū Yūsuf Ya'qūb b. Yazīd b. Ḥammād al-Anbārī al-Sulamī, a chancellor (*kātib*) at the court of the Abbasid Caliph al-Muntaṣir (r. 861–62) in Baghdad and a close associate of the eighth Imam 'Alī b. Mūsā al-Riḍā. He is considered very reliable in his narrations. See Ḥillī, *Khulāṣat al-aqwāl*, 298 (nr. 1107).

٦. عن عمّار بن موسى، عن أبي عبد الله عليه السلام قال: سُئل عن الحكومة؟ قال: من حَكَم برأيه بين اثنين فقد كَفَر، ومن فسَّر آيةً من كتاب الله فقد كَفَر.

كراهيَة الجِدال في القرآن

١. عن زُرارة، عن أبي جعفر عليه السلام، قال: إيّاكم والخُصومة، فإنَّها تُحبِط العمل، وتَمْحَق الدِّين، وإنّ أحدكم لينزِع بالآية يقع منها أبعد من السّماء.

٢. عن القاسم بن سليمان، عن أبي عبد الله عليه السلام، قال: قال أبي عليه السلام: ما ضَرَب رجلٌ القرآن بعضه ببعضٍ إلا كفر.

٣. عن يعقوب بن يزيد، عن ياسر، عن أبي الحسن الرِّضا عليه السلام يقول: المِراء في كتاب الله كُفر.

٤. عن داود بن فَرْقَد، عن أبي عبد الله عليه السلام، قال: لا تقولوا لكلّ آية هذه رجل وهذه رجل، إنّ من القرآن حلالاً ومنه حرامًا، وفيه نبأ مَن قبلكم، وخبر مَن بعدكم، وحكم ما بينكم، فهكذا هو، كان رسول الله صلى الله عليه وآله مفوِّضٌ فيه، إن شاء فعل الشيء، وإن شاء تَذكّر، حتّى إذا فُرِضت فرائضه، وخُمِّست أخماسه، حقٌّ على النّاس أن يأخُذُوا به، لأنّ الله قال: ﴿مَا آتَاكُمُ الرَّسُولُ فَخُذُوهُ وَمَا نَهَاكُمْ عَنْهُ فَانْتَهُوا﴾.

or kept it to himself until its obligations had been issued and its five foundations established. So people are supposed to accept from him, for God has said: ﴾ *So accept whatever the Messenger gives you, and abstain from whatever he forbids you.* ﴿'(59: 7)

The Opening

1. The Opening[1]

1. From al-Ḥasan b. ʿAlī b. Abī Ḥamza al-Baṭāʾinī[2], from his father who reported that Abū ʿAbd Allāh عليه السلام said, 'The Greatest Name of God (*al-ism al-aʿẓam*) is a syllable within the Mother of the Book[3].'

2. From Muḥammad b. Sinān [who reported] from Abū al-Ḥasan Mūsā b. Jaʿfar عليه السلام from his father who asked Abū Ḥanīfa, 'Which is the chapter of the Qurʾan whose beginning is praise of God, whose middle a declaration of exclusive worship, and whose end is a supplication?' He was perplexed at this and admitted he did not know. So Abū ʿAbd Allāh عليه السلام said, 'The chapter whose beginning is praise, whose middle is a declaration of exclusive worship, and whose end is a supplication is the Chapter of Praise (*sūrat al-ḥamd*).'

3. From Yūnus b. ʿAbd al-Raḥmān[4] from whoever cited this without giving a source, saying, 'I asked Abū ʿAbd Allāh عليه السلام about the verse: ﴿ *We have given*

---

1 Also known as the Chapter of Praise (*sūrat al-ḥamd*).

2 His full name is Abū Muḥammad al-Ḥasan b. ʿAlī b. Abī Ḥamza (=Sālim) al-Baṭāʾinī, an adherent of the Wāqifī sect whose followers considered the fifth Imam Muḥammad al-Bāqir to have been raised by God only to return in the future as the promised Mahdī. Kishshī describes him as a cursed liar (*kadhdhāb malʿūn*). See Ḥillī, *Khulāṣat*, 334 (no. 1320); Modarressi, *Tradition and Survival*, 250–4 (nr. 81).

3 The Arabic phrase used here is *umm al-kitāb*, literally 'mother of the Scripture'. It appears in the Qurʾan at 3:7 and is interpreted by Muslim exegetes as a reference to the first chapter of the Qurʾan (i.e. *sūrat al-fātiḥa*).

4 Abū Muḥammad Yūnus b. ʿAbd al-Raḥmān (d. 208/823–4), the client of ʿAlī b. Yaqṭīn, was a prominent figure of the Shīʿī community in his day and a transmitter of the eighth Imam's traditions. He is reported to have been especially praised for his knowledge by Imam ʿAlī b. Mūsā al-Riḍā and enstrusted by him with endowment monies on behalf of the Muslim community. He is regarded as one of the major transmitters (*ruwāt*) of the Imams' traditions and an individual about whom the Shīʿī tradition records a statement from the eighth

بِسْمِ اللَّهِ الرَّحْمَٰنِ الرَّحِيمِ

من سورة أُمّ الكتاب

١. بأسانيد عن الحسن بن علي بن أبي حمزة البطائني، عن أبيه، قال: قال أبو عبد الله عليه السلام: اسم الله الأعظم مُقَطّع في أُمّ الكتاب.

٢. عن محمّد بن سِنان، عن أبي الحسن موسى بن جعفر، عن أبيه عليهما السلام، قال: قال لأبي حنيفة: ما سورة أوّلها تحميد، وأوسطها إخلاص، وآخرها دُعاء؟ فبقي مُتحيِّرًا، ثمّ قال: لا أدري.

فقال أبو عبد الله عليه السلام: السُّورة التي أوّلها تحميد، وأوسطها إخلاص، وآخرها دُعاء، سورة الحمد.

٣. عن يُونُس بن عبد الرّحمن، عمّن رفعه، قال: سألتُ أبا عبد الله عليه السلام: ﴿وَلَقَدْ آتَيْنَاكَ سَبْعًا مِنَ الْمَثَانِي وَالْقُرْآنَ الْعَظِيمَ﴾؟ قال: هي سورة الحمد، وهي سبع آيات، منها ﴿بِسْمِ اللَّهِ الرَّحْمَٰنِ الرَّحِيمِ﴾ وإنّما سُمِّيَت المثاني لأنّها تُثنى في الرّكعتين.

you the seven oft-repeated verses and the whole glorious Qur'an.﴿(15:87) He replied, "This refers to the Chapter of Praise *(sūrat al-ḥamd)* which contains seven verses, and ﴾*In the name of God, the Lord of Mercy, the Giver of Mercy*﴿ is a part of it. It has been named 'oft-repeated' because it is recited in the first two units of every prayer."'

4. From Abū Ḥamza, from Abū Ja'far عليه السلام who said, 'They have stolen the most valuable verse of God's Scripture: ﴾*In the name of God, the Lord of Mercy, the Giver of Mercy.*﴿'

5. From Ṣafwān al-Jammāl[5] who narrated, 'Abū 'Abd Allāh عليه السلام said, 'Every single Divine Scripture that God has revealed from above contains ﴾*In the name of God, the Lord of Mercy, the Giver of Mercy*﴿ as its opening. Indeed the end of a previous chapter was marked by the revelation of ﴾*In the name of God, the Lord of Mercy, the Giver of Mercy*﴿ signalling the beginning of the next chapter.'

6. From Abū Ḥamza, from Abū Ja'far عليه السلام who narrated, 'The Messenger of God صلى الله عليه وآله used to recite ﴾*In the name of God, the Lord of Mercy, the Giver of Mercy*﴿ loudly, raising his voice. When the polytheists would hear it they would turn their backs to him, so God revealed: ﴾*When you mention your Lord in the Qur'an, and Him alone, they turn their backs and run away.*﴿'(17:46)

7. From al-Ḥasan b. Khurrazād from Abū 'Abd Allāh عليه السلام that he said, 'When a man stands to lead the community in prayer, a devil comes to the devil that is attached to the imam, and says to him, 'Did he remember God?' [i.e: did he say ﴾*In the name of God, the Lord of Mercy, the Giver of Mercy*﴿?] If he replies 'yes' the devil runs away. If not, then he climbs onto the imam's neck, dangling his legs onto his chest, such that it's actually the devil leading the people until they finish their prayers.'

Imam in which he is promised a place in paradise. See Ḥillī, *Khulāṣat al-aqwāl*, 296–7 (nr. 1103); Khū'ī, *Mu'jam*, 21: 209–33 (nr. 13863).

5 Abū Muḥammad Ṣafwān b. Mihrān b. al-Mughīra al-Asadī, Kufan in origin, is regarded a reliable (*thiqa*) narrator. See Ḥillī, *Khulāṣat al-aqwāl*, 171 (nr. 501); Modarressi, *Tradition and Survival*, 365 (nr. 181).

٤. عن أبي حمزة، عن أبي جعفر عليه السلام، قال: سرقوا أكرم آية في كتاب الله ﴿بِسْمِ اللَّهِ الرَّحْمَنِ الرَّحِيمِ﴾.

٥. عن صفوان الجمّال، قال: قال أبو عبد الله عليه السلام: ما أنزل الله من السّماء كتابًا إلاّ وفاتحته ﴿بِسْمِ اللَّهِ الرَّحْمَنِ الرَّحِيمِ﴾، وإنّما كان يُعرف انقضاء السورة بنزول ﴿بِسْمِ اللَّهِ الرَّحْمَنِ الرَّحِيمِ﴾ ابتداءً للأخرى.

٦. عن أبي حمزة، عن أبي جعفر عليه السلام، قال: كان رسول الله صلى الله عليه وآله وسلم يجهر بـ﴿بِسْمِ اللَّهِ الرَّحْمَنِ الرَّحِيمِ﴾ ويرفع صوته بها، فإذا سمعها المشركون ولّوا مدبرين، فأنزل الله ﴿وَإِذَا ذَكَرْتَ رَبَّكَ فِي الْقُرْآنِ وَحْدَهُ وَلَّوْا عَلَى أَدْبَارِهِمْ نُفُورًا﴾.

٧. قال الحسن بن خُرّزاد: ورُوي عن أبي عبد الله عليه السلام، قال: إذا أمّ الرجل القوم، جاء شيطان إلى الشيطان الذي هو قَرِين الإمام، فيقول: هل ذكر الله؟ يعني هل قرأ ﴿بِسْمِ اللَّهِ الرَّحْمَنِ الرَّحِيمِ﴾؟ فإن قال: نعم، هَرَب منه، وإن قال: لا، رَكِبَ عُنُق الإمام، ودلّى رجليه في صدره، فلم يزل الشيطان إمام القوم حتى يَفْرَغُوا من صلاتهم.

8. From ʿAbd al-Malik b. ʿUmar, from Abū ʿAbd Allāh عليه السلام who said, ʿIblīs (Satan) let out a groan on four occasions – the first on the day he was cursed; the second when he was demoted to earth; then when Muḥammad ﷺ was sent down as a messenger a while after other prophets; and lastly when the cornerstone of the Scripture – the opening chapter of the Qur'an was revealed. He let out a sigh of satisfaction twice – when Ādam عليه السلام ate from the tree and when he managed to get Ādam demoted to earth.' He said, 'He was cursed for doing that.'

9. From Ismāʿīl b. Abān who, without mentioning his source, cited the Prophet ﷺ. He said, 'The Messenger of God ﷺ said to Jābir b. ʿAbd Allāh, "Jābir, shall I teach you the best chapter that God has revealed in His Scripture?" Jābir replied, "Of course – may my father and mother be your ransom, O Messenger of God, teach it to me." So he taught him the Praise (*sūrat al-ḥamd*) – the cornerstone of the Scripture. Then he asked him, "Jābir, shall I tell you more about it?" He replied, "Of course – may my father and mother be your ransom, please tell me." So he said, "It is a cure for every ailment save poison, i.e. death."'

10. From Salama b. Muḥriz who narrated, 'I heard Abū ʿAbd Allāh عليه السلام say, "He who is not given relief by the Chapter of Praise will not be relieved by anything else."'

11. From Abū Bakr al-Ḥaḍramī[6] who narrated, 'Abū ʿAbd Allāh عليه السلام said, "When you have a particular need, read the oft-repeated verses and another chapter of the Qur'an, and perform two units of prayer then supplicate God." I said, "May God make you prosper – what are the oft-repeated verses?" He replied, "The Chapter of the Opening (*sūrat al-fātiḥa*): ﴾*In the name of God, the Lord of Mercy, the Giver of Mercy. Praise belongs to God, Lord of the worlds*﴿'

12. From ʿĪsā b. ʿAbd Allāh, on his father's authority, on his grandfather's authority from ʿAlī عليه السلام that he came to know of a group of people who were

---

6 Abū Bakr ʿAbd Allāh b. Muḥammad al-Ḥaḍramī, about whom there is scant information. He is reported to have been involved in a famous debate with Zayd b. ʿAlī. See Ḥillī, *Khulāṣat*, 200 (nr. 621).

٨. عن عبد الملك بن عُمر، عن أبي عبد الله عليه السلام، قال: إنّ إبليس رَنّ أربع رنّات: أولهنّ يوم لُعِن، وحين هَبَط إلى الأرض، وحين بُعث محمّد صلى الله عليه وآله على فترةٍ من الرُّسُل، وحين أُنزلت أُمّ الكتاب ﴿الْحَمْدُ لِلَّهِ رَبِّ الْعَالَمِينَ﴾، ونخر نخرتين: حين أكل آدم عليه السلام من الشجرة، وحين أُهبط آدم إلى الأرض. قال: ولُعِن من فعل ذلك.

٩. عن إسماعيل بن أبان، يرفعه إلى النبي صلى الله عليه وآله، قال: قال رسول الله صلى الله عليه وآله لجابر بن عبد الله: يا جابر، ألا أعلّمُك أفضل سورة أنزلها الله في كتابه؟ قال: فقال جابر: بلى —بأبي أنت وأُمّي يا رسول الله— علّمنيها، قال: فعلّمه ﴿الْحَمْدُ لِلَّهِ﴾ أمّ الكتاب.

قال: ثمّ قال له: يا جابر ألا أُخبِرُك عنها؟ قال: بلى — بأبي أنت وأُمّي — فأخبرني. قال: هي شِفاء من كلّ داء، إلاّ السام، يعني الموت.

١٠. عن سَلَمة بن مُحْرِز، قال: سَمِعتُ أبا عبد الله عليه السلام يقول: من لم تُبرِئه الحمد لم يُبرِئه شيء.

١١. عن أبي بكر الحَضْرمي، قال: قال أبو عبد الله عليه السلام: إذا كانت لك حاجة، فاقرأ المثاني وسورة أُخرى، وصَلِّ ركعتين، وادعُ الله.

قلت: أصلحك الله، وما المثاني؟ قال: فاتحة الكتاب ﴿بِسْمِ اللَّهِ الرَّحْمَٰنِ الرَّحِيمِ ۝ الْحَمْدُ لِلَّهِ رَبِّ الْعَالَمِينَ﴾.

١٢. عن عيسى بن عبد الله، عن أبيه، عن جدِّه، عن عليّ عليه السلام، قال: بلغه أنّ أُناسًا يَنزِعُون ﴿بِسْمِ اللَّهِ الرَّحْمَٰنِ الرَّحِيمِ﴾، فقال: هي آيةٌ من كتاب الله، أنساهم إيّاها الشيطان.

leaving out ﴾*In the name of God, the Lord of Mercy, the Giver of Mercy*﴿, so he said, 'This is a verse from God's Scripture and Shayṭān has made you forget it.'

13. From Ismāʿīl b. Mihrān who narrated, 'Abū al-Ḥasan al-Riḍā عليه السلام said, "Indeed, ﴾*In the name of God, the Lord of Mercy, the Giver of Mercy*﴿ is closer to the Greatest Name of God than the iris is to the sclera in the eye."'

14. From Sulaymān al-Jaʿfarī[7] who narrated, 'I heard Abū al-Ḥasan [i.e. al-Riḍā عليه السلام] say, "When any of you approaches his wife, let there be caressing beforehand for that will soften her heart and take away any resentment in her. And when he is ready to have his need fulfilled, he should say ﴾*In the name of God, the Lord of Mercy, the Giver of Mercy*﴿ three times, then any other verse of the Qur'an that comes to his mind, if he can. If not, then saying ﴾*In the name of God, the Lord of Mercy, the Giver of Mercy*﴿ is enough." A man in the gathering asked him, "So if he recites ﴾*In the name of God, the Lord of Mercy, the Giver of Mercy*﴿ it will really be enough for him?" He retorted, "And is there any verse more honourable in God's Book than ﴾*In the name of God, the Lord of Mercy, the Giver of Mercy*﴿?"'

15. From al-Ḥasan b. Khurrazād who narrated, 'I wrote to al-Ṣādiq عليه السلام to ask about the meaning of 'God,' to which he replied, "He has absolute authority over the tiniest as well as the greatest of all things."'

16. From Khālid b. al-Mukhtār who narrated, 'I heard Jaʿfar b. Muḥammad عليه السلام exclaim, "What is wrong with them? May God combat them – they have a vendetta against the greatest verse in God's Book and claim that it is an innovation when it has been made so clear to them. It is: ﴾*In the name of God, the Lord of Mercy, the Giver of Mercy.*﴿"'

17. From Muḥammad b. Muslim who narrated, 'I asked Abū 'Abd Allāh عليه السلام about God's verse: ﴾*We have given you the seven oft-repeated verses and the*

---

7 Abū Muḥammad Sulaymān b. Jaʿfar b. Ibrāhīm b. Muḥammad b. ʿAlī b. ʿAbd Allāh b. Jaʿfar al-Ṭayyār al-Ṭālibī al-Jaʿfarī, a reliable (*thiqa*) narrator of traditions from the eighth Imam ʿAlī b. Mūsā al-Riḍā. See Ḥillī, *Khulāṣat al-aqwāl*, 154 (nr. 446).

١٣. عن إسماعيل بن مهران، قال: قال أبو الحسن الرّضا عليه السلام: إنّ ﴿بِسْمِ اللَّهِ الرَّحْمَٰنِ الرَّحِيمِ﴾ أقرب إلى اسم الله الأعظم من سواد العين إلى بياضها.

١٤. عن سليمان الجعفري، قال: سَمِعتُ أبا الحسن عليه السلام يقول: إذا أتى أحدكم أهله، فليكن قبل ذلك مُلاطَفَةٌ، فإنّه أبرّ لقلبها، وأسلّ لسَخِيْمَتها، فإذا أفضى إلى حاجته قال: ﴿بِسْمِ اللَّهِ﴾ ثلاثًا، فإن قدر أن يقرأ أيّ آيةٍ حَضَرَتْهُ من القرآن فعل، وإلا قد كَفَتْهُ التسمية، فقال له رجل في المجلس: فإن قرأ ﴿بِسْمِ اللَّهِ الرَّحْمَٰنِ الرَّحِيمِ﴾ أُجِرَ به؟ فقال: وأيُّ آيةٍ في كتاب الله أكرم من ﴿بِسْمِ اللَّهِ الرَّحْمَٰنِ الرَّحِيمِ﴾.

١٥. عن الحسن بن خُرَّزَاد، قال: كَتَبتُ إلى الصّادق عليه السلام أسأَلُ عن معنى الله، فقال: استولى على ما دَقَّ وجَلَّ.

١٦. عن خالد بن المُخْتَار، قال: سَمِعتُ جعفر بن محمّد عليهما السلام يقول: ما لهم – قاتلهم الله – عمدوا إلى أعظم آيةٍ في كتاب الله، فزعموا أنّها بِدْعَةٌ إذا أظهروها، وهي ﴿بِسْمِ اللَّهِ الرَّحْمَٰنِ الرَّحِيمِ﴾.

١٧. عن محمّد بن مسلم، قال: سألت أبا عبد الله عليه السلام عن قول الله عزّوجلّ ﴿وَلَقَدْ آتَيْنَاكَ سَبْعًا مِنَ الْمَثَانِي وَالْقُرْآنَ الْعَظِيمَ﴾، فقال: فاتحة الكتاب يُثنّى فيها القول.

قال: وقال رسول الله صلّى الله عليه وآله: إنّ الله منَّ عليَّ بفاتحة الكتاب من كنز الجنّة، فيه ﴿بِسْمِ اللَّهِ الرَّحْمَٰنِ الرَّحِيمِ﴾، الآية التي يقول فيها: ﴿وَإِذَا ذَكَرْتَ رَبَّكَ فِي الْقُرْآنِ وَحْدَهُ

whole glorious Qur'an. ﴿'(15:87) So he replied, "It refers to the Opening of the Qur'an (*sūrat al-fātiḥa*), which is often recited." He continued, "The Messenger of God ﷺ said, 'God has gifted me with the Opening from the treasures of Paradise. Within it is: ﴾*In the name of God, the Lord of Mercy, the Giver of Mercy*﴿, regarding which He says: ﴾*When you mention your Lord in the Qur'an, and Him alone, they turn their backs and run away.*﴿(17:46) Then: ﴾*Praise belongs to God, Lord of the worlds*﴿ – this will be the exclamation of the people of Paradise in expressing thanks to God for their good reward. ﴾*Master of the Day of Judgement*﴿ – Jibra'īl said that no sooner does a Muslim affirm this than God and the inhabitants of the heavens attest to his sincerity. ﴾*It is You we worship*﴿ – the exclusivity of His worship; ﴾*It is You we ask for help*﴿ – this is the best way that the servants can ask for their needs. ﴾*Guide us to the straight path: the path of those You have blessed*﴿ – the path of the prophets. They are the ones whom God has blessed; ﴾*not of those who incur anger*﴿ – the Jews; ﴾*nor those who have gone astray*﴿ – the Christians."'

18. From 'Abd Allāh b. Sinān, from Abū 'Abd Allāh (عليه السلام) regarding the interpretation of: ﴾*In the name of God, the Lord of Mercy, the Giver of Mercy*﴿. He said, 'The letter *bā'* stands for God's magnificence (*bahā'*), the *sīn* stands for God's splendour (*sanā'*), and the *mīm* stands for God's majesty (*majd*).'

19. Others have narrated on his authority, adding that *mīm* stands for God's kingdom (*mulk*); 'God' being the God of all creatures; '*al-Raḥmān*' – Lord of Mercy, in that He is merciful to the whole world, and '*al-Raḥīm*' – Giver of extra mercy particularly to the believers.

20. Others have also narrated this on his authority, and God is the God of everything.

21. From Muḥammad b. 'Alī al-Ḥalabī[8], from Abū 'Abd Allāh (عليه السلام), that he used to recite – ﴾*Master of the Day of Judgement*﴿ (*māliki yawm al-dīn*).

---

8 Abū Ja'far Muḥammad b. 'Alī b. Abī Shu'ba al-Ḥalabī (d. before 148/765) was a noteworthy companion of the fifth and sixth Imams and the brother of 'Ubayd Allāh b. 'Alī, 'Imrān b. 'Alī and 'Abd al-A'lā, all of whom are deemed reliable and trustworthy narrators according

وَلَّوْا عَلَىٰ أَدْبَارِهِمْ نُفُورًا﴾، ﴿الْحَمْدُ لِلَّهِ رَبِّ الْعَالَمِينَ﴾. دعوى أهل الجنة، حين شكروا الله حسن الثواب، ﴿مَالِكِ يَوْمِ الدِّينِ﴾ قال جبرئيل ما قالها مسلم قطّ إلاّ صدّقه الله وأهل سماواته ﴿إِيَّاكَ نَعْبُدُ﴾ إخلاص العبادة ﴿وَإِيَّاكَ نَسْتَعِينُ﴾ أفضل ما طلب به العباد حوائجهم ﴿اهْدِنَا الصِّرَاطَ الْمُسْتَقِيمَ﴾ صراط الأنبياء، وهم الذين أنعم الله عليهم ﴿غَيْرِ الْمَغْضُوبِ عَلَيْهِمْ﴾ اليهود (وَغَيْرِ الضَّالِّينَ) النّصارى.

١٨. عن عبدالله بن سِنان، عن أبي عبدالله عليه السلام، في تفسير ﴿بِسْمِ اللَّهِ الرَّحْمَٰنِ الرَّحِيمِ﴾، فقال: الباء بهاء الله، والسين سَناء الله، والميم مجد الله.

١٩. وروى غيره عنه: مُلكُ الله، الله إله الخلق، الرّحمن بجميع العالم، الرّحيم بالمؤمنين خاصّة.

٢٠. وروى غيره عنه: والله إله كلّ شيء.

٢١. عن محمّد بن عليّ الحلبيّ، عن أبي عبدالله عليه السلام، أنّه كان يقرأ: ﴿مَالِكِ يَوْمِ الدِّينِ﴾.

22. From Dāwūd b. Farqad who narrated, 'I heard Abū 'Abd Allāh عليه السلام recite ﴾*Sovereign of the Day of Judgement*﴿ (*maliki yawm al-dīn*) countlessly.'

23. From al-Zuhrī who narrated, "'Alī b. al-Ḥusayn عليه السلام said, 'If everything from the east to the west were to die, I would not feel alone if the Qur'an was with me.' When he used to recite ﴾*Master of the Day of Judgement*﴿, he used to repeat it continuously as if he was on the verge of death.'

24. From al-Ḥasan b. Muḥammad al-Jammāl[9], from one of our associates who said, "'Abd al-Malik b. Marwān[10] sent a message to the governor of Medina, asking him to bring Muḥammad b. 'Alī b. al-Ḥusayn عليه السلام, without provoking him or alarming him, and to fulfil any needs that he had. This was because a man from among the Qadariyya[11] had come to 'Abd al-Malik, and all the people of Shām had gathered to debate with him, but he had defeated them all. So he said that there is one last resort and that is Muḥammad b. 'Alī عليه السلام. So he wrote to the governor of Medina to bring Muḥammad b. 'Alī to him, so the governor took his letter to him, and the Imam said to him, "I am an old man now and am not healthy enough to travel. Here is my son Ja'far عليه السلام – he can go instead of me," and he sent him off. When he approached the Umayyad caliph, he scorned him عليه السلام because of his youthful age, and was averse to the idea of a debate between him and the Qadarī lest the latter should defeat him. Word got around, and people in Shām soon came to know that Ja'far عليه السلام had come to debate with the Qadarī. The next

---

to Shī'ī tradition. See Ḥillī, *Khulāṣat al-aqwāl*, 243 (nr. 829); Modarressi, *Tradition and Survival*, 337–8 (nr. 147).

9 Some manuscripts have it on the authority of al-Ḥusayn b. Muḥammad al-Jammāl instead, which appears more likely.

10 'Abd al-Malik b. Marwān (r. 685–705) was the fifth Umayyad Caliph.

11 The Qadariyya or Qadarites were a theological branch of the early Mu'tazila whose followers denied God's predetermination of human actions, instead believing that all humans are free to act however they please. Their origins are supposedly traced back to Ma'bad b. 'Abd Allāh al-Juhanī (d. 80/699) of Basra and Ghaylān b. Muslim al-Dimishqī (d. 105/723): the former an associate and student (possibly) of al-Ḥasan al-Baṣrī while the latter was a contemporary of the Umayyad Caliphs Hishām b. 'Abd al-Malik (r. 105–125/724–743) and 'Umar b. 'Abd al-'Azīz (r. 95–98/717–720). Generally regarded as a heretical movement, the Qadariyya are condemned in a tradition attributed to the Prophet in which he states: "The Qadariyya are the *majūs* of this *umma*." See s.v. "Ḳadariyya," *Encyclopaedia of Islam*, Second Edition, iv, 368a (J v. Ess).

٢٢ . عن داود بن فَرْقَد، قال: سمعت أبا عبد الله عليه السلام يقرأ مالا أُحصي: ﴿مَـٰلِكِ يَوۡمِ ٱلدِّينِ﴾ .

٢٣ . عن الزُّهريّ، قال: قال عليّ بن الحسين عليه السلام: لو مات ما بين المشرق والمغرب لما استوحشتُ بعد أن يكون القرآن معي؛ وكان إذا قرأ ﴿مَـٰلِكِ يَوۡمِ ٱلدِّينِ﴾ يُكرّرها، ويكاد أن يموت.

٢٤ . عن الحسن بن محمّد الجمّال، عن بعض أصحابنا، قال: بعث عبد الملك بن مروان إلى عامل المدينة أن وَجِّه إليّ محمّد بن عليّ بن الحسين ولا تُهيّجه، ولا تروّعه، واقضِ له حوائجه، وقد كان ورد على عبد الملك رجلٌ من القدرية، فحضر جميع من كان بالشام فأعياهم جميعًا، فقال: ما لهذا إلاّ محمّد بن عليّ، فكتب إلى صاحب المدينة أن يحْمِل محمّد بن عليّ عليهما السلام إليه، فأتاه صاحب المدينة بكتابه، فقال له أبو جعفر عليه السلام: إنّي شيخٌ كبيرٌ، لا أقوى على الخُروج، وهذا جعفر ابني يقوم مقامي، فوجّهه إليه، فلمّا قَدِم على الأموي ازدراه لِصغره، وكَرِه أن يجمع بينه وبين القدريّ، مخافة أن يغْلِبه، وتسامع النّاس بالشّام بقُدُوم جعفر لمخاصمة القَدَريّ.

فلمّا كان من الغد اجتمع النّاس لخُصومتهما. فقال الأمويّ لأبي عبد الله عليه السلام: إنّه قد أعيانا أمر هذا القَدَريُّ، وإنّما كتبتُ إليك لأجمع بينك وبينه، لم يَدَع عندنا أحدًا إلاّ خَصَمه، فقال: إنّ الله يكفيناه.

day, people gathered to watch the debate, and the Umayyad caliph said to Abū ʿAbd Allāh عليه السلام, "This Qadarī's argument has thwarted us all. That is why I wrote to you, to bring you two together, for he has not left anyone here undefeated." He replied, "God suffices us." So when they had all gathered together, the Qadarī said to Abū ʿAbd Allāh, "Ask me whatever you want." He replied, "Recite the Opening Chapter of the Qur'an." So he recited it. The Umayyad – and I was with him – exclaimed, "What has the Opening Chapter got against us? To God we belong, and to Him we will return!" So the Qadarī started to recite the Opening until he reached God's verse: ﴾*It is You we worship, and it is You we ask for help.*﴿ At this point, Jaʿfar عليه السلام told him to stop, and said, "Who do you seek help from? Moreover why would you need provision, since the matter is in your own control?" The infidel was left dumbstruck. God does not guide people who are unjust.'

25. From Dāwūd b. Farqad, from Abū ʿAbd Allāh عليه السلام, who said, ﴾*Guide us to the straight path*﴿ refers to ʿAlī b. Abī Ṭālib – may God's blessings be upon him."'

26. Muḥammad b. ʿAlī al-Ḥalabī narrated, 'I have heard him reciting ﴾*Guide us to the straight path*﴿ a countless number of times when I am praying behind him.'

27. From Muʿāwiya b. Wahb who narrated, 'I asked Abū ʿAbd Allāh عليه السلام about God's verse: ﴾*not of those who incur anger, nor of those who have gone astray.*﴿ He replied, "They are the Jews and the Christians."'

28. From a man who narrated it from Ibn Abī ʿUmayr who, without mentioning his source, cited an Imam عليه السلام as having said about the verse: ﴾*not of those who incur anger, nor of those who have gone astray.*﴿[12] 'Those who incur anger are [Abū Bakr, ʿUmar and ʿUthmān] and the *nāṣibīs*,[13] and the ones who are astray are the skeptics who do not acknowledge the Imam.'

12 In this particular narration, a variant reading of the verse is quoted: *ghayr al-ḍāllīn* instead of *wa-la l-ḍāllīn*, which is a very rare reading of the script transmitted on the authority of ʿUmar b. al-Khaṭṭāb and some of the Imams.

13 The word *nāṣibī* (pl. *nuṣṣāb*) is a pejorative term frequently encountered in Shīʿī literature to refer to the enemies of the Household of the Prophet and their followers.

قال: فلمّا اجتمعوا، قال القَدَريُّ لأبي عبدالله عليه السلام: سَل عمّا شِئتَ، فقال له: اقرأ سورة الحمد. قال: فقرأها، وقال الأُمويُّ ــ وأنا معه ــ : ما في سورة الحمد علينا، إنّا لله وإنّا إليه راجعون!

فجعل القدريُّ يقرأ سورة الحمد حتّى بلغ قول الله تبارك وتعالى: ﴿إِيَّاكَ نَعْبُدُ وَإِيَّاكَ نَسْتَعِينُ﴾، فقال له جعفر عليه السلام: قِف، مَنْ تستعين، وما حاجتك إلى المعونة، إن الأمر إليك؟! فبُهِت الذي كفر، والله لا يهدي القوم الظّالمين.

٢٥. عن داود بن فَرْقَد، عن أبي عبدالله عليه السلام، قال: ﴿اهْدِنَا الصِّرَاطَ الْمُسْتَقِيمَ﴾ يعني أمير المؤمنين صلوات الله عليه.

٢٦. قال محمّد بن عليّ الحلبيّ: سمعته مالا أحصي، وأنا أُصلّي خلفه يقرأ ﴿اهْدِنَا الصِّرَاطَ الْمُسْتَقِيمَ﴾.

٢٧. عن معاوية بن وَهْب، قال: سألتُ أبا عبدالله عليه السلام، عن قول الله تعالى: ﴿غَيْرِ الْمَغْضُوبِ عَلَيْهِمْ وَلَا الضَّالِّينَ﴾؟ قال: هم اليهود والنّصارى.

٢٨. عن رجل، عن ابن أبي عُمير، رفعه في قوله: ﴿غَيْرِ الْمَغْضُوبِ عَلَيْهِمْ وَغَيْرِ الضَّالِّينَ﴾ هكذا نزلت، قال: المغضوب عليهم: فلان وفلان وفلان والنُصّاب، والضّالّين: الشُكّاك الذين لا يعرفون الإمام.

The Cow

2. The Cow

1. From Sa'd al-Iskāf[1]: 'I heard Abū Ja'far ﵇ say, "The Messenger of God ﷺ said: 'I have been given the lengthy chapters (*al-ṭiwāl*)[2] [of the Qur'an] in lieu of the Torah (*al-tawrā*), [the chapters comprising] a hundred verses of more (*al-mi'ūn*) as a substitute for the Gospel (*al-injīl*), the middle frequently-recited chapters (*al-mathānī*) in equivalent standing to the Psalms [of David] (*al-zabūr*), and to my distinction I have been privileged with the last sixty-seven chapters (*al-mufaṣṣal*) [of the Qur'an].'"'

2. From Abū Baṣīr, from Abū 'Abd Allāh ﵇ who said, 'Whoever recites the Chapter of the Cow (*sūrat al-baqara*) and The Family of 'Imrān (*sūrat āl 'imrān*) will be shaded by them on the Day of Judgement like two clouds or canopies above their heads.'

3. From 'Umar b. Jumay'[3] who, without mentioning his source, cited 'Alī ﵇ as narrating the following: 'The Messenger of God ﷺ stated, "Whoever

1 Sa'd b. Ṭarīf al-Ḥanẓalī al-Iskāf, a weak and unreliable narrator according to Najāshī and Ibn al-Ghaḍā'irī. He was a renowned story-teller in the late Umayyad period and known supporter of 'Alī b. Abī Ṭālib. See Ḥillī, *Khulāṣat al-aqwāl*, 352–3 (nr. 1390); Modarressi, *Tradition and Survival*, 118–21 (nr. 12).

2 According to Muḥsin Fayḍ al-Kāshānī (d. 1091/1680–81), the *al-ṭiwāl* or 'long chapters' refer to the seven or eight longest chapters of the Qur'an after the Opening (*sūrat al-fātiḥa*) up to and including the Repentance (*sūrat al-tawba*). Similarly the *al-mi'ūn* refer to those chapters of the Qur'an which contain one hundred verses or more, while the *al-mathānī* are those chapters which are shorter than a hundred verses but greater in length than the *al-mufaṣṣal* chapters, i.e. chapters 40–114 of the Qur'an.

3 This is more than likely a transcription error for Abū 'Uthmān 'Amr b. Jumay' al-Azdī since neither Ḥillī nor Khū'ī have an entry for the name 'Umar b. Jumay' in their respective works. For 'Amr b. Jumay' see Khū'ī, *Mu'jam*, 14:90 (no. 8884); Ḥillī, *Khulāṣat al-aqwāl*, 386 (nr. 1513); Modarressi, *Tradition and Survival*, 200–2 (nr. 41). He was a Sunnī narrator

بسم الله الرحمن الرحيم

من سورة البقرة

١. عن سعد الإسكاف، قال: سَمعت أبا جعفر عليه السلام يقول: قال رسول الله صلى الله عليه وآله: أعطيت الطِوال مكان التوراة، وأُعطيت المِئين مكان الإنجيل، وأعطيت المثاني مكان الزَبُور، وفُضِّلت بالمفَصّل سبع وستّين سورة.

٢. عن أبي بصير، عن أبي عبدالله عليه السلام، قال: من قرأ البقرة وآل عِمران، جاء يوم القيامة تُظلاَّنه على رأسه مثل الغَمامَتين، أو غَيابَتَين.

٣. عن عمر بن جُمَيع، رفعه إلى عليّ عليه السلام، قال: قال رسول الله صلى الله عليه وآله: من قرأ أربع آيات من أوّل البقرة، وآية الكُرسيّ، وآيتين بعدها، وثلاث آياتٍ من آخرها، لم يرَ في نفسه وأهله وماله شيئًا يَكْرَهه، ولم يَقْرَبه الشيطان ولم يَنْسَ القرآن.

قوله تعالى: ﴿الٓمٓ . ذَٰلِكَ ٱلۡكِتَٰبُ لَا رَيۡبَۛ فِيهِۛ هُدٗى لِّلۡمُتَّقِينَ﴾ الآية.

recites the first four verses of the Chapter of the Cow, the Verse of the Throne (*āyat al-kursī*) accompanied by the two verses following it, and the last three verses of the Chapter of the Cow, then he shall never see in himself, his family or his wealth anything which causes displeasure in him. Neither shall he be approached by Shayṭān nor shall he ever forget the Qur'an."'

4. From Sa'dān b. Muslim, from one of his associates, from Abū 'Abd Allāh ﵇ that regarding the verses ﴾*Alif Lām Mīm. This is the Scripture in which there is no doubt*﴿ he ﵇ said: 'The Book of 'Alī has no doubt in it.' Regarding the verse ﴾*containing guidance for those who are mindful of God*﴿ he ﵇ said: 'Those who are mindful of God are our followers (*shī'atunā*).' Regarding the verse ﴾*who believe in the unseen, keep up the prayer, and give out of what We have provided for them*﴿ he ﵇ said: 'and spread [to others] of what we have taught them.' (2:1–3)

5. From Muḥammad b. Qays[4]: 'I heard Abū Ja'far ﵇ narrate the following: 'Ḥuyyī and Abū Yāsir, the sons of Akhṭab, as well as some other Jews and a group of individuals from Khaybar came to the Messenger of God ﷺ and asked him, "Is this *alif lām mīm* which you recite part of what has been sent down to you?"

After the Messenger ﷺ confirmed that they were indeed part of the revelation they asked him, "Did Jibra'īl bring it down to you from God?"

He ﷺ again replied yes.

They said, "Before you there have been many other prophets, and apart from you we know not of a single one among them except he had informed [the people of his community] about the length of his mission and the appointed lifespan of their nation."

---

with Shī'ī tendencies and served as a judge in Ḥulwān and Ray at different periods of his life. He is considered a weak (*ḍa'īf*) narrator in his reports of the Imams' traditions.

4 Abū Naṣr Muḥammad b. Qays al-Asadī, a reliable Sunnī narrator from Imams Muḥammad al-Bāqir and Ja'far al-Ṣādiq. See Ḥillī, *Khulāṣat al-aqwāl*, 236 (nr. 805); cf. Modarressi, *Tradition and Survival*, 345–7 (nr. 155).

٤. عن سعدان بن مسلم، عن بعض أصحابه، عن أبي عبد الله عليه السلام، في قوله ﴿الٓمٓ . ذَٰلِكَ الْكِتَابُ لَا رَيْبَ فِيهِ﴾، قال: كتاب عليّ لا ريب فيه ﴿هُدًى لِّلْمُتَّقِينَ﴾ قال: المتّقون شيعتنا ﴿الَّذِينَ يُؤْمِنُونَ بِالْغَيْبِ وَيُقِيمُونَ الصَّلَاةَ وَمِمَّا رَزَقْنَاهُمْ يُنفِقُونَ﴾ وممّا علّمناهم يبثّون.

٥. عن محمّد بن قيس، قال: سَمِعتُ أبا جعفر عليه السلام يُحدّث، قال: أن حُيَيًّا وأبا ياسر ابني أخْطَب، ونفرًا من اليهود أهل خيبر، أتَوَا رسول الله صلى الله عليه وآله وسلم، فقالوا له: أليس فيما تَذكُر فيما أُنزِل عليك ﴿الٓمٓ﴾؟ قال: بلى، قالوا: أتاك بها جبْرَئيل من عند الله؟ قال: نعم، قالوا: لقد بُعِثت أنبياء قبلك، ما نعلم نبيًّا منهم أخبر ما مدّة مُلكه، وما أجل أُمّته غيرك! فأقبل حُيي على أصحابه، فقال لهم: الألِف واحدٌ، واللام ثلاثُون، والميم أربعون، فهي إحدى وسبعون سنةً، فعجب ممّن يدْخُل في دين مدّة مُلكه وأجل أُمّته إحدى وسبعون سنة!

Then Ḥūyyī turned to his companions and stated, "My friends, the *alif* stands for one, the *lām* equals thirty and the *mīm* equals forty, which makes their sum equal to seventy-one."[5]

Astonished at why anyone would consider entering a religion whose lifespan and whose community would only survive for seventy-one years, he turned towards the Messenger of God ﷺ and asked, "O Muḥammad, is there anything else apart from this?"

He ﷺ replied, "Yes, ﴾*Alif Lām Mīm Ṣād*﴿.(7:1)"

He [Ḥuyyī] said, "This is much longer and more weighty: the *alif* is equal to one, the *lām* equals thirty [...].[6]

* * *

5 The Abjad numerals are a decimal system wherein the twenty-eight letters of the Arabic alphabet are assigned numerical values. The Abjad system of numerals was used among the Arabic speaking peoples of the Near East since before the eighth century for, among other things, the purpose of numerology, and are equivalent to the earlier Hebrew numerals; s.v. "Abdjad," *Encyclopaedia of Islam*, Second Edition, i, 97a (G. Wiel [G. S. Colin]).

6 The editors of the Arabic editions of 'Ayyāshī's *Tafsīr* each remark that in the original manuscript the report abruptly cuts off here and that there is a lacuna of at least a few pages. 'Ayyāshī himself also comments in the marginal note of at least one manuscript that the version from which he was copying was defective and that some pages had probably fallen out of the original source text. However al-'Allāma al-Majlisī in his *Biḥār al-anwār* and similarly Shaykh al-Ṣadūq in his *Ma'ānī al-akhbār* report the tradition in full as follows: "'[...] the *mīm* equals forty and the *ṣād* equals ninety, the total sum of which is one hundred and sixty-one years.' Then he asked the Messenger of God ﷺ, 'Is there anything more?' He replied, 'Yes,' to which they said, 'Go ahead.' He ﷺ said, '﴾*Alif Lām Rā*﴿.' He [Ḥuyyī] said, 'Yes, this is even longer and weightier: the *alif* is equal to one, the *lām* to thirty, the *mīm* to forty and the *rā'* to two hundred. Do you have any others [O Muḥammad]?' He ﷺ replied, 'Yes.' So they said, 'You are confusing us, and we cannot make sense of what it is you have been given exactly.' They then got up to leave, and Abū Yāsir said to his brother, Ḥuyyī, 'Do you not wonder if perhaps Muḥammad has been given the sum of all these and more?' [...]."

ثمّ أقبل على رسول الله ﷺ، فقال له: يا محمّد، هل مع هذا غيره؟ فقال: نعم، قال: ﴿الٓمٓصٓ﴾ قال: هذه أثقل وأطول، الألف واحدٌ، واللام ثلاثون، [والميم أربعون، والصاد تسعون، فهذه مائة وإحدى وستّون سنة!

ثمّ قال لرسول الله ﷺ: فهل مع هذا غيره؟ قال: نعم. قال: هَاتِه، قال ﷺ: ﴿الٓر﴾ ، قال: هذه أثقل وأطول، الألف واحدٌ، واللام ثلاثون، والراء مائتان!

ثمّ قال لرسول الله ﷺ: فهل مع هذا غيره؟ قال: نعم. قال: هَاتِه، قال ﷺ: ﴿الٓمٓر﴾، قال: هذه أثقل وأطول، الألف واحدٌ، واللام ثلاثون، الميم أربعون، والراء مائتان! ثم قال له: هل مع هذا غيره؟ قال: نعم. قالوا: قد التبس علينا أمرك، فما ندري ما أُعطيت! ثم قاموا عنه، ثمّ قال أبو ياسر لحُيّي أخيه: ما يُدريك، لعلّ محمّدًا قد جُمِع له هذا كُلّه وأكثر منه. قال: فذكر أبو جعفر عليه السلام: أنّ هذه الآيات أُنزلت فيهم ﴿مِنْهُ آيَاتٌ مُحْكَمَاتٌ هُنَّ أُمُّ الْكِتَابِ وَأُخَرُ مُتَشَابِهَاتٌ﴾، قال: وهي تجري في وجهٍ آخر تأويل حُيي وأبي ياسر وأصحابهما].

6. ʿAlī b. Ibrāhīm al-Qummī narrates in his *Tafsīr*: 'My father narrated to me from al-Ḥasan b. Maḥbūb[7], from ʿAmr b. Abī al-Miqdām[8] from Thābit al-Ḥidhā'[9] from Jābir b. Yazīd al-Juʿfī[10] from Abū Jaʿfar Muḥammad b. ʿAlī b. al-Ḥusayn عليه السلام, on his father's authority, from his forefathers from the Commander of the Faithful ʿAlī عليه السلام who said: "God, Blessed and most High, wished to originate a creation with His own Hands after some seven thousand years had passed since the Jinn and the *nasnās*[11] had started inhabiting the earth. When He felt like creating Ādam عليه السلام He uncovered the strata of the heavens and told the angels to look down and observe His creation of the Jinn and *nasnās*. So when they saw the extent of sinning, bloodshed and corruption they were perpetrating on the earth, it was too much for them to bear. They became angry with God and distressed at the state of the land. Being unable to control their sense of outrage they said: 'Our Lord, You are the Mightiest, the Omnipotent, the Conqueror and Subjugator, of great Majesty, and yet You have these weak and base creatures in the palm of

---

7 Abū ʿAlī al-Ḥasan b. Maḥbūb al-Sarād (d. 224/839), a reliable (*thiqa*) narrator and close companion of Imam ʿAlī b. Mūsā al-Riḍā. He is regarded as one of four major reporters of Imāmī *ḥadīth* during the eighth Imam's lifetime. See Ḥillī, *Khulāṣat al-aqwāl*, 97 (nr. 222).

8 There is disagreement among the *rijāl* authors as to whether this is a reference to ʿAmr b. Abī al-Miqdām Thābit b. Hirmiz or ʿAmr b. Thābit b. Haram al-Ḥaddād and whether or not these are in fact the same individual. See the editor's footnote in Ḥillī, *Khulāṣat al-aqwāl*, 212 (nr. 696).

9 Thābit b. Hirmiz al-Ḥidhā', on whom there is scant information, was a frequent narrator of the traditions of Jābir b. Yazīd al-Juʿfī. See Khū'ī, *Muʿjam*, 4:307 (nr. 1983).

10 Jābir b. Yazīd b. al-Ḥārith al-Juʿfī (d. 128/745–6) was a companion of the fifth and sixth Imams. He was highly regarded in his day as a fount of knowledge and learning, with whom many scholars – Shīʿī and Sunnī alike – studied. He relayed thousands of *ḥadīth* and is reported to have spent 18 years studying under Imam Muḥammad al-Bāqir. He is variously described by the likes of Najāshī and others as being weak and unreliable, except that the majority of these reports are based on unreliable narrators. According to Ibn al-Ghaḍā'irī the reason for the negative opinion surrounding him is due more to the fact that those who reported from Jābir are unreliable transmitters, not that he himself was unreliable. This opinion is the one which later scholars of *rijāl* have adopted, thereby absolving Jābir of any blameworthy characteristics. However, there are many reports in heresiographical texts that Jābir may have joined, or at least sympathized with, the extremist Shīʿī sect known as the Mughīriyya, founded by Mughīra b. Saʿīd al-Bajalī (d. 119/737). See Ḥillī, *Khulāṣat al-aqwāl*, 94–5 (nr. 213); Modarressi, *Tradition and Survival*, 86–103 (nr. 7).

11 In Arabic folklore the *nasnās* are said to have been monstrous creatures, described by Edward Lane as being 'half a human being; having half a head, half a body, one arm, one leg, with which it hops with much agility.'

٦. عن الحسن بن محبوب، عن عمرو بن أبي المِقدام، عن جابر، عن أبي جعفر عليه السلام قال: قالَ أمير المؤُمنين عليه السلام: إنَّ الله تبارك وتعالى لمَا أحبَّ أن يخلُق خَلقًا بيده، وذلك بعد ما مضى من الجنّ والنَّسْنَاس في الأرض سبعة آلاف سنة، قال: ولمَّا كان من شأن الله أن يَخْلق آدم عليه السلام للذي أراد من التدبير والتقدير لما هو مكوّنه في السماوات والأرض، وعلمه لما أراد من ذلك كُلَّه، كَشَط عن أطباق السماوات، ثم قال للملائكة: انظُروا إلى أهل الأرض من خَلقي من الجنِّ والنَّسْنَاس، فلمّا رأوا ما يعملون فيها من المعاصي وسَفْك الدماء والفساد في الأرض بغير الحقّ، عظُمَ ذلك عليهم، وغَضِبوا لله، وأسِفُوا على الأرض، ولم يَملِكوا غضبهم أن قالوا: ياربّ، أنت العزيز القادر الجبَّار القاهر العظيم الشأن، وهذا خلقك الضعيف الذليل في أرضك يتقلَّبون في قَبْضَتك، ويعيشون برِزْقك، ويستمتعون بعافيتك، وهم يَعْصُونك بمثل هذه الذنوب العِظام، لا تأسَف ولا تَغْضَب ولا تنتقم لنفسك لما تسمع منهم وترى، وقد عَظُم ذلك علينا وأكبرناه فيك!

Your hand doing as they please, living off Your sustenance and enjoying Your bounties, whilst continuing to disobey You by committing such grave sins. You neither get distressed nor angry with them, nor do You avenge Yourself against them in spite of everything that You see and hear happening! This is too much for us to bear and we admire You for it.'

When He heard the angels say this He said, '﴾*I am putting a successor on earth*﴿ who will be My proof therein over My creation.'

So the angels retorted, '﴾*How can You put someone there who will cause damage and bloodshed*﴿ like the Jinn have done? They will be jealous and hateful towards each other. Make this successor from one of us, for we are never jealous or hateful towards one another and neither do we spill blood. It is we who ﴾*celebrate Your praise and proclaim Your holiness*﴿.'

So God, Mighty and Exalted, said '﴾*I know things you do not*﴿. I want to originate a creation with My own hands and make prophets, messengers, righteous servants and rightly-guided leaders from his progeny, and I will make them the inheritors of My earth over My creatures. They will prevent them from wrongdoing and warn them of My chastisement, and they will guide them to My obedience, show them the path to Me. I will make them My authority over them, be it as a warning or as proof. I will free the earth of the *nasnās* and cleanse it of them. I will move the wrongdoing Jinn away from My human creation and My chosen ones, and will inhabit them in the air and the far corners of the Earth so that they do not come anywhere near the progeny of My creation. I will place a barrier between the Jinn and My creation so that they can neither see the Jinn nor sit with them, nor frequent them. Whoever from the progeny of this creation of mine that I have chosen disobeys Me, I will make them inhabit the dwelling places of those who sin and make them their inmates without a second thought.'

So the angels said, 'Our Lord, do as You wish, ﴾*we have knowledge only of what You have taught us. You are the All-Knowing and All-Wise*﴿.' Then God, Blessed and most High, said '﴾*I will create a mortal out of dried clay, formed from dark mud. When I have fashioned him and breathed My spirit into him, bow down before him*﴿'(15:28–29). This was both a mark of distinction for Ādam before he had even been created as well as an argument that He could use against them.

فلمّا سَمِع الله عزّ وجلّ ذلك من الملائكة قال ﴿إِنِّي جَاعِلٌ فِي الأَرْضِ خَلِيفَةً﴾ لي عليهم، فيكون حُجّةً لي في أرضي على خلقي. فقالت الملائكة: سبحانك ﴿أَتَجْعَلُ فِيهَا مَنْ يُفْسِدُ فِيهَا وَيَسْفِكُ الدِّمَاءَ وَنَحْنُ نُسَبِّحُ بِحَمْدِكَ وَنُقَدِّسُ لَكَ﴾، وقالوا: فاجعله منا، فإنّا لا نُفْسد في الأرض ولا نَسْفِك الدماء.

قال جلّ جلاله: يا ملائكتي ﴿إِنِّي أَعْلَمُ مَا لَا تَعْلَمُونَ﴾، إنّي أريد أن أخلُق خَلقًا بيدي، أجعل ذُرّيته أنبياء مرسلين وعبادًا صالحين وأئمّةً مهتدين، أجعلهم خلفائي على خَلقي في أرضي، يَنْهَوْنَهم عن المعاصي، ويُنذرونهم عذابي، ويهدونهم إلى طاعتي، ويَسْلُكون بهم طريق سبيلي، وأجعلهم حُجّةً لي عُذرًا أو نُذرًا، وأُبين النَّسْنَاس من أرضي، فأُطّهرها منهم، وأنقل مَرَدَةَ الجِنّ العُصاة عن بريّتي وخَلقي وخيرتي، وأسكنهم في الهواء وفي أقطار الأرض، لا يجاورون نسل خلقي، وأجعل بين الجنّ وبين خَلقي حِجابًا، ولا يرى نَسل خَلقي الجِنّ، ولا يُؤانسونهم ولا يُخالطونهم ولا يُجالسونهم، فمن عصاني من نَسل خَلقي الذين اصطفيتهم لنفسي أسكنتهم مساكن العُصاة، وأوردتهم مواردهم ولا أُبالي.

فقالت الملائكة: يا ربّنا افعل ما شئت ﴿لَا عِلْمَ لَنَا إِلَّا مَا عَلَّمْتَنَا إِنَّكَ أَنْتَ الْعَلِيمُ الْحَكِيمُ﴾، فقال الله جلّ جلاله للملائكة ﴿إِنِّي خَالِقٌ بَشَرًا مِنْ صَلْصَالٍ مِنْ حَمَإٍ مَسْنُونٍ ۝ فَإِذَا سَوَّيْتُهُ وَنَفَخْتُ فِيهِ مِنْ رُوحِي فَقَعُوا لَهُ سَاجِدِينَ﴾، وكان ذلك من أمر الله عزّ وجلّ تقدّم إلى الملائكة في آدم عليه السلام من قبل أن يَخْلُقه احتجاجًا منه عليهم.

Then Our Lord, Blessed and most High, took a handful of sweet, fresh water in His right Hand – and both His Hands are right – and he kneaded it all together until it had formed. Then He said addressing it, "From you I am going to create prophets and messengers, righteous servants and rightly-guided leaders who usher others to the Garden, as well as all their followers until the Day of Judgement. I cannot be taken to task nor questioned for what I do, but they will be questioned." Then He took another handful][12] of salty, bitter water, and kneaded it all in His Hand until it formed, then said to it, "From you, I am going to create the tyrants, the pharaohs, the insolent ones, the associates of Shayṭān, the leaders of disbelief and those who call others to the Fire, and all their followers until the Day of Judgement. I cannot be taken to task nor questioned about what I do, but they will be asked."'

[Imam 'Alī] says, 'He reserved the right to alter the decree regarding them though this is not necessarily the case about the people of the Right.'

Then he kneaded the two types of waters in His Palm altogether and made it into sounding clay, then laid it out in front of His Throne while it was still wet mud. He commanded the four angels of the northerly, westerly, easterly and southerly winds to blow back and forth around the essence of this clay. So they prepared it, straightened it, burnished it, then departed, leaving the four humors to flow within it: air, phlegm, bile and blood. Then the angels of the northerly, southerly, westerly and easterly winds swept around it and made the four humors flow within it. The air in the four humors corresponds to the northerly wind, phlegm to the easterly, bile to the westerly, and blood to the southerly wind. Then the soul wafted upwards and the body was complete. The air in it brought about the love of life, high hopes and avidity in him; the phlegm injected a love of food, drink, and clothing, as well as softness, clemency and leniency; the bile brought about anger, folly, devilishness, high-handedness, rebellion and haste; and the blood brought about a desire for women, pleasures, and a taste for the forbidden.'

---

12 As mentioned above some of the pages of 'Ayyāshī's original manuscript from which he was copying are no longer extant, and hence this tradition starts midway from this point forwards. The whole tradition can however be found in the *Tafsīr* of 'Alī b. Ibrāhīm al-Qummī, and is cited here in full. Shaykh al-Ṣadūq quotes the full narration in *'Ilal al-Sharā'i'* as does al-'Allāma al-Majlisī in his *Biḥār al-anwār*, relying on the works of his two predecessors.

قال: فاغترف تبارك وتعالى غُرفةً من الماء العَذْب الفُرات فَصَلْصَلَها فَجَمَدَت، ثمّ قال لها: منك أخلُقُ النبيّين والمرسلين، وعبادي الصالحين، والأئمّة المهتدين الدُّعاة إلى الجنّة وأتباعهم إلى يوم القيامة ولا أبالي، ولا أُسأل عمّا أفعل وهم يُسألون — يعني بذلك خَلقَه — . ثمّ اغترف غُرفة ﴿من الماء المِلح الأُجاج، فصَلْصلها في كفّه فجَمَدَت، ثمّ قال لها: منك أخلُقُ الجبّارين والفَراعِنة والعُتاة إخوان الشياطين، وأئمّة الكفر، والدُّعاة إلى النّار وأتباعهم إلى يوم القيامة ولا أُبالي، ولا أُسأل عمّا أفعل وهم يُسألون، وأشترط في ذلك البَدَاء فيهم، ولم يشترط في أصحاب اليمين البَدَاء لله فيهم، ثمّ خلط الماءين في كفّه جميعًا فصَلْصَلَهما ثمّ اكفأهما قُدّام عرشه، وهم بَلّةٌ من طين.

ثمّ أمر الملائكة الأربعة: الشّمال، والدَّبُور، والصَّبا، والجَنُوب أن جولوها على هذه البَلّة الطين، فأبْرِئوها وأنْشئوها ثمّ جَزّئوها وفصّلوها، وأجروا فيها الطبائع الأربع: الرّيح، والبَلغم، والمِرّة، والدّم، قال: فجالت عليها الملائكة الشّمال، والجَنُوب، والدَّبُور، والصَّبَا، وأجروا فيها الطبائع، فالرّيح في الطبائع الأربع من قبل الشّمال، والبَلْغَم في الطبائع الأربع في البَدَن من ناحية الصَّبَا، قال: والمِرّة في الطبائع الأربع من ناحية الدَّبور، قال: والدم في الطبائع الأربع من ناحية الجَنُوب.

قال فاستعلت النَّسمة وكَمَل البدن، قال: فلزمها من ناحية الرّيح: حبُّ الحياة، وطول الأمل والحِرص، ولَزِمها من ناحية البَلْغَم: حبُّ الطعام والشراب واللباس واللين والحِلم والرفق، ولَزِمها من ناحية المِرّة: الغضب والسَفَه والشّيطنة والتجبّر والتمرُّد والعَجَلة، ولَزِمها من ناحية الدم: الشّهوة للنساء واللّذات ورُكوب المحارم في الشهوات. قال أبو

Abū ʿAlī al-Ḥasan b. Maḥbūb said, reporting from ʿAmr, from Jābir that Abū Jaʿfar عليه السلام narrated to him, 'We found this discourse written in one of the books of ʿAlī b. Abī Ṭālib.'

7. He [the same narrator] reported, 'Hishām b. Sālim said, "Abū ʿAbd Allāh عليه السلام said, 'The angels could not have said "﴾*How can You put someone there* [*on the earth*] *who will cause damage and bloodshed?*﴿"(2:30) had it not been for the fact that they had already seen someone cause corruption and bloodshed therein previously.'"'

8. From Muḥammad b. Marwān[13], from Jaʿfar b. Muḥammad عليه السلام that he said the following: 'I was circumambulating the House [of God] with my father when, all of a sudden, a tall abrasive looking man wearing a turban approached us. He said, "I bid you peace, O son of the Messenger of God," so my father replied him. He continued, "There were a few things I wanted to ask you about, things no longer known except perhaps to maybe one or two individuals." My father completed his circumambulation, entered the *ḥijr* [of Ismāʿīl][14] offering two units of prayer there, and then, when he had finished, said to me, "Let's go, Jaʿfar" and moved in the direction of the man saying to him, "You seem to be a stranger around here."

The man replied, "That is right, [and if you would be so courteous as to oblige a stranger] please tell me about this circumambulation, how did it come about and why?"

So he عليه السلام replied, 'When God told the angels ﴾*I am putting a successor on earth. They asked, 'How can You put someone there who will cause damage and bloodshed. When we celebrate Your praise and proclaim Your holiness?' but He said, 'I know things you do not*﴿(2:30) He was referring to the unruly ones from among them, so He veiled Himself from them for seven years, whereupon they would seek refuge at the Throne saying, 'Acknowledge us, O Lord of the lofty ranks, acknowledge us,' until He turned to them

13 Muḥammad b. Marwān al-Jallāb, a reliable (*thiqa*) transmitter of the eighth Imam's traditions. See Ḥillī, *Khulāṣat al-aqwāl*, 242 (nr. 824).

14 The *ḥijr* of Ismāʿīl is an area beside the north side of the Kaʿba where Prophet Ismāʿīl is said to have been buried.

عليّ الحسن بن محبوب: وأخبرني عمرو، عن جابر أنَّ أبا جعفر عليه السلام أخبره أنّه قال: وجدنا هذا الكلام مكتوبًا في كتاب من كتب عليَّ بن أبي طالب عليه السلام.

٧. قال: قال هِشام بن سالم، قال أبو عبد الله عليه السلام: وما علم الملائكة بقولهم: ﴿أَتَجْعَلُ فِيهَا مَنْ يُفْسِدُ فِيهَا وَيَسْفِكُ الدِّمَاءَ﴾ لولا أنَّهم قد كانوا رأوا مَن يُفسِد فيها ويَسفِك الدماء.

٨. عن محمّد بن مَروان عن جعفر بن محمّد عليهما السلام، قال: إنّي لأطوف بالبيت مع أبي عليه السلام، إذ أقبل رجلٌ طُوَال جُعشُم مُتعمِّم بعمامةٍ، فقال: السلام عليك يا بن رسول الله صلّى الله عليه وآله وسلّم، قال: فردَّ عليه أبي، فقال: أشياء أردت ان أسألك عنها، ما بقي أحدٌ يعلمها إلاّ رجل أو رجلان. قال: فلمّا قضى أبي الطواف دخل الحِجر فصلّى ركعتين، ثمَّ قال: ها هنا يا جعفر، ثمَّ أقبل على الرجل، فقال له أبي: كأنّك غريب؟ فقال: أجل، فأخبرني عن هذا الطّواف، كيف كان؟ ولم كان؟ قال: إنَّ الله لمّا قال للملائكة ﴿إِنِّي جَاعِلٌ فِي الأَرْضِ خَلِيفَةً قَالُوا أَتَجْعَلُ فِيهَا مَنْ يُفْسِدُ فِيهَا﴾ إلى آخر الآية، كان ذلك من يعصي منهم، فاحتجب عنهم سبع سنين، فلاذوا بالعرش يلوذون، يقولون: لبَّيك ذا المعارج لبَّيك؛ حتّى تاب عليهم، فلمّا أصاب آدم الذّنب طاف بالبيت حتّى قَبِل الله منه، قال: صَدَقت، فعَجِب أبي من قوله: صَدَقت. قال: فأخبرني عن: ﴿ن ۚ وَالْقَلَمِ وَمَا يَسْطُرُونَ﴾، قال: نون نهرٌ في الجنَّة أشدُّ بياضًا من اللّبَن، قال: فأمر الله القلم،فجرى بما

mercifully. Then, when Ādam عليه السلام committed the error he circumambulated the House until God accepted him.'

[The man] said, 'You speak the truth.'

My father was surprised at his statement, "You speak the truth."

Then he asked, "Now tell me about the verse ﴾*Nūn. By the pen and what they write*﴿"(68:1).

So he replied, "*Nūn* is a river in Paradise, whiter than milk. God has commanded the Pen to write whatever happens, and whatever will come to be, so it is established before Him, and He adds to it whatever He wills and omits whatever He wills. Whatever He wills comes to pass and whatever He does not will does not come to be."

[The man] said, "You speak the truth."

Again my father was surprised at his statement, "You speak the truth."

Then he asked, "Now tell me about the verse ﴾*those who give a due share of their wealth*﴿(70:24), what is this due share?"

He replied, "It is referring to a portion of a man's wealth that he gives away but which does not constitute the obligatory alms tax (*zakāt*) and is thus specifically reserved for either one afflicted by misfortune or one who is a close relative."

[The man] said, "You speak the truth."

My father was again surprised at his statement, "You speak the truth."

Then the man got up and left.

My father exclaimed, "Bring that man back!"

So I went to look for him but did not find him anywhere.' [2:30]

9. From Muḥammad b. Marwān who narrated, 'I heard Abū 'Abd Allāh عليه السلام say, "I was with my father at the *ḥijr* [of Ismā'īl], and while he was standing in prayer a man came and sat beside him. When he had finished he greeted him saying, "I want to ask you about three things that only you and one other man know the answer to."

My father asked him, "And what are these?"

He continued, "Tell me, what is it that explains the reason why people circumambulate this House?"

هوكائن ومايكون، فهو بين يديه موضوعٌ ما شاء منه زاد فيه، وما شاء نقص منه، وما شاء كان، وما لا يشاء لا يكون. قال: صدقت، فعَجِب أبي من قوله صدقت.

قال: فأخبرني عن: ﴿وَفِيٓ أَمۡوَٰلِهِمۡ حَقٞ مَّعۡلُومٞ﴾، ما هذا الحقّ المعلوم؟ قال: هو الشيء يُخرِجه الرجل من ماله ليس من الزكاة، فيكون للنائبة والصِّلة، قال: صدقت. قال: فعَجِب أبي من قوله صَدَقت. قال: ثمّ قام الرجل، فقال أبي: عليَّ بالرجل، قال: فطَلَبته فلم أجِدْه.

٩. عن محمّد بن مرْوان، قال: سمِعتُ أبا عبد الله عليه السلام يقول: كنتُ مع أبي في الحِجْر، فبينا هو قائم يصلّي إذا أتاه رجل فجلس إليه، فلمّا انصرف سلّم عليه، قال: إنّي أسألك عن ثلاثة أشياء، لا يعلمها إلاّ أنت ورجلٌ آخر، قال: ماهي؟ قال: أخبرني أيّ شيء كان سبب الطّواف بهذا البيت؟

So he عليه السلام replied, “When God, the Sublime, commanded the angels to prostrate before Ādam they retorted saying, ﴾*How can You put someone there who will cause damage and bloodshed when we celebrate Your praise and proclaim Your holiness?’ But He said, ‘I know things you do not*﴿. When they said this He became angry with them, so they asked to be forgiven. Thereupon He commanded them to circumambulate the shrine which is the Oft-Visited House (*al-bayt al-maʿmūr*), and doing so they stayed there circumambulating it for seven years seeking God’s forgiveness for what they had said; then He forgave them and was pleased with them. So this was the origin of the circumambulation, after which He established the Sacred House directly under the shrine as a means of repentance and purification for whoever has committed a sin from the progeny of Ādam.”

The man said, “You speak the truth,” and went on to ask the other two questions in the aforementioned narration.

Afterwards the man got up and left, and I asked my father, “Who was that man, father?”

He replied, “My son, that was Khiḍr.”’ [2:30]

10. From ʿAlī b. al-Ḥusayn عليه السلام regarding the verse ﴾*When your Lord told the angels, ‘I am putting a successor on earth,’ they said, ‘How can You put someone there who will cause damage and bloodshed?*﴿: ‘They retorted to God saying ﴾*How can You put someone there who will cause damage and bloodshed?*﴿ referring to the previous creation of the Jinn. By saying ﴾*when we celebrate Your praise and proclaim Your holiness?*﴿ they were reminding God of their worship of Him, so He turned away from them.

Then ﴾*He taught Ādam all the names, then He showed them to the angels and said, ‘Tell me the names of these if you truly* [*think you can*]*.’ They said, ‘May You be glorified! We have knowledge only of what You have taught us. You are the All-Knowing and All-Wise.’ Then He said, ‘Ādam, tell them the names of these.’ When he told them their names, God said, ‘Bow down before Ādam’, so they bowed down*﴿ and in the course of their bowing they thought to themselves, “We never imagined that God would create a being dearer to Him than us, when we are the keepers of His treasures, His neighbours, and the closest in proximity to Him.” So when they raised their heads God said ﴾*I know what you reveal and what you conceal*﴿ – that is to say, I know

فقال: إنّ الله تبارك وتعالى لمّا أمر الملائكة أن يَسْجُدوا لآدم، ردّت الملائكة فقالت: ﴿أَتَجْعَلُ فِيهَا مَن يُفْسِدُ فِيهَا وَيَسْفِكُ الدِّمَاءَ وَنَحْنُ نُسَبِّحُ بِحَمْدِكَ وَنُقَدِّسُ لَكَ قَالَ إِنِّي أَعْلَمُ مَا لَا تَعْلَمُونَ﴾، فغَضِب عليهم، ثمّ سألوه التوبة فأمرهم أن يطوفوا بالضُراح، — وهو البيت المعمور — فمكثوا به يطوفون به سبع سنين، يستغفرون الله ممّا قالوا، ثمّ تاب عليهم من بعد ذلك ورضي عنهم، فكان هذا أصل الطّواف. ثم جعل الله البيت الحرام حِذاء الضُّرَاح، توبةً لمن أذنب من بني آدم وطَهُورًا لهم، فقال: صدقت.

ثمّ ذكر المسألتين نحو الحديث الأوّل، ثمّ قام الرجل، فقلت: من هذا الرجل يا أبه؟ فقال: يا بنيّ هذا الخِضر عليه السلام.

١٠. عليّ بن الحسين، في قوله: ﴿وَإِذْ قَالَ رَبُّكَ لِلْمَلَائِكَةِ إِنِّي جَاعِلٌ فِي الْأَرْضِ خَلِيفَةً قَالُوا أَتَجْعَلُ فِيهَا مَن يُفْسِدُ فِيهَا وَيَسْفِكُ الدِّمَاءَ﴾ ردّوا على الله فقالوا ﴿أَتَجْعَلُ فِيهَا مَن يُفْسِدُ فِيهَا وَيَسْفِكُ الدِّمَاءَ﴾، وإنّما قالوا ذلك بخلق مضى يعني الجانّ بن الجِنّ ﴿وَنَحْنُ نُسَبِّحُ بِحَمْدِكَ وَنُقَدِّسُ لَكَ﴾ فمَنُّوا على الله بعبادتهم إيّاه، فأعرض عنهم.

ثمّ علَّم آدم الأسماء كلّها، ثمّ قال للملائكة: ﴿أَنبِئُونِي بِأَسْمَاءِ هَؤُلَاءِ﴾ قالوا: لا علم لنا، قال: ﴿يَا آدَمُ أَنبِئْهُم بِأَسْمَائِهِمْ﴾، فأنبأهم، ثمّ قال لهم: ﴿اسْجُدُوا لِآدَمَ﴾ فسجدوا، وقالوا في سُجُودهم في أنفسهم — : ما كُنّا نَظُنّ أن يخلق الله خلقًا أكرم عليه منّا، نحن خُزّان الله وجِيرانه، وأقرب الخلق إليه! فلمّا رفعوا رؤوسهم، قال: الله يعلم ما تُبدون من ردّكم عليّ وما كنتم تَكْتُمون، ظننّا أن لا يخلُق خَلقًا أكرم عليه منّا.

what you reveal in your retort to Me and what you conceal inside yourselves, thinking that God will not create a being dearer to Him than you.

When the angels realised the mistake they had made, those in close proximity to the Throne (and not all of the angels who had thought God could not create a creation dearer to Him than them) and they were the ones who had been commanded to prostrate. So they sought refuge with God, beseeching Him at the Throne by motioning to it with their hands. Thereupon He signalled to them by rotating His finger that they were to circumambulate around the Throne until the Day of Judgement. When Ādam slipped and committed his mistake, God established this House for anyone who made a mistake from his progeny to come to it and resort to it, just as those angels had resorted to the Throne previously.

Thus when Ādam was sent down to the earth, he circumambulated the House. When he arrived at the sanctuary he approached the House and raised his hands to the heavens crying, "O Lord, forgive me," whereupon a voice informed him, "I have forgiven you." Then he exclaimed, "O Lord, forgive my progeny," to which the response he was given was: "O Ādam, whoever from among your progeny comes to Me confessing his sin at this place, I will forgive him."' [2:30]

11. From 'Īsā b. Ḥamza[15]: 'A man asked Abū 'Abd Allāh ﵇, "May I be your ransom – people allege that the world is seven thousand years old." He replied, "No, it is not as they say. God decreed fifty thousand years for it and left it as a barren, empty plain for ten thousand years. Then God decided to originate a creation on it, so He created something that was neither Jinn nor angelic nor human. He decreed ten thousand years for them, and when they were approaching the end of their term they caused corruption on it, so God completely obliterated them and left [the Earth] as a barren, empty plain for another ten thousand years.

Then He created the Jinn and decreed ten thousand years for them. When they neared the end of their term they caused corruption and bloodshed therein too, as evidenced by the angels' retort: ﴾*How can You put someone there who will cause damage and bloodshed?*﴿, and the Jinn had shed

15 There is no record of this individual in Ḥillī's *Khulāṣat al-aqwāl*. It is more than likely a transcription error for 'Īsā b. Abī Ḥamza.

فلمّا عرفت الملائكة أنّها وقعت في خطيئةٍ لاذوا بالعرش، وإنّها كانت عِصابة من الملائكة، وهم الذين كانوا حول العرش، لم يكُن جميع الملائكة الذين قالوا: ما ظَنَنّا أن يَخلُق خَلقًا أكرم عليه منّا، وهم الذين أُمِروا بالسجود، فلاذوا بالعرش وقالوا بأيديهم — وأشار بإصبعه يديرها — فهم يَلُوذون حول العرش إلى يوم القيامة، فلمّا أصاب آدم الخطيئة، جعل الله هذا البيت لمن أصاب من ولده خطيئةً أتاه فلاذ به من وُلد آدم عليه السلام كما لاذ أولئك بالعرش

.فلمّا هَبَط آدم إلى الأرض طاف بالبيت، فلمّا كان عند المُستَجار دنا من البيت، فرفع يديه إلى السماء، فقال: ياربّ، اغفر لي، فنُودي: إنّي قد غفرتُ لك، قال: ياربّ، ولوُلدي، قال: فنُودي يا آدم، من جاءني من وُلدِك فباء بذنبه بهذا المكان، غَفَرت له.

١١. عن عيسى بن حمزة، قال: قال رجلٌ لأبي عبدالله عليه السلام: جُعِلت فداك، إنّ النّاس يزعُمُون أنّ الدنيا عُمرها سبعة آلاف سنةٍ! فقال: ليس كما يقولون، إنّ الله خلق لها خمسين ألف عامٍ فتركها قاعًا قَفراءَ خاويةً عشرة آلاف عام، ثمّ بدا الله بداء، فخلق فيها خَلقًا ليس من الجنّ ولا من الملائكة ولا من الإنس، وقدّر لهم عشرة آلاف عامٍ، فلمّا قَرُبت آجالهم أفسدوا فيها، فدمّر الله عليهم تدميرًا، ثم تركها قاعًا قَفْراءَ خاويةً عشرة آلاف عام.

ثمّ خلق فيها الجِنّ، وقدّر لهم عشرة آلاف عام، فلمّا قَرُبت آجالهم أفسدوا فيها، وسفكوا الدماء، وهو قول الملائكة: ﴿أَتَجْعَلُ فِيهَا مَن يُفْسِدُ فِيهَا وَيَسْفِكُ الدِّمَاءَ﴾ كما سَفَكَت بنو الجانّ، فأهلكهم الله، ثمّ بدا لله فخلق آدم، وقرّر له عشرة آلاف عامٍ، وقد مضى من ذلك سبعة آلاف عام ومائتان، وأنتم في آخر الزمان.

blood. So God destroyed them, then originated the creation of Ādam and decreed ten thousand years [as the length of time man shall tarry on this Earth]. Of this duration 7200 years have passed already, and you are now in the end of times."

12. He [the same narrator] reported that Zurāra narrated the following: 'I had visited Abū Jaʿfar عليه السلام, and during my visit he asked me, 'Which narrations of the Shiʿa do you have, Zurāra?'

So I replied, 'I have many, and I am thinking of lighting a fire to burn them all.'

He replied, 'Bury them instead, for you will forget whatever you decided to reject from among them.'

Then I remembered the fate of the humans,[16] so he said to me, 'The angels did not know anything when they said ﴾*How can You put someone there who will cause damage and bloodshed*﴿."'

He [the same narrator] reported the following: 'Abū 'Abd Allāh عليه السلام used to say, "Whenever this *ḥadīth* is narrated, it is a rebuttal against the Qadariyya [i.e. believers in absolute free-will]."

13. Abū 'Abd Allāh عليه السلام then said, "Ādam had a friend from among the angels in the heavens, and when he was made to descend to Earth the angel felt lonely and complained to God and asked Him for permission to descend to him. So He granted him his request and he, the angel, descended upon the Earth.

Upon descending the angel found Ādam sitting on some desolate wasteland, and when Ādam saw him he placed his hand on his head and heaved such a deep sigh that it was heard by the whole of creation.

So the angel said to him, 'O Ādam, I can see that you have disobeyed your Lord and are carrying a burden that you cannot bear. Do you know what God told us about you, and how we contradicted Him?'

He said, 'No.'

So he continued: He said: ﴾*I am putting a successor on earth* [...]﴿ We said ﴾*How can You put someone there who will cause damage and bloodshed?*﴿ So

16 The word *ādamiyyūn* may refer to humans in general (as in the progeny of Ādam) or to all of the previous Ādams as noted in several narrations in which it has been reported that there have been thousands of other worlds and thousands of other Ādams prior to this one.

١٢. قال: قال زُرارة: دخلتُ على أبي جعفر عليه السلام فقال: أيُّ شيءٍ عندك من أحاديث الشيعة؟ فقلت: إنَّ عندي منها شيئًا كثيرًا، قد هَمَمتُ أن أوقد لها نارًا، ثمّ أُحرقها، فقال: أرِها وبيّنّا ما أنكرت منها. فخَطَر على بالي الآدميّون، فقال لي: ما كان علم الملائكة حيث قالوا: ﴿أَتَجْعَلُ فِيهَا مَنْ يُفْسِدُ فِيهَا وَيَسْفِكُ الدِّمَاءَ﴾.

قال: وكان يقول أبو عبد الله عليه السلام: إذا حدّث بهذا الحديث: هو كسرٌ على القَدَريَّة.

١٣. ثمّ قال أبو عبد الله عليه السلام: إنَّ آدم كان له في السماء خليلٌ من الملائكة، فلما هبط آدم من السماء إلى الأرض استوحش الملك، وشكا إلى الله، وسأله أن يأذن له فيهبِطَ عليه، فأذن له فَهَبَطَ عليه، فوجده قاعدًا في قفرة من الأرض، فلمّا رآه آدم وضع يده على رأسه وصاح صيحةً، قال أبو عبد الله عليه السلام: يروون أنّه أسمع عامّة الخلق.

فقال له الملك: يا آدم، ما أراك إلاّ قد عَصَيت ربَّك، وحملتَ على نفسك ما لا تُطيق، أتدري ما قال الله لنا فيك فرددنا عليه؟ قال: لا. قال: قال: ﴿إِنِّي جَاعِلٌ فِي الأَرْضِ خَلِيفَةً﴾، قلنا: ﴿أَتَجْعَلُ فِيهَا مَنْ يُفْسِدُ فِيهَا وَيَسْفِكُ الدِّمَاءَ﴾، فهو خَلَقَك أن تكون في الأرض، يستقيم أن تكون في السماء؟ فقال أبو عبد الله عليه السلام: والله، عزّى بها آدم ثلاثًا.

if He created you to be on the Earth, would it have been right for you to stay in the heavens?'"

Abū 'Abd Allāh then said, "By God, he consoled Ādam thus three times."'

14. From Abū al-'Abbās[17] from Abū 'Abd Allāh ﷺ: 'I asked him about the verse ﴿*He taught Ādam all the names*﴾ – what did He teach him? He replied, "He taught him about the plains, the mountains, the canyons, and the valleys. Then he looked down at the various levels of the heavens under him, and that too was part of what He taught him."' [2:31]

15. From al-Faḍl b. 'Abbās[18] from Abū 'Abd Allāh ﷺ: 'I asked him about the verse ﴿*He taught Ādam all the names*﴾ – what are they? He replied, "The names of the valleys, plants, trees, and mountains on the Earth."'

16. From Dāwūd b. Sirḥān al-'Aṭṭār[19] who narrated, 'I was with Abū 'Abd Allāh ﷺ when he called for the table to be set, and we ate lunch. Then they brought the washbasin for us to wash our hands, so I asked him: "May I be your ransom, in the verse ﴿*He taught Ādam all the names*﴾ – was the washbasin and the water part of them?" So he replied, "[Yes], and the ravines and valleys," motioning with his hands as he spoke.'

17. From Ḥarīz[20], from whoever narrated it to him, from Abū 'Abd Allāh ﷺ who said: 'When God created Ādam, He commanded the angels to bow down before him. So the angels thought to themselves, "We never imagined that God would create a being dearer to Him than us when we have been His neighbours and the closest of creation in proximity to Him." So God said: ﴿*I know what you reveal and what you conceal*﴾ – referring to what

17 This in all likelihood is referring to Abū al-'Abbāṣ al-Ṭabarnānī, a known liar and exaggerator (*min al-ghulāt*) of the Imams' status. See Ḥillī, *Khulāṣat al-aqwāl*, 423 (nr. 1726).

18 There is no record of this individual in Ḥillī's *Khulāṣat al-aqwāl.*

19 Dāwūd b. Sirḥān al-'Aṭṭār, a reliable (*thiqa*) narrator of the sixth and seventh Imams. See Ḥillī, *Khulāṣat al-aqwāl*, 143 (nr. 397); Modarressi, *Tradition and Survival*, 215–6 (nr. 54).

20 Abū Muḥammad Ḥarīz b. 'Abd Allāh al-Azdī al-Sijistānī, a companion of the sixth and seventh Imams. Though controversial – he apparently set out with the aim of killing the Khawārij in Sijistān without the Imam's permission – he is generally deemed a trustworthy narrator of their *ḥadīths*. See Ḥillī, *Khulāṣat al-aqwāl*, 134 (nr. 360); Modarressi, *Tradition and Survival*, 244–7 (nr. 77).

١٤. عن أبي العبّاس، عن أبي عبدالله عليه السلام، سألته عن قول الله: ﴿وَعَلَّمَ آدَمَ الأَسْمَاءَ كُلَّهَا﴾ ماذا علّمه؟ قال: الأرضين، والجِبال، والشِعاب، والأودية. ثم نظر إلى بِساط تحته، فقال: وهذا البِساط ممّا علّمه.

١٥. عن الفضل بن عباس، عن أبي عبدالله عليه السلام، قال: سألتُهُ عن قول الله: ﴿وَعَلَّمَ آدَمَ الأَسْمَاءَ كُلَّهَا﴾، ما هي؟ قال: أسماء الأودية، والنبات، الشجر والجِبال من الأرض.

١٦. عن داود بن سرحان العطّار، قال: كنتُ عند أبي عبدالله عليه السلام، فدعا بالخِوَان فتغدّينا، ثم جاءوا بالطَّشت والدَّست سنانه، فقلت: جعلت فداك، قوله: ﴿وَعَلَّمَ آدَمَ الأَسْمَاءَ كُلَّهَا﴾، الطَشْت والدست سنانه منه؟ فقال: والفُجاج والأودية. وأهوى بيده، كذا وكذا.

١٧. عن حريز، عمّن أخبره، عن أبي عبدالله عليه السلام، قال: لمّا أن خلق الله آدم، أمر الملائكة أن يسجدوا له. فقالت الملائكة في أنفسها: ما كنّا نظنّ أنّ الله خلق خلقًا أكرم عليه منّا، فنحن جيرانه، ونحن أقرب خلقه إليه. فقال الله: ﴿قَالَ أَلَمْ أَقُلْ لَكُمْ إِنِّي أَعْلَمُ ...... مَا تُبْدُونَ وَمَا .... تَكْتُمُونَ﴾ فيما أبدوا من أمر بني الجانّ، وكتموا ما في أنفسهم، فلاذت الملائكة الذين قالوا ما قالوا بالعرش.

they betrayed of themselves concerning the plight of the Jinn and what they concealed within themselves. So the angels who had uttered that resorted to the Throne.'

18. From Jamīl b. Darrāj[21] who narrated: 'I asked Abū 'Abd Allāh عليه السلام about Iblīs and whether he was one of the angels or whether he was simply in charge of some affair or other in the heavens? He replied, "He was not an angel, but the angels considered him one of them, yet God knew that he was not really one of them; nor was he in charge of any particular affair in the heavens nor did he have any special prestige."

So I went to al-Ṭayyār[22] and informed him of what I had heard, but he refused to believe it saying, "How could he not have been an angel when God told the angels: ﴾*Bow down before Ādam, they all bowed. But not Iblīs?*﴿"

So al-Ṭayyār went to him [the Imam] and asked him while I was also there, 'May I be your ransom – does the verse ﴾*O you who believe* [...]﴿ include the hypocrites also when it is not referring exclusively to the believers?" He عليه السلام replied, "Yes, the hypocrites and those who have been led astray are included in it too, as well as all those who make an outward claim of belief."

19. From Jamīl b. Darrāj from Abū 'Abd Allāh عليه السلام: 'I asked him عليه السلام about Iblīs and if he was one of the angels or whether he was in charge of one of the affairs of the heavens. He عليه السلام replied, 'He was neither one of the angels nor was he in charge of any affair of the heavens. He was one of the Jinn, but because he frequented the angels they used to consider him one of them, yet God knew that he was not one of them. So when He issued the command to bow down, it included whoever was present.'

---

21 Abū 'Alī Jamīl b. Darrāj b. 'Abd Allāh al-Nakha'ī, the author of an *aṣl* (one of the pre-canonical works of the Imams' *ḥadīths*) and a companion of the sixth and seventh Imams. A leading figure of the Imāmī community and notable jurist of the latter part of the second century, he is reported to have concealed his allegiance to the Imams through the practice of precautionary dissimulation (*taqiyya*). He lost his eyesight in later life and died during Imam al-Riḍā's imamate. See Ḥillī, *Khulāṣat al-aqwāl*, 92–3 (nr. 209); Modarressi, *Tradition and Survival*, 307–8 (nr. 119).

22 This is the nickname of Muḥammad b. 'Abd Allāh, a companion of Imam al-Bāqir and Imam al-Ṣādiq. It is also used to refer to his son, Ḥamza b. Muḥammad b. 'Abd Allāh, who was a companion of Imam al-Ṣādiq. See Khū'ī, *Mu'jam*, 24:136 (no. 15413).

١٨. عن جميل بن درّاج، قال: سألتُ أبا عبد الله عليه السلام عن إبليس، أكان من الملائكة، أو كان يلي شيئًا من أمر السّماء؟ فقال: لم يكن من الملائكة، وكانت الملائكة ترى أنّه منها، وكان الله يعلمُ أنّه ليس منها، ولم يكُن يلي شيئًا من أمر السّماء، ولا كرامة.

فأتيت الطيّار فأخبرته بما سَمعت فأنكر، وقال: كيف لا يكون من الملائكة والله يقول للملائكة: ﴿اسْجُدُوا لِآدَمَ فَسَجَدُوا إِلاَّ إِبْلِيسَ﴾؟

فدخل عليه الطيّار فسأله — وأنا عنده — فقال له: جُعلت فداك، قول الله عز وجلّ: ﴿يَا أَيُّهَا الَّذِينَ آمَنُوا﴾ في غير مكان في مخاطبة المؤمنين، أيَدْخُل في هذه المنافقون؟ فقال: نعم يَدْخُلُ في هذه المنافقون والضُّلال وكلّ من أقرّ بالدعوة الظاهرة.

١٩. عن جميل بن دَرّاج، عن أبي عبد الله عليه السلام، قال: سألتُه عن إبليس أكان من الملائكة، أو هل كان يلي شيئًا من أمر السّماء؟ قال: لم يكن من الملائكة، ولم يكن يلي شيئًا من أمر السّماء، وكان من الجنّ وكان مع الملائكة، وكانت الملائكة ترى أنّه منها، وكان الله يعلَمُ أنّه ليس منها، فلمّا أُمِرَ بالسُّجود كان منه الذي كان.

20. From Abū Baṣīr who narrated the following: 'Abū 'Abd Allāh عليه السلام said, "The first time anyone committed an act of defiance (*kufr*) against God was when God created Ādam and Iblīs defiantly refused [to bow down], rejecting His command. The first time anyone committed an act of jealousy was when Ādam's son was jealous of his brother. The first time anyone committed an act of greed was Ādam's greed when he was forbidden from the tree but still ate from it, so his greed caused him to be expelled from the garden."'

21. From Badr b. Khalīl al-Asadī[23], from a man from Syria (*al-shām*) who narrated the following: 'The Commander of the Faithful عليه السلام said, "The first place in which God was worshipped [in the heavens] was directly above Kufa when God commanded the angels to prostrate before Ādam. So they bowed down, directly above Kufa."'

22. From Mūsā b. Bakr al-Wāsiṭī[24] who narrated the following: 'I asked Abū al-Ḥasan Mūsā عليه السلام about disbelief (*kufr*) and associating partners to God (*shirk*) – which of them came first? He replied, "My long-standing acquaintance with you does not befit us to discuss matters suited for the disputes of a layman." I responded by saying that Hishām b. al-Ḥakam[25] told me to ask you about it. He replied, "Disbelief is prior [to polytheism] because it is defiance. God says about Iblīs: ﴾*who refused and was arrogant: he was one of the disbelievers*﴿."'

23. From Sallām b. al-Mustanīr[26], from Abū Ja'far عليه السلام regarding the verse: ﴾*but do not go near this tree*﴿ (2:35) – he said: 'It means do not eat from it.'

---

23 Abū al-Khalīl Badr b. al-Khalīl al-Asadī, on whom there is scant information, was a companion of fifth and sixth Imams. See Khū'ī, *Mu'jam*, 4:180 (nr. 1646).

24 Mūsā b. Bakr al-Wāsiṭī, a companion of the seventh Imam who belonged to the Wāqifiyya. See Ḥillī, *Khulāṣat al-aqwāl*, 406 (nr. 1639); Modarressi, *Tradition and Survival*, 354 (nr. 163).

25 See fn. 44

26 Sallām b. al-Mustanīr al-Ju'fī al-Kūfī, on whom there is scant information, was a companion of the fourth, fifth and sixth Imams. See Khū'ī, *Mu'jam*, 9:181 (nr. 5286).

٢٠. عن أبي بَصير، قال: قال أبو عبد الله عليه السلام: إنّ أوّل كُفرٍ كُفرٌ بالله – حيث خلق الله آدم – كُفْر إبليس، حيث ردّ على الله أمره، وأوّل الحسد حيث حَسَد ابن آدم أخاه، وأوّل الحِرص حِرص آدم، نُهي عن الشجرة فأكل منها، فأخرجه حرصه من الجنّة.

٢١. عن بدر بن خليل الأسديّ، عن رجل من أهل الشّام، قال: قال أمير المؤمنين صلوات الله عليه: أوّل بُقعةٍ عُبِدَ الله عليها ظَهر الكُوفة، لمـّا أمر الله الملائكة أن يَسْجُدوا لآدم، سَجَدوا على ظَهر الكُوفة.

٢٢. عن موسى بن بكر الواسطي، قال: سألت أبا الحسن موسى صلى الله عليه وآله وسلم عن الكُفر الشّرك، أيُّهما أقدم؟ فقال: ما عهدي بك تُخاصِم النّاس. قلت: أمرني هِشام بن الحكم أن أسألك عن ذلك، فقال لي: الكُفر أقدم – وهو الجُحود – قال [الله عزّ وجلّ]: ﴿إِلاَّ إِبْلِيسَ أَبَى وَاسْتَكْبَرَ وَكَانَ مِنَ الْكَافِرِينَ﴾.

٢٣. عن سلاّم بن المُسْتَنير، عن أبي جعفر عليه السلام، في قوله: ﴿وَلا تَقْرَبَا هَـٰذِهِ الشَّجَرَةَ﴾ يعني لا تأكُلا منها.

24. From ʿAṭāʾ[27] who narrated from Abū Jaʿfar عليه السلام who reported on his father's authority, who reported from his forefathers that ʿAlī عليه السلام reported that the Messenger of God ﷺ stated: ʿĀdam and Ḥawwā were residing in the garden until they left it. Seven earthly hours passed from the time they ate from the tree to the moment when God had sent them down to live on the earth henceforth.

So Ādam beseeched his Lord saying, "My Lord, tell me, did You decree this sin of mine even before You created me, and am I simply proceeding with your decree of affairs? Or is my sin something that You did not decree for me previously but my desire overpowered me, making this action of mine entirely from me and not from You, or is it an action of Yours?"

He told him, "O Ādam, I created you and I informed you that I would make you and your wife reside in the garden. It is due to My bounty and My strength which I placed in you that your limbs felt empowered to disobey Me. Nothing is hidden from My sight, nor are any of your past or future actions unknown to Me."

Ādam exclaimed, "My Lord, You have proof against me, from when You created me and fashioned me and blew Your spirit into me."

God most High then added, "I made the angels bow down before you, extolled your name in My heavens, initiated your existence with My kindness from the start and allowed you to reside in My Garden. I did not do any of this except out of My pleasure towards you and to test you through the bounties, without any effort on your part towards Me to deserve all that I have done for you."

Ādam replied, "My Lord, all good is from You, and evil from me."

God said, "O Ādam, I am God, the Kind One. I have created good before evil, My mercy before My wrath. My kindness precedes My disgrace, and I advance My arguments [in favour of My servant] before My punishment. O Ādam, did I not forbid you from the tree and inform you that Shayṭān is an enemy to you and your wife? I warned you both before you entered the garden and I taught you both that if you eat from the tree you would be wronging yourselves and disobeying Me. O Ādam, no wrongdoer or disobedient person can reside in My proximity in My garden." So he replied, "Of course

27 There are several narrators whose first name is ʿAṭāʾ and thus we cannot be certain which of these is being referred to in this tradition.

٢٤. عن عَطاء، عن أبي جعفر، عن أبيه، عن آبائه، عن عليّ عليهم السلام، عن رسول الله ﷺ، قال: إنّما كان لبث آدم وحوّاء في الجنَّة حتّى خرجا منها سبع ساعات من أيّام الدنيا حتّى أكلا من الشجرة، فأهبطهما الله إلى الأرض من يومهما ذلك.

قال:فحاجَّ آدم ربَّه، فقال: يا ربّ، أرأيتك قبل أن تخلُقني كُنتَ قدّرت عليَّ هذا الذنب وكُلّ ما صرتُ وأنا صائرٌ إليه، أو هذا شيءٌ فعلته أنا من قبل أن تُقدّره عليَّ، غَلَبت عليَّ شِقْوَتي، فكان ذلك منّي وفعلي، لا منك ولا من فعلك؟

قال له: يا آدم، أنا خَلَقْتُك، وعلّمتك أنّي أسكنتك وزَوْجَتَكَ الجنَّة، وبنعمتي وما جعلت فيك من قوّتي، قويت بجوارحك على معصيتي، ولم تَغِب عن عيني، ولم يَخْلُ علمي من فعلك، ولا ممّا أنت فاعله.

قال آدم: يا ربّ، الحُجّة لك عليَّ. يا ربّ،فحين خلقتني وصوّرتني ونَفَخت فِيَّ من روحك!

قال الله تعالى: يا أدم، إنّي أسجدتُ لك ملائكتي، ونوّهت باسمك في سماواتي، وابتدأتك بكرامتي، واسكنتك جنّتي، ولم أفعل ذلك إلاّ برضًا مِنّي عليك، أَبْلُوك بذلك من غير أن يكون عَلِمت لي عملاً تستوجب به عندي ما فعلتُ بِك؟

قال آدم: يا ربّ، الخير منك، والشرُّ منّي.

قال الله تعالى: يا آدم، أنا الله الكريم، خلقتُ الخير قبل الشرّ، وخلقتُ رحمتي قبل غضبي، وقدّمت بكرامتي قبل هواني، وقدّمت باحتجاجي قبل عذابي. يا آدم، ألم أنهَكَ عن الشجرة؟ وأُخْبِركَ أنّ الشيطان عَدُوٌّ لكَ ولزوجتك؟ وأُحذّركما قبل أن تصيرا إلى

my Lord, you have proof against us. We have indeed wronged ourselves and disobeyed. And if You do not forgive us and have mercy on us, we will certainly be lost." So when they both admitted their sin to their Lord and admitted that He had full proof against them, the mercy of the all-Merciful, the Compassionate One enveloped them, and God accepted their repentance; indeed He is ever-Relenting and all-Merciful.

God said, "O Ādam, go down to the earth with your wife, and when you have set yourselves aright I shall rectify the both of you. If you work well for Me, I will strengthen you both, and if you apply yourselves to what pleases Me, I will hasten to compensate you both, and if you are wary [of displeasing] Me, I will protect you from My displeasure."

Upon hearing this they both wept and said, "Our Lord, help us to rectify ourselves and to work at that which earns us Your pleasure." God replied to them, "Whenever you do wrong, turn back to Me immediately, and I will accept your repentance, for I am God, the ever-Relenting, all-Compassionate One."

He responded, "By Your mercy, send us down to wherever is most beloved to You."

So God revealed to Jibra'īl to deliver them to the blessed land of Mecca. Thus Jibra'īl took them there, dropping Ādam at the mount of Ṣafā and Ḥawwā at the mount of Marwa.[28] When they landed, they both stood and lifted their heads up to the sky and began lamenting and crying to God, then bowing their heads in shame. So God called out to them, "Why are the two of you still crying when I am satisfied with you?"

So they said, "Our Lord, we are weeping on account of our sin, for it has expelled us from the proximity of our Lord; the angels' reverence of You is now hidden from us. Lord, our nakedness is now manifest to us. Our sin has compelled us to till the land for food and drink. And a terrible loneliness has overcome us due to Your separating us."

Thereupon the all-Merciful and all-Compassionate One had mercy on them and revealed to Jibra'īl, "I am God, the all-Merciful and all-Compassionate, and I show mercy to Ādam and Ḥawwā when they complain to Me thus, so take down to them a tent from the tents of Paradise, console them on My behalf on account of their detachment from the Garden and bring

28 Ṣafā and Marwa are two hills adjacent to the Sacred Mosque in Mecca.

الجنة؟ وأُعلِّمْكما أنَّكما إن أكلتما من الشجرة، كنتما ظالِمَين لأنفسكما عاصِيَين لي؟ يا آدم، لا يجاورني في جنّتي ظالمٌ عاصٍ لي.

قال: فقال: بلى يا ربّ؟ الحُجّة لك علينا، ظَلَمْنا أنفسنا وعَصَيْنا، وإن لم تَغْفِر لنا وتَرحَمْنا نكنْ من الخاسرين. قال: فلمّا أقرّا لربّهما بذنبهما، وأنَّ الحُجّة من الله لهما، تَدارَكَتْهُما رحمةُ الرَّحمن الرحيم، فتاب عليهما ربُّهما، إنَّه هو التوّاب الرّحيم.

قال: يا آدم، اهبط أنت وزوجتك إلى الأرض، فإذا أصلحتما أصلحتكما، وإن عَمِلتما لي قوّيتكما، وإن تعرّضتما لرضاي تسارعتْ إلى رضاكما، وإن خِفتما منّي آمنتكما من سَخَطي.

قال: فبكيا عند ذلك، وقالا: ربّنا، فأعِنّا على صلاح أنفسنا وعلى العمل بما يُرضيك عنّا. قال الله تعالى لهما: إذا عَمِلتُم سُوءًا فتُوبا إليَّ منه أتُبْ عليكما وأنا التوّاب الرّحيم.

قالا: فأهبطنا برحمتك إلى أحبّ البقاع إليك.

قال: فأوحى الله إلى جَبْرَئيل أن أهبِطهُما إلى البلدة المباركة مكّة. قال: فهَبَط بهما جَبْرَئيل، فألقى آدم عليه السلام على الصَّفا، وألقى حوّاء على المَرْوة، فلما ألقِيا قاما على أرجلهما، ورفعا رؤوسهما إلى السماء، وضجّا بأصواتهما بالبكاء إلى الله تعالى، وخضعا بأعناقهما.

قال: فهَتَف الله بهما: ما يُبكيكما بعد رضاي عنكما؟

قال: فقالا: ربّنا أبكتنا خَطيئَتُنا، وهي أخرجتنا من جِوار ربّنا، وقد خفي علينا تقديس ملائكتك لك، ربّنا وبَدَت لنا عَوْراتُنا، واضطرّتنا ذنبنا إلى حَرْث الدنيا ومَطْعَمها ومَشْرَبها، ودخلتنا وَحْشَةٌ شديدةٌ لتفريقك بيننا.

them both together in the tent, for indeed I have mercy on them for their weeping and their fear and their loneliness. Pitch the tent for them on the raised clearing between the hills of Mecca." (He explained that the clearing was the actual location where the foundations of the Kaʿba had been raised by the angels beforehand).

So Jibra'īl brought down the tent and pitched it exactly as per the height of the Kaʿba at that particular spot. Then Jibra'īl brought Ādam down from Ṣafā and Ḥawwā from Marwa to the tent. The centre pole of the tent was a pillar made of red rubies whose glow and light radiated out as far as the hills of Mecca and their surroundings. As far as the light extended God made a sanctuary, and these are still part of the sanctuary of the House today. Every corner radiated by that initial glow. God designated it as a sanctuary in honour of the tent and the pole, as they were from Paradise. That is why God has multiplied the reward for all good deeds performed within the Sanctuary, as well as the sanction for all misdeeds committed therein. The ropes of the tent extended around them until the edge of the pegs, which encompassed the area of the Sacred Mosque [today]. Its pegs were made out of the branches of Paradise and its ropes were deep reddish-purple tresses.[29]

God then commanded Jibra'īl to gather seventy thousand angels to roam the tent and guard the two of them against rebellious Jinn, to keep Ādam and Ḥawwā company and to circumambulate the tent in reverence of the House and the tent. So the angels descended to the tent, guarding it against rebellious devils and Jinn, circumambulating around the cornerstones of the House and the tent night and day just as they had been doing in the heavens around the Oft-Visited House. The cornerstones of the Sacred House on the earth are directly below the Oft-Visited House in the heavens.

Then after that God revealed to Jibra'īl, "Descend to Ādam and Ḥawwā and move them away from the area of the foundations of My House as I myself wish to descend to My earth in the shade of My angels so that I can raise the cornerstones of My House for My angels and My creatures from the progeny of Ādam."

So Jibra'īl descended to Ādam and Ḥawwā and took them away from the tent, prohibiting them from nearing the vicinity of the Sacred House. Then

29 The word used here is *urjuwān* and may refer to certain flowers that were of a deep reddish purple colour, said to be similar to jacinth.

قال: فرَحِمَهُما الرّحمن الرّحيم عند ذلك، وأوحى إلى جبْرَئيل: أنا الله الرّحمن الرّحيم، وإنّي قد رحِمت آدم وحوّاء لِما شكيا إليَّ. فاهبط عليهما بخَيمةٍ مَن خِيام الجنّة، وعزِّهما عنّي بفِراق الجنّة، واجمع بينهما في الخَيمة، فإنّي قد رَحِمتهما لِبُكائهما ووَحْشتهما ووَحْدَتهما، وانصِب لهما الخَيمة على التُرْعَة التي بين جِبال مكّة، قال والتُرعَة مكان البيت وقواعده التي رفعتها الملائكة قبل ذلك.

فهبَط جبْرَئيل عليه السلام على أدم بالخَيمة على مكان أركان البيت وقواعده فنَصَبها. قال: وأنزل جبْرَئيل آدم من الصّفا، وأنزل حوّاء من المَروة، وجمع بينهما في الخَيمة، قال: وكان عَمُود الخَيمة قضيب ياقوتٍ أحمر، فأضاء نُوره وضَوؤه جِبال مكّة وما حولها، قال: وامتدَّ ضوء العَمُود،فجعله الله حَرَمًا، فهو مواضع الحَرَم اليوم، كلّ ناحية من حيث بلغ ضوء العَمُود،فجعله الله حَرَمًا لحُرمَة الخَيمة والعَمُود، لأنّهنَّ من الجنّة. قال: ولذلك جعل الله الحسنات في الحَرَم مضاعفةً، والسيِّئات فيه مضاعفة. قال: ومدّت أطناب الخَيمة حولها، فمنتهى أوتادها ما حول المسجد الحرام، قال: وكانت أوتادها من غُصون الجَنّة، وأطنابها من ضفائر الأُرجوان.

قال: فأوحى الله إلى جبْرَئيل: أهْبِط على الخَيمة سبعين ألف مَلَك يحْرُسونها من مَرَدَة الجنّ، ويُؤنسون آدم وحوّاءً، ويطُوفون حول الخَيمة تعظيمًا للبيت والخَيمة. قال: فَهَبَطت الملائكة، فكانوا بحضرة الخَيمة يحْرُسونها من مَرَدَة الشياطين والعُتاة، ويطوفون حول أركان البيت والخَيمة كلّ يوم وليلة، كما كانوا يطوفون في السّماء حول البيت المعْمُور، وأركان البيت الحرام في الأرض حِيال البيت المعْمُور الذي في السّماء.

he vacated the tent away from the clearing, took Ādam to Ṣafā and Ḥawwā to Marwa, and raised the tent back up to the heavens.

Ādam and Ḥawwā asked, "Jibra'īl, have you moved us back here and separated us again due to God's displeasure, or is it with His decree and pleasure with us?"

So he replied to them, saying, 'It was not out of any displeasure towards you both, but no one has the right to question God about what He does. Ādam, the seventy thousand angels that God has sent down to earth to keep your company and to circumambulate the cornerstones of the House and the tent have asked God to replace it with a House on the blessed clearing directly above the Oft-Visited House. They wish to circumambulate it just as they had been doing in the heavens around the Oft-Visited House. So God revealed to me to move you and Ḥawwā away from there, and to take the tent back up to the heavens."

Then Ādam said, 'We are resigned to God's decree, so carry out whatever He wills regarding us."

Then, when Ādam and Ḥawwā were on Ṣafā and Marwa respectively, Ādam felt an intense anguish and sorrow enter his heart at being separated from her. So he went down the hill of Ṣafā towards Marwa longing to see Ḥawwā and greet her. Between Ṣafā and Marwa was a valley; where before he was able to see Marwa from atop Ṣafā, he found when he reached the bottom of the valley that Marwa was no longer visible to him. So he ran in the valley confused as to why he could no longer see Marwa, fearing that he had lost his way. When, however, he crossed the valley and started climbing away from it, he spotted Marwa and carried on walking until he reached the summit. He climbed and greeted Ḥawwā. Then they both turned to face the clearing to see if the foundations of the House had been raised yet, beseeching God to send them back to their original place. Then he climbed back down from Marwa and went back to Ṣafā. There he stood on its summit facing the raised clearing between the hills of Mecca and supplicating God. Then he longed for Ḥawwā again, so he again descended from Ṣafā and made for Marwa just like he had done before, and went back and forth thus three times.

Finally back at Ṣafā, he climbed atop its mount and supplicated God to reunite him with his partner, Ḥawwā. His to-ing and fro-ing between the two hills made six laps in total, and when they finally beseeched God

قال: ثمّ إنّ الله أوحى إلى جِبْرَئيل بعد ذلك: أن اهْبِط إلى آدم وحوّاء، فنحِّهما عن مواضع قواعد بيتي، فإنّي أريد أن اهبط في ظِلال من ملائكتي إلى أرضي، فأرفع أركان بيتي لملائكتي ولِخَلقي من ولد آدم.

قال: فهَبَط جِبْرَئيل على آدم وحَوّاء فأخرجهما من الخَيمة، ونحّاهما عن تُرعَة البيت الحرام، ونحّى الخيمة عن موضع التُرعة، قال: ووضع آدم على الصّفا، ووضع حَوّاء على المَرْوة ورفع الخيمة إلى السماء. فقال آدم وحَوّاء: يا جَبْرَئيل، أبِسَخَط من الله حوّلتنا وفرّقت بيننا، أم برضًا تقديرًا من الله علينا؟ فقال لهما: لم يَكُن ذلك سَخَطًا من الله عليكما، ولكن الله لا يُسأل عمّا يفعل. يا آدم، إنّ السبعين ألف مَلَك الذين أنزلهم الله إلى الأرض ليؤُنسوك ويطوفوا حول أركان البيت والخيمة، سألوا الله أن يبني لهم مكان الخيمة بيتًا على موضع التُرعة المباركة حيال البيت المعمُور، فيطوفون حوله كما كانوا يطوفون في السّماء حول البيت المعمُور، فأوحى الله إليّ أن أُنحّيك وحَوّاء وأرفع الخيمة إلى السماء، فقال آدم: رضينا بتقدير الله ونافذ أمره فينا، فكان آدم على الصّفا وحَوّاء على المَرْوة.

قال: فدخل آدم لفراق حَوّاء وحشةٌ شديدةٌ وحزن، قال: فهَبَط من الصّفا يريد المَرْوة شوقًا إلى حَوّاء وليُسلّم عليها، وكان فيما بين الصّفا والمَرْوة وادٍ، وكان آدم يرى المَرْوة من فوق الصّفا، فلمّا انتهى إلى موضع الوادي غابت عنه المَرْوة، فسعى في الوادي حذرًا لمّا لم ير المَرْوة، مخافة أن يكون قد ضلّ عن طريقه، فلمّا أن جاز الوادي وارتفع عنه نظر إلى المَرْوة، فمشى حتى انتهى إلى المَرْوة، فصَعِد عليها، فسلّم على حَوّاء، ثمّ أقبلا بوجههما نحو موضع التُرعة ينظُران هل رفع قواعد البيت، ويسألان الله أن يرُدَّهما إلى مكانهما، حتى

together and wept in front of Him asking Him to reunite them, God answered them in that very moment on the very same day in the afternoon.

So Jibra'īl came and found him on Ṣafā standing and facing the raised clearing calling upon God, and he said to him, "Ādam, climb down from Ṣafā now and go and meet Ḥawwā." So Ādam climbed down from Ṣafā and went towards Marwa just as he had done the previous three times. There he climbed up and told Ḥawwā the good news that Jibra'īl had told him, and they rejoiced jubilantly praising and thanking God. This is how the practice of performing *sa'y*[30] between Ṣafā and Marwa seven times came about. This is also why God says in the Qur'an: ﴾*Ṣafā and Marwa are among the rites of God, so for those who make major or minor pilgrimage to the House it is no offence to circulate between the two*﴿(2:158).[31]

After that Jibra'īl brought them down from Marwa and informed them that the all-Conqueror, Blessed and most High, had descended [angels] to the earth to raise the foundations of the Sacred House with a stone from Ṣafā, another from Marwa, a third from Mount Sinai and a fourth from Mount Salām, which is now in Kufa. So God inspired Jibra'īl to build it to completion, whereupon he went and picked the four stones from their locations by God's will. He carried them back on his wings fixing them on the cornerstones of the House just as he had been commanded by God. And upon the foundations that the all-Conqueror had decreed he mounted its supports.

Then God commanded Jibra'īl to build it and to complete it with a stone from Mount Abū Qubays, which he was to place between the eastern and western door. So Jibra'īl built it, and when he had completed it the angels began to circumambulate it. When Ādam and Ḥawwā saw the angels circumambulating the House they too began to do the same, circumambulating it seven times. Then they left to go and look for something to eat. All this happened on the same day that they were brought down to earth.'

---

30 The 'walk' (*sa'y*) is one of the ritual obligations performed at Hajj in which pilgrims walk between the hills of Ṣafā and Marwa seven times, praising and glorifying God.

31 The Muslims were initially reluctant to perform this rite due to the fact that some of the polytheists (*mushrikūn*) of Mecca had installed two idols on these hills. Here it is reclaimed for God.

هَبَط من المَرْوة، فرجع إلى الصّفا فقام عليه، وأقبل بوجهه نحو موضع التُرعة فدعا الله، ثمّ إنّه اشتاق إلى حَوّاء فهَبَط من الصّفا يريد المَرْوة، ففعل مثل ما فعله في المرّة الأوْلى، ثمّ رجع إلى الصّفا ففعل عليه مثل ما فعله في المرّة الأوْلى، ثمّ إنّه هَبَط من الصّفا إلى المَرْوة ففعل مثل ما فعل في المرّتين الأُوْليين.

ثمّ رجع إلى الصّفا فقام عليه، ودعا الله أن يجمع بينه وبين زوجته حَوّاء، قال: فكان ذهاب آدم من الصّفا إلى المَرْوة ثلاث مرّات، ورجوعه ثلاث مرّات، فذلك ستّة أشواط، فلمّا أن دعيا الله وبكيا إليه وسألاه أن يجمع بينهما، استجاب الله لهما من ساعتهما من يومهما ذلك مع زوال الشّمس.

فأتاه جَبْرَئيل وهو على الصّفا واقف يدعو الله مقبلاً بوجهه نحو التُرعة، فقال له جَبْرَئيل: انزِل يا آدم من الصّفا فالحَق بحَوّاء فنزل آدم من الصّفا إلى المَرْوة، ففعل مثل ما فعل في الثلاث مرّات حتىّ انتهى إلى المَرْوة، فصَعِد عليها وأخبر حَوّاء بما أخبرهُ جَبْرَئيل ففرِحا بذلك فرَحًا شديدًا، وحمِدا الله وشَكراه، فلذلك جرت السُنّة بالسعي بين الصّفا والمرْوة، ولذلك قال الله ﴿إِنَّ ٱلصَّفَا وَٱلْمَرْوَةَ مِن شَعَآئِرِ ٱللَّهِ فَمَنْ حَجَّ ٱلْبَيْتَ أَوِ ٱعْتَمَرَ فَلَا جُنَاحَ عَلَيْهِ أَن يَطَّوَّفَ بِهِمَا﴾.

قال: ثمّ إن جَبْرَئيل أتاهما فأنزلهما من المَرْوة، وأخبرهما أن الجبار تبارك وتعالى قد هَبَط إلى الأرض، فرفع قواعد البيت الحرام بحَجَر من الصّفا، وحجر من المَرْوة، وحجر من طور سيناء، وحجر من جبل السّلام، وهو ظهر الكوفة، فأوحى الله إلى جَبْرَئيل أن ابنِه وأتمّه،

25. From Jābir [b. Yazīd] al-Juʿfī, from Jaʿfar b. Muḥammad ﷺ who narrated the following from his forefathers: 'God distinguished Mecca out of [all] the [other places on] Earth, and from Mecca He chose Bakka, upon which He poured a pavilion of light encrusted with pearls and rubies. Then He sent down four pillars to stand in the middle of the pavilion and placed a white pearl in their midst. Each pillar was seven cubits tall and stood in one of the quarters of the House. He placed therein light from the light of the pavilion like candlesticks. The pillars originated from the stars, with their tops just under the Throne. The first of the four was made of emerald, the second of red ruby, the third was made of white pearl and the fourth of piercing light. The House rested between them but was suspended above the Earth, and the light from the candlesticks radiated over the entire area of the Sanctuary. The largest candlestick was at what is now the Station of Ibrāhīm (*maqām Ibrāhīm*), and there were three hundred and sixty candlesticks in total. The corner of the Black Stone was the gateway of mercy, then the Syrian corner, which was the gateway of pleas. The door at the Syrian corner was the gateway of intercession, and the door at the Yemeni corner which extends up to the Black Stone was the gateway of repentance – and this is the gateway reserved for the Family of Muḥammad ﷺ and their followers. This House is God's proof on the Earth over His creation. When Ādam came down to Earth he descended onto the mount of Ṣafā, and God derived its name from one of Ādam's titles,[32] in accordance with the verse of the Qur'an: ﴾*God chose Ādam* […]﴿(3:33). Ḥawwā descended onto the mount of Marwa, whose name God derived from the word for woman (*mar'a*). Ādam had descended from the Garden with a woman, but Ādam did not create woman next to the Station [of Ibrāhīm]; and while leaning against it he asked his Lord to send the House down to the Earth. So He sent it down and it landed on the surface of the Earth, wherewith Ādam would resort to. Its height from the ground was seven cubits high, and it had four doors. Its surface area was twenty-five square cubits, while the pavilion measured two hundred square cubits.'

32 Ādam is known in Islamic literatures as *ṣafī Allāh* or *ṣafwat Allāh*, meaning 'God's chosen one'.

قال: فاقتلع جَبْرَئيل الأحجار الأربعة بأمر الله من مواضعهنّ بجَناحيه، فوضعهما حيث أمره الله في أركان البيت على قواعده التي قدّرها الجبّار، ونصب أعلامها.

ثمّ أوحى الله إلى جَبْرَئيل عليه السلام أن ابْنِه وأتِمّه بحجارة من أبي قُبيس، واجْعل له بابَين: باب شرقيّ وباب غربي، قال: فأتمّه جَبْرَئيل، فلمّا أن فرغ منه طافت الملائكة حوله، فلمّا نظر آدم وحَوّاء إلى الملائكة يطوفون حول البيت، انطَلَقا فطافا بالبيت سبعة أشواط، ثمّ خرجا يطلُبان ما يأكلان، وذلك من يومهما الذي هُبِط بهما فيه.

٢٥. عن جابر الجُعفي، عن جعفر بن محمّد، عن آبائه عليهم السلام، قال: إنّ الله اختار من الأرض جميعًا مَكّة، واختار من مَكّة بَكّة، فأنزل في بَكّة سُرادقًا من نور محفوفًا بالدُّرّ والياقوت، ثمّ أنزل في وسط السُّرادِق عَمَدًا أربعة، وجعل بين العَمَد الأربعة لؤلؤةً بيضاء، وكان طولها سبعة أذرع في ترابيع البيت، وجعل فيها نورًا من نور السُّرادِق بمنزلة القناديل، وكانت العَمَد أصلها في الثّرى والرؤوس تحت العرش. وكان الربع الأوّل من زُمُرُّد أخضر، والربع الثاني من ياقوتٍ أحمر، والربع الثالث من لؤلؤٍ أبيض، والربع الرابع من نورٍ ساطع، وكان البيت ينزِل فيما بينهم مرتفعًا من الأرض، وكان نور القناديل يبلُغ إلى موضع الحرم، وكان أكبر القناديل مقام إبراهيم، فكانت القناديل ثلاثمائة وستّين قنديلاً، فالركُن الأسود باب الرّحمة، إلى الركُن الشّاميّ، فهو باب الإنابة، وبابُ الركُن الشّاميّ باب التوسّل، وباب الركّن اليماني باب التّوبة، وهو باب آل محمّد صلى الله عليه وآله وشيعتهم إلى الحجر، فهذا البيت حُجّة الله في أرضه على خلقه.

26. From Jābir b. ʿAbd Allāh[33], from the Messenger of God ﷺ that he said: ‘Iblīs was the first one ever to sing, the first ever to lament, and the first ever to dance. He sang when Ādam ate from the tree, he danced upon setting foot on the Earth when he was sent down there, and when made to settle there he lamented at the remembrance of the pleasures he had enjoyed in the Garden previously.’

27. From Jābir who reports from Abū Jaʿfar عليه السلام, who narrated the following: ‘The Messenger of God ﷺ said, “When God sent Ādam down to earth He commanded him to cultivate the land with his own hands and eat the fruits of his own labour, after having enjoyed the bounties of the Garden. However, he kept lamenting and crying for the Garden for two hundred years. Then he prostrated to God for three days and nights without lifting his head saying, ‘My Lord, did You not create me?’

So God replied, ‘Indeed I did.’

He asked, ‘Did You not blow Your Spirit into me?’

He again responded, ‘Indeed I did.’

So Ādam asked, ‘Did Your mercy not supersede Your wrath against me?’

He said, ‘Indeed it did. However, did you have patience? Were you grateful?’

Ādam replied, ‘There is no god but You, glory be to You. I have indeed wronged myself so forgive me, for You are the all-Forgiving, the Compassionate.’

So God had mercy on him and accepted his repentance, for He is the ever-Relenting and Compassionate One.”’

33 Jābir b. ʿAbd Allāh b. ʿAmr b. Haram al-Anṣārī (d. 78/697), a highly revered companion of the Prophet whose merits are extensively extolled in both Sunnī and Shīʿī literature. Besides also being a famous narrator of *ḥadīth* among Sunnī Muslims, he is especially revered among Shīʿī scholars for his allegiance and support for the cause of ʿAlī and his followers after the death of the Prophet. According to Shīʿī legend, the Prophet had informed Jābir that he would live a long life, so long in fact that he would live to see the Prophet's grandson, the fifth Imam, Muḥammad al-Bāqir (d. 117/733). Upon finally meeting Imam, Jābir conveyed the Prophet's greetings to him as the Prophet had requested thus fulling the prophecy. He died at the age of 94 after being poisoned by the notoriously ruthless Umayyad governor al-Ḥajjāj b. Yūsuf (d. 95/714) because of his support for the ʿAlid Imams. See Ḥillī, *Khulāṣat al-aqwāl*, 93–4 (nr. 212); s.v. “Djābir b. ʿAbd Allāh al-Anṣārī,” *Encyclopaedia of Islam*, Second Edition, Supplement (J. M. Kister).

فلمّا هَبَط آدم إلى الأرض هَبَط على الصّفا، ولذلك اشتقّ الله له اسماً من اسم آدم، لقوله تعالى: ﴿إِنَّ اللَّهَ اصْطَفَىٰ آدَمَ﴾، ونزلت حَوّاء على المرْوة، فاشتقّ الله لها اسماً من اسم المرأة، وكان آدم نزل بمرأة من الجنّة، فلمّا لم يخلق آدم المرأة إلى جنب المقام، وكان يركن إليه، سأل ربّه أن يُهبِط البيت إلى الأرض، فأُهْبِط فصار على وجه الأرض، فكان آدم يركن إليه، وكان ارتفاعها من الأرض سبعة أذرُع، وكانت له أربعة أبواب، وكان عرضها خمسة وعشرين ذِراعًا في خمسة وعشرين ذِراعًا ترابيعة، وكان السُّرادِقُ مائتي ذِراع في مائتي ذِراع.

٢٦. عن جابر بن عبدالله، عن النبي ﷺ، قال: كان إبليس أوّل من تغنّى، وأوّل من ناح، وأوّل من حدا، لمّا أكَلَ آدم من الشجرة تغنّى، فلمّا هَبَط حدا، فلمّا استقرّ على الأرض ناح يُذكِّره ما في الجنّة.

٢٧. عن جابر، عن أبي جعفر عليه السلام، قال: قالَ رَسول الله ﷺ: إن الله حين أهَبَط آدم إلى الأرض، أمره أن يَحْرُث بيده فيأكلَ من كَدّه بعد الجنّة ونعيمها، فلبث يجأر ويبكي على الجنّة مائتي سنة، ثمّ إنّه سجد لله سجدةً فلم يرْفعْ رأسه ثلاثة أيّام ولياليها.

ثمّ قال: أي ربّ ألم تخلُقني؟

فقال الله: قد فعلت. فقال: ألم تنفُخ فيّ من روحك؟ قال: قد فعلت، قال: ألم تُسكنّي جنتك؟ قال: قد فعلت، قال: ألم تسبِق لي رحمتك غضبك؟ قال الله: قد فعلت، فهل صبرتَ أو شكرتَ؟

28. From Muḥammad b. Muslim, from Abū Jaʿfar عليه السلام that he said, 'The words that Ādam received from His Lord after which God accepted his repentance and guided him were:

"Glory and all praise be to You, O God. I have committed a sin and wronged myself so forgive me, for You are the all-Forgiving, the Compassionate One.

O God, indeed there is no god but You, glory and praise be to You: I have committed a sin and wronged myself so forgive me, for You are the best of those who forgive.

O God, indeed there is no god but You, glory and praise be to You: I have committed a sin and wronged myself so forgive me, for You are the all-Forgiving, the Compassionate One."'

29. [Abū ʿAlī] al-Ḥasan b. Rāshid[34] narrated, 'When you awake from your sleep, recite the words that Ādam received from his Lord:

"Holy and Sanctified Lord of the angels and Spirit,
Your mercy supersedes Your wrath.
There is no god but You [Glory be to You].
Truly I have wronged myself,
so forgive me and have mercy on me,
for surely You are the ever-Relenting,
the Compassionate, and the all-Forgiving One."'

30. From ʿAbd al-Raḥmān b. Kathīr [al-Hāshimī][35], from Abū ʿAbd Allāh عليه السلام who narrated the following: 'God, Blessed and most High, showed Ādam his progeny when taking the covenant, so the Prophet صلى الله عليه وآله passed by him leaning on ʿAlī عليه السلام with Fāṭima following close behind, and al-Ḥasan عليه السلام

---

34 Abū ʿAlī al-Ḥasan b. Rāshid, the client (*mawlā*) of the Āl al-Mihlab clan, was a reliable (*thiqa*) narrator of the ninth Imam Muḥammad al-Jawād's traditions. See Ḥillī, *Khulāṣat al-aqwāl*, 100 (nr. 226).

35 ʿAbd al-Raḥmān b. Kathīr al-Hāshimī, a client (*mawlā*) of ʿAbbās b. Muḥammad b. ʿAlī b. ʿAbd Allāh b. al-ʿAbbās (d. 186/802), the brother of the Abbasid Caliph al-Manṣūr, is regarded weak (*ḍaʿīf*) in his narrations, a fabricator of *ḥadīth*, and a transmitter of obscure and esoteric narrations. See Ḥillī, *Khulāṣat al-aqwāl*, 374 (nr. 1490); Modarressi, *Tradition and Survival*, 171–4 (nr. 24).

قال آدم: لا إله إلاّ أنت سُبحانك إنّي ظلمتُ نفسي، فاغْفِر لي إنّك أنت الغفور الرّحيم.
فرحِمه الله بذلك وتاب عليه، إنّه هو التوّاب الرّحيم.

٢٨. عن محمّد بن مسلم، عن أبي جعفر ﷺ قال: قال: الكلمات التي تلقّاهنّ آدم من ربّه فتاب عليه وهدى، قال: سُبحانك اللّهمّ وبحمدك إنّي عمِلت سُوءًا وظلمتُ نفسي، فاغْفِر لي إنّك أنت الغفور الرّحيم، اللّهم إنّه لا إله إلا أنت سُبحانك وبِحمدك، إنّي عمِلتُ سُوءًا وظلمتُ نفسي، فاغْفر لي إنّك خير الغافرين، اللّهم إنّه لا إله إلاّ أنت سُبحانك وبِحمدك، إنّي عمِلتُ سوءًا وظلمتُ نفسي، فاغْفر لي إنّك أنت الغفور الرّحيم.

٢٩. وقال الحسن بن راشد: إذا استيقظتَ من منامك، فقل الكلمات التي تلقّى بها آدم من ربّه: سُبّوح قُدّوس ربّ الملائكة والرُوح، سبقت رحمتك غضبك، لا إلَه إلاّ أنت سُبحانك إنّي ظلمت نفسي، فاغفر لي وارحمني، إنّك أنت التوّاب الرّحيم الغفور.

٣٠. عن عبدالرّحمن بن كَثير، عن أبي عبدالله ﷺ، قال: إنّ الله تبارك وتعالى عرض على آدم في الميثاق ذُرّيّته، فمرّ به النبيّ ﷺ وهو مُتّكئ على علي ﷺ، وفاطمة صلوات الله عليها تتلوهما والحسن والحسين ﷺ يتلوان فاطمة – عليها السلام –، فقال الله: يا آدم، إيّاك أن تَنْظُر إليهم بحَسَد، أُهبِطك من جِواري.

فلمّا أسكنه الله الجنّة مثّل له النبيّ وعليّ وفاطمة والحسن والحسين صلوات الله عليهم، فنظر إليهم بحَسَدٍ، ثمّ عُرضت عليه الولاية فأنكرها، فَرَمَتْهُ الجنّة بأوراقها، فلمّا تاب إلى

and al-Ḥusayn عليه السلام behind her. God told him, "Ādam, be wary of looking at them with envy for I will demote you from My proximity."

Then when he made him reside in the Garden, the Prophet, ʿAlī, Fāṭima, al-Ḥasan and al-Ḥusayn appeared to him and he looked at them with envy. Then when it was time for him to pledge his allegiance to their authority (*walāya*) he refused, and thus the Garden began throwing its leaves at him. God forgave him only after he repented to God on account of his envy, attested to their authority and beseeched Him in the name of these five: Muḥammad, ʿAlī, Fāṭima, al-Ḥasan and al-Ḥusayn. This is the purport of the verse: ﴾*Then Ādam received some words from his Lord*﴿.' [2:37]

31. From Muḥammad b. ʿĪsā b. ʿAbd Allāh al-ʿAlawī[36] from his father from his grandfather from ʿAlī عليه السلام who said: 'The words that Ādam received from his Lord were: "O Lord, I ask you for the sake of Muḥammad ﷺ that you accept my repentance." So God asked him, "And who has taught you about Muḥammad?" He replied, "I saw his name inscribed on Your loftiest pavilion when I was in the Garden."'

32. From Jābir who reported, 'I asked Abū Jaʿfar عليه السلام about the inner meaning of the verse: ﴾*But when guidance comes from Me, as it certainly will, there will be no fear for those who follow My guidance nor will they grieve*﴿. He replied, "The inner meaning of guidance here is ʿAlī عليه السلام, for God has said about him ﴾*there will be no fear for those who follow My guidance nor will they grieve*﴿."' [2:38]

33. From Samāʿa b. Mihrān who reported, 'I asked Abū ʿAbd Allāh عليه السلام about [the meaning of] the verse ﴾*Honour your pledge to Me and I will honour My pledge to you*﴿. He replied, "Honour your pledge to the authority of ʿAlī عليه السلام as an obligation imposed by God and I will honour My pledge to you of Paradise."' [2:40]

34. From Jābir al-Juʿfī who reported, 'I asked Abū Jaʿfar عليه السلام about the inner meaning of the verse: ﴾*Believe in the message I have sent down confirming what you already possess. Do not be the first to disbelieve in it*﴿. [He said:]

36 There is no record of this individual in Ḥillī's *Khulāṣat al-aqwāl*.

الله من حسده، وأقرّ بالولاية، ودعا بحقّ الخمسة، محمّد وعليّ، وفاطمة، والحسن والحسين صلوات الله عليهم، غفر الله له، وذلك قوله: ﴿فَتَلَقَّىٰ آدَمُ مِن رَّبِّهِ كَلِمَاتٍ﴾ الآية.

٣١. عن محمّد بن عيسى بن عبدالله العلوي، عن أبيه، عن جدّه، عن عليّ عليه السلام قال: الكلمات التي تلقّاها آدم من ربّه قال: يا ربّ، أسألك بحقّ محمد لمّا تُبت عليّ، قال: وما عِلمك بمحمّد؟ قال: رأيتُهُ في سُرادِقك الأعظم مكتوبًا وأنا في الجنّة.

٣٢. عن جابر، قال: سألتُ أبا جعفر عليه السلام عن تفسير هذه الآية في باطن القرآن: ﴿فَإِمَّا يَأْتِيَنَّكُم مِّنِّي هُدًى فَمَن تَبِعَ هُدَايَ فَلَا خَوْفٌ عَلَيْهِمْ وَلَا هُمْ يَحْزَنُونَ﴾.
قال: تفسيرها عليّ عليه السلام الهُدى، قال الله فيه: ﴿فَمَن تَبِعَ هُدَايَ فَلَا خَوْفٌ عَلَيْهِمْ وَلَا هُمْ يَحْزَنُونَ﴾.

٣٣. عن سَماعة بن مِهران، قال: سألتُ أبا عبدالله عليه السلام عن قول الله عزّ وجلّ: ﴿وَأَوْفُوا بِعَهْدِي أُوفِ بِعَهْدِكُمْ﴾ قال: أوفوا بولاية عليّ فرضًا من الله أُوفِ لكم الجنّة.

٣٤. عن جابر الجُعفي، قال: سألتُ أبا جعفر عليه السلام عن تفسير هذه الآية في باطن القرآن: ﴿وَآمِنُوا بِمَا أَنزَلْتُ مُصَدِّقًا لِّمَا مَعَكُمْ وَلَا تَكُونُوا أَوَّلَ كَافِرٍ بِهِ﴾ يعني عليًا عليه السلام.

"He is addressing so-and-so [Abū Bakr] and his companion ['Umar b. al-Khaṭṭāb], and those who follow them and adhere to their religion. And when He tells them ﴾*Do not be the first to disbelieve in it*﴿ the 'it' refers to [the authority of] 'Alī."' [2:41]

35. From Isḥāq b. 'Ammār[37] who said, 'I asked Abū 'Abd Allāh عليه السلام about the verse ﴾*Keep up the prayer, and pay the prescribed alms*﴿. He said, 'This is the obligatory almsgiving (*fiṭra*) that God has made incumbent upon the believers.' [2:43]

36. From Ibrāhīm b. 'Abd al-Ḥamīd[38] who narrated from Abū al-Ḥasan عليه السلام the following: 'I asked him [Abū al-Ḥasan] about the *fiṭra* almsgiving – is it just as obligatory as the alms tax (*zakāt*)? He replied, "Yes. It is included in the commandment in which God says: ﴾*Keep up the prayer, and pay the prescribed alms*﴿ and it is obligatory."' [2:43]

37. From Zurāra [b. A'yan] who reported, 'I asked Abū Ja'far عليه السلام when he was alone with his son Ja'far b. Muḥammad عليه السلام about the *fiṭra* alms. He said, "A man should fulfil the obligation on behalf of himself, his family and his slaves, male and female, young and old. He should give either a measure of dates or half a measure of wheat for every individual [in his household]. This is the almsgiving that God has made obligatory on the believers alongside the prayer, be they rich or poor, for they [the poor] are greater in number while the rich greater in means of giving." I asked, "Is it even obligatory on the poor who is himself a beneficiary of the alms?" He replied, "Yes. He gives out of what has been donated to him."'

---

37 Abū Ya'qūb Isḥāq b. 'Ammār b. Ḥayyān al-Ṣayrafī is said to have belonged to the Faṭḥiyya, a sect within Shi'ism which claimed that the imamate after Imam Ja'far al-Ṣādiq had not passed to either of his sons Ismā'īl or Mūsā al-Kāẓim but rather to his eldest son 'Abd Allāh al-Afṭaḥ (d. 148/765), whence their name the Faṭḥiyya (= Afṭaḥiyya). He is still considered a reliable (*thiqa*) narrator nonetheless. See Ḥillī, *Khulāṣat al-aqwāl*, 317 (nr. 1244); Modarressi, *Tradition and Survival*, 299 (nr. 111).

38 Ibrāhīm b. 'Abd al-Ḥamīd al-Asadī, a companion of the sixth Imam (though possibly Wāqifī) who is generally considered reliable (*thiqa*). See Ḥillī, *Khulāṣat al-aqwāl*, 313 (nr. 1128; see also editor's remark in fn. 1).

٣٥. عن إسحاق بن عمّار، قال: سألتُ أبا عبدالله عليه السلام عن قول الله عزّ وجلّ: ﴿وَأَقِيمُوا الصَّلاةَ وَآتُوا الزَّكَاةَ﴾ قال: هي الفِطرة التي افترض الله على المؤمنين.

٣٦. عن إبراهيم بن عبدالحَميد، عن أبي الحسن عليه السلام، قال: سألتُهُ عن صدقةِ الفِطر، أواجبة هي بمنزلة الزكاة؟ فقال: هي ممّا قال الله: ﴿وَأَقِيمُوا الصَّلاةَ وَآتُوا الزَّكَاةَ﴾ هي واجبة.

٣٧. عن زُرارة، قال: سألتُ أبا جعفر عليه السلام ــ وليس عنده غير ابنه جعفر ــ عن زكاةِ الفطرةِ؟ فقال: يؤدّي الرجلَّ عن نفسه وعياله، وعن رقيقه الذّكر منهم والأُنثى، والصغير منهم والكبير، صاعًا من تمرٍ عن كلّ إنسان، أو نصف صاعٍ من حِنطة، وهي الزكاة التي فرضها الله على المؤمنين مع الصلاة على الغنيّ والفقير منهم، وهم جُلّ النّاس، وأصحاب الأموال أجلّ الناس.

قال: قلتُ: وعلى الفقير الذي يُتَصَدَّق عليه؟ قال: نعم يُعطي ما يُتَصدّق به عليه.

38. From Hishām b. al-Ḥakam, from Abū 'Abd Allāh عليه السلام who said, 'The injunction to pay the alms tax came at a time when people had little or no wealth, but it was actually referring to the *fiṭra*.'

39. From Sālim b. Mukarram al-Jammāl[39], from Abū 'Abd Allāh عليه السلام who said, 'Give the *fiṭra* before the 'Īd prayer, and that is the meaning of the verse: ﴾*Keep up the prayer, and pay the prescribed alms*﴿. The one who receives *fiṭra* must also give it on behalf of himself and his family. If he pays it after performing the 'Īd prayer, then that would not count as *fiṭra*.' [2:43]

40. From Ya'qūb b. Shu'ayb[40] who narrated the following from Abū 'Abd Allāh عليه السلام: 'I asked him regarding the verse: ﴾*How can you tell people to do what is right and forget to do it yourselves, even though you recite the Scripture?*﴿. So he placed his hand on his throat and said, "One might as well kill himself."' [2:44]

41. Al-Hajjāl narrated from Ibn Isḥāq who mentioned it from whoever narrated it to him, that the verse ﴾[...] *and forget to do it yourselves*﴿ meant 'abandoning [doing what is right].' [2:44]

42. From Misma'[41] who narrated the following: 'Abū 'Abd Allāh عليه السلام said to me, "O Misma', when any one of you is afflicted with a worldly sorrow, what is it that prevents him from performing the ablution, entering his place of prayer, offering two units of prayer and supplicating God? Haven't you heard God say: ﴾*Seek help with steadfastness and prayer*﴿?"' [2:45]

---

39 Abū Khadīja Sālim b. Mukarram al-Jammāl, about whom there are divergent opinions concerning his reliability. 'Allāma al-Ḥillī, *Khulāṣat al-aqwāl*, 354 (nr. 1404) is non-committal on his status, preferring instead to abstain (*tawaqquf*) from passing judgement on him. Khū'ī, *Mu'jam*, 8:25 on the other hand believes him to have been a reliable (*thiqa*) narrator. See also Modarressi, *Tradition and Survival*, 368 (nr. 187).

40 Abū Muḥammad Ya'qūb b. Shu'ayb b. Maytham b. Yaḥyā al-Tammār, a client of the Banū Asad and a descendant of Maytham al-Tammār is regarded a reliable (*thiqa*) narrator of the sixth Imam's traditions. See Ḥillī, *Khulāṣat al-aqwāl*, 299 (nr. 1112); Modarressi, *Tradition and Survival*, 398 (nr. 224).

41 A reference most likely to Abū Sayyār Misma' b. Mālik. See Ḥillī, *Khulāṣat al-aqwāl*, 279–80 (nr. 1024).

٣٨. عن هِشام بن الحكم، عن أبي عبدالله عليه السلام، قال: نزلت الزكاة وليس للنّاس الأموال، وإنّما كانت الفِطرة.

٣٩. عن سالم بن مُكرَّم الجمّال، عن أبي عبدالله عليه السلام، قال: أعطِ الفِطرة قبل الصّلاة، وهو قول الله: ﴿وَأَقِيمُوا الصَّلَاةَ وَآتُوا الزَّكَاةَ﴾ والّذي يأخُذ الفِطرة عليه أن يؤدّي عن نفسهِ وعن عِياله، وإن لم يُعطِها حتّى يَنصَرِف من صلاته فلا تُعدّ فِطرة.

٤٠. عن يعقوب بن شُعيب، عن أبي عبدالله عليه السلام، قال: قلت قوله تعالى: ﴿أَتَأْمُرُونَ النَّاسَ بِالْبِرِّ وَتَنسَوْنَ أَنفُسَكُمْ﴾؟ قال: فوضع يده على حَلْقه، قال: كالذابح نفسه.

٤١. وقال الحجّال، عن أبي إسحاق، عمّن ذكره: ﴿وَتَنسَوْنَ أَنفُسَكُمْ﴾، أي تترُكون.

٤٢. عن مِسمع، قال: قال أبو عبدالله عليه السلام: يا مِسمَع، ما يمنع أحدكم إذا دخل عليه غمٌّ من غُموم الدنيا أن يتوضّأ، ثمّ يدخُل مسجده فيركع ركعَتينِ فيدعو الله فيهما؟ أما سَمِعت الله يقول: ﴿وَاسْتَعِينُوا بِالصَّبْرِ وَالصَّلَاةِ﴾.

43. From ʿAbd Allāh b. Ṭalḥa[42], from Abū ʿAbd Allāh عليه السلام regarding the verse: ﴾*Seek help with steadfastness and prayer*﴿, he said, 'Steadfastness refers to fasting.' [2:45]

44. From Sulaymān al-Farrā[43], from Abū al-Ḥasan عليه السلام regarding the verse: ﴾*Seek help with steadfastness and prayer*﴿ he said, 'Steadfastness is fasting. Whenever any difficulty or hardship befalls upon a man then he should fast, for God has stated: ﴾*Seek help with steadfastness and prayer*﴿ where "steadfastness" refers to fasting.' [2:45]

45. From Abū Maʿmar [al-Saʿdī][44], from ʿAlī عليه السلام regarding the verse: ﴾*those who know that they will meet their Lord*﴿. He said, 'They are absolutely certain that they will be raised from their graves; their supposition (*ẓann*) [mentioned in the verse] is in fact certainty (*yaqīn*).' [2:46]

46. From Hārūn b. Muḥammad al-Ḥalabī[45] who narrated the following: 'I asked Abū ʿAbd Allāh عليه السلام about the verse: ﴾*Children of Israel, remember how I blessed you and favoured you over other people*﴿. He replied, "More specifically it means us [the Ahl al-Bayt]."' [2:47]

47. From Muḥammad b. ʿAlī[46] who narrated the following from Abū ʿAbd Allāh عليه السلام: 'I asked him about the verse: ﴾*Children of Israel, remember how I blessed you and favoured you over other people*﴿. He replied, "It addresses specifically the family of Muḥammad."' [2:47]

---

42 ʿAbd Allāh b. Ṭalḥa al-Nahdī, on whom there is scant information, was a narrator of Imam Jaʿfar al-Ṣādiq's traditions. See Khūʾī, *Muʿjam*, 11:243 (nr. 6946); Modarressi, *Tradition and Survival*, 161 (nr. 16).

43 A transcription error possibly of Salīm al-Farrāʾ. See Ḥillī, *Khulāṣat al-aqwāl*, 163 (nr. 474).

44 There is no record of any individual by this name in Ḥillī's *Khulāṣāt al-aqwāl*.

45 There is no record of this individual in either Ḥillī's *Khulāṣat al-aqwāl* or Khūʾī's *Muʿjam*.

46 There are 18 individuals carrying this name in Ḥillī's *Khulāṣat al-aqwāl* alone and hence impossible to know without further detail which of these, if any, is being referred to in this narration.

٤٣. عن عبدالله بن طلحة، عن أبي عبدالله عليه السلام، [في قوله تعالى]: ﴿وَاسْتَعِينُوا بِالصَّبْرِ وَالصَّلَاةِ﴾ قال: الصّبر هو الصوم.

٤٤. عن سُليمان الفرّاء، عن أبي الحسن عليه السلام، في قول الله تعالى: ﴿وَاسْتَعِينُوا بِالصَّبْرِ وَالصَّلَاةِ﴾، قال: الصّبر: الصوم، إذا نزلت بالرجل الشدّة أو النازلة فَليَصُم، فإنّ الله يقول: ﴿وَاسْتَعِينُوا بِالصَّبْرِ وَالصَّلَاةِ﴾ الصبر: الصوم.

٤٥. وعن أبي مَعْمَر، عن علي عليه السلام، في قوله: ﴿الَّذِينَ يَظُنُّونَ أَنَّهُم مُّلَاقُوا رَبِّهِمْ﴾، يقول عليه السلام: يُوقنون أنّهم مبعوثون، والظنّ منهم يقين.

٤٦. عن هارون بن محمّد الحلبي، قال: سألتُ أبا عبدالله عن قول الله عزّ وجلّ: ﴿يَا بَنِي إِسْرَائِيلَ﴾، قال: هم نحن خاصّة .

٤٧. عن محمّد بن علي، عن أبي عبدالله عليه السلام، قال: سألته عن قوله تعال ﴿يَا بَنِي إِسْرَائِيلَ﴾، قال: هي خاصّة بآل محمّد عليه السلام .

48. From Abū Dāwūd[47], from whoever heard the Messenger of God ﷺ say, 'I am the servant of God, my name is Aḥmad, and I am the son of the servant of God whose name was Israel. Whatever He commanded him to do, He has commanded me too, and whatever concerned him concerns me.'

49. From Muḥammad b. Muslim, from Abū Ja'far عليه السلام regarding the verse: ﴾*We appointed forty nights for Mūsā* [on Mount Sinai]﴿. He said, 'Originally it had been decreed in the knowledge [of God] as thirty nights, but God altered (*badā*[48]) His decree and added another ten, so the time appointed by His Lord between the first night and the last was forty nights.' [2:51]

50. From Sulaymān al-Ja'farī who said, 'I heard Abū al-Ḥasan al-Riḍā عليه السلام narrate concerning the verse: ﴾*and say, 'Relieve us!' Then We shall forgive you your sins*﴿ that Abū Ja'far عليه السلام would say, "We are the gate through which you seek relief."' [2:58]

51. From Abū Isḥāq, from whoever mentioned it to him, that the verse: ﴾*and say, 'Relieve us!'*﴿ means to seek forgiveness; that is, 'relieve us!' means 'forgive us!' [2:58]

52. From Zayd al-Shaḥḥām[49], from Abū Ja'far عليه السلام who said: 'Jibra'īl brought down this verse:[50] ﴾*But those who wronged **the family of Muḥammad of their rights** substituted a different word from the one that they had been given.*

---

47 Although unlikely, this could possibly be referring to Abū Dāwūd Sulaymān b. Sufyān al-Mustaraq (d. 231/845–46). See the entry for Sulaymān b. Sufyān in Ḥillī, *Khulāṣat al-aqwāl*, 154–5 (nr. 447).

48 Considered by many Shī'ī scholars to be a genuine part of the Imams' teachings, the doctrine of *badā'* (literally, 'to change or alter') holds the view that some of God's decrees may change according to His Wisdom (*ḥikma*). Whether this also implies a change in God's knowledge or not is a matter of interpolemic debate among Shī'a and Sunnī theologians; s.v. "Badā'," *Encyclopaedia of Islam*, Second Edition, i, 850a (Goldzier, I. and A. S. Tritton).

49 Abū Usāma Zayd b. Yūnus al-Shaḥḥām, of Kufan origin, was the client (*mawlā*) of Shadīd b. 'Abd al-Raḥmān b. Nu'aym/Na'īm al-Azdī al-Ghāmidi and a reliable (*thiqa*) narrator of traditions. See Ḥillī, *Khulāṣat al-aqwāl*, 148 (nr. 422); Modarressi, *Tradition and Survival*, 401–2 (nr. 230).

50 Qur'anic citations marked with the asterisk symbol (*) indicate that a verse quoted in the main body of 'Ayyāshī's *Tafsīr* differs from its equivalent in the official standardized 'Uthmānic codex of the Qur'an.

٤٨. عن أبي داوود، عمّن سَمِع رسول الله ﷺ يقول: أنا عبد الله اسمي أحمد، وأنا عبد الله اسمي إسرائيل، فما أمره فقد أمرني، وما عنَاه فقد عنَاني.

٤٩. عن محمّد بن مسلم، عن أبي جعفر عليه السلام، في قوله تعالى ﴿وَإِذْ وَاعَدْنَا مُوسَى أَرْبَعِينَ لَيْلَةً﴾، قال: كان في العلمِ والتقدير ثلاثين ليلةً، ثمّ بدا لله فزاد عشرًا، فتمّ ميقات ربه للأوّل والآخر أربعين ليلةً.

٥٠. عن سُليمان الجعفري، قال: سَمِعت أبا الحسن الرضا عليه السلام، في قول الله: ﴿وَقُولُوا حِطَّةٌ نَّغْفِرْ لَكُمْ خَطَايَاكُمْ﴾، قال: أبو جعفر عليه السلام: نحن باب حِطّتكم.

٥١. عن أبي إسحاق، عمّن ذكره: ﴿وَقُولُوا حِطَّةٌ﴾ مغفرة، حُطّ عنّا: أي اغفِرْ لنا.

٥٢. عن زيد الشحّام، عن أبي جعفر عليه السلام، قال: نزل جبرئيل بهذه الآية: ﴿فَبَدَّلَ الَّذِينَ ظَلَمُوا آلَ مُحَمَّدٍ حَقَّهُمْ غَيْرَ الَّذِي قِيلَ لَهُمْ فَأَنزَلْنَا عَلَى الَّذِينَ ظَلَمُوا آلَ مُحَمَّدٍ حَقَّهُمْ رِجْزًا مِنَ السَّمَاءِ بِمَا كَانُوا يَفْسُقُونَ﴾.

So, because they persistently disobeyed, We sent a plague down from the heavens upon those who wronged ***the family of Muḥammad of their rights*** ﴿.' [2:59*]

53. From Ṣafwān al-Jammāl, from Abū 'Abd Allāh عليه السلام who said, 'God told Mūsā's people: ﴾[...] *enter its gate humbly and say, 'Relieve us!' Then We shall forgive you your sins and increase the rewards of those who do good. But the wrongdoers substituted a different word from the one they had been given. So, because they persistently disobeyed, We sent a plague down from the heavens upon the wrongdoers*﴿.' [2:58–59]

54. From Isḥāq b. 'Ammār, from Abū 'Abd Allāh عليه السلام that he recited the verse: ﴾[...] *They were struck with humiliation and wretchedness, and they incurred the wrath of God because they persistently rejected His messages and killed prophets contrary to all that is right. All this was because they disobeyed and were lawbreakers*﴿ and then said, 'By God, they did not merely strike them with their hands and kill them with their swords, but upon hearing their messages they would divulge their teachings [to the people falsely]. Therefore, they [the prophets] were consequently incriminated and killed as a result. So it was murder, assault, and rebellion.' [2:61]

55. From Isḥāq b. 'Ammār who narrated the following: 'I asked Abū 'Abd Allāh عليه السلام about the verse: ﴾*And hold with might what We have given you*﴿ and whether this is referring to physical might or a might in their hearts? He replied, "It refers to both of them."' [2:63]

56. From 'Abd ['Ubayd] Allāh al-Ḥalabī[51] that he said regarding the verse: ﴾[...] *and bear its contents in mind*﴿ that it means to keep in mind whatever would lead to chastisement if it was abandoned. [2:63]

---

51 A transcription error possibly for Abū 'Alī 'Ubayd Allāh b. 'Alī b. Abī Shu'ba al-Ḥalabī, a reliable and noteworthy companion of Imam al-Ṣādiq and the author of a work (*kitāb*) about which the Imam is reported to have said, 'They [i.e. the proto-Sunnī community] have nothing like it in *fiqh*.' According to Ḥillī it was the first work authored by a Shī'ī scholar. See Ḥillī, *Khulāṣat al-aqwāl*, 203 (nr. 644).

٥٣. عن صَفوان الجمّال، عن أبي عبد الله عليه السلام، قال: قال الله تعالى لقوم موسى: ﴿ادْخُلُوا الْبَابَ سُجَّدًا وَقُولُوا حِطَّةٌ ... فَبَدَّلَ الَّذِينَ ظَلَمُوا قَوْلًا غَيْرَ الَّذِي قِيلَ لَهُمْ﴾ الآية.

٥٤. عن إسحاق بن عمّار، عن أبي عبد الله عليه السلام، أنّه تلا هذه الآية: ﴿ذَٰلِكَ بِأَنَّهُمْ كَانُوا يَكْفُرُونَ بِآيَاتِ اللَّهِ وَيَقْتُلُونَ النَّبِيِّينَ بِغَيْرِ الْحَقِّ ذَٰلِكَ بِمَا عَصَوا وَكَانُوا يَعْتَدُونَ﴾، فقال: والله ما ضربُوهم بأيديهم، ولا قتلوهم بأسيافهم، ولكن سَمِعوا أحاديثهم فأذاعوها، فأُخذوا عليها، فقُتِلوا، فصار قتلاً واعتداءً ومعصيةً.

٥٥. عن إسحاق بن عمّار، قال: سألتُ أبا عبد الله عليه السلام عن قول الله عزّ وجلّ: ﴿خُذُوا مَا آتَيْنَاكُمْ بِقُوَّةٍ﴾، أقوّة في الأبدان، أم قوّة في القلوب؟ قال: فيهما جميعًا.

٥٦. عن عبد الله الحلبي، قال: قال: ﴿اذْكُرُوا مَا فِيهِ﴾ واذْكروا ما في ترْكِه من العُقوبة.

57. From Muḥammad b. Abī Ḥamza[52], from one of our associates from Abū ʿAbd Allāh عليه السلام who said regarding the verse: ﴾[...] *And hold with might what We have given you*﴿: 'It is the act of prostration and placing the hands on the knees while bowing [*rukūʿ*] in prayer.' [2:63]

58. From ʿAbd al-Ṣamad b. Barrār[53] who narrated the following: 'I heard Abū al-Ḥasan عليه السلام say, 'The apes are the Jews who broke the Sabbath, so God turned them into apes.'

59. From Zurāra, from Abū Jaʿfar عليه السلام and Abū ʿAbd Allāh عليه السلام concerning the verse: ﴾*We made this an example to those people who were there at the time and to those who came after them, and a lesson to all who are mindful of God*﴿. They (peace be upon them) said, 'So that their contemporaries in the villages would look at them [and take heed], and those who were to come after them would say, "Surely in this there is a lesson for us."' [2:66]

60. From Aḥmad b. Muḥammad b. Abī Naṣr al-Bizanṭī[54] who said, 'I heard Abū al-Ḥasan al-Riḍā عليه السلام say that a man from among the Children of Israel killed one of his relatives and after so doing took the body and [secretly] placed it on the doorstep of one of the best young men from among their nation, the Children of Israel. Then he came seeking revenge and blood money, so they came to the Prophet Mūsā and asked him, "The grandson of so-and-so has [allegedly] killed this man, so please inform us who [actually] killed him."

So he replied by saying, "Bring me a cow."

Upon hearing this ﴾*They said, "Are you making fun of us?" He answered, "God forbid that I should be so ignorant"*﴿(2:67). If they had just brought any cow it would have sufficed, but they were reluctant in heeding the command; and so God made things more difficult for them. ﴾*They said, "Call on your Lord for us, to show us what sort of cow it should be." He answered, "God*

52 Muḥammad b. Abī Ḥamza, a notable (*fāḍil*) and reliable (*thiqa*) narrator of traditions. See Ḥillī, *Khulāṣat al-aqwāl*, 255 (nr. 869).

53 There is no individual with this name in either Ḥillī's *Khulāṣat al-aqwāl* or Khūʾī's *Muʿjam*.

54 Abū Jaʿfar Aḥmad b. Muḥammad b. Abī Naṣr al-Bizanṭī (d. 220/835 or 224/838), a praiseworthy and reliable (*thiqa*) companion of the eighth Imam whose character and companionship are commended by all of the *rijāl* authors. See Ḥillī, *Khulāṣat al-aqwāl*, 61 (nr. 66).

٥٧. عن محمّد بن أبي حمزة، عن بعض أصحابنا، عن أبي عبدالله ؏، عن قول الله عزّ وجلّ: ﴿خُذُوا مَا آتَيْنَاكُمْ بِقُوَّةٍ﴾، قال: السُّجود، ووضْع اليدين على الرُّكبتين في الصّلاة وأنت راكِع.

٥٨. عن عبد الصمد بن برار، قال: سَمِعتُ أبا الحسن ؏ يقول: كانت القِردَة وهم اليهود الذين اعتدوا في السبت، فمسخهم الله قُرُودًا.

٥٩. عن زُرارة، عن أبي جعفر وأبي عبدالله ؏، في قوله: ﴿فَجَعَلْنَاهَا نَكَالًا لِمَا بَيْنَ يَدَيْهَا وَمَا خَلْفَهَا وَمَوْعِظَةً لِلْمُتَّقِينَ﴾، قال: لِمَا معها ينْظُر إليها من أهل القُرى، ولِمَا خلفها قال: ونحن، ولنا فيها موعظة.

٦٠. عن أحمد بن محمّد بن أبي نصر البِزَنْطِي، قال: سَمِعتُ أبا الحسن الرضا ؏ يقول: إنّ رجلاً من بني إسرائيل قتل قرابةً له، ثمّ أخذه فطرحه على طريق أفضل سِبط من أسباط بني إسرائيل، ثمّ جاء يطلُب بدمه. فقالوا لموسى ؏: إنّ سِبط آل فلان قتل فلانًا، فأخبرنا من قتله؟ فقال: أئتوني ببقرة. ﴿قَالُوا أَتَتَّخِذُنَا هُزُوًا قَالَ أَعُوذُ بِاللَّهِ أَنْ أَكُونَ مِنَ الْجَاهِلِينَ﴾، قال: ولو عَمَدوا إلى بقرةٍ أجزأتهم، ولكن شدّدوا فشدّد الله عليهم ﴿قَالُوا ادْعُ لَنَا رَبَّكَ يُبَيِّنْ لَنَا مَا هِيَ قَالَ إِنَّهُ يَقُولُ إِنَّهَا بَقَرَةٌ لَا فَارِضٌ وَلَا بِكْرٌ عَوَانٌ بَيْنَ ذَلِكَ﴾ لا صغيرة ولا كبيرة، ولو أنهّم عمَدوا إلى بقرةٍ لأجزأتهم، ولكن شدّدوا فشدّد الله عليهم. ﴿قَالُوا ادْعُ لَنَا رَبَّكَ يُبَيِّنْ لَنَا مَا لَوْنُهَا قَالَ إِنَّهُ يَقُولُ إِنَّهَا بَقَرَةٌ صَفْرَاءُ فَاقِعٌ لَوْنُهَا تَسُرُّ النَّاظِرِينَ﴾ ولو أنهّم عمَدوا إلى بقرة

says it should be neither too old nor too young, but in between"﴾(2:68) – that is, neither too old nor too young.

If only then they had brought any cow it would have sufficed, but still they continued to be obstinate in heeding the command, so God made things even more difficult for them. ﴿*They said, "Call on your Lord for us, to show us what colour it should be." He answered, "God says it should be a bright yellow cow, pleasing to the eye"*﴾(2:69).

If only then they had brought any cow it would have sufficed, but they were obstinate in heeding the command, so God made things even more difficult for them. ﴿*They said, "Call on your Lord for us, to show us* [*exactly*] *what it is: all cows are more or less alike to us. With God's will, we shall be guided." He replied, "It is a perfect and unblemished cow, not trained to till the earth or water the fields." They said, "Now you have brought the truth"*﴾(2:70–71).

So they began searching for a cow of this description and found one belonging to a young man from among the Children of Israel. He said, "I shan't sell it to you until I receive its hide's fill of gold in exchange for it."

So again they came to Mūsā and informed him of the young man's demands, and he told them to purchase it.

He continued, 'One of Prophet Mūsā's companions said to him, "This cow, there is something you are not telling us about it." So he [Mūsā] replied, "There was a young man from the Children of Israel who was particularly kind to his father. He had a commodity for which an opportunity arose for a good trade, but the keys to where it was kept were under his father's head [while he rested]. He did not want to disturb his father's sleep, so he left it. When his father awoke he told him about it, and he in turn commended him and gave him this cow in exchange for the loss that he had incurred." Then God's messenger ﷺ said, "See how kindness rewards itself?"'

61. From al-Ḥasan b. 'Alī b. Yaqṭīn[55] who narrated the following: 'I heard Abū al-Ḥasan ؑ say, "When God commanded the Children of Israel to slaughter a cow, all they needed to take from it was its tail. But because they complicated the matter so much God complicated the matter for them."'

55 Al-Ḥasan b. 'Alī b. Yaqṭīn b. Mūsā, a client (*mawlā*) of the Banū Hāshim tribe, was a religious scholar (*faqīh*), *mutakallim* and reliable (*thiqa*) narrator of Imam al-Riḍā's traditions. See Ḥillī, *Khulāṣat al-aqwāl*, 100 (nr. 225).

لأجزأتهم، ولكن شدّدوا فشدّد الله عليهم. ﴿قَالُوا ادْعُ لَنَا رَبَّكَ يُبَيِّنْ لَنَا مَا هِيَ إِنَّ الْبَقَرَ تَشَابَهَ عَلَيْنَا وَإِنَّا إِنْ شَاءَ اللَّهُ لَمُهْتَدُونَ ﴿﴾ قَالَ إِنَّهُ يَقُولُ إِنَّهَا بَقَرَةٌ لَا ذَلُولٌ تُثِيرُ الْأَرْضَ وَلَا تَسْقِي الْحَرْثَ مُسَلَّمَةٌ لَا شِيَةَ فِيهَا قَالُوا الْآنَ جِئْتَ بِالْحَقِّ﴾.

فطلبوها، فوجدوها عند فتىً من بني إسرائيل، فقال: لا أبيعها إلاّ بِمِلء مَسْكِها ذهبًا، فجاءوا إلى موسى عليه السلام فقالُوا له: قال: فاشتروها.

قال: وَقَالَ لِرَسُوْلِ الله مُوْسَى (عليه السلام) بَعْضُ أَصْحَابِهِ: إنّ هذه البقرة لها نبأ. فقال: وما هو؟ قال: إنّ فتىً من بني إسرائيل كان بارًّا بأبيه، وأنّه اشترى تَبِيعًا، فجاء إلى أبيه والإقليد تحت رأسه، فكَرِه أن يُوقظه، فترك ذلك، فاستيقظ أبوه، فأخبره، فقال له: أحسنت، فخُذ هذه البقرة فهي لك عِوضٌ لما فاتك. قال: فقال رسول الله عليه السلام: انْظُروا إلى البرّ ما بلغ بأهله!

٦١. عن الحسن بن علي بن فضّال، قال: سَمِعتُ أبا الحسن عليه السلام يقول: إنّ الله أمر بني إسرائيل أن يذبحوا بقرةً، وإنّما كانوا يحتاجون إلى ذَنَبها، فشدّد الله عليهم.

62. From al-Faḍl b. Shādhān[56] from one of our associates who, without mentioning his source, cited Abū ʿAbd Allāh عليه السلام as having said the following: 'Whoever wears yellow sandals will remain cheerful until he wears them out, for God has stated: ﴾*a bright yellow cow, pleasing to the eye*﴿'. [2:69]

63. He also said, 'Whoever wears yellow sandals will benefit either from knowledge or wealth before they get worn out.'

64. From Yūnus b. Yaʿqūb[57] who narrated the following: 'I said to Abū ʿAbd Allāh عليه السلام, "The Meccans slaughter cows from the upper part of their chest. What is your opinion about eating their meat?" He remained silent for a while and then replied, "God says ﴾*so they slaughtered it, though they almost failed to do so*﴿, so eat only that which has been slaughtered from its proper place."' [2:71]

65. From Muḥammad b. Sālim[58], from Abū Baṣīr who said that Jaʿfar b. Muḥammad عليه السلام narrated that "ʿAbd Allāh b. ʿAmr b. al-ʿĀṣ left ʿUthmān's house one day and met the Commander of the Faithful. He said to him, "O ʿAlī, we have spent the entire night discussing a matter which we hope God will use to fortify this community (*umma*)." The Commander of the Faithful replied, "What you have spent the whole night doing I am well aware of. You distorted and twisted and changed nine hundred letters [of the Qur'an]; three hundred of which you distorted, three hundred of which you twisted, and three hundred of which you changed around, ﴾*So woe to those who write something down with their own hands and then claim, 'This is from God,' in order to*

56 Abū Muḥammad al-Faḍl b. Shādhān al-Azdī al-Naysābūrī was a scholar and *mutakallim* of high-standing and a companion of the eighth Imam who is described by al-ʿAllāma al-Ḥillī as 'The leader of our sect' (*ra'īs ṭā'ifatinā*). He is reported to have authored approximately 180 works. See Ḥillī, *Khulāṣat al-aqwāl*, 229 (nr. 769).

57 Abū ʿAlī Yūnus b. Yaʿqūb b. Qays al-Jallāb al-Duhnī, of Kufan origin, about whom there are varying opinions among the *rijāl* authors, especially regarding his religious affiliations. Some claim he was a Faṭḥī, an advocate of ʿAbd Allāh al-Afṭaḥ's imamate after the death of Jaʿfar al-Ṣādiq. He died in Medina and was according to Kishshī's account wrapped in burial garments (*kafan*) by the eighth Imam ʿAlī b. Mūsā al-Riḍā. See Ḥillī, *Khulāṣat al-aqwāl*, 297 (nr. 1104); Modarressi, *Tradition and Survival*, 399–400 (nr. 227).

58 Abū Ismāʿīl Muḥammad b. Sālim b. Sharīḥ al-Ashjaʿī al-Ḥadhā' al-Kūfī (d. 192/808), a reliable (*thiqa*) companion of Imam Jaʿfar al-Ṣādiq. See Ḥillī, *Khulāṣat al-aqwāl*, 236 (nr. 806).

٦٢. عن الفضل بن شاذان، عن بعض أصحابنا، رفعه إلى أبي عبدالله عليه السلام، أنّه قال: من لَبِس نَعلاً صفراء لم يزَل مسرورًا حتّى يُبليها، كما قال الله: ﴿صَفْرَاءُ فَاقِعٌ لَوْنُهَا تَسُرُّ النَّاظِرِينَ﴾.

٦٣. وقال: من لَبِس نَعلاً صفراء لم يُبلِها حتّى يستفيد عِلمًا أو مالاً.

٦٤. عن يُونُس بن يعقوب، قال: قلتُ لأبي عبدالله عليه السلام: إنّ أهل مكّة يذبحون البقرة في اللَّبَب، فما ترى في أكل لحُومها؟ قال: فسكت هُنيئة، ثمّ قال: قال الله: ﴿فَذَبَحُوهَا وَمَا كَادُوا يَفْعَلُونَ﴾ لا تأْكُل إلاّ ما ذُبح من مَذبحه.

٦٥. عن محمّد بن سالم، عن أبي بصير، قال: قال جعفر بن محمّد عليه السلام: خرج عبدالله بن عمرو بن العاص من عند عُثمان، فلقي أمير المؤمنين صلوات الله عليه، فقال له: يا عليّ، بيَّتنا الليلة في أمرٍ، نرجو أن يُثبت الله هذه الأُمة.

فقال أمير المؤمنين عليه السلام: لن يخفى عليّ ما بيَّتهم فيه، حرَّفتم وغيَّرتم وبدَّلتم تسعمائة حرف: ثلاثمائة حرَّفتم، وثلاثمائة غيَّرتم، وثلاثمائة بدَّلتم ﴿فَوَيْلٌ لِلَّذِينَ يَكْتُبُونَ الْكِتَابَ بِأَيْدِيهِمْ ثُمَّ يَقُولُونَ هَذَا مِنْ عِنْدِ اللَّهِ﴾ إلى آخر الآية ﴿مِمَّا يَكْسِبُونَ﴾.

make some small gain. Woe to them for what their hands have written! Woe to them for all that they have earned!﴾."' [2:79]

66. From Jābir, from Abū Ja'far ﷺ regarding the verse ﴿[...] *and speak good words to all people*﴾ that he said, 'Speak to people in whatever way you yourselves wish to be spoken to, for God despises the foul-mouthed person who is lewd and abusive to others, who insults believers and uses obscene language, as well as the insistent beggar. Rather He loves those who are reserved [in their speech], compassionate, gentle and virtuous.' [2:83]

67. From Ḥarīz, from Burayd [b. Mu'āwiya][59] who narrated the following: 'I asked Abū 'Abd Allāh ﷺ, "Should I feed a beggar if I do not know whether he is a Muslim or not?" He replied, "Yes, feed him, even if you are not aware whether he is an adherent [of ours] or an enemy, for God has stated: ﴿*and speak good words to all people*﴾. However, do not feed one who rejects the truth or openly encourages falsehood."' [2:83]

68. From 'Abd Allāh b. Sinān who narrated the following from Abū 'Abd Allāh ﷺ: 'I heard him say, "Be mindful of God and do not bear grudges against people, for God has said: ﴿*and speak good words to all people*﴾. Visit the sick among them, attend their funerals and pray with them in their mosques for as long as you are alive, even if differences exist between you."' [2:83]

69. From Ḥafṣ b. Ghiyāth[60], from Ja'far b. Muḥammad ﷺ that he said: 'God sent Muḥammad ﷺ with five specific ordinances in which the sword could

---

59 Abū al-Qāsim Burayd b. Mu'āwiya al-'Ijlī (d. 150/767) was a companion of the fifth and sixth Imams and a leading figure of the Imāmī community, who is counted among their close associates by all major authorities of Shī'ī *rijāl* and included in the category of those individuals who are collectively referred to as the People of Consensus (*aṣḥāb al-ijmā'*). A reliable (*thiqa*) narrator, he is reported to have been promised Paradise by Imam Ja'far al-Ṣādiq. See Ḥillī, *Khulāṣat al-aqwāl*, 81–2 (nr. 164); Modarressi, *Tradition and Survival*, 213–4 (nr. 51).

60 Abū 'Umar Ḥafṣ b. Ghiyāth b. Ṭalq b. Mu'āwiya al-Nakha'ī (d. 194/809) was a Kufan judge (*qāḍī*) in service of the Abbasid Caliph Hārūn al-Rashīd (r. 786–809). Despite being Sunnī (*'āmmī*), he is mentioned in Shī'a *rijāl* books as a narrator of Imam al-Ṣādiq's traditions and

٦٦. عن جابر، عن أبي جعفر ﷺ، في قوله ﴿وَقُولُوا لِلنَّاسِ حُسْنًا﴾، قال: قولوا للنّاس أحسن ما تُحبّون أن يُقال لكم، فإنّ الله يُبْغِض اللعّان السبّاب الطعّان على المؤمنين، المتُفَحّش، السائل المُلْحِف، ويُحبُّ الحييَّ الحليم، العَفيف المتعفّف.

٦٧. عن حَرِيز، عن بُريد، قال: قلت لأبي عبدالله ﷺ: أُطعِمُ رجلاً سائلاً لا أعرفه مسلماً؟ قال: نعم أطعمْه ما لم تَعْرِفه بولايته ولا بعداوة، إنّ الله تعالى يقول: ﴿وَقُولُوا لِلنَّاسِ حُسْنًا﴾ ولا تُطعم مَن ينَصِب لشيءٍ من الحقّ، أودعا إلى شيء من الباطل.

٦٨. عن عبدالله بن سِنان، عن أبي عبدالله ﷺ، قال: سَمِعتُهُ يقول: اتّقوا الله ولا تَحْمِلوا الناس على أكتافكم، إنّ الله تعالى يقُول في كتابه: ﴿وَقُولُوا لِلنَّاسِ حُسْنًا﴾، قال ﷺ: وعودوا مرضاهم، واشهدوا جنائزهم، وصلّوا معهم في مساجدهم حتّى النَّفَس، وحتّى تكون المباينة.

٦٩. عن حَفص بن غِياث، عن جعفربن محمّد ﷺ، قال: إنّ الله بعث محمّدًا ﷺ بخمسة أسياف، فسَيف على أهل الذمّة، قال الله ﴿وَقُولُوا لِلنَّاسِ حُسْنًا﴾ نزلت في أهل الذمّة، ثم نَسَخَتها أُخرى، قوله: ﴿قَاتِلُوا الَّذِينَ لا يُؤْمِنُونَ بِاللهِ﴾ الآية.

be raised, one of which is against the *dhimmīs*[61]. The verse: ﴾*and speak good words to all people*﴿ was initially revealed concerning the *dhimmīs*, but was later abrogated by the verse: ﴾*Fight those of the People of the Book who do not* [*truly*] *believe in God* [...]﴿(9:29).' [2:83]

70. From Abū ʿAmr al-Zubayrī[62], from Abū ʿAbd Allāh عليه السلام who said, 'There are five instances of disbelief (*kufr*) in the Qur'an. Among these is that which occurs due to repudiation [and it is of two types:] [(i)] repudiation of [God's] favours and [(ii)] repudiation of God's command. The latter can also be referred to as wrongful action and forsaking the command of God, the Mighty and Exalted, as stated in the verse ﴾*We took a pledge from you, 'Do not shed one another's blood or drive one another from your homelands. You acknowledged it at the time, and you can testify to this. Yet here you are, killing one another and driving some of your own people from their homes, helping one another in sin and aggression against them. If they come to you as captives, you still pay to set them free, although you had no right to drive them out. So do you believe in some parts of the Scripture and not in others?*﴿. Here God brands them as disbelievers because of their rejection of His command. And even though He relates them to faith [referring to the part ﴾*do you believe*﴿] it was not accepted from them nor was it of any avail to them. Hence for that reason He says ﴾[...] *The punishment for those of you who do this will be nothing but disgrace in this life, and on the Day of Resurrection they will be condemned to the harshest torment: God is not unaware of what you do*﴿.' [2:84–85]

71. From Jābir, from Abū Jaʿfar عليه السلام who said, 'The verse ﴾*So how is it that, whenever a messenger brings you something you do not like* [...]﴿ is speaking about Mūsā and the other prophets who came after him including ʿĪsā (may God's blessings be upon all of them) as a way putting forth an example to

---

as the author of a commendable and noteworthy book. See Ḥillī, *Khulāṣat al-aqwāl*, 340 (nr. 1349).

61 Dhimmīs (*ahl al-dhimma* in Arabic) refers to the protected minorities within the Islamic state; s.v. "Dhimma," *Encyclopaedia of Islam*, Second Edition, ii, 227a (C. Chehata).

62 Although his name occurs in the chains of transmission (*isnād*) of numerous Shīʿī traditions, not much is known about Abū ʿAmr al-Zubayrī. See Khūʾī, *Muʿjam*, 22: 284–5 (nr. 14652).

٧٠. عن أبي عمرو الزُّبيري، عن أبي عبد الله عليه السلام، قال: الكُفر في كتاب الله على خمسة أوجه: فمنها كُفر البراءة، وكفر النِّعَم، والكُفر بترك أمر الله، فالكفر بما نقول من أمر الله فهو كُفر المعاصي، وترك ما أمر الله عزّ وجلّ، وذلك قوله تعالى: ﴿وَإِذْ أَخَذْنَا مِيثَاقَكُمْ لَا تَسْفِكُونَ دِمَاءَكُمْ﴾ إلى قوله: ﴿أَفَتُؤْمِنُونَ بِبَعْضِ الْكِتَابِ وَتَكْفُرُونَ بِبَعْضٍ﴾ فكفّرهم بتركهم ما أمر الله، ونسبهم إلى الإيمان ولم يقبله منهم، ولم ينفعهم عنده، فقال: ﴿فَمَا جَزَاءُ مَنْ يَفْعَلُ ذَلِكَ مِنْكُمْ إِلَّا خِزْيٌ﴾ الآية إلى قوله: ﴿عَمَّا تَعْمَلُونَ﴾.

٧١. عن جابر، عن أبي جعفر عليه السلام، قال: أمّا قوله: ﴿أَفَكُلَّمَا جَاءَكُمْ رَسُولٌ بِمَا لَا تَهْوَى أَنْفُسُكُمُ﴾ الآية، قال أبو جعفر عليه السلام: ذلك مثل موسى عليه السلام والرُّسل من بعده وعيسى صلوات الله عليه، ضُرِب مثلاً لأمّة محمّد صلى الله عليه وآله، فقال الله لهم: فإن جاءكم محمّد بما لا تهوى أنفسكم بموالاة عليّ استكبرتم، ففريقًا من آل محمّد كذّبتم، وفريقًا تقتُلون، فذلك تفسيرها في الباطن.

Muḥammad's community, as if God were saying to them: 'When Muḥammad brings you something you do not like, you become arrogant with respect to 'Alī's authority over you and you call some of Muḥammad's progeny impostors, and you kill others'; that is its inner meaning.' [2:87]

72. From Abū Baṣīr, from Abū 'Abd Allāh ﷺ who stated in respect of the verse ﴾ *When a Scripture came to them from God confirming what they already had, and when they had been praying for victory against the disbelievers, even when there came to them something they knew [to be true], they disbelieved in it* [...] ﴿: 'The Jews [in pre-Islamic Arabia] found in their scriptures that Muḥammad's settlements would be located somewhere between the mountains of 'Ayr and Uḥud. So they left in search of this location, passing by a mountain called Ḥaddād which they said was the same as the mount of Uḥud. Satisfied they had found the place they were looking for they decided to disperse themselves in that region, some choosing to settle in Fadak, some in Khaybar and others in Taymā'. Those settling in Taymā' soon began to miss their brethren in the other regions, so when a Bedouin from Qays passed them by they hired him, and he offered to take them to the place between 'Ayr and Uḥud. They requested him to point out the location described in their scriptures for them, and so when they reached the oasis of Medina between the two mountains, he told them which mountain was 'Ayr and which Uḥud. They got down from his camel and informed him that since they had reached their destination, they had no further need of him and that he was free to go wherever he pleased. They then wrote to their fellow brothers in Fadak and Khaybar informing them that they had found the place [destined in their scriptures as the place where Muḥammad's settlements would be found] and requested the remaining Jewish tribes to join them there. They wrote back saying that they had settled in their homes and were prospering and that when such time [as the advent of the Prophet] came, they would rush there. So they settled in Medina and prospered, and when they were at the peak of their prosperity, the Tubba'[63] came and attacked them. They protected themselves against his army but were subsequently captured and

63 Referring to the Himyarite Kings of Yemen who ruled over Southwest Arabia between the late 3rd and early 6th centuries of the common era. See "Tubba'," *Encyclopaedia of Islam*, Second Edition, x, 575a (A. F. L. Beeston).

٧٢. عن أبي بصير، عن أبي عبدالله عليه السلام، في قوله: ﴿وَكَانُوا مِن قَبۡلُ يَسۡتَفۡتِحُونَ عَلَى ٱلَّذِينَ كَفَرُواْ﴾، فقال عليه السلام: كانت اليهود تجد في كتبها أنّ مَهاجِر محمّد صلى الله عليه وآله ما بين عَير وأُحد، فخرجوا يطلبُون الموضوع، فمرّوا بجبلٍ يسمى حداداً، فقالوا حداد وأحد سَواء، فتفرّقوا عنده، فنزل بعضهم بفَدَك، وبعضهم بخيبر، وبعضهم بتَيماء، فاشتاق الذين بتَيماء إلى بعض إخوانهم، فمرّ بهم أعرابيّ من قيس فتكارَوا منه، وقال لهم: أمُرّ بكم ما بين عَير وأُحد؟ فقالوا له: إذا مررت بهما فآرناهما، فلمّا توسّط بهم أرض المدينة، قال لهم: ذاك عَير وهذا أُحد، فنزلوا عن ظهر إبله، فقالوا له: قد أصبنا بُغيتنا، فلا حاجة لنا في إبلك، فاذهب حيث شئت.

وكتبوا إلى إخوانهم الذين بفَدَك وخَيبر: إنّا قد أصبنا الموضع، فهلمّوا إلينا. فكتبوا إليهم: إنّا قد استقرّت بنا الدّار، واتّخذنا الأموال، وما أقرَبنا منكم، وإذا كان ذلك فما أسرعنا إليكم!

فاتّخذوا بأرض المدينة الأموال، فلمّا كثُرت أموالهم بلغ تُبّع فغزاهم، فتحصّنوا منه فحاصرهم، فكانوا يرِقّون لضعفى أصحاب تُبّع فيَلقُونَ إليهم بالليل التمر والشعير، فبلغ ذلك تُبّع فَرَقّ لهم وآمنهم، فنزلوا إليه، فقال لهم: إنّي قد استطبت بلادكم ولا أراني إلاّ مقيماً فيكم.

فقالوا له: إنّه ليس ذلك لك، إنها مَهاجِر نبيّ، وليس ذلك لأحدٍ حتىّ يكون ذلك.

فقال لهم: فإنّي مخلّف فيكم من أُسرتي من إذا ذلك ساعده ونصره.

enslaved by the weakest of his men, who would throw dates and barley at them to eat at night. The news reached Tubbaʿ himself, so he set them free and gave them protection. The Jews went to him saying, "This land does not belong to you. It is going to be the settlement of a prophet and cannot be owned by anyone." So he told them that in that case he would leave two of his tribes behind to help and support him, the tribes of Aws and Khazraj. When these tribes flourished, they began to dominate the Jews' wealth. The Jews would often despair saying, "If only God would send Muḥammad, then we would drive you out of our territories and possessions." When God eventually sent Muḥammad ﷺ down, the *anṣār* [the Prophet's supporters in Medina] believed in him whilst the Jews belied him. This is what was intended in the verse: ﴾*and when they had been praying for victory against the disbelievers, even when there came to them something they knew* [*to be true*], *they disbelieved in it: God rejects those who disbelieve*﴿.' [2:89]

73. From Jābir who narrated, 'I asked Abū Jaʿfar عليه السلام about the verse ﴾*even when there came to them something they knew* [*to be true*], *they disbelieved in it*﴿. He said: "Its inner meaning is that when there came to them something which they knew to be true about ʿAlī عليه السلام, they disbelieved in it. For this reason, God says to them, ﴾*so God rejects those who disbelieve*﴿, meaning the Umayyads (*banū Umayya*). According to the inner meaning of the Qur'an, they, the Umayyads, are the disbelievers."

74. Abū Jaʿfar عليه السلام said, 'This verse was revealed to the Messenger of God thus: ﴾*Low indeed is the price for which they have sold their souls by denying that which God has sent down* ***concerning ʿAlī*** *out of envy that God should send His bounty to any of His servants He pleases . The disbelievers* (referring to the Umayyads) *have ended up with wrath upon wrath and a humiliating torment awaits them*﴿ [2:89–90].

75. Jābir reports that Abū Jaʿfar عليه السلام said the following: 'By God, this verse was revealed to Muḥammad ﷺ as follows: ﴾***When it is said to them, 'What has your Lord revealed about ʿAlī?' they reply, 'We believe in what was revealed to us***﴿ – so in their hearts they believe in what was revealed to the Prophet – ﴾*but they do not believe in what came afterwards*﴿ – namely that which God

فخلف فيهم حَيّين: الأوس والخَزْرج، فلمّا كثُروا بها كانوا يتناولون أموال اليهود، فكانت اليهود تقول لهم: أما لو بُعث محمّد لُنخرجنّكم من ديارنا وأموالنا، فلمّا بعث الله محمّدًا ﷺ آمنت به الأنصار، وكفرت به اليهود، وهو قول الله عزّ وجلّ: ﴿وَكَانُوا مِن قَبْلُ يَسْتَفْتِحُونَ عَلَى الَّذِينَ كَفَرُوا﴾ إلى ﴿فَلَعْنَةُ اللهِ عَلَى الْكَافِرِينَ﴾.

٧٣. عن جابر، قال: سألتُ أبا جعفر عليه السلام عن هذه الآية من قول الله: ﴿فَلَمَّا جَاءَهُم مَّا عَرَفُوا كَفَرُوا بِهِ﴾. قال: تفسيرها في الباطن لما جاءهم ما عرفوا في عليّ عليه السلام كفروا به، فقال الله [فيهم ﴿فَلَعْنَةُ اللهِ عَلَى الْكَافِرِينَ﴾] يعني بني أُميّة، هم الكافرون في باطن القرآن.

٧٤. قال أبو جعفر عليه السلام: نزلت هذه الآية على رسول الله ﷺ هكذا: ﴿بِئْسَمَا اشْتَرَوْا بِهِ أَنفُسَهُمْ أَن يَكْفُرُوا بِمَا أَنزَلَ اللهُ﴾ في عليّ ﴿بَغْيًا﴾، وقال الله في عليّ عليه السلام: ﴿أَن يُنَزِّلَ اللهُ مِن فَضْلِهِ عَلَى مَن يَشَاءُ مِنْ عِبَادِهِ﴾ يعني عليًا، قال الله: ﴿فَبَاءُوا بِغَضَبٍ عَلَى غَضَبٍ﴾ يعني بني أُمية ﴿وَلِلْكَافِرِينَ﴾ يعني بني أُمية ﴿عَذَابٌ مُّهِينٌ﴾.

٧٥. وقال جابر: قال أبو جعفر عليه السلام: نزلت هذه الآية على محمّد ﷺ هكذا والله (وإذا قِيل لَهُم ماذا أنزل ربّكم في عَليٍّ) يعني بني أُمّية ﴿قَالُوا نُؤْمِنُ بِمَا أُنزِلَ عَلَيْنَا﴾ يعني في قلوبهم بما أنزل الله عليه ﴿وَيَكْفُرُونَ بِمَا وَرَاءَهُ﴾ بما أنزل الله في عليٍّ ﴿وَهُوَ الْحَقُّ مُصَدِّقًا لِّمَا مَعَهُمْ﴾ يعني عليًّا عليه السلام.

has revealed about ʿAlī – ﴾*though it is the truth confirming what they already have*﴿ – referring to ʿAlī.' [2:91*]

76. From Abū ʿAmr al-Zubayrī, from Abū ʿAbd Allāh عليه السلام who said, 'God narrates about the Jews in His Book that they used to say: ﴾*God has commanded us not to believe in any messenger unless he brings us an offering that fire [from heaven] consumes* [...]﴿(3:183). In response to them He replied: ﴾*Then why did you kill God's prophets in the past if you were true believers?*﴿. This verse was revealed addressing the Jewish community at the time of Muḥammad ﷺ despite the fact that they were not physically persecuting any prophets at that time nor were they the ones living at the time of those prophets [referenced in the verse]. Rather it was their ancestors before them who perpetrated the killing. But since they had descended from these original murderers, God includes them in their midst and addresses them for their forefathers' actions because they followed them and took over from them [in allowing wrongdoing].' [2:91]

77. From Abū Baṣīr, from Abū Jaʿfar عليه السلام who narrated the following regarding the verse ﴾*and through their disbelief they were made to drink [the love of] the calf deep into their hearts*﴿: 'When Mūsā was conversing with His Lord, God revealed to Him: "O Mūsā, I am testing your community."

He asked, "With what, my Lord?"

"With al-Sāmirī," replied God.

"But what has he done?" asked Mūsā.

"He has moulded a calf out of all their gold," replied God.

So Mūsā replied, "But my Lord, their gold would have been moulded into a gazelle or a statue or a calf in any case, so how is it that You are testing them?"

God replied, "He has moulded a calf that makes a mooing sound."

"But my Lord, what is making it moo?" he asked.

"Me," God replied.

Upon hearing this Mūsā exclaimed, "﴾*This is only a trial from You – through it, You cause whoever You will to stray and guide whoever You will* [...]﴿(7:155)."

When Mūsā returned to his community and saw them worshipping the calf, he threw the tablets on the ground, and they broke.'

٧٦. عن أبي عمرو الزُبيري، عن أبي عبد الله ، قال: قال الله تعالى في كتابه يحكي قول اليهود: ﴿إِنَّ اللَّهَ عَهِدَ إِلَيْنَا أَلَّا نُؤْمِنَ لِرَسُولٍ حَتَّىٰ يَأْتِيَنَا بِقُرْبَانٍ﴾ الآية، فقال: ﴿فَلِمَ تَقْتُلُونَ أَنبِيَاءَ اللَّهِ مِن قَبْلُ إِن كُنتُم مُّؤْمِنِينَ﴾ وإنّما نزل هذا في قومٍ [من] اليهود، وكانوا على عهد محمّد لم يقتُلوا الأنبياء بأيديهم ولا كانوا في زمانهم، وإنّما قتل أوائلهم الذين كانوا من قبلهم، فنزّلوا بهم أُولئك القَتلة، فجعلهم الله منهم وأضاف إليهم فعل أوائلهم بما تَبِعوهم وتولّوهم.

٧٧. عن أبي بَصير، عن أبي جعفر ، في قول الله عزّ وجلّ: ﴿وَأُشْرِبُوا فِي قُلُوبِهِمُ الْعِجْلَ بِكُفْرِهِمْ﴾. قال: لمّا ناجى موسى ربّه أوحى الله إليه: أن يا موسى، قد فتنتُ قومك. قال: بماذا، يا ربّ؟ قال: بالسامري قال: وما فعل السامري؟ قال: صاغ لهم من حُليّهم عِجلاً.

قال: يا ربّ، إنّ حُليّهم لتحتمل أن يُصاع منه غَزال أو تمثال أو عِجل، فكيف فتنتهم؟ قال: إنهُ صاغ لهم عِجلاً فخار. قال: يا ربّ، ومن أخاره؟ قال: أنا. فقال عندها موسى: ﴿إِنْ هِيَ إِلَّا فِتْنَتُكَ تُضِلُّ بِهَا مَن تَشَاءُ وَتَهْدِي مَن تَشَاءُ﴾.

قال: فلمّا انتهى موسى إلى قومه ورآهم يَعبُدون العِجل، ألقى الألواح من يده فتكسّرت. فقال أبو جعفر : كان ينبغي أن يكون ذلك عند إخبار الله إيّاه.

قال: فعمدَ موسى فَبرَد العِجل من أنفه إلى طرَف ذَنَبه، ثم أحرقه بالنّار، فذَرّه في اليمّ، قال: فكان أحدهم ليقع في الماء وما به إليه من حاجة، فيتعرّض لذلك الرماد فيشربه، وهو قول الله تعالى ﴿وَأُشْرِبُوا فِي قُلُوبِهِمُ الْعِجْلَ بِكُفْرِهِمْ﴾.

Abū Ja'far عليه السلام continued, 'This must have been something about which God had already informed him. So Mūsā took the calf, pulverized it from head to tail, burnt it in the fire and scattered the ashes in the sea. One of them was near the water at that moment about to drink some, so he rushed instead towards the ashes and drank them in, and this is the meaning of the verse ﴿ *and through their disbelief they were made to drink* [*the love of*] *the calf deep into their hearts* ﴾.' [2:93]

78. From Abū Baṣīr, from Abū Ja'far عليه السلام who said, 'When Sulaymān passed away Iblīs formulated a magical spell which he inscribed into a scroll. He rolled it up and on its front he wrote: "This is [the spell] that 'Āsif b. Barkhiyā formulated from the kingdom of Sulaymān, the son of Dāwūd, and it [is the key to] the storehouses and treasures of knowledge. Whosoever wishes anything should chant what is written inside this scroll." Then he buried it under the throne and indicated to the wrongdoers where it was. The disbelievers claimed that it was only through witchcraft that Sulaymān had been able to defeat them, whereas the believers asserted that he was a servant of God and a prophet. So God revealed the verse: ﴿ *they followed what the evil ones had fabricated about the Kingdom of Sulaymān instead* [...] ﴾ – meaning magic.' [2:102]

79. From Muḥammad b. Qays who narrated, 'I was with Abū Ja'far عليه السلام in Mecca when 'Atā' asked him about Hārūt and Mārūt.[64]

He replied by saying, "The angels used to descend from the heavens to the Earth every night and day, monitoring the deeds of the inhabitants of the Earth, men and Jinn. Then they would record them down and take them back up to the heavens. The heavenly beings were astonished at the sins of these earthly creatures, and they would deliberate with each other about all the sins they had seen and heard being committed against God, and about their audacity to disobey Him. They would then declare God's sanctity far beyond what these creatures were saying about Him and describing Him to be. Then a group of angels asked God, 'Our Lord, how is it that You are not

64 Hārūt and Mārūt are the names of two fallen angels in the legend of Solomon. The Qur'an condemns them for teaching men the forbidden occult sciences; s.v. "Hārūt wa-Mārūt," *Encyclopaedia of Islam*, Second Edition, iii, 236b (G. Vajda).

٧٨. عن أبي بصير، عن أبي جعفر عليه السلام، قال: لمّا هلك سُليمان عليه السلام وضع إبليس السِّحر، ثمّ كتبه في كتاب فطواه، وكتب على ظهره: هذا ما وضع آصف بن بَرخيا من مُلك سليمان بن داود عليه السلام، من ذخائر كُنُوز العلم، من أراد كذا وكذا فليقل كذا وكذا، ثمّ دفنه تحت السرير، ثمّ استبانه فقرأه لهم، فقال الكافرون: ما كان يَغْلِبنا سُليمان إلاّ بهذا. وقال المؤمنون: هو عبدالله ونبيّه. فقال الله في كتابه ﴿وَاتَّبَعُوا مَا تَتْلُوا الشَّيَاطِينُ عَلَى مُلْكِ سُلَيْمَانَ﴾ أي السحر.

٧٩. عن محمّد بن قيس، سَمِعتُ أبا جعفر عليه السلام وسأله عطاء — ونحن بمكّة — عن هاروت وماروت، فقال أبو جعفر عليه السلام: إنّ الملائكة كانوا يَنْزِلون من السّماء إلى الأرض في كلّ يوم وليلةٍ، يَحْفَظون أعمال أهل أوساط الأرض من ولد آدم والجنّ، فيَكْتُبون أعمالهم ويَعْرُجون بها إلى السماء، قال: فضجّ أهل السماء من معاصي أهل أوساط الأرض، فتآمروا بينهم بما يسمعون ويَرَون من افترائِهم الكَذِب على الله وجُرأتهم عليه، ونزّهوا الله ممّا يقول فيه خلقه ويصفون.

قال: فقالت طائفةٌ من الملائكة: يا ربّنا، ما تَغْضَب ممّا يعمل خلقك في أرضك، ممّا يفترون عليك الكَذِب، ويقولن الزُور، ويرتكبون المعاصي وقد نهيتهم عنها، ثمّ أنت تَحْلُم عنهم، وهم في قبضتك وقُدرتك وخلال عافيتك!

قال: أبو جعفر عليه السلام وأحبَّ الله أن يُري الملائكة قُدرته ونافذ أمره في جميع خلقه، ويعرف الملائكة ما منَّ به عليهم ممّا عَدَله عنهم من جميع خلقه، وما طبعهم عليه من الطاعة، وعصمهم به من الذنوب.

angered at what Your creatures on earth are doing, inventing lies about you, spreading falsehood and committing sins when You have expressly forbidden them from doing so? Not only that but You are so clement towards them when You have them in the Palm of Your Hand and have all power over them while they subsist only through You.'"

Abū Ja'far عليه السلام continued, "So God wanted to show the angels His power and the way His plan worked with respect to all His creatures. He wanted to make them realise the bounty that He had bestowed on them by keeping them away from what the rest of His creatures were prone to, having created them naturally inclined to obedience and immune from sinning. So God commanded the angels to elect two angels from among themselves who would be sent down to Earth with natural urges for food and drink, desire, greed, and hope, just as He had placed in humans. Then He would test them for their obedience to Him."

The Imam continued, "So they elected Hārūt and Mārūt, for they had been the most vehement of all the angels in their criticism of humans. Then God revealed to them both: 'Descend to the earth, for I have placed in you natural urges for food and drink, desire, greed, and hope just as I have placed in humans.' Then God told them: 'Do not associate anything with Me, nor shall you kill an innocent soul, nor commit fornication, nor shall you drink wine.' Then He exposed the seven heavens to them [in all their glory] to show them His power and sent them down to Earth in human form and clothing. They descended somewhere near Babylon where they saw a lofty and grand building, so they approached it and noticed a lovely, beautiful, well-adorned and perfumed, unveiled woman walking towards them. When they looked at her, took in her beauty and thought about her, an overwhelming feeling flooded their hearts, which was the desire that had been placed in them. They discussed with each other and reminded themselves of the fact that they had been forbidden from committing the act of illicit fornication (*zinā*). So they walked past her, but their desire drove them to turn back on their heels in temptation and self-betrayal. So they sought to seduce her, and she said to them, 'I follow a religion that does not allow me to fulfil your desires unless you both enter my religion with me.'

So they asked her which religion that was, and she replied, 'I have a god who enables me to fulfil each and every desire of the one who worships him and prostrates to him.'

قال: فأوحى الله إلى الملائكة: أن انْدُبوا منكم مَلَكين حتّى أُهْبِطهما إلى الأرض، ثمّ أجعل فيهما من طبائع المطعم والمشرب والشهوة والحِرص والأمل مثل ما جعلت في ولد آدم، ثمّ أختبرهما في الطاعة لي.

قال: فندبوا لذلك هاروت وماروت، وكانا من أشدّ الملائكة قولاً في العيب لولد آدم، واستئثار غضب الله عليهم.

قال: فأوحى الله إليهما أن اهبِطا إلى الأرض، وقد جعلتُ فيكما من طبائع المطعم والمشرب والشهوة والحِرص والأمل مثل ما جعلتُ في ولد آدم.

قال: ثمّ أوحى الله إليهما: انظُرا أن لا تُشرِكا بي شيئًا، ولا تَقْتُلا النفس التي حرّمت، ولا تَزْنِيا ولا تَشْرَبا الخمر.

قال: ثمّ كَشَط عن السماوات السبع ليرُيهما قُدرته، ثمّ أهبطهما إلى الأرض في صُورة البشر ولباسهم، فهَبَطا برَحْبة بابل مهرود، فرفع لهما بناء مشرف فأقبلا نحوه، فإذا بحضرته امرأة جميلة حسناء مزيّنة مُعطّرة مسفرة مقبلة نحوهما، فلمّا نظرا إليها وناطقاها وتأمّلاها، وقعت في قلوبهما موقعًا شديدًا لموضع الشهوة التي جُعِلت فيهما، ثمّ أنّهما ائتمرا بينهما، وذكرا ما نُهِيا عنه من الزنا فمضيا.

ثمّ حرّكتهما الشّهوة التي جُعِلت فيهما، فرجعا إليها رُجُوع فتنةٍ وخِذلان، فراوداها عن نفسها. فقالت لهما: إنّ لي دينًا أدينُ به، ولستُ أقدر في دِيني الذي أدين به على أن أُجيبكما إلى ما تُريدان إلاّ أن تَدْخُلا في ديني الذي أدين به.

So they asked her who that god was, and she replied, 'This statue here is my god.'

So they both looked at each other and said, 'These are both vices that are explicitly prohibited to us – polytheism and fornication. If we prostrate before this statue and worship it, we will have associated another with God, and we will be doing that to fornicate. Here we want to fornicate, and the only way to it is through polytheism!'

So they deliberated between themselves, but the desire in them overpowered them, whereupon they said to her, 'We will do as you say.'

So she said, 'Come here and drink this wine as an offering to him, and through this you will achieve whatever you both want.'

So they discussed it among themselves again saying, 'These are three vices that our Lord expressly forbade us: polytheism, fornication and wine. Moreover, we are drinking wine to be able to fornicate!'

After further discussion they said to her, 'How severely we are being tested through you! We will do as you say.'

So she said, 'Here you go – drink this wine, worship this statue and prostrate before it.'

So they did as they were told. Then they were ready to seduce her, and just as she was preparing herself for them and they for her, a beggar walked in on them. Upon seeing the beggar the two angels were startled, and he said to them, 'Why are you so startled and frightened? It is because you are both alone with this beautifully adorned and perfumed woman. You are both evil men!' With that, he left.

She exclaimed, 'No, by my god! You cannot touch me or come near me now that this man has seen your state and knows your whereabouts. He has gone to tell people about you. Run and catch him and kill him before he gets a chance to expose you both and me also. Then come back here and fulfil your needs when you are reassured and safe.'

So they went after the man, found him and killed him. Then they returned to her but failed to find her anywhere. That is when they realised their sins; their wings fell off and they fell on to their hands.

God revealed to them saying, 'It has only been an hour since I sent you down to Earth and already you have disobeyed me with four sins, all of which I expressly forbade you beforehand. Neither were you careful of your duty to Me, nor were you ashamed before Me, when you were the ones most

فقالا لها: وما دينك؟ فقالت: لي إله مَن عَبَدَه وسَجَد له كان لي السبيل إلى أن أُجيبه إلى كلّ ما سألني. فقالا لها: وما إلهك؟ قالت: إلهي هذا الصنم.

قال: فنظر أحدهما إلى صاحبه، فقالا: هاتان الخَصْلتان ممّا نُهينا عنه: الشّرك، والزّنا، لأنّا إنْ سجدنا لهذا الصنم وعبدناه أشركنا بالله، وإنّما نُشرِك بالله لنصل إلى الزّنا، وهو ذا نحن نَطْلُبُ فليس نعطاه إلاّ بالشّرك. قال: فأتمرا بينهما فغلبتهما الشّهوة التي جُعِلت فيهما، فقالا لها: نُجيبك إلى ما سألت. قالت: فدونكما، فاشربا هذا الخمر فإنّه قُربان لكما عنده، وبه تَصِلان إلى ما تُريدان.

قال: فأتمرا بينهما فقالا: هذه ثَلاثُ خِصال ممّا قد نهانا ربُّنا عنه: الشِرك، والزنا وشُرب الخمر، وإنّما ندخلُ في شُرب الخمر حتّى نَصِل إلى الزِنا. فأتمرا بينهما، ثمّ قالا لها: ما أعظم البليّة بك! قد أجبناك إلى ما سألتِ، قالت: فدُونكما فاشربا من هذا الخمر، واعْبُدا الصَّنم، واسْجُدا له.

قال: فشَرِبا الخمر، وسجدا له، ثمّ راوداها عن نفسها، فلمّا تهيّأت لهما وتهيّئا لها، دخل عليهما سائلٌ يسأل، فلمّا أن رأياه ذعِرا منه، فقال لهما: إنّكما لمريبان ذَعِران، قد خَلَوتُما بهذه المرأة المعطّرة الحسناء، إنّكما لرجلا سُوء، وخرج عنهما. فقالت لهما: لا وإلهي لا تصلان إليّ، ولا تقربان، وقد اطّلع هذا الرجل على حالكما وعَرَف مكانكما، خرج الآن فيُخبر بخبركما، ولكن بادرا إلى هذا الرجل فاقْتُلاه قبل أن يَفْضَحَكما ويَفضَحني، ثمّ دُونكما فاقضيا حاجتكما وأنتما مطمئنّان آمنان.

critical of My humans' sins, and quickest to incite My disappointment and anger towards them when I had not yet placed that same nature in you, and kept you immune from sins. So how now would you like to experience My disappointment with you both? Choose either chastisement in this world or the Hereafter.'

So one replied, 'We can enjoy ourselves in this world now that we are here until we get to the chastisement of the Hereafter.'

The other one said, 'The chastisement of the world is temporary and limited, whereas the chastisement of the Hereafter will be eternal and unlimited, so we would rather choose to be punished in this temporal, finite world instead of the intense, eternal punishment in the Hereafter.'

So God said, 'Then you shall have punishment in this world.' So they used to teach witchcraft to people in Babylon, and when they had done that they were raised from the earth and suspended in the air, tormented and hung upside down until the Day of Judgement.'"

80. From Zurāra, from Abū al-Ṭufayl[65] who narrated, 'I was in the mosque of Kufa listening to 'Alī عليه السلام on the pulpit when Ibn al-Kawwā[66] shouted out to him from the back of the mosque, "O Commander of the Faithful, what is guidance?"

So he عليه السلام said, too low for the man to hear, "May God curse you, you are asking what guidance is but it is really misguidance that you are after." He told him to come nearer, so the man approached and asked him several questions, which he duly answered.

Then he said, "Tell me about this red star," meaning the planet Venus.

So he عليه السلام said, "God let the angels observe the humans [he had created and placed on Earth] whilst they were committing sins, and the angels

65 Abū al-Ṭufayl 'Āmir b. Wāthila has been recorded by various biographers sometimes as a companion of the Prophet, sometimes of 'Alī b. Abī Ṭālib, sometimes of Imam al-Ḥasan and sometimes as a companion of Imam 'Alī b. al-Ḥusayn. According to Barqī he was one of the foremost companions of 'Alī b. Abī Ṭālib and the fourth Imam 'Alī b. al-Ḥusayn. Some reports claim that 'Āmir b. Wāthila was a follower of the Kaysāniyya, a movement which believed in the imamate of Muḥammad b. al-Ḥanafiyya, whom the Kaysāniyya claimed was still alive. See Khū'ī, *Mu'jam*, 10:219–22 (nr. 6116).

66 'Abd Allāh b. 'Amr Ibn al-Kawwā', a Khārijī adversary of 'Alī known for his persistent questioning and rebuking. See Ḥillī, *Khulāṣat al-aqwāl*, 369 (nr. 1454).

قال: فقاما إلى الرجل فأدركاه فقتلاه، ثمّ رجعا إليها، فلم يرياها، وبَدَت لهما سَوآتهما، ونُزِع عنهما رِياشهما، وأُسقِطا في أيديهما.

قال: فأوحى الله إليهما: إنّما أهبطتُكما إلى الأرض مع خلقي ساعةً من نهار، فعصيتماني بأربع معاصٍ كُلّها قد نهيتُكما عنها، وتقدّمتُ إليكما فيها، فلم تُراقباني، ولم تستحيا منّي، وقد كُنتما أشدّ من نَقَم على أهل الأرض من المعاصي، وأسجر سعير غَضَبي عليهم، لما جعلت فيكما من طبع خلقي وعصمتي إيّاكما من المعاصي، فكيف رأيتما موضع خِذلاني فيكما؟ اختارا عذاب الدنيا أو عذاب الآخرة.

فقال أحدهما: نتمتّع من شهواتنا في الدنيا إذ صرنا إليها إلى أن نصير إلى عذاب الآخرة. وقال الآخر: إنّ عذاب الدنيا له مدّة وانقطاع، وعذاب الآخرة دائم لا انقطاع له، فلسنا نختارُ عذاب الآخرة الدائم الشّديد على عذاب الدنيا الفاني المنقطع.

قال: فاختارا عذاب الدنيا، فكانا يُعلّمان السحر بأرض بابل، ثمّ لما علّما الناس رُفِعا من الأرض إلى الهواء، فهما معذّبان منكّسان معلّقان في الهواء إلى يوم القيامة.

٨٠. عن زُرارة، عن أبي الطفيل، قال: كنتُ في مسجد الكوفة، فسَمِعتُ عليًّا ﵇ وهو على المِنبَر وناداه ابن الكوّاء وهو في آخر المسجد، فقال: يا أمير المؤمنين، ما الهُدى؟ فقال ﵇: لعنك الله — ولم يسمعه — ما الهُدى تُريد ولكن العمى تُريد. ثمّ قال له: ادنُ. فدنا منه، فسأله عن أشياء فأخبره، فقال أخبرني عن هذه الكوكبة الحمراء — يعني الزُّهرَة.

Hārūt and Mārūt objected by retorting, 'These are the very creatures whose father You created with Your own Hands, whom You made the angels prostrate to, and now they dare to disobey You?' So He replied, 'If I were to try you the same way that I have tried them, then maybe you would disobey Me too just like them.' They retorted, 'No! By Your might!'

So He tried them with the same desire with which He tries humans, then commanded them not to associate anything with Him nor to kill an innocent soul, nor fornicate or drink wine. Then he sent them both down to Earth where they used to adjudicate between people and resolve their disputes. Then one day, whilst they were occupied doing that, this star came to one of them [in human form] to present her plea. She was most beautiful, and he liked her, so he told her that although she was in the right he would not decree in her favour until she had made herself available to him. So she arranged an appointment with him on a particular day. Then she went to the other one, presenting her plea to him. He too was taken by her beauty and attracted to her, and said the same thing to her as his friend had done. So she agreed to meet him at the same time as she had told the other. So they both met each other at her residence at the agreed time, and each one was ashamed in front of the other, and they both bowed their heads in shame.

Eventually their shame vanished and one said to the other, 'We are both in the same boat now.' So they both told her [of their desires] and tried to seduce her. She refused unless they prostrated to her idol and drank her drink. They refused at first, but upon her insistence they agreed to do as she said, and just as they had drunk and prayed to her idol, a beggar walked in on them and saw them.

She exclaimed, 'This man will go and tell people about you, so go and kill him.'

Then after that they tried to seduce her again, but she refused unless they told her how they fly up to the sky, for they used to adjudicate during the day and go back up to the sky at night. They refused to tell her at first, but when she declined to do as they wanted they told her.

She stated that all this had been to test them and she flew upwards. They lifted their gazes up to see her and noticed all the inhabitants of the heavens looking down at them, while she reached the sky and transformed into the star that you now see."'

قال: إنّ الله اطّلع ملائكته على خلقه، وهم على معصيةٍ من معاصيه، فقال المَلَكان هاروت وماروت: هؤلاء الذين خَلَقتَ أباهم بيدك، وأسجدت له ملائكتك يَعْصُونك!

قال: فلعلّكم لو ابتُلِيتُم بمثل الذي ابتليتُهم به عصيتموني كما عَصَوني. قالا: لا وعزّتك.

قال: فابتلاهما بمثل الّذي ابتلى به بني آدم من الشهوة، ثمّ أمرهما أن لا يُشْرِكا به شيئًا، ولا يَقْتُلا النّفس التي حرّم الله، ولا يزنيا ولا يشربا الخمر، ثمّ أهبطهما إلى الأرض، فكانا يقضيان بين الناس، هذا في ناحية، وهذا في ناحية، فكانا بذلك حتى أتت أحدهما هذه الكوكبة تُخاصم إليه، وكانت من أجمل الناس. فأعْجَبَتْهُ، فقال لها: الحقُّ لك ولا أقضي لك حتّى تمكّنيني من نفسك، فواعدت يومًا، ثمّ أتت الآخر، فلمّا خاصمت إليه وقعت في نفسه، وأعجبته، كما أعجبت الآخر، فقال لها مثل مقالة صاحبه، فواعدته الساعة التي واعدت صاحبه، فاتّفقا جميعًا عندها في تلك الساعة، فاستحيا كلّ واحدٍ من صاحبه حيث رآه وطأطآ رؤوسهما ونكّسا، ثمّ نُزِع الحَيَاء عنهما، فقال أحدهما لصاحبه: يا هذا، جاء بي الذي جاء بك.

قال: ثم أعلماها وراوداها عن نفسها، فأبت عليهما حتى يسجدا لوثنها، ويشربا من شرابها، فأبيا عليها وسألاها، فأبت إلا أن يشربا من شرابها، فلمّا شربا صلّيا لِوثنها، ودخل مسكينٌ فرآهما، فقالت لهما: يَخرج هذا فيُخبر عنكما. فقاما إليه فقتلاه، ثم راوداها عن نفسها فأبت حتّى يُخبراها بما يصعدان به إلى السماء، وكانا يقضيانِ بالنهار، فإذا كان الليل صَعِدا إلى السماء فأبيا عليها وأبت أن تفعل فأخبراها، فقالت ذلك لتُجرّب مقالتهما وصعدت، فرفعا أبصارهما إليها، فرأيا أهل السماء مشرفين عليهما ينظرون إليهما، وتناهت إلى السماء فُسِخت، فهي الكوكبة التي ترى.

81. From Muḥammad b. Muslim, from Abū Jaʿfar عليه السلام who said regarding the verse ﴾*Any revelation We cause to be superseded or forgotten, We replace with something better or similar*﴿: '[It is] the verse which abrogates another that He causes to be forgotten, like the unseen which has not yet come to pass, as per His saying: ﴾*God erases or confirms whatever He wills, and the source of Scripture is with Him*﴿(13:39). Thus God does whatever He wills and transforms whatever He wishes, as He had done with the community of Yūnus, whose fate He altered and whom He forgave, as mentioned in His verse: ﴾*so ignore them, for you are not to blame*﴿(51:54), but then they were encompassed by His mercy.' [2:106]

82. From 'Umar b. Yazīd[67] who narrated, 'I asked Abū 'Abd Allāh عليه السلام about God's verse in the Qur'an: ﴾*Any revelation We cause to be superseded or forgotten, We replace with something better or similar*﴿, so he said, "They lie, it is not really like that. He can cause it to be superseded and forgotten, but were it to be similar then wherefore the need to abrogate it?"

So I retorted, "But that is what God has said."

He said, "No, that is not what God, Blessed and most High, has said. There is no 'or' in the verse. It is supposed to be ﴾***Any revelation We cause to be superseded or forgotten, We replace with something better [yet] similar***﴿. He عليه السلام continued, "Whenever an Imam dies or his mention is forgotten, we replace him with one like him, better than him from his own lineage."' [2:106*]

83. From Muḥammad b. Yaḥyā[68] regarding the verse: ﴾*Such people should not enter them without fear*﴿, that it means that they do not accept faith until and unless their lives are at stake.' [2:114]

---

67 Abū al-Aswad 'Umar [b. Muḥammad] b. Yazīd Bayāʿ al-Sābirī (d. after 148/765), a reliable (*thiqa*) and trustworthy companion of the sixth and seventh Imams. He is the author of a book on the rites and obligations of Hajj, all of which is reported to have been based on statements heard directly from Imam al-Ṣādiq. He is so highly praised in some accounts that Imam al-Ṣādiq is reported to have stated: 'O 'Umar, by God you are part of our household' (*anta minnā ahl al-bayt*). See Ḥillī, *Khulāṣat al-aqwāl*, 210 (686); Khū'ī, *Muʿjam*, 14:59 (nr. 8806); Modarressi, *Tradition and Survival*, 388 (nr. 211).

68 Given the presence of several individuals by this name in the works of *rijāl*, it is impossible to know from this *ḥadīth* alone who exactly is being referred to.

٨١. عن محمّد بن مسلم، عن أبي جعفر عليه السلام، في قوله: ﴿مَا نَنسَخْ مِنْ آيَةٍ أَوْ نُنسِهَا نَأْتِ بِخَيْرٍ مِنْهَا أَوْ مِثْلِهَا﴾. قال الناسخ: ما حوّل، وما ينساها: مثل الغيب الذي لم يكن بعد، كقوله: ﴿يَمْحُوا اللَّهُ مَا يَشَاءُ وَيُثْبِتُ وَعِندَهُ أُمُّ الْكِتَابِ﴾، قال: يفعل الله ما يشاء، ويحوّل ما يشاء، مثل قوم يونس إذ بدا له فرحمهم، ومثل قوله: ﴿فَتَوَلَّ عَنْهُمْ فَمَا أَنْتَ بِمَلُومٍ﴾ قال: أدركتهم رحمتُه.

٨٢. عن عمر بن يزيد، قال: سألت أبا عبد الله عليه السلام، عن قول الله: ﴿مَا نَنسَخْ مِنْ آيَةٍ أَوْ نُنسِهَا نَأْتِ بِخَيْرٍ مِنْهَا أَوْ مِثْلِهَا﴾، فقال: كذبوا ما هكذا هي، إذا كان ينسخها ويأتي بمثلها لم يَنسخْها.

قلت: هكذا قال الله، قال: ليس هكذا قال تبارك وتعالى. قلت: فكيف؟

قال: قال: ليس فيها ألف ولا واو، قال: (ما ننسخ من آيةٍ أو نُنسها نأتِ بخيرٍ منها مثلها) يقول: ما نُميت من إمامٍ أو نُنسِ ذكرَه نأتِ بخير منه من صُلبه مثله.

٨٣. عن محمّد بن يحيى، في قوله تعالى: ﴿مَا كَانَ لَهُمْ أَنْ يَدْخُلُوهَا إِلاَّ خَائِفِينَ﴾ يعني الإيمان لا يقبلونه إلاّ والسيف على رؤوسهم.

84. From Ḥarīz who narrated, 'Abū Ja'far ﷺ said that the verse: ﴿ *Wherever you turn, there is His Face. God is all-pervading and all-knowing* ﴾ was specifically revealed for optional supererogatory prayers: namely, that the Messenger of God ﷺ used to pray while sitting on his mount whichever way it happened to be facing on his way to Khaybar, even as he was riding away from Mecca and the Ka'ba was behind him.' [2:115]

85. Zurāra narrated, 'I asked Abū 'Abd Allāh ﷺ, "Does one pray aboard a ship the same as he would on a riding beast?"

He replied, "The supererogatory prayers are all the same: you can pray with gestures wherever your riding beast or your ship turns. For obligatory prayers, though, you must dismount if you are riding and pray standing, unless you fear for your life – in which case you would gesture. On a ship you must pray standing and make every effort to face the Qibla. Nūḥ ﷺ performed his obligatory prayers aboard the ark standing and facing the Qibla when it was hidden from sight."

I asked, "But how did he know the direction of the Qibla when it was not in view?"

He replied, "Jibra'īl would make him stand towards it."

So I asked, "So I should face it every time I raise my hands in *takbīr*?"

He replied, "[Yes,] but not in supererogatory prayers where it is not incumbent on you to face the Qibla, for every direction is Qibla for the one who offers supererogatory prayers. This is what the verse: ﴿ *Wherever you turn, there is His Face. God is all-pervading and all-knowing* ﴾ means.' [2:115]

86. From Ḥammād b. 'Uthmān who narrated from Abū 'Abd Allāh ﷺ: 'I asked him about how someone should prostrate in the prayer while sitting astride his mount. He replied, "He would prostrate towards whichever direction it was facing. The Messenger of God ﷺ used to offer his supererogatory prayers while riding his camel on the way to Medina. God says: ﴿ *Wherever you turn, there is His Face. God is all-pervading and all-knowing* ﴾.' [2:115]

٨٤. عن حريز، قال: قال أبو جعفر عليه السلام: أنزل الله هذه الآية في التطوّع خاصّة ﴿فَأَيْنَمَا تُوَلُّوا فَثَمَّ وَجْهُ اللَّهِ إِنَّ اللَّهَ وَاسِعٌ عَلِيمٌ﴾، وصلّى رسول الله صلى الله عليه وآله إيماءً على راحلته أينما توجّهت به حيث خرج إلى خيبر، وحين رَجَع من مكة، وجعل الكعبة خلف ظهره.

٨٥. قال زُرارة: قلت لأبي عبدالله عليه السلام: الصّلاة في السفر في السفينة والمَحمِل سواء؟ قال: النافلة كلّها سواء، تُومئ إيماءً أينما توجّهت دابّتك وسفينتك، والفريضة تنزل لها من المَحمل إلى الأرض إلا من خوف، فإن خفت أومأت، وأمّا السفينة فصَلِّ فيها قائمًا وتَوخّ القبلة بجُهدك، فإنّ نوحًا عليه السلام قد صلّى الفريضة فيها قائمًا متوجّهًا إلى القبلة وهي مُطبقة عليهم.

قال: قلت: وما كان علمه بالقبلة فيتوجّهها وهي مُطبقة عليهم؟ قال: كان جبريل عليه السلام يقوّمه نحوها.

قال: قلت فأتوجّه نحوها في كلّ تكبيرة؟ قال: أمّا في النافلة فلا، إنّما يُكبّر في النافلة على غير القبلة أكثر، ثم قال: كلّ ذلك قبلة للمُتنفّل، إنّه قال: ﴿فَأَيْنَمَا تُوَلُّوا فَثَمَّ وَجْهُ اللَّهِ إِنَّ اللَّهَ وَاسِعٌ عَلِيمٌ﴾.

٨٦. عن حمّاد بن عثمان، عن أبي عبدالله عليه السلام، قال: سألته عن رجلٍ يقرأ السجدة وهو على ظهر دابّته، قال: يسجُد حيث توجّهت به فإنّ رسول الله صلى الله عليه وآله كان يُصلّي على ناقته النافلة وهو مستقبل المدينة، يقول: ﴿فَأَيْنَمَا تُوَلُّوا فَثَمَّ وَجْهُ اللَّهِ إِنَّ اللَّهَ وَاسِعٌ عَلِيمٌ﴾.

87. From Abū Wallād[69] who said, 'I asked Abū 'Abd Allāh عليه السلام about the verse: ﴾*Those to whom We have given the Scripture, who follow it as it deserves, are the ones who truly believe in it*﴿. He replied, "They are the Imams."' [2:121]

88. From Manṣūr, from Abū Baṣīr, from Abū 'Abd Allāh عليه السلام regarding the verse: ﴾*who follow it as it deserves*﴿, 'It is to pause when the Garden and the Fire are mentioned.' [2:121]

89. From Ya'qūb al-Aḥmar[70], from Abū 'Abd Allāh عليه السلام that he said, 'Compensation (*'adl*) means the obligatory prayer.' [2:123]

90. From Ibrāhīm b. al-Fuḍayl[71], from Abū 'Abd Allāh عليه السلام who said, 'Compensation (*'adl*) according to Abū Ja'far عليه السلام is sacrifice.' [2:123]

91. He said, 'Asbāṭ al-Zuṭṭī[72] also narrated that he asked Abū 'Abd Allāh عليه السلام about the meaning of the divinely-attributed saying: ﴾*God will accept neither compensation nor penalty from him*﴿. He said, 'Penalty (*ṣarf*) here means the supererogatory prayer, and compensation (*'adl*) the obligatory prayer.' [2:123]

---

69 Abū Wallād Ḥafṣ b. Sālim al-Ḥannāṭ, a client of the Banū Makhzūm, was a reliable (*thiqa*) narrator and author of one of the pre-canonical works (*aṣl*) of *ḥadīth*. See Ḥillī, *Khulāṣat al-aqwāl*, 127 (nr. 333); Modarressi, *Tradition and Survival*, 235 (nr. 68).

70 Ya'qūb b. Sālim al-Aḥmar, a reliable companion of Imam Ja'far al-Ṣādiq. See Ḥillī, *Khulāṣat al-aqwāl*, 298 (nr. 1108); Khū'ī, *Mu'jam*, 21:136 (nr. 13753); Modarressi, *Tradition and Survival*, 397 (nr. 222).

71 We have not been able to identify this individual.

72 Abū al-Ḥasan 'Alī b. Asbāṭ b. Sālim Bayyā' al-Zuṭṭī, about whom there are conflicting reports about his allegiances. While Kishshī and Najāshī both agree he was originally of the Faṭḥiyya school of thought, they disagree on whether or not he ever converted his allegiance to the later Imams. According to Kishshī he died believing in his original Faṭḥī allegiances, while according to Najāshī he died having abandoned the Faṭḥiyya and converted to the proto-Imāmī school of thought. Biographical sources recount that 'Alī b. Mahziyār authored a substantial rebuttal of his views and those of the Faṭḥiyya in general. According to Najāshī he was one the most reliable companions of the eighth Imam and a trustworthy narrator of his traditions. See Ḥillī, *Khulāṣat al-aqwāl*, 185–6 (nr. 549).

٨٧. عن أبي ولاّد، قال: سألت أبا عبدالله، عن قوله تعالى: ﴿الَّذِينَ آتَيْنَاهُمُ الْكِتَابَ يَتْلُونَهُ حَقَّ تِلاوَتِهِ أُولَئِكَ يُؤْمِنُونَ بِهِ﴾، قال: فقال: هم الأئمة عليهم السلام.

٨٨. عن منصور، عن أبي بصير، عن أبي عبدالله عليه السلام، في قول الله تعالى: ﴿الَّذِينَ آتَيْنَاهُمُ الْكِتَابَ يَتْلُونَهُ حَقَّ تِلاوَتِهِ أُولَئِكَ يُؤْمِنُونَ بِهِ﴾، فقال: الوقوف عند ذِكر الجنّة والنّار.

٨٩. عن يعقوب الأحمر، عن أبي عبدالله عليه السلام، قال: العدل: الفريضة.

٩٠. عن إبراهيم بن الفُضيل، عن أبي عبدالله عليه السلام، قال: العَدل في قول أبي جعفر عليه السلام: الفِداء.

٩١. قال: ورواه أسباط الزّطّي، قال: قلت لأبي عبدالله عليه السلام: قول الله: (لا يقبلُ اللهُ منه صرفًا ولا عدلاً) قال: الصّرف: النافلة، والعدل: الفريضة.

92. He narrated with numerous chains from Ṣafwān al-Jammāl, who said, 'We were in Mecca discussing the verse: ﴾*When Ibrāhīm's Lord tested him with certain commandments, which he fulfilled*﴿(2:124). He said, "He fulfilled it in the name of Muḥammad and 'Alī and the Imams from 'Alī's lineage in accordance with the verse: ﴾*in one line of descent – God hears and knows all*﴿(3:34). Then God goes on to say: ﴾*He said, 'I will make you a leader of people.' Ibrāhīm asked, 'And will You make leaders from my descendants too?' God answered, 'My pledge does not hold for those who do evil'*﴿(2:124).

Thereupon Ibrāhīm asked, 'My Lord, will there be evil-doers from among my descendants?'

He replied, 'Yes, these three and their followers.'

So he said, 'My Lord, hasten Muḥammad and 'Alī and that which you have promised me regarding them both, and hasten your support of them both.' This is an indication to the verse: ﴾*Who but a fool would forsake the religion of Ibrāhīm? We have chosen him in this world and he will rank among the righteous in the Hereafter*﴿(2:130). So the religion [of Ibrāhīm] is the Imamate.

Moreover, when he settled one of his offspring in Mecca he said, ﴾*Our Lord, I have established some of my offspring in an uncultivated valley, close to Your Sacred House, Lord, so that they may keep up the prayer. Make people's hearts turn to them, and provide them with produce*﴿(14:37) and ﴾*those of them who believe in God and the Last Day*﴿(2:62), omitting the phrase "those of them who believe" out of fear that his request would be rejected as it had been previously when he had asked about his descendants, and God had said: ﴾*My pledge does not hold for those who do evil*﴿(2:123).

So when God replied: ﴾*As for those who disbelieve, I will grant them enjoyment for a short while and then subject them to the torment of the Fire – an evil destination*﴿(2:124), Ibrāhīm asked, 'Who are the people to whom You will grant temporary enjoyment?'

He replied, 'Those who disbelieve in My communications – then He mentioned the names of three individuals."'

93. From Ḥarīz, from whoever mentioned it to him from Abū Ja'far عليه السلام who said, regarding the verse ﴾*My pledge does not hold for those who do evil*﴿, that it means that he would not be an evil leader.

٩٢. رواه بأسانيد عن صفوان الجمّال، قال: كُنّا بمكّة فجَرى الحديث في قول الله تبارك وتعالىٰ: ﴿وَإِذِ ابْتَلَى إِبْرَاهِيمَ رَبُّهُ بِكَلِمَاتٍ فَأَتَمَّهُنَّ﴾، قال: أتمّهنّ بمحمّدٍ وعليّ والأئمّة من وُلد عليّ ﷺ، في قول الله: ﴿ذُرِّيَّةً بَعْضُهَا مِن بَعْضٍ وَاللَّهُ سَمِيعٌ عَلِيمٌ﴾، ثمّ قال: ﴿إِنِّي جَاعِلُكَ لِلنَّاسِ إِمَامًا قَالَ وَمِن ذُرِّيَّتِي قَالَ لَا يَنَالُ عَهْدِي الظَّالِمِينَ﴾ قال: يا ربّ، ويكون من ذرّيتي ظالم؟ قال: نعم فلان وفلان وفلان ومَن اتّبَعَهم.

قال: يا ربّ، فعجّل لمحمّد وعليّ ما وعدتَني فيهما، وعجّل نَصرَك لهما، وإليه أشار بقوله تعالى: ﴿وَمَن يَرْغَبُ عَن مِّلَّةِ إِبْرَاهِيمَ إِلَّا مَن سَفِهَ نَفْسَهُ وَلَقَدِ اصْطَفَيْنَاهُ فِي الدُّنْيَا وَإِنَّهُ فِي الْآخِرَةِ لَمِنَ الصَّالِحِينَ﴾ فالمِلّة: الإمامة.

فلمّا أسكن ذُرّيّته بمكّة قال: ﴿وَإِذْ قَالَ إِبْرَاهِيمُ رَبِّ اجْعَلْ هَٰذَا بَلَدًا آمِنًا وَارْزُقْ أَهْلَهُ مِنَ الثَّمَرَاتِ مَنْ آمَنَ﴾ فاستثنَى ﴿مَنْ آمَنَ﴾ خوفًا أن يقول له: لا، كما قال له في الدعوة الأولى: ﴿وَمِن ذُرِّيَّتِي قَالَ لَا يَنَالُ عَهْدِي الظَّالِمِينَ﴾، فلمّا قال الله: ﴿وَمَن كَفَرَ فَأُمَتِّعُهُ قَلِيلًا ثُمَّ أَضْطَرُّهُ إِلَىٰ عَذَابِ النَّارِ وَبِئْسَ الْمَصِيرُ﴾ قال: يا ربّ، ومن الذين مَتّعتَهم؟ قال: الّذين كفروا بآياتي فلان وفلان وفلان.

٩٣. عن حَريز، عمّن ذكره، عن أبي جعفر ﷺ، في قول الله تعالى: ﴿لَا يَنَالُ عَهْدِي الظَّالِمِينَ﴾ أي لا يكون إمامًا ظالمًا.

94. From Hishām b. al-Hakam, from Abū ʿAbd Allāh عليه السلام, with respect to the verse ﴾*I will make you a leader* [Imam] *of people*﴿, he said, 'Were there to be a better word for God to use than that [i.e. Imam], He would have called us by that instead.' [2:124]

95. From Muḥammad b. al-Fuḍayl[73], from Abū al-Ṣabbāḥ who narrated the following: 'Abū ʿAbd Allāh عليه السلام was asked about the ruling for someone who had forgotten to offer the two units of prayer incumbent at the Station of Ibrāhīm عليه السلام after the circumambulation of Hajj and *ʿumra*. He replied, "If he is still in Mecca, he must go and offer the two units of prayer at the Station of Ibrāhīm, for God says ﴾*Take the spot where Ibrāhīm stood as your place of prayer*﴿. If, however, he has left and travelled on, I would not ask him to come back [and perform it]."' [2:125]

96. From al-Ḥalabī, who states from Abū ʿAbd Allāh عليه السلام: 'I asked him عليه السلام about someone who performs the obligatory circumambulation, be it in Hajj or *ʿumra*, then forgets to offer the two units of prayer at the Station of Ibrāhīm عليه السلام. He replied, "He should go and offer them even if it is a few days later, for God says ﴾*Take the spot where Ibrāhīm stood as your place of prayer*﴿.' [2:125]

97. From al-Mundhir al-Thawrī who reports from Abū Jaʿfar عليه السلام that he said: 'I asked him عليه السلام about the Black Stone, so he said, "Three stones descended from heaven: the Black Stone which Ibrāhīm set in place, the platform on which Ibrāhīm stood, and the rock of the Children of Israel." Abū Jaʿfar عليه السلام continued, "God sent Ibrāhīm a stone that was whiter than paper but it blackened due to the sins of humankind."'

98. From Jābir al-Juʿfī who narrated, 'Muḥammad b. ʿAlī [al-Bāqir] عليه السلام exclaimed to me, "Jābir, how audaciously the people of Shām slander God! They claim that when God, Blessed and most High, climbed to the sky, He placed His

73 Abū Jaʿfar al-Azraq Muḥammad b. al-Fuḍayl b. Kathīr al-Azdī al-Ṣayrafī, a well-known associate of the eight Imam accused of exaggerating the status of the Imams. See Ḥillī, *Khulāṣat al-aqwāl*, 395 (nr. 1593); Khūʾī, *Muʿjam*, 18: 151–4 (nr. 11591).

٩٤. عن هشام بن الحكم، عن أبي عبدالله ﷺ، في قول الله: ﴿إِنِّي جَاعِلُكَ لِلنَّاسِ إِمَامًا﴾، قال: فقال: لو علم الله أنّ اسمًا أفضل منه لسمّانا به.

٩٥. عن محمّد بن الفُضَيل، عن أبي الصبّاح، قال: سُئل أبو عبدالله ﷺ عن رجلٍ نَسي أن يُصلّي الركعتين عند مقام إبراهيم ﷺ في الطّواف في الحجّ أو العُمرة. فقال: إن كان بالبلد صلّى ركعتين عند مقام إبراهيم ﷺ، فإنّ الله يقول: ﴿وَاتَّخِذُوا مِنْ مَقَامِ إِبْرَاهِيمَ مُصَلًّى﴾، وإن كان ارتحل وسار، فلا آمُره أن يرجع.

٩٦. عن الحلبي، عن أبي عبدالله ﷺ، قال: سألتُه عن رجلٍ طاف بالبيت طواف الفريضة في حجّ كان أو عُمرةٍ، وجَهِل أن يُصلّي ركعتين عند مقام إبراهيم ﷺ، قال: يُصلّيهما ولو بعد أيّام، لأنّ الله يقول: ﴿وَاتَّخِذُوا مِنْ مَقَامِ إِبْرَاهِيمَ مُصَلًّى﴾.

٩٧. عن المُنذر الثوري، عن أبي جعفر ﷺ، قال: سألتُه عن الحَجَر، فقال ﷺ: نزلت ثلاثة أحجارٍ من الجنّة، الحَجر الأسود استودعه إبراهيم، ومقام إبراهيم، وحَجَر بني إسرائيل.

قال أبو جعفر ﷺ: إنّ الله تعالى استودع إبراهيم ﷺ الحَجر الأبيض، وكان أشدّ بياضًا من القراطيس، فاسْودَّ من خطايا بني آدم.

٩٨. عن جابر الجُعفي، قال: قال محمّد بن عليّ عليهما السلام: يا جابر، ما أعظم فِرْيَة أهل الشام على الله! يزعمون أنّ الله تبارك وتعالى حيث صَعِد على السماء وَضَع قدمه على صخرةِ بيت

foot on the rock of Bayt al-Muqaddas.[74] When one of God's mere servants placed his foot on a rock, God, Blessed and most High, commanded us to take it as a place of prayer. Jābir, God has no match nor anything similar to Him. He is beyond the description of those who attempt to describe Him, and too lofty is He to be comprehended by the imaginations of the fanciful ones. He is veiled from the sight of the onlookers, and neither does He cease with all those who die, nor fade away with the temporary ones. There is nothing like unto Him, and He is the all-Hearing, Omniscient."'

99. From al-Ḥalabī who reports from Abū 'Abd Allāh عليه السلام the following: 'I asked him, "Does a woman have to perform the ritual washing (*ghusl*) before coming to the Ka'ba?" He replied, "Yes, for God has stated ﴿*Purify My House for those who walk round it, those who stay there, and those who bow and prostrate themselves in worship*﴾. The servant cannot enter unless he is in a state of purity, having washed away the sweat and the stress, and purified himself."' [2:125]

100. From 'Abd Allāh b. Ghālib[75], on his father's authority, from a man who narrated from 'Alī b. al-Ḥusayn عليه السلام, regarding Ibrāhīm's supplication in the Qur'an: ﴿*My Lord, make this land secure and provide with produce those of its people who believe in God and the Last Day*﴾. He said, 'We are the ones that he meant here, and his own vicegerents and the followers of his successor. In the verse ﴿*As for those who disbelieve, I will grant them enjoyment for a short while and then subject them to the torment of the Fire – an evil destination*﴾ he means those who rebelled against his successor, and those of his community who refused to follow him. By God, this is the same state of affairs in this community.' [2:126]

101. Aḥmad b. Muḥammad narrated on his authority that he said, 'When Ibrāhīm supplicated to his Lord to provide his offspring with produce, a plot of land from Jordan came and started to circumambulate the Ka'ba seven times;

74 Bayt al-Muqaddas (or al-Maqdis), the Aqsa mosque in Jerusalem. Shām refers to Greater Syria or the Levant, including Palestine.

75 Abū 'Alī 'Abd Allāh b. Ghālib b. al-Hudhayl al-Asadī, a reliable narrator of the fifth and sixth Imams as well a renowned poet. See Ḥillī, *Khulāṣat al-aqwāl*, 192 (nr. 599); Modarressi, *Tradition and Survival*, 141–2 (nr. 9).

المقَدِس، ولقد وضع عبدٌ من عباد الله قدمه على حَجَرٍ، فأمرنا الله تبارك وتعالى أن نتّخذها مُصلّى.

يا جابر، إنّ الله تبارك وتعالى لا نظيرَ له ولا شبيه، تعالى عن صفة الواصفين، وجلّ عن أوهام المتوهّمين، واحتجب عن أعيُن الناظرين، لا يزول مع الزائلين، ولا يأفُلُ مع الآفلين، ليس كمثلِه شيء، وهو السميع العليم.

٩٩. عن الحلبي، عن أبي عبد الله عليه السلام، قال: سألتُه: أتغتسِل النساء إذ أتين البيت؟ قال: نعم، إنّ الله يقول: ﴿طَهِّرَا بَيْتِيَ لِلطَّائِفِينَ وَالْعَاكِفِينَ وَالرُّكَّعِ السُّجُودِ﴾. ينبغي للعبد أن لا يدخُل إلاّ وهو طاهر، قد غسل عنه العرَق والأذى وتطهّر.

١٠٠. عن عبد الله بن غالب، عن أبيه، عن رجلٍ، عن عليّ بن الحسين عليهما السلام، في قول إبراهيم عليه السلام: ﴿رَبِّ اجْعَلْ هَٰذَا بَلَدًا آمِنًا وَارْزُقْ أَهْلَهُ مِنَ الثَّمَرَاتِ مَنْ آمَنَ مِنْهُم بِاللَّهِ﴾ إيّانا عنَى بذلك وأولياءه وشيعة وصيّه، ﴿قَالَ وَمَن كَفَرَ فَأُمَتِّعُهُ قَلِيلًا ثُمَّ أَضْطَرُّهُ إِلَىٰ عَذَابِ النَّارِ وَبِئْسَ الْمَصِيرُ﴾ قال: عنَى بذلك من جحد وصيّه ولم يتّبِعهُ من أُمّته، وكذلك والله حال هذه الأمّة.

١٠١. عن أحمد بن محمّد، عنه عليه السلام، قال: إنّ إبراهيم عليه السلام لمّا أن دعا ربّه أن يرزُق أهله من الثّمرات، قطعَ قِطعةً من الأُردُن، فأقبلت حتّى طافت بالبيت سبعًا، ثم أقرّها الله في موضعِها، وإنّما سُمّيت الطائف للطواف بالبيت.

then God settled it down in its place and called it al-Ṭā'if, because of its circumambulation around the House.'

102. From Abū Salama, from Abū ʿAbd Allāh عليه السلام who said, 'God sent down the Black Stone from the Garden to Ādam when the House was a white pearl. Then God raised it up to the heavens and only its foundation remained, which is the entourage of this House as it is now.' He continued, 'Every day seventy thousand new angels would come to visit it, never to return. Then God commanded Ibrāhīm and Ismāʿīl to build the House up from its foundations.'

103. Al-Ḥalabī narrated that Abū ʿAbd Allāh عليه السلام was asked about the House and whether it was a site of pilgrimage even before the advent of the Prophet ﷺ. He replied, 'Yes, and the proof of that in the Qur'an is Shuʿayb's statement when he says to Mūsā when he marries him [to his daughter]: ﴿*on condition that you serve me for eight years*﴾(28:27), where he did not use the word *sinīn* for 'years' [but *ḥijaj*]. Ādam and Nūḥ both performed the Hajj, as did Sulaymān, the son of Dāwūd, with Jinn, humans, birds and the winds. Mūsā too went for Hajj on a red camel, saying '*Labbayk, Labbayk.*'[76] It is, as per the verse ﴿*The first House* [*of worship*] *to be established for people was the one at Mecca. It is a blessed place; a source of guidance for all people*﴾(3:96). He also said ﴿*and Purify My House for those who walk round it, those who stay there, and those who bow and prostrate themselves in worship*﴾. God sent down the Black Stone to Ādam, which was at the House.' [2:125]

104. From Abū al-Warqā' who narrated, 'I asked ʿAlī b. Abī Ṭālib عليه السلام what the first thing to be sent down from the heavens was. He replied, "The first thing to come down from the heavens to the earth was the House in Mecca, which God sent down as a red ruby, but the community of Nūḥ caused so much corruption in the land that He raised it up again, until, that is, ﴿*Ibrāhīm and Ismāʿīl built up the foundations of the House*﴾."' [2:127]

76 This phrase forms the basis of the *talbiya*, the only vocal utterances which are obligatory to recite during the Hajj and the meaning of which signify: 'At Your service, Lord'.

١٠٢. عن أبي سلمة، عن أبي عبدالله عليه السلام: أنّ الله أنزل الحَجَر الأسود من الجنّة لآدم عليه السلام، وكان البيتُ دُرّةً بيضاء فرفعه الله إلى السماء وبقي أساسه، فهو حِيال هذا البيت.

وقال: يدخُله كلّ يوم سبعون ألف ملكٍ لا يرجِعون إليه أبدًا، فأمر الله إبراهيم وإسماعيل عليهما السلام أن يَبْنيا البيت على القواعد.

١٠٣. قال الحلبي: سُئل أبو عبدالله عليه السلام عن البيت، أكان يُحجّ قبل أنْ يُبعثَ النبي صلى الله عليه وآله وسلم؟ قال: نعم، وتصديقه في القرآن قول شعيب عليه السلام حين قال لِموسى عليه السلام، حيث تزوّج: ﴿عَلَىٰٓ أَن تَأۡجُرَنِي ثَمَٰنِيَ حِجَجٖ﴾ ولم يقُل ثماني سنين، وإنّ آدم ونوحًا عليهما السلام حجّا، وسليمان بن داود عليه السلام قد حجّ البيت بالجنّ والإنس والطير والريح، وحجّ موسى عليه السلام على جملٍ أحمر، يقول: لبّيك، لبّيك، وإنّه كما قال الله تعالى: ﴿إِنَّ أَوَّلَ بَيۡتٖ وُضِعَ لِلنَّاسِ لَلَّذِي بِبَكَّةَ مُبَارَكٗا وَهُدٗى لِّلۡعَٰلَمِينَ﴾، وقال: ﴿وَإِذۡ يَرۡفَعُ إِبۡرَٰهِـۧمُ ٱلۡقَوَاعِدَ مِنَ ٱلۡبَيۡتِ وَإِسۡمَٰعِيلُ﴾، وقال: ﴿أَن طَهِّرَا بَيۡتِيَ لِلطَّآئِفِينَ وَٱلۡعَٰكِفِينَ وَٱلرُّكَّعِ ٱلسُّجُودِ﴾ وإنّ الله أنزل الحَجَر لآدم وكان البيت.

١٠٤. عن أبي الوَرقاء، قال: قُلت لعليّ بن أبي طالب عليه السلام: أوّل شيء نَزل من السماء، ما هو؟ قال: أوّل شيء نَزل من السماء إلى الأرض فهو البيت الذي بمكّة أنزل الله ياقوتةً حمراء، ففَسق قوم نُوح في الأرض، فرفعه حيث يقول: ﴿وَإِذۡ يَرۡفَعُ إِبۡرَٰهِـۧمُ ٱلۡقَوَاعِدَ مِنَ ٱلۡبَيۡتِ وَإِسۡمَٰعِيلُ﴾.

105. From Abū 'Amr al-Zubayrī who narrates the following from Abū 'Abd Allāh ﷺ: 'I asked him, "Tell me about the community of Muḥammad: who are they?" He replied, "The community of Muḥammad is specifically the Banū Hāshim." So I asked, "What is the proof that the community of Muḥammad are the specific members of his Household that you have mentioned, to the exclusion of all others?" He replied, "It is the Qur'anic verse ﴾*As Ibrāhīm and Ismā'īl built up the foundations of the House* [*they prayed*], *'Our Lord, accept* [*this*] *from us. You are the All-Hearing, the All Knowing. Our Lord, make us devoted to You; make our descendants into a community devoted to You. Show us how to worship and accept our repentance, for You are the Ever Relenting, the Most Merciful. Our Lord, make a messenger of their own rise up from among them, to recite Your revelations to them, teach them the Scripture and wisdom, and purify them: You are the Mighty, the Wise*﴿(2:126–129)." So when God answered their prayer by making their descendants into a devoted community and raising a prophet from among them who would recite His revelations to them, purify them and teach them the Scripture and wisdom, they added another supplication to their first. They asked for Him to keep them immaculate and devoid of all polytheism and idolatry, for His will to be done through them, and that none may be followed aside from them. He [Ibrāhīm] said ﴾*Preserve me and my offspring from idolatry. Lord, the* [*idols*] *have led many people astray! Anyone who follows me is with me, but as for anyone who disobeys me – You are surely forgiving and merciful*﴿(14:35–36). So this is a proof that both the Imams as well as the devoted community to whom Muhammad (peace and blessings upon him) had been sent can only have been from the progeny of Ibrāhīm, because of his prayer ﴾*Preserve me and my offspring from idolatry*﴿(14:35).'

106. From Jābir who reports the following from Abū Ja'far ﷺ: 'I asked him about the interpretation of the verse ﴾*When he* [*Ya'qūb*] *said to his sons, 'What will you worship after I am gone?' they replied, 'We shall worship your God and the God of your fathers, Ibrāhīm, Ismā'īl, and Isḥāq, one single God*﴿. He replied, "This applies to the one who will rise (*al-Qā'im*)."' [2:133]

107. From al-Walīd, from Abū 'Abd Allāh ﷺ that he said whilst referring to the verse: ﴾*They say, 'Become Jews or Christians, and you will be rightly guided.'*

١٠٥. عن أبي عمرو الزبيري، عن أبي عبد الله عليه السلام، قال: قلتُ له: أخبرني عن أمّة محمّد صلى الله عليه وآله، من هم؟ قال: أمّة محمّد بنو هاشم خاصّة.

قلتُ: فما الحجّة في أمّة محمّد أنّهم أهل بيته الذين ذكرتَ دون غيرهم؟ قال: قول الله: ﴿وَإِذْ يَرْفَعُ إِبْرَاهِيمُ الْقَوَاعِدَ مِنَ الْبَيْتِ وَإِسْمَاعِيلُ رَبَّنَا تَقَبَّلْ مِنَّا إِنَّكَ أَنْتَ السَّمِيعُ الْعَلِيمُ ﴿١٢٧﴾ رَبَّنَا وَاجْعَلْنَا مُسْلِمَيْنِ لَكَ وَمِنْ ذُرِّيَّتِنَا أُمَّةً مُسْلِمَةً لَكَ وَأَرِنَا مَنَاسِكَنَا وَتُبْ عَلَيْنَا إِنَّكَ أَنْتَ التَّوَّابُ الرَّحِيمُ﴾ فلما أجاب الله إبراهيم وإسماعيل، وجعل من ذُرّيّتهما أمّةً مسلمةً، وبعث فيها رسولاً منها — يعني من تلك الأمّة — يتلو عليهم آياته ويزكّيهم ويُعلّمهم الكتاب والحكمة، رَدَف إبراهيم عليه السلام دعوته الأولى بدعوةٍ أخرى، فسأل لهم تطهيرًا من الشّرك ومن عبادة الأصنام ليصحّ أمره فيهم، ولا يتّبعوا غيرهم، فقال: ﴿وَاجْنُبْنِي وَبَنِيَّ أَنْ نَعْبُدَ الْأَصْنَامَ ﴿٣٥﴾ رَبِّ إِنَّهُنَّ أَضْلَلْنَ كَثِيرًا مِنَ النَّاسِ فَمَنْ تَبِعَنِي فَإِنَّهُ مِنِّي وَمَنْ عَصَانِي فَإِنَّكَ غَفُورٌ رَحِيمٌ﴾ فهذه دلالة على أنّه لا يكون الأئمّة والأُمّة المسلمة التي بُعث فيها محمّد صلى الله عليه وآله إلاّ من ذرّيّة إبراهيم عليه السلام، لقوله: ﴿وَاجْنُبْنِي وَبَنِيَّ أَنْ نَعْبُدَ الْأَصْنَامَ﴾.

١٠٦. عن جابر، عن أبي جعفر عليه السلام، قال: سألتُه عن تفسير هذه الآية من قول الله تعالى: ﴿إِذْ قَالَ لِبَنِيهِ مَا تَعْبُدُونَ مِنْ بَعْدِي قَالُوا نَعْبُدُ إِلَٰهَكَ وَإِلَٰهَ آبَائِكَ إِبْرَاهِيمَ وَإِسْمَاعِيلَ وَإِسْحَاقَ إِلَٰهًا وَاحِدًا﴾ قال: جرَت في القائم عليه السلام.

١٠٧. عن الوليد، عن أبي عبد الله عليه السلام، قال: إنّ الحنيفيّة هي الإسلام.

Say [Prophet], 'No, [ours is] the religion of Ibrāhīm, the upright, who did not worship any god besides God﴿, 'The upright religion is Islam.' [2:135]

108. From Zurāra, from Abū Jaʿfar عليه السلام that he said, 'The upright religion [of Ibrāhīm] did not leave anything out, to the extent that it even included guidelines for trimming the moustache, clipping nails and circumcision.'

109. From al-Mufaḍḍal b. Ṣāliḥ, from one of his associates, that the verse ﴾*So [you believers] say, 'We believe in God and in what was sent down to us and what was sent down to Ibrāhīm, Ismāʿīl, Isḥāq, Yaʿqūb and the Tribes, and what was given to Mūsā, ʿĪsā, and all the prophets by their Lord. We make no distinction between any of them, and we devote ourselves to Him"*﴿ was a reference to the household of Muḥammad (peace be upon them), whereas the verse ﴾*So if they believe like you do, they will be rightly guided*﴿ addresses the rest of people.' [2:136–7]

110. From Ḥanān b. Sadīr who reports the following on his father's authority, from Abū Jaʿfar عليه السلام. He said, 'I asked him, "Were the sons of Yaʿqūb prophets?" He replied, "No, but they were tribes descended from prophets, and they all departed this world felicitous, after having repented to their Lord and acknowledged how they had behaved."'

111. From Sallām, from Abū Jaʿfar عليه السلام regarding His verse ﴾*We believe in God and in what was sent down to us*﴿. He said, 'By this He was referring to ʿAlī, al-Ḥasan, al-Ḥusayn, and Fāṭima, and it also applied to the Imams after them. Then it continues with God's address to the rest of people, whereby He says: ﴾*So if they believe* – i.e. the people – *like you do* – i.e. ʿAlī, Fāṭima, al-Ḥasan, al-Ḥusayn – *then they will be rightly guided. But if they turn their backs, then they will be entrenched in opposition*﴿.' [2:136–7]

112. From Zurāra, from Abū Jaʿfar عليه السلام, and from Ḥumrān from Abū ʿAbd Allāh عليه السلام, that the colour [from God] refers to Islam. [2:138]

١٠٨. عن زرارة، عن أبي جعفر عليه السلام: ما أبقت الحنيفيّة شيئًا حتّى إنّ منها قصّ الشارِب وقلم الأظفار والخِتان.

١٠٩. عن المُفضّل بن صالح، عن بعض أصحابه، في قوله تعالى: ﴿قُولُوا آمَنَّا بِاللَّهِ وَمَا أُنزِلَ إِلَيْنَا وَمَا أُنزِلَ إِلَىٰ إِبْرَاهِيمَ وَإِسْمَاعِيلَ وَإِسْحَاقَ وَيَعْقُوبَ وَالْأَسْبَاطِ﴾، أمّا قوله: ﴿قُولُوا﴾ فهم آل محمّد صلى الله عليه وآله، وقوله: ﴿فَإِنْ آمَنُوا بِمِثْلِ مَا آمَنتُم بِهِ فَقَدِ اهْتَدَوا﴾ سائر الناس.

١١٠. عن حَنان بن سدير، عن أبيه، عن أبي جعفر عليه السلام، قال: قلتُ له: كان وُلد يعقوب أنبياء؟ قال: لا، ولكنّهم كانوا أسباط أولاد الأنبياء، ولم يكونوا يُفارقوا الدنيا إلاّ سُعداء، تابوا وتذكّروا ما صَنَعوا.

١١١. عن سَلاّم، عن أبي جعفر عليه السلام، في قوله تعالى: ﴿آمَنَّا بِاللَّهِ وَمَا أُنزِلَ إِلَيْنَا﴾. قال: عنَى بذلك عليًّا والحسن والحُسين وفاطمة عليهم السلام، وجرَت بعدهم في الأئمّة عليهم السلام قال: ثمّ رَجَع القول من الله عزّ وجلّ في النّاس، فقال: ﴿فَإِنْ آمَنُوا﴾ يعني النّاس ﴿بِمِثْلِ مَا آمَنتُم بِهِ﴾ يعني عليًّا وفاطمة والحسن والحُسين والأئمّة عليهم السلام من بعدهم ﴿فَقَدِ اهْتَدَوا وَّإِن تَوَلَّوْا فَإِنَّمَا هُمْ فِي شِقَاقٍ﴾.

١١٢. عن زُرارة، عن أبي جعفر عليه السلام، وحُمران، عن أبي عبدالله، قال: الصِّبغة: الإسلام.

113. From ʿAbd al-Raḥmān b. Kathīr al-Hāshimī, a protégé of Abū Jaʿfar, who narrated from Abū ʿAbd Allāh عليه السلام regarding the verse ﴾ [*Our life*] *takes its colour from God, and who gives a better colour than God? It is Him we worship* ﴿ that he said, 'The colour here signifies the acknowledgment of the authority of the Commander of the Faithful [i.e. ʿAlī عليه السلام] within the covenant.' [2:137]

114. From Burayd b. Muʿāwiya al-ʿIjlī who reports from Abū Jaʿfar عليه السلام that he said, 'I asked him to whom this verse was referring: ﴾ *We have made you* [*believers*] *into a just community, so that you may bear witness* [*to the truth*] *before others and so that the Messenger may bear witness* [*to it*] *before you* ﴿, to which he replied, 'We are the just community, as well as God's witnesses over His creation and His proofs on the earth.' [2:143]

115. From Abū Baṣīr who narrated, 'I heard Abū Jaʿfar عليه السلام saying, "We are as the Ḥijāz highway." So I asked, "And what is the Ḥijāz highway?" He replied, "It is the straightest road, for God has said: ﴾ *We have made you* [*believers*] *into a just community* ﴿. He continued, "The extremist [who has veered off track] returns to us, and the one lagging behind catches up with us."' [2:143]

116. ʿUmar b. Ḥanẓala narrated the same from Abū ʿAbd Allāh that he said, "They are the Imams."

117. Abū Baṣīr narrated from Abū ʿAbd Allāh عليه السلام regarding the verse: ﴾ *so that you may bear witness* [*to the truth*] *before others* ﴿ that he said, 'It is due to the knowledge which we have about the permissible and the prohibited, and all that they have lost from it.' [2:143]

118. From Abū ʿAmr al-Zubayrī, from Abū ʿAbd Allāh عليه السلام who narrated, 'God says: ﴾ *We have made you* [*believers*] *into a just community, so that you may bear witness* [*to the truth*] *before others and so that the Messenger may bear witness* [*to it*] *before you* ﴿. If you think that God is addressing all the believing monotheists here, then consider the one whose testimony is rejected in this world and is not even worth a few dates. Would God actually seek his testimony on the Day of Judgement and accept it in front of all the past communities? Never! God does not address those types of people, but rather the

١١٣. عن عبد الرحمن بن كَثِير الهاشمي – مولى أبي جعفر –، عن أبي عبدالله ﷺ، في قول الله تعالى: ﴿صِبْغَةَ اللهِ وَمَنْ أَحْسَنُ مِنَ اللهِ صِبْغَةً﴾، قال: الصّبغة معرِفة أمير المؤمنين ﷺ بالولاية في الميثاق.

١١٤. عن يزيد بن معاوية العِجلي، عن أبي جعفر ﷺ، قال: قلت له: قوله: ﴿وَكَذَٰلِكَ جَعَلْنَاكُمْ أُمَّةً وَسَطًا لِتَكُونُوا شُهَدَاءَ عَلَى النَّاسِ وَيَكُونَ الرَّسُولُ عَلَيْكُمْ شَهِيدًا﴾، قال: نحن الأُمّة الوسطى، ونحن شُهداءُ الله على خَلقه، وحُجّته في أرضه.

١١٥. عن أبي بصير، قال سمعتُ أبا جعفر ﷺ يقول: نحنُ نَمَط الحجاز. فقلتُ: وما نمُط الحجاز؟ قال: أوسط الأنماط، إنّ الله تعالى يقول: ﴿وَكَذَٰلِكَ جَعَلْنَاكُمْ أُمَّةً وَسَطًا﴾، قال: ثمّ قال: إلينا يرجِعُ الغالي، وبنا يلحقُ المقصِّر.

١١٦. وروى عمر بن حَنْظَلة، عن أبي عبدالله ﷺ، قال: هم الأئمّة.

١١٧. وقال أبو بصير، عن أبي عبدالله ﷺ: ﴿تَكُونُوا شُهَدَاءَ عَلَى النَّاسِ﴾، قال: بما عندنا من الحلال والحرام، وبِما ضَيّعوا منه.

١١٨. عن أبي عَمرو الزُبيري، عن أبي عبدالله ﷺ، قال: قال الله: ﴿وَكَذَٰلِكَ جَعَلْنَاكُمْ أُمَّةً وَسَطًا لِتَكُونُوا شُهَدَاءَ عَلَى النَّاسِ وَيَكُونَ الرَّسُولُ عَلَيْكُمْ شَهِيدًا﴾ فإن ظَننتَ أنّ الله عنى بهذه الآية جميع أهل القِبلة من المُوحّدين، افترى أنّ من لا تجوز شهادته في الدنيا على صاعٍ من تَمرٍ، يطلُبُ الله شهادتَه يوم القيامة ويقبلها منه بحضرةِ

just community refers to the best of people that have been placed among them.' [2:143]

119. Abū 'Amr al-Zubayrī narrated from Abū 'Abd Allāh عليه السلام that he asked him, 'Can you tell me about faith – is it testimony coupled with action or mere testimony without action?' He replied, 'Faith is all action, and testifying it is only a part of that action that has been made incumbent by God. He has clarified this and elucidated it in His Book. Its proof is established and the Book itself calls upon us to be mindful of it. When the Prophet ﷺ was told to turn from Jerusalem to the Ka'ba [as the new direction for prayer], the Muslims said to him, "What happens to the prayers that we had performed facing Jerusalem – will they still be counted? And what about the prayers performed towards Jerusalem by our deceased relatives?" So God revealed the verse: ﴾ *God would never let your faith go to waste [believers], for God is most compassionate and most merciful towards people* ﴿. He called prayer 'faith', so whoever is mindful of his duty to God, preserving his limbs for His worship and using every limb to fulfil the duty that God has made incumbent upon it, he shall meet with God among the people of the Garden as one whose faith is completed. But whoever is treacherous in his duties or transgresses God's commands, such a person shall meet Him with a deficient faith.' [2: 143]

120. From Ḥarīz who narrated the following: 'Abū Ja'far عليه السلام said, "Face the Qibla [in prayer] and do not turn your face away from it as doing so will invalidate your prayer, for God tells His Prophet ﷺ regarding the obligatory prayer: ﴾ *Turn your face in the direction of the Sacred Mosque: wherever you [believers] may be, turn your faces to it* ﴿."' [2:144]

121. From Jābir al-Ju'fī, from Abū Ja'far عليه السلام who said, 'Remain in this land and do not move an arm or a leg from here until you see the signs that I am about to tell you concerning what shall occur within a year:

You will see a caller calling out in Damascus, where one of its villages will crumble and part of its mosque will collapse. Then the Turks will pass through Damascus and continue until they reach this peninsula [Hijaz], and the Romans will advance to Ramla and camp there. This will be a year of chaos in every Arab land. The people of Shām will be divided between three banners: the banners of al-Aṣhab, al-Abqa' and al-Sufyānī. The tribe

جميع الأُمم الماضية؟ كلاّ، لمَ يعنِ الله مثل هذا من خلقِه، يعني الأمّة الّتي وَجَبت لها دعوة إبراهيم ﵇: ﴿كُنتُمْ خَيْرَ أُمَّةٍ أُخْرِجَتْ لِلنَّاسِ﴾ وهم الأُمّة الوُسطى، وهم خير أمّةٍ أُخرِجت للنّاس.

١١٩. قال أبوعمرو الزبيري: قلت لأبي عبد الله ﵇ ألا تُخبرُني عن الإيمان، أقولٌ هو وعَمل، أم قولٌ بلا عَمل؟ فقال ﵇: الإيمان عملٌ كلّه، والقولُ بعض ذلك العَمل، مفترضٌ من الله مبيّنٌ في كتابه، واضحٌ نورُه، ثابتةٌ حُجّته، يَشهد له بها الكتاب ويَدعو إليه.

ولمّا أن صرف نبيّه ﵇ إلى الكعبة عن بيت المَقدِس، قال المسلمون للنّبي ﷺ: أرأيت صلاتنا الّتي كنّا نُصلّي إلى بيت المَقدِس ما حالُنا فيها، وما حال مَن مضىٰ من أمواتِنا وهم يُصلّون إلى بيت المَقدِس؟ فأنزل الله: ﴿وَمَا كَانَ اللَّهُ لِيُضِيعَ إِيمَانَكُمْ إِنَّ اللَّهَ بِالنَّاسِ لَرَءُوفٌ رَحِيمٌ﴾ فسمّى الصّلاة إيمانًا، فمن لَقي الله حافظًا لجوارِحه مُوفيًا كُلّ جارحةٍ من جَوارِحه ما فَرض الله عليه، لقي الله مُستكمِلاً لإيمانه من أهل الجنّة، ومن خان في شيء منها، أو تعدّى ما أمر الله فيها، لَقي الله ناقِص الإيمان.

١٢٠. عن حريز، قال: قال أبو جعفر ﵇: استَقبِل القِبلة بِوجهك، ولا تقلِب وجهَك من القِبلة فتُفسِد صلاتك، فإنّ الله يقول لنبيّه ﷺ في الفريضة: ﴿فَوَلِّ وَجْهَكَ شَطْرَ الْمَسْجِدِ الْحَرَامِ وَحَيْثُ مَا كُنتُمْ فَوَلُّوا وُجُوهَكُمْ شَطْرَهُ﴾.

١٢١. عن جابر الجُعفي، عن أبي جعفر ﵇: يقول الزَم الأرض لا تُحرّكَنّ يدَك ولا رِجلك أبدًا حتّى ترى علاماتٍ أذكرُها لك في سنة، وترى مُناديًا يُنادي بدِمشق، وخَسفًا بِقرية من

of Muḍarr will join the Banī Dhanb al-Ḥimār, and al-Sufyānī will be accompanied by his uncles from the tribe of Banī Kalb. Al-Sufyānī and his people will attack the Banī Dhanb al-Ḥimār and kill them barbarically. A man from Damascus will rise to counter them, but he and his men will also be killed in the most barbaric manner. This is the meaning of the verse ﴾*But factions have differed among themselves. What suffering will come to those who obscure the truth when a dreadful Day arrives!*﴿(19:37).

Thereafter al-Sufyānī and his army shall appear with no ambition except to target the descendants of Muḥammad ﷺ and their followers (*shīʿa*), so he will dispatch a contingent towards Kufa, where a large number of Shīʿa will be killed and massacred. An army will come from Khurasan and set up camp by the river Tigris, and a man with weak followers will rise, but he will be attacked and killed near Kufa. Then a contingent will be sent to Medina where a man will be killed, wherefrom al-Mahdī and al-Manṣūr will flee. The descendants of Muḥammad and his Household will be attacked, and everyone old and young will be captured and imprisoned. The army will be hell-bent on finding the two men, and al-Mahdī will escape as Mūsā had done fearing for his life, until he will reach Mecca. The army will follow him until they reach the desert, where they will perish and sink into the ground, and only a single person will survive from among them to tell the tale. Then the Qā'im will rise between the *rukn* and the *maqām*. He will pray two units of prayer there accompanied by his assistant, and he will address the people saying:

"O people, we resort to God to grant us victory over those who have oppressed us and snatched away our rights. Whoever disputes our rights with God, know that we are more worthy of those rights. Whoever disputes with us concerning Ādam, we are the worthiest of all people [to claim proximity to Ādam]. And whoever disputes with us about Nūḥ, then know again that we are the worthiest of Nūḥ. And whoever disputes our claim to Ibrāhīm, indeed we are the worthiest of Ibrāhīm. And whoever disputes with us about Muḥammad, indeed we are the worthiest of Muḥammad and the rest of the prophets. Whoever disputes our claim to the Qur'an, know that we are the worthiest of the Qur'an. We bear witness on this day along with every Muslim that we are the ones who have been oppressed, cast out, persecuted, driven out of our homes, usurped of our property and our families, and

قُراها، وتَسقُط طائفةٌ من مسجدِها، فإذا رأيتَ التُرك جازُوها، فأقبلَت التُرك حتّى نزلت الجزيرة، وأقبلَت الرّوم حتى نزلَت الرَّملة، وهي سنة اختِلاف في كلّ أرض من أرضِ العَرَب.

وإنّ أهلَ الشام يختلِفون عند ذلك على ثلاث راياتٍ: الأصهَب، والأبقع، والسُّفياني، مع بني ذنَب الحِمار مُضَر، ومع السُّفياني أخوالُه من كَلب، فيظهر السُّفياني ومن معه على بني ذَنبِ الحِمار، حتّى يُقتلوا قتلاً لم يُقتلْه شيءٌ قطّ. ويحضُر رجلٌ بدِمشق، فيُقتَل هو ومن معه قتلاً لم يُقتلْه شيءٌ قطّ، وهو من بني ذنَب الحِمار، وهي الآية التي يقول الله تبارك وتعالى: ﴿فَاخْتَلَفَ الْأَحْزَابُ مِنْ بَيْنِهِمْ فَوَيْلٌ لِلَّذِينَ كَفَرُوا مِنْ مَشْهَدِ يَوْمٍ عَظِيمٍ﴾.

ويَظهر السُّفياني ومن معه حتّى لا يكون له هِمّة إلاّ آل محمّد صلى الله عليه وآله وشيعتهم، فيبعث -والله- بَعثًا إلى الكوفة، فيُصاب بأناسٍ من شيعة آل محمّد بالكوفة قتلاً وصَلبًا، وتُقبل رايةٌ من خراسان حتى تنزِل ساحل الدِّجلة، يخرج رجل من المَوالي ضَعيف ومن تبِعَه، فيُصاب بظَهر الكوفة، ويبعث بعثًا إلى المدينة فيَقتل بها رجلاً، ويهرُب المهدي والمنصُور منها، ويؤخذُ آل محمّد صلى الله عليه وآله صغيرهم وكبيرهم، لا يُترك منهم أحدٌ إلا حُبِس، ويَخرُج الجيش في طلب الرّجلين. ويخرج المهدي عليه السلام منها على سُنّة موسى عليه السلام خائفًا يترقّب حتّى يَقدِم مكّة ويُقبِل الجيش حتّى إذا نزل البيداء -وهو جيش الهملاتِ- خُسِفَ بهم، فلا يَفلِتُ منهم إلاّ مُخبِر، فيقومُ القائمُ بين الرُّكنِ والمَقام فيُصلّي ويَنصَرف، ومعه وزيرُه، فيقول: يا أيّها الناس، إنّا نستنصِر الله على من ظَلَمنا وسَلَب حقّنا، من يحاجّنا في الله فإنّا أولى بالله، ومن يحاجّنا في آدم فإنّا أولى النّاس بآدم، ومن حاجّنا في نوحٍ فإنّا أولى النّاس بنوحٍ، ومن حاجّنا في إبراهيم فإنّا أولى النّاس بإبراهيم، ومن حاجّنا بمحمّد صلى الله عليه وآله فإنّا أولى النّاس بمحمّد صلى الله عليه وآله،

harassed. However today we resort only to God to grant us victory, along with every Muslim."

I swear upon God that some three hundred and ten odd men, including fifty women, will all gather together in Mecca as storm clouds gather in the sky, as per the verse ﴾*wherever you are, God will bring you together. God has power to do everything*﴿(2:148).

Then a man from among the descendants of Muḥammad ﷺ will exclaim that this is the town that originally oppressed its people, and he and his three hundred odd companions will leave Mecca after pledging allegiance to the Qā'im between the *rukn* and the *maqām*. He will have with him the covenant of the Prophet, his banner and his weapons, and will be accompanied by his chief minister. Then the man in Mecca will announce his name and it will be broadcast from the sky to be heard by every single person on earth, and his name will be that of the Prophet's ﷺ. Even if you were to doubt him there would be no doubting the Prophet's ﷺ covenant, banner and sword that he will carry, nor the innocent man (*al-nafs al-zakiyya*) from the lineage of al-Ḥusayn [who will be killed there]. Even if you doubt about that, there will be no doubting the voice from the sky announcing his name and his mission. Beware of impostors from the descendants of Muḥammad, for Muḥammad and 'Alī's banner are different to their banners. So remain steadfast in this land and do not follow anyone until and unless you are sure of his lineage from al-Ḥusayn and he carries with him the covenant, the banner, and the weapons of the Prophet ﷺ, and these were passed down from him to 'Alī b. al-Ḥusayn, and then to Muḥammad b. 'Alī, and God does as He wills. So hold fast to them, and beware of those whom I mentioned to you earlier.

This man will leave Mecca accompanied by three hundred and ten odd men carrying the banner of the Messenger ﷺ headed for Medina, until he will pass by a place in the desert where the army was to be destroyed, and will recite the verse: ﴾*Are those who plan evil so sure that God will not make the earth swallow them up, that punishment will not come on them from some unimagined direction, that it will not catch them suddenly in the midst of their comings and goings*﴿(16:45–46). When he reaches Medina, Muḥammad b. al-Shajarī shall emerge as [Prophet] Yūsuf had done, and they will stay in Kufa for some time for as long as God wills, after which he will head towards al-'Adhrā'. There a large number of people will join him, at which

ومن حاجّنا في النّبيّين فنحن أولى النّاس بالنّبيّين، ومن حاجّنا في كتاب الله فنحنُ أولى النّاس بكتابِ الله، إنّا نشهد وكلّ مُسلم اليوم أنا قد ظُلِمنا وطُرِدنا وبُغي علينا، وأُخرِجنا من ديارنا وأموالنا وأهلينا وقُهرنا، إلاّ أنّا نستنصِر الله اليوم وكلّ مسلم.

ويجيءُ – واللهِ – ثلاثمائة وبضعة عشر رجلاً، فيهم خمسون امرأة، يجتمعون بمكّة على غير ميعادٍ قزعًا كقزع الخريف يتْبعُ بعضُهم بعضًا، وهي الآية الّتي قال الله تبارك وتعالى: ﴿أَيْنَ مَا تَكُونُوا يَأْتِ بِكُمُ اللَّهُ جَمِيعًا إِنَّ اللَّهَ عَلَىٰ كُلِّ شَيْءٍ قَدِيرٌ﴾ فيقول رجلٌ من آل محمّد صلى الله عليه وآله: وهي القرية الظالمة أهلها. ثمّ يخرج من مكّة هو ومن معه الثلاثمائة وبضعة عشر، يُبايِعونه بين الرُّكن والمقَام، ومعه عَهد نبيّ الله صلى الله عليه وآله ورَايته، وسِلاحه، ووزيره معه، فينادي المنادي بمكّة باسمِه وأمرِه من السماء، حتّى يسمعه أهل الأرض كلّهم: اسمُه اسم النّبي صلى الله عليه وآله، ما أشكل عليكم فلم يُشكل عليكم عَهد نبيّ الله صلى الله عليه وآله، ورَايته وسِلاحه، والنّفس الزكيّة من وُلد الحُسين عليه السلام، فإن أشكل عليكم هذا فلا يُشكل عليكم الصّوت من السماء باسمِه وأمرِه.

وإيّاك وشُذاذًا من آل محمّد، فإنّ لآل محمّد وعليّ عليه السلام راية، ولِغيرهم راياتٍ، فالزَم الأرض ولا تتّبع منهم رجُلاً أبدًا حتّى ترى رجلاً من وُلد الحُسين عليه السلام، معه عهد نبيّ الله صلى الله عليه وآله ورايته وسِلاحه، فإنّ عهد نبيّ الله صلى الله عليه وآله صار عند عليّ بن الحسين عليه السلام، ثم صار عند محمّد بن علي عليه السلام، ويفعل الله ما يشاء، فالزَم هؤلاء أبدًا وإيّاك ومن ذكرتُ لك.

فإذا خرج رجلٌ منهم معه ثلاثمائة وبضعة عشر رجلاً، ومعه راية رسول الله صلى الله عليه وآله، عامدًا إلى المدينة حتّى يمرّ بالبَيداء، حتّى يقول: هنا مكان القوم الّذين يُخسَف بهم، وهي

point al-Sufyānī's army will be in the valley of Ramla. When the two armies meet, it will be a day of exchange where the Shīʿas from al-Sufyānī's army will leave and join al-Mahdī's army, and people who are with him will go and join al-Sufyānī and become his followers. All the people will gather beneath their respective banners, and that will be the day of exchange.

The Commander of the Faithful عليه السلام said, 'Al-Sufyānī and his army will be killed on that day, and no one will survive to tell the tale, and the one who will be worst off will be the one who hoped to gain something from the war booty of Banū Kalb. Then he [al-Mahdī] will advance towards Kufa and establish his residence there. He will not leave a single Muslim enslaved, but will purchase him and set him free. He will help repay their debts and settle their liabilities. He will pay the blood money due to a family for any slave that had been killed, and repay the debts left by any free man killed, as well as financially support his family after him. Thus will he fill the earth with equity and justice just as it had been filled with injustice, oppression and aggression previously. He and his family will reside in Ruḥba, which is the place where Nūḥ settled, and it will be a pure land. Every man from the Household of Muḥammad عليه السلام only lives and dies on pure land, for they are the pure successors.'

122. From Abū Samīna, from a protégé of Abū al-Ḥasan's who said, 'I asked Abū al-Ḥasan عليه السلام about His verse ﴿*wherever you are, God will bring you together*﴾. He replied, "By God this applies to when the Qā'im will rise, and God will gather together with him all our Shīʿa from all different countries."' [2:148]

الآية الّتي قال الله: ﴿أَفَأَمِنَ الَّذِينَ مَكَرُوا السَّيِّئَاتِ أَنْ يَخْسِفَ اللهُ بِهِمُ الأَرْضَ أَوْ يَأْتِيَهُمُ الْعَذَابُ مِنْ حَيْثُ لا يَشْعُرُونَ أَوْ يَأْخُذَهُمْ فِي تَقَلُّبِهِمْ فَمَا هُمْ بِمُعْجِزِينَ﴾.

فإذا قدِم المدينة أخرَج محمّد بن الشجَري على سُنّة يوسف عليه السلام، ثم يأتي الكوفة فيُطيل بها المكث ما شاء الله أن يمكُث حتّى يظهرَ عليها، ثمّ يسير حتّى يأتي العذراء هو ومَن معه، وقد لحَق به ناسٌ كثير، والسُّفياني يومئذٍ بوادي الرَّملة، حتّى إذا التقوا — وهو يوم الأبدال — يخرُج أناس كانوا مع السُّفياني من شيعة آل محمّد إلى آل محمّد عليهم السلام، ويخرج ناس كانوا مع آل محمّد إلى السُّفياني، فهم من شيعته حتّى يلحقوا بهم، ويخرج كلّ ناس إلى رايتهم، وهو يوم الأبدال.

قال أمير المؤمنين عليه السلام: ويُقتل يومئذٍ السُّفياني ومَن معه حتّى لا يُترك منهم مخبِرٌ، والخائِب يومئذٍ من خاب من غنيمة كلب، ثم يُقبِل إلى الكوفة فيكون منزلُه بها، فلا يترُك عبدًا مسلمًا إلا اشتراه وأعتقَه، ولا غارمًا إلاّ قضى دَينه، ولا مظلِمة لأحدٍ من النّاس إلاّ ردّها، ولا يُقتل منهم عبدٌ إلا أدّى ثمَنه، دِية مُسلَّمة إلى أهلها، ولا يُقتل قتيلٌ إلاّ قضى عنه دَينه، وألحقَ عِياله في العَطاء، حتّى يملأ الأرض قِسطًا وعدلًا كما مُلئَت ظُلمًا وجورًا وعُدوانًا.

ويَسكن هو وأهل بيته الرُّحبة، والرُّحبة إنّما كانت مَسكن نوح عليه السلام وهي أرض طيّبة، ولا يسكُن رجلٌ من آل محمّد صلى الله عليه وآله ولا يُقتَل إلاّ بأرضٍ طّيبةٍ زاكيةٍ فهم الأوصياء الطيّبون.

١٢٢. عن أبي سَمينة، عن مولًى لأبي الحسن عليه السلام، قال: سألتُ أبا الحسن عليه السلام عن قوله عزّ وجلّ: ﴿أَيْنَ مَا تَكُونُوا يَأْتِ بِكُمُ اللهُ جَمِيعًا﴾ قال: وذلك — واللهِ — أن لو قَد قام قائِمنا يجمَعُ اللهُ إليه شيعتَنا من جميع البُلدان.

123. From al-Mufaḍḍal b. ʿUmar[77] who narrated, ʻAbū ʻAbd Allāh عليه السلام said, "When the Imām['s advent] is announced, God will call out his name in Hebrew, and three hundred and thirteen people will be selected to gather towards him as storm clouds gather. They will be the people who attest to his authority. Some of them will go missing from their beds at night and wake up in Mecca the next morning, and some of them will be seen to be travelling on clouds during the day. He will know them by name, their father's name, their surname, and lineage." I asked, "May I be your ransom - which of them will have the greatest faith?" He replied, 'Those who travel on clouds by day, and are anonymous [to people]. It is about them that the verse was revealed ﴿*wherever you are, God will bring you together*﴾."' [2:148]

124. From Jābir, from Abū Jaʿfar عليه السلام who narrated, 'The Prophet ﷺ said, "The angel comes down with the scroll of deeds at the start of each day and writes down man's deeds therein at the beginning of the night. So work diligently at the beginning and at the end of the day, for God will forgive you what is in between, if He so wills, for God says ﴿*So remember Me; I will remember you*﴾."' [2:152]

125. From Samāʿa b. Mihrān who stated, from Abū ʻAbd Allāh عليه السلام, 'I asked him, "Is there a specific manner defined for someone to express his gratitude in order for him to be considered among the 'grateful'?" He replied, "Yes." I asked, "What is it?" He replied, "Say: 'Praise be to God for every bounty that He has bestowed on me.' Moreover, it is to fulfil the use of that bounty in the rightful manner. This is the purport of the verse ﴿*Glory be to Him who has given us control over this; we could not have done it by ourselves*﴾(43:13)"; and he went on to list other verses.'

126. From Abū ʻAmr al-Zubayrī, from Abū ʻAbd Allāh عليه السلام who said, 'Disbelief (*kufr*) features in the Qur'an in five different forms, of which one is ingratitude for bounties, and this is as per the verse in which God says, narrating Sulaymān's statement, ﴿*This is a favour from my Lord, to test whether I am*

---

77 Abū ʻAbd Allāh Mufaḍḍal b. ʻUmar al-Juʿfī, leader of the extremist *mufawwiḍa* sect of Shīʿism. There is considerable debate regarding his reliability as a narrator of Imam Jaʿfar al-Ṣādiq in Shīʿī works of *rijāl*. See Modarressi, *Tradition and Survival*, 333–6 (nr. 146).

١٢٣. عن المُفضَّل بن عُمَر، قال: قال أبو عبد الله عليه السلام: إذا أُذن الإمام دعا الله باسمِه العِبرانيّ الأكبر فانتُجِب له أصحابه الثلاثمائة والثلاثة عشر، قزعًا كقزعِ الخريفِ، وهُم أصحاب الولاية، ومنهم من يُفتقَد من فراشه ليلاً فيُصبِح بمكّة، ومنهم من يُرى يسير في السّحاب نهارًا، يُعرَف باسمه واسم أبيه وحَسَبه ونَسَبه.

قلتُ: جُعِلتُ فداك، أيّهم أعظَم إيمانًا؟ قال: الّذي يسير في السّحاب نهارًا، وهُم المَفقودون، وفيهم نزلت هذه الآية: ﴿أَيْنَ مَا تَكُونُوا يَأْتِ بِكُمُ اللَّهُ جَمِيعًا﴾.

١٢٤. عن جابر، عن أبي جعفر عليه السلام، قال: قال النبي صلى الله عليه وآله: إنّ المَلَك يُنزِل الصحيفة أوّل النّهار وأوّل الليل، يكتُبُ فيها عمل ابن آدم، فأملوا في أوّلها خيرًا، وفي آخرها خيرًا، فإنّ الله يَغفِر لكم ما بين ذلك إن شاء الله، فإنّ الله يقول: ﴿فَاذْكُرُونِي أَذْكُرْكُمْ﴾.

١٢٥. عن سَماعة بن مِهران، عن أبي عبد الله عليه السلام، قال: قلتُ له: للشُّكر حدّ إذا فعلهُ الرجل كان شاكرًا؟ قال: نعم، قُلت: ما هو؟ قال: الحمد لله على كلّ نِعمةٍ أنعمها عليّ وإن كان لكم فيما أنعم حقّ أدّاه، قال: ومنه قول الله تعالى: (الحمدُ لله الّذي سخّر لنَا هذا): حتّى عدّ آياتٍ.

١٢٦. عن أبي عَمرو الزُبيري، عن أبي عبد الله عليه السلام، قال: الكُفر في كتاب الله على خَمسة أوجُه، فمنها: كُفر النعم، وذلك قول الله تعالى يحكي قول سُليمان عليه السلام: ﴿هَٰذَا مِن فَضْلِ رَبِّي لِيَبْلُوَنِي أَأَشْكُرُ أَمْ أَكْفُرُ﴾ الآية، وقال الله: ﴿لَئِن شَكَرْتُمْ لَأَزِيدَنَّكُمْ﴾، وقال: ﴿فَاذْكُرُونِي أَذْكُرْكُمْ وَاشْكُرُوا لِي وَلَا تَكْفُرُونِ﴾.

grateful or not: if anyone is grateful, it is for his own good, if anyone is ungrateful, then my Lord is self-sufficient and most generous ﴿(27:40) and the verse ﴾ *If you are thankful, I will give you more, but if you are thankless, My punishment is terrible indeed* ﴿(14:7). He also says ﴾ *So remember Me; I will remember you. Be thankful to Me, and never ungrateful* ﴿(2:152).'

127. From Muḥammad b. Muslim, from Abū Jaʿfar عليه السلام who said, 'Fāṭima's glorification (*tasbīḥ*) is an example of an abundant remembrance of God, as per the verse ﴾ *So remember Me; I will remember you* ﴿.' [2:152]

128. From al-Fuḍayl, from Abū Jaʿfar عليه السلام who said, 'Fuḍayl, convey our greetings of peace to whomever you meet from among our adherents, and give them this message from me: "Nothing you do is of any avail to God unless done with piety. So guard your tongues, restrain yourselves from harming others, and adhere to steadfastness and prayer, for God is with the steadfast."'

129. From ʿAbd Allāh b. Ṭalḥa who said, 'Abū ʿAbd Allāh عليه السلام said [concerning 2:153] that steadfastness refers to fasting.'

130. From [Abū Hamza] al-Thumālī[78] who narrated, 'I asked Abū Jaʿfar عليه السلام about the verse in which God says ﴾ *We shall certainly test you with fear and hunger* ﴿. He replied, "There will be a specific hunger and a general hunger. Shām will be afflicted with a general widespread hunger and Kufa with a specific one afflicting the enemies of Muḥammad's Household whom God will destroy by means of starvation. As for fear, it will be widespread in Shām when the Qā'im عليه السلام rises, just as it will be afflicted with hunger before his uprising. And this is the meaning of the verse ﴾ *We shall certainly test you with fear and hunger* ﴿."' [2:155]

78 Abū Ḥamza Thābit b. Abī Ṣafiyya b. Dīnār al-Thumālī al-Kūfī (d. 150/767) was a reliable and highly praised companion of the fourth, fifth, sixth and seventh Imams. His three sons Ḥamza, Nūḥ and Manṣūr were each killed in the revolt of Zayd b. ʿAlī. See Ḥillī, *Khulāṣat al-aqwāl*, 85–6 (nr. 179); Modarressi, *Tradition and Survival*, 377–9 (nr. 201).

١٢٧. عن محمّد بن مسلم، عن أبي جعفر عليه السلام، قال: تسبيح فاطمة عليها السلام من ذِكر الله الكثير الّذي قال تعالى: ﴿فَاذْكُرُونِي أَذْكُرْكُمْ﴾.

١٢٨. عن الفُضَيل، عن أبي جعفر عليه السلام، قال: قال: يا فُضَيل، بلّغ من لَقيتَ من مَوالينا عنّا السلام، وقُل لهم: إنّي أقول إنّي لا أُغني عنكم من الله شيئًا إلاّ بِورعٍ. فاحفَظوا ألسِنتَكم، وكُفُّوا أيديكم، وعليكم بالصّبر والصّلاة، إنّ الله مع الصّابرين.

١٢٩. عن عبدالله بن طَلحة، قال أبو عبدالله عليه السلام: الصّبر هو الصّوم.

١٣٠. عن الثُّماليّ، قال: سألتُ أبا جعفر عليه السلام: عن قول الله عزّ وجلّ: ﴿وَلَنَبْلُوَنَّكُمْ بِشَيْءٍ مِنَ الْخَوْفِ وَالْجُوعِ﴾. قال: ذلك جُوع خاصّ، وجُوع عامّ، فأمّا بالشام فإنّه عامٌّ، وأما الخاصّ فهو بالكوفة يَخُصُّ ولا يُعمّ، ولكنّه يَخصّ بالكوفة أعداء آل محمّد عليه الصّلاة والسّلام، فيُهلكُهم الله بالجُوع، وأمّا الخوف فإنّه عامٌّ بالشّام، وذاك الخوف إذا قام القائم عليه السلام، وأمّا الجُوع فقبلَ قِيام القائم عليه السلام، وذلك قوله تعالى: ﴿وَلَنَبْلُوَنَّكُمْ بِشَيْءٍ مِنَ الْخَوْفِ وَالْجُوعِ﴾.

131. From Isḥāq b. ʿAmmār who narrated, ʿWhen Abū Jaʿfar عليه السلام passed away we went to give our condolences to Abū ʿAbd Allāh عليه السلام, and someone sitting with us in the gathering said, "May God bless and have mercy on this servant who used to narrate traditions to us, saying: 'The Messenger of God ﷺ said..." upon which Abū ʿAbd Allāh عليه السلام fell silent for a long time, tapping the ground in deep thought. Then he turned to us and said, "The Messenger of God ﷺ said that God, Blessed and Exalted, says, 'I have placed the whole world at the disposal of My servants as a barter, so whoever lends Me part of it, for every single part of that loan, I repay him between ten and seven hundred times what it is worth, and whatever else I want. However, whoever refuses to lend Me anything I take it from him forcefully, and yet give him three things in return for it, of which but a single one given to My angels would elicit their satisfaction with it.'" He continued by reciting the verse ﴾*those who say, when afflicted with a calamity, 'We belong to God and to Him we shall return.' These will be given blessings and mercy from their Lord, and it is they who are rightly guided*﴿."' [2:156–157]

132. From Ismāʿīl b. [Abī Ziyād] al-Sakūnī, from Jaʿfar b. Muḥammad عليه السلام, on his father's authority, from his forefathers who narrated, 'The Messenger of God ﷺ said, "Whoever has four habits in him, God will decree him to be among the people of Paradise: to safeguard oneself [from sin] through the testimony that there is no god but God; whenever bestowed with a bounty, to say 'All praise be to God'; whenever afflicted with a sin, to say: 'I seek God's forgiveness'; and whenever afflicted with a calamity to say ﴾*We belong to God and to Him we shall return*﴿.'" [2:156]

133. From Abū ʿAlī al-Lahabī, from Abū ʿAbd Allāh عليه السلام who narrated, 'The Messenger of God ﷺ said, "Whoever has four habits in him will be included in God's greatest light: he safeguards himself [from sin] through the testimony that there is no god but God and that Muḥammad is the Messenger of God; that whenever afflicted with a calamity, he says ﴾*We belong to God and to Him we shall return*﴿; that whenever bestowed with anything good, he says: 'All praise be to God'; and that whenever he is afflicted with a sin, he says: 'I seek God's forgiveness, and turn to Him penitently'." [2:156]

١٣١. عن إسحاق بن عمّار، قال: لمّا قُبِض أبو جعفر عليه السلام جَعلنا نُعزّي أبا عبد الله عليه السلام، فقال بعض من كان معنا في المجلس: رحِمَه الله عبدًا وصلّى عليه، كان إذا حدّثنا قال: قال رسول الله صلى الله عليه وآله، قال: فسكَت أبو عبد الله عليه السلام طويلاً ونكَت في الأرض، قال: ثمّ التفت إلينا، فقال: قال رسول الله صلى الله عليه وآله: قال الله تبارك وتعالى: إنّي أعْطيتُ الدنيا بين عبادي قيضًا، فمن أقرَضَني منها قرضًا أعطيتُه لكلّ واحدةٍ منهنّ عشرًا إلى سبعمائة ضعف، وما شئت، ومن لم يُقرِضْني منها قرضًا فأخذتُها منه قسرًا، أعطيتُه ثلاث خصالٍ، لو أعطيتُ واحدةً منهنّ ملائكتي لَرضُوا بها عنّي، ثمّ قال: ﴿الَّذِينَ إِذَا أَصَابَتْهُم مُّصِيبَةٌ قَالُوا إِنَّا لِلَّهِ وَإِنَّا إِلَيْهِ رَاجِعُونَ﴾ إلى قوله: ﴿وَأُولَئِكَ هُمُ الْمُهْتَدُونَ﴾.

١٣٢. عن إسماعيل بن أبي زياد السّكوني، عن جعفر بن محمّد، عن أبيه، عن آبائه عليهم السلام، قال: قال رسول الله صلى الله عليه وآله: أربعٌ من كُنّ فيه كَتَبه الله من أهل الجنّة: من كانت عِصمَته شهادة أن لا إله إلاّ الله، ومن إذا أنعَم الله عليه النِعمة، قال: الحمدُ لله، ومن إذا أصاب ذنبًا، قال: استغفِرُ الله، ومن إذا أصابته مُصيبةٌ، قال: إنّا لله وإنّا إليه راجعون.

١٣٣. عن أبي عليّ اللّهبيّ، عن أبي عبد الله عليه السلام، قال: قال رسول الله صلى الله عليه وآله: أربع من كنّ فيه كان في نور الله الأعظَم: من كان عِصمَةَ أمره شهادة أن لا إله إلاّ الله، وأنّ محمّدًا رسول الله، ومن إذا أصابته مُصيبةٌ، قال: إنّا لله وإنّا إليه راجعون، ومن إذا أصاب خيرًا، قال: الحمدُ لله، ومن إذا أصاب خطيئةً، قال: أستغفر الله وأتوب إليه.

134. From ʿAbd Allāh b. Ṣāliḥ al-Khathʿamī, from Abū ʿAbd Allāh عليه السلام who narrated, 'The Messenger of God ﷺ said that God says, "When I bestow everything on My believing servant, give him [whatever he wants] and provide him with sustenance, I expect him to lend Me something thereof. If he lends it to Me spontaneously of his own accord, for every single offering I repay him a hundred thousand times what it is worth and more. If he refuses, I take it from him forcefully through afflictions in his wealth. Then if he bears them steadfastly I give him three qualities, of which but a single one given to My angels would elicit their satisfaction." Then he went on to recite the verse ﴾*those who say, when afflicted with a calamity, 'We belong to God and to Him we shall return.' These will be given blessings and mercy from their Lord, and it is they who are rightly guided*﴿.' [2:156–157]

135. Isḥāq b. ʿAmmār narrated that Abū ʿAbd Allāh ﷺ said, 'This is only the case when God takes something away from him and he remains steadfast and says ﴾*We belong to God and to Him we shall return*﴿.' [2:156]

136. From Abū Baṣīr, from Abū Jaʿfar عليه السلام who, regarding the verse ﴾*Ṣafā and Marwa are among the rites of God, so for those who make major or minor pilgrimage to the House it is no offence to circulate between the two*﴿ said, 'It means that there is no blame on him for circulating between them.' [2:158]

137. From ʿĀṣim b. Ḥumayd[79], from Abū ʿAbd Allāh عليه السلام who, regarding the verse ﴾*Ṣafā and Marwa are among the rites of God, so for those who make major or minor pilgrimage to the House it is no offence to circulate between the two*﴿ said, 'It means that there is no blame on him for circulating between them, and that is when this verse was revealed.' So I asked him, 'Is it specific to them or general?' He replied, 'It is like the verse ﴾*We gave the Scripture as a heritage to Our chosen servants: some of them wronged their own souls, some stayed between [right and wrong], and some, by God's leave, were foremost in good deeds*﴿(35:32). So whoever joined them from among the people was on their level. God also says ﴾*Whoever obeys God and the Messenger*

79 Abū al-Faḍl ʿĀṣim b. Ḥumayd al-Kūzī al-Ḥanafī, a reliable Sunnī narrator of Imam Jaʿfar al-Ṣādiq's traditions. See Ḥillī, *Khulāṣat al-aqwāl*, 220 (nr. 727); Modarressi, *Tradition and Survival*, 210–1 (nr. 48).

١٣٤. عن عبدالله بن صالح الخَثْعَميّ، عن أبي عبدالله عليه السلام، قال: قال رسول الله صلى الله عليه وآله: قال الله تعالى: عبدي المؤمن، إن خوّلته وأعطيتُه ورزقته استقرضتُه، فإن أقرضني عفوًا أعطيتُه مكان الواحد مائة ألف فما زاد، وإن لا يفعَل أخذتُه قسرًا بالمَصائب في ماله، فإن يَصْبِر أعطيتُه ثلاث خِصالٍ، إن أخيّر الواحدة منهنّ ملائكتي اختاروها، ثمّ تلا هذه الآية: ﴿الَّذِينَ إِذَا أَصَابَتْهُم﴾ إلى قوله: ﴿هُمُ الْمُهْتَدُونَ﴾.

١٣٥. قال إسحاق بن عمّار، قال أبو عبدالله عليه السلام: هذا إن أخذ الله منه شيئًا فصبر واسترجع.

١٣٦. عن أبي بصير، عن أبي جعفر عليه السلام، في قول الله تعالى: ﴿إِنَّ الصَّفَا وَالْمَرْوَةَ مِن شَعَائِرِ اللَّهِ فَمَنْ حَجَّ الْبَيْتَ أَوِ اعْتَمَرَ فَلَا جُنَاحَ عَلَيْهِ أَن يَطَّوَّفَ بِهِمَا﴾ أي لا حَرَج عليه أن يطّوّف بهما.

١٣٧. عن عاصِم بن حُمَيد، عن أبي عبدالله عليه السلام: ﴿إِنَّ الصَّفَا وَالْمَرْوَةَ مِن شَعَائِرِ اللَّهِ﴾ يقول: لا حَرَجَ عليه أن يَطّوّف بهما، فنزلت هذه الآية. فقلت: هي خاصّة، أو عامّة؟ قال: هي بمنزلة قوله: ﴿ثُمَّ أَوْرَثْنَا الْكِتَابَ الَّذِينَ اصْطَفَيْنَا مِنْ عِبَادِنَا﴾، فمن دخل فيهم من الناس كان بمنزِلَتهم، يقول الله تعالى: ﴿وَمَن يُطِعِ اللَّهَ وَالرَّسُولَ فَأُولَٰئِكَ مَعَ الَّذِينَ أَنْعَمَ اللَّهُ عَلَيْهِم مِّنَ النَّبِيِّينَ وَالصِّدِّيقِينَ وَالشُّهَدَاءِ وَالصَّالِحِينَ وَحَسُنَ أُولَٰئِكَ رَفِيقًا﴾.

will be among those He has blessed: the messengers, the truthful, those who bear witness to the truth, and the righteous – what excellent companions these are!﴾ (4:69).”’ [2:158]

138. From one of our associates, from Abū ʿAbd Allāh عليه السلام; he said, ‘I asked him about circulating between Ṣafā and Marwa, as to whether this was a mandatory practice or a recommended one? He replied, “It is an obligation.” So I asked, “But does God not say ﴿*it is no offence to circulate between the two*﴾?” He replied, “That was only for the *ʿumra* performed late after the designated time for it had elapsed, at which time when the Messenger of God صلى الله عليه وآله had stipulated that the idols be removed from there. One particular man was prevented from being able to perform it along with his companions [within the designated period] until they had been replaced there anew. So they came to the Messenger of God صلى الله عليه وآله and asked him, ‘So and so has not circumambulated, and now the idols are back in their place.’ So God, the All-Mighty, revealed the verse ﴿*Ṣafā and Marwa are among the rites of God, so for those who make major or minor pilgrimage to the House it is no offence to circulate between the two*﴾, meaning while the idols were atop them.”’ [2:158]

139. From [ʿAbd Allāh] Ibn Muskān, from al-Ḥalabī who said, ‘I asked him the reason for running between Ṣafā and Marwa. He replied, “Iblīs appeared before Ibrāhīm عليه السلام in that valley, so Ibrāhīm عليه السلام ran away from him in aversion that he should speak to him, as therein lay the abodes of the devils.”’

140. According to a report by Ḥammād b. ʿUthmān, Abū ʿAbd Allāh عليه السلام said that there were idols on Ṣafā and Marwa, so when the Muslims went for Hajj they did not know what to do about it, so God revealed this verse [i.e. 2:158], and the people were running to and fro whilst the idols were in their place. When the Prophet صلى الله عليه وآله went for Hajj, he stoned them.

141. From Ibn Abī ʿUmayr, from whoever mentioned it from Abū ʿAbd Allāh عليه السلام that the verse ﴿*As for those who hide the proofs and guidance We send down, after We have made them clear to people in the Scripture, God rejects them, and so do others*﴾ was revealed about ʿAlī عليه السلام. [2:159]

١٣٨. عن بعض أصحابنا، عن أبي عبدالله ﵇، قال: سألتُهُ عن السّعي بين الصّفا والمرْوَة، فَريضة هو أو سُنّة؟ قال: فَريضة.

قال: قلتُ: أليس الله يقول: ﴿فَلَا جُنَاحَ عَلَيْهِ أَنْ يَطَّوَّفَ بِهِمَا﴾؟ قال: كان ذلك في العُمرةِ القضاء، وذلك أنّ رسول الله ﷺ كان شَرْطُهُ عليهم أن يَرْفَعُوا الأصنام، فتَشَاغَلَ رجلٌ من أصحابه حتّى أُعيدَت الأصنام. فجاءوا إلى رسول الله ﷺ فسألوه، وقيل له: إنّ فلانًا لم يُطُف، وقد أُعيدَت الأصنام، قال: فأنزل الله: ﴿إِنَّ الصَّفَا وَالْمَرْوَةَ مِنْ شَعَائِرِ اللهِ فَمَنْ حَجَّ الْبَيْتَ أَوِ اعْتَمَرَ فَلَا جُنَاحَ عَلَيْهِ أَنْ يَطَّوَّفَ بِهِمَا﴾ أي والأصنام عليهما.

١٣٩. عن ابن مُسكان، عن الحَلَبيّ، قال: سألتُهُ فقلت: وَلِمَ جُعِل السّعي بين الصّفا والمرْوَة؟ قال: إنّ إبليس تراءى لإبراهيم ﵇ في الوادي، فسعى إبراهيم ﵇ منه كراهيّة أن يُكلّمه، وكان مَنازِل الشياطين.

١٤٠. وقال: قال أبو عبدالله في خَبر حمّاد بن عثمان: إنّه كان على الصّفا والمرْوَة أصنام، فلمّا أن حَجّ الناس لم يَدْرُوا كيف يَصْنعَون، فأنزل الله هذه الآية، فكان الناس يَسْعَون والأصنام على حالِها، فلمّا حجّ النبيّ ﷺ رمى بها.

١٤١. عن ابن أبي عُمَير، عمّن ذكره، عن أبي عبد الله ﵇: ﴿إِنَّ الَّذِينَ يَكْتُمُونَ مَا أَنْزَلْنَا مِنَ الْبَيِّنَاتِ وَالْهُدَى﴾ في عليّ ﵇.

142. From Ḥumrān, from Abū Jaʿfar عليه السلام who said with regard to the verse ﴿*As for those who hide the proofs and guidance We send down, after We have made them clear to people in the Scripture, God rejects them, and so do others*﴾, 'By this He means us, and God is the One to whom we resort.' [2:159]

143. From Zayd al-Shaḥḥām who narrated, 'Abū 'Abd Allāh عليه السلام was once asked about the punishment in the grave. So he said, "Abū Jaʿfar عليه السلام narrated to us that a man once came to Salmān al-Fārsī saying, 'Narrate to me a *ḥadīth* of the Prophet,' but he remained silent. So he asked again, and again he stayed silent. So the man turned away, muttering the verse ﴿*As for those who hide the proofs and guidance We send down, after We have made them clear to people in the Scripture*﴾. So Salmān called him back saying, 'When we find someone worthy of this trust, we narrate it to him. Be prepared for Munkar and Nakīr though when they come to you in your grave and ask you about the Messenger of God صلى الله عليه وآله; for if you doubt or try to squirm out of answering, they will clobber you on the head with a hammer that they carry, which will pulverize you into dust.'" Then I asked, 'Then what?' He replied, 'Then you will be brought back [on the Day of Resurrection] and shall be punished.' Then I asked, 'Who are Munkar and Nakīr?' He replied, 'They are the guardians of the grave.' 'So angels will punish humans in their graves?' I asked again, to which he replied, 'Yes'."' [2:159]

144. From one of our associates, from Abū 'Abd Allāh عليه السلام: 'I asked him عليه السلام to explain to me the verse ﴿*As for those who hide the proofs and guidance We send down, after We have made them clear to people in the Scripture*﴾. He عليه السلام replied, 'By this He means us, and God is the one to whom we resort. When one of us [Imams] goes back to Him, he never does so without specifying for the people who is to succeed him.' [2:159]

145. Muḥammad b. Muslim also narrated the same, saying that they [i.e. those who hide the proofs] are the People of the Book.'

١٤٢. عن حُمران، عن أبي جعفر ﷺ، فيقول الله تعالى: ﴿إِنَّ الَّذِينَ يَكْتُمُونَ مَا أَنزَلْنَا مِنَ الْبَيِّنَاتِ وَالْهُدَى مِن بَعْدِ مَا بَيَّنَّاهُ لِلنَّاسِ فِي الْكِتَابِ﴾. يعني بذلك نحنُ، والله المُستعَان.

١٤٣. عن زَيد الشَّحّام، قال: سُئِل أبو عبدالله ﷺ عن عذابِ القَبر؟ قال: إنّ أبا جعفر ﷺ حدّثنا أنّ رجلاً أتى سلمان الفارسيّ، فقال: حدّثني، فسكتَ عنه ثمّ عاد فسَكت، فأدْبَر الرجل وهو يقول، ويتلو هذه الآية: ﴿إِنَّ الَّذِينَ يَكْتُمُونَ مَا أَنزَلْنَا مِنَ الْبَيِّنَاتِ وَالْهُدَى مِن بَعْدِ مَا بَيَّنَّاهُ لِلنَّاسِ فِي الْكِتَابِ﴾.

فقال له: أقبِل، إنّا لو وجَدنا أمينًا لحَدّثناه، ولكن أعِدَّ لمُنكَرٍ ونَكيرٍ إذا أتياك في القبر فسألاك عن رسول الله ﷺ، فإن شككت أو التوَيت ضَرَبَاكَ على رأسِك بمِطْرَقَة معهما تصير منها رَمادًا، فقُلتُ: ثمّ مَه؟ قال: تعود، ثمّ تُعذَّب.

قلتُ: وما مُنْكَر ونَكير؟ قال: هما قَعيدا القَبر. قلتُ: أمَلَكان يُعذِّبان الناس في قُبورهم؟ فقال: نعم.

١٤٤. عن بعض أصحابنا، عن أبي عبدالله ﷺ، قال: قلتُ له: أخبرني عن قوله تعالى: ﴿إِنَّ الَّذِينَ يَكْتُمُونَ مَا أَنزَلْنَا مِنَ الْبَيِّنَاتِ وَالْهُدَى مِن بَعْدِ مَا بَيَّنَّاهُ لِلنَّاسِ فِي الْكِتَابِ﴾. قال: نحنُ يعني بها والله المُستَعان؛ إنّ الرجل منّا إذا صارت إليه، لم يكُن له – أو لم يَسَعه – إلاّ أن يبيّن للناس من يكون بعده.

١٤٥. ورواه محمّد بن مسلم، قال: هم أهل الكتاب.

146. From ʿAbd Allāh b. Bukayr, from whoever narrated it from Abū ʿAbd Allāh عليه السلام regarding the verse ﴾*As for those who disbelieve and die as disbelievers, God rejects them, as do the rejecters*﴿. He said, 'We are these [rejecters] even though they used to say it was the reptiles of the earth.' [2:161]

147. From Jābir who narrated, 'I asked Abū ʿAbd Allāh عليه السلام about the verse in which God states ﴾*Even so, there are some who choose to worship others besides God as rivals to Him, loving them with the love due to God*﴿. So he replied, "They are the adherents of those three individuals[80] whom they have adopted as their leaders besides the Imam rightly appointed by God to be a leader over the people. This is why God, Blessed and most High, says ﴾*If only the idolaters could see – as they will see when they face the torment – that all power belongs to God, and that God punishes severely. When those who have been followed disown their followers, when they all see the suffering, when all bonds between them are severed, the followers will say, 'If only we had one last chance, we would disown them as they now disown us.' In this way, God will make them see their deeds as a source of bitter regret: they shall not leave the Fire*﴿. Then Abū Jaʿfar عليه السلام continued, "By God, O Jābir, they and their followers are leaders of wrongdoing."' [2:165–7]

148. From Zurāra, Ḥumrān and Muḥammad b. Muslim, from Abū Jaʿfar and Abū ʿAbd Allāh regarding the verse ﴾*there are some who choose to worship others besides God as rivals to Him, loving them with the love due to God, but the believers have greater love for God*﴿. They said, 'They are Muḥammad's صلى الله عليه وآله Household.' [2:165]

149. From ʿUthmān b. ʿĪsā[81], from whoever narrated it from Abū ʿAbd Allāh عليه السلام, that regarding the verse in which God says ﴾*In this way, God will make them see their deeds as a source of bitter regret*﴿ he عليه السلام said, 'This pertains to someone who stingily hoards his wealth, refusing to spend it in acts of obedience to God, then dies leaving it to be inherited by others who either use it

80 No doubt referring to the first three Caliphs, Abū Bakr, ʿUmar and ʿUthmān.

81 Abū ʿAmr ʿUthmān b. ʿĪsā al-Rawwāsī al-ʿĀmirī al-Kilābī, described by the majority of his biographers as Wāqifī, was a companion and narrator of the eighth Imam. See Ḥillī, *Khulāṣat al-aqwāl*, 382–3 (nr. 1535).

١٤٦. عن عبد الله بن بُكير، عمّن حدّثه، عن أبي عبد الله عليه السلام، في قوله تعالى: ﴿أُولَئِكَ يَلْعَنُهُمُ اللهُ وَيَلْعَنُهُمُ اللاَّعِنُونَ﴾، قال: نحنُ هم، وقد قالوا: هَوامّ الأرض.

١٤٧. عن جابر، قال: سألتُ أبا عبد الله عليه السلام عن قول الله: ﴿وَمِنَ النَّاسِ مَنْ يَتَّخِذُ مِنْ دُونِ اللهِ أَنْدَادًا يُحِبُّونَهُمْ كَحُبِّ اللهِ وَالَّذِينَ آمَنُوا أَشَدُّ حُبًّا لِلَّهِ﴾. قال: فقال: هم أولياء فُلانٍ وفُلانٍ وفُلانٍ، اتّخذوهم أئمّةً من دون الإمام الّذي جعَلَهُ الله للناس إماماً، فلذلك قال الله تبارك وتعالى: ﴿وَلَوْ يَرَى الَّذِينَ ظَلَمُوا إِذْ يَرَوْنَ الْعَذَابَ أَنَّ الْقُوَّةَ لِلَّهِ جَمِيعًا وَأَنَّ اللهَ شَدِيدُ الْعَذَابِ ۝ إِذْ تَبَرَّأَ الَّذِينَ اتُّبِعُوا مِنَ الَّذِينَ اتَّبَعُوا﴾ إلى قوله ﴿مِنَ النَّارِ﴾.

قال: ثمّ قال أبو جعفر عليه السلام: والله — يا جابر — هم أئمّة الظُلم وأشياعهم.

١٤٨. عن زُرارَة، وحُمران، ومحمّد بن مسلم، عن أبي جعفر وأبي عبد الله عليهما السلام، قوله: ﴿وَمِنَ النَّاسِ مَنْ يَتَّخِذُ مِنْ دُونِ اللهِ أَنْدَادًا يُحِبُّونَهُمْ كَحُبِّ اللهِ وَالَّذِينَ آمَنُوا أَشَدُّ حُبًّا لِلَّهِ﴾ قالا: هم آل محمّد صلى الله عليه وآله وسلم.

١٤٩. عن عُثمان بن عيسى، عمّن حدّثه، عن أبي عبد الله عليه السلام، في قول الله تعالى: ﴿كَذَلِكَ يُرِيهِمُ اللهُ أَعْمَالَهُمْ حَسَرَاتٍ عَلَيْهِمْ﴾، قال: هو الرجل يَدَعُ المال لا يُنفِقُه في طاعة الله بُخلاً، ثمّ يموت فيدَعُه لِمَن يعمل به في طاعة الله، أو في مَعصِيَتِه، فإن عَمِل به في طاعة الله رآه في ميزان غيره، فزادَهُ حَسْرَةً وقد كان المالُ له، وإن عَمِلَ به في معصية الله قوّاه بذلك المال حتّى عَمِل به في معاصي الله.

towards God's obedience or transgression. So if it is spent in the way of God, he will see it [on the Day of Judgement] on someone else's scale of deeds, which will fill him with even deeper regret since the wealth was initially his. However, if it is being used to transgress against God, then it will be counted as his own wealth that facilitated acts of transgressions against God.' [2:167]

150. From Manṣūr b. Ḥāzim[82] who narrated, 'I asked Abū 'Abd Allāh عليه السلام about the verse ﴾*they shall not leave the Fire*﴿. He said, "'Alī's عليه السلام enemies are those that will remain in the Fire indefinitely and for all eternity."' [2:167]

151. From al-'Alā b. Razīn[83], from Muḥammad b. Muslim, from one of the two [either al-Bāqir or al-Ṣādiq عليهما السلام], that he was once asked about the case of a woman who gives all her wealth away in charity and sets every slave of hers free to not have to speak to her sister ever again. He said, 'She must speak to her, for these kinds of things are nothing but following in Shayṭān's footsteps.' [2:168]

152. From Muḥammad b. Muslim that there was once a woman from the family of al-Mukhtār who made her sister or another close relative to swear an oath. She had asked her to come and join her for a meal, upon which the other refused. So she said, 'If you do not come and eat with me, then I bind you to an oath to walk to the Ka'ba on foot and to free your slaves; otherwise I will not live under the same roof as you, and you will never again eat with me.' So the other retorted with a similar thing. So 'Umar b. Hanẓala took the matter to Abū Ja'far عليه السلام and he said, 'I will rule on this issue. Tell her to eat together with her and live under the same roof, and neither walk on foot [to Mecca] nor free slaves, but to be mindful of their duty to God and to never do such a thing again, for these are just Shayṭān's footsteps.' [2:168]

---

82 Abū Ayyūb Manṣūr b. Ḥāzim al-Bajalī, a high-standing companion and narrator of traditions from Imams Muḥammad al-Bāqir and Ja'far al-Ṣādiq. See Ḥillī, *Khulāṣat*, 275 (nr. 1001); Modarressi, *Tradition and Survival*, 317–8 (nr. 135).

83 'Alā' b. Razīn al-Qallā', a client of Thaqīf, was a narrator of Imam Ja'far al-Ṣādiq's traditions. He was the disciple and student of the prominent Shī'ī jurist Muḥammad b. Muslim b. Rabāḥ, from whom this tradition has been narrated.

١٥٠. عن مَنْصُور بن حَازِم، قال: قلتُ لأبي عبدالله عليه السلام: ﴿وَمَا هُمْ بِخَارِجِينَ مِنَ النَّارِ﴾؟ قال: أعداء عليّ عليه السلام هم المُخلّدون في النار أبد الآبدين ودَهْر الدَّاهِرين.

١٥١. عن العلاء بن رَزِين، عن محمّد بن مُسلم، عن أحدهما عليه السلام: أنّه سُئِل عن امرأةٍ جَعَلت مالَها هَديًا، وكُلّ مملوكٍ لها حُرًّا، إن كلّمت أُخْتَها أبدًا؟ قال: تُكَلّمُها وليس هذا بشيء، إنّما هذا وأشباهه من خُطوات الشيطان.

١٥٢. عن محمّد بن مُسلم: إنّ امرأةً من آل المُختار حلّفت على أُختِها، أو ذات قرابةٍ لها، قالت: ادني يا فلانة، فكُلي معي. فقالت: لا آكُل [قالت:] فحَلَفتُ عليها بالمشي إلى بيت الله، وعِتقِ ما تَملِك إن لم تَدني فتأكُلي معي ألاّ أُظِلَّ وإيّاك سقف بيتٍ، أو أكلتُ مَعَكِ على خِوانٍ أبداً؟ قال: فقالت الأخرى مثل ذلك.

فحمل عُمر بن حَنظَلة إلى أبي جعفر عليه السلام مقالتَهُما، فقال عليه السلام: أنا أقضي في ذا، قل لها: فلتأكُل وليُظِلّها وإيّاها سقف بيتٍ، ولا تَمشي ولا تَعتِق ولتَتّقِ الله ربَّها ولا تَعود إلى ذلك، فإن هذا من خُطُوات الشيطان.

153. From Manṣūr b. Ḥāzim who narrated, ʿAbū ʿAbd Allāh عليه السلام said, ʿHave you not heard about Ṭāriq? Ṭāriq was a coppersmith in Medina who came to Abū Jaʿfar عليه السلام saying, "O Abū Jaʿfar, I am doomed for I have taken an oath to divorce, to free slaves and pledged offerings." So he said to him, "Ṭāriq, these are footsteps of Shayṭān."ʾ [2:168]

154. From ʿAbd al-Raḥmān b. Abī ʿAbd Allāh who narrated, ʿI asked Abū ʿAbd Allāh عليه السلام about a man who took an oath to sacrifice his son. He replied, "That is considered among the footsteps of Shayṭān."ʾ [2:168]

155. From Muḥammad b. Muslim who narrated, ʿI heard Abū Jaʿfar عليه السلام say ﴾*do not follow Shayṭān's footsteps*﴿. Every oath sworn for other than God counts as [following in] Shayṭān's footsteps.ʾ [2:168]

156. From Muḥammad b. Ismāʿīl who, without mentioning his source, cited Abū ʿAbd Allāh عليه السلام as having said regarding the verse ﴾*But if anyone is forced* [*to eat such things by hunger*], *rather than desire or excess*﴿: ʿThe excessive one is the oppressor, and the one wanton to desire is the usurper.ʾ [2:173]

157. From Abū Baṣīr who narrated, ʿI heard Abū ʿAbd Allāh عليه السلام say [regarding 2:173]: "No one is ever compelled to drink wine, for it will only increase evil in him, and if he drinks it, it will end up killing him, so do not even drink a drop of it."ʾ

158. From Muḥammad b. Muslim, from Abū Jaʿfar عليه السلام, that he was asked about a situation in which a man or a woman loses their sight and is advised by physicians to remain lying down for a month or forty days in order for it to be restored, and how such a person would pray. He recited the verse ﴾*But if anyone is forced, neither by desire nor excess, he commits no sin: God is most merciful and forgiving*﴿. [2:173]

١٥٣. عن مَنْصُور بن حَازِم، قال: قال أبو عبد الله ﵇: أما سَمِعتَ بطارِق؟ إنّ طارقًا كان نخّاسًا بالمدينة فأتى أبا جعفر ﵇ فقال: يا أبا جعفر، إنّي هالك، إنّي حَلَفتُ بالطّلاق والعِتاق والنُذور، فقال له: يا طارق، إنّ هذه من خُطُوات الشيطان.

١٥٤. عن عبد الرّحمن بن أبي عبد الله، قال: سألتُ أبا عبد الله ﵇ عن رجلٍ حلَفَ أن يَنْحَرَ وَلَده. فقال: ذلك من خُطوات الشّيطان.

١٥٥. عن محمّد بن مسلم، قال: سمِعتُ أبا جعفر ﵇ يقول: ﴿وَلَا تَتَّبِعُوا خُطُوَاتِ الشَّيْطَانِ﴾، قال: كلّ يمين بغير الله فهي من خُطُوات الشّيطان.

١٥٦. عن محمّد بن إسماعيل، رفعه إلى أبي عبد الله ﵇، في قوله: ﴿فَمَنِ اضْطُرَّ غَيْرَ بَاغٍ وَلَا عَادٍ﴾، قال: الباغي: الظالم، والعادي: الغاصب.

١٥٧. عن أبي بصير، قال: سِمعتُ أبا عبد الله ﵇ يقول: المُضطّر لا يَشْرَبُ الخَمرَ، لأنّها لا تَزيدُه إلاّ شَرًّا، فإن شَرِبهَا قَتَلته، فلا يَشْرَبَنّ منها قَطْرةً.

١٥٨. عن محمّد بن مسلم، عن أبي جعفر ﵇، في المرأة أو الرّجُل يذهَبُ بصَره، فيأتيه الأطِبّاء، فيقولون: نُداويك شهرًا أو أربعين ليلةً مُستَلقيًا، كذلك يُصلّي؟ فرَجَعتُ إليه لهُ، فقال: ﴿فَمَنِ اضْطُرَّ غَيْرَ بَاغٍ وَلَا عَادٍ﴾.

159. From Ḥammād b. ʿUthmān, from Abū ʿAbd Allāh ﵇, as having said concerning the verse ﴾*But if anyone is forced* [*to eat such things by hunger*], *rather than desire or excess*﴿, 'The excessive one is the one who revolts against the Imam, and the one wanton to desire is the thief.' [2:173]

160. From one of our associates who narrated, 'A woman once came to ʿUmar saying, "O Commander of the Faithful, I have committed an indecency so sentence me accordingly." So he gave the order for her to be stoned to death, while the Commander of the Faithful ʿAlī ﵇ was also present there. So he ﵇ said to him, "At least ask what kind of indecency she has committed?" So she said, "I was in the desert when an intense thirst overcame me. I saw a tent in the distance, to which I went and found a Bedouin there. So I asked him for some water, but he refused to give me any unless I made myself available to him. So I turned and ran away from him, but my thirst intensified until my eyes sunk in and my tongue became parched. At this point I had to go back to him, and he gave me some water and had his way with me." So ʿAlī ﵇ said to him, "It is her that the Qur'an means in the verse ﴾*But if anyone is forced, neither by desire nor excess he commits no sin: God is most merciful and forgiving*﴿; she was neither desiring nor exceeding the bounds, so let her go." ʿUmar said, "Were it not for ʿAlī, ʿUmar would have perished."' [2:173]

161. From Ḥammād b. ʿUthmān, from Abū ʿAbd Allāh ﵇ regarding the verse ﴾*But if anyone is forced, neither by desire nor excess*﴿. He said, 'The one driven by desire is the exploiting opportunist whereas the one given to excess is the thief. Neither of them is allowed the concession to shorten the prayers, nor to eat unlawful meat if compelled, nor anything that is lawful for the rest of people in times of compulsion.' [2:173]

162. From Ibn Muskān who, without mentioning his source, cited Abū ʿAbd Allāh ﵇ as having said about the verse ﴾*What can make them patient in the face of the Fire?*﴿: 'What has made them persist in that which they know is only going to drive them into the Fire?' [2:175]

١٥٩. عن حمّاد بن عُثمان، عن أبي عبدالله عليه السلام، في قوله: ﴿فَمَنِ اضْطُرَّ غَيْرَ بَاغٍ وَلَا عَادٍ﴾، قال: الباغي: الخارج على الإمام، والعادِي: اللّصّ.

١٦٠. عن بعض أصحابنا، قال: أتتْ امرأةٌ إلى عمر، فقالت: يا أمير المؤمنين، إنّي فَجَرتُ، فأقِم فيّ حدّ الله، فأمَرَ بِرَجْمِها، وكان عليّ أمير المؤمنين عليه السلام، حاضِرًا، قال: فقال له: سَلها كيف فَجَرَت؟

قالت: كنتُ في فَلاةٍ من الأرض، أصابني عَطَشٌ شديدٌ، فرفِعت لي خيمةٌ فأتَيْتُها، فأصَبْتُ فيها رجُلاً أعرابيًّا، فسألتُهُ الماء فأبى عليّ أن يَسْقِيني إلاّ أن أُمكّنَه من نفسي، فولّيتُ عنه هاربةً، فاشتَدّ بي العَطَش حتّى غارَت عيناي وذَهب لساني، فلمّا بلغ ذلك منّي أتَيتُه فَسقاني ووقع عليّ.

فقال له عليّ عليه السلام: هذه الّتي قال الله: ﴿فَمَنِ اضْطُرَّ غَيْرَ بَاغٍ وَلَا عَادٍ﴾ وهذه غير باغيةٍ ولا عاديةٍ، فخلِّ سبيلها.

فقال عمر: لولا عليّ لهلَك عُمر.

١٦١. عن حمّاد بن عُثمان، عن أبي عبدالله عليه السلام، في قوله تعالى: ﴿فَمَنِ اضْطُرَّ غَيْرَ بَاغٍ وَلَا عَادٍ﴾، قال: الباغي: طالب الصَّيد، والعادي: السّارِق، ليس لهما أن يُقصِّرا من الصَّلاة، وليس لهما إذا اضطُرّا إلى المَيْتَة أن يأكُلاها، ولا يَحِلّ لهما ما يَحِلّ للناس إذا اضْطُرّوا.

١٦٢. عن ابن مُسكان، رفعه إلى أبي عبدالله عليه السلام، في قوله تعالى: ﴿فَمَا أَصْبَرَهُمْ عَلَى النَّارِ﴾، قال: ما أصبرهم على فِعل ما يعلمون أنّه يُصيّرهم إلى النار.

163. From Samā'a b. Mihrān, from Abū 'Abd Allāh عليه السلام, that he said regarding the verse ﴾*You who believe, fair retribution is prescribed for you in cases of murder: the free man for the free man, the slave for the slave, the female for the female*﴿: 'A free man cannot be killed [in retribution] for a slave's life, but he should be severely beaten and made to pay the blood money of the slave. If a man kills a woman, however, and the relatives of the victim wish for him to be killed [in retribution], they have to pay half of the blood money back to the man's family.' [2:178]

164. From Muḥammad b. Khālid al-Barqī[84], from one of his associates, from Abū 'Abd Allāh عليه السلام, that he was asked regarding the verse ﴾*You who believe, fair retribution is prescribed for you*﴿: He said, 'It pertains to the whole body of Muslims and is not specific to the believers.' [2:178]

165. From al-Ḥalabī, from Abū 'Abd Allāh عليه السلام; 'I asked him about the verse ﴾*But if the culprit is pardoned by his aggrieved brother, this shall be adhered to fairly, and the culprit shall pay what is due in a good way*﴿, to which he replied, "The one with the right [to whom the blood money is owed] should not harass his brother [the culprit] if he can pay the retribution, and the culprit should not tarry in the payment of it if he can pay it, and he should do so with goodwill." He continued, "This means that if retaliation has been granted, they should immediately pay the blood money to the family of the murdered so that the blood of a fellow Muslim is not spilled in vain."' [2:178]

166. From Abū Baṣīr, from one of the two Imams عليه السلام, regarding the verse in which God states ﴾*But if the culprit is pardoned by his aggrieved brother, this shall be adhered to fairly, and the culprit shall pay what is due in a good way*﴿ – what would that be? He said, 'This refers to the man who accepts the retribution, so God commands the payee to pursue it courteously and

84 Abū 'Abd Allāh Muḥammad b. Khālid b. 'Abd al-Raḥmān b. Muḥammad b. 'Alī, the client of Abū Mūsā al-Ash'arī, was a reliable companion of Imam 'Alī b. Mūsā al-Riḍā. According to Ibn al-Ghaḍā'irī he is unreliable and would frequently narrate traditions from individuals who are deemed weak, often without complete chains of narration; likewise according to Najāshī. Ḥillī relies on the opinion of Shaykh al-Ṭūsī, who exonerates him from any malicious wrongdoing on his own part. See Ḥillī, *Khulāṣat al-aqwāl*, 237–8 (nr. 813).

١٦٣. عن سَماعة بن مِهران، عن أبي عبد الله ﵇، في قوله تعالى: ﴿الْحُرُّ بِالْحُرِّ وَالْعَبْدُ بِالْعَبْدِ وَالْأُنثَى بِالْأُنثَى﴾: قال: لا يُقتَل حرٌّ بعَبْد، ولكن يُضرَبُ ضَربًا شديدًا، ويُغرّم دِيَة العبد، وإن قتَل رجل امرأةً، فأراد أولياء المقتول أن يَقتُلوا أدّوا نِصف دِيَته إلى أهل الرّجلُ.

١٦٤. محمّد بن خالد البرقيّ، عن بعض أصحابه، عن أبي عبد الله ﵇، في قول الله تعالى: ﴿يَا أَيُّهَا الَّذِينَ آمَنُوا كُتِبَ عَلَيْكُمُ الْقِصَاصُ﴾ هي لجماعة المسلمين، ما هي للمؤمنين خاصّة.

١٦٥. عن الحَلَبيّ، عن أبي عبد الله ﵇، قال: سألتُهُ عن قول الله: ﴿فَمَنْ عُفِيَ لَهُ مِنْ أَخِيهِ شَيْءٌ فَاتِّبَاعٌ بِالْمَعْرُوفِ وَأَدَاءٌ إِلَيْهِ بِإِحْسَانٍ﴾، قال ﵇: ينبغي للذي له الحَقّ أن لا يَعْسُرُ أخاه إذا كان قادرًا على دِيَةٍ، وينبغي للّذي عليه الحقّ أن لا يَمْطُل أخاه إذا قَدَر على ما يُعطيه، ويُؤدّي إليه بإحسانٍ.

قال: يعني إذا وَهَب القَود أتبعوه بالدِّيَة إلى أولياء المقتول، لكيلا يَبْطُل دمُ امرئٍ مسلم.

١٦٦. عن أبي بصير، عن أحدهما ﵇، في قوله تعالى: ﴿فَمَنْ عُفِيَ لَهُ مِنْ أَخِيهِ شَيْءٌ﴾ ما ذلك؟ قال: هو الرجل يقبل الدِّية، فأمر الله الذي له الحقّ أن يَتْبَعَه بمعروفٍ ولا يَعْسُره، وأمَر الله الذي عليه الدِّية ألاّ يَمْطُله، وأن يؤدّي إليه بإحسانٍ إذا أيسر.

not coercively, and He commands the culprit not to tarry in his remittance of the blood money if he is able to, and to do so with goodwill.' [2:178]

167. From al-Ḥalabī, from Abū 'Abd Allāh عليه السلام; 'I asked him about the verse in which God states ﴾*If anyone then exceeds these limits, grievous suffering awaits him*﴿. He replied, "This is referring to someone who accepts responsibility for paying the blood money, or one who forgives or makes peace, then turns around and kills instead. For him is a grievous punishment."' An alternative narration adds: "So he attacks his companion after having feigned peace-making with him, and for him is a grievous punishment." [2:178]

168. From 'Ammār b. Marwān[85], from Abū 'Abd Allāh عليه السلام; 'I asked him about the meaning of the verse in which God states ﴾*it is prescribed that he should make a proper bequest*﴿. He replied, "This is a right that God has given to people regarding their wealth [to be able to bequeath it]." So I asked, "Is there a defined proportion for this?" He replied, "Yes – a minimum of a sixth and a maximum of a third [of his estate]."' [2:180]

169. From Muḥammad b. Muslim, from Abū Ja'far عليه السلام; 'I asked him about the bequest and whether one can include an [automatic] heir therein? He replied, 'Yes,' then recited the verse ﴾*it is prescribed that he should make a proper bequest to parents and close relatives*﴿.' [2:180]

170. From Muḥammad b. Qays, from Abū Ja'far عليه السلام, that he said, 'Whoever makes a bequest to someone other than his heir, be it young or old, courteously and not wrongfully, then his bequest is in order.'

171. From al-Sakūnī, from Ja'far b. Muḥammad عليه السلام, on his father's authority, from 'Alī عليه السلام who said, 'Whoever does not make a bequest upon his death for those of his relatives who do not automatically inherit from him, has sealed his [life's] work with wrongdoing.'

---

85 'Ammār b. Marwān, along with his brother 'Amr b. Marwān, are both regarded reliable and trustworthy narrators of Imam Ja'far al-Ṣādiq. See Ḥillī, *Khulāṣat al-aqwāl*, 223 (nr. 743); Modarressi, *Tradition and Survival*, 198–9 (nr. 39).

١٦٧. عن الحَلَبيّ، عن أبي عبدالله عليه السلام، قال: سألتُه عن قول الله: ﴿فَمَنِ اعْتَدَى بَعْدَ ذَلِكَ فَلَهُ عَذَابٌ أَلِيمٌ﴾. قال: هو الرجل يَقْبَل الدِّيَة، أو يعفو، أو يُصالح، ثم يعتدي فيقتُل ﴿فَلَهُ عَذَابٌ أَلِيمٌ﴾.

وفي نُسخةٍ أُخرى: فيلقى صاحبه بعد الصُلح فيُمثّل به ﴿فَلَهُ عَذَابٌ أَلِيمٌ﴾.

١٦٨. عن عمّار بن مَروان، عن أبي عبدالله عليه السلام، قال: سألتُهُ عن قول الله عزّ وجلّ: ﴿إِنْ تَرَكَ خَيْرًا الْوَصِيَّةُ﴾، قال: حقّ جعلَه الله في أموال الناس لصاحب هذا الأمر.

قال: قلت: لذلك حدٌّ محدود؟ قال: نعم. قال: قلت: كم؟ قال: أدناه السُّدُس، وأكثره الثُّلث.

١٦٩. عن محمّد بن مُسلم، عن أبي جعفر عليه السلام، قال: سألتُهُ عن الوصيّة، تجوز للوارِث؟ قال: نعم، ثمّ تلا هذه الآية: ﴿إِنْ تَرَكَ خَيْرًا الْوَصِيَّةُ لِلْوَالِدَيْنِ وَالأَقْرَبِينَ﴾.

١٧٠. عن محمّد بن قَيس، عن أبي جعفر عليه السلام، قال: مَن أوصى بوصيّة لغير الوارِث من صغيرٍ أو كبيرٍ بالمَعْروف غير المُنْكَر، فقد جازَت وصيّتُه.

١٧١. عن السَّكُوني، عن جعفر بن محمّد، عن أبيه، عن عليّ عليه السلام، قال: من لم يُوصِ عند موته لِذوي قرابته ممّن لا يَرِث، فقدختَم عمله بمعصية.

172. From Ibn Muskān, from Abū Baṣīr, from one of the two [Imams al-Bāqir or al-Ṣādiq] عليه السلام regarding the verse in which God states ﴾*When death approaches one of you who leaves wealth, it is prescribed that he should make a proper bequest to parents and close relatives*﴿. He said, 'This verse has been abrogated by the verse of incumbent duties dealing with inheritance: ﴾*If anyone alters the bequest after hearing it, the guilt of the alteration will fall on them*﴿, by which He means the beneficiary.' [2:180–1]

173. From Samā'a, from Abū 'Abd Allāh عليه السلام, that he stated regarding the verse ﴾*It is prescribed that he should make a proper bequest to parents and close relatives – a duty incumbent on those who are mindful of God*﴿, 'It refers to that amount which God had placed at the disposal of the decedent.' So I asked, 'Is there a specific proportion to it?' He replied, 'Yes, a minimum of a ninth [of his estate].' [2:180]

174. From Muḥammad b. Muslim, from Abū Ja'far عليه السلام; he said, 'I asked him about a man who bequeaths his wealth towards a good cause in the way of God?' He replied, 'You have to give it to whomever he bequeathed it to, even if they were Jewish or Christian, for indeed God says, ﴾*If anyone alters the bequest after hearing it, the guilt of the alteration will fall on them*﴿.' [2:181]

175. From Abū Sa'īd, from Abū 'Abd Allāh عليه السلام, that he was asked about a man who makes a will and makes a bequest for a Hajj to be performed by a person, as the beneficiary of his will. He replied, 'Then it must be paid to his beneficiary as per his will, and he must spend it on Hajj as per the bequest, for God says, ﴾*If anyone alters the bequest after hearing it, the guilt of the alteration will fall on them*﴿.' [2:181]

176. From Muthannā b. 'Abd al-Salām[86], from Abū 'Abd Allāh عليه السلام; he said, 'I asked him about a man who was entitled to something in a will, but died before he could receive it, and he himself has no kin [to inherit from him]. He replied, "Find an heir or protégé of his and give it to him, for God says, ﴾*If anyone alters the bequest after hearing it, the guilt of the alteration will fall on*

86 Muthannā b. 'Abd al-Salām, on whom there is scant information, is not considered a problematic narrator. See Ḥillī, *Khulāṣat al-aqwāl*, 275 (nr. 1004).

١٧٢. عن ابن مُسكان، عن أبي بصير، عن أحدهما عليه السلام في قوله تعالى: ﴿كُتِبَ عَلَيْكُمْ إِذَا حَضَرَ أَحَدَكُمُ الْمَوْتُ إِن تَرَكَ خَيْرًا الْوَصِيَّةُ لِلْوَالِدَيْنِ وَالْأَقْرَبِينَ﴾. قال: هي منسوخة، نَسَخَتْها آية الفرائض التي هي المواريث ﴿فَمَن بَدَّلَهُ بَعْدَمَا سَمِعَهُ فَإِنَّمَا إِثْمُهُ عَلَى الَّذِينَ يُبَدِّلُونَهُ﴾ يعني بذلك الوصيّ.

١٧٣. عن سَماعة، عن أبي عبدالله عليه السلام، في قوله تعالى: ﴿إِن تَرَكَ خَيْرًا الْوَصِيَّةُ لِلْوَالِدَيْنِ وَالْأَقْرَبِينَ بِالْمَعْرُوفِ حَقًّا عَلَى الْمُتَّقِينَ﴾، قال: شيءٌ جعله الله لصاحب هذا الأمر.

قال: قلتُ: فهل لذلك حدّ؟ قال: نعم. قلت: وما هو؟ قال: أدنى ما يكون ثُلُثُ الثُلث.

١٧٤. عن محمّد بن مُسلم، عن أبي جعفر عليه السلام، قال: سألتُهُ عن رجل أوصى بماله في سبيل الله.

قال عليه السلام: أعطِه لمن أوصَى له، وإن كان يهوديًّا أو نصرانيًّا، لأنّ الله يقول: ﴿فَمَن بَدَّلَهُ بَعْدَمَا سَمِعَهُ فَإِنَّمَا إِثْمُهُ عَلَى الَّذِينَ يُبَدِّلُونَهُ﴾.

١٧٥. عن أبي سعيد، عن أبي عبدالله عليه السلام، أنه سُئِل عن رجل أوصى في حجّةٍ، فجعلها وصيُّه في نَسَمةٍ. قال: يَغرَمُها وصيّه، ويجعلَها في حجّة كما أوصى، أنّ الله تعالى يقول: ﴿فَمَن بَدَّلَهُ بَعْدَمَا سَمِعَهُ فَإِنَّمَا إِثْمُهُ عَلَى الَّذِينَ يُبَدِّلُونَهُ﴾.

١٧٦. عن مُثنّى بن عبد السلام، عن أبي عبدالله عليه السلام، قال: سألتُه عن رجلٍ أُوصِيَ له بوصيّةٍ، فمات قبل أن يَقْبِضَها، ولم يَتْرُك عَقِبًا. قال: اطلُب له وارثًا أو مَولىً، فادفعها إليه، فإنّ الله تعالى يقول: ﴿فَمَن بَدَّلَهُ بَعْدَمَا سَمِعَهُ فَإِنَّمَا إِثْمُهُ عَلَى الَّذِينَ يُبَدِّلُونَهُ﴾.

them﴿." Then I said, "The man was from Persia and had recently embraced Islam without having identified a next-of-kin or an heir." He said, "Try to find some kin of his, and then if you are still unable to do so, God will know that you have tried and you can give it away in charity."' [2:181]

177. From Muḥammad b. Sūqa[87] who narrated, 'I asked Abū 'Abd Allāh عليه السلام about the verse ﴾*If anyone alters the bequest after hearing it, the guilt of the alteration will fall on them*﴿. He replied, 'It has been abrogated by the verse after it ﴾*But if anyone knows that the testator has made a mistake, or done wrong, and so puts things right between the parties, he will incur no sin*﴿. This means that if the executor [of the will] knows that the testator has made a mistake in the appropriation of the third that he has made a bequest in, and that it would not please God and would be misappropriated, then there is no sin upon the executor to change it to that which is rightful and pleasing to God for a good cause.' [2: 181–2]

178. From Yūnus who, without mentioning his source, cited Abū 'Abd Allāh عليه السلام as having said about the verse ﴾*But if anyone knows that the testator has made a mistake, or done wrong, and so puts things right between the parties, he will incur no sin*﴿, 'This means when he has transgressed beyond the bequest allowed and bequeathed more than a third [of his estate].' [2:182]

179. From al-Barqī, from one of our associates, from Abū 'Abd Allāh عليه السلام, that regarding the verse ﴾*You who believe, fasting is prescribed for you, as it was prescribed for those before you, so that you may be mindful of God*﴿ he said, 'This is specifically for the believers.' [2:183]

180. From Jamīl b. Darrāj who said, 'I asked Abū 'Abd Allāh عليه السلام about the verses ﴾*Fighting has been ordained for you*﴿(2:214) and ﴾*You who believe, fasting is prescribed for you*﴿(2:183). He said, "In all these verses, God addresses everyone including the deviants, the hypocrites and all those who make even a superficial claim to belief."'

87 Muḥammad b. Sūqa, on whom there is virtually no information, is deemed a reliable narrator. See Ḥillī, *Khulāṣat al-aqwāl*, 271 (nr. 981).

قلتُ: إنّ الرَّجُل كان من أهل فارس، دخَل في الإسلام، لم يُسَمِّ، ولا يُعْرَف له وليّ؟ قال: اجْهَد أن تَقْدِر له على وَليّ، فإن لم تَجِده وعَلِم الله مِنك الجَهد تتصدّق بها.

١٧٧. عن محمّد بن سُوقَة، قال: سألتُ أبا جعفر عليه السلام عن قول الله عزّ وجلّ: ﴿فَمَنۢ بَدَّلَهُۥ بَعۡدَمَا سَمِعَهُۥ فَإِنَّمَآ إِثۡمُهُۥ عَلَى ٱلَّذِينَ يُبَدِّلُونَهُۥٓ﴾. قال: نَسَختْها التي بعدها: ﴿فَمَنۡ خَافَ مِن مُّوصٖ جَنَفًا أَوۡ إِثۡمٗا﴾ يعني المُوصي إليه إن خاف جَنَفًا من المُوصي إليه في ثُلثه جميعًا، فيما أوصى به إليه، ممّا لا يرضى الله به من خِلاف الحقّ، فلا إثم على المُوصي إليه أن يُبدّله إلى الحقّ، وإلى ما يرضى الله به من سبيل الخير.

١٧٨. عن يُونُس، رفعه إلى أبي عبد الله عليه السلام، في قوله تعالى: ﴿فَمَنۡ خَافَ مِن مُّوصٖ جَنَفًا أَوۡ إِثۡمٗا فَأَصۡلَحَ بَيۡنَهُمۡ فَلَآ إِثۡمَ عَلَيۡهِۚ﴾. قال: يعني إذا ما اعتدى في الوصيّة وزاد في الثُلُث.

١٧٩. عن البَرْقيّ، عن بعض أصحابنا، عن أبي عبد الله عليه السلام في قوله: ﴿يَٰٓأَيُّهَا ٱلَّذِينَ ءَامَنُواْ كُتِبَ عَلَيۡكُمُ ٱلصِّيَامُ﴾، قال: هي للمؤمنين خاصّة.

١٨٠. عن جَميل بن درّاج، قال: سألتُ أبا عبد الله عليه السلام عن قول الله تبارك وتعالى: ﴿كُتِبَ عَلَيۡكُمُ ٱلۡقِتَالُ﴾ و ﴿يَٰٓأَيُّهَا ٱلَّذِينَ ءَامَنُواْ كُتِبَ عَلَيۡكُمُ ٱلصِّيَامُ﴾، قال: فقال: هذه كلّها تجْمَع الضُّلاّل والمُنافقين وكُلّ من أقرّ الدَّعْوَة الظاهِرَة.

181. From Muḥammad b. Muslim, from Abū Jaʿfar عليه السلام, that with respect to the verse ﴿*For those who can fast only with extreme difficulty, there is a way to compensate – feed a needy person*﴾, he said, 'This refers to the aged person or one who suffers from extreme thirst.' [2:184]

182. From Samāʿa, from Abū Baṣīr who narrated, 'I asked him عليه السلام about the verse ﴿*For those who can fast only with extreme difficulty, there is a way to compensate – feed a needy person*﴾. He said, 'This is the aged person who is unable to fast, and the sick.' [2:184]

183. From Abū Baṣīr who narrated, 'I asked him about a man who is ill from one Ramadan to the next, and is not well enough to fast in between. He said, "He should give charity for every fast missed by feeding a needy person one *mudd* of food, if not wheat then dates. This is as per God's command ﴿*a way to compensate – feed a needy person*﴾. If he can fast the following Ramadan, well and good, but if not then he should wait till the Ramadan after that to make up the fasts. However, if he is still no better in his health by the following Ramadan, then he should give in charity as he did previously, one *mudd* for every fast missed. If he does get better between the two Ramadans, then he should slowly and gradually make up the fasts before the next Ramadan comes, because he has both the fasts to make up as well as the charity to give – he makes up the fasts and gives charity because he lost out on those fasts."' [2:184]

184. From al-ʿAlā, from Muḥammad, from Abū Jaʿfar عليه السلام; he said, 'I asked him about the verse ﴿*For those who can fast only with extreme difficulty, there is a way to compensate – feed a needy person*﴾. He said, 'It is the aged person and the one afflicted with extreme thirst.' [2:184]

185. From Rifāʿa, from Abū ʿAbd Allāh عليه السلام, who said regarding the verse ﴿*For those who can fast only with extreme difficulty, there is a way to compensate – feed a needy person*﴾, '[They are] the pregnant woman who fears harm to her unborn child, and the aged person.' [2:184]

١٨١. عن محمّد بن مسلم، عن أبي جعفر ﷺ، في قوله تعالى: ﴿وَعَلَى الَّذِينَ يُطِيقُونَهُ فِدْيَةٌ طَعَامُ مِسْكِينٍ﴾ قال: الشيخ الكبير، والذي يأخُذُهُ العُطاش.

١٨٢. عن سَماعة، عن أبي بصير، قال: سألتُهُ عن قول الله: ﴿وَعَلَى الَّذِينَ يُطِيقُونَهُ فِدْيَةٌ طَعَامُ مِسْكِينٍ﴾، قال: هو الشيخ الكبير الذي لا يستطيع، والمريض.

١٨٣. عن أبي بصير، قال: سألتُهُ عن رجل مَرِض من رمضان إلى رَمضان قابل، ولم يَصِحّ بينهما، ولم يُطِق الصوم. قال: يَتَصَدّق مكان كلِّ يومٍ أفطر على مسكينٍ مُدّاً من طعام، وإن لم يكن حِنطة فبِمُدٍّ من تَمر، وهو قول الله: ﴿فِدْيَةٌ طَعَامُ مِسْكِينٍ﴾، فإن استطاع أن يصوم رَمَضان الذي يستقبل، وإلاّ فليتربَّص إلى رَمَضان قابِل فيَقضيه، فإن لم يَصِحّ حتّى جاء رمضان قابل، فليتصدّق كما تصدّق مكان كُلّ يوم أفطر مُدّاً، وإن صحّ فيما بين الرّمضانين فتوانى أن يقضيه حتّى جاء الرمضان الآخر، فإنّ عليه الصّوم والصَدَقة جميعًا، يقضي الصّوم ويَتصدّق، من أجل أنّه ضيّع ذلك الصيّام.

١٨٤. عن العلاء، عن محمّد بن مسلم، عن أبي جعفر ﷺ، قال: سألتُهُ عن قول الله: ﴿وَعَلَى الَّذِينَ يُطِيقُونَهُ فِدْيَةٌ طَعَامُ مِسْكِينٍ﴾. قال: الشيخ الكبير، والذي يأخُذُه العُطاش.

١٨٥. عن رِفاعة، عن أبي عبدالله ﷺ، في قوله: ﴿وَعَلَى الَّذِينَ يُطِيقُونَهُ فِدْيَةٌ طَعَامُ مِسْكِينٍ﴾، قال: المرأةُ تخَافُ على وَلَدِها، والشيخُ الكبير.

186. From Muḥammad b. Muslim who narrated, 'I heard Abū Ja'far عليه السلام say, 'There is no blame on the aged person or the one afflicted with extreme thirst if they cannot fast in Ramadan, and each of them should give one *mudd* of food to charity for every fast missed. They do not have to make up the fasts, and if they are unable [to give in charity], then there is no obligation on them.'

187. From al-Ḥārith al-Baṣrī, from Abū 'Abd Allāh عليه السلام who on the last day of Sha'bān said, 'This blessed month has come upon us, in which You revealed the Qur'an, and which You have made a guide for mankind, with clear messages of guidance and distinction [between right and wrong]. So keep us healthy therein, and make it a source of health for us, and welcome it on our behalf, with ease and vitality.'

188. From 'Abdwuss al-'Aṭṭār, from Abū Baṣīr, from Abū 'Abd Allāh عليه السلام who said, 'When the month of Ramadan starts, say "O God, the month of Ramadan has come, and You have made fasting incumbent upon us therein and have revealed the Qur'an as a guide for mankind, with clear messages of guidance and distinction [between right and wrong]. O God, assist us to observe the fasts and accept them from us. Keep us healthy therein and make it a source of health for us, and welcome it on our behalf, with ease and well-being. You have power over all things, most Merciful of all."'

189. From Ibrāhīm, from Abū 'Abd Allāh عليه السلام; he said, 'I made a comment to him about the verse ﴿*It was in the month of Ramadan that the Qur'an was revealed*﴾ as to how the Qur'an was revealed in one month and yet at the same time revealed over the course of twenty years from start to finish. He replied, "The Qur'an came down as a whole unto the Oft-Visited House (*al-bayt al-ma'mūr*) in the month of Ramadan, then it was revealed from there gradually over the course of twenty years. The Prophet ﷺ said, 'The scriptures of Ibrāhīm were revealed on the first night of Ramadan, the Torah on the sixth, the Injīl (Gospel) on the thirteenth, the Zabūr (Psalms) on the eighteenth and the Qur'an on the twenty-fourth night of Ramadan.'" [2:185]

١٨٦. عن محمّد بن مسلم، قال: سَمِعتُ أبا جعفر عليه السلام يقول: الشيخ الكبير، والذي به العُطاش، لا حرَج عليهما أن يُفطرا في رَمضان، وتصدَّق كلُّ واحدٍ منهما في كلّ يومٍ بمُدٍّ من طعام، ولا قَضاء عليهما، وإن لم يَقْدِرا فلا شيء عليهما.

١٨٧. عن الحارث البَصريّ، عن أبي عبد الله عليه السلام، قال: قال في آخر شَعبان: إنّ هذا الشَهر المُبارَك الذي أنزَلتَ فيه القرآن، وجعَلتَه هُدىً للناسِ وبيّناتٍ من الهُدى والفُرقانِ قد حضَر، فسلِّمنا فيه، وسلِّمهُ لنا، وسلِّمه منّا في يُسرٍ منك وعافيةٍ.

١٨٨. عن عَبْدوُس العَطّار، عن أبي بصير، عن أبي عبد الله عليه السلام، قال: إذا حضَر شَهُر رَمَضان، فقُل: اللّهمَّ قد حضَر شهر رَمضان. وقد افترضتَ علينا صِيامه، وأنزَلتَ فيه القُرآن هُدىً للنّاسِ، وبيّناتٍ من الهُدى والفُرقان، اللّهمَّ أعِنّا على صِيامِه وتَقَبّلهُ منّا، وسلِّمنا فيه، وسلِّمه منّا، وسلِّمنا له في يسرٍ منك وعافيةٍ، إنّك على كلّ شيءٍ قدير، يا أرحَمَ الرّاحمين.

١٨٩. عن إبراهيم، عن أبي عبد الله عليه السلام، قال: سألتُهُ عن قوله تبارك وتعالى: ﴿شَهْرُ رَمَضَانَ الَّذِي أُنزِلَ فِيهِ الْقُرآنُ﴾ كيف أُنزِل فيه القُرآن، وإنّما أُنزِل القُرآنُ في عشرينَ سنةً من أوّله إلى آخره؟ فقال عليه السلام: نزل القُرآنُ جُملةً واحدةً في شَهرِ رَمَضان إلى البيت المَعمور، ثمّ أُنزِل من البَيتِ المعمور في طُول عشرين سنةً. ثم قال: قال النّبي صلى الله عليه وآله وسلم: نزلت صُحُف إبراهيم في أوّل ليلةٍ من شَهرِ رَمَضان، وأنزِلَتِ التوراة لستّ مَضَين من شَهرِ رَمَضَان، وأُنزِلَ الإنجيل لثلاث عشر ليلةٍ خَلَت من شَهرِ رَمَضان، وأُنزِلَ الزّبور لثماني عشرة من رَمَضَان، وأُنزِلَ القُرآن لأربع وعشرين من رَمَضان.

190. From Ibn Sinān, from whoever mentioned it saying, 'I asked Abū 'Abd Allāh عليه السلام about the Qur'an and the Criterion (*furqān*) – are they two separate things or one and the same?' He replied, 'The Qur'an is the whole scripture, whereas the Criterion refers to the decisive part of it, the practice of which is incumbent.'

191. From Ṣabbāḥ b. Sayāba who narrated, 'I said to Abū 'Abd Allāh عليه السلام, "Ibn Abī Ya'fūr[88] has requested me to ask you about certain matters." He responded, "What are they?" I said, "He is asking: When the month of Ramadan comes, I am at home but intend to travel, [what do I do]?" He replied, "God says ﴿*So any one of you who is present that month should fast*﴾. So whoever is present at home when the month of Ramadan sets in should not travel, unless it is to go for Hajj or *'umra* or to recuperate property whose loss is feared."' [2:185]

192. From Zurāra, from Abū Ja'far عليه السلام, about the verse ﴿*So any one of you who is present that month should fast, and anyone who is ill or on a journey should make up for the lost days by fasting on other days later. God wants ease for you, not hardship. He wants you to complete the prescribed period and to glorify Him for having guided you, so that you may be thankful*﴾. He said, 'How clear it is for those who comprehend it! Whoever is present when Ramadan comes fasts, and whoever is travelling does not.' [2:185]

193. Regarding the phrase ﴿*he should fast*﴾, Abū 'Abd Allāh عليه السلام said, 'Fasting is a mouth that utters only good.' [2:185]

194. From Abū Baṣīr who narrated, 'I asked Abū 'Abd Allāh عليه السلام about the severity of the illness required for one to eat [rather than fast] as one is supposed to do when travelling, as per the verse ﴿*and anyone who is ill or on a journey should make up for the lost days by fasting on other days later*﴾. He replied, "It is at his discretion and left to him to decide – if he finds himself

88 Abū Muḥammad 'Abd Allāh b. Abī Ya'fūr Wāqid al-'Abdī (d. 131/748), a notable scholar and very reliable companion of Imam Ja'far al-Ṣādiq. See Ḥillī, *Khulāṣat al-aqwāl*, 195 (nr. 610); Modarressi, *Tradition and Survival*, 103–4 (nr. 8).

١٩٠. عن ابن سِنان، عمّن ذكره، قال: سألتُ أبا عبدالله عليه السلام عن القُرآن والفُرقان، أهما شيئان، أو شيء واحد؟ قال: فقال: القُرآن: جُملة الكتاب، والفُرقان: المُحكم الواجب العمل به.

١٩١. عن الصَّبّاح بن سَيابة، قال: قلتُ لأبي عبدالله عليه السلام: إنّ ابن أبي يَعفور أمَرني أن اسألك عن مَسائِل، فقال عليه السلام: وما هي؟ قال: يقول لك: إذا دخل شهر رَمَضان وأنا في منزلي، إلى أن أسافر؟ قال: إنّ الله يقول: ﴿فَمَنْ شَهِدَ مِنكُمُ الشَّهْرَ فَلْيَصُمْهُ﴾ فمن دخل عليه شَهرُ رَمَضان وهو في أهله، فليس له أن يُسافر إلاّ لحجّ أو عُمرة، أو في طلب مالٍ يخاف تَلَفه.

١٩٢. عن زُرارة، عن أبي جعفر عليه السلام، في قوله تعالى ﴿فَمَنْ شَهِدَ مِنكُمُ الشَّهْرَ فَلْيَصُمْهُ﴾، قال: فقال: ما أبيَنَها لمن عَقَلها! قال: من شَهِد رَمَضان فليَصُمهُ، ومن سافَر فيه فليُفطِر.

١٩٣. وقال أبو عبدالله: ﴿فَلْيَصُمْهُ﴾، قال: الصوم فُوهُ لا يتكلّم إلاّ بالخير.

١٩٤. عن أبي بصير، قال: سألتُ أبا عبدالله عليه السلام عن حدّ المرَض الذي يجب على صاحبه فيه الإفطار كما يجب عليه في السفر، في قوله ﴿وَمَن كَانَ مَرِيضًا أَوْ عَلَىٰ سَفَرٍ﴾. قال: هو مؤتَمَنٌ عليه، مفوّض إليه، فإن وجَد ضَعفًا فليُفطِر، وإن وجَد قُوّةً فليصُم، كان المريض على ما كان.

too weak, then he eats, and if he finds himself able to, then he fasts, whatever the illness may be."' [2:185]

195. From Muḥammad b. Muslim, from Abū ʿAbd Allāh عليه السلام who said, 'The Messenger of God ﷺ did not fast on a journey, neither optional fasts nor obligatory ones, but they lie about the Messenger of God ﷺ. This verse came down when he was at Kurāʿ al-Ghamīm[89] at the time of the dawn prayer. So the Prophet ﷺ called for a drink and ordered the people not to fast either. A group of them said, "It is already daylight, so we may as well fast today." So the Messenger of God ﷺ called them 'the rebels', and they continued to be known as such until the Prophet ﷺ passed away.'

196. From [Abū Hamza] al-Thumālī, from Abū Jaʿfar عليه السلام, that he said regarding the verse ﴿*God wants ease for you, not hardship*﴾, 'Ease is ʿAlī عليه السلام, and those two [Abū Bakr and ʿUmar] are hardship, and no one from the progeny of Ādam should acquiesce to the authority of those two.' [2:185]

197. From al-Zuhrī, from ʿAlī b. al-Ḥusayn عليه السلام who said, 'The common folk [i.e. the Ahl al-Sunnah] differ concerning fasting during travel and illness. Some say they should fast and some say they should not. Others say that they can fast if they wish, and not fast if they so wish. We, however, say that in both cases they must not fast, and if one were to fast during illness or travel, then he must still make up for them afterwards, for God has said ﴿*and anyone who is ill or on a journey should make up for the lost days by fasting on other days later. God wants ease for you, not hardship*﴾.' [2:185]

198. From Saʿīd al-Naqqāsh who narrated, 'I heard Abū ʿAbd Allāh عليه السلام say, "ʿĪd al-Fiṭr has a special *takbīr*,[90] but it is recommended to recite privately at sunset on the eve of ʿĪd al-Fiṭr, just before dawn and at dawn, and during the ʿĪd prayer, as per the verse ﴿*He wants you to complete the prescribed period and to glorify Him for having guided you*﴾. The *takbīr* is to say: 'God is greater!

89 Kurāʿ al-Ghamīm is the name of a locality in modern-day Saudi Arabia situated between Mecca and Medina. See Yāqūt al-Ḥamawī, *Muʿjam al-buldān* (Beirut: Dār Ṣādir, 1993), 4:443.

90 *takbīr*: the statement '*Allāhu akbar*' meaning 'God is greater'.

١٩٥. عن محمّد بن مسلم، عن أبي عبدالله عليه السلام، قال: لم يَكُن رسول الله صلى الله عليه وآله يصوم في السفر تطوّعًا ولا فريضةً، يَكْذِبون على رسول الله صلى الله عليه وآله، نزلت هذه الآية ورسول الله صلى الله عليه وآله بِكُرَاعِ الغَمِيم عند صلاة الفجر، فدعا رسول الله صلى الله عليه وآله بإناءٍ فشَرِب، وأمر الناس أن يُفطِروا، فقال قوم: قد توجّه النهار ولوصُمنا يومنا هذا! فسمّاهم رسول الله صلى الله عليه وآله العُصاة، فلم يزالوا يُسمّون بذلك الاسم حتّى قُبِضَ رسول الله صلى الله عليه وآله.

١٩٦. عن الثُّماليّ، عن أبي جعفر عليه السلام، في قول الله تعالى: ﴿يُرِيدُ اللَّهُ بِكُمُ الْيُسْرَ وَلَا يُرِيدُ بِكُمُ الْعُسْرَ﴾ قال اليُسر: عليّ عليه السلام، وفُلان وفُلان العُسر، فمن كان من وُلدِ آدم لم يدخُل في ولاية فُلان وفُلان.

١٩٧. عن الزُّهري، عن عليّ بن الحسين عليه السلام، قال: صوم السَفَر والمرَض، إنّ العامة اختلَفت في ذلك، فقال قوم: يصومُ، وقال قوم: لا يصومُ، وقال قوم: إن شاء صام، وإن شاء أفطر.
وأمّا نحنُ فنقول: يُفطِر في الحالين جميعًا، فإن صامَ في السَّفر أو في المرَض فعليه القضاء، ذلك بأنّ الله يقول: ﴿وَمَن كَانَ مَرِيضًا أَوْ عَلَىٰ سَفَرٍ فَعِدَّةٌ مِّنْ أَيَّامٍ أُخَرَ﴾ إلى آخر قوله تعالى: ﴿يُرِيدُ اللَّهُ بِكُمُ الْيُسْرَ وَلَا يُرِيدُ بِكُمُ الْعُسْرَ﴾.

١٩٨. عن سَعيد النقّاش، قال: سَمِعتُ أبا عبدالله عليه السلام يقول: إنّ في الفِطرِ لتكبيرًا، ولكنّه مَسْتُور، يكبّر في المغرب ليلةَ الفِطر، وفي العَتَمة والفَجر، وفي صلاة العيد، وهو قول الله تبارك وتعالى: ﴿وَلِتُكْمِلُوا الْعِدَّةَ وَلِتُكَبِّرُوا اللَّهَ عَلَىٰ مَا هَدَاكُمْ﴾ والتكبير أن

God is greater! There is no god but God, and God is greater, and to God belongs all praise."'

In another narration from Abū 'Amr, the last *takbīr* is to be recited four times. [2:185]

199. From Ibn Abī 'Umayr, from someone who narrated from Abū 'Abd Allāh عليه السلام who said, 'I said to him, "May I be your ransom – what is being narrated in our midst is that the Prophet ﷺ used to fast for 29 days [in Ramadan] more often than he would fast for 30 days. Is that correct?" He replied, "God has never created a word implying such a thing, and the Prophet ﷺ only ever fasted 30 days, for God has said ﴾*He wants you to complete the prescribed period*﴿ so why would the Messenger of God ﷺ curtail it?"' [2:185]

200. From Sa'īd, from Abū 'Abd Allāh عليه السلام who said, 'There is a *takbīr* to be recited on 'Īd al-Fiṭr.' I asked, 'Is it the same as the *takbīr* on the Day of Sacrifice ['Īd al-Aḍḥā]?' He replied, 'Yes, but it is to be recited privately at the time of the *maghrib* (sunset), *'ishā'* (evening), *fajr* (dawn), *dhuhr* (noon), and *'aṣr* (afternoon) prayers, and during the two units of the 'Īd prayer.'

201. From Ibn Abī Ya'fūr, from Abū 'Abd Allāh عليه السلام who said, regarding the verse ﴾*so let them respond to Me, and believe in Me*﴿, 'They should know that I can give them whatever they ask for.' [2:186]

202. From Samā'a, from Abū 'Abd Allāh عليه السلام; he said, 'I asked him about the verse ﴾*You [believers] are permitted to lie with your wives during the night of the fast: they are [close] as garments to you, as you are to them. God was aware that you were betraying yourselves, so He turned to you in mercy and pardoned you: now you can lie with them – seek what God has ordained for you – eat and drink until the white thread of dawn becomes distinct from the black. Then fast until nightfall*﴿. He said, "It was revealed about Khawwāt b. Jubayr who was with the Messenger of God ﷺ at the trench [during the Battle of Khandaq] and he was fasting. Evening came, and he was still fasting. Before this verse came down, if anyone fell asleep [before breaking his fast] then food became prohibited for him. So Khawwāt went back home to his family when evening fell, and asked for some food. They said, 'Do not go to sleep while we prepare some food for you.' So he sat down but fell asleep. They asked

تقول: الله أكبر، الله أكبر، الله أكبر، لا إله إلا الله، والله أكبر، الله أكبر، ولله الحمد. قال: في رواية أبي عمرو: التكبير الأخير أربع مرّات.

١٩٩. عن ابن أبي عُمير، عن رجل، عن أبي عبد الله ﵇، قال: قلتُ له: جُعِلت فِداك، ما يُتَحَدّث به عندنا أنّ النبي ﷺ صام تِسعة وعِشرين أكثر ممّا صام ثلاثين، أحقٌّ هذا؟ قال: ما خَلَق الله هذا حرْفًا، ما صامَه النّبيّ ﷺ إلاّ ثلاثين، لأنّ الله تعالى يقول: ﴿وَلِتُكْمِلُوا الْعِدَّةَ﴾ فكان رسول الله ﷺ يُنقصه!

٢٠٠. عن سعيد، عن أبي عبد الله ﵇، قال: إنّ في الفِطر تكبيرًا. قال: قلتُ: ما تكبيرٌ إلاّ في يوم النَّحر. قال: فيه تكبيرٌ ولكنّه مستور، في المغرب والعِشاء والفجر والظُّهر والعصر وركعتَي العِيد.

٢٠١. عن ابن أبي يَعفُور، عن أبي عبد الله ﵇، في قوله تبارك وتعالى: ﴿فَلْيَسْتَجِيبُوا لِي وَلْيُؤْمِنُوا بِي﴾ يعلمون أنّي أقدِرُ على أن أُعطِيَهُم ما يسألون.

٢٠٢. عن سَماعة، عن أبي عبد الله ﵇، قال: سألتُهُ عن قول الله عزّ وجلّ: ﴿أُحِلَّ لَكُمْ لَيْلَةَ الصِّيَامِ الرَّفَثُ إِلَى نِسَائِكُمْ هُنَّ لِبَاس﴾ إلى ﴿وَكُلُوا وَاشْرَبُوا﴾. قال: نَزَلت في خوّات بن جُبَير، وكان مع رسول الله ﷺ في الخَنْدَقِ وهو صائم، فأمسى على ذلك، وكانوا من قَبلِ أن تَنزِلَ هذه الآية، إذا نام أحدهُم حُرِّم عليه الطَّعام، فَرَجَعَ خوّات إلى أهله حين أمسى، فقال: عندكم طعام؟ فقالوا: لا تَنَم حتّى نصنعَ لك طعامًا، فاتّكأ فنام، فقالوا: قد فَعَلت؟

him if he had indeed fallen asleep and he said yes. So he slept hungry, woke up the next morning and went to the trench, and fainted. When the Messenger of God ﷺ passed by and saw his state, he asked him what had happened, and the latter informed him. So this verse came down saying ﴾*You [believers] are permitted to lie with your wives during the night of the fast: they are [close] as garments to you, as you are to them. God was aware that you were betraying yourselves, so He turned to you in mercy and pardoned you: now you can lie with them – seek what God has ordained for you – eat and drink until the white thread of dawn becomes distinct from the black*﴿."' [2:187]

203. From Sa'd, from one of his associates, from one of the two [Imams al-Bāqir or al-Ṣādiq ؑ], who was asked about a man who eats *suḥūr*[91] before the fast and doubts whether the time for the dawn prayer has set in or not. He said, 'It does not matter, ﴾*eat and drink until the white thread of dawn becomes distinct from the black*﴿, and I believe that in Ramadan he should exercise caution, and stop eating *suḥūr* before then.' [2:187]

204. From Abū Baṣīr who narrated, 'I asked Abū 'Abd Allāh ؑ about two men who wake up in the month of Ramadan and one says to the other, "It is time for the dawn prayer," while the other says, "I do not see anything [to suggest that]." He replied, "The one who is unconvinced of it being dawn can continue eating, whereas eating is prohibited for the one who sees it as dawn, for God says ﴾*eat and drink until the white thread of dawn becomes distinct from the black. Then fast until nightfall*﴿."' [2:187]

205. From Abū Baṣīr who narrated, 'I asked Abū 'Abd Allāh ؑ about people who are fasting in the month of Ramadan, then dark clouds at sunset lead them to believe that night has fallen in, so they break their fast, or some of them break their fast. Then the clouds disperse in the sky and they realize that the sun had not yet set. He replied, "The one who broke his fast has to make up for it on another day, for God says, ﴾*Then fast until nightfall*﴿. So whoever eats before night has fallen in has to make up the fast because he ate intentionally."' [2:187]

91 The *suḥūr* is a light meal one is recommended to eat in the hours before dawn prior to fasting.

قال: نعم. فباتَ على ذلك وأصبح، فغَدا إلى الخَندَق،فجعل يُغشَى عليه، فمرّ به رسول الله ﷺ، فلمّا رأى الذي به سأله، فأخبره كيف كان أمْره، فنزلَت هذه الآية: ﴿أُحِلَّ لَكُمْ لَيْلَةَ الصِّيَامِ الرَّفَثُ إِلَى نِسَائِكُمْ﴾ إلى ﴿وَكُلُوا وَاشْرَبُوا حَتَّى يَتَبَيَّنَ لَكُمُ الْخَيْطُ الأَبْيَضُ مِنَ الْخَيْطِ الأَسْوَدِ مِنَ الْفَجْرِ﴾.

٢٠٣. عن سَعْد، عن بعض أصحابه، عنهما عليهما السلام، في رَجُلٍ تسحَّر وهو شاكٌّ في الفجر؟ قال: لا بأس: ﴿وَكُلُوا وَاشْرَبُوا حَتَّى يَتَبَيَّنَ لَكُمُ الْخَيْطُ الأَبْيَضُ مِنَ الْخَيْطِ الأَسْوَدِ مِنَ الْفَجْرِ﴾ وأرَى أن يَستَظْهِر في رَمَضان، ويتَسَحرَّ قبل ذلك.

٢٠٤. عن أبي بصير، قال: سألتُ أبا عبدالله عليه السلام عن رَجُلين قاما في شهر رَمَضان، فقال أحدُهما: هذا الفجر، وقال الآخر: ما أرى شيئًا. قال: لِيأكُل الّذي لم يَستَيقِن الفَجر، وقد حُرِّم الأكلُ على الّذي زعَم قد رأى، إنّ الله يقول: ﴿وَكُلُوا وَاشْرَبُوا حَتَّى يَتَبَيَّنَ لَكُمُ الْخَيْطُ الأَبْيَضُ مِنَ الْخَيْطِ الأَسْوَدِ مِنَ الْفَجْرِ ثُمَّ أَتِمُّوا الصِّيَامَ إِلَى اللَّيْلِ﴾.

٢٠٥. عن أبي بَصير، قال: سألتُ أبا عبدالله عليه السلام عن أُناسٍ صاموا في شهر رَمَضان، فَغشِيَهُم سَحَاب أسود عند مَغرب الشَّمس، فظَنّوا أنّه اللّيل، فأفطَروا أو أفطر بعضُهم، ثمّ إنّ السّحاب فَصَل عن السّماء، فإذا الشمس لم تَغِب.

قال: على الّذي أفطر قَضاء ذلك اليوم، إنّ الله يقول: ﴿ثُمَّ أَتِمُّوا الصِّيَامَ إِلَى اللَّيْلِ﴾، فمن أكَلَ قبل أن يَدْخُلَ اللّيل فعليه قَضاؤه، لأنّه أكل مُتعَمِّدًا.

206. From al-Qāsim b. Sulaymān, from Jarrāḥ from al-Ṣādiq عليه السلام who said, 'God, most High, says ﴾ *Then fast until nightfall* ﴿, meaning the fast of Ramadan. So whoever sees the new moon during the day should complete his fast.' [2:187]

207. From Samā'a who said, 'The one who breaks his fast must make up for it because God says, ﴾ *Then fast until nightfall* ﴿. So whoever eats before night has fallen must make up for it because he ate intentionally.' [2:187]

208. From 'Abd Allāh al-Ḥalabī, from Abū 'Abd Allāh عليه السلام; he said, 'I asked him about the meaning of the white thread of dawn becoming distinct from the black. He replied, "The brightness of daylight from the darkness of night."' [2:187]

209. From Ziyād b. 'Īsā who narrated, 'I asked Abū 'Abd Allāh عليه السلام about the verse ﴾ *Do not consume your property wrongfully* ﴿. He replied, "The Quraysh used to gamble with each other, with family and property at stake, so God prohibited them from doing that.' [2:188]

210. From Abū Baṣīr, from Abū 'Abd Allāh عليه السلام; he said, 'I asked him about the verse ﴾ *Do not consume your property wrongfully, nor use it to bribe judges* ﴿. So he replied, "Abū Baṣīr, God knows only too well that there are judges in the community who are unjust. Here He does not mean the equitable judges, but rather those judges who deal unjustly. Abū Muḥammad,[92] Imagine if you had a right over someone that was due to you, whom you invited to settle the matter before an equitable judge. However, he refused unless you agreed to take the case to unjust judges so that they could rule in his favour; then such a person would be among those who take their cases to tyrants."' [2:188]

211. From al-Ḥasan b. 'Alī who narrated, 'I read in a letter that Abū al-Asad[93] wrote to the second Abū al-Ḥasan [i.e. al-Riḍā عليه السلام], as well as the latter's

---

92 One of Abū Baṣīr's agnomens.

93 According to Kishshī, he was among those who narrated from Imam al-Riḍā and was a close companion of 'Alī b. Yaqṭīn. See 'Alī al-Ardabīlī, *Jāmi' al-Ruwāt* (Qum: Manshūrāt Maktabat al-Mar'ashī, 1982), 2:366.

٢٠٦. عن القاسم بن سُليمان، عن جرّاح، عن الصادق ﴿عليه السلام﴾، قال: قول الله تعالى: ﴿ثُمَّ أَتِمُّوا الصِّيَامَ إِلَى اللَّيْلِ﴾ يعني صيام رَمَضان، فمن رأى الهلال بالنهار فليُتِمّ صِيامَه.

٢٠٧. عن سَماعة، قال: على الذي أفطر القَضاء، لأنّ الله تعالى يقول: ﴿ثُمَّ أَتِمُّوا الصِّيَامَ إِلَى اللَّيْلِ﴾ فمن أكل قبل أن يَدخُل الليل، فعليه قَضاؤه، لأنّه أكل مُتعَمّدًا.

٢٠٨. عن عبدالله الحلبي، عن أبي عبدالله ﴿عليه السلام﴾، قال: سألتُهُ عن الخَيطِ الأبيض وعن الخَيْطِ الأَسْوَدِ. فقال: بَياض النّهار من سَواد اللّيل.

٢٠٩. عن زياد بن عيسى، قال: سألتُ أبا عبدالله ﴿عليه السلام﴾ عن قول الله تعالى: ﴿وَلَا تَأْكُلُوا أَمْوَالَكُم بَيْنَكُم بِالْبَاطِلِ﴾، قال: كانت قُرَيش تُقامِرُ الرجُلَ في أهله وماله، فنَهاهم الله.

٢١٠. عن أبي بصير، عن أبي عبدالله ﴿عليه السلام﴾، قال: قلتُ له: قول الله تبارك وتعالى: ﴿وَلَا تَأْكُلُوا أَمْوَالَكُم بَيْنَكُم بِالْبَاطِلِ وَتُدْلُوا بِهَا إِلَى الْحُكَّامِ﴾؟ فقال: يا أبا بصير، إنّ الله قد عَلِمَ أنّ في الأُمّة حُكّامًا يَجُورون، أما إنّه لم يَعْنِ حُكام أهلِ العَدل، ولكنّه عنى حُكّام أهل الجور. يا أبا محمّد، أما إنّه لو كان لك على رجلٍ حقّ، فدعَوْتَه إلى حُكّام أهل العدل، فأبى عليك إلاّ أن يُرافِعك إلى أهل الجَور ليَقضُوا له، كان مِمّن يُحاكم إلى الطاغُوت.

٢١١. عن الحسن بن عليّ، قال: قرأتُ في كتاب أبي الأسد إلى أبي الحسن الثاني ﴿عليه السلام﴾ وجوابه بخَطِّه، سأل ما تفسير قوله تعالى: ﴿وَلَا تَأْكُلُوا أَمْوَالَكُم بَيْنَكُم بِالْبَاطِلِ وَتُدْلُوا بِهَا إِلَى

reply in his own handwriting, where he asked about the meaning of the verse ﴾*Do not consume your property wrongfully, nor use it to bribe judges*﴿. So he عليه السلام wrote back to him saying, "This refers to the judges." Then under it he wrote, "This refers to when a person knows that a judge is unjust and corrupt, in which case he has no excuse to accept a ruling in his favour if he knows full well that he is unjust."' [2:188]

212. From Samāʿa who said, 'I asked Abū ʿAbd Allāh عليه السلام that if a man has just enough money to subsist on and a debt that is due to be paid, does he feed his family first until God gives him prosperity to be able to repay his debt, or does he take on another loan? He said, "He should repay the debt upon him, and not consume others' wealth when he has the means to repay them. God says, ﴾*Do not consume your property wrongfully*﴿."' [2:188]

213. From Abū Usāma Zayd [al-Shaḥḥām] who narrated, 'Abū ʿAbd Allāh عليه السلام was once asked about 'the crescent moons', so he replied, "They are the months, so when you see the crescent, fast, and when you see it [again], stop fasting." I asked, "If the month is twenty-nine days long, does one have to make up that [extra] day?" He replied, "No, unless three just individuals bear witness that they saw the crescent before that, then he has to make up the fast for that day."' [2:189]

214. From Ziyād b. al-Mundhir [=Abū al-Jārūd] who said, 'I heard Abū Jaʿfar عليه السلام say, "Fast when the people fast, and stop fasting when they stop, for God has made the crescent moons appointed times."'

215. From Saʿd, from Abū Jaʿfar عليه السلام; he said, 'I asked him about the verse ﴾*Goodness does not consist of entering houses by the back* [*door*]; *the truly good person is the one who is mindful of God. So enter your houses by their* [*main*] *doors*﴿. He replied, "The family of Muḥammad ﷺ are the doors of God, the path to Him, and the callers to Paradise, who will lead the way to it and guide towards it on the Day of Resurrection."' [2:189]

الْحُكَّامِ﴾؟ قال: فكتب عليه السلام إليه: الحكّام القُضاة، قال: ثمّ كتب تحته: هو أن يعلمَ الرجُل أنّه ظالمٌ عاصٍ، هو غير مَعْذُورٍ في أخذه ذلك الذي حَكَم له به إذا كان قد عَلِم أنّه ظالم.

٢١٢. عن سَماعة، قال: قلتُ لأبي عبدالله عليه السلام: الرجل يكون عنده الشيء يَتَبَلّغ به وعليه الدَّين، أيُطعِمه عِيالَه حتّى يأتيه الله بمَيسَرَة فيقضي دَينه، أو يستقرض على ظهره؟ فقال: يقضي بما عنده دَينه، ولا يأكُلوا أموال الناس إلاّ وعنده ما يُؤدّي إليهم حُقوقهم، إنّ الله تعالى يقول: ﴿وَلَا تَأْكُلُوا أَمْوَالَكُم بَيْنَكُم بِالْبَاطِلِ﴾.

٢١٣. عن زَيد أبي أُسامة، قال: سُئِل أبو عبدالله عليه السلام عن الأهِلّة؟ قال هي الشهور، فإذا رأيتَ الهلال فَصُم، وإذا رأيتَه فأفطِرْ. قلتُ: أرأيتَ إن كان الشهر تِسعة وعشرين، أيُقضى ذلك اليوم؟ قال: لا، إلاّ أن يَشْهَد ثَلاثة عُدول، فإنّهم إن شَهِدوا أنّهم رأوا الهِلال قبل ذلك، فإنّه يُقضى ذلك اليوم.

٢١٤. عن زياد بن المُنذر، قال: سمِعتُ أبا جعفر عليه السلام يقول: صُم حين يَصومُ الناس، وأفْطِرْ حين يُفْطِرُ الناس، فإنّ الله جعل الأهِلّة مواقيت.

٢١٥. عن سَعد، عن أبي جعفر عليه السلام، قال، سألتُهُ عن هذه الآية: ﴿وَلَيْسَ الْبِرُّ بِأَنْ تَأْتُوا الْبُيُوتَ مِنْ ظُهُورِهَا وَلَٰكِنَّ الْبِرَّ مَنِ اتَّقَىٰ وَأْتُوا الْبُيُوتَ مِنْ أَبْوَابِهَا﴾. فقال عليه السلام: آل محمّد صلى الله عليه وآله أبواب الله وسَبيله، والدُّعاة إلى الجَنّة، والقادَة إليها، والأدِلاّء عليها إلى يوم القيامة.

216. From Jābir b. Yazīd, from Abū Jaʿfar عليه السلام who said regarding the verse ﴾*Goodness does not consist of entering houses by the back door*﴿, 'It means to tackle issues head on, whatever they may be.' [2:189]

217. Saʿīd b. Munakhkhal narrated in a report, without mentioning his source, saying, 'The houses refer to the Imams عليهم السلام and the doors are their doorways.'

218. From Jābir, from Abū Jaʿfar عليه السلام who said, regarding the verse ﴾*So enter your houses by their* [*main*] *doors*﴿, 'Tackle issues head on.' [2:189]

219. From al-Ḥasan, the salesman of al-Harawī, who, without mentioning his source, cited one of the two [Imams al-Bāqir or al-Ṣādiq عليهما السلام] as having said regarding the verse ﴾*there can be no* [*further*] *hostility, except towards aggressors*﴿, '[This means] except towards the progeny of the killers of al-Ḥusayn عليه السلام.' [2:193]

220. From al-ʿAlā b. al-Fuḍayl who narrated, 'I asked him about the polytheists and whether the Muslims could initiate an attack on them in the sacred month? So he replied, "[Only] if the polytheists initiate by declaring war against them and the Muslims can see that they will vanquish them otherwise, and this is as per the verse ﴾*A sacred month for a sacred month: violation of sanctity* [*calls for*] *fair retribution*﴿."' [2:194]

221. From Ibrāhīm who said that someone, who narrated from one of the two [Imams] عليهما السلام, reported to him asking about the verse ﴾*there can be no* [*further*] *hostility, except towards aggressors*﴿. He عليه السلام said, 'God is not hostile towards anyone except the descendants of the killers of al-Ḥusayn عليه السلام.' [2:193]

٢١٦. عن جابر بن يزيد، عن أبي جعفر ﵇، في قوله: ﴿وَلَيْسَ الْبِرُّ بِأَنْ تَأْتُوا الْبُيُوتَ مِنْ ظُهُورِهَا﴾ الآية، قال: يعني أن تُأتى الأُمور من وَجْهِها، أيّ الأُمور كان.

٢١٧. قال: وروى سعيد بن مُنَخَّل، في حديث رفعه، قال: البيوت الأئمة ﵈، والأبواب أبوابها.

٢١٨. عن جابر، عن أبي جعفر ﵇: ﴿وَأْتُوا الْبُيُوتَ مِنْ أَبْوَابِهَا﴾، قال: ائتوا الأُمور من وَجْهِها.

٢١٩. عن الحسن بيّاع الهَرَوي، يرفعه، عن أحدهما عليهما السلام، في قوله: ﴿فَلَا عُدْوَانَ إِلَّا عَلَى الظَّالِمِينَ﴾، قال: إلاّ على ذُرّيّة قَتَلة الحسين ﵇.

٢٢٠. عن العَلاء بن الفُضيل، قال: سألتُهُ عن المُشركين، أيبتدئهم المُسلمون بالقِتال في الشّهر الحَرام؟ فقال: إذا كان المُشركون ابتَدءُوهُم باستِحلالِهم، ورأى المُسلمون أنّهم يظهرون عليه فيه، وذلك قوله سبحانه ﴿الشَّهْرُ الْحَرَامُ بِالشَّهْرِ الْحَرَامِ وَالْحُرُمَاتُ قِصَاص﴾.

٢٢١. عن إبراهيم، قال: أخبرني من رَواه عن أحدِهما عليهما السلام، وقال: قلت: ﴿فَلَا عُدْوَانَ إِلَّا عَلَى الظَّالِمِينَ﴾ قال: لا يعتدي الله على أحدٍ إلاّ على نَسلِ وُلد قَتَلة الحسين ﵇.

222. From Ḥammād, the butcher, from Abū 'Abd Allāh ﷺ who said, 'If a man spends everything he has on one of God's causes, he is not considered to have done good nor been successful, for has God not said, ﴿*do not contribute to your destruction with your own hands, but do good, for God loves those who do good*﴾, meaning those who spend moderately.' [2:195]

223. From Ḥudhayfa who narrated ﴿*do not contribute to your destruction with your own hands*﴾ – he ﷺ said, 'This pertains to spending.' [2:195]

224. From Zurāra, from Abū Ja'far ﷺ who said, ''*Umra* is obligatory just like Hajj because God says, ﴿*Complete the pilgrimages, major and minor, for the sake of God*﴾. It is obligatory like the Hajj, and it is sufficient for one to perform the *'umra* with a break from the state of *iḥrām*[94] in between, and the *'umra* performed during the months of Hajj counts as *mut'a*[95].' [2:196]

225. From Zurāra, from Abū 'Abd Allāh ﷺ who said regarding the verse ﴿*Complete the pilgrimages, major and minor, for the sake of God*﴾, 'Completion means to fulfil them both whereby he abstains from all that the *muḥrim*[96] must abstain during both.' [2:196]

226. From Abū 'Ubayda[97], from Abū 'Abd Allāh ﷺ who said regarding the verse ﴿*Complete the pilgrimages, major and minor, for the sake of God*﴾, 'Hajj incorporates all the rituals whereas *'umra* does not require one to leave Mecca.' [2:196]

---

94 The *iḥrām* is a state of ritual consecration upon embarking on the Hajj, during which the pilgrim wears two seamless white sheets, and where worldly things such as women, perfume, and hunting become prohibited during the pilgrimage.

95 The *mut'a* or *tamattu'* of Hajj/*'umra* means 'enjoyment' and refers to the *'umra* (minor pilgrimage) performed upon entering Mecca, after which the pilgrim comes out of the state of *iḥrām*, when women, perfume and other worldly things were prohibited to him. He is free to enjoy them until the days of Hajj start a few days later.

96 The *muḥrim* is a pilgrim in the state of *iḥrām*.

97 Abū 'Ubayda Ziyād b. 'Īsā al-Ḥadhdhā', originally of Kufa, was a reliable narrator of the fifth and sixth Imams. See Ḥillī, *Khulāṣat al-aqwāl*, 148–9 (nr. 427); Modarressi, *Tradition and Survival*, 116–8 (nr. 11).

٢٢٢. عن حمّاد اللحّام، عن أبي عبدالله ﷺ، قال: لو أنّ رجلاً أنفقَ ما في يدَيه في سبيل من سُبُل الله ما كان أحسَنَ ولا وُفّق، أليس الله يقول: ﴿وَلَا تُلْقُوا بِأَيْدِيكُمْ إِلَى التَّهْلُكَةِ وَأَحْسِنُوا إِنَّ اللَّهَ يُحِبُّ الْمُحْسِنِينَ﴾ يعني المُقْتَصِدين.

٢٢٣. عن حُذَيفة، قال: ﴿وَلَا تُلْقُوا بِأَيْدِيكُمْ إِلَى التَّهْلُكَةِ﴾، قال: هذا في النفقة.

٢٢٤. عن زُرارة، عن أبي جعفر ﷺ، قال: إنّ العُمرة واجبةٌ بمنزلة الحجّ لأنّ الله تعالى يقول: ﴿وَأَتِمُّوا الْحَجَّ وَالْعُمْرَةَ لِلَّهِ﴾ ما ذلك؟ هي واجبةٌ مثل الحَجّ، ومن تمتّع أجزأته، والعُمرة في أشهر الحَجّ مُتعةٌ.

٢٢٥. عن زُرارة، عن أبي عبدالله ﷺ، في قوله تعالى: ﴿وَأَتِمُّوا الْحَجَّ وَالْعُمْرَةَ لِلَّهِ﴾، قال: إتمامُها إذا أدّاهُما، يتّقي ما يتّقي المُحرِم فيهما.

٢٢٦. عن أبي عُبيدة، عن أبي عبدالله ﷺ، في قول الله: ﴿وَأَتِمُّوا الْحَجَّ وَالْعُمْرَةَ لِلَّهِ﴾، قال: الحَجّ جَميع المَناسك، والعُمرة لا يُجاوز بها مكّة.

227. From Yaʿqūb b. Shuʿayb, from Abū ʿAbd Allāh عليه السلام, 'I asked him about the verse ﴾*Complete the pilgrimages, major and minor, for the sake of God*﴿ – does it suffice for a man to perform the *ʿumra* with a break joining it to the Hajj, instead of performing a separate *ʿumra* by itself?' He replied, 'Yes, that is how the Messenger of God ﷺ commanded it to be.' [2:196]

228. From Muʿāwiya b. ʿAmmār al-Duhānī[98], from Abū ʿAbd Allāh عليه السلام who said, '*ʿUmra* is obligatory on people just like Hajj because God says, ﴾*Complete the pilgrimages, major and minor, for the sake of God*﴿. The command to perform *ʿumra* came down in Medina, and the best time to perform *ʿumra* is in the month of Rajab.' [2:196]

229. From Abān, from al-Faḍl Abū al-ʿAbbās;[99] He عليه السلام said regarding the verse ﴾*Complete the pilgrimages, major and minor, for the sake of God*﴿, 'They are both incumbent.' [2:196]

230. From Zurāra, Ḥumrān and Muḥammad b. Muslim, on the authority Abū Jaʿfar and Abū ʿAbd Allāh عليه السلام; they said, 'We asked them both about the verse ﴾*Complete the pilgrimages, major and minor, for the sake of God*﴿, to which they said, "The completion of the Hajj and the *ʿumra* means to refrain from indecent speech, misbehaviour and quarrelling [for that duration]."' [2:196]

231. From ʿAbd Allāh b. Farqad, from Abū Jaʿfar عليه السلام who said, 'The sacrificial animal can be a camel, a cow, or a sheep, and it does not become obligatory until it is decorated, meaning it is garlanded; then it becomes obligatory [to sacrifice it].' He continued, ﴾*then [send] whatever offering for sacrifice you can afford*﴿ such as an ewe.' [2:196]

---

98 Abū al-Qāsim Muʿāwiya b. ʿAmmār b. Abī Muʿāwiya (=Khabbāb) b. ʿAbd Allāh al-Duhānī (d. 175/791–2) was a prominent figure of the Kufan Shīʿī community and a highly venerated narrator of the Imams' traditions. See Ḥillī, *Khulāṣat al-aqwāl*, 273–4 (nr. 995); Modarressi, *Tradition and Survival*, 327–32 (nr. 143).

99 Other sources quote it from al-Faḍl b. Abī al-ʿAbbās or Abū al-Faḍl b. Abī al-ʿAbbās, but the above selection in the text seems most likely, as Abū al-ʿAbbās was the agnomen used for al-Faḍl al-Baqbāq who narrated from al-Ṣādiq; see Khūʾī, *Muʿjam*, 14:299 (no. 9354).

٢٢٧. عن يعقوب بن شُعيب، عن أبي عبدالله عليه السلام ﴿وَأَتِمُّوا الْحَجَّ وَالْعُمْرَةَ لِلَّهِ﴾، قُلتُ: يكتَفي الرجل إذا تمتّع بالعُمرة إلى الحجّ مكان ذلك العُمرة المُفرَدة؟ قال: نعم، كذلك أمر رسول الله صلى الله عليه وآله.

٢٢٨. عن مُعاوية بن عمّار الدُّهنيّ، عن أبي عبدالله عليه السلام، قال: إنّ العُمرَة واجبةٌ على الخَلق بمنزِلَة الحَجّ، لأنّ الله تعالى يقول: ﴿وَأَتِمُّوا الْحَجَّ وَالْعُمْرَةَ لِلَّهِ﴾ وإنّما نزَلتِ العمرةُ بالمدينة، وأفضَل العُمرَة عُمرة رَجَب.

٢٢٩. عن أبان، عن الفضل أبي العبّاس في قوله تعالى: ﴿وَأَتِمُّوا الْحَجَّ وَالْعُمْرَةَ لِلَّهِ﴾ قال: هما مفروضان.

٢٣٠. عن زُرارة وحُمران ومحمّد بن مسلم، عن أبي جعفر وأبي عبدالله عليهما السلام، قالوا: سألناهما عن قوله تعالى: ﴿وَأَتِمُّوا الْحَجَّ وَالْعُمْرَةَ لِلَّهِ﴾. قالا: فإنّ تمام الحَجّ والعُمرة أن لا يَرفُثَ، ولاَ يفسُق، ولا يجادِل.

٢٣١. عن عبدالله بن فرقَد، عن أبي جعفر عليه السلام، قال: الهَدْي من الإبل والبَقَر والغَنَم، ولا يَجِبُ حتّى يُعلَّقَ عليه – يعني إذا قَلّده فقد وَجب – وقال: ﴿فَمَا اسْتَيْسَرَ مِنَ الْهَدْيِ﴾ شاة.

232. From al-Ḥalabī, from Abū ʿAbd Allāh ﵇, that he said regarding the verse ﴾*If you are prevented [from doing so], then [send] whatever offering for sacrifice you can afford*﴿, 'An ewe is enough, but a fattened camel or a cow is better.' [2:196]

233. From Abū Usāma Zayd [b. Shahhām] who narrated, 'Abū ʿAbd Allāh ﵇ was asked about a man who sends a sacrificial animal with pilgrims [on his behalf] and fixes an appointed day with them when they will be garlanding their animals and entering the state of *iḥrām*. He replied, "The same things that are prohibited to them in the state of *iḥrām* apply to him on the appointed day, until the animal is sacrificed." Then I asked, "What if they end up changing the designated time or get delayed on the way, would it be a sin for him to come out of the state of *iḥrām* on the day that they had agreed?" He replied, "No."'

234. From al-Ḥalabī, from Abū ʿAbd Allāh ﵇ who narrated, 'The Messenger of God ﷺ left to go on his farewell pilgrimage [before his passing away] about four days before the end of the month of Dhū l-Qaʿda, until he reached al-Shajara.[100] He performed two units of prayer there, then drove his mount until al-Baydāʾ[101] and entered the state of *iḥrām* from there, commencing the glorifications of God specific to Hajj. He drove one hundred bulls and made all the people enter the state of *iḥrām* from there, who neither made an intention for *ʿumra* nor knew anything about the *mutʿa* [break between *ʿumra* and Hajj]. When the Messenger of God ﷺ reached Mecca, he circumambulated the Kaʿba and so did the people accompanying him. Then he performed two units of prayer at the Station of Ibrāhīm ﵇, and saluted the Black Stone, then said, "I begin with what God initiated." Then he went to Ṣafā and started from there, and circulated between Ṣafā and Marwa. When he had completed his rounds, he ended up at Marwa and stood to address his companions, commanding them to come out of the state of *iḥrām*, and

100 Literally 'the tree', it is today known as Masjid al-Shajara (the Mosque of the Tree). This was originally an acacia tree at Dhū l-Ḥulayfa, and the Prophet it is said used to stop there on his way from Medina to Mecca and enter the state of *iḥrām* from there. It lies about six kilometers from Medina. See Ḥamawī, *Muʿjam al-buldān*, 3:323.

101 Al-Baydāʾ is the name of a flat area of land between Mecca and Medina, but closer to Mecca. See Yāqūt al-Ḥamawī, *Muʿjam al-buldān*, 1:523.

٢٣٢ . عن الحلبيّ، عن أبي عبدالله عليه السلام، في قوله ﴿فَمَا اسْتَيْسَرَ مِنَ الْهَدْيِ﴾، قال: يُجزيه شاة، والبَدنَة والبَقَرة أفضل.

٢٣٣ . عن زيد أبي أُسامة، قال: سُئل أبو عبدالله عليه السلام عن رجُلٍ بعثَ بِهَدي مع قَومٍ يُساق، فواعَدهم يوم يُقَلّدون فيه هَديَهم ويُحرِمون فيه؟ قال: يُحرِّم عليه ما يُحرّم على المُحرِمِ في اليوم الذي واعَدَهم حتّى يَبْلُغ الهَديُ مَحِلّه.

قلتُ: أرأيتَ إن اختَلفوا في ميعادِهم، أو أبطئُوا في السَّير، عليه جُناح أن يُحِلّ في اليوم الذي واعدهم؟ قال: لا.

٢٣٤ . عن الحلبيّ، عن أبي عبدالله عليه السلام، قال: خرج رسول الله صلى الله عليه وآله حين حَجّ حِجّة الوَداع، خرج في أربع بقين من ذي القعدة حتّى أتى الشَجَرة فصلّى، ثم قادَ راحِلته، حتّى أتى البَيْداء فأحرم، وأهلَّ بالحَجّ، وساق مائة بَدَنة، وأحرَم الناس كُلهم بالحجّ، لا يُريدون عُمرةً، ولا يدرون ما المُتعَة، حتّى إذا قَدِم رسول الله صلى الله عليه وآله مكّة، طافَ بالبيت، وطاف الناسُ معه، ثمّ صلّى عند مقام إبراهيم عليه السلام فاستلم الحجر، ثمّ قال أبدأ بما بدأ الله به ثمّ أتى الصَّفَا فبدأ بها، ثمّ طاف بين الصَّفا والمَرْوَة، فلمّا قضى طَوافَه ختم بالمَرْوَة، قام يَخْطُبُ أصحابه، وأمرهم أن يُحِلّوا ويجعَلوها عُمرةً، وهو شيء أمر الله به، فأحَلّ الناس.

وقال رسول الله صلى الله عليه وآله: لو كنتُ استقبلتُ من أمري ما استَدْبرتُ، لفعلتُ ما أمرتكُم، ولم يكُن يستطيع أن يُحِلّ من أجل الهَدي الذي معه، لأنّ الله يقول: ﴿وَلَا تَحْلِقُوا رُءُوسَكُمْ حَتَّىٰ يَبْلُغَ الْهَدْيُ مَحِلَّهُ﴾. فقال سُراقة بن جُعشُم الكِنانيّ: يا رسول الله،

to designate it as an *'umra*, for it was something that God had commanded. Thus the people came out of the state of *iḥrām*.

The Messenger of God ﷺ said, "If I could carry out this rite instead of delaying it, I would do exactly what I have told you to do," as he could not come out of the state of *iḥrām* because the animals that were with him had not yet been sacrificed, because God says ﴾ *and do not shave your heads until the offering has reached the place of sacrifice* ﴿. So Surāqa b. Ju'shum al-Kināni asked him, "O Messenger of God, you have indeed taught us our religion [gradually] like we are new-borns. This ruling that you have commanded us, is it only applicable this year or every year henceforth?" The Messenger of God ﷺ replied, "No, forever and ever."' [2:196]

235. From Ḥarīz, from whoever reported it from Abū 'Abd Allāh عليه السلام regarding the verse ﴾ *If any of you is ill, or has an ailment of the scalp* ﴿, he عليه السلام said, 'The Messenger of God ﷺ saw Ka'b b. 'Ujra[102] with lice falling out of his head while he was in the state of *iḥrām*, so he asked him, "Are these critters irritating you?"[103] He replied, "Yes." Then God revealed this verse ﴾ *If any of you is ill, or has an ailment of the scalp, he should compensate by fasting, or feeding the poor, or offering sacrifice* ﴿. Hence the Messenger of God ﷺ commanded him to shave off his head [while still in the state of *iḥrām*] and compensate by either fasting for three days, or feeding six poor people two *mudd* of food each, or sacrificing an ewe.' [2:196]

He also narrated, 'Abū 'Abd Allāh عليه السلام said, "Everything in the Qur'an that has the clause 'or', one is free to choose between the options given. Everything is found in the Qur'an, and if at first he does not find it he must strive until he does."'

236. From Abū Baṣīr, from one of the Imams عليه السلام who said, 'If you come out of the state of *iḥrām* as *mut'a* between *'umra* and Hajj, then you must sacrifice

---

102 Ka'b b. 'Ujra b. Umayya b. 'Udayy al-Balawī was an ally of the *ansār* and a companion of the Prophet, with the agnomen Abū Muḥammad. He witnessed all the major events and lived in Kufa. He died in Medina in the year 51 AH. See Ibn al-Athīr, *Usd al-ghāba fī ma'rifat al-ṣaḥāba* (Beirut: Dār Ibn Ḥazm, 2012) 4:243 (henceforth shortened to *Usd al-ghāba*); Ibn al-Athīr, *al-Kāmil fī al-tārīkh*, (Beirut: Dār Ṣādir, 1981), 3:191 and 492.

103 While in the state of *iḥrām* it is prohibited to kill any living creature, or to scratch the skin vigorously.

عُلّمنا ديننا كأنّما خُلقنا اليوم، أرأيتَ لهذا الذي أمرتنا به لعامِنا هذا أو لِكُلِّ عام؟ فقال رسول الله ﷺ: لا بل لأبد الأبد.

٢٣٥. عن حَريز، عمّن رواه، عن أبي عبدالله عليه السلام، في قول الله تبارك وتعالى: ﴿فَمَن كَانَ مِنكُم مَّرِيضًا أَوْ بِهِۦٓ أَذًى مِّن رَّأْسِهِۦ﴾. قال: مرّ رسول الله ﷺ على كَعب بن عُجْرَة، والقمل يتناثر من رأسه وهو مُحرم، فقال له: أتؤذيك هوامُّك؟ قال: نعم، فأُنزِلت هذه الآية: ﴿فَمَن كَانَ مِنكُم مَّرِيضًا أَوْ بِهِۦٓ أَذًى مِّن رَّأْسِهِۦ فَفِدْيَةٌ مِّن صِيَامٍ أَوْ صَدَقَةٍ أَوْ نُسُكٍ﴾. فأمره رسول الله ﷺ أن يَحلِق رأسه، وجعل الصيام ثلاثة أيّام، والصدقة على ستّة مساكين، مُدَّين لِكلّ مسكين، والنُّسك شاة. قال: وقال أبو عبدالله عليه السلام: كلّ شيء في القرآن (أو) فصاحبُه بالخِيار يختار ما يشاء، وكلّ شيء في القرآن (فإن لم يَجِد) فعليه ذلك.

٢٣٦. عن أبي بصير، عنه عليه السلام، قال: إن استَمْتَعتَ بالعُمرة إلى الحجّ، فإنّ عليك الهَدي ﴿فَمَا اسْتَيْسَرَ مِنَ الْهَدْيِ﴾ إمّا جَزُور، وإمّا بقرة، وإمّا شاة، فإن لم تَقدِر فعليكَ الصِّيام كما قال الله.

﴾*whatever offering for sacrifice you can afford*﴿, either a she-camel, a cow or an ewe. If you cannot afford it, then you must fast as God has commanded.' [2:196]

237. Abū Baṣīr also mentioned this on his authority, 'The command for *mut'a* was revealed to the Messenger of God ﷺ while he was on the mount of Marwa having already completed the *sa'ī*.'

238. From Mu'āwiya b. 'Ammār, from Abū 'Abd Allāh عليه السلام who said regarding the verse ﴾*When you are in safety, anyone wishing to take a break between the minor pilgrimage and the major one must make whatever offering he can afford*﴿, 'It should be a plump ram, and if he does not have one then a calf, though a ram is better. If he does not find a young ram then an older one, and when even this is not possible then the most affordable sacrificial animal would be an ewe.' [2:196]

239. From 'Abd al-Raḥmān b. al-Ḥajjāj who narrated, 'I was standing in prayer and unbeknownst to me Abū al-Ḥasan Mūsā b. Ja'far عليه السلام was sitting ahead of me. Then 'Abbād al-Baṣrī came and greeted him, sat down beside him and asked, "O Abū al-Ḥasan, what do you say about a man who takes a break between Hajj and *'umra* but does not have an animal to sacrifice?"

He replied, "He must fast for the three days that God has commanded."'

As he continued I started listening to their conversation, and 'Abbād asked, "Which days are they?"

He عليه السلام replied, "The day before *tarwiya,*[104] the day of *tarwiya*, and the day of 'arafa."[105]

He then asked, "And if he misses them?"

He replied, "Then he fasts the day of *ḥaṣba*[106] and the two days after it."

---

104 The day of *tarwiya* (lit. quenching) is the 8th day of Dhū l-Ḥijja when pilgrims quench themselves and make preparations to go onwards to Mina for the rites of Hajj the next day.

105 The day of 'arafa is the 9th day of Dhū l-Ḥijja and is the day which marks the beginning of the actual Hajj when pilgrims spend the day in Mina on the outskirts of Mecca, fulfilling the rites of Hajj.

106 The day of *ḥaṣba* is the 14th of Dhū l-Ḥijja.

٢٣٧. وذكر أبو بصير، عنه ﷷ، قال: نزلت على رسول الله ﷺ المُتعَة وهو على المَروة بعد فَراغِه من السّعي.

٢٣٨. عن مُعاوية بن عمار، عن أبي عبد الله ﷷ في قوله: ﴿فَمَن تَمَتَّعَ بِالْعُمْرَةِ إِلَى الْحَجِّ فَمَا اسْتَيْسَرَ مِنَ الْهَدْيِ﴾، قال: ليَكُن كَبشًا سمينًا، فإن لم يَجد فعِجْلاً من البَقَر، والكبش أفضل، فإن لم يَجِد فمُوجَأً من الضأن، وإلاّ ما استَيْسَرَ من الهَدي شاة.

٢٣٩. عن عبد الرّحمن بن الحجّاج، قال: كنتُ قائمًا أُصلّي، وأبو الحسن موسى بن جعفر ﷷ قاعدًا قُدّامي، وأنا لا أعلم، قال: فجاء عبّاد البصري، فسلّم عليه، وجَلَس وقال: يا أبا الحسن، ما تقول في رجُل تمتّع ولم يَكن له هَدْي؟ قال: يصوم الأيّام الّتي قال الله.

قال: فجَعلتُ سمعي إليهما، قال عبّاد: وأيّ أيّام هي؟

قال: قبل التَّروِيَة، ويوم التروية، ويوم عَرَفَة.

قال: فإن فاته؟

قال: يصوم صبيحة الحَصبة ويومين بعده.

قال: أفلا تقول كما قال عبد الله بن الحسن؟

قال: قال: يصوم أيّام التَشريق.

قال: إنّ جعفرًا ﷷ كان يقول: إنّ رسول الله ﷺ أمر بلالاً ينادي: أنّ هذه أيّام أكلٍ وشِرب، فلا يَصومَنَّ أحد.

So he asked, "Do you not say the same thing as ʿAbd Allāh b. al-Ḥasan then?"

"And what is it that he says?" He عليه السلام asked.

He replied, "That he must fast the days of *tashrīq*."[107]

He said, "Jaʿfar عليه السلام used to say, 'The Messenger of God ﷺ requested Bilāl to announce that these were the days of feasting and that no one should fast.'"

So ʿAbbād then said, "Abū al-Ḥasan, God says ﴾*If he lacks the means, he should fast for three days during the pilgrimage, and seven days on his return, making ten days in all*﴿."

So he replied, "Jaʿfar عليه السلام used to say, 'Dhū l-Qaʿda and Dhū l-Ḥijja are both the months of Hajj.'" [2:196]

240. From Manṣūr b. Ḥāzim, from Abū ʿAbd Allāh عليه السلام who said, 'If someone takes a break between *ʿumra* and Hajj and does not have an animal to sacrifice, he must fast the day before *tarwiya*, the day of *tarwiya*, and the day of ʿarafa. If he does not fast these three days, then he should fast [any other days] in Mecca. However, if he is in a hurry, he can fast on the way. If he is staying in Mecca for a while before heading back home, then he can fast the seven there if he wishes to.'

241. From Ribʿī b. ʿAbd Allāh b. al-Jārūd[108] who narrated the following from Abū al-Ḥasan عليه السلام: 'I asked him about the verse: ﴾*he should fast for three days during the pilgrimage*﴿. He عليه السلام answered, "He should fast the day before *tarwiya*, the day of *tarwiya*, and the day of ʿarafa. If he misses these, then he can make up for them during the rest of Dhū l-Ḥijja, for God has stated ﴾*The pilgrimage takes place during the prescribed months*﴿."' [2:196]

---

107 The days of *tashrīq* are the 11– 13th Dhū l-Ḥijja, the days immediately following the Hajj when people are free to eat the meat that they have sacrificed.

108 Abū Nuʿaym Ribʿī b. ʿAbd Allāh b. al-Jārūd b. Abī Sabra al-Hadhalī, a reliable narrator of Imam Jaʿfar al-Ṣādiq and Imam Mūsā al-Kāẓim, and a close associate of al-Fuḍayl b. Yasār from whom he took the majority of his traditions. See Ḥillī, *Khulāṣat al-aqwāl*, 146 (nr. 410); Modarressi, *Tradition and Survival*, 361–2 (nr. 175).

فقال: يا أبا الحسن، إنّ الله قال: ﴿فَصِيَامُ ثَلَاثَةِ أَيَّامٍ فِي الْحَجِّ وَسَبْعَةٍ إِذَا رَجَعْتُمْ﴾، قال: كان جعفر ﷺ يقول: ذو القَعدة وذو الحِجّة كلتين أشهر الحجّ.

٢٤٠. عن مَنصور بن حازم، عن أبي عبدالله ﷺ، قال: إذا تمتّع بالعُمرة إلى الحَجّ ولم يكن معه هَدي، صام قبل التّروية، ويوم التّروية ويوم عَرَفَة، فإن لم يَصُم هذه الأيّام صام بمكّة، فإن أعجلوا صام في الطريق، وإن أقام بمكّة قدر مسيره إلى منزلة فشاء أن يصوم السبعة الأيّام فَعَل.

٢٤١. عن ربعي بن عبدالله بن الجارود، عن أبي الحسن ﷺ، قال: سألته عن قول الله عزّ وجلّ: ﴿فَصِيَامُ ثَلَاثَةِ أَيَّامٍ فِي الْحَجِّ﴾. قال: قبل التّروية يصوم، ويوم التّروية، ويوم عرفة، فمن فاته ذلك فليَقضِ ذلك في بقيّة ذي الحجّة، فإنّ الله تعالى يقول في كتابه: ﴿الْحَجُّ أَشْهُرٌ مَعْلُومَاتٌ﴾.

242. From Mu'āwiya b. 'Ammār, from Abū 'Abd Allāh عليه السلام who said regarding the verse ﴾*he should fast for three days during the pilgrimage, and seven days on his return*﴿, 'When you return to your family.' [2:196]

243. From Ḥafṣ b. al-Bakhtarī[109], from Abū 'Abd Allāh عليه السلام who was asked about an individual who did not perform the three fasts in Dhū l-Ḥijja until the next month had set in. He said, 'He must offer a sacrifice, for God says, ﴾*he should fast for three days during the pilgrimage*﴿ in Dhū l-Ḥijja.' Ibn Abī 'Umayr said, 'He no longer has to fast the seven days [after the sacrifice].' [2:196]

244. From 'Alī b. Ja'far who narrated the following from his brother Mūsā b. Ja'far عليه السلام: 'I asked him about fasting the three days in Hajj, and then seven afterwards, whether one must fast them all consecutively or separate between them both? He replied, "He should fast the three together and the seven altogether, but should not combine the three and the seven days consecutively."'

245. From 'Alī b. Ja'far, from his brother [Mūsā b. Ja'far]. He said, 'I asked him about fasting the three days in Hajj, and then seven afterwards, whether one should fast them consecutively or separate between the two? He replied, "He should fast each of the three days and the seven days altogether without a gap, but not combine the three days and the seven days altogether consecutively."'

246. From 'Abd al-Raḥmān b. Muḥammad al-'Arzamī[110], from Abū 'Abd Allāh عليه السلام from his father from 'Alī عليه السلام regarding the three days of fasting during Hajj.

---

109 Ḥafṣ b. al-Bakhtarī, resident of Baghdad but originally of Kufa, was a reliable narrator of the sixth and seventh Imams' traditions. He was accused by the prominent Kufan Shī'ī family of the Āl A'yan clan of lacking religiosity and judicious temperament as evinced by his fondness of playing chess. Najāshī claims that this allegation was motivated by personal grudge. See Ḥillī, *Khulāṣat al-aqwāl*, 128 (nr. 335); Modarressi, *Tradition and Survival*, 230–1 (nr. 66).

110 Abū Muḥammad 'Abd al-Raḥmān b. Muḥammad b. 'Ubayd Allāh al-Fazārī al-'Arzamī, a narrator of Imam Ja'far al-Ṣādiq with Shī'ī symphathies. See Modarressi, *Tradition and Survival*, 174–5 (nr. 25).

٢٤٢. عن معاوية بن عمّار، عن أبي عبد الله عليه السلام، في قول الله: ﴿فَصِيَامُ ثَلَاثَةِ أَيَّامٍ فِي الْحَجِّ وَسَبْعَةٍ إِذَا رَجَعْتُمْ﴾، قال: إذا رجعتَ إلى أهلك.

٢٤٣. عن حَفْص بن البختريّ، عن أبي عبد الله عليه السلام، فيمَن لم يصُم الثلاثة الأيام في ذي الحجّة حتّى يهِلّ الهلال؟ قال عليه السلام: عليه دَم، لأنّ الله سبحانه وتعالى يقول: ﴿فَصِيَامُ ثَلَاثَةِ أَيَّامٍ فِي الْحَجِّ﴾ في ذي الحجّة. قال ابن أبي عُمير: وسقط عنه السبعة الأيّام.

٢٤٤. عن عليّ بن جعفر، عن أخيه موسى بن جعفر عليهما السلام، قال: سألتُه عن صوم ثلاثة أيّام في الحجّ والسبعة، أيَصومها مُتوالية، أم يفرّق بينهما؟ قال: يصوم الثلاثة لا يفرّق بينها، ولا يجمع الثلاثة والسبعة جميعًا.

٢٤٥. عن عليّ بن جعفر، عن أخيه عليه السلام، قال: سألتُه عن صوم الثلاثة الأيّام في الحجّ والسبعة، أيَصومهما متوالية أو يفرّق بينهما؟ قال: يصوم الثلاثة والسبعة لا يُفرّق بينها، ولا يجمع السبعة والثلاثة جميعًا.

٢٤٦. عن عبد الرّحمن بن محمّد العَرزميّ، عن أبي عبد الله، عن أبيه، عن علي عليه السلام، في صيام ثلاثة أيّام في الحجّ، قال: قبل الترّوية بيومٍ، ويوم الترّوية، ويوم عَرفة، فإن فاتَه ذلك تَسحّر ليلة الحَصبة.

He عليه السلام said, '[They are] the day before *tarwiya*, the day of *tarwiya*, and the day of 'arafa. If he misses them, he should wake up before the dawn of the 14th day (*al-ḥaṣba*) intending to fast.'

247. From Ghiyāth b. Ibrāhīm[111], on his father's authority, from 'Alī عليه السلام who said, 'The three days of fasting during the Hajj are the day before *tarwiya*, the day of *tarwiya*, and the day of 'arafa. If he misses them, he should wake up before dawn of the 14th day (*al-ḥaṣba*) and fast for three [consecutive] days, then seven when he returns home.'

248. He also narrated that 'Alī عليه السلام said, 'If a person misses these fasts, then he should start fasting from the eve of *al-nafar*[112].'

249. From Ibrāhīm b. Abī Yaḥyā, from Abū 'Abd Allāh عليه السلام, on his father's authority, from 'Alī عليه السلام who said, 'Anyone who takes a break between *'umra* and Hajj should fast on the day before *tarwiya*, the day of *tarwiya*, and the day of 'arafa, and if he fails to fast the three days during the Hajj and has no animal to sacrifice, then he should fast straight after the days of *tashrīq*, wake up to eat before dawn on the day of the fourteenth (*al-ḥaṣba*), and fast from that morning.'

250. From Ḥarīz, from Zurāra who said, 'I asked Abū Ja'far عليه السلام about the meaning of the verse ﴿ *This applies to those whose household is not near the Sacred Mosque* ﴾. He replied, "This is referring to those whose households are in Mecca and to whom the rule of *mut'a* does not apply; and nor do they perform *'umra*." I asked, "What is the boundary of that [area]?" He replied, "It is forty-eight miles from the boundaries of Mecca itself, and thus includes everyone within 'Usfān and Dhāt 'Irq, and these are the people whose households are 'near' the Sacred Mosque."' [2:196]

---

111 A reference possibly to Abū Muḥammad Ghiyāth b. Ibrāhīm al-Tamīmī al-Dārimī al-Asbadhī, a Zaydī transmitter of Imam Ja'far al-Ṣādiq's narrations. There are however multiple entires under the name Ghiyāth b. Ibrāhīm in Shī'ī *rijāl* works. See Modarressi, *Tradition and Survival*, 227–30 (nr. 65).

112 The day of *nafar* is synonymous with the day of *ḥaṣba*, when people finally depart from Mina to Mecca.

٢٤٧. عن غياث بن إبراهيم، عن أبيه، عن علي عليه السلام قال: صيام ثلاثة أيّام في الحجّ: قبل التّروية بيوم، ويوم التّروية، ويوم عَرفة، فإن فاته ذلك تَسحّر ليلة الحَصبة، فصِيام ثلاثة أيّام، وسبعة إذا رجع.

٢٤٨. وقال: قال عليّ عليه السلام: إذا فات الرّجل الصيام، فليبدأ صيامه من ليلة النّفر.

٢٤٩. عن إبراهيم بن أبي يحيى، عن أبي عبدالله، عن أبيه، عن عليّ عليه السلام، قال: يصوم المتَمتّع قبل التّروية بيوم، ويوم التّروية، ويوم عَرفة، فإن فاته أن يصوم ثلاثة أيّام في الحجّ ولم يكن عنده دمٌ، صام إذا انقضت أيّام التّشريق، يتَسحّر ليلة الحَصبة ثمّ يُصبح صائمًا.

٢٥٠. عن حَريز، عن زُرارة، قال: سألت أبا جعفر عليه السلام عن قول الله تعالى: ﴿ذَٰلِكَ لِمَن لَّمْ يَكُنْ أَهْلُهُ حَاضِرِي الْمَسْجِدِ الْحَرَامِ﴾؟ قال: هؤلاء أهل مكّة، ليست لهم مُتعةٌ، ولا عليهم عُمرة.

قلت: فما حدّ ذلك؟ قال: ثمانية وأربعين ميلاً من نواحي مكّة، كلّ شيءٍ دون عُسفَان دون ذات عِرق فهو من حاضري المسجد الحرام.

251. From Ḥammād b. ʿUthmān, from Abū ʿAbd Allāh عليه السلام who said regarding the verse ﴾*those near the Sacred Mosque*﴿, '[Those who reside] within the places of *mīqāt*[113] on the way to Mecca, and they are the people about whom it is said they are "near" to the Sacred Mosque; and *mutʿa* does not apply to them.' [2:196]

252. From ʿAlī b. Jaʿfar, from his brother Mūsā عليه السلام; he said, 'I asked him about the people of Mecca and whether they are allowed the *mutʿa* of taking a break between *ʿumra* and Hajj? He replied, "The people of Mecca are not allowed to do *mutʿa*, and this is what was intended in the verse ﴾*This applies to those whose household is not near the Sacred Mosque*﴿"' [2:196]

253. From Saʿīd al-Aʿraj[114], on his authority عليه السلام saying, 'The people of Sarif, Marr,[115] and Mecca are not allowed *mutʿa* [between *ʿumra* and Hajj], as God states ﴾*This applies to those whose household is not near the Sacred Mosque*﴿' [2:196]

254. From Muʿāwiya b. ʿAmmār, from Abū ʿAbd Allāh عليه السلام who said regarding the verse ﴾*The pilgrimage takes place during the prescribed months*﴿, 'These are Shawwāl, Dhū l-Qaʿda, and Dhū l-Ḥijja.' [2:196]

255. From Zurāra, from Abū Jaʿfar عليه السلام who said, ﴾*The pilgrimage takes place during the prescribed months*﴿, they are the months of Shawwāl, Dhū l-Qaʿda, and Dhū l-Ḥijja, and one cannot enter the state of *iḥrām* for the purpose of Hajj in any other month.' [2:196]

256. From al-Ḥalabī, from Abū ʿAbd Allāh عليه السلام who said regarding the verse ﴾*The pilgrimage takes place during the prescribed months so for anyone undertaking the pilgrimage*﴿, '[These are the lunar months] marked by the crescent moons.' [2:196]

---

113 *mīqāt*: specific places on the way to Mecca, where one enters the state of *iḥrām*.

114 Abū ʿAbd Allāh Saʿīd b. ʿAbd Allāh al-Taymī al-Aʿraj, on whom there is scant information, was a narrator of the sixth and seventh Imam's traditions. See Modarressi, *Tradition and Survival*, 365–6 (nr. 182).

115 Sarif and Marr are localities about 6 and 5 miles away from Mecca respectively.

٢٥١. عن حمّاد بن عُثمان، عن أبي عبد الله عليه السلام في: ﴿حَاضِرِي الْمَسْجِدِ الْحَرَامِ﴾، قال: دون المواقيت إلى مكّة، فهم من حاضري المسجد الحرام، وليس لهم مُتعة.

٢٥٢. عن عليّ بن جعفر، عن أخيه موسى عليه السلام، قال: سألتُه عن أهل مكّة، هل يَصلُح لهم أن يتمتّعوا في العُمرة إلى الحجّ؟ قال: لا يَصلُح لأهل مكّة المُتعة، وذلك قول الله تعالى: ﴿ذَلِكَ لِمَن لَّمْ يَكُنْ أَهْلُهُ حَاضِرِي الْمَسْجِدِ الْحَرَامِ﴾.

٢٥٣. عن سعيد الأعرج، عنه عليه السلام، قال: ليس لأهل سَرِف، ولا لأهل مَرّ، ولا لأهل مكّة مُتعة، يقول الله تعالى: ﴿ذَلِكَ لِمَن لَّمْ يَكُنْ أَهْلُهُ حَاضِرِي الْمَسْجِدِ الْحَرَامِ﴾.

٢٥٤. عن مُعاوية بن عمّار، عن أبي عبد الله عليه السلام، في قوله تعالى: ﴿الْحَجُّ أَشْهُرٌ مَّعْلُومَاتٌ﴾ هو شوّال، وذو القَعدة، وذو الحجّة.

٢٥٥. عن زُرارة، عن أبي جعفر عليه السلام، قال: ﴿الْحَجُّ أَشْهُرٌ مَّعْلُومَاتٌ﴾، قال: شوّال، وذو القَعدة، وذو الحجّة، وليس لأحد أن يُحرِم بالحجّ فيما سِواهنّ.

٢٥٦. عن الحَلبي، عن أبي عبد الله عليه السلام، في قوله تعالى: ﴿الْحَجُّ أَشْهُرٌ مَّعْلُومَاتٌ فَمَن فَرَضَ فِيهِنَّ الْحَجَّ﴾، قال: الأهلّة.

257. From Muʿāwiya b. ʿAmmār, from Abū ʿAbd Allāh ﷺ who said regarding the verse ﴾*The pilgrimage takes place during the prescribed months so for anyone undertaking the pilgrimage*﴿, 'The duty incumbent when undertaking the pilgrimage is the *talbiya, ishʿār,*[116] and garlanding the animal. Whichever one of these he performs, he has undertaken the Hajj. Hajj is only incumbent in these months, for God has stated ﴾*The pilgrimage takes place during the prescribed months*﴿, which are Shawwāl, Dhū l-Qaʿda and Dhū l-Ḥijja.' [2:196–7]

258. From Ibrāhīm b. ʿAbd al-Ḥamīd, from Abū al-Ḥasan who said, 'Whoever quarrels during the Hajj must feed six poor people half a measure (*ṣāʿ*) regardless of whether he is in the right or wrong. If he resumes the quarrel, then the one in the right must sacrifice an ewe, and the one in the wrong a cow, because God, Mighty and Exalted, says ﴾*There should be no indecent speech, misbehaviour, or quarrelling for anyone undertaking the pilgrimage*﴿. "Misbehaviour" refers to sexual intercourse, "indecent speech" means lying, and "quarrelling" is when someone argues and swears by God [to make his point against someone else who is his adversary], and boasting.' [2:197]

259. From Muʿāwiya b. ʿAmmār, from Abū ʿAbd Allāh ﷺ who said, 'In the verse ﴾*The pilgrimage takes place during the prescribed months. There should be no indecent speech, misbehaviour, or quarrelling for anyone undertaking the pilgrimage*﴿, 'misbehaviour' means sexual intercourse, 'indecent speech' means lying and cursing, and 'quarrelling' is when someone argues and swears by God [to make his point], and boasting.' [2:197]

260. From Muḥammad b. Muslim who narrated, 'I asked Abū Jaʿfar ﷺ about the meaning of the verse ﴾*There should be no indecent speech, misbehaviour, or quarrelling for anyone undertaking the pilgrimage*﴿. He said, "Dear Muḥammad, God has imposed a condition on people, [in exchange for which] he stipulates a provision for them. Whoever fulfils it for Him, God fulfils it for him." I asked, "So what is the condition that is imposed on them, and what is stipulated as a provision for them?"

116 The *ishʿār* was the practice of marking the sacrificial animal to distinguish it as being meant for slaughter, so it would not be harmed.

٢٥٧. عن مُعاوية بن عمّار، عن أبي عبدالله عليه السلام، قال في قول الله تعالى: ﴿الْحَجُّ أَشْهُرٌ مَعْلُومَاتٌ فَمَنْ فَرَضَ فِيهِنَّ الْحَجَّ﴾، والفرض فرضُ الحجّ: التّلبية، والإشعار، والتقليد، فأيّ ذلك فَعل فقد فَرَض الحجّ، ولا يُفرَض الحجّ إلاّ في هذه الشهور الّتي قال الله تعالى: ﴿الْحَجُّ أَشْهُرٌ مَعْلُومَاتٌ﴾، وهي: شوّال، وذو القعدة، وذو الحجّة.

٢٥٨. عن إبراهيم بن عبد الحميد، عن أبي الحسن عليه السلام، قال: من جادل في الحجّ فعليه إطعام ستّة مساكين، لكلّ مسكين نِصف صاعٍ، إن كان صادقًا أو كاذبًا، فإن عاد مرّتين، فعلى الصّادق شاةٌ، وعلى الكاذب بَقرة، لأنّ الله عزّ وجلّ يقول: ﴿فَلَا رَفَثَ وَلَا فُسُوقَ وَلَا جِدَالَ فِي الْحَجِّ﴾ والرّفث: الجماع، والفُسوق: الكَذب، والجِدال: قول الرجل: لا واللهِ، وبلى واللهِ، والمفُاخرة.

٢٥٩. عن مُعاوية بن عمّار، عن أبي عبدالله عليه السلام، قال: قول الله: ﴿الْحَجُّ أَشْهُرٌ مَعْلُومَاتٌ فَمَنْ فَرَضَ فِيهِنَّ الْحَجَّ فَلَا رَفَثَ وَلَا فُسُوقَ وَلَا جِدَالَ فِي الْحَجِّ﴾ والرّفث: هو الجماع، والفُسوق: الكَذِب، والسِّباب، والجِدال: قول الرّجل: لا واللهِ، وبلى واللهِ والمفُاخرة.

٢٦٠. عن محمّد بن مسلم، قال: سألتُ أبا جعفر عليه السلام عن قول الله عزّ وجلّ: ﴿فَمَنْ فَرَضَ فِيهِنَّ الْحَجَّ فَلَا رَفَثَ وَلَا فُسُوقَ وَلَا جِدَالَ فِي الْحَجِّ﴾. قال: يا محمّد، إنّ الله اشترط على النّاس شرطًا، وشَرط لهم شرطًا، فمن وفَى لله وفَى الله له. قلتُ: فما الّذي اشترط عليهم، وما الذي شَرط لهم؟

He replied, "The condition that is imposed on them is mentioned in the verse ﴾ *The pilgrimage takes place during the prescribed months. There should be no indecent speech, misbehaviour, or quarrelling for anyone undertaking the pilgrimage* ﴿, and the provision stipulated for them [in exchange] is mentioned where He says, ﴾ *If anyone is in a hurry to leave after two days, there is no blame on him, nor is there any blame on anyone who stays on, so long as they are mindful of God* ﴿, i.e., he goes back sin-free."' [2:197]

261. From Abū Baṣīr, from Abū ʿAbd Allāh عليه السلام who said, 'If someone rightfully swears an oath [in the course of argumentation] three consecutive times, then he is considered to have quarrelled and must sacrifice an animal; if he wrongfully swears once, then he has quarrelled and must sacrifice an animal [to compensate].'

262. From Muḥammad b. Muslim, from one of the two [Imams, i.e. either al-Bāqir or al-Ṣādiq عليه السلام] who was asked about a man in the state of *iḥrām* who swears by his life. He عليه السلام said, 'That does not count as quarrelling. Quarrelling here is to say, 'I swear by God' to make a point.'

263. From Muḥammad b. Muslim who narrated, 'I asked Abū Jaʿfar عليه السلام about the meaning of the verse ﴾ *The pilgrimage takes place during the prescribed months. There should be no indecent speech, misbehaviour, or quarrelling for anyone undertaking the pilgrimage* ﴿ (2:197).

He replied by saying, "Muḥammad, God has imposed a condition on people, [in exchange for which] he stipulates a provision for them. Whoever fulfils it for Him, God fulfils it for him."

I asked, "So what is the condition that is imposed on them, and what is stipulated as a provision for them?"

He replied, "The condition that is imposed on them is found in the verse ﴾ *The pilgrimage takes place during the prescribed months. There should be no indecent speech, misbehaviour, or quarrelling for anyone undertaking the pilgrimage* ﴿, whereas the provision stipulated for them is that ﴾ *If anyone is in a hurry to leave after two days, there is no blame on him, nor is there any blame on anyone who stays on, so long as they are mindful of God* ﴿, i.e., he goes back sin-free."

قال: أمّا الّذي اشترط عليهم فإنّه قال: ﴿الْحَجُّ أَشْهُرٌ مَعْلُومَاتٌ فَمَنْ فَرَضَ فِيهِنَّ الْحَجَّ فَلَا رَفَثَ وَلَا فُسُوقَ وَلَا جِدَالَ فِي الْحَجِّ﴾ وأمّا ما شَرط لهم، فإنّه قال: ﴿فَمَنْ تَعَجَّلَ فِي يَوْمَيْنِ فَلَا إِثْمَ عَلَيْهِ وَمَنْ تَأَخَّرَ فَلَا إِثْمَ عَلَيْهِ لِمَنِ اتَّقَى﴾، قال: يَرجِع لا ذنبَ له.

٢٦١. عن أبي بصير، عن أبي عبد الله عليه السلام، قال: إذا حَلَفَ ثلاث أيمانٍ متتابعاتٍ صادقًا فقد جادل، فعليه دمٌ، وإذا حلف بواحدةٍ كاذبًا فقد جادل، فعليه دمٌ.

٢٦٢. عن محمّد بن مسلم، عن أحدهما عليه السلام، عن رجلٍ مُحرِمٍ قال لرجلٍ: لا، لَعُمري، قال عليه السلام: ليس ذلك بِجدال، إنّما الجِدال: لا واللهِ، وبلى واللهِ.

٢٦٣. عن محمّد بن مسلم، قال: سألتُ أبا جعفر عليه السلام، عن قول الله عزّ وجلّ: ﴿الْحَجُّ أَشْهُرٌ مَعْلُومَاتٌ فَمَنْ فَرَضَ فِيهِنَّ الْحَجَّ فَلَا رَفَثَ وَلَا فُسُوقَ وَلَا جِدَالَ فِي الْحَجِّ﴾، فقال: يا محمّد، إنّ الله اشترط على النّاس، وشَرط لهم، فمن وفى لله وفى الله له.

قال: قلتُ: ما الّذي اشترط عليهم، وشَرَط لهم؟

قال: أمّا الّذي اشترط في الحجّ، فإنّه قال: ﴿الْحَجُّ أَشْهُرٌ مَعْلُومَاتٌ فَمَنْ فَرَضَ فِيهِنَّ الْحَجَّ فَلَا رَفَثَ وَلَا فُسُوقَ وَلَا جِدَالَ فِي الْحَجِّ﴾ وأمّا الذي شَرط لهم، فإنّه قال: ﴿فَمَنْ تَعَجَّلَ فِي يَوْمَيْنِ فَلَا إِثْمَ عَلَيْهِ وَمَنْ تَأَخَّرَ فَلَا إِثْمَ عَلَيْهِ لِمَنِ اتَّقَى﴾ يَرجِع لا ذنبَ له.

Then I asked, "What if someone commits a misbehaviour, I mean sexual intercourse – what is the compensation due on him?"

He said, "He must drive the sacrificial animal, and separate from his wife until they have completed the rest of the rites, then they can return to the place where they were tried with their temptation."

I asked, "Do they have to take a different route to the one on which they fell into temptation?"

He said, "They can come together again after they have completed the rites."

Then I asked, "What about the one who commits an indecency by lying – has there not been a penalty imposed for that?"

He replied, "He should beseech God for forgiveness and recite the *talbiya*."

I asked, "What about the one who quarrels, and tried to prove a point by saying, 'I swear by God' – how does he compensate?"

He said, "If he quarrels with someone twice, then the victim must sacrifice an ewe, and the perpetrator a cow."' [2:197]

264. From Muḥammad b. Muslim, from Abū Jaʿfar عليه السلام who was asked about a man in the state of *iḥrām* quarrelling with his brother, saying, 'By my life.' He replied, 'That does not count as quarrelling. Quarrelling here is to say 'No, by God' or 'Yes, by God' [to make a point].'

265. From ʿUmar b. Yazīd Bayyāʿ al-Sābirī, from Abū ʿAbd Allāh عليه السلام who said regarding the verse ﴿*it is no offence to seek some bounty from your Lord*﴾, 'It refers to provisions. When a person has come out of the state of *iḥrām* and completed the sacrifice, it becomes permissible for him to buy and sell during the festive season.' [2:198]

266. From Zayd al-Shaḥḥām, from Abū ʿAbd Allāh عليه السلام: 'I asked him about God's statement, Mighty and Exalted, ﴿*Surge down where the rest of the people do*﴾. He said, 'This refers to the Quraysh who used to say, "We are worthier of the Kaʿba than everyone else" and as a result used to come down

قلتُ: أرأيتَ من ابتُلِيَ بالرّفث، والرّفث: هو الجماع ما عليه؟ قال: يسوق الهَدي، ويُفرّق ما بينه وبين أهله حتّى يقضيا المناسِك، وحتّى يعودا إلى المكان الّذي أصابا فيه ما أصابا.

قلتُ: أرأيتَ إن أرادا أن يرجِعا في غير ذلك الطريق الّذي ابتُليا فيه؟ قال: فليجتَمِعا، إذا قَضَيا المناسك.

قلتُ: فمن ابتُلي بالفُسوق — والفسوق: الكَذِب — فلم يُجعل له حدّ؟ قال: يستغفر الله ويُلبّي.

قلتُ: فمن ابتُلي بالجِدال — والجِدال: قول الرّجل: لا واللهِ، وبلى واللهِ — ما عليه؟ قال: إذا جادل قومًا مرّتين، فعلى المُصيب دَم شاةٍ، وعلى المُخطِئ دم بقرةٍ.

٢٦٤. عن محمّد بن مسلم، عن أبي جعفر عليه السلام، عن الرّجل المُحرم قال لأخيه: لا لَعُمري. قال: ليس هذا بجِدال، إنّما الجدال: لا واللهِ، وبلى واللهِ.

٢٦٥. عن عمر بن يزيد بيّاع السّابري، عن أبي عبد الله عليه السلام، في قول الله تعالى: ﴿لَيْسَ عَلَيْكُمْ جُنَاحٌ أَنْ تَبْتَغُوا فَضْلاً مِنْ رَبِّكُمْ﴾ يعني الرِّزق، إذا أحلّ الرجل من إحرامه وقضى نُسُكه، فلْيشترِ ولْيبع في المَوْسم.

٢٦٦. عن زيد الشحّام، عن أبي عبد الله عليه السلام، قال: سألتُه عن قول الله عزّ وجلّ: ﴿أَفِيضُوا مِنْ حَيْثُ أَفَاضَ النَّاسُ﴾. قال: أولئك قُريش، كانوا يقولون: نحنُ أَولى الناس بالبيت، ولا يُفيضون إلاّ من المُزدلِفة، فأمَرَهم الله أن يُفيضوا من عرفة.

from Muzdalifa[117] [and not ʿArafa with the rest], so God commanded them to surge down from ʿArafa altogether.' [2:199]

267. From Rifāʿa from Abū ʿAbd Allāh عليه السلام: 'I asked him about the meaning of the verse ﴿*Surge down where the rest of the people do*﴾. He replied, "The people of the Sacred House would stay at the Sacred Place [Muzdalifa] while the rest of the people would be staying at ʿArafa, and they would not set off until they saw the people of ʿArafa come into view. There was a man known as Abū Sayyār who had a swift donkey, on whom he used to race ahead of the people of ʿArafa. When they would see that he has ridden ahead they would say, 'There is Abū Sayyār,' then they would surge down. But God commanded them all to stay at ʿArafa and to all surge down together from it."' [2:199]

268. From Muʿāwiya b. ʿAmmār, from Abū ʿAbd Allāh عليه السلام who said about the verse ﴿*Surge down where the rest of the people do*﴾, 'It refers to Ibrāhīm and Ismāʿīl عليه السلام.' [2:199]

269. From ʿAlī who said, 'I asked Abū ʿAbd Allāh عليه السلام about the meaning of the verse ﴿*Surge down where the rest of the people do*﴾. He said, "The Quraysh used to come down from Muzdalifa in times of pagan ignorance saying, 'We are worthier of the Kaʿba than everyone else,' so God commanded them to surge down from ʿArafa where the rest of the people surged down from."' [2:199]

270. In another narration from Abū ʿAbd Allāh عليه السلام he said, 'The tribe of Quraysh used to surge down from Jamʿ, and the tribes of Muḍarr and Rabīʿa from ʿArafāt.'

271. From Abū al-Ṣabbāḥ, from Abū ʿAbd Allāh عليه السلام who said, 'Ibrāhīm عليه السلام took Ismāʿīl to the station [at ʿArafa] and they both came down from it together. Subsequently, the people who came after them would surge down altogether from there too, until their numbers increased and the Quraysh refused to surge down from where the rest of the people did, coming down instead from Muzdalifa. They also prevented other people from joining

117 So as to reach the Kaʿba faster and earlier than the rest of the people.

٢٦٧. عن رِفاعة، عن أبي عبد الله عليه السلام، قال: سألتُه عن قول الله تعالى: ﴿ثُمَّ أَفِيضُوا مِنْ حَيْثُ أَفَاضَ النَّاسُ﴾. قال: إنّ أهل الحَرم كانوا يقِفون على المشعر الحَرام، ويقِف الناس بعرفة، ولا يُفيضون حتّى يطلُع عليهم أهل عَرفة، وكان رجل يُكنّى أبا سيّار، وكان له حِمارٌ فارِهٌ، وكان يسبِق أهل عَرفة، فإذا طَلَع عليهم، قالوا: هذا أبو سيّار، ثم أفاضوا، فأمرَهم الله أن يقِفوا بعَرفة وأن يُفيضوا منه.

٢٦٨. عن مُعاوية بن عمّار، عن أبي عبد الله عليه السلام، في قوله تعالى: ﴿ثُمَّ أَفِيضُوا مِنْ حَيْثُ أَفَاضَ النَّاسُ﴾ قال: يعني إبراهيم وإسماعيل.

٢٦٩. عن عليّ قال: سألتُ أبا عبد الله عليه السلام، عن قوله تعالى: ﴿ثُمَّ أَفِيضُوا مِنْ حَيْثُ أَفَاضَ النَّاسُ﴾. قال: كانت قُريش تُفيض من المُزدلِفة في الجاهلية، يقولون: نحنُ أَولى بالبيت من النّاس، فأمرهُم الله أن يُفيضوا من حيثُ أفاض الناس من عرفة.

٢٧٠. وفي رواية أُخرى، عن أبي عبد الله عليه السلام، قال: إنّ قُريشًا كانت تُفيض من جَمع، ومُضر وربَيعة من عَرفات.

٢٧١. عن أبي الصّبّاح، عن أبي عبد الله عليه السلام، قال: إنّ إبراهيم عليه السلام أخرج إسماعيل إلى الموَقف فأفاضا منه، ثمّ إنّ النّاس كانوا يُفيضون منه، حتّى إذا كثُرت قُريش، قالوا: لا نُفيض من حيث أفاض النّاس، وكانت قُريش تُفيض من المُزدلِفة، ومنعوا الناس أن يُفيضوا معهم

them, restricting them to surge down only from ʿArafāt. But when God sent Muḥammad ﷺ as a Messenger, He commanded him to surge down from where the people did, meaning Ibrāhīm and Ismāʿīl.'

272. From Jābir, from Abū Jaʿfar عليه السلام who stated about the verse ﴾*Surge down where the rest of the people do*﴿, 'They are the people of Yemen.' [2:199]

273. From Muḥammad b. Muslim who narrated, 'I asked Abū Jaʿfar عليه السلام about the verse ﴾*remember God as much as you remember your own fathers, or even more*﴿. He عليه السلام replied: "People in the pagan times of ignorance would boast, 'My father was like this and my father was like that,' so this verse was revealed about that."' [2:200]

274. From Muḥammad b. Muslim, from Abū ʿAbd Allāh عليه السلام; and also from al-Ḥusayn [b. Saʿīd], from Faḍāla b. Ayyūb, from al-ʿAlā, from Muḥammad b. Muslim, from Abū Jaʿfar عليه السلام saying a similar thing about the context of the above verse, that whilst staying in Mina after the sacrifice people would boast about their fathers saying, 'My father was the one in charge of all the blood-money' or 'My father was the one who fought so and so,' and they also used to swear by their fathers in argumentation.

275. From Zurāra from Abū Jaʿfar عليه السلام: 'I asked him about the meaning of the verse ﴾*remember God as much as you remember your own fathers, or even more*﴿. He replied by saying, "The people in times of pagan ignorance used to swear by each other's fathers saying, 'No, by your father' or 'Yes, by your father.' So they were commanded to say, 'No, by God' and 'Yes, by God' instead."' [2:200]

إلاّ من عرَفات، فلمّا بعث الله محمّدًا عليه الصلاة والسلام أمَره أن يُفيض من حيث أفاض الناس، وعنى بذلك إبراهيم وإسماعيل عليهما السلام.

٢٧٢. عن جابر، عن أبي جعفر عليه السلام، في قوله: ﴿ثُمَّ أَفِيضُوا مِنْ حَيْثُ أَفَاضَ النَّاسُ﴾، قال: هم أهل اليمن.

٢٧٣. عن محمّد بن مسلم، قال: سألتُ أبا جعفر عليه السلام، في قول الله تعالى: ﴿فَاذْكُرُوا اللَّهَ كَذِكْرِكُمْ آبَاءَكُمْ أَوْ أَشَدَّ ذِكْرًا﴾، قال: كان الرّجل في الجاهلية يقول: كان أبي، وكان أبي، فأُنزِلت هذه الآية في ذلك.

٢٧٤. عن محمّد بن مسلم، عن أبي عبدالله عليه السلام، والحُسين، عن فَضالة بن أيّوب عن العلاء، عن محمّد بن مسلم، عن أبي جعفر عليه السلام، في قول الله تعالى، مثله سواء. أي كانوا يفتَخرون بآبائهم، يقولون أبي الّذي حمل الدِّيات، والّذي قاتل كذا وكذا، إذا قاموا بِمنًى بعد النَّحر، وكانوا يقولون أيضًا —يحلفون بآبائهم— : لا وأبي، لا وأبي.

٢٧٥. عن زُرارة، عن أبي جعفر عليه السلام، قال: سألتُه عن قوله تعالى: ﴿فَاذْكُرُوا اللَّهَ كَذِكْرِكُمْ آبَاءَكُمْ أَوْ أَشَدَّ ذِكْرًا﴾. قال: إنّ أهل الجاهليّة كان من قولهم: كلاّ وأبيك، بلى وأبيك، فأُمِروا أن يقولوا: لا واللهِ، وبلى واللهِ.

276. Muḥammad b. Muslim narrated from Abū Jaʿfar عليه السلام regarding the verse ﴾*remember God as much as you remember your own fathers, or even more*﴿, that he said, 'People used to boast "My father was such" and "My father was such," so this verse came down about that.' [2:200]

277. From 'Abd al-A'lā[118] who narrated, 'I asked Abū 'Abd Allāh عليه السلام about the meaning of the verse ﴾*Our Lord, give us good in this world and in the Hereafter, and protect us from the torment of the Fire*﴿. He replied, 'It is [asking for] God's pleasure and Paradise in the Hereafter, prosperity in one's livelihood and good character in the life of this world.' [2:201]

278. From 'Abd al-A'lā, from Abū 'Abd Allāh عليه السلام who said regarding the verse ﴾*Our Lord, give us good in this world and in the Hereafter, and protect us from the torment of the Fire*﴿, '[It is] the pleasure of God, ampleness in one's livelihood, good company [in this world] and Paradise in the Hereafter.'

279. From Rifāʿa, from Abū 'Abd Allāh عليه السلام: 'I asked him about the appointed days (*ayyām maʿdūdāt*) [in the verse] ﴾*Remember God on the appointed days*﴿. He replied by saying, "They are the days of *tashrīq*."' [2:203]

280. From Zayd al-Shaḥḥām, from Abū 'Abd Allāh عليه السلام who said, 'The "appointed days" and the "specified days" (*ayyām maʿlūmāt*) [22:28] are one and the same; they are the days of *tashrīq*.'

281. From Ḥammād b. 'Īsā[119] who narrated, 'I heard Abū 'Abd Allāh عليه السلام say that 'Alī عليه السلام said about the verse ﴾*Remember God on the appointed days*﴿, "They are the days of *tashrīq*."' [2:203]

---

118 'Abd al-A'lā, protégé of the Āl Sām, on whom there is very little information in Ḥillī's *Khulāṣat al-aqwāl*. See Ḥillī, *Khulāṣat al-aqwāl*, 222 (nr. 734).

119 Abū Muḥammad Ḥammād b. 'Īsā al-Juhnī al-Baṣrī (d. 209/824–5), a prominent companion of the sixth, seventh and eighth Imams whom the biographical sources report as being extremely careful and cautious in transmitting the *ḥadīth*. He performed the Hajj on 50 occasions and died as a result of drowning at an old age of 95 years. He is regarded very reliable in his reports of the Imams' traditions. See Ḥillī, *Khulāṣat al-aqwāl*, 124–5 (nr. 323); Khū'ī, *Muʿjam*, 7: 236–51 (nr. 3972).

٢٧٦. وروى محمّد بن مسلم، عن أبي جعفر ﴿عليه السلام﴾، في قوله تعالى: ﴿فَاذْكُرُوا اللَّهَ كَذِكْرِكُمْ آبَاءَكُمْ أَوْ أَشَدَّ ذِكْرًا﴾. قال: كان الرجل يقول: كان أبي، وكان أبي، فنزلت عليهم في ذلك.

٢٧٧. عن عبد الأعلى، قال: سألتُ أبا عبد الله ﴿عليه السلام﴾، عن قول الله عزّ وجلّ: ﴿رَبَّنَا آتِنَا فِي الدُّنْيَا حَسَنَةً وَفِي الْآخِرَةِ حَسَنَةً وَقِنَا عَذَابَ النَّارِ﴾. قال ﴿عليه السلام﴾: رضوان الله والجنّة في الآخرة، والسّعة في المِعيشة وحُسن الخُلق في الدنيا.

٢٧٨. عن عبد الأعلى، عن أبي عبد الله ﴿عليه السلام﴾، قال: رضوان الله، والتّوسِعة في المَعيشة، وحُسن الصُّحبة، وفي الآخرة الجنّة.

٢٧٩. عن رِفاعة، عن أبي عبد الله ﴿عليه السلام﴾، قال: سألتُه عن الأيّام المعدودات، قال: هي أيّام التّشريق.

٢٨٠. عن زيد الشحّام، عن أبي عبد الله ﴿عليه السلام﴾، قال: المعدودات والمعلومات هي واحدة، أيّام التّشريق.

٢٨١. عن حمّاد بن عيسى، قال: سمِعتُ أبا عبد الله ﴿عليه السلام﴾، يقول: قال: عليّ ﴿عليه السلام﴾ في قول الله تعالى: ﴿وَاذْكُرُوا اللَّهَ فِي أَيَّامٍ مَعْدُودَاتٍ﴾ قال: أيّام التّشريق.

282. From Muḥammad b. Muslim who narrated, 'I asked Abū 'Abd Allāh ﷺ about the verse ﴾*Remember God on the appointed days*﴿. He replied by saying, "It is the glorification (*takbīr*) after the prayer on the days of *tashrīq*."' [2:203]

283. From Sallām b. al-Mustanīr, from Abū Ja'far ﷺ who, regarding the verse ﴾*If anyone is in a hurry to leave after two days, there is no blame on him, nor is there any blame on anyone who stays on, so long as they are mindful of God*﴿ said, 'He must stay away from hunting, misbehaviour, indecent speech, quarrelling and whatever else God has prohibited in the state of *iḥrām*.' [2:203]

284. From Mu'āwiya b. 'Ammār, from Abū 'Abd Allāh ﷺ who, about verse ﴾*If anyone is in a hurry to leave after two days, there is no blame on him, nor is there any blame on anyone who stays on*﴿ said, 'He goes back forgiven, free of sin.' [2:203]

285. From Abū Ayyūb al-Khazzāz[120] who narrated, 'I said to Abū 'Abd Allāh ﷺ: "We are in a hurry to depart." He replied, "Do not leave immediately on the second day [after the Hajj] until after sunset. On the third day, you can leave halfway through the day, for God says, ﴾*If anyone is in a hurry to leave after two days, there is no blame on him*﴿. If He had remained silent about the matter, everyone would hurry to depart and no one would remain, but God, Mighty and Exalted, says ﴾*nor is there any blame on anyone who stays on*﴿."' [2:203]

286. From Abū Baṣīr, from Abū 'Abd Allāh ﷺ who said: 'When the believing servant leaves his home to embark on the Hajj, God records a good deed for every step he takes and erases one sin for every other step he takes. The more he walks, the higher God raises his rank. When he arrives at the plains of 'Arafāt, whatever sins he has accumulated, regardless of their quantity, he returns back in the state in which his mother gave him birth [i.e. sinless]. It

120 Abū Ayyūb Ibrāhīm b. 'Īsā (or 'Uthmān) b. Ayyūb al-Khazzāz, a reliable companion of the sixth and seventh Imams. See Ḥillī, *Khulāṣat al-aqwāl*, 50 (nr. 13); Modarressi, *Tradition and Survival*, 285–6 (nr. 102).

٢٨٢. عن محمّد بن مسلم، قال: سألتُ أبا عبد الله عليه السلام، عن قول الله سبحانه: ﴿وَاذْكُرُوا اللَّهَ فِي أَيَّامٍ مَعْدُودَاتٍ﴾، قال: التّكبير في أيّام التّشريق في دُبر الصلاة.

٢٨٣. عن سلاّم بن المُستَنير، عن أبي جعفر عليه السلام في قوله: ﴿فَمَنْ تَعَجَّلَ فِي يَوْمَيْنِ فَلَا إِثْمَ عَلَيْهِ وَمَنْ تَأَخَّرَ فَلَا إِثْمَ عَلَيْهِ لِمَنِ اتَّقَى﴾ منهم الصّيد، واتّقى الرّفث والفُسوق والجِدال وما حرّم الله عليه في إحرامه.

٢٨٤. عن مُعاوية بن عمّار، عن أبي عبد الله عليه السلام، في قول الله تعالى: ﴿فَمَنْ تَعَجَّلَ فِي يَوْمَيْنِ فَلَا إِثْمَ عَلَيْهِ﴾، قال: يَرجِع مغفُورًا له، لا ذنب له.

٢٨٥. عن أبي أيّوب الخزّاز، قال: قلتُ لأبي عبد الله عليه السلام: إنّا نُريد أن نتعجّل؟ فقال عليه السلام: لا تَنفِروا في اليوم الثّاني حتّى تزول الشمس، فأمّا اليوم الثالث، فإذا انتصَف فانفِروا، فإنّ الله تعالى يقول: ﴿فَمَنْ تَعَجَّلَ فِي يَوْمَيْنِ فَلَا إِثْمَ عَلَيْهِ﴾، فلو سكت لم يبق أحدٌ إلا تعجّل، ولكنّه قال جلّ وعزّ: ﴿وَمَنْ تَأَخَّرَ فَلَا إِثْمَ عَلَيْهِ﴾.

٢٨٦. عن أبي بصير، عن أبي عبد الله عليه السلام، قال: إنّ العبد المؤمن حين يخرُج من بيته حاجًّا لا يخطو خُطوةً ولا تخطو به راحِلتُه، إلا كتَبَ الله لها بها حَسنةً، ومحا عنه سيّئةً، ورفع له بها درجةً، فإذا وقف بعَرفات، فلو كانت له ذُنُوبٌ عدد الثرى، رجع كما ولدته أُمّه، يقال له: استأنِف العمل، يقول الله: ﴿فَمَنْ تَعَجَّلَ فِي يَوْمَيْنِ فَلَا إِثْمَ عَلَيْهِ وَمَنْ تَأَخَّرَ فَلَا إِثْمَ عَلَيْهِ لِمَنِ اتَّقَى﴾.

will be said to him, "Perform your deeds afresh." God says, ﴾ *Then he who hurries in two days shall bear no sin, and he who delays shall have no sin; that for whoever fears [God]* ﴿.'

287. Abū Baṣīr related a similar narration adding: 'And when he shaves his head, for every hair that falls, God erects a light for him on the Day of Resurrection. Every penny that he spends is recorded for him as a good deed, and when he has circumambulated the Kaʿba, he returns home like a new-born baby.'

288. From Abū Ḥamza al-Thumālī, from Abū Jaʿfar عليه السلام regarding the verse ﴾ *If anyone is in a hurry to leave after two days, there is no blame on him, nor is there any blame on anyone who stays on, so long as they are mindful of God* ﴿ that he said, 'By God, you are the ones meant here. The Messenger of God ﷺ said, "Only those who are mindful of God will remain steadfast upon ʿAlī's authority (*walāya*)."' [2:203]

289. From Ḥammād, from one of the Imams who said regarding the verse ﴾ *so long as they are mindful of God* ﴿ that 'It means to refrain from hunting, and if he does hunt, then he must offer a sacrifice for it, for he should not just hurry off in two days.' [2:203]

290. From al-Ḥusayn b. Bashshār[121] who narrated, 'I asked Abū al-Ḥasan عليه السلام about the verse ﴾ *There is [a kind of] man whose views on the life of this world may please you [Prophet], he even calls on God to witness what is in his heart, yet he is the bitterest of opponents. When he leaves, he sets out to spread corruption in the land, destroying crops and livestock – God does not like corruption.* ﴿ He said, "It refers to so and so; and the word *al-nasl* in ﴾ *destroying crops (ḥarth) and livestock (nasl)* ﴿ refers to progeny, while *ḥarth* is crops."'

---

121 Al-Ḥusayn b. Bashshār al-Madāʾinī, a reliable and trustworthy companion of Imam ʿAlī b. Mūsā al-Riḍā. See Ḥillī, *Khulāṣat al-aqwāl*, 114 (nr. 280).

٢٨٧. عن أبي بصير، في رواية أُخرى عنه عليه السلام نحوه، وزاد فيه: فإذا حلق رأسه لم تَسقُط شَعرةٌ إلاّ جَعَلَ الله له بها نوراً يوم القيامة، وما أنفَقَ من نفقةٍ كُتِبت له، فإذا طاف بالبيت رجَع كما وَلَدَتْه أمّه.

٢٨٨. عن أبي حمزة الثّمالي، عن أبي جعفر عليه السلام، في قوله: ﴿فَمَن تَعَجَّلَ فِي يَوْمَيْنِ فَلَا إِثْمَ عَلَيْهِ﴾ الآية، قال: أنتم — واللهِ — هم، إنّ رسول الله صلى الله عليه وآله وسلم قال: لا يثبُت على ولاية عليّ عليه السلام إلا المتّقون.

٢٨٩. عن حمّاد، عنه عليه السلام، في قوله: ﴿لِمَنِ اتَّقَىٰ﴾ الصّيد، فإن ابتُلي بشيءٍ من الصّيد ففداه، فليس له أن ينفِر في يومين.

٢٩٠. عن الحُسين بن بشّار، قال: سألتُ أبا الحسن عليه السلام عن قول الله عزّ وجلّ: ﴿وَمِنَ النَّاسِ مَن يُعْجِبُكَ قَوْلُهُ فِي الْحَيَاةِ الدُّنْيَا﴾. قال: فلان وفلان ﴿وَيُهْلِكَ الْحَرْثَ وَالنَّسْلَ﴾ النّسل: هم الذُّرّية، والحَرث: الزّرع.

291. From Zurāra, from Abū Jaʿfar عليه السلام and Abū ʿAbd Allāh عليه السلام. He said, ‘I asked them both about the verse ﴾*When he leaves, he sets out to spread corruption in the land*﴿. They said, “*Nasl* refers to progeny and *ḥarth* to the land.”’ [2:205]

292. Abū ʿAbd Allāh عليه السلام has said that *ḥarth* is progeny.

293. From Abū Isḥāq al-Sabīʿī, from the Commander of the Faithful ʿAlī عليه السلام regarding the verse ﴾*When he leaves, he sets out to spread corruption in the land, destroying crops and livestock*﴿ that he عليه السلام said, ‘[He does this] with his injustice and his evil character, and ﴾*God does not like corruption*﴿.’ [2:205]

294. From Saʿd al-Iskāf, from Abū Jaʿfar عليه السلام who said, ‘God says in His Book ﴾*he is the bitterest of opponents*﴿, and yet they still oppose.’ I asked him, ‘What does bitterest mean here?’ He replied, ‘Having intense animosity.’ [2:204]

295. From Jābir, from Abū Jaʿfar عليه السلام who said, ‘The verse ﴾*But there is also a kind of man who gives his life away to please God, and God is most compassionate to His servants*﴿ was revealed about ʿAlī b. Abī Ṭālib عليه السلام and the willingness he showed to be sacrificed for God and His Messenger ﷺ on the night when he lay in the Prophet’s bed as the Quraysh pursued the Messenger of God seeking his blood.’ [2:207]

296. From Ibn ʿAbbās who narrated, “ʿAlī عليه السلام was the one who gave his life; he wore the Prophet’s robe, then slept in his place while the polytheists were trying to target the Messenger of God ﷺ.’

He continued, ‘Then Abū Bakr entered while ʿAlī عليه السلام was sleeping, thinking that it was the Prophet ﷺ, so he asked him, “Where is the Prophet of God ﷺ?” ʿAlī عليه السلام replied, “God’s prophet has left in the direction of Biʾr Maymūn[122] so go and catch up with him.”

So Abū Bakr set off and entered the cave with him. On that night ʿAlī عليه السلام had stones thrown at him just like they used to throw stones at the Messenger of God ﷺ, and he would wince in pain, having bandaged his head.

122 Biʾr Maymūn, the name of a well in Mecca named after Maymūn b. Khālid b. ʿĀmir b. al-Ḥaḍramī. See Yāqūt al-Ḥamawī, *Muʿjam al-buldān*, 1:302.

٢٩١. عن زُرارة، عن أبي جعفر عليه السلام، وأبي عبدالله عليه السلام، قال: سألتُهما عن قوله سبحانه: ﴿وَإِذَا تَوَلَّى سَعَى فِي الأَرْضِ﴾ إلى آخر الآية. فقالا: النّسل: الولد، والحَرث: الأرض.

٢٩٢. وقال أبو عبدالله عليه السلام: الحرث: الذُّرية.

٢٩٣. عن أبي إسحاق السّبيعيّ، عن أمير المؤمنين عليّ عليه السلام، في قوله تبارك وتعالى: ﴿وَإِذَا تَوَلَّى سَعَى فِي الأَرْضِ لِيُفْسِدَ فِيهَا وَيُهْلِكَ الْحَرْثَ وَالنَّسْلَ﴾ بِظُلمه وسُوء سيرته: ﴿وَاللَّهُ لَا يُحِبُّ الْفَسَادَ﴾.

٢٩٤. عن سعد الإسكاف، عن أبي جعفر عليه السلام قال: إنّ الله يقول في كتابه: ﴿وَهُوَ أَلَدُّ الْخِصَامِ﴾ بل هم يختصمون. قال: قلتُ: ما ألَدّ؟ قال: شديد الخُصومة.

٢٩٥. عن جابر، عن أبي جعفر عليه السلام، قال: فأمّا قوله: ﴿وَمِنَ النَّاسِ مَنْ يَشْرِي نَفْسَهُ ابْتِغَاءَ مَرْضَاةِ اللَّهِ وَاللَّهُ رَءُوفٌ بِالْعِبَادِ﴾ فإنّها أُنزلت في عليّ بن أبي طالب عليه السلام حين بذَل نفسه لله ولرسوله ليلة اضطَجَعَ على فِراش رسول الله صلى الله عليه وآله لمّا طلبتُه كُفّار قريش.

٢٩٦. عن ابن عبّاس، قال: شرى عليّ عليه السلام نفسه، لبس ثوب النّبيّ صلى الله عليه وآله، ثمّ نام مكانه، فكان المُشركون يَرمون رسول الله صلى الله عليه وآله.

قال: فجاء أبو بكر، وعليّ عليه السلام نائم، وأبو بكر يحسبُ أنّه نبيّ الله، فقال: أين نبيّ الله؟ فقال عليّ: إنّ نبيّ الله قد انطلق نحوَ بئر ميمون فأدرِك.

Once they [found him] they exclaimed, "It is you! We would not have known any better were it not for the fact that your companion, Muḥammad, never winced."'

297. From Abū Baṣīr who narrated, 'I once heard Abū 'Abd Allāh عليه السلام recite the verse ﴾*You who believe, enter wholeheartedly into submission to God and do not follow in Satan's footsteps, for he is your sworn enemy*﴿ whereupon he asked, "Do you know what submission is?" I replied, "You know better [than us]." He said, "It is the authority of 'Alī and the vicegerency of the Imams after him." He continued, "By God, Satan's footsteps are [to follow] the authority of those two [a reference to Abū Bakr and 'Umar b. al-Khaṭṭāb]."' [2:208]

298. From Zurāra, Ḥumrān and Muḥammad b. Muslim, from Abū Ja'far and Abū 'Abd Allāh عليهما السلام. They said, 'We asked them both about the meaning of the verse ﴾*You who believe, enter wholeheartedly into submission to God and do not follow in Satan's footsteps, for he is your sworn enemy*﴿. Their response was that, "They [the believers] have been commanded to acknowledge us."' [2:208]

299. From Jābir, from Abū Ja'far عليه السلام that regarding the verse ﴾*You who believe, enter wholeheartedly into submission to God and do not follow in Satan's footsteps*﴿ he said, 'The submission that God has commanded you all to enter into is the family of Muḥammad صلى الله عليه وآله.'[2:208]

300. From Abū Bakr al-Kalbī, from Ja'far عليه السلام, on his father's authority who, regarding the verse ﴾*enter wholeheartedly into submission to God*﴿ said, 'It is our authority.' [2:208]

301. Jābir narrated from Abū Ja'far عليه السلام who said, 'The submission that God commands you all to enter into is [submission to] the family of Muḥammad صلى الله عليه وآله. They are the rope of God that He has commanded to hold fast to, when He says, ﴾*Hold fast to God's rope all together; do not split into factions*﴿(3:103).'

قال: فانطلق أبو بكر، فدخَل معه الغار، وجعل يُرمَى بالحِجارة كما كان يُرمى رسول الله ﷺ، وهو يتضوّر، قد لفّ رأسه، فقالوا، إنّك! لكنّه كان صاحبك لا يتضوّر، قد استنكرنا ذلك.

٢٩٧. عن أبي بصير، قال: سمعتُ أبا عبد الله عليه السلام يقول: ﴿يَا أَيُّهَا الَّذِينَ آمَنُوا ادْخُلُوا فِي السِّلْمِ كَافَّةً وَلَا تَتَّبِعُوا خُطُوَاتِ الشَّيْطَانِ﴾ قال: أتدري ما السِّلم؟ قلتُ: أنت أعلم. قال: ولاية عليّ والأئمّة الأوصياء من بعده، قال: وخُطُوات الشيطان والله ولاية فلان وفلان.

٢٩٨. عن زُرارة، وحُمران، ومحمّد بن مسلم، عن أبي جعفر، وأبي عبد الله عليهما السلام، قالوا: سألناهما عن قول الله جلّ وعزّ: ﴿يَا أَيُّهَا الَّذِينَ آمَنُوا ادْخُلُوا فِي السِّلْمِ كَافَّةً﴾، قال: أُمِروا بمعرفتنا.

٢٩٩. عن جابر، عن أبي جعفر عليه السلام في قول الله تعالى: : ﴿يَا أَيُّهَا الَّذِينَ آمَنُوا ادْخُلُوا فِي السِّلْمِ كَافَّةً وَلَا تَتَّبِعُوا خُطُوَاتِ الشَّيْطَانِ﴾، قال: السِّلم هم آل محمّد ﷺ، أمر الله بالدخول فيه.

٣٠٠. عن أبي بكر الكلبي، عن جعفر، عن أبيه عليه السلام، في قوله تعالى: ﴿ادْخُلُوا فِي السِّلْمِ كَافَّةً﴾ هو ولايتنا.

٣٠١. وروى جابر، عن أبي عبد الله عليه السلام، قال: السِّلم: هو آل محمّد ﷺ أمر الله بالدخول فيه، وهم حَبل الله الّذي أمر بالاعتصام به، قال الله تعالى: ﴿وَاعْتَصِمُوا بِحَبْلِ اللَّهِ جَمِيعًا وَلَا تَفَرَّقُوا﴾.

302. In a narration by Abū Baṣīr from Abū ʿAbd Allāh عليه السلام regarding the verse ﴾*and do not follow in Satan's footsteps*﴿ that he عليه السلام said, 'This is the authority of the second and the first [caliphs].' [2:208]

303. From Masʿada b. Ṣadaqa, from Jaʿfar b. Muḥammad, on his father's authority, on his grandfather's authority, that he narrated, 'The Commander of the Faithful عليه السلام said, "All the knowledge which was bestowed upon Ādam and with which he came down, as well that which all the prophets have been endowed with up until the Seal of the Prophets and Messengers, all of it is with the family of the Seal of the Prophets and Messengers. So how can you be led astray? Where would you go? O people who have let go of the strong masts that are the People of the Ship,[123] this is a similitude right in front of you. Just as some people were saved on that one, thus will some of you be saved on this one, upon the pledge of my word. Woe! Damned be anyone who tarries behind them, for they live amongst you like the People of the Cave, and they are an embodiment of the door to forgiveness. They are the door of submission so ﴾*enter wholeheartedly into submission to God and do not follow in Satan's footsteps.*"'﴿ [2:208]

304. From Jābir who narrated, 'Abū Jaʿfar عليه السلام stated regarding the verse ﴾*Are these people waiting for God to come to them in the shadows of the clouds, together with the angels?*﴿ that 'He descends amid seven domes of light; which one of them precisely is unknown. This takes place when He descends directly above Kufa.' [2:210]

305. From Abū Ḥamza, from Abū Jaʿfar عليه السلام who said, 'Abū Ḥamza, it is as if I see the Avenger (*al-qāʾim*) of my Household towering over Najaf. When he عليه السلام rises above Najaf and unfurls the banner of the Messenger of God ﷺ, the angels from the Battle of Badr will descend upon him.' [2:210]

306. Abū Jaʿfar عليه السلام said, 'He will descend amid domes of light when he comes down above Kufa to distinguish between truth and falsehood. The phrase ﴾*But the matter would already have been decided*﴿ refers to the day on which

123 An allusion to those traditions which mention the likeness of the Household of the Prophet (*ahl al-bayt*) to the Arc or Ship of Nūḥ.

٣٠٢. وفي رواية أبي بصير، عن أبي عبد الله عليه السلام، في قوله: ﴿وَلا تَتَّبِعُوا خُطُوَاتِ الشَّيْطَانِ﴾، قال: هي ولاية الثاني والأوّل.

٣٠٣. عن مَسعدة بن صَدقة، عن جعفر بن محمّد عن أبيه، عن جدّه، قال: قال أمير المؤمنين عليه السلام: ألا إنّ العلم الّذي هَبط به آدم، وجميع ما فُضِّلت به النبيّون إلى خاتَم النّبيّين والمُرسلين في عِترة خاتَم النّبيّين والمُرسَلين، فأين يُتاه بكم؟ وأين تذهبون؟ يا معاشر من نُسِخ من أصاب السفينة، فهذا مثل ما فيكم، فكما نجا في هاتيك منهم من نجا، وكذلك ينجو في هذه منكم من نجا ورهن ذمّتي، وويل لمن تَخلّف عنهم، إنّهم فيكم كأصحاب الكَهف، ومَثلهم باب حِطّة، وهم باب السِّلم، فادخُلوا في السِّلم كافّة ولا تتّبعوا خُطوات الشيطان.

٣٠٤. عن جابر، قال: قال أبو جعفر عليه السلام، في قول الله تعالى: ﴿فِي ظُلَلٍ مِنَ الْغَمَامِ وَالْمَلَائِكَةُ وَقُضِيَ الْأَمْرُ﴾، قال: ينزل في سبع قِباب من نور، لا يُعلم في أيّها هو، حين ينزل في ظهر الكوفة، فهذا حين ينزل.

٣٠٥. عن أبي حمزة، عن أبي جعفر عليه السلام، قال: قال: يا أبا حمزة، كأنّي بقائم أهل بيتي قد علا نجفكم، فإذا علا فوق نجفِكم نَشَر راية رسول الله صلّى الله عليه وآله، فإذا نشَرَها انحطّت عليه ملائكة بدر.

٣٠٦. وقال أبو جعفر عليه السلام: إنّه نازلٌ في قِباب من نورٍ، حين ينزل بِظهر الكوفة على الفاروق، فهذا حين ينزل، وأمّا قوله: ﴿قُضِيَ الْأَمْرُ﴾ فهو الوسم على الخُرطوم، يوم يُوسم الكافر.

the infidel's noses will be branded [to distinguish them from the true believers].' [2:210]

307. From Abū Baṣīr, from Abū 'Abd Allāh عليه السلام who regarding the verse ﴾*Ask the Children of Israel how many clear signs We brought them*﴿ stated, 'Some of them believed, some rebelled, some attested and some rejected, and there were some who altered the favour of God.' [2:211]

308. From Zurāra, Ḥumrān and Muḥammad b. Muslim, on the authority Abū Ja'far and Abū 'Abd Allāh عليه السلام regarding the verse ﴾*Mankind was a single community, then God sent prophets*﴿ that both of them said, 'They were misguided, so God sent prophets from among them, and if you were to have asked the people themselves, they would have said, "There was nothing that needed to be redressed."' [2:213]

309. From Ya'qūb b. Shu'ayb who narrated, 'I asked Abū 'Abd Allāh عليه السلام about the meaning of the verse ﴾*Mankind was a single community*﴿. He عليه السلام replied, "They had been a single community before Nūḥ, until which time God decided to send prophets from before Nūḥ."

I asked, "Were the people rightly-guided or had they been led astray?" He replied, "They had gone astray, neither believers nor disbelievers, but not polytheists either."' [2:213]

310. From Ya'qūb b. Shu'ayb who narrated, 'I asked Abū 'Abd Allāh عليه السلام about the meaning of the verse ﴾*Mankind was a single community*﴿. He عليه السلام said, "Between Ādam and Nūḥ the people had gone astray, therefore God decided to send prophets to bring good news and to warn them. But had you met these people and asked them they would have said, 'This was not the case.' But they would be lying as God had decided this."' [2:213]

٣٠٧. عن أبي بصير، عن أبي عبدالله عليه السلام، في قوله: ﴿سَلْ بَنِي إِسْرَائِيلَ كَمْ آتَيْنَاهُم مِّنْ آيَةٍ بَيِّنَةٍ﴾ فمنهم من آمن، ومنهم من جَحَد، ومنهم من أقرّ، ومنهم من أنكر، ومنهم من يُبدّل نعمة الله.

٣٠٨. عن زُرارة، وحُمران، ومحمّد بن مسلم، عن أبي جعفر، وأبي عبدالله عليهما السلام، عن قوله تعالى: ﴿كَانَ النَّاسُ أُمَّةً وَاحِدَةً فَبَعَثَ اللهُ النَّبِيِّينَ﴾. قال: كانوا ضُلاّلاً، فبعث الله فيهم أنبياء، ولو سألتَ النّاس لقالوا: قد فرغ من الأمر.

٣٠٩. عن يعقوب بن شُعيب، قال: سألتُ أبا عبدالله عليه السلام، عن قول الله تعالى: ﴿كَانَ النَّاسُ أُمَّةً وَاحِدَةً فَبَعَثَ اللهُ النَّبِيِّينَ﴾، قال: كان هذا قبل نوح عليه السلام أمّة واحدة، فبدا الله فأرسل الرُّسل قبل نوح.

قلتُ: أعَلَى هدًى كانوا أم ضلالة؟ قال: بل كانوا ضُلاّلاً، كانوا لا مؤمنين، ولا كافرين، ولا مشركين.

٣١٠. عن يعقوب بن شُعيب، قال: سألتُ أبا عبدالله عليه السلام عن هذه الآية: ﴿كَانَ النَّاسُ أُمَّةً وَاحِدَةً﴾، قال: بعد آدم وبعد نوح عليهما السلام ضُلاّلاً، فبدا الله فبعث النّبيّين مُبشّرين ومُنذرين، أمّا إنّك إن لقيت هؤلاء، قالوا: إنّ ذلك لم يزل، وكذبوا إنّما هو شيءٌ بدا الله فيه.

311. From Muḥammad b. Muslim, from Abū Ja'far عليه السلام who regarding the verse ﴾*Mankind was a single community, then God sent prophets to bring good news and warning*﴿ said, 'These are verses referring to how it was before Nūḥ when people were astray, so God sent prophets as bearers of glad tidings and as warners.' [2:213]

312. From Mas'ada, from Abū 'Abd Allāh عليه السلام regarding the verse ﴾*Mankind was a single community, then God sent prophets to bring good news and warning*﴿ (2:213) said, 'This was before Nūḥ.' He was asked, 'Were they rightly-guided?'

He replied, 'No, they were led astray, and that was because when Ādam passed away after making peace between his offspring, Shīth was his vicegerent after him, who was not able to openly profess God's creed that Ādam and his righteous children had adhered to. That was because Qābīl was determined on killing him just as he had killed his brother Ḥābīl, so he lived in fear and secrecy. With each day the misguided ones increased in number, either opposing or lagging behind the vicegerent, until there were only a few people left who worshipped God on a small island in the sea. God, Blessed and most High, decided to send prophets. Were these ignorant people to be asked about it, they would say that there was no such command, but they would be lying, as this is something that God decrees every year.' Then he went on to recite ﴾*a night when every matter of wisdom was made distinct*﴿ (44:4), 'God, Blessed and most High, decrees all that is to happen in that year: hardship and ease, rainfall or drought.'

I asked, 'So were they astray or rightly-guided before the prophets came?'

He replied, 'They were not guided, but rather followed their natural instincts which God had instilled in them, and there is no altering God's creation. There was no way for them to be guided save by God guiding them. Have you not heard Ibrāhīm's statement ﴾*If my Lord does not guide me, I shall be one of those who go astray*﴿ (6:77), meaning he would forget the covenant [between him and his Lord].'

٣١١. عن محمّد بن مسلم عن أبي جعفر عليه السلام، في قول الله تعالى: ﴿كَانَ النَّاسُ أُمَّةً وَاحِدَةً فَبَعَثَ اللهُ النَّبِيِّينَ مُبَشِّرِينَ وَمُنذِرِينَ﴾، فقال: كان هذا قبل نوح عليه السلام كانوا ضُلاّلاً، فبعث الله النّبيّين مُبشّرين ومُنذرين.

٣١٢. عن مَسعدة، عن أبي عبدالله عليه السلام، في قول الله تعالى: ﴿كَانَ النَّاسُ أُمَّةً وَاحِدَةً فَبَعَثَ اللهُ النَّبِيِّينَ مُبَشِّرِينَ وَمُنذِرِينَ﴾، فقال عليه السلام: كان ذلك قبل نوح عليه السلام. قيل: فعلى هُدًى كانوا؟

قال عليه السلام: بل كانوا ضُلاّلاً، وذلك أنه لمّا انقرض آدم عليه السلام وصالح ذُرّيته بقي شيث وصيّه لا يقدر على إظهار دين الله الذي كان عليه آدم وصالح ذُرّيته، وذلك أنّ قابيل تواعده بالقتل، كما قتل أخاه هابيل، فسار فيهم بالتّقية والكِتمان، فازدادوا كلّ يوم ضلالاً حتّى لم يبقَ على الأرض معهم إلاّ من هو سلف، ولحق الوصّي بجزيرةٍ في البحر يعبُد الله، فبدا الله تبارك وتعالى أن يبعث الرّسل، ولو سُئل هؤلاء الجُهّال لقالوا: قد فرغ من الأمر، وكذبوا، إنّما شيء يحكم به الله في كلّ عام، ثمّ قرأ: ﴿فِيهَا يُفْرَقُ كُلُّ أَمْرٍ حَكِيمٍ﴾ فيحكم الله تبارك وتعالى ما يكون في تلك السّنة من شدّةٍ أو رخاءٍ أو مطرٍ أو غير ذلك.

قلتُ: أفضُلاّلاً كانوا قبل النّبيّين، أم على هدًى؟

قال: لم يكونوا على هدًى، كانوا على فِطرة الله التي فطرهم عليها، لا تبديل لخلق الله، ولم يكونوا ليهتدوا حتّى يهديَهم الله، أما تسمع بقول إبراهيم: ﴿لَئِن لَّمْ يَهْدِنِي رَبِّي لَأَكُونَنَّ مِنَ الْقَوْمِ الضَّالِّينَ﴾ أي ناسيًا للميثاق.

313. From Muḥammad b. Sinān who said, 'Al-Mu'āfī b. Ismā'īl made a comment to me saying, "When al-Walīd[124] was killed, many people from this sect rose up and people sought change." He continued, "So we went to see Abū 'Abd Allāh عليه السلام and he asked, 'What has caused you to come here besides Hajj and *'umra*?'

Thus a spokesman from among them said, 'God's exposure of the stance of the people of Shām, their killing of their own Caliph, and the disputes going on between them.'

He said, 'Do you think you will find what you are looking for with them?'

Then he went on to elaborate their state of affairs, 'Is it not the case that a man from among you can leave his house, go to the market to get his provisions and return home quite easily? Is it not also true that had it been before your time and someone was to go about their business as you do now, he would have been arrested, amputated, sawed to pieces and crucified on the branches of palm trees. He would not have been allowed to practice.'

Then he stopped talking and turned instead to a verse in God's Book: ﴿*Do you suppose that you will enter the Garden without first having suffered like those before you? They were afflicted by misfortune and hardship, and they were so shaken that even [their] messenger and the believers with him cried, 'When will God's help arrive?' Truly, God's help is near*﴾."' [2:214]

314. From Ḥamduwayh[125], from Muḥammad b. 'Īsā who said, 'I heard him say that Ibrāhīm b. 'Anbasa wrote to 'Alī b. Muḥammad عليه السلام saying, "Would my chief and my master please tell me about the meaning of the verse ﴿*They ask you [Prophet] about intoxicants and gambling: say, 'There is great sin in both, and some benefit for people: the sin is greater than the benefit*﴾: What is considered gambling? May I be your ransom." He wrote back saying, "It includes anything that can be used to gamble; and every intoxicant is prohibited."' [2:219]

---

124 This is Walīd b. Yazīd b. Abd al-Malik (r. 126–7/743–4), the Umayyad ruler, who is said to have set out for Hajj in order to drink alcohol in the vicinity of the Ka'ba, for which reason people despised him, rose up against him and killed him.

125 Abū al-Ḥasan Ḥamduwayh b. Naṣīr b. Shāhī, a prominent figure known for his learning and erudition. He is considered a reliable narrator of traditions. See Ḥillī, *Khulāṣat al-aqwāl*, 133 (nr. 359).

٣١٣. عن محمّد بن سِنان، قال: حدّثني المُعافى بن إسماعيل، قال: لما قُتل الوليد، خرج من هذه العِصابة نفرٌ بحيث أحدث القوم، قال: فدخلنا على أبي عبدالله ﷺ فقال: ما الذي أخرجكم من غير الحجّ والعُمرة؟

قال: فقال القائل منهم: الذي شتّت الله من كلمة أهل الشّام، وقتلهم خليفتهم، واختلافهم فيما بينهم.

قال: قال: ما تجدون أعينكم إليهم؟ — فأقبل يذكر حالاتهم — أليس الرجل منكم يخرُج من بيته إلى سوقه فيقضي حوائجه، ثُمّ يرجِع لم يختلف، إن كان لمن كان قبلكم أتى هو على مثل ما أنتم عليه، ليأخُذ الرّجل منهم فيقطع يديه ورجليه ويُنشَر بالمناشير ويُصلَب على جذع النخلة، ولا يَدع ما كان عليه.

ثمّ ترك هذا الكلام، ثمّ انصرف إلى آيةٍ من كتاب الله: ﴿أَمْ حَسِبْتُمْ أَنْ تَدْخُلُوا الْجَنَّةَ وَلَمَّا يَأْتِكُمْ مَثَلُ الَّذِينَ خَلَوْا مِنْ قَبْلِكُمْ مَسَّتْهُمُ الْبَأْسَاءُ وَالضَّرَّاءُ وَزُلْزِلُوا حَتَّىٰ يَقُولَ الرَّسُولُ وَالَّذِينَ آمَنُوا مَعَهُ مَتَىٰ نَصْرُ اللَّهِ أَلَا إِنَّ نَصْرَ اللَّهِ قَرِيبٌ﴾.

٣١٤. عن حَمدوَيه، عن محمّد بن عيسى، قال: سمعتُه يقول: كتب إليه إبراهيم بن عَنبسة — يعني إلى عليّ بن محمّد ﷺ: إن رأى سيّدي ومولاي أن يُخبرني عن قول الله تعالى: ﴿يَسْأَلُونَكَ عَنِ الْخَمْرِ وَالْمَيْسِرِ﴾ الآية، فما الميسِر، جُعلت فداك؟ فكتب: كلّ ما قُومر به فهو المَيسِر، وكلّ مُسكر حرام.

315. From al-Ḥusayn, from Mūsā b. al-Qāsim al-Bajalī,[126] from Muḥammad b. ʿAlī b. Jaʿfar b. Muḥammad, on his father's authority, from his brother Mūsā, on his father's authority Jaʿfar عليه السلام who said, 'Backgammon and chess count as gambling.' [2:219]

316. From ʿĀmir b. al-Samṭ, from ʿAlī b. al-Ḥusayn عليه السلام who said, 'Wine can be made from six things: dates, raisins, wheat, barley, honey, and corn.' [2:219]

317. From Jamīl b. Darrāj, from Abū ʿAbd Allāh عليه السلام. He said, 'I asked him about the meaning of the verse ﴾*They ask you what they should give: say, 'Give what you can spare.'*﴿. He replied, "What you can spare in moderation."' [2:219]

318. From ʿAbd al-Raḥmān who narrated, 'I asked Abū ʿAbd Allāh عليه السلام about the meaning of the verse ﴾*They ask you what they should give: say, 'Give what you can spare.'*}. He replied by saying '﴾*They are those who are neither wasteful nor niggardly when they spend, but keep to a just balance*﴿(25:67). This one was revealed after that one, and it is to give in moderation."' [2:219]

319. From Yūsuf, from Abū ʿAbd Allāh عليه السلام or Abū Jaʿfar عليه السلام regarding the verse ﴾*They ask you what they should give: say, 'Give what you can spare.'*﴿. He عليه السلام said, 'To have sufficiency.' [2:219]

320. In a narration from Abū Baṣīr, 'It is frugality.' [2:219]

321. From Zurāra, from Abū Jaʿfar عليه السلام. He said, 'I asked him about the words of God, Blessed and most High, ﴾*If you combine their affairs with yours, remember they are your brothers and sisters*﴿. He replied, "You should take out from their wealth an amount that will suffice them, and from your wealth an amount that will suffice you." I asked, "Is that the same for both older and younger orphans when the clothing needs of some may be more than others?" He replied, "Clothing is specific to each person, but when it comes to food, combine it all together since a youngster may well eat as much as an adult."' [2:220]

---

126 Mūsā b. al-Maʿmar al-ʿIjlī in one source, and Mūsā b. al-Qāsim al-ʿIjlī in another.

٣١٥. عن الحُسين، عن موسى بن القاسم البجلي، عن محمّد بن عليّ بن جعفر بن محمّد عن أبيه عن أخيه موسى، عن أبيه جعفر عليه السلام، قال: النَّرد والشَّطرنج من المَيسِر.

٣١٦. عن عامر بن السّمط، عن عليّ بن الحُسين عليه السلام، قال: الخمر من ستّة أشياء: التّمر، والزّبيب، والحِنطَة، والشَّعير، والعَسل، والذُّرّة.

٣١٧. عن جميل بن درّاج، عن أبي عبدالله عليه السلام، قال: سألتُه عن قوله: ﴿وَيَسْأَلُونَكَ مَاذَا يُنفِقُونَ قُلِ الْعَفْوَ﴾، قال: العفو: الوسط.

٣١٨. عن عبد الرّحمن، قال: سألتُ أبا عبدالله عليه السلام، عن قوله تعالى: ﴿وَيَسْأَلُونَكَ مَاذَا يُنفِقُونَ قُلِ الْعَفْوَ﴾ قال: ﴿وَالَّذِينَ إِذَا أَنفَقُوا لَمْ يُسْرِفُوا وَلَمْ يَقْتُرُوا وَكَانَ بَيْنَ ذَٰلِكَ قَوَامًا﴾، قال: نزلت هذه بعد هذه، هي الوسط.

٣١٩. عن يوسف، عن أبي عبدالله عليه السلام — أو أبي جعفر عليه السلام — في قول الله تعالى: ﴿وَيَسْأَلُونَكَ مَاذَا يُنفِقُونَ قُلِ الْعَفْوَ﴾ قال: الكفاف.

٣٢٠. وفي رواية أبي بصير: القَصد.

٣٢١. عن زُرارة، عن أبي جعفر عليه السلام، قال: سألتُه عن قول الله تبارك وتعالى: ﴿وَإِنْ تُخَالِطُوهُمْ فَإِخْوَانُكُمْ﴾، قال: تُخرج من أموالهم قدر ما يكفيهم، وتُخرج من مالِكَ قَدر ما يكفيك.

322. From Samā'a, from Abū 'Abd Allāh عليه السلام or Abū al-Ḥasan عليه السلام; he said, 'I asked him about the meaning of the verse ﴿*If you combine their affairs with yours, remember they are your brothers and sisters*﴾, and he said, "This refers to the orphans, in that when a person is a guardian of orphans under his care he should spend on them from his wealth the same as what he would spend on any other human being. He should combine their affairs such that they all eat together, and there should be no loss incurred on their property, for that is [tantamount to] Hellfire."' [2:220]

323. From al-Kāhilī who narrated, 'I was with Abū 'Abd Allāh عليه السلام when a blind man asked him, "We go to visit a brother in a house where there are orphans living, and a servant there too. We sit on their carpet and drink their water, and their servant serves us. We may even eat there with our host, of food that may include their portion. What would you say about this? May God grant you goodness."

He replied, "God has said, ﴿*Truly, man is a clear witness against himself*﴾ (75:14), so you should take heed. He has also said, ﴿*If you combine their affairs with yours, remember they are your brothers and sisters. God knows those who spoil things and those who improve them. Had He so willed, He could have made you vulnerable too*﴾." He continued, "If your visiting them is a source of benefit for them, then there is no problem. If it is to their disadvantage, then no."' [2:220]

324. From Abū Ḥamza, from Abū Ja'far عليه السلام who said, 'A man once came to the Prophet صلى الله عليه وآله saying, "O Messenger of God, my brother has died and left orphans. They also have cattle. What am I allowed to consume from them?" Then the Messenger of God صلى الله عليه وآله replied, "If you are the one to refill their watering trough, round up their strays and tend to them, then you can drink from their milk, but be careful not to over-milk them nor cause any harm to their young. Then he said, ﴿*And God knows those who spoil things and those who improve them*﴾."' [2:220]

قال: قلتُ: أرأيت أيتامًا صغارًا وكبارًا، وبعضهم أعلى في الكُسوة من بعض؟ فقال: أمّا الكُسوة فعلى كلّ إنسان من كسوته، وأمّا الطعام فاجعله جميعًا، فأمّا الصغير فإنّه أوشك أن يأكل كما يأكل الكبير.

٣٢٢. عن سماعة، عن أبي عبد الله — أو أبي الحسن عليه السلام — قال: سألتُه عن قول الله تعالى: ﴿وَإِنْ تُخَالِطُوهُمْ﴾. قال يعني اليتامى، يقول: إذا كان الرجل يلي يتامى وهم في حِجره، فلْيُخرج من ماله على قدر ما يُخرج لكلّ إنسان منهم، فيُخالطهم، فيأكلون جميعًا، ولا يَرزأنّ من أموالهم شيئًا، فإنّما هو نار.

٣٢٣. عن الكاهليّ، قال: كنتُ عند أبي عبد الله عليه السلام، فسأله رجل ضَرير البصر، فقال: إنّا ندخل على أخٍ لنا في بيت أيتامٍ معهم خادم لهم، فنقعُد على بِساطهم، ونَشرب من مائهم، ويخدِمُنا خادمهم، وربما أطعمنا فيه الطعام من عند صاحبنا وفيه من طعامهم، فما ترى، أصْلَحَكَ الله؟ فقال عليه السلام: قد قال الله: ﴿بَلِ الإِنسَانُ عَلَىٰ نَفْسِهِ بَصِيرَةٌ﴾ فأنتم لا يخفى عليكم، وقد قال الله تعالى: ﴿وَإِنْ تُخَالِطُوهُمْ فَإِخْوَانُكُمْ﴾ إلى قوله: ﴿لَأَعْنَتَكُمْ﴾. ثمّ قال: إن يكُن دُخولكم عليهم فيه مَنفعة لهم فلا بأس، وإن كان فيه ضَرر فلا.

٣٢٤. عن أبي حمزة، عن أبي جعفر عليه السلام، قال: جاء رجل إلى النبي صلى الله عليه وآله، فقال: يا رسول الله، إنّ أخي هَلك، وترك أيتامًا ولهم ماشيةٌ، فما يحِلّ لي منها؟ فقال: رسول الله صلى الله عليه وآله: إن كنت تَليط حَوضها وتَرُدّ نادّتها، وتقوم على رعيّتها، فأشرب من ألبانها غير مجتهدٍ للحَلْب، ولا ضارٍّ بالولد ﴿وَاللَّهُ يَعْلَمُ الْمُفْسِدَ مِنَ الْمُصْلِحِ﴾.

325. From Muḥammad b. Muslim who narrated, 'I asked him about a man who has cattle that belongs to his orphaned nephew in his care and whether he can combine them with his own livestock? He replied, "If he is refilling their watering troughs, tarring their hooves, and rounding up their strays, then he can drink from their milk, being careful not to over-milk them nor cause any harm to their young." Then he recited the verse ﴾*if the guardian is well off he should abstain from the orphan's property, and if he is poor he should use only what is fair*﴿ (4:6) and the verse ﴾*And God knows those who spoil things and those who improve them*﴿.' [2:220]

326. From Muḥammad al-Ḥalabī who narrated, 'I asked Abū 'Abd Allāh عليه السلام about the meaning of the verse ﴾*If you combine their affairs with yours, remember they are your brothers and sisters. God knows those who spoil things and those who improve them*﴿. He replied, "You should take out from their wealth enough to suffice them, and from your own wealth enough to suffice you, then spend it."

Muḥammad b. Muslim narrates a similar report from Abū Ja'far عليه السلام. [2:220]

327. From 'Alī, from Abū 'Abd Allāh عليه السلام. He said, 'I asked him about the meaning of the verse regarding orphans ﴾*If you combine their affairs with yours, remember they are your brothers and sisters*﴿. He replied, "They should have as much milk and dates as you do, according to what suffices them and what suffices you. Then he said, ﴾*And God is well aware of those who spoil things and those who improve them*﴿."' [2:220]

328. From 'Abd al-Raḥmān b. al-Ḥajjāj, from Abū al-Ḥasan Mūsā عليه السلام. He said, 'I asked him, "The orphan in my care owns wealth out of which I spend on him. Sometimes I get confused between the food [bought] from this money and that which I spend on him [from my money], as to which is more." He replied, "There is no problem there; ﴾*And God is well aware of those who spoil things and those who improve them*﴿."' [2:220]

٣٢٥. عن محمّد بن مسلم، قال: سألتُه عن رجل بيده الماشية لابن أخٍ له يتيم في حِجره، أيَخلط أمرها بأمره ماشيته؟ قال: فإن كان يَليط حوضها، ويقوم على هَنائها، ويردّ نادّتها، فلْيشرب من ألبانها، غير مجتهد للحلاب، ولا مضرّ بالولد، ثمّ قال: ﴿وَمَن كَانَ غَنِيًّا فَلْيَسْتَعْفِفْ وَمَن كَانَ فَقِيرًا فَلْيَأْكُلْ بِالْمَعْرُوفِ﴾ ﴿وَاللَّهُ يَعْلَمُ الْمُفْسِدَ مِنَ الْمُصْلِحِ﴾.

٣٢٦. عن محمّد الحلبي، قال: قلتُ لأبي عبدالله عليه السلام، قول الله تعالى: ﴿وَإِن تُخَالِطُوهُمْ فَإِخْوَانُكُمْ وَاللَّهُ يَعْلَمُ الْمُفْسِدَ مِنَ الْمُصْلِحِ﴾، قال: تُخرج من أموالهم قدر ما يكفيهم، وتُخرج من مالك قدر ما يكفيك، ثمّ تُنفِقه.

عن محمّد بن مسلم، عن أبي جعفر عليه السلام، مثله.

٣٢٧. عن علي، عن أبي عبدالله عليه السلام، قال: سألتُه عن قول الله تعالى في اليتامى: ﴿وَإِن تُخَالِطُوهُمْ فَإِخْوَانُكُمْ﴾؟ قال: يكون لهم التمر واللّبن، ويكون لك مثله، على قدر ما يكفيك ويكفيهم، ولا يَخفى على الله المُفسد من المُصلح.

٣٢٨. عن عبد الرّحمن بن الحجّاج، عن أبي الحسن موسى عليه السلام، قال: قلتُ له: يكون لليتيم عندي الشيء، وهو في حِجري أُنفق عليه منه، وربما أُصيب ممّا يكون له من الطعام، وما يكون منّي إليه أكثر؟ فقال: لا بأس بذلك، إنّ الله يعلم المُفسد من المُصلح.

329. From Jamīl who said, 'I heard Abū 'Abd Allāh say, "People used to clean themselves with stones or leaves after relieving themselves. Then washing with water came about, which is a good practice that the Messenger of God ﷺ commanded and initiated, and that has been revealed by God in His Book in the verse ﴾*God loves those who turn to Him, and He loves those who keep themselves clean*﴿."' [2:222]

330. From Sallām who said, 'I was with Abū Ja'far عليه السلام when Ḥumrān b. A'yan came in to ask him about some things. Then when Ḥumrān got ready to leave, he said to Abū Ja'far عليه السلام, "May God prolong your life and grant us the joy of your company. For whenever we come to you, we always go back with our hearts softened and our souls detached from this world, and the material wealth that people have in their possessions seems insignificant to us. Then we leave your presence and associate with people and traders, and we start inclining towards worldly matters again."

Abū Ja'far عليه السلام replied, "That is just how the hearts are; one minute something is difficult for them and the next easy."

Then Abū Ja'far continued, "The Prophet's ﷺ companions said to him, 'O Messenger of God, we fear that we may be hypocritical.'

So he asked, 'And why do you fear that?'

They replied, 'When we are with you, and you remind us, we are in awe, and we tremble and forget the world. We lose all interest in it, and it is as if we see the Hereafter and the Garden and the Fire with our own eyes when we are with you. Then we leave your presence, enter our houses, and interact with our children, see our families, relatives and possessions, it is almost as if we are transformed from the state that we were in your presence, to an extent whereby it is as if we had never experienced that in the first place. Do you fear that this might be hypocrisy on our part?'

So the Messenger of God ﷺ replied, 'Absolutely not. These are the footsteps of Satan to entice you into worldliness. By God, if you were to remain perpetually in the state that you are in when you are with me, in the way that you described yourselves, the angels themselves would come and greet you, and you would be able to walk on water! If you did not commit sins to warrant seeking God's forgiveness subsequently, then He would create others to commit sins, that they may seek His forgiveness and that He may forgive them. The believer is afflicted and penitent. Have you not heard His words

٣٢٩. عن جميل، قال: سمعتُ أبا عبد الله ﵇ يقول: كان الناس يستنجُون بالحجار والكُرسُف، ثمّ أُحدِث الوضوء، وهو خُلق حسن، فأمر به رسول الله ﷺ، وأنزله الله في كتاب: ﴿إِنَّ اللَّهَ يُحِبُّ التَّوَّابِينَ وَيُحِبُّ الْمُتَطَهِّرِينَ﴾.

٣٣٠. عن سلاّم، قال: كنتُ عند أبي جعفر ﵇ فدخل عليه حُمران بن أعين، فسأله عن أشياء، فلمّا همّ حُمران بالقيام، قال لأبي جعفر ﵇: أخبرك – أطال الله بقاك، وأمتَعَنا بك – أنّا نأتيك فما نخرُج من عندك حتّى ترَقّ قلوبنا، وتَسلو أنفسنا عن الدنيا، ويَهُون علينا ما في أيدي الناس من هذه الأموال، ثمّ نخرُج من عندك فإذا صِرنا مع الناس والتُجّار أحببنا الدنيا.

قال: فقال أبو جعفر ﵇: إنّما هي القلوب مرّةً يَصعب عليها الأمر، ومرّةً يَسهل.

ثمّ قال أبو جعفر ﵇: أمّا إنّ أصحاب رسول الله ﷺ قالوا: يا رسول الله، نخاف علينا النِّفاق قال: فقال لهم، ولِمَ تخافون ذلك؟ قالوا: إنّا إذا كنّا عندك فذكّرتنا، رُوِّعنا ووجِلنا، ونَسِينا الدنيا، وزَهِدنا فيها حتّى كأنّا نُعاين الآخرة، والجنّة، والنّار، ونحنُ عندك، فإذا خرجنا من عندك، ودخلنا هذه البيوت، وشَمَمنا الأولاد، ورأينا العِيال، والأهل، والمال، يكاد أن نُحوِّل عن الحال التي كنّا عليها عندك، وحتّى كأنّا لم نكُن على شيء، أفتخاف علينا أن يكون هذا النِّفاق؟

فقال لهم رسول الله ﷺ: كلاّ، هذا من خُطُوات الشيطان ليُرغِّبَكم في الدنيا، واللهِ لو أنّكم تدومون على الحال التي تكونون عليها، وأنتم عندي في الحال التي وَصفتم أنفسكم بها، لَصافحَتْكم الملائكة، ومشَيتم على الماء، ولولا أنّكم تُذنبون فتَستغفرون الله، لَخَلَقَ الله خلقًا

﴾*God loves those who turn to Him*﴿(2:222)?' Then he said, ﴾*Ask forgiveness from your Lord, and turn to Him in repentance*﴿(11:90).'''

331. From Abū Khadīja, from Abū 'Abd Allāh ﷺ who narrated, 'People used to clean themselves with three stones after relieving themselves because they would eat dates which were not yet ripe and consequently have hard bowel movements. Once a man from among the *anṣār* ate some pumpkin which upset his stomach, so he used water to wash himself. Upon receiving news of this the Prophet ﷺ sent for him, and the man came apprehensively, thinking that something negative had been revealed about him condemning him for having used water to clean himself.'

He continued, 'The Messenger of God ﷺ asked him, "Have you done anything significant today?" He replied, "Yes, O Messenger of God. I swear by God, I was only compelled to use water to clean myself because I had eaten something that made my stomach upset, and stones were of no avail, so I used water." At that point the Messenger of God ﷺ said, "Well done! God has revealed a verse about you: ﴾*God loves those who turn to Him, and He loves those who keep themselves clean*﴿; for you are the first one to do this, the first one from among those who turn to Him, and the first from among those who keep themselves clean."' [2:222]

332. From 'Īsā b. 'Abd Allāh[127]: 'Abū 'Abd Allāh ﷺ said, "When a woman is menstruating her husband is prohibited from having sexual intercourse with her, as per the command of God: ﴾*Do not approach them until they are cleansed*﴿. Be this as it may, it is all well and good for a man to be close to his wife [intimately] while she is menstruating so long as he avoids her private parts."' [2:222]

333. From 'Abd Allāh b. Abī Ya'fūr who said, 'I asked Abū 'Abd Allāh ﷺ about entering women from behind. He replied, "There is no problem with that,

127 'Īsā b. 'Abd Allāh b. Sa'd b. Mālik al-Ash'arī al-Qummī, a beloved companion and narrator of Imam Ja'far al-Ṣādiq whom the latter praised as one of the *ahl al-bayt*. See Ḥillī, *Khulāṣat al-aqwāl*, 216–7 (nr. 708 and 712; Ḥillī regards each entry as two separate individuals, though in fact they are the same individual.)

لكي يُذنِبوا ثمّ يستغفروا فيغفر لهم، إنّ المؤمن مُفتّن توّاب، أما تسمع لقوله تعالى: ﴿إِنَّ اللهَ يُحِبُّ التَّوَّابِينَ﴾ ﴿وَاسْتَغْفِرُوا رَبَّكُمْ ثُمَّ تُوبُوا إِلَيْهِ﴾؟

٣٣١. عن أبي خَديجة، عن أبي عبدالله عليه السلام، قال: كانوا يستنجُون بثلاثة أحجار، لأنّهم كانوا يأكلون البُسر، وكانوا يبْعَرون بَعرًا، فأكل رجل من الأنصار الدُّبّاء، فَلان بطنُه واستنجى بالماء، فبعث إليه النبي صلى الله عليه وآله، قال: فجاء الرجل وهو خائفٌ أن يكون قد نزل فيه أمر يسُوءُه في استنجائه بالماء.

قال: فقال رسول الله صلى الله عليه وآله: هل عَمِلت في يومك هذا شيئًا؟ فقال: نعم يا رسول الله، إنّي واللهِ ما حملني على الاستنجاء بالماء إلاّ أنّي أكلتُ طعامًا فَلان بطني، فلم تُغنِ عنّي الحجارة، فاستنجيتُ بالماء. فقال رسول الله صلى الله عليه وآله: هنيئًا لك، فإنّ الله عزّ وجلّ قد أنزل فيك آية: ﴿إِنَّ اللهَ يُحِبُّ التَّوَّابِينَ وَيُحِبُّ الْمُتَطَهِّرِينَ﴾ فكنتَ أوّل من صَنَع ذا، أوّل التوّابين، وأوّل المتطهرين.

٣٣٢. عن عيسى بن عبدالله، قال: قال أبو عبدالله عليه السلام: المرأة تحيض يحَرُم على زوجها أن يأتيَها في فرجِها، لقول الله تعالى: ﴿وَلَا تَقْرَبُوهُنَّ حَتَّىٰ يَطْهُرْنَ﴾ فيستقيم للرجل أن يأتي امرأته وهي حائض فيما دون الفرج.

٣٣٣. عن عبدالله بن أبي يعفور، قال: سألتُ أبا عبدالله عليه السلام: عن إتيان النساء في أعجازهنّ، قال: لا بأس، ثمّ تلا هذ الآية: ﴿نِسَاؤُكُمْ حَرْثٌ لَكُمْ فَأْتُوا حَرْثَكُمْ أَنَّىٰ شِئْتُمْ﴾.

and recited this verse ﴿ *Your wives are your fields, so go into your fields whichever way you like* ﴾."' [2:223]

334. From Zurāra, from Abū Jaʿfar عليه السلام regarding the verse ﴿ *Your wives are your fields, so go into your fields whichever way you like* ﴾, he said, 'From wherever he wishes.' [2:223]

335. From Ṣafwān b. Yaḥyā[128], from one of our associates who said, 'I asked Abū ʿAbd Allāh عليه السلام about the verse ﴿ *Your wives are your fields, so go into your fields whichever way you like* ﴾. He replied, "From the front as well as from behind, but in the front part."' [2:223]

336. From Maʿmar b. Khallād[129], from Abū al-Ḥasan al-Riḍā عليه السلام who was asked, 'What is your opinion about approaching women from behind, as I have heard from the people of Medina that they do not see anything wrong with that.' He replied, 'The Jews believed that if a man entered from behind, the resulting child would be born with a squint. That is why God revealed this verse, ﴿ *Your wives are your fields, so go into your fields whichever way you like* ﴾, intending by that [that a man can enter the sexual organ of his wife, the vagina,] while facing her or from behind [her], contrary to the Jews' belief; but it does not mean from their anuses.'

There is a similar narration from al-Ḥasan b. ʿAlī, from Abū ʿAbd Allāh عليه السلام. [2:223]

337. From Zurāra, from Abū Jaʿfar عليه السلام. He said, 'I asked him about the meaning of the verse ﴿ *Your wives are your fields, so go into your fields whichever way you like* ﴾. He replied, "It means the front part [i.e. the vagina]."' [2:223]

338. From Abū Baṣīr, from Abū ʿAbd Allāh عليه السلام. He said, 'I asked him about a man who enters his wife from her anus. He was repulsed by that and said, "Keep away from women's anuses." He continued, "The verse ﴿ *Your wives are your*

128 Abū Muḥammad Ṣafwān b. Yaḥyā al-Bajalī Bayyāʿ al-Sāburī, a renowned pietist and ascetic who was a leading companion of Imam al-Riḍā whose traditions are considered reliable and trustworthy. See Ḥillī, *Khulāṣat al-aqwāl*, 170–1 (nr. 500).

129 Abū Khallād Maʿmar b. Khallād al-Baghdādī was a reliable companion and narrator of the eighth Imam's traditions. See Ḥillī, *Khulāṣat al-aqwāl*, 277 (nr. 1010).

٣٣٤. عن زُرارة عن أبي جعفر عليه السلام، في قول الله تعالى: ﴿نِسَاؤُكُمْ حَرْثٌ لَّكُمْ فَأْتُوا حَرْثَكُمْ أَنَّىٰ شِئْتُمْ﴾، قال: حيثُ شاء.

٣٣٥. عن صفوان بن يحيى، عن بعض أصحابنا، قال: سألتُ أبا عبدالله عليه السلام عن قول الله: ﴿نِسَاؤُكُمْ حَرْثٌ لَّكُمْ فَأْتُوا حَرْثَكُمْ أَنَّىٰ شِئْتُمْ﴾، فقال: من قُدّامها ومن خلفها في القُبُل.

٣٣٦. عن مَعمَر بن خلّاد، عن أبي الحسن الرضا عليه السلام، أنّه قال: أيّ شيء يقولون في إتيان النساء في أعجازهنّ؟ قلتُ: بلغني أنّ أهل المدينة لا يرَون به بأسًا. قال: إنّ اليهود كانت تقول: إذا أتى الرجل من خلفها خرج ولده أحول، فأنزل الله: ﴿نِسَاؤُكُمْ حَرْثٌ لَّكُمْ فَأْتُوا حَرْثَكُمْ أَنَّىٰ شِئْتُمْ﴾ يعني من خلف أو قدّام خلافًا لقول اليهود، ولم يَعنِ في أدبارهنّ.

عن الحسن بن علي عن أبي عبدالله عليه السلام، مثله.

٣٣٧. عن زُرارة، عن أبي جعفر عليه السلام، قال: سألتُه عن قول الله: ﴿نِسَاؤُكُمْ حَرْثٌ لَّكُمْ فَأْتُوا حَرْثَكُمْ أَنَّىٰ شِئْتُمْ﴾، قال: من قُبُل.

٣٣٨. عن أبي بصير، عن أبي عبدالله عليه السلام، قال: سألتُه عن الرجل يأتي أهله في دُبُرها، فكرِه ذلك، وقال: وإيّاكم ومحاشّ النساء. قال: إنّما معنى ﴿نِسَاؤُكُمْ حَرْثٌ لَّكُمْ فَأْتُوا حَرْثَكُمْ أَنَّىٰ شِئْتُمْ﴾ أي ساعةٍ شئتم.

fields, so go into your fields whichever way you like ﴿ means at whichever time you like."' [2:223]

339. From al-Fatḥ b. Yazīd al-Jurjānī[130] who said, 'I wrote to al-Riḍā ﵇ for a similar issue, and the reply that came from him said, "You have asked about one who enters his servant-girl from her back passage, and woman is for man to enjoy, but she must not be hurt, and she is a field as God, most High, has said."' [2:223]

340. From Muḥammad b. Muslim who narrated, 'I asked Abū 'Abd Allāh ﵇ about the words of God, Blessed and most High, there is no god but Him ﴾ *[Believers], do not allow your oaths in God's name to hinder you from doing good, being mindful of God and making peace between people* ﴿. He replied, "It is when a man says 'Yes, by God!' and 'No, by God' [in vain]."' [2:224]

341. From Zurāra, Ḥumrān and Muḥammad b. Muslim, from Abū Ja'far ﵇ and Abū 'Abd Allāh ﵇ regarding the verse: ﴾ *[Believers], do not allow your oaths in God's name to hinder you from doing good, being mindful of God and making peace between people* ﴿. They said, "This refers to a man who makes peace with another, and consequently relieves both of the burden of sin." [2:224]

342. From Manṣūr b. Ḥāzim, from Abū 'Abd Allāh ﵇; and from Muḥammad b. Muslim, from Abū Ja'far ﵇, regarding the verse ﴾ *[Believers], do not allow your oaths in God's name to hinder you from doing good, being mindful of God and making peace between people* ﴿. He said, 'It is referring to when a man swears an oath that he will not speak to his brother or his mother, and other such things.' [2:224]

343. From Ayyūb who narrated, saying, 'I heard him say, "Do not swear by God, neither in truth nor in jest, for God has said ﴾ *[Believers], do not allow your oaths in God's name to hinder you from doing good, being mindful of God and making peace between people* ﴿. When a man solicits someone's help in

---

130 Al-Fatḥ b. Yazīd al-Jurjānī is described in biographical sources as an unknown (*majhūl*) individual. He apparently sent a series of questions to the eighth Imam. See Ḥillī, *Khulāṣat al-aqwāl*, 388 (nr. 1557).

٣٣٩. عن الفَتح بن يزيد الجُرجانيّ، قال: كتبتُ إلى الرضا عليه السلام في مثله، فورد منه الجواب: سألتَ عمّن أتى جارِيَته في دُبُرها، والمرأة لُعبةٌ لا تؤذى، وهي حرثٌ كما قال الله تعالى.

٣٤٠. عن محمّد بن مسلم قال: سألتُ أبا عبدالله عليه السلام عن قول الله تبارك وتعالى ولا إله غيره: ﴿وَلَا تَجْعَلُوا اللَّهَ عُرْضَةً لِأَيْمَانِكُمْ أَنْ تَبَرُّوا وَتَتَّقُوا﴾، قال: هو قول الرجل: لا واللهِ، وبلى واللهِ.

٣٤١. عن زُرارة، وحُمران، ومحمّد بن مسلم، عن أبي جعفر وأبي عبدالله عليهما السلام: ﴿وَلَا تَجْعَلُوا اللَّهَ عُرْضَةً لِأَيْمَانِكُمْ﴾، قالا: هو الرجل يُصلِح بين الرجلين فيَحمِل ما بينهما من الإثم.

٣٤٢. عن مَنصور بن حازم، عن أبي عبدالله عليه السلام، ومحمّد بن مسلم، عن أبي جعفر عليه السلام، في قول الله: ﴿وَلَا تَجْعَلُوا اللَّهَ عُرْضَةً لِأَيْمَانِكُمْ﴾، قال: يعني الرجل يحلف أن لا يُكلّم أخاه، وما أشبه ذلك، أولا يُكلّم أُمّه.

٣٤٣. عن أيّوب قال: سمعتُه يقول: لا تحلِفوا بالله صادقين ولا كاذبين، فإنّ الله يقول: ﴿وَلَا تَجْعَلُوا اللَّهَ عُرْضَةً لِأَيْمَانِكُمْ﴾، قال: إذا استعان رجلٌ برجلٍ على صُلحٍ بينه وبين رجلٍ، فلا يقولنّ: إنّ عليّ يمينًا أن لا أفعل، وهو قول الله: ﴿وَلَا تَجْعَلُوا اللَّهَ عُرْضَةً لِأَيْمَانِكُمْ أَنْ تَبَرُّوا وَتَتَّقُوا وَتُصْلِحُوا بَيْنَ النَّاسِ﴾.

reconciling between him and another person, then the latter must not say: 'I have sworn an oath not to do that,' for these are God's words: ﴾*Do not allow your oaths in God's name to hinder you from doing good, being mindful of God and making peace between people*﴿."' [2:224]

344. From Abū al-Ṣabbāḥ who said, 'I asked Abū 'Abd Allāh عليه السلام about the meaning of the verse ﴾*God will not call you to account for oaths you have uttered unintentionally*﴿. He replied, "It is to say: 'No, by God', 'Yes, by God' and 'Never, by God' [in vain], where one is not really bound by it or by anything."' [2:225]

345. From Burayd b. Mu'āwiya who narrated, 'I heard Abū 'Abd Allāh عليه السلام speak about *īlā'*,[131] "When a man swears not to sleep with his wife, not to touch her, nor to embrace her, he can do this for a maximum of four months. When this period has elapsed, he is at liberty if she remains silent about the matter. If, however, she asks for her right after the four months, then [suspending his oath] he must either fulfil it and touch her again, or decide to divorce. In that case, he must separate from her until she menstruates and becomes cleansed of her menses, then he can divorce her with a single pronouncement of the divorce in the presence of two just witnesses, without first sleeping with her. After that he has the right to take her back within three months."' [2:226]

346. From al-Ḥalabī, from Abū 'Abd Allāh عليه السلام who said, 'Any man who forswears his wife by saying, "By God, I shall never sleep with you because of such and such," or "By God, I am exasperated with you," because he is infuriated by her, or "I am going to torment you," thus neglecting her by not sleeping with her, he is at liberty to do this for four months. After that, he can return to her through reconciliation, for God is Oft-Forgiving and Merciful. If he does not return, then he should divorce her, and this is not effective until he suspends his oath. If he does decide to divorce, then it is by a single pronouncement.' [2:226]

131 A pre-Islamic practice in which the husband could take an oath to refrain from sexual intimacy with his wife thereby leaving her in a state of uncertainty for an indefinite period.

٣٤٤. عن أبي الصَّبّاح، قال: سألتُ أبا عبدالله ﵇ عن قوله تعالى: ﴿لا يُؤَاخِذُكُمُ اللهُ بِاللَّغْوِ فِي أَيْمَانِكُمْ﴾، قال: هو (لا واللهِ)، (وبلى واللهِ)، (وكلاّ واللهِ) لا يَعقِد عليها، أولا يَعقِد على شيء.

٣٤٥. عن بُريد بن معاوية، قال: سمعتُ أبا عبدالله ﵇ يقول في الإيلاء: إذا آلى الرجل من امرأته، لا يَقربُها، ولا يَمسّها، ولا يجمع رأسَه ورأسَها، فهو في سَعةٍ ما لم يمضِ الأربعة الأشهر، فإذا مضى الأربعة الأشهر فهو في حلّ ما سكتتْ عنه، فإذا طلبتْ حقّها بعد الأربعة الأشهر وقف، فإمّا أن يفي فَيَمسّها، وإمّا أن يعزِم على الطّلاق فيُخلّي عنها، حتّى إذا حاضت وتطهّرت من محيضها، طلّقها تطليقةً من قبل أن يجامعها بشهادة عدلَين، ثمّ هو أحقّ برجعتها ما لم يمضِ الثلاثة الأقراء.

٣٤٦. عن الحلبي عن أبي عبدالله ﵇، قال: أيّما رجل آلى من امرأته ــ والإيلاء: أن يقول الرجل: واللهِ، لا أجامِعُكِ كذا وكذا ويقول: واللهِ، لأغيظنّكِ، ثمّ يُغايظها، ولأسوئنّكِ، ثمّ يهجُرها فلا يُجامعها ــ فإنّه يتربّص بها أربعة أشهر، فإن فاء ــ والإيفاء: أن يُصالح ــ ﴿فَإِنَّ اللهَ غَفُورٌ رَحِيمٌ﴾، وإن لم يفئ جُبر على الطّلاق فهي تطليقة.

347. From Abū Baṣīr, who asked about a man who forswears his wife until four months pass. He [either Imam al-Ṣādiq ﷺ or Imam al-Bāqir ﷺ] said, 'If he decides to divorce her, then she observes the waiting period after the divorce as a regular divorcee. If he takes her back, then there is no problem.' [2:226]

348. From Manṣūr b. Ḥāzim who narrated, 'I asked Abū 'Abd Allāh ﷺ about a man who forswears his wife and four months pass. He replied, "He must suspend it, and either decide to divorce her, in which case she must part from him and observe the waiting period of a divorcee, or he can rescind his oath and take her back."' [2:226]

349. From al-'Abbās b. Hilāl[132], from al-Riḍā ﷺ; 'He mentioned to us that the time limit for *īlā'* was four months, after they have been to the ruler (*sulṭān*) [to officialise it]. When four months have passed, he can take her back if he wills, or divorce her if he so wishes; and she can be taken back by mere touch.' [2:226]

350. Abū 'Abd Allāh ﷺ was asked, 'When a woman separates from her husband, does he have to contract a marriage with her again [to take her back]?' He replied, 'He need only contract a marriage with her [when taking her back] after two pronouncements of divorce. However, he cannot be intimate with her until he has rescinded his oath.' [2:228–229]

351. From Ṣafwān, from one of his associates, from Abū 'Abd Allāh ﷺ regarding a slave who refuses to divorce [his wife]. He said, "Alī ﷺ would make an enclosure out of long cane stalks, and keep him there without food or drink until he agreed to divorce [her].' [2:228–229]

352. From Abū Baṣīr, from Abū 'Abd Allāh ﷺ regarding a man who forswears his wife and four months pass without him returning to her, then she is divorced. Then if he rescinds his oath and returns, then she still has two

132 There is no record of al-'Abbās b. Hilāl in Ḥillī's *Khulāṣat al-aqwāl*. For a brief mention about him see Khū'ī, *Mu'jam*, 10: 271 (nr. 6219).

٣٤٧. عن أبي بصير في رجلٍ آلى من امرأته حتّى مضت أربعة أشهر. قال: يُوقَف فإن عَزم الطَّلاق اعتدّت امرأته كما تعتدّ المُطلَّقة، وإن أمسَك فلا بأس.

٣٤٨. عن منصور بن حازِم، قال: سألتُ أبا عبدالله عليه السلام عن رجلٍ آلى من امرأته، فمضت أربعة أشهر، قال: يُوقَف، فإن عَزم الطَّلاق بانتْ منه، وعليها عدّة المُطلَّقة، وإلا كفَّر يمينه وأمسكها.

٣٤٩. عن العبّاس بن هلال، عن الرضا عليه السلام، أنّه ذكر لنا أنّ أجل الإيلاء أربعة أشهر بعد ما يأتيان السّلطان، فإذا مضَت الأربعة الأشهر، فإن شاء أمسك، وإن شاء طلّق، والإمساك: المسيس.

٣٥٠. سُئل أبو عبدالله عليه السلام: إذا بانت المرأة من الرجُل، هل يَخطُبها مع الخُطّاب؟ قال: يَخطُبها على تطليقَتَين، ولا يَقرَبها حتّى يُكفِّر يمينه.

٣٥١. عن صَفوان، عن بعض أصحابه، عن أبي عبدالله عليه السلام، في المولي إذا أبى أن يُطلّق، قال: كان عليّ عليه السلام يجعل له حظيرة قَصَب، ويحبِسُه فيها، ويمنعُه من الطَّعام والشَّراب حتّى يُطلّق.

٣٥٢. عن أبي بصير، عن أبي عبدالله عليه السلام، في الرجل إذا آلى من امرأته، فمضَت أربعة أشهر ولم يفئ، فهي مُطلّقة، ثمّ يُوقَف، فإن فاء فهي عنده على تطليقَتَين، وإن عَزم فهي بائنةٌ منه.

pronouncements of divorce left [before it is irrevocable]. If he decides to divorce her, then she is to separate from him. [2:228–229]

353. From Muḥammad b. Muslim and Zurāra, both of whom said that Abū Jaʿfar عليه السلام said, 'A month [of the waiting period] (*qurʾ*) is equivalent to one menstrual cycle between two periods.' [2:228–229]

354. From Zurāra who said, 'I heard Rabīʿa al-Raʾy say, "According to my opinion, the monthly waiting periods (*qurʾ*) that God has designated in the Qurʾan is the time when a woman is clean between two menstrual periods and does not include the duration of the period itself." I went to Abū Jaʿfar عليه السلام and narrated to him what Rabīʿa had said. He replied, "He is lying. That is not his opinion, but rather one that he has heard from ʿAlī عليه السلام." So I asked, "May God do you good; was ʿAlī the one to say that?" He replied, "Yes. He used to say: 'One month of the waiting period is the time from when the blood stops and gathers inside her until she menstruates and it flows again.'" I asked, "May God do you good; [what about] if a man divorces his wife while she is clean, and without having slept with her, testified by two just witnesses?" He replied, "When she starts her third menstrual period, her waiting period is over and she is free to remarry." I asked, "The people of Iraq believe ʿAlī عليه السلام used to say that he can still take her back as long as she has not taken her ritual bath (*ghusl*) after the completion of her third menstrual period." He said, "They are wrong. ʿAlī used to say: 'When she sees the blood of her third menstrual period, her waiting period is over.'" [2:228–229]

In the report of Rabīʿa al-Raʾy he does not have access to her, and that one month of the waiting period is the time between two menstrual periods; a woman cannot remarry until she has performed the ritual bath (*ghusl*) after completion of her third period. If you investigate the matter, you will find that these waiting periods are actually three months. If she has irregular periods, where she may see blood more than once in one month, and only once in another month, then her waiting period [after divorce] is the waiting period of one who has irregular periods for three calendar months. If she has regular periods, where she bleeds once a month, and there is a month's duration between two cycles, then that counts as one month's waiting period (*qurʾ*).' [2:228–229]

٣٥٣. عن محمّد بن مسلم، وعن زُرارة قالا: قال أبو جعفر ﵇: القُرء: ما بين الحَيضَتَين.

٣٥٤. عن زُرارة، قال: سمعتُ ربيعة الرأي وهو يقول: إنّ الأقراء التي سمّى الله في القرآن إنّما هي الطّهر فيما بين الحَيضَتَين، وليس بالحَيض. قال: فدخلتُ على أبي جعفر ﵇فحدّثتُه بما قال ربيعة، فقال: كَذَب ولم يقُل برأيه، وإنّما بلغه عن عليّ ﵇. فقلتُ: أصلحك الله، أكان عليّ ﵇ يقول ذلك؟ قال: نعم، كان يقول: «إنّما القُرء الطُّهر، تقرأ فيه الدمّ فتجمعه، فإذا جاءت قذفته». قلتُ: أصلحك الله، رجلٌ طلّق امرأته طاهرًا من غير جِماعٍ بشهادة عدلَين؟ قال: إذا دخلَت في الحيضة الثالثة، فقد انقضَت عِدّتُها، وحلّت للأزواج. قال: قلتُ: إنّ أهل العراق يرَوون عن عليّ ﵇ أنّه كان يقول: هو أحقّ برجعتِها ما لم تَغتسِل من الحيضة الثالثة؟ فقال: كَذَبوا، قال: وكان عليّ ﵇ يقول: «إذا رأَت الدم من الحيضة الثالثة، فقد انقضَت عِدَّتها».

وفي رواية ربيعة الرأي: ولا سبيل له عليها، وإنّما القُرء ما بين الحيضَتَين، وليس لها أن تتزوّج حتّى تَغتسِل من الحيضة الثالثة، فإنّك إذا نظرتَ في ذلك لم تجِد الأقراء إلاّ ثلاثة أشهر، فإذا كانت لا تستقيم، ممّا تَحيض في الشهر مرارًا وفي الشهر مرّة، كان عِدّتها عدّة المُستحاضة ثَلاثة أشهر، وإن كانت تَحيض حيضًا مستقيمًا، فهو في كلّ شهرٍ حَيضة، بين كلّ حيضَتَين شهر، وذلك القُرء.

355. From Ibn Muskān, from Abū Baṣīr who said, 'The waiting period [after divorce] of a woman who has regular periods is three menstrual cycles.' [2:228–229]

356. Aḥmad b. Muḥammad said, 'The monthly waiting period is the duration between when the menstrual blood stops until when the next period starts and flows again.' [2:228–229]

357. From Muḥammad b. Muslim who said, 'I asked Abū Ja'far عليه السلام about a man who divorces his wife and when she ought to separate from him? He replied, "When the blood of the third menstrual period starts flowing."' [2:228–229]

358. From Abū Baṣīr, from Abū 'Abd Allāh عليه السلام who regarding the verse ﴾*Divorced women must wait for three monthly periods before remarrying, and, if they really believe in God and the Last Day, it is not lawful for them to conceal what God has created in their wombs*﴿ said, 'This means that she is not allowed to conceal her pregnancy if she was divorced while having conceived already without the husband's knowledge of it. She is not allowed to conceal her pregnancy, and he is responsible for her [maintenance] during that pregnancy until she gives birth.' [2:228]

359. From Zurāra, from Abū Ja'far عليه السلام who said, 'The divorced woman can leave as soon as the first drop of blood from her third menstrual period begins.' [2:228–229]

360. From 'Abd al-Raḥmān b. Abī 'Abd Allāh, from Abū 'Abd Allāh عليه السلام regarding a woman who is divorced by her husband and becomes responsible for herself, he said, 'When she sees the blood of her third menstrual period, she parts ways.' [2:228–229]

361. Zurāra narrated that Abū Ja'far عليه السلام said, 'The monthly waiting periods are equivalent to the times of cleanliness [from menstrual blood].' He also said, 'It is the cycle between two menstrual periods.' [2:228–229]

362. From 'Abd al-Raḥmān who said, 'I heard Abū Ja'far عليه السلام say, "When a man marries a woman, he should say: 'She has attested to the covenant that God

٣٥٥. قال ابن مُسكان عن أبي بصير، قال: عِدّة الّتي تَحيض ويستقيم حيضها ثلاثة أقراء، وهي ثَلاث حِيَض.

٣٥٦. وقال أحمد بن محمّد: القُرء: هو الطُّهر، إنّما تقرأ فيه الدّم حتّى إذا جاء الحيض دفعتها.

٣٥٧. عن محمّد بن مسلم، قال: سألتُ أبا جعفر عليه السلام في رجلٍ طلّق امرأته، متى تَبين منه؟ قال: حين يَطْلُع الدّم من الحَيْضَة الثالثة.

٣٥٨. عن أبي بصير، عن أبي عبدالله عليه السلام، في قوله تعالى: ﴿وَالْمُطَلَّقَاتُ يَتَرَبَّصْنَ بِأَنفُسِهِنَّ ثَلَاثَةَ قُرُوءٍ وَلَا يَحِلُّ لَهُنَّ أَن يَكْتُمْنَ مَا خَلَقَ اللهُ فِي أَرْحَامِهِنَّ﴾ يعني لا يَحِلُّ لها أن تَكْتُم الحَمْل إذا طُلِّقت وهي حُبلى، والزوج لا يعلم بالحُمْل، فلا يَحِلّ لها أن تَكْتُم حَمْلها، وهو أحقُّ بها في ذلك الحَمْل ما لم تَضَع.

٣٥٩. عن زُرارة، عن أبي جعفر عليه السلام، قال: المُطَلَّقة تَبين عند أوّل قطرةٍ من الحيضة الثالثة.

٣٦٠. عن عبد الرّحمن بن أبي عبدالله، عن أبي عبدالله عليه السلام، في المرأة إذا طلّقها زوجُها، متى تكون أملك بنفسها؟ قال: إذا رأت الدم من الحيضة الثالثة فقد بانت.

٣٦١. قال زُرارة: قال: أبو جعفر عليه السلام: الأقراء: هي الأطهار، وقال: القُرء: ما بين الحَيْضَتين.

٣٦٢. عن عبد الرّحمن، قال: سَمِعتُ أبا جعفر عليه السلام يقول في الرجل إذا تزوّج المرأة: قال: أقررتُ بالمِيثاق الذي أخَذَ الله: ﴿إِمْسَاكٌ بِمَعْرُوفٍ أَوْ تَسْرِيحٌ بِإِحْسَانٍ﴾.

has taken, namely to ﴾*either be kept on in an acceptable manner or released in a good way*﴿."'' [2:229]

363. From Abū Baṣīr, from Abū ʿAbd Allāh ﵇ who said, 'The woman who is not allowed to go back to her husband unless she has married another husband [in the meantime] is she who has been divorced, gone back, then divorced again and gone back a second time, and then finally divorced for a third time. After that, he is not allowed to take her back until she marries another husband. God, Mighty and Exalted, says, ﴾*Divorce can happen twice, and* [*each time*] *wives either be kept on in an acceptable manner or released in a good way*﴿. "Release" here refers to the third divorce.' [2:229]

364. Regarding the verse ﴾*If a husband re-divorces his wife after the second divorce, she will not be lawful for him until she has taken another husband*﴿, he narrated that Abū ʿAbd Allāh ﵇ said, 'Here it refers to the third divorce, and if her latest husband divorces her, then there will be no blame on them both if they return to one another again in a new marriage.' [2:230]

365. From Abū Baṣīr, from Abū Jaʿfar ﵇ who said, 'God, most High, says ﴾*Divorce can happen twice, and* [*each time*] *wives either be kept on in an acceptable manner or released in a good way*﴿. "Release in a good way" refers to the third divorce.' [2:229]

366. From Samāʿa b. Mihrān who narrated, 'I asked him about the woman who is not allowed to go back to her husband unless she has married another husband. He replied, "She is one who has been divorced, then gone back, then divorced again and gone back again, and finally divorced a third time. She is the one who is not allowed to go back to her husband until she marries another husband, and has sexual relations with him. These are God's words in the verse ﴾*Divorce can happen twice, and* [*each time*] *wives either be kept on in an acceptable manner or released in a good way*﴿. 'Release in a good way' is the third divorce."' [2:229]

367. From Abū al-Qāsim al-Fārisī who narrated, 'I asked al-Riḍā ﵇, "May I be your ransom; God says in His Book ﴾*either be kept on in an acceptable manner or released in a good way*﴿. What does He mean by that?" He replied,

٣٦٣. عن أبي بصير، عن أبي عبدالله عليه السلام، قال: المرأة الّتي لا تَحِلّ لزوجها حتّى تَنْكِح زوجًا غيره، الّتي تُطلّق، ثمّ تُراجع، ثمّ تُطلّق، ثمّ تُراجع، ثمّ تُطّلق الثالثة، فلا تَحِلّ له حتى تَنْكِح زوجًا غيره، إنّ الله جلّ وعزّ يقول: ﴿الطَّلَاقُ مَرَّتَانِ فَإِمْسَاكٌ بِمَعْرُوفٍ أَوْ تَسْرِيحٌ بِإِحْسَانٍ﴾ والتسريح: هو التطليقة الثالثة.

٣٦٤. قال: قال أبو عبدالله عليه السلام، في قوله تعالى: ﴿فَإِنْ طَلَّقَهَا فَلَا تَحِلُّ لَهُ مِنْ بَعْدُ حَتَّىٰ تَنْكِحَ زَوْجًا غَيْرَهُ﴾ ها هنا التطليقة الثالثة، فإن طلّقها الأخير فلا جناح عليهما أن يتراجعا بتزويج جديد.

٣٦٥. عن أبي بصير، عن أبي جعفر عليه السلام، قال: إنّ الله تعالى يقول: ﴿الطَّلَاقُ مَرَّتَانِ فَإِمْسَاكٌ بِمَعْرُوفٍ أَوْ تَسْرِيحٌ بِإِحْسَانٍ﴾ والتسريح بالإحسان: هي التطليقة الثالثة.

٣٦٦. عن سماعة بن مهران، قال: سألته عن المرأة التي لا تحلّ لزوجها حتّى تنكح زوجًا غيره. قال: هي التي تُطلَّق ثم تُراجَع، ثم تُطلَّق، ثم تُراجَع، ثم تُطلَّق الثالثة، فهي الّتي لا تحلّ لزوجها حتّى تنكح زوجا غيره، وتذُوق عُسيلَته، ويذوق عُسَيلتها، وهو قول الله: ﴿الطَّلَاقُ مَرَّتَانِ فَإِمْسَاكٌ بِمَعْرُوفٍ أَوْ تَسْرِيحٌ بِإِحْسَانٍ﴾ أن تُسرَّح بالتطليقة الثالثة.

٣٦٧. عن أبي القاسم الفارسيّ، قال: قلت للرضا عليه السلام: جُعِلت فداك، إنّ الله تعالى يقول في كتابه: ﴿فَإِمْسَاكٌ بِمَعْرُوفٍ أَوْ تَسْرِيحٌ بِإِحْسَانٍ﴾ وما يعني بذلك؟ قال: أمّا

"To keep on in an acceptable manner means to desist harming her and to provide for her upkeep without reproach or demand of repayment; and to release in a good way refers to divorce, according to what the Book has revealed."' [2:229]

368. From Zurāra, from Abū Ja'far ﴿عليه السلام﴾ who said, 'One who has given something for the sake of God must not take it back.' [He continued]: 'And whatever he has not given for God or for the sake of God, he can take back, be it a bridal gift or a present, whether [the marriage] was consummated or not. A man is not allowed to take back whatever he gave to his wife as a gift, and a woman is not allowed to take back whatever she gave her husband as a gift, whether it has been consummated or not. Has God not said, ﴾*It is not lawful for you to take back anything that you have given [your wives]*﴿(2:229) and ﴾*Give women their bridal gift upon marriage, though if they are happy to give up some of it for you, you may enjoy it with a clear conscience*﴿(4:4)?'

369. From Abū Baṣīr, from Abū 'Abd Allāh ﴿عليه السلام﴾. He said, 'I asked him about the woman who initiates a divorce of *khul'*, how is she to be divorced?[133] He replied, "It is not lawful to divorce her unless she says something along the lines of, 'By God, I will not keep a single promise to you,' or 'I refuse to obey any of your commands,' and not the like of, 'I refuse to make your bed from now on,' or 'I will walk in on you without your permission.' If she says things of the former type, then one can divorce her, and he is allowed to take back a portion of her bridal gift or even more. This is in accordance with God's words ﴾*then there will be no blame on either of them if the woman opts to give something for her release*﴿. When he has done so, she can separate from him after he pronounces the divorce and she is responsible for herself. If she wishes, she may or may not re-marry, that is at her discretion. If she does remarry him, then she still has two [divorces] left."' [2:229]

370. From Muḥammad b. Muslim, from Abū Ja'far ﴿عليه السلام﴾ who regarding the verse ﴾*These are the bounds set by God: do not overstep them. It is those who overstep*

133 In Islamic Law, *khul'* is a divorce proceeding initiated by the wife if she wants her husband to divorce her, by mutual consent, for compensation (usually monetary) paid back to the husband.

الإمساك بالمعروف فكفُّ الأذى وإحباء النفقة، وأمّا التسريح بإحسان فالطلاق على ما نزل به الكتاب.

٣٦٨. عن زُرارة، عن أبي جعفر عليه السلام، قال: لا ينبغي لمن أعطى لله شيئًا أن يرجع فيه، وما لم يُعطِ لله وفي الله، فله أن يرجع فيه، نِحلة كانت أو هِبةً، جَرَت أو لم تجرِ، أليس الله يقول: ﴿وَلَا يَحِلُّ لَكُمْ أَنْ تَأْخُذُوا مِمَّا آتَيْتُمُوهُنَّ شَيْئًا﴾، وقال: ﴿إِنْ طِبْنَ لَكُمْ عَنْ شَيْءٍ مِنْهُ نَفْسًا فَكُلُوهُ هَنِيئًا مَرِيئًا﴾.

٣٦٩. عن أبي بصير، عن أبي عبدالله عليه السلام، قال: سألتُه عن المُختلَعة، كيف يكون خُلعها؟ فقال: لا يحلّ خُلعها حتّى تقول: واللهِ لا أبرّ لك قَسَمًا، ولا أُطيع لك أمرًا، ولأُوطِئنّ فِراشك، ولأُدخِلنّ عليك بغير إذنك، فإذا هي قالت ذلك حلّ خُلعها، وحلّ له ما أخذ منها من مهرِها وما زاد، وهو قول الله تعالى: ﴿فَلَا جُنَاحَ عَلَيْهِمَا فِيمَا افْتَدَتْ بِهِ﴾ وإذا فعل ذلك فقد بانت منه بِتطليقة، وهي أملكُ بنفسها، إن شاءت نَكحتْهُ، وإن شاءت فلا، فإن نَكحتْهُ فهي عنده على ثِنتَين.

٣٧٠. عن محمّد بن مسلم، عن أبي جعفر عليه السلام، في قول الله تبارك وتعالى: ﴿تِلْكَ حُدُودُ اللَّهِ فَلَا تَعْتَدُوهَا وَمَنْ يَتَعَدَّ حُدُودَ اللَّهِ فَأُولَئِكَ هُمُ الظَّالِمُونَ﴾. فقال: إنّ الله غَضِب على الزاني فجعل له جلد مائة، فمن غَضِبَ عليه فزاد، فأنا إلى الله منه بريء، فذلك قوله: ﴿تِلْكَ حُدُودُ اللَّهِ فَلَا تَعْتَدُوهَا﴾.

God's bounds who are doing wrong﴿ said, 'God is angered by the fornicator and has decreed his punishment to be one hundred lashes. Whoever increases the number of lashes angers God, and I disassociate myself from him, for those are His words ﴾*These are the bounds set by God: do not overstep them*﴿.' [2:229]

371. From 'Abd Allāh b. Faḍāla, from al-'Abd al-Ṣāliḥ [Imam al-Kāẓim ﵇], he said, 'I asked him about a man who divorces his wife the first time and does not take her back straight away, then pronounces the divorce again in the third month of her waiting period and she separates from him. Can he take her back? He replied, "Yes." I asked, "Before she marries another husband?" He replied, "Yes." So I asked him, "So what about a man who divorces his wife then takes her back, then divorces her again and takes her back, then divorces her [for a third time]." He replied, "He is not allowed to take her back until she marries another husband first."' [2:230]

372. From Abū Baṣīr who said, 'I asked Abū Ja'far ﵇ about that divorce after which a woman is no longer permissible for him until she marries another husband. He said to me, "Let me tell you what I did with a wife I had, whom I wanted to divorce. I let her be until she had had her menstrual period and become cleansed thereof. Then I divorced her in the presence of two witnesses, without sleeping with her. Then I left her alone until her waiting period was almost over, and took her back by having sexual relations with her. Then I left her alone again until she menstruated and became cleansed thereof, after which I divorced her again in the presence of two witnesses, without sleeping with her. Then I left her alone again until just before her waiting period was coming to an end, at which time I took her back by having sexual relations with her. Then again I left her alone until she menstruated and became cleansed, and then divorced her in front of witnesses, without having slept with her. I did this with her because I had no more need of her."' [2:230]

٣٧١. عن عبدالله بن فَضالة، عن العبد الصالح ﵇، قال: سألتُه عن رجلٍ طلّق امرأته عند قُرئها تطليقةً، ثمّ لم يُراجعها، ثم طلّقها عند قُرئها الثالثة، فبانت منه أله أن يُراجعها؟ قال: نعم. قلت: قبل أن تتزوّج زوجًا غيره؟ قال: نعم. قلت له: فرجلٌ طلّق امرأته تطليقة، ثمّ راجعها، ثم طلّقها، ثمّ راجعها، ثم طلّقها؟ قال: لا تحلُّ له حتّى تنكح زوجًا غيره.

٣٧٢. عن أبي بصير، قال: سألتُ أبا جعفر ﵇ عن الطّلاق الّتي لا تحلّ له حتّى تنكح زوجًا غيره؟ قال لي: أُخبرك بما صنعتُ أنا بامرأةٍ كانت عندي، فأردتُ أن أطلِّقها، فتركتُها حتّى إذا طَمثَت ثمّ طهُرتْ، طلّقتُها من غير جِماعٍ بشاهِدين، ثمّ تركتُها حتّى طمثتْ وطهرتْ، ثمّ طلّقتها بغير جِماعٍ بشاهدَين، ثمّ تركتُها حتّى إذا كادت أن تنقضي عِدّتها، راجعتُها ودخلتُ بها ومسستُها، ثمّ تركتُها حتّى طمثَتْ وطهُرتْ، ثمّ طلّقتُها بشهود من غير جِماعٍ، وإنّما فعلتُ ذلك بها، لأنّه لم يكن لي بها حاجة.

373. From al-Ḥasan b. Ziyād[134] who narrated, 'I asked him [i.e. one of the Imams] about a man who divorced his wife, and she contracted a temporary marriage (*mut'a*) with someone else. Is she permissible for her first husband now?' He replied, 'No, she is not permissible for him until she enters into a marriage like her previous marriage. This is according to the verse ﴿*If a husband re-divorces his wife after the second divorce, she will not be lawful for him until she has taken another husband; if that one divorces her, there will be no blame if she and the first husband return to one another, provided they feel that they can keep within the bounds set by God*﴾. There is no divorce in temporary marriage.' [2:230]

374. From Abū Baṣīr, from Abū 'Abd Allāh ﷺ. He said, 'I asked him about the divorce after which a woman is no longer permissible for a man until she marries another husband. He said, "This is when a man divorces a woman, then they return to each other, and the return is by having sexual relations together. Then he divorces her again and takes her back. Then divorces her the third time, after which she is no longer permissible for him until she marries another husband." He continued, "Getting back together is by having sexual relations; otherwise it counts as a single divorce."' [2:230]

375. From 'Umar b. Ḥanẓala, from the Imam who said, 'When a man says to his wife: "You are now divorced," then takes her back, then again pronounces "You are now divorced," then takes her back again, and then says to her a third time "You are now divorced," this woman is no longer permissible to him until she marries another husband. If he divorces her without getting it witnessed, he can remain married to her if he so wishes.' [2:230]

376. From Muḥammad b. Muslim, from Abū 'Abd Allāh ﷺ who says regarding a man who divorced his wife, then left her alone until her waiting period was complete and then married her again and once again divorced her without having consummated the marriage—doing this on three complete occasions—that, 'She is no longer permissible for him until she marries another husband.' [2:230]

---

134 Al-Ḥasan b. Ziyād al-'Aṭṭār, reliable transmitter from Imam Ja'far al-Ṣādiq. See Ḥillī, *Khulāṣat al-aqwāl*, 103 (nr. 234).

٣٧٣. عن الحسن بن زياد، قال: سألتُه عن رجلٍ طلّق امرأته فتزوّجت بالمُتعَة، أتحلّ لزوجها الأوّل؟ قال: لا، لا تحلّ له حتّى تدخل في مثل الذي خرجت من عنده، وذلك قوله تعالى: ﴿فَإِنْ طَلَّقَهَا فَلَا تَحِلُّ لَهُ مِنْ بَعْدُ حَتَّىٰ تَنْكِحَ زَوْجًا غَيْرَهُ فَإِنْ طَلَّقَهَا فَلَا جُنَاحَ عَلَيْهِمَا أَنْ يَتَرَاجَعَا إِنْ ظَنَّا أَنْ يُقِيمَا حُدُودَ اللَّهِ﴾ والمُتعة ليس فيها طلاق.

٣٧٤. عن أبي بصير، عن أبي عبدالله عليه السلام، قال: سألتُه عن الطلاق الذي لا تحلّ له حتّى تنكح زوجًا غيره. قال: هوالّذي يطلّق، ثمّ يُراجع – والرّجعة: هي الجِماع – ثمّ يطلّق، ثمّ يُراجع، ثمّ يطلّق الثالثة، فلا تحلّ له حتّى تنكح زوجًا غيره، وقال: الرجعة: الجِماع، وإلاّ فهي واحدة.

٣٧٥. عن عُمر بن حنظلة، عنه عليه السلام، قال: إذا قال الرّجل لامرأته: أنتِ طالقة، ثمّ راجعها، ثم قال: أنتِ طالقة. ثمّ راجَعها، ثمّ قال: أنتِ طالقة. لم تحلّ له حتّى تنكح زوجًا غيره، فإن طلّقها ولم يُشهِدْ فهو يتزوّجها إذا شاء.

٣٧٦. محمّد بن مسلم، عن أبي عبدالله عليه السلام، في رجل طلّق امرأته، ثمّ تركها حتّى انقضت عِدّتها، ثمّ تزوّجها، ثمّ طلّقها من غير أن يدخل بها حتّى فعل ذلك بها ثلاثًا، قال: لا تحلّ له حتّى تنكح زوجًا غيره.

377. From Isḥāq b. ʿAmmār who narrated, 'I asked Abū ʿAbd Allāh عليه السلام about a man who divorces his wife to the point she is no longer permissible for him until she marries another husband, and a slave marries her then divorces her, whether the [previous] divorce is overturned? He replied, "Yes, because of God's words ﴾*until she has taken another husband*﴿, and he counts as someone marriageable."' [2:230]

378. From ʿAbd Allāh b. Sinān, from Abū ʿAbd Allāh عليه السلام from the Commander of the Faithful عليه السلام who said, 'When a man wants to divorce his wife, he should divorce her before her waiting period is over without sleeping with her. If he divorces her the first time, then leaves her alone until her waiting period is over, he can contract a marriage with her anew if he so wishes. However, if he takes her back before her waiting period comes to an end, then she remains his wife despite one pronouncement of divorce. If he divorces her a second time, he can again contract a second marriage to her if he so wishes after her waiting period has already passed. Otherwise, if he wishes, he can take her back before her waiting period comes to an end, in which case she remains with him after two pronouncements of divorce. If he divorces her a third time, then she is no longer permissible for him until and unless she marries another husband. They inherit from each other as long as she is still in her waiting period of the first two divorces.' [2:230]

379. From Zurāra and Ḥumrān, the two sons of Aʿyan, and Muḥammad b. Muslim, from Abū Jaʿfar عليه السلام and Abū ʿAbd Allāh عليه السلام. They said, 'We asked them both about the verse ﴾*Do not hold on to them with intent to harm them and commit aggression: anyone who does this wrongs himself*﴿. They said, "It refers to someone who divorces his wife the first time, then leaves her alone until the very last moment of her waiting period, then takes her back again, then divorces her again, and leaves her again as before. So He [God] is prohibiting him from doing that."' [2:231]

380. From al-Ḥalabī, from Abū ʿAbd Allāh عليه السلام. He said, 'I asked him about the verse ﴾*Do not hold on to them with intent to harm them and commit aggression: anyone who does this wrongs himself*﴿. He said, "It refers to someone who divorces his wife, then when her waiting period is almost over takes her

٣٧٧. عن إسحاق بن عمّار، قال: سألتُ أبا عبدالله عليه السلام عن رجلٍ طلّق امرأته طلاقاً لا تحلّ له حتّى تنكح زوجاً غيره، فتزوّجها عبدٌ، ثمّ طلّقها، هل يهدم الطلاق؟ قال: نعم، لقول الله تعالى: ﴿حَتَّىٰ تَنكِحَ زَوْجًا غَيْرَهُ﴾ وهو أحد الأزواج.

٣٧٨. عن عبدالله بن سنان، عن أبي عبدالله، عن أمير المؤمنين عليه السلام، قال: إذا أراد الرجل الطلاق طلّقها من قبل عِدّتها في غير جِماعٍ، فإنّه إذا طلّقها واحدةً، ثمّ تركها حتّى يخلو أجلها، وشاء أن يخطُب مع الخِطاب فعل، فإن راجعها قبل أن يخلو الأجَل أو العِدّة فهي عنده على تطليقة، فإن طلّقها الثانية، فشاء أيضا أن يخطُب مع الخِطاب، إن كان تركها حتّى يخلو أجلها، وإن شاء راجَعها قبل أن ينقضي أجلها، فإن فعل فهي عنده على تطليقتين، فإن طلّقها ثلاثاً فلا تحلّ له حتّى تنكح زوجاً غيره، وهي ترِث وتُورَث ما كانت في الدم في التطليقتين الأوّلتين.

٣٧٩. عن زُرارة وحُمران ابني أعين، ومحمّد بن مسلم، عن أبي جعفر عليه السلام وأبي عبدالله عليه السلام، قالوا: سألناهما عن قوله تعالى: ﴿وَلَا تُمْسِكُوهُنَّ ضِرَارًا لِّتَعْتَدُوا﴾، فقالا: هو الرجل يطلّق المرأة تطليقة واحدة، ثمّ يدعها حتّى إذا كان آخر عِدّتها راجعها، ثمّ يطلّقها أخرى، فَيتركها مثل ذلك، فنُهي عن ذلك.

٣٨٠. عن الحَلَبي، عن أبي عبدالله عليه السلام، قال: سألتُه عن قول الله عزّ وجلّ: ﴿وَلَا تُمْسِكُوهُنَّ ضِرَارًا لِّتَعْتَدُوا﴾ قال: الرجل يطلِّق، حتّى إذا كادت أن يخلو أجلُها راجَعها، ثم طلّقها ثمّ راجعها، يفعل ذلك ثلاثَ مرّاتٍ، فنَهى الله عنه.

back, but divorces her again and then takes her back again, and does this three times. God has prohibited this."' [2:231]

381. From 'Amr b. Jumay' who, without mentioning his source, cited the Commander of the Faithful عليه السلام as having said, 'It is written in the Torah that whoever wakes up in the morning disappointed with the world, then it is as if he has woken up displeased with God's decree. Whoever wakes up complaining of a tribulation that has afflicted him, it is as if he is complaining about God. The one who disgraces himself before a wealthy man because of his wealth, God does away with two-thirds of his faith. If anyone from this community reads the Qur'an and nevertheless still ends up in the Fire, it is because he was among those who took God's signs for a mockery. Those who do not accept good counsel end up regretting it; and poverty is the greatest annihilation.' [2:232]

382. From Dāwūd b. al-Ḥuṣayn, from Abū 'Abd Allāh عليه السلام who recited: ﴾*Mothers suckle their children for two whole years*﴿, and said, 'As long as a child is still suckling both parents have equal right over him. When he is weaned, the father has a greater right to him than the mother; but if the father dies, then the mother has a greater right over him than the extended family. If the father can find someone to suckle him for four *dirhams* if his mother refuses to suckle him for less than five *dirhams*, then he can take him away from her, even though it is better, more considerate and kinder of him to let the child stay with its mother.' [2:233]

383. From Jamīl b. Darrāj who said, 'I asked Abū 'Abd Allāh عليه السلام about the verse: ﴾*No mother shall be made to suffer harm on account of her child, nor any father on account of his*﴿. He replied, "[This refers to] sexual intercourse."'[135] [2:233]

135 The Meccans used to think that having sexual intercourse during pregnancy would lead to another child being conceived thereby causing the death of the unborn foetus already in the womb. According to this *ḥadīth*, this verse came down as a reassurance that neither the man nor the woman would have to suffer abstinence on account of their child, thus permitting the married couple to have sexual relations even whilst being pregnant and giving reassurance that their as yet unborn child would not be harmed.

٣٨١. عن عمرو بن جُمَيع، رفعه إلى أمير المؤمنين عليه السلام، أنّه قال: مكتوبٌ في التوراة: من أصبح على الدنيا حَزِينًا، فقد أصبح لقضاء الله ساخِطًا، ومن أصبح يشكو مُصيبةً نزلت به، فقد أصبح يشكو الله، ومن أتى غنيًّا فتواضع لغنائِه، ذهب الله بثُلثَي دينه، ومن قرأ القرآن من هذه الأمة ثمّ دخل النار، فهو ممّن كان يتّخذ آيات الله هُزُوًا، ومن لم يستشِر يندُم، والفقرُ الموتُ الأكبر.

٣٨٢. عن داود بن الحُصين، عن أبي عبد الله عليه السلام، قال: ﴿وَالْوَالِدَاتُ يُرْضِعْنَ أَوْلَادَهُنَّ حَوْلَيْنِ كَامِلَيْنِ﴾. قال: ما دام الولد في الرَّضاع فهو بين الأبوين بالسّويّة، فإذا فُطِمَ فالأب أحقُّ من الأمّ، فإذا مات الأب فالأمّ أحقّ به من العَصَبة، وإن وجد الأب مَن يُرضِعه بأربعة دراهم، وقالت الأمّ: لا أُرضِعه إلاّ بخمسة دراهم، فإنّ له أن يَنزِعه منها، إلاّ أنّ ذلك خير له وأقدم وأرفق به أن يُترَك مع أمّه.

٣٨٣. عن جميل بن درّاج، قال: سألتُ أبا عبد الله عليه السلام، عن قول الله تعالى: ﴿لَا تُضَارَّ وَالِدَةٌ بِوَلَدِهَا وَلَا مَوْلُودٌ لَهُ بِوَلَدِهِ﴾، قال: الجِماع.

384. From al-Ḥalabī who narrated that Abū ʿAbd Allāh عليه السلام said regarding the verse: ﴾*No mother shall be made to suffer harm on account of her child, nor any father on account of his*﴿, 'Women used to raise up their hands to [block] their husbands from sleeping with them, saying, "I will not let you [have intercourse with me] for I fear that I shall conceive on top of this child," or the husband would say to his wife, "I will not sleep with you for fear that you will conceive, and I will be killing my own child." But God refused for men and women to suffer [unnecessarily] on account of their child.' [2:233]

385. From al-ʿAlā, from Muḥammad b. Muslim, from one of the two [Imams al-Ṣādiq عليه السلام or al-Bāqir عليه السلام]. He said, 'I asked him about the verse: ﴾*The same duty is incumbent on the father's heir*﴿. He said, "The responsibility of maintenance incumbent upon the heir is the same as the father's [upon the latter's death]."'

A similar narration has been reported from Jamīl, from Sawra, from Abū Jaʿfar عليه السلام. [2:233]

386. From Abū al-Ṣabbāḥ who said, 'Abū ʿAbd Allāh was asked about God's verse: ﴾*The same duty is incumbent on the father's heir*﴿, so he عليه السلام said, "The [father's] heir must not distress the mother by refusing her access to her son, nor distress her son by withholding what rightfully belongs to him, and he must not be miserly in his maintenance of him."' [2:233]

387. From al-Ḥalabī, from Abū ʿAbd Allāh عليه السلام who said, 'The [expectant] divorcee must be maintained financially until she gives birth, and she has a greater right to suckle her child over another woman, for God says: ﴾*No mother shall be made to suffer harm on account of her child, nor any father on account of his, and the same duty is incumbent on the father's heir*﴿. He has prohibited for a child or his mother to suffer harm as a result of his suckling. She must not suckle him for more than two whole years, and if they want to wean the child before that time, with mutual consent from both, then that is fine. Weaning means to stop suckling.' [2:233]

٣٨٤. عن الحلبيّ، قال أبو عبد الله عليه السلام: ﴿لا تُضَارَّ وَالِدَةٌ بِوَلَدِهَا وَلا مَوْلُودٌ لَهُ بِوَلَدِهِ﴾، قال: كانت المرأة ممّن تَرفع يدها إلى الرجل إذا أراد مُجامَعتها، فتقول: لا أدَعُك، إنّي أخاف أنْ أحملَ على ولدي. ويقول الرجل للمرأة: لا أجامعُكِ إنّي أخاف أن تَعلَقي، فأقتل ولدي، فنهى الله عن أن يُضارّ الرّجُل المرأةَ، والمرأةُ الرجلَ.

٣٨٥. عن العلاء، عن محمّد بن مسلم، عن أحدهما عليه السلام، قال: سألته عن قوله تعالى: ﴿وَعَلَى الْوَارِثِ مِثْلُ ذَلِكَ﴾، قال: هو في النَّفقة، على الوارث مثل ما على الوالد.

وعن جميل، عن سَورَة، عن أبي جعفر عليه السلام، مثله.

٣٨٦. عن أبي الصَّبّاح، قال: سُئل أبو عبد الله عليه السلام عن قول الله تعالى: ﴿وَعَلَى الْوَارِثِ مِثْلُ ذَلِكَ﴾ قال: لا ينبغي للوارث أن يضارّ المرأة، فيقول: لا أدَعُ ولدها يأتيها، ويُضارّ ولدها إن كان لهم عنده شيء، ولا ينبغي له أن يُقتِّر عليه.

٣٨٧. عن الحَلبيّ، عن أبي عبد الله عليه السلام، قال: المُطلَّقة يُنفَق عليها حتّى تَضع حَملها، وهي أحقُّ بولدها أن تُرضِعه ممّا تَقبَله امرأة أُخرى، إنّ الله يقول: ﴿لا تُضَارَّ وَالِدَةٌ بِوَلَدِهَا وَلا مَوْلُودٌ لَهُ بِوَلَدِهِ وَعَلَى الْوَارِثِ مِثْلُ ذَلِكَ﴾ إنّه نهى أن يُضارّ بالصّبي، أو يضارّ بأمّه في رِضاعه، وليس لها أن تأخُذ في رَضاعه فوق حَولين كاملين، فإن أرادا الفِصال قبل ذلك عن تراضٍ منهما كان حَسَنا، والفِصال: هو الفِطام.

388. From Abū Bakr al-Ḥaḍramī, from Abū ʿAbd Allāh عليه السلام who said, 'When this verse was revealed: ﴾*If any of you die and leave widows, the widows should wait for four months and ten nights before remarrying*﴿, some women came to the Messenger of God صلى الله عليه وآله objecting by saying to him, "We will not wait." So the Messenger of God صلى الله عليه وآله said to them, "[In past times] When a woman's husband would die, she would have to take some dung and throw it behind her in her private chamber and wait. After a whole year had passed, she would take it, crumble it and then apply it to her eyes as kohl, and then remarry. God has absolved you of eight months [of waiting]."' [2:234]

389. From ʿAbd Allāh b. Sinān who narrates the following from Abū ʿAbd Allāh عليه السلام: 'I heard him say: "A woman whose husband dies without him having touched her, cannot marry until she has waited for four months and ten nights, i.e. the waiting period of one whose husband dies."' [2:234]

390. From Abū Baṣīr, from Abū Jaʿfar عليه السلام: 'I asked him about the verse: ﴾*a year's maintenance and no expulsion from their homes [for that time]*﴿(2:240). He replied, "It has been abrogated by the verse: ﴾*the widows should wait for four months and ten nights before remarrying*﴿(2:234); and the verse of inheritance has also abrogated it."'

391. From Muḥammad b. Muslim, from Abū Jaʿfar al-Bāqir عليه السلام: 'I said to him, "May I be your ransom, how is it that the waiting period of a divorcee is three menstrual periods or three months whilst the waiting period of a widow is four months and ten days?"

He replied, "The waiting period of a divorcee is three months to disclose any child in her womb. As for the waiting period of the widow, God has ordained one stipulation in women's favour, and one against them, and He has neither been unfair in the stipulation that is in their favour, nor in the one against them. The one that is in their favour is that in the practice of *īlāʾ*, their waiting period is four months, where He says: ﴾*For those who swear that they will not approach their wives, there shall be a waiting period of four months*﴿(2:226). Therefore no man is allowed to stay away from his wife for more than four months in *īlāʾ*, for He, Blessed and most High, knows that this is the upper limit of a woman's patience towards a man. As for the stipulation that is not in her favour, it is that He has commanded her to wait for

٣٨٨. عن أبي بكر الحضرميّ، عن أبي عبدالله عليه السلام قال: لمّا نزلت هذه الآية: ﴿وَالَّذِينَ يُتَوَفَّوْنَ مِنكُمْ وَيَذَرُونَ أَزْوَاجًا يَتَرَبَّصْنَ بِأَنفُسِهِنَّ أَرْبَعَةَ أَشْهُرٍ وَعَشْرًا﴾ جئن النّساء يخاصمن رسول الله صلى الله عليه وآله، وقُلن: لا نَصبر. فقا لهنّ رسول الله صلى الله عليه وآله: كانت إحداكنّ إذا مات زوجها، أخذت بعرةً فألقتها خلفها في دُويرها في خدرها، ثمّ قعدت، فإذا كان مثل ذلك اليوم من الحول، أخذتها ففتّتها، ثمّ اكتحلت بها، ثمّ تزوّجت، فوضع الله عنكنّ ثمانية أشهر.

٣٨٩. عن عبدالله بن سِنان، عن أبي عبدالله عليه السلام، قال: سمعتُه يقول: في امرأة تُوفّي عنها زوجُها لم يَمسَّها. قال: لا تنكِح حتّى تعتدّ أربعة أشهر وعشرًا، عِدّة المُتوفّى عنها زوجها.

٣٩٠. عن أبي بصير، عن أبي جعفر عليه السلام، قال: سألتُه عن قوله تعالى: ﴿مَتَاعًا إِلَى الْحَوْلِ غَيْرَ إِخْرَاجٍ﴾، قال: منسوخة، نسختها: ﴿يَتَرَبَّصْنَ بِأَنفُسِهِنَّ أَرْبَعَةَ أَشْهُرٍ وَعَشْرًا﴾ ونسختها آية الميراث.

٣٩١. عن محمّد بن مسلم، عن أبي جعفر الباقر عليه السلام، قال: قلتُ له: جُعِلت فداك، كيف صارت عِدّة المطلّقة ثلاث حِيَض أو ثلاثة أشهر، وصارت عِدّة المتوفّى عنها زوجها أربعة أشهُرٍ وعشرًا؟

فقال: أمّا عدّة المُطلّقة ثلاثة قُروء، فلاستبراء الرّحِم من الولد، وأمّا عِدّة المُتوفّى عنها زوجها، فإنّ الله تعالى شَرَط للنّساء شرطًا، وشرط عليهنّ شرطًا، فلم يجُر فيما شرط لهنّ، ولم يجُر فيما شرط عليهنّ. أمّا ما شرط لهنّ، ففي الإيلاء أربعة أشهرٍ، إذ يقول تعالى: ﴿لِّلَّذِينَ يُؤْلُونَ مِن نِّسَائِهِمْ تَرَبُّصُ أَرْبَعَةِ أَشْهُرٍ﴾ فلن يجوز لأحدٍ أكثر من أربعة أشهر في الإيلاء،

four months and ten nights after her husband has died [before remarrying]; so the same thing that was imposed on him in her favour during his lifetime is now imposed on her after his death."' [2:234]

392. From ʿAbd Allāh b. Sinān, on his father's authority who narrated, 'I asked Abū ʿAbd Allāh عليه السلام about God's verse: ﴾*Do not make a secret arrangement with them;* [*unless you*] *speak to them honourably*﴿. He replied, "It is when seeking a lawful marriage, ﴾*and do not confirm the marriage tie until the prescribed period reaches its end*﴿. It is that the man should not arrange to meet at a particular place before her waiting period has ended, where he asks her not to engage in marriage with someone else when her waiting period is over." I asked, "What about the verse: ﴾[*unless you*] *speak to them honourably*﴿?" He replied, "It is to seek lawful marriage without making explicit arrangements to marry before the prescribed period reaches its end."' [2:235]

393. In a narration by Rifāʿa, on his عليه السلام authority regarding the phrase: ﴾*speak to them honourably*﴿, he عليه السلام said, 'It is for you to speak what is beneficial.' [2:235]

394. In another narration from Abū Baṣīr, on his authority regarding the verse: ﴾*Do not make a secret arrangement with them*﴿, he عليه السلام said, 'It is when a man arranges to meet a woman at a specified place before her waiting period is over for them both to indulge in indecent acts with each other.' [2:235]

395. In a report from ʿAbd Allāh b. Sinān, in which he narrated that Abū ʿAbd Allāh عليه السلام said, 'It is when a man tells a woman to meet him at a specified place before her waiting period is over, then asks her not to engage in marriage with someone else whenever her waiting period ends.' [2:235]

396. From Abū Baṣīr, from Abū ʿAbd Allāh عليه السلام regarding the verse ﴾*Do not make a secret arrangement with them;* [*unless you*] *speak to them honourably*﴿, that he عليه السلام said, 'When a woman is still in her waiting period, speak to her in a pleasant manner that would attract her to yourself, rather than list all the objectionable and obscene things that you do.' [2:235]

لعلمه تبارك وتعالى أنّها غاية صبر المرأة من الرجل. وأمّا ما شرط عليهنّ، فإنّه أمرها أن تعتدّ إذا مات زوجها أربعة أشهر وعشرا، فأخذ له منها عند موته ما أخذ لها منه في حياته.

٣٩٢. عن عبدالله بن سِنان، عن أبيه، قال: سألتُ أبا عبدالله ﵇ عن قول الله تعالى: ﴿لا تُوَاعِدُوهنَّ سِراً إِلاَّ أَنْ تَقُولُوا قَوْلاً مَعْرُوفاً﴾. قال: هو طلبُ الحلال: ﴿ولا تَعْزِمُوا عُقْدَةَ النِّكَاحِ حَتَّى يَبْلُغَ الْكِتَابُ أَجَلَهُ﴾ أليس يقول الرجل للمرأة قبل أن تنقضي عِدّتها: موعدُك بيت آل فُلان، ثمّ يطلُب إليها أن تسبِقه بنفسها إذا انقضت عدّتها؟! قلتُ: فقوله: ﴿إِلاَّ أَنْ تَقُولُوا قَوْلاً مَعْرُوفاً﴾؟ قال: هو طلب الحلال في غير أن يعزم عُقدة النِّكاح حتّى يبلغ الكتّاب أجله.

٣٩٣. وفي خبر رِفاعة، عنه ﵇ ﴿قَوْلاً مَعْرُوفاً﴾، قال: يقول خيرًا.

٣٩٤. وفي رواية أبي بصير، عنه ﵇ ﴿لا تُوَاعِدُوهُنَّ سِراً﴾، قال: هو الرّجل يقول للمرأة قبل أن تنقضي عِدّتها: أوعِدُك بيت آل فلان لترفُثَ ويرفُث معها.

٣٩٥. وفي رواية عبدالله بن سِنان، قال: أبو عبدالله ﵇: هو قول الرّجل للمرأة قبل أن تنقضي عِدّتها: مَوعِدك بيت آل فلان، ثمّ يطلُب إليها أن تسبِقه بنفسها إذا انقضت عِدّتها.

٣٩٦. عن أبي بصير، عن أبي عبدالله ﵇، في قول الله تعالى: ﴿لا تُوَاعِدُوهُنَّ سِراً إِلاَّ أَنْ تَقُولُوا قَوْلاً مَعْرُوفاً﴾، قال: المرأة في عِدّتها تقول لها قولاً جميلاً، ترغبها في نفسك، ولا تقول: إنّي أصنع كذا، وأصنع كذا، القَبيح من الأمر في البُضع، وكلّ أمرٍ قبيح.

397. From Mas'ada b. Ṣadaqa, from Abū 'Abd Allāh عليه السلام that he said regarding the verse of God, Blessed and most High: ﴾*unless you speak to them honourably*﴿, 'It is for a man to say to a woman when she is still in her waiting period, 'I only want to make you happy, and when your waiting period is over and if God wills, do not pass me up and proceed with marriage with someone else.' All this is without formally confirming the marriage tie.' [2:235]

398. From Ḥafṣ b. al-Bakhtarī, from Abū 'Abd Allāh عليه السلام who was asked whether a man who had divorced his wife could contract a temporary marriage with her. He replied, 'Yes, would you not want to be included among the doers of good? Would you not want to be included among the righteous?' [2:235]

399. From Abū al-Ṣabbāḥ, from Abū 'Abd Allāh عليه السلام who said, 'If a man divorces his wife before having consummated the marriage, then she is due half of her bride-gift. If he had not yet fixed a bride-gift for her, then he should make fair provision for her, the rich according to his means and the poor according to his. There is no waiting period for her, and she is free to marry whomever she pleases from that point on.' [2:236]

400. From al-Ḥalabī, from Abū 'Abd Allāh عليه السلام who said, 'The rich man should make provision by offering a male and female servant, and the poor man by offering wheat, grapes, clothing, and money.' [2:236]

401. He also narrated that al-Ḥusayn (or al-Ḥasan) b. 'Alī, may peace be upon them both, offered a maidservant to a wife whom he divorced. He never divorced a woman without providing for her. [2:236]

402. From Ibn Bukayr who narrated, 'I asked Abū 'Abd Allāh عليه السلام about the verse: ﴾*make fair provision for them, the rich according to his means and the poor according to his*﴿, what is the value of the rich man and the poor man's means? He replied, "'Alī b. al-Ḥusayn, may peace be upon them both, used to provide as much as his riding beast could carry."' [2:236]

٣٩٧. عن مسعدة بن صدقة، عن أبي عبد الله عليه السلام، في قول الله تبارك وتعالى: ﴿إِلَّآ أَن تَقُولُوا قَوْلًا مَّعْرُوفًا﴾، قال: يقول الرجل للمرأة وهي في عِدّتها: يا هذه، ما أحبّ إليّ ما أسرّك! ولو قد مضى عِدّتك لا تفوتيني إن شاء الله، فلا تَسبِقيني بنفسك، وهذا كلّه من غير أن يعزِموا عُقدة النِّكاح.

٣٩٨. عن حَفص بن البَختريّ، عن أبي عبد الله عليه السلام، في الرجل يُطلّق امرأته، أيُمتّعها؟ فقال: نعم، أما تُحبّ أن تكون من المُحسِنين، أما تُحبّ أن تكون من المتُّقين؟

٣٩٩. عن أبي الصّبّاح، عن أبي عبد الله عليه السلام، قال: إذا طلّق الرجل امرأته قبل أن يدخل بها، فلها نِصف مهرها، وإن لم يكن سمّى لها مهرًا، فمتاعٌ بالمعروف على المُوسع قدرُه، وعلى المُقترِ قدرُه، وليس لها عِدّة، وتزوّج من شاءت في ساعتها.

٤٠٠. عن الحلبيّ، عن أبي عبد الله عليه السلام، قال: المُوسِع يُمتّع بالعبد والأمة، ويُمتّع المُعسِر بالحِنطة والزبيب والثوب والدراهم.

٤٠١. وقال: إنّ الحسين بن عليّ عليه السلام متّع امرأةً طلّقها أَمَةً، ولم يكُن يُطلِق امرأة إلاّ متّعها بشيء.

٤٠٢. عن ابن بُكَير، قال: سألتُ أبا عبد الله عليه السلام عن قوله تعالى: ﴿وَمَتِّعُوهُنَّ عَلَى الْمُوسِعِ قَدَرُهُ وَعَلَى الْمُقْتِرِ قَدَرُهُ﴾ ما قدر المُوسع والمُقتِر؟ قال: كان عليّ بن الحسين عليه السلام يُمتّع براحلتِه، يعني حِملها الذي عليها.

403. From Muḥammad b. Muslim who narrated, 'I asked him about a man who wanted to divorce his wife. He replied, "He must provide for her before he divorces her, for God says in His Book, ﴿*make fair provision for them, the rich according to his means and the poor according to his*﴾."' [2:236]

404. From Usāma b. Ḥafṣ[136], a caretaker of Mūsā b. Jaʿfar عليه السلام, who narrated, 'I was told to ask him about a man who marries a woman but does not fix a bride gift for her. He replied, "She inherits, and she has to observe the waiting period even though she did not get a bride gift. Have you not read what God has said in His Book: ﴿*If you divorce wives before consummating the marriage but after fixing a bride-gift for them, then give them half of what you had previously fixed*﴾."' [2:237]

405. From Manṣūr b. Ḥāzim who said, 'I asked about a man who marries a woman, fixing a bride gift for her, then dies before consummating the marriage. He said, "She receives the bride gift in full as well as the inheritance." I asked, "But they are narrating on your authority that she gets half of the bride gift." He replied, "They are not memorizing from me [properly]; for that is the case for the divorcee."' [2:237]

406. From ʿAbd Allāh b. Sinān, from Abū ʿAbd Allāh عليه السلام who said, 'The one who holds the marriage tie is the executor of it.' [2:237]

407. From Zurāra, Ḥumrān and Muḥammad b. Muslim, from Abū Jaʿfar عليه السلام and Abū ʿAbd Allāh عليه السلام regarding the verse: ﴿*unless they waive* [*their right*], *or unless the one who holds the marriage tie waives* [*his right*]﴾. He عليه السلام said, 'This refers to the executor, and the ones who waive their right at the time of receiving the bride gift or acquit him of some or all of it.' [2:237]

---

136 Usāma b. Ḥafṣ, on whom there is scant information, was one of the caretakers of Imam al-Riḍā. See Ḥillī, *Khulāṣat al-aqwāl*, 76 (nr. 132).

٤٠٣. عن محمّد بن مسلم، قال: سألتُه عن الرّجل يُريد أن يطلّق امرأته. قال ﴿عليه السلام﴾: يُمتّعها قبل أن يُطلّقها، قال الله تعالى في كتابه: ﴿وَمَتِّعُوهُنَّ عَلَى ٱلْمُوسِعِ قَدَرُهُۥ وَعَلَى ٱلْمُقْتِرِ قَدَرُهُۥ﴾.

٤٠٤. عن أُسامة بن حَفص، قيّم موسى بن جعفر ﴿عليه السلام﴾ قال: قلتُ له: سَلهُ عن رجلٍ يتزوّج المرأة ولم يُسمِّ لها مهرًا؟ قال: لها الميراث، وعليها العِدّة ولا مهرَ لها، وقال: أما تقرأ ما قال الله في كتابه: ﴿وَإِن طَلَّقْتُمُوهُنَّ مِن قَبْلِ أَن تَمَسُّوهُنَّ وَقَدْ فَرَضْتُمْ لَهُنَّ فَرِيضَةً فَنِصْفُ مَا فَرَضْتُمْ﴾؟

٤٠٥. عن مَنصور بن حازِم، قال: قلتُ: رجلٍ تزوّج امرأةً، وسمّى لها صداقًا، ثمّ مات عنها ولم يدخُل بها؟ قال: لها المهر كملاً، ولها الميراثُ. قلتُ: فإنّهم رووا عنك أنّ لها نِصف المهر؟ قال: لا يحفَظون عنّي، إنّما ذاك المُطلّقة.

٤٠٦. عن عبدالله بن سِنان، عن أبي عبدالله ﴿عليه السلام﴾، قال: الذي بيده عُقدة النّكاح هو وليّ أمره.

٤٠٧. عن زُرارة، حُمران، ومحمّد بن مسلم، عن أبي جعفر، وأبي عبدالله ﴿عليهما السلام﴾، في قوله تعالى: ﴿إِلَّآ أَن يَعْفُونَ أَوْ يَعْفُوَا۟ ٱلَّذِى بِيَدِهِۦ عُقْدَةُ ٱلنِّكَاحِ﴾، قال: هو الوليّ والّذين يعفون عن الصّداق، أو يحُطّون عنه، بعضه أوكلّه.

408. From Abū Baṣīr, from Abū Jaʿfar عليه السلام who said regarding the verse ﴿*unless the one who holds the marriage tie waives* [*his right*]﴾, 'This can be the father, the brother who is the legal representative, and anyone else who has been authorised to transact property for a woman, so he can buy and sell on her behalf. It is thus permissible for any of them to waive it.' [2:237]

409. From Rifāʿa, from Abū 'Abd Allāh عليه السلام who said, '﴿*the one who holds the marriage tie*﴾ is the legal guardian who married her [to him], who can keep some and waive the rest, and he should not waive all of it.' [2:237]

410. From Abū Baṣīr, from Abū 'Abd Allāh عليه السلام who said regarding the verse ﴿*unless the one who holds the marriage tie waives* [*his right*]﴾, 'This can be the brother, the father, or a legal representative who is authorised to transact her property for a fee.' I asked him, 'What if she says that she does not approve of what he is doing?' He replied, 'That is not up to her; how can she approve of him to transact on her behalf and yet not approve of this?' [2:237]

411. From Rifāʿa, from Abū 'Abd Allāh عليه السلام who narrated, 'I asked him who ﴿*the one who holds the marriage tie*﴾ refers to, and he replied, "It is the one who marries her [to him]: he can keep some of it and relinquish some, but should not relinquish all of it."' [2:237]

412. From Isḥāq b. 'Ammār who narrated, 'I asked Jaʿfar b. Muḥammad عليه السلام about God's verse ﴿*unless they waive* [*their right*]﴾. He عليه السلام said, "The woman can waive half of her bride gift." Then I asked him about ﴿*or unless the one who holds the marriage tie waives* [*his right*]﴾, and he said, "If her father waives it, it is permissible for him to do so, as too is her brother if he is the one who maintains her and is responsible for her, in which case he holds the same position as a father and is allowed [to waive it]. However, if the brother does not maintain her and is not responsible for her, then he has no such authority over her."' [2:237]

413. From Muḥammad b. Muslim, from Abū Jaʿfar عليه السلام who, regarding God's verse ﴿*unless they waive* [*their right*], *or unless the one who holds the marriage tie waives* [*his right*]﴾ said, 'This is the one who can waive the bride gift, or relinquish part of it or all of it.' [2:237]

٤٠٨. عن أبي بصير، عن أبي جعفر عليه السلام، في قول الله تعالى: ﴿أَوْ يَعْفُوَ الَّذِي بِيَدِهِ عُقْدَةُ النِّكَاحِ﴾، قال: هو الأب والأخ الموصى إليه، والّذي يجوز أمره في مال المرأة، فيبتاع لها ويشتري، فأيّ هؤلاء عفا فقد جاز .

٤٠٩. عن رِفاعة، عن أبي عبد الله عليه السلام، قال: ﴿الَّذِي بِيَدِهِ عُقْدَةُ النِّكَاحِ﴾ وهو الوليّ الذي أنكَحَ، يأخُذ بعضًا ويَدَع بعضًا، وليس له أن يَدَع كلّه .

٤١٠. عن أبي بصير، عن أبي عبد الله عليه السلام، في قول الله: ﴿أَوْ يَعْفُوَ الَّذِي بِيَدِهِ عُقْدَةُ النِّكَاحِ﴾، قال: هو الأخ والأب والرجل يوصى إليه، والذي يجوز أمره في مالٍ بقيمته. قلتُ: أرأيت إن قالت: لا أُجيز ما يصنع؟ قال: ليس ذلك لها، أتُجيز بيعه في مالها، ولا تُجيز هذا؟!

٤١١. عن رِفاعة، عن أبي عبد الله عليه السلام، قال: سألتُه عن الّذي بيده عُقدة النِكاح، فقال: هو الّذي يُزوّج، يأخذ بعضًا ويترك بعضًا، وليس له أن يترك كلّه.

٤١٢. عن إسحاق بن عمّار، قال: سألتُ جعفر بن محمّد عليهما السلام عن قول الله عزّ وجلّ: ﴿إِلاَّ أَنْ يَعْفُونَ﴾، قال: المرأة تعفو عن نِصف الصَّداق. قلتُ: ﴿أَوْ يَعْفُوَ الَّذِي بِيَدِهِ عُقْدَةُ النِّكَاحِ﴾؟ قال: أبوها إذا عفا جاز له، وأخوها إذا كان يُقيم بها، وهو القائم عليها، فهو بمنزلة الأب يجوز له، وإذا كان الأخ لا يُقيم بها، ولا يقوم عليها، لم يجُز عليها أمره.

٤١٣. عن محمّد بن مسلم، عن أبي جعفر عليه السلام، في قوله تعالى: ﴿إِلاَّ أَنْ يَعْفُونَ أَوْ يَعْفُوَ الَّذِي بِيَدِهِ عُقْدَةُ النِّكَاحِ﴾، قال: الذي يعفو عن الصَّداق، أو يحطّ بعضه أو كلّه.

414. From Samāʿa, from Abū ʿAbd Allāh عليه السلام who said regarding ﴾*or unless the one who holds the marriage tie waives* [*his right*]﴿: 'This can be the father, the brother, the legal representative, and anyone who has been authorised to transact the property of a woman, so he can buy and sell on her behalf. It is thus permissible for any of them to waive it.' I asked him, 'What if she says that she does not approve of what he is doing?' He replied, 'That is not up to her; how can she approve of him to transact on her behalf and yet not approve of this?' [2:237]

415. From one of the sons of ʿAṭiyya, from Abū ʿAbd Allāh عليه السلام who said regarding someone investing the wealth of the orphan [in his guardianship], 'He must procure some of the profit for him, for God says, ﴾*do not forget to be generous towards one another*﴿.' [2:237]

416. From Ibn Abī Ḥamza, from Abū Jaʿfar عليه السلام who narrated, 'The Messenger of God ﷺ said, "A rapacious time will come upon people when every man will devour whatever comes into his possession, forgetting to be generous towards each other. God says, ﴾*do not forget to be generous towards one another*﴿."' [2:237]

417. From Muḥammad b. Muslim, from Abū Jaʿfar عليه السلام. He said, 'I asked him about the middle prayer and he said: ﴾*Take care to do your prayers, including the middle prayer*﴿; and the afternoon (*ʿaṣr*) prayer, ﴾*and stand before God in devotion*﴿. The middle prayer is the noon (*ẓuhr*) prayer, and this is how the Messenger of God ﷺ used to recite it.' [2:238]

418. From Zurāra, from Abū Jaʿfar عليه السلام who said, '﴾*Take care to do your prayers, including the middle prayer*﴿, the middle prayer is the first prayer that the Messenger of God ﷺ prayed, and it is the one in the middle of two daytime prayers, the early morning prayer and the afternoon prayer; ﴾*and stand before God in devotion*﴿ in the middle prayer.'

He continued, 'This verse was revealed on a Friday whilst the Messenger of God ﷺ was on a journey. So he devoted himself to it and kept it whole, whether he was travelling or staying in town. He added two units of prayer to that act of standing in devotion, and in fact, these two units that he had added that Friday came to be prescribed for anyone who attends the Friday

٤١٤. عن سماعة، عن أبي عبدالله عليه السلام: ﴿أَوْ يَعْفُوَ الَّذِي بِيَدِهِ عُقْدَةُ النِّكَاحِ﴾. قال: هو الأب والأخ والرجل الذي يُوصى إليه، والذي يجوز أمره في مال المرأة، فيبتاع لها ويشتري، فأيّ هؤلاء عفا فقد جاز. قلتُ: أرأيت إن قالت: لا أُجيز ما يصنع؟ قال: ليس لها ذلك، أتُجيز بيعه في مالها، ولا تُجيز هذا.

٤١٥. عن بعض بني عطيّة، عن أبي عبدالله عليه السلام، في مال اليتيم يعمَل به الرجل، قال: يُنيله من الرّبح شيئًا، إنّ الله يقول: ﴿وَلَا تَنسَوُا الْفَضْلَ بَيْنَكُمْ﴾.

٤١٦. عن ابن أبي حمزة، عن أبي جعفر عليه السلام، قال: قال رسول الله صلى الله عليه وآله: يأتي على الناس زمان عَضُوض يعضُّ كلّ امرئٍ على ما في يديه، وينسَون الفضل بينهم، قال الله: ﴿وَلَا تَنسَوُا الْفَضْلَ بَيْنَكُمْ﴾.

٤١٧. عن محمّد بن مسلم، عن أبي جعفر عليه السلام، قال قلتُ له: الصلاة الوُسطى؟ فقال: (حَافِظُوا عَلَى الصَّلَوَاتِ وَالصَّلَوةِ الوُسْطَى وصلاةُ العَصْرِ، وَقُومُوا لِلهِ قَانِتِينَ) والوُسطى: هي الظُّهر، وكذلك كان يَقرؤها رسول الله صلى الله عليه وآله.

٤١٨. عن زُرارة، عن أبي جعفر عليه السلام قال: ﴿حَافِظُوا عَلَى الصَّلَوَاتِ وَالصَّلَاةِ الْوُسْطَى﴾ الوُسطى: هي اوّل صلاة صلاّها رسول الله، وهي وَسَط صلاتَين بالنّهار: صلاة الغداة، وصلاة العصر ﴿وَقُومُوا لِلَّهِ قَانِتِينَ﴾ في الصلاة الوُسطى.

prayer but misses the two sermons given by the imam. Whoever misses the performance of the Friday prayer in congregation must perform it as four units, like the noon (*ẓuhr*) prayer that he prays every day.'

He continued, 'The verse ﴾*and stand before God in devotion*﴿ means 'obediently and eagerly.'' [2:238]

419. From Zurāra and Muḥammad b. Muslim that they asked Abū Jaʿfar عليه السلام about God's verse: ﴾*Take care to do your prayers, including the middle prayer*﴿. He replied, 'It is the noon (*ẓuhr*) prayer, being the one during which God has prescribed the Friday prayer. He has also designated it to be a time wherein it is impossible for a Muslim to ask for goodness and it is not granted to him by God.' [2:238]

420. From ʿAbd Allāh b. Sinān, from Abū ʿAbd Allāh عليه السلام who said, 'The middle prayer is the noon prayer, and standing before God in devotion means for a man to be attentive to his prayer, maintaining its performance on time, and not allowing anything to distract him or preoccupy him from it.' [2:238]

421. From Muḥammad b. Muslim, from Abū ʿAbd Allāh عليه السلام who said, 'The middle prayer is the one that comes in the middle of the day, and it is the noon prayer. And that is precisely why our companions are so mindful of when noontime is.' [2:238]

422. In a narration from Samāʿa, he is quoted to have said, '[The phrase:] ﴾*stand before God in devotion*﴿ refers to supplication.' [2:238]

423. From ʿAbd al-Raḥmān b. Kathīr, from Abū ʿAbd Allāh عليه السلام who said regarding the verse: ﴾*Take care to do your prayers, including the middle prayer, and stand before God in devotion*﴿, 'The prayers are the Messenger of God, the Commander of the Faithful, Fāṭima, al-Ḥasan and al-Ḥusayn (peace be upon them), and the middle prayer is the Commander of the Faithful عليه السلام. As for ﴾*stand before God in devotion*﴿, it means to be obedient to the Imams (peace be upon them).' [2:238]

وقال: نزلت هذه الآية يوم الجمعة، ورسول الله ﷺ في سفرٍ، فقَنت فيها وتركها على حالها في السَّفر والحضر، وأضاف لمقامه رَكعتين، وإنّما وُضِعت الرَّكعتان اللّتان أضافهما يوم الجمعة للمُقيم لمكان الخُطبَتين مع الإمام، فمن صلّى الجُمعة في غير الجماعة، فليُصلِّها أربعًا كصلاة الظُّهر في سائر الأيّام.

قال: قوله تعالى: ﴿وَقُومُوا لِلَّهِ قَانِتِينَ﴾ قال: مُطيعين راغِبين.

٤١٩. عن زُرارة، ومحمّد بن مسلم أنّهما سألا أبا جعفر عليه السلام عن قول الله تعالى: ﴿حَافِظُوا عَلَى الصَّلَوَاتِ وَالصَّلَاةِ الْوُسْطَى﴾، قال عليه السلام: صلاة الظُّهر، وفيها فَرَض الله الجُمعة، وفيها الساعة الّتي لا يوافقها عبدٌ مسلمٌ فيسأل خيرًا إلاّ أعطاه الله إيّاه.

٤٢٠. عن عبدالله بن سِنان، عن أبي عبدالله، قال: الصلاة الوُسطى الظُّهر، ﴿وَقُومُوا لِلَّهِ قَانِتِينَ﴾ إقبال الرجل على صلاته، ومُحافظته على وقتها، حتّى لا يلهيه عنها ولا يشغله شيءٌ.

٤٢١. عن محمّد بن مسلم، عن أبي عبدالله عليه السلام، قال: صلاة الوُسطى هي الوُسطى من صلاة النهار، وهي الظُّهر، وإنّما يُحافظ أصحابنا على الزَّوال من أجلها.

٤٢٢. وفي رواية سَماعة: ﴿وَقُومُوا لِلَّهِ قَانِتِينَ﴾، قال: هو الدُّعاء.

٤٢٣. عبد الرّحمن بن كَثير، عن أبي عبدالله عليه السلام، في قوله تعالى: ﴿حَافِظُوا عَلَى الصَّلَوَاتِ وَالصَّلَاةِ الْوُسْطَى وَقُومُوا لِلَّهِ قَانِتِينَ﴾، قال: الصّلوات: رسول الله ﷺ

424. From Zurāra, from Abū Ja'far ﷺ. He said, 'I said to him: "Tell me about the prayer while in combat." He replied, "If there is no sign of justice from your enemy [to afford you a pause for prayer], you pray by gesturing, be it on foot or mounted, for God says: ﴿*If you are in danger, pray when you are out walking or riding*﴾. In the bowing (*rukū'*) say: 'I bow before You and You are my Lord,' and in prostration, 'I prostrate for You and You are my Lord.' You can pray in whichever direction your mount is facing as long as you continue to face there from your first *takbīr* onwards."'[137] [2:239]

425. From Abān b. Manṣūr[138], from Abū 'Abd Allāh ﷺ who said, 'The Commander of the Faithful and the people spent a whole day at Ṣiffīn, through the noon (*ẓuhr*), afternoon (*'aṣr*), sunset (*maghrib*) and evening (*'ishā'*) prayers. So the Commander of the Faithful ﷺ ordered them to glorify God by saying *Subḥān Llāh, Allāhu Akbar,* and *Lā Ilāha illa Llāh.* God says: ﴿*If you are in danger, pray when you are out walking or riding*﴾, which is what 'Alī ﷺ commanded them to do, which they then did, on foot as well as mounted.'

Al-Ḥalabī narrated from Abū 'Abd Allāh ﷺ saying, 'The people missed their prayer with 'Alī on the day of Ṣiffīn.' [2:239]

426. From 'Abd al-Raḥmān [b. Abī 'Abd Allāh], from Abū 'Abd Allāh ﷺ stating: 'I asked him about God's verse: ﴿*If you are in danger, pray when you are out walking or riding*﴾, how should he do it and what should he say? And for one who fears a predator or a robber, how should he pray?' He replied, 'He starts the prayer with the *takbīr*, then gestures with his head.' [2:239]

---

137 The *takbīr* referred to in this *ḥadīth* is the first raising of the hands while saying 'God is greater' to mark the beginning of prayer.

138 We were unable to locate any individual by this name in either Ḥillī's *Khulāṣat al-aqwāl* or Khū'ī's *Mu'jam*.

وأمير المؤمنين، وفاطمة والحسن والحسين عليهم السلام: والوسطى: أمير المؤمنين عليه السلام ﴿وَقُومُوا لِلَّهِ قَانِتِينَ﴾ طائعين للأئمّة عليهم السلام؟

٤٢٤. عن زُرارة، عن أبي جعفر عليه السلام قال: قلتُ له: صلاة المُواقَفة. فقال: إذا لم يكن النِّصفُ من عدوّك صلّيت إيماءً، راجلاً كنت أو راكبًا، فإنّ الله تعالى يقول: ﴿فَإِنْ خِفْتُمْ فَرِجَالًا أَوْ رُكْبَانًا﴾ تقول في الرّكوع: لك ركعتُ وأنت ربّي، وفي السّجود: لك سجدتُ، وأنت ربّي. أينما توجّهت بك دابّتك، غير أنّك توجّه حين تُكبّر أوّل تكبيرة.

٤٢٥. عن أبان بن مَنصُور، عن أبي عبدالله عليه السلام، قال: فات أمير المؤمنين عليه السلام والناس يومًا – يعني في صفّين – صلاة الظُّهر، والعصر، والمغرب، والعِشاء، فأمرهم أمير المؤمنين عليه السلام أن يُسبّحوا ويُكبّروا، ويُهلّلوا، قال: وقال الله تعالى: ﴿فَإِنْ خِفْتُمْ فَرِجَالًا أَوْ رُكْبَانًا﴾ فأمرهم عليّ عليه السلام، فصنعوا ذلك رُكبانًا ورِجالاً.

ورواه الحَلَبيّ، عن أبي عبدالله عليه السلام قال: فات النّاس الصلاة مع عليّ يوم صفّين إلى آخره.

٤٢٦. عن عبد الرّحمن بن أبي عبدالله، عن أبي عبدالله عليه السلام، قال: سألتُهُ عن قول الله تعالى ﴿فَإِنْ خِفْتُمْ فَرِجَالًا أَوْ رُكْبَانًا﴾، كيف يفعل، وما يقول؟ ومن يخاف سبُعًا أو لِصًّا كيف يُصلّي؟ قال عليه السلام: يُكبّر ويومئ إيماءً برأسه.

427. From ʿAbd al-Raḥmān, from Abū ʿAbd Allāh عليه السلام who said about the prayer whilst marching [in battle], 'He says *Allāhu Akbar* and *Lā ilāha illa Llāh*, for God says: ﴾*If you are in danger, pray when you are out walking or riding*﴿ [2:239].'

428. From Ibn Abī ʿUmayr, from Muʿāwiya who said, 'I asked him about God's verse: ﴾*If any of you die and leave widows, make a bequest for them: a year's maintenance*﴿(2:240). He replied, "It has been abrogated by the verse ﴾*the widows should wait for four months and ten nights*﴿(2:234) and by the verse of inheritance."'

429. From Abū Baṣīr who narrated, 'I asked him about God's verse: ﴾*If any of you die and leave widows, make a bequest for them: a year's maintenance and no expulsion from their homes [for that time]*﴿. He عليه السلام replied, "It has been abrogated." I asked, "So how did it used to be?" He replied, "When a man would die, his widow would be maintained for a year from his estate, then she would be made to leave without any inheritance. Then this was abrogated by the verse about quarters and eighths [of inheritance], so the widow would be maintained from her own share."' [2:240]

430. From Abū Baṣīr who said, 'I asked Abū Jaʿfar عليه السلام, "In the verse: ﴾*Divorced women shall also have such maintenance as is considered fair: this is a duty for those who are mindful of God*﴿, what is the minimum requirement of maintenance incumbent upon the man if he is poor and cannot afford it?" He replied, "The head-covering and the likes of that."' [2:241]

431. From Abū Baṣīr, from Abū ʿAbd Allāh عليه السلام who said about the verse: ﴾*Divorced women shall also have such maintenance as is considered fair: this is a duty for those who are mindful of God*﴿: 'Her maintenance after the completion of her waiting period is for the rich man according to his means and the poor man according to his. As for the waiting period itself, how he may provide for her whilst she still has hope in him, and he still has hope in her, [is up to him]; and God will do whatever He pleases between them both. The rich man should make provision by offering a male and female servant, and the poor man by offering wheat, grapes, clothing and money. Al-Ḥasan

٤٢٧. عن عبد الرّحمن عن أبي عبد الله عليه السلام، في صلاة الزّحف، قال: يُكبّر، ويُهلّل، يقول: الله أكبر، يقول الله تعالى: ﴿فَإِنْ خِفْتُمْ فَرِجَالًا أَوْ رُكْبَانًا﴾.

٤٢٨. عن ابن أبي عُمَير، عن مُعاوية، قال: سألتُه عليه السلام عن قول الله تعالى: ﴿وَالَّذِينَ يُتَوَفَّوْنَ مِنكُمْ وَيَذَرُونَ أَزْوَاجًا وَصِيَّةً لِّأَزْوَاجِهِم مَّتَاعًا إِلَى الْحَوْلِ﴾. قال: منسوخةٌ، نسخَتها، آية: ﴿يَتَرَبَّصْنَ بِأَنفُسِهِنَّ أَرْبَعَةَ أَشْهُرٍ وَعَشْرًا﴾ ونسختها آية الميراث.

٤٢٩. عن أبي بصير، قال: سألتُه عليه السلام عن قول الله تعالى: ﴿وَالَّذِينَ يُتَوَفَّوْنَ مِنكُمْ وَيَذَرُونَ أَزْوَاجًا وَصِيَّةً لِّأَزْوَاجِهِم مَّتَاعًا إِلَى الْحَوْلِ غَيْرَ إِخْرَاجٍ﴾. قال: هي منسوخة. قلت: وكيف كانت؟ قال: كان الرّجل إذا كان أنفق على امرأته من صُلبِ المال حولاً، ثمّ أخرجت بلا ميراث، ثمّ نَسخَتها آية الرُّبع والثّمن، فالمرأة يُنفق عليها من نصيبها.

٤٣٠. عن أبي بصير قال: قلتُ لأبي جعفر عليه السلام: ﴿وَلِلْمُطَلَّقَاتِ مَتَاعٌ بِالْمَعْرُوفِ حَقًّا عَلَى الْمُتَّقِينَ﴾ ما أدنى ذلك المتاع، إذا كان الرجل مُعسرًا لا يجد؟ قال: الخِمار وشِبهه.

٤٣١. عن أبي بصير، عن أبي عبد الله عليه السلام، في قول الله تعالى: ﴿وَلِلْمُطَلَّقَاتِ مَتَاعٌ بِالْمَعْرُوفِ حَقًّا عَلَى الْمُتَّقِينَ﴾. قال: متاعُها بعد ما تنقضي عِدّتها، على المُوسع قَدرُه، وعلى المُقتِر قدرُه، فأمّا في عِدّتها، فكيف يُمتّعها وهي تَرجوه، وهو يَرجُوها، ويُجري الله بينهما ما شاء؟ أمّا إنّ الرجل المُوسِر يُمتّع المرأة العبد والأَمَة، ويُمتّع الفقير بالحِنطة والزّبيب، والثوب، والدّراهم، وإنّ الحسن بن عليّ عليه السلام متّع امرأةً كانت له بأمةٍ، ولم يُطلّق امرأةً إلاّ متّعها.

b. 'Alī عليه السلام offered a maidservant to a wife that he used to have, and he never divorced a woman without providing for her.' [2:241]

432. Al-Ḥalabī narrated, 'Her maintenance after the completion of her waiting period is for the rich man according to his means and the poor man according to his.' [2:241]

433. From Abū 'Abd Allāh and Abū al-Ḥasan, Mūsā b. Ja'far, may peace be upon them both. He said, 'I asked one of them about the divorcee and what she receives by way of maintenance. He replied, "According to her husband's means."' [2:241]

434. From al-Ḥasan b. Ziyād, from Abū 'Abd Allāh عليه السلام who was asked about a man who divorces his wife before he has consummated the marriage. He said, 'If he had fixed a bride gift for her, then she receives half of it and does not have to observe a waiting period. And if he did not fix a bride gift for her, then she does not receive a bride gift but he must provide for her, for God has said in His Book: ﴾*Divorced women shall also have such maintenance as is considered fair: this is a duty for those who are mindful of God.*﴿.' [2:241]

435. Aḥmad b. Muḥammad narrated from one of our associates that providing for the divorcee is an obligation. [2:241]

436. From Ḥumrān b. A'yan, from Abū Ja'far عليه السلام. He said, 'I asked him to explain to me God's verse: ﴾*[Prophet], consider those people who abandoned their homeland in fear of death, even though there were thousands of them. God said to them, 'Die!' and then brought them back to life again*﴿, did He bring them back to life long enough for people to see and then caused them to die again on the same day? Or did he return them to the life of this world whereby they lived in houses, ate food, and married women again? He replied, "Yes, God returned them to live in houses, eat food, and marry women and they stayed thus for as long as God willed, then died their destined deaths."' [2:243]

٤٣٢. قال: وقال: الحلبيّ: مَتاعُها بعدما تنقضي عِدّتها، على المُوسع قَدرُه، وعلى المُقتِر قدرُه.

٤٣٣. عن أبي عبدالله وأبي الحسن موسى عليهما السلام، قال: سألتُ أحدهما عن المُطلَّقة ما لها من المُتعة؟ قال: على قَدرِ مال زَوجِها.

٤٣٤. عن الحسن بن زياد، عن أبي عبدالله عليه السلام، عن رجلٍ طلّق امرأته قبل أن يدخل بها، قال: فقال عليه السلام: إن كان سمّى بها مهرًا، فلها نِصفُ المهَر، ولا عِدّة عليها، وإن لم يَكُن سمّى لها مهرًا فلا مَهر لها، ولكن يُمتّعُها، فإنّ الله تعالى يقول في كتابه: ﴿وَلِلْمُطَلَّقَاتِ مَتَاعٌ بِالْمَعْرُوفِ حَقًّا عَلَى الْمُتَّقِينَ﴾.

٤٣٥. قال أحمد بن محمّد، عن بعض أصحابنا: إنّ مُتعة المُطلَّقة فرِيضةٌ.

٤٣٦. عن حُمران بن أعين، عن أبي جعفر عليه السلام، قال: قلتُ له: حدّثني عن قول الله تعالى: ﴿أَلَمْ تَرَ إِلَى الَّذِينَ خَرَجُوا مِنْ دِيَارِهِمْ وَهُمْ أُلُوفٌ حَذَرَ الْمَوْتِ فَقَالَ لَهُمُ اللَّهُ مُوتُوا ثُمَّ أَحْيَاهُمْ﴾ قلتُ: أحياهُم حتّى نظر الناس إليهم، ثمّ أماتهم من يومهم، أوردهم إلى الدنيا حتّى سكنُوا الدُّور، وأكلوا الطعام، ونكحُوا النساء؟قال: بل ردّهم الله حتّى سكنُوا الدُّور، وأكلوا الطعام، ونكحُوا النساء، ولَبِثوا بذلك ما شاء الله، ثمّ ماتوا بآجالهم.

437. From 'Alī b. 'Ammār[139] who narrated, 'Abū 'Abd Allāh عليه السلام narrated that when this verse: ﴾*Whoever comes with a good deed will be rewarded with something better*﴿(27:89) was revealed, the Messenger of God ﷺ said, "My Lord, give me more," so God revealed: ﴾*Whoever has done a good deed will have it ten times to his credit*﴿(6:160). Again the Messenger of God ﷺ said, "My Lord, give me more," so God revealed: ﴾*Who will give God a good loan, which He will increase for him many times over?*﴿(2:245). 'Many times over' by God's count is innumerable.'

438. From Isḥāq b. 'Ammār who narrated, 'I asked Abū al-Ḥasan about the verse: ﴾*Who will give God a good loan, which He will increase for him many times over?*﴿. He replied, "It is the link with the Imam."' [2:245]

439. From Muḥammad b. 'Īsā b. Ziyād who narrated, 'I was in the office of Ibn Ziyād when I noticed a scribe copying something, so I asked about it. They said, "It is a letter that al-Riḍā wrote to his son, may peace be upon them both, from Khurasan." I asked them to pass it to me, so they did, and it read as follows: 'In the name of God, the Lord of Mercy, the Giver of Mercy. May God give you a long life and protect you from your enemies, my son. May your father be your ransom. I have placed my wealth at your disposal while still alive and well, in the hope that God will grant you strong ties with your relatives and with the protégés of Mūsā and Ja'far, may God be pleased with them both. As for Sa'īda,[140] she is a woman of strong resolve on her creed and on the truth, with a gentle disposition, which is not usually the case. This is what God means: ﴾*Who will give God a good loan, which He will increase for him many times over?*﴿(2:245), and ﴾*and let the wealthy man spend according to his wealth. But let him whose provision is restricted spend according to what God has given him*﴿(65:7). God has made you very wealthy, my son; may your father be your ransom. Let matters not be overlooked

139 We could not find any individual by this name in Ḥillī's *Khulāṣāt al-aqwāl* or Khū'ī's *Mu'jam*.

140 Sa'īda was one of the trusted and reliable female *ḥadīth* narrators at the time of Imam al-Kāẓim. See Muḥammad al-Ḥassūn, *A'lām al-nisā' al-mu'mināt* (Qum: Dār al-uswa li-l-maṭbū'āt wa-l-nashr, 2001), 487. Kishshī narrates from al-'Abbās b. Hilāl that Sa'īda was a client of Imam Ja'far al-Ṣādiq and a woman of virtue. She used to teach whatever she heard from the sixth Imam to others. See Ṭūsī, *Rijāl al-Kishshī*, 366 (nr. 681).

٤٣٧. عن عليّ بن عمّار، قال: قال أبو عبد الله ﵇: لمّا نزلت هذه الآية: ﴿مَن جَآءَ بِٱلْحَسَنَةِ فَلَهُۥ خَيْرٌ مِّنْهَا﴾، قال رسول الله ﷺ: ربّ زِدني فأنزل الله تعالى: ﴿مَن جَآءَ بِٱلْحَسَنَةِ فَلَهُۥ عَشْرُ أَمْثَالِهَا﴾، قال رسول الله ﷺ: ربّ زِدني فأنزل الله تعالى: ﴿مَّن ذَا ٱلَّذِى يُقْرِضُ ٱللَّهَ قَرْضًا حَسَنًا فَيُضَٰعِفَهُۥ لَهُۥٓ أَضْعَافًا كَثِيرَةً﴾ والكثير عند الله لا يُحصى.

٤٣٨. عن إسحاق بن عمّار، قال: قلتُ لأبي الحسن ﵇ قوله تعالى: ﴿مَّن ذَا ٱلَّذِى يُقْرِضُ ٱللَّهَ قَرْضًا حَسَنًا﴾؟ قال: هي صِلة الإمام.

٤٣٩. عن محمّد بن عيسى بن زيد، قال: كنتُ في ديوان ابن عبّاد. فرأيتُ كتابًا يُنْسَخ فسألت عنه؟ فقالوا: كتاب الرضا إلى ابنه ﵇ من خُراسان، فسألتهم أن يدفعوه إليّ، فدفعوه إليّ، فإذا فيه: بسم الله الرّحمن الرّحيم، أبقاك الله طويلاً، وأعاذك من عدوّك يا ولدي، فداك أبوك، قد فسَّرتُ لك مالي وأنا حيّ سويّ، رجاء أن يُميك الله بالصِّلة لقرابتك، ولموالي موسى وجعفر رضي الله عنهما، فأمّا سعيدة فإنّها امرأة قويّة الجزم في النّحل، والصواب في دقّة النّظر، وليس ذلك كذلك، قال الله تعالى: ﴿مَّن ذَا ٱلَّذِى يُقْرِضُ ٱللَّهَ قَرْضًا حَسَنًا فَيُضَٰعِفَهُۥ لَهُۥٓ أَضْعَافًا كَثِيرَةً﴾ وقال: ﴿لِيُنفِقْ ذُو سَعَةٍ مِّن سَعَتِهِۦ وَمَن قُدِرَ عَلَيْهِ رِزْقُهُۥ فَلْيُنفِقْ مِمَّآ ءَاتَىٰهُ ٱللَّهُ﴾ وقد أوسع الله عليك كثيرًا. يابنيّ، فداك أبوك، لا تستردني الأُمور بحسبها فتحظى حظّك، والسلام.

regarding her and you will enjoy the favours of your good fortune. With peace.'"'

440. From Muḥammad al-Ḥalabī, from Abū 'Abd Allāh ﷺ who recited: ﴾*[Prophet], consider the leaders of the Children of Israel who came after Mūsā, when they said to one of their prophets, 'Set up a king for us and we shall fight in God's cause.'*﴿ The king at that time would be the one to march out with the armies, while the prophet would handle all the affairs and inform him of what his Lord had revealed. So when they said this to their prophet, he told them: 'You have neither loyalty nor sincerity nor a real desire to fight.' They retorted, 'We used to be afraid of fighting when we would leave our homes with our sons, but now we must necessarily fight and obey our Lord in [His command] to fight our enemies.'

He recited: ﴾*God has now appointed Ṭālūt to be your king*﴿. So the elders of the Children of Israel exclaimed, 'And what special quality does Ṭālūt have over us in the domain of prophethood and kingship? You know very well that both prophethood and kingship have been in the lineage of the households of al-Lāwī and Yahūdā, whereas Ṭālūt is a descendant of Yāmīn, son of Ya'qūb.' ﴾*He said, 'God has chosen him over you, and has given him great knowledge and stature*﴿. The kingdom belongs to God, and He designates it wherever He wishes it to be; it is not up to you to choose. ﴾*The sign of his authority will be that the Ark* [*of the Covenant*] *will come to you* from God. *In it there will be* [*the gift of*] *tranquillity from your Lord and relics of the House of Mūsā and the House of Hārūn, carried by the angels*﴿. He is the one whom you used to defeat your opponents that you encountered.' So they replied, 'If the Ark of the Covenant truly comes, then we will accept and submit.' [2:247–8]

441. From Abū Baṣīr, from Abū Ja'far ﷺ who said regarding the verse ﴾*Yet when they were commanded to fight, all but a few of them turned away*﴿, 'The few of them numbered sixty thousand.' [2:246]

442. From Abū Baṣīr, from Abū Ja'far ﷺ who said about the verse: '﴾*God has now appointed Ṭālūt to be your king,' but they said, 'How can he be king over us when we have a greater right to rule than he?*﴿. He was neither in the lineage of prophethood nor kingship. ﴾*God has chosen him over you, and has given*

٤٤٠. عن محمّد الحلبيّ، عن أبي عبدالله عليه السلام في قوله تعالى: ﴿أَلَمْ تَرَ إِلَى الْمَلَإِ مِن بَنِي إِسْرَاءِيلَ مِن بَعْدِ مُوسَى إِذْ قَالُوا لِنَبِيٍّ لَّهُمُ ابْعَثْ لَنَا مَلِكًا نُّقَاتِلْ فِي سَبِيلِ اللَّهِ﴾. قال عليه السلام: وكان المَلِك في ذلك الزمان هو الذي يَسير بالجنود، والنبيّ يُقيم له أمره، ويُنَبِّئه بالخبر من عند ربّه، فلمّا قالوا ذلك لنبيّهم، قال لهم: إنّه ليس عندكم وفاء ولا صِدق ولا رغبة في الجِهاد. فقالوا: إنّا كنّا نَهابُ الجِهاد، فإذا أُخرِجنا من ديارنا وأبنائنا فلا بدّ لنا من الجِهاد، ونُطِيع ربّنا في جِهاد عدّونا.

قال: ﴿فَإِنَّ اللَّهَ قَدْ بَعَثَ لَكُمْ طَالُوتَ مَلِكًا﴾ فقالت عُظماء بني إسرائيل: وما شأن طالُوت يُملّك علينا، وليس في بيت النُّبوّة والمملكة، وقد عَرَفت أنّ النبوّة والمملكة، في آل لاوي ويَهُودا، وطالُوت من سِبط بِنْيامين بن يعقوب. فقال لهم: ﴿إِنَّ اللَّهَ قَدِ اصْطَفَاهُ عَلَيْكُمْ وَزَادَهُ بَسْطَةً فِي الْعِلْمِ وَالْجِسْمِ﴾ والمُلك بيد الله يجعله حيث يشاء، ليس لكم أن تختاروا و ﴿إِنَّ ءَايَةَ مُلْكِهِ أَن يَأْتِيَكُمُ التَّابُوتُ﴾ من قِبل الله تحمِلهُ الملائكة ﴿فِيهِ سَكِينَةٌ مِّن رَّبِّكُمْ وَبَقِيَّةٌ مِّمَّا تَرَكَ ءَالُ مُوسَى وَءَالُ هَارُونَ﴾ وهو الذي كنتم تَهزِمون به من لَقِيتم، فقالوا: إن جاء التابوت رضينا وسلّمنا.

٤٤١. عن أبي بصير، عن أبي جعفر عليه السلام، في قوله تعالى ﴿فَلَمَّا كُتِبَ عَلَيْهِمُ الْقِتَالُ تَوَلَّوْا إِلَّا قَلِيلًا مِّنْهُمْ﴾، قال: كان القليل ستّين ألفًا.

٤٤٢. عن أبي بصير، عن أبي جعفر عليه السلام، في قول الله تعالى: ﴿إِنَّ اللَّهَ قَدْ بَعَثَ لَكُمْ طَالُوتَ مَلِكًا قَالُوا أَنَّى يَكُونُ لَهُ الْمُلْكُ عَلَيْنَا وَنَحْنُ أَحَقُّ بِالْمُلْكِ مِنْهُ﴾. قال: لم يَكُن من سِبط

him great knowledge and stature ﴿ and ﴾ *The sign of his authority will be that the Ark [of the Covenant] will come to you. In it there will be [the gift of] tranquillity from your Lord and relics of the House of Mūsā and the House of Hārūn, carried by the angels.* ﴿. The angels carried it and brought it forth.' [2:247–8]

443. From Ḥarīz, from a man who narrated from Abū Jaʿfar عليه السلام regarding the verse: ﴾ *that the Ark [of the Covenant] will come to you. In it there will be [the gift of] tranquillity from your Lord and relics of the House of Mūsā and the House of Hārūn, carried by the angels* ﴿. He said, 'They were broken pieces of the tablets inscribed with wisdom and knowledge. Knowledge was revealed from the heavens, inscribed on the tablets and placed inside the Ark of the Covenant.' [2:248]

444. From Abū al-Muḥsin [or Abū al-Ḥasan], from Abū ʿAbd Allāh عليه السلام who was asked about the verse: ﴾ *And relics of the House of* Mūsā *and the House of Hārūn, carried by the angels* ﴿. He said, '[From] the progeny of the prophets.' [2:248]

445. From al-ʿAbbās b. Hilāl, who narrated from Abū al-Ḥasan al-Riḍā عليه السلام saying, 'I heard him ask al-Ḥasan: "According to you, what does the 'tranquillity' (*al-sakīna*) refer to in the verse: ﴾ *God sent His tranquillity down on to His Messenger* ﴿ (48:26)?"

Al-Ḥasan replied, "May I be your ransom, I do not know. What is it?"

He replied, "A pleasant fragrance that emanates from the Garden, having a form like the form of a human face; and it accompanies the prophets."

ʿAlī b. al-Asbāṭ asked him, "Does it descend upon the vicegerents as well as the prophets?"

He replied, "[Yes] it descends upon the prophets [and the vicegerents]. And this is what descended upon Ibrāhīm عليه السلام when he was building the Kaʿba, and it is what inspired him to pick up the relevant [stones] and to build the foundation according to it."

So Muḥammad b. ʿAlī asked him, "What about the verse: ﴾ *In it there will be [the gift of] tranquillity from your Lord* ﴿ (2:248)?"

He replied, "Yes, that too." Then he turned towards al-Ḥasan and said, "According to you, what was in the Ark [of the Covenant]?"

He replied, "Weapons."

النبوّة، ولا من سِبط المملكة ﴿قَالَ إِنَّ اللهَ اصْطَفَاهُ عَلَيْكُمْ﴾ قال: ﴿إِنَّ ءَايَةَ مُلْكِهِ أَن يَأْتِيَكُمُ التَّابُوتُ فِيهِ سَكِينَةٌ مِّن رَّبِّكُمْ وَبَقِيَّةٌ مِّمَّا تَرَكَ ءَالُ مُوسَى وَءَالُ هَـٰرُونَ تَحْمِلُهُ الْمَلَـٰئِكَةُ﴾ فجاءت به الملائكة تحمله.

٤٤٣. عن حَرِيز، عن رَجُلٍ، عن أبي جعفر عليه السلام، في قول الله تعالى: ﴿يَأْتِيَكُمُ التَّابُوتُ فِيهِ سَكِينَةٌ مِّن رَّبِّكُمْ وَبَقِيَّةٌ مِّمَّا تَرَكَ ءَالُ مُوسَى وَءَالُ هَـٰرُونَ تَحْمِلُهُ الْمَلَـٰئِكَةُ﴾. قال: رُضَاض الألواح، فيها العلم والحِكمة، العِلم جاء من السَّماء فكُتِب في الألواحِ وجُعِل في التابُوت.

٤٤٤. عن أبي المُحسن، عن أبي عبدالله عليه السلام، أنّه سُئِل عن قول الله تعالى: ﴿وَبَقِيَّةٌ مِّمَّا تَرَكَ ءَالُ مُوسَى وَءَالُ هَـٰرُونَ تَحْمِلُهُ الْمَلَـٰئِكَةُ﴾، فقال عليه السلام: ذُرِّيّة الأنبياء.

٤٤٥. عن العبّاس بن هِلال، عن أبي الحسن الرضا عليه السلام، قال: سمِعتُهُ وهو يقول للحسن: أيّ شيءٍ السَّكِينة عندكم؟ وقرأ: ﴿فَأَنزَلَ اللهُ سَكِينَتَهُ عَلَىٰ رَسُولِهِ﴾. فقال له الحسن: جُعِلت فِداك، لا أدري فأيّ شيءٍ هي؟

قال: ريحٌ تخرُج من الجنّة طيّبة لها صُورة كصُورة وجه الإنسان، قال: فتكون مع الأنبياء.

فقال له عليّ بن أسباط: تَنزِل على الأنبياء والأوصياء؟ فقال: تَنزِل على الأنبياء.

قال: وهي الّتي نَزَلت على إبراهيم عليه السلام حيث بنى الكعبة فجعلت تأخُذ كذا وكذا، وبنى الأساس عليها.

فقال له محمّد بن عليّ: قول الله تعالى: ﴿فِيهِ سَكِينَةٌ مِّن رَّبِّكُمْ﴾؟ قال: هي من هذا.

He said, "Yes, that is what is in your ark."

So he inquired, "So what was in the Ark which was in the possession of the Children of Israel?"

He replied, "In it were broken pieces of Mūsā's tablets, and the bowl that was used to wash the hearts of the prophets."'

446. From Abū Baṣīr, from Abū Ja'far عليه السلام who said about the verse: ﴾*God will test you with a river. Anyone who drinks from it will not belong with me*﴿, 'All of them drank from it except for three hundred and thirteen men. Some of them drank just a handful and some did not drink at all. So when they marched out to encounter [the enemy], those who had drunk just a handful said, ﴾*We have no strength today against Jālūt and his warriors*﴿; whereas those who had not drunk at all said, ﴾*How often a small force has defeated a large army with God's permission! God is with those who are steadfast.*﴿.' [2:249]

447. From Ḥammād b. 'Uthmān who narrated, 'Abū 'Abd Allāh عليه السلام said, 'The Avenger (*al-qā'im*) عليه السلام will not rise until there is at least a force present, and a force numbers no less than ten thousand.' [2:249]

448. From Muḥammad al-Ḥalabī, from Abū 'Abd Allāh عليه السلام who narrated, 'Dāwūd lived with his four brothers and their father, who was an old man. Dāwūd stayed behind to help his father with the sheep when Ṭālūt set forth with his army. Dāwūd was the youngest of them all, and his father called him saying, 'My son, go to your brothers with this [food] that I have made for them to strengthen them against their enemy.' Dāwūd himself was a short young man, blue-eyed with thin hair and pure of heart. He set out towards the barracks while the army had regrouped together.'

The narrator continued from Abū Baṣīr saying, 'I heard him say, "Dāwūd passed by a rock and the rock said to him, 'Dāwūd, pick me up and use me to kill Jālūt, for I have indeed been created to kill him.'

So he picked it up and put it in his feedbag, which contained other stones that he would use to throw at his sheep with his catapult. So when he entered the barracks, he heard them all talking dramatically about facing Jālūt.

So Dāwūd said to them, 'Why are you all making a big deal out of facing him? By God, if I were to see him I would certainly kill him.'

ثمّ أقبل على الحسن، فقال: أيّ شيءٍ التابُوت فيكم؟ فقال: السِّلاح. فقال عليه السلام: نعم، هوتابُوتكم.

فقال: فأيّ شيء في التابُوت الذي كان في بني إسرائيل؟ قال: كان فيه ألواح موسى الّتي تكسّرت، والطَّست التي تُغسل فيها قلوب الأنبياء.

٤٤٦. عن أبي بصير، عن أبي جعفر عليه السلام، في قول الله: ﴿ إِنَّ اللّٰهَ مُبْتَلِيكُم بِنَهَرٍ فَمَن شَرِبَ مِنْهُ فَلَيْسَ مِنِّي ﴾ فَشَربوا منه إلاّ ثَلاثمائة وثَلاثَة عشر رجلاً، منهم من اغتَرَف، ومنهم من لم يَشْرَب، فلمّا برزوا، قال الّذين اغترفوا: ﴿ لَا طَاقَةَ لَنَا الْيَوْمَ بِجَالُوتَ وَجُنُودِهِ ﴾ وقال الذين لم يَغْتَرِفوا: ﴿ كَم مِّن فِئَةٍ قَلِيلَةٍ غَلَبَتْ فِئَةً كَثِيرَةً بِإِذْنِ اللّٰهِ واللّٰه مَعَ الصَّابِرِين ﴾.

٤٤٧. عن حَمّاد بن عُثمان، قال: قال أبو عبد الله عليه السلام: لا يَخْرُج القائم عليه السلام في أقلّ من الفِئة، ولا تكون الفِئة أقلّ من عَشَرة آلاف.

٤٤٨. عن محمّد الحَلَبيّ، عن أبي عبد الله عليه السلام، قال: كان داود وإخوة له أربعة ومعهم أبوهم شيخ كبير، وتخلّف داود في غنمٍ لأبيه، فَفَصَل طالُوت بالجنود، فدعا أبو داود [داود] وهو أصغرهم، فقال: يابنيّ، إذهب إلى إخوتِك بهذا الذي قد صَنَعناه لهم يتقوّون به على عَدوّهم، وكان رجلاً قصيرًا أزرق، قليل الشّعر، طاهر القلب، فخرج وقد تقارَب القوم بعضهم من بعض.

فذكر عن أبي بصير، قال: سَمِعته يقول: فمّر داود على حَجَرٍ، فقال الحَجَر: يا داود خُذني فاقْتُل بي جالوت، فإنّي إنّما خُلِقتُ لقَتله، فأخذه فوضعه في مِخْلاَته الّتي تكون فيها حِجارته

So they all talked about his statement until it reached Ṭālūt, and he said, 'Young man, what special strength or experience do you possess?'

He replied, 'A lion had attacked one of the ewes from my flock, so I caught it and took it by the head. I cleaved its jaws apart and released her from its mouth.'

So he said, 'Call for a large-sized armour.'

He continued, 'So he was brought an armour, which he hung from his neck, and which fit him so perfectly that Ṭālūt and all the Children of Israel watched in amazement.

Ṭālūt said, 'By God, maybe God does want him to kill him [after all]!'"

He continued, "So the next morning when they all turned to Ṭālūt and he met the people, Dāwūd said, 'Show me Jālūt.'

When he saw him, he took the rock, placed it in his catapult, aimed and struck him between his eyes. His head split open and he fell from his horse.

The people exclaimed, 'Dāwūd has killed Jālūt!'

The people pronounced him king until there was no mention of Ṭālūt, and the Children of Israel all united under Dāwūd. God revealed to him the Zabūr (Psalms) and taught him how to wield iron, making it pliant in his hands. He commanded the mountains and the birds to glorify with him."

He continued, "No one has ever been given a voice like his. So He subtly established Dāwūd as a leader of the Children of Israel, and he was given a special strength for worship."' [2:251]

449. From Yūnus b. Ẓibyān[141], from Abū 'Abd Allāh ﷺ who said, 'God uses those who pray from among our followers to drive back those of our followers who do not pray. If they all unanimously agreed to abandon the prayer, they would perish. Similarly, God uses those who fast from among them to drive back those who do not fast, for if they all agreed not to fast they would all perish. God uses those of our followers who pay the alms to drive back those who do not, and if they all united to abolish the alms, they would all perish. God also uses those of our followers who perform the Hajj to drive back those of them who do not. And if they unanimously agreed to abandon the Hajj, they would all perish. This is the meaning of the verse: ﴾*If God did not*

141 Yūnus b. Ẓibyān is someone all of the major scholars of Shīʿī *rijāl* regard as a known liar and fabricator of the Imams' traditions. See Ḥillī, *Khulāṣat al-aqwāl*, 419 (nr. 1701).

التي كان يرمي بها عن غنمه بمِقْذَافه.

فلمّا دخل العسكر سَمِعهم يتعظّمون أمر جالُوت، فقال: لهم داود: ما تُعظّمون من أمره؟ فوا لله لئن عايَنْتُه لأقتلنَّه. فتحدّثوا بخَبَرِه حتّى أُدخِل على طالُوت، فقال: يا فتى، وما عندك من القُوّة وما جرّبت من نفسك؟ قال: كان الأسد يعدو على الشاة من غَنَمي، فأُدرِكُه فآخذ برأسه، فأفُكّ لَحْيِيه عنها، فآخُذها من فيه، قال: فقال: ادعُ لي بدرع سَابِغَة، قال: فأُتِيَ بِدرع فقذفها في عُنُقه، فتملّأ منها حتّى راع طالُوت من حضره من بني إسرائيل. فقال طالُوت: والله لعسى الله أن يَقْتُلَه به.

قال: فلمّا أن أصبحوا ورجعوا الى طالُوت والتقى الناس، قال داود: أروني جالُوت، فلمّا رآه أخذ الحَجَر فجعله في مِقْذَافِه، فرماه فصَكَّ به بين عَيْنَيه فدَمَغَه ونَكّس عن دابّته. وقال الناس: قتل داودُ جالُوتَ، وملّكهُ النّاس حتّى لم يَكُن يُسْمَع لطالُوت ذِكرٌ، واجتمعت بنو إسرائيل على داود، وأنزل الله عليه الزَّبُور، وعلّمه صنعة الحديد فليَّنه له، وأمر الجبال والطير يُسَبّحن معه.

قال: ولم يُعطَ أحدٌ مثل صوته، فأقام داود في بني إسرائيل مُستخفيًا، وأعطي قوّةً في عبادته.

٤٤٩. عن يُونُس بن ظِبيان، عن أبي عبدالله ﵇، قال: إنَّ الله يدفع بمن يُصلّي من شيعتنا، ولو أجمعوا على ترك الصلاة لَهَلَكُوا، وإنّ الله يدفع بمن يصوم منهم عمّن لا يصوم من شيعتنا، ولو أجمعوا على ترك الصيّام لهلَكوا، وإنّ الله يدفع بمن يزكّي من شيعتنا عمّن لا يُزكّي من شيعتنا، ولو أجمعوا على ترك الزكاة لَهَلَكُوا، وإنّ الله ليدفع بمن يَحُجّ من شيعتنا عمّن لا

drive some back by means of others the earth would be completely corrupt, but God is bountiful to all﴿. By God, this was only revealed about you [my followers], and He did not intend anyone else by it.' [2:251]

450. From Abū ʿAmr al-Zubayrī, from Abū ʿAbd Allāh عليه السلام who said, 'By increasing in their faith, the believers contend with each other for precedence in their rankings with God.'

I asked, 'Does faith have degrees and stations through which believers can compete for God's favour?'

He replied, 'Yes.'

I asked, 'Please describe these for me, God have mercy on you, so that I may better understand.'

He replied, 'It is how God had favoured some of His friends over others when He says: ﴾*We favoured some of these messengers above others. God spoke to some; others He raised in rank; We gave ʿĪsā, son of Maryam, Our clear signs and strengthened him with the holy spirit. If God had so willed, their successors would not have fought each other after they had been brought clear signs. But they disagreed: some believed and some disbelieved. If God had so willed, they would not have fought each other, but God does what He will.*﴿ (2:253). He continued by reciting: ﴾*We gave some prophets more than others: We gave Dāwūd a book [of Psalms]*﴿ (17:55) and ﴾*see how We have given some more than others – but the Hereafter holds greater ranks and greater favours*﴿ (17:21); and ﴾*They are in a different class in God's eyes; God sees exactly what they do*﴿ (3:163). This is God's statement about varying degrees of faith and their rankings with God.'

451. From al-Aṣbagh b. al-Nubāta who narrated, 'I was standing with the Commander of the Faithful ʿAlī b. Abī Ṭālib عليه السلام on the day of the Battle of the Camel, when a man approached and stood in front of him and said, "O Commander of the Faithful, the people [in the opposite camp] magnify God, and so do we. They proclaim that there is no god but God, and so do we. They pray, and so do we. So what are we fighting them for?"

He replied, "According to this verse: ﴾*We favoured some of these messengers above others. God spoke to some; others He raised in rank; We gave ʿĪsā, son of Maryam, Our clear signs and strengthened him with the holy spirit. If God had so willed, their successors would not have fought each other*﴿ (2:253)

يَحُجّ من شيعتنا ولو أجمعوا على ترك الحج لَهلَكُوا، وهو قول الله تعالى: ﴿وَلَوْلَا دَفْعُ اللَّهِ النَّاسَ بَعْضَهُم بِبَعْضٍ لَّفَسَدَتِ الْأَرْضُ وَلَٰكِنَّ اللَّهَ ذُو فَضْلٍ عَلَى الْعَالَمِينَ﴾ فوالله ما أُنزلت إلاّ فيكم، ولا عنى بها غيركم.

٤٥٠. عن أبي عَمرو الزُّبيريّ، عن أبي عبدالله عليه السلام، قال: بالزيادة بالإيمان تَفَاضَل المؤمنون بالدّرجات عند الله.

قلتُ: وإنّ للإيمان درجات ومنازل يتفاضل بها المؤمنون عند الله؟

قال: نعم.

قلتُ: صِف لي ذلك — رحمك الله — حتّى أفهمه.

قال: ما فضّل الله به أولياءه بعضهم على بعض، فقال: ﴿تِلْكَ الرُّسُلُ فَضَّلْنَا بَعْضَهُمْ عَلَىٰ بَعْضٍ مِّنْهُم مَّن كَلَّمَ اللَّهُ وَرَفَعَ بَعْضَهُمْ دَرَجَاتٍ﴾ الآية، وقال: ﴿وَلَقَدْ فَضَّلْنَا بَعْضَ النَّبِيِّينَ عَلَىٰ بَعْضٍ﴾، وقال: ﴿انظُرْ كَيْفَ فَضَّلْنَا بَعْضَهُمْ عَلَىٰ بَعْضٍ وَلَلْآخِرَةُ أَكْبَرُ دَرَجَاتٍ﴾ وقال: ﴿هُمْ دَرَجَاتٌ عِندَ اللَّهِ﴾ فهذا ذِكرُ درجات الإيمان ومنازله عند الله.

٤٥١. عن الأصبغ بن نُباتة، قال: كنتُ واقفًا مع أمير المؤمنين عليّ بن أبي طالب عليه السلام يوم الجمل، فجاء رجلٌ حتّى وقف بين يديه، فقال: يا أمير المؤمنين، كَبَّرَ القومُ وكبّرنا، وهلّل القوم وهَلّلنا، وصلّى القوم وصلّينا، فعلامَ نُقاتِلهم؟

فقال عليّ عليه السلام: على هذه الآية: ﴿تِلْكَ الرُّسُلُ فَضَّلْنَا بَعْضَهُمْ عَلَىٰ بَعْضٍ

– we are their successors; ﴾*after they had been brought clear signs. But they disagreed: some believed and some disbelieved. If God had so willed, they would not have fought each other, but God does what He will*﴿(2:254) – we are the ones who believed, and they are the people who disbelieved."

Thereupon the man exclaimed, "Those people have disbelieved indeed, by the Lord of the Kaʿba." Then he attacked and fought until he was killed, may God have mercy on him.'

452. From 'Abd al-Ḥamīd b. Farqad, from Jaʿfar b. Muḥammad ﷷ who said, 'The Jinn say that everything has a zenith, and the zenith of the Qur'an is the Verse of the Throne.' [2:255]

453. From Muʿāwiya b. 'Ammār, from Abū 'Abd Allāh ﷷ. 'I asked: ﴾*Who is there that can intercede with Him except by His leave?*﴿. He replied, "We are those intercessors."' [2:255]

454. From 'Abd Allāh b. Sinān, from Abū 'Abd Allāh ﷷ who said, '[The devils say that] Everything has a zenith, and the zenith of the Qur'an is the Verse of the Throne. Whoever recites the Verse of the Throne once, God wards off a thousand adversities away from him in this world, and a thousand adversities in the Hereafter, the most basic of the worldly ones being poverty, and the most basic of the ones in the Hereafter being the chastisement in the grave. Indeed, I use it to rise in rank.' [2:255]

455. From Ḥammād, on his authority [i.e. one of the Imams] saying, 'I saw him sitting, leaning his leg on his thigh when a man seated with him asked him, "May I be your ransom, is this manner of sitting not considered abominable (*makrūh*)?" He replied, "No. The Jews used to say that when God had completed the creation of the heavens and the earth, He sat on the Throne in this manner to relax. So God revealed the verse: ﴾*God: there is no god but Him, the Ever Living, the Ever Watchful. Neither slumber nor sleep overtakes Him*﴿. He did not lean back like that."' [2:255]

﴿مِنْهُم مَّن كَلَّمَ اللَّهُ وَرَفَعَ بَعْضَهُمْ دَرَجَاتٍ وَءَاتَيْنَا عِيسَى ابْنَ مَرْيَمَ الْبَيِّنَاتِ وَأَيَّدْنَاهُ بِرُوحِ الْقُدُسِ وَلَوْ شَاءَ اللَّهُ مَا اقْتَتَلَ الَّذِينَ مِن بَعْدِهِم﴾ فنحنُ الّذين من بعدهم ﴿مِّن بَعْدِ مَا جَاءَتْهُمُ الْبَيِّنَاتُ وَلَٰكِنِ اخْتَلَفُوا فَمِنْهُم مَّنْ ءَامَنَ وَمِنْهُم مَّن كَفَرَ وَلَوْ شَاءَ اللَّهُ مَا اقْتَتَلُوا وَلَٰكِنَّ اللَّهَ يَفْعَلُ مَا يُرِيدُ﴾ فنحنُ الذين آمنّا وهُم الذين كفروا.

فقال الرجل: كَفَرَ القوم وربِّ الكعبة، ثمّ حَمَل فقاتل حتّى قُتِل رَحمه الله.

٤٥٢. عن عبد الحميد بن فَرْقَد، عن جعفر بن محمّد عليه السلام، قال: قالت الجنّ: إنّ لكلّ شيءٍ ذُروة، وذُرْوَةُ القرآن آية الكُرسيّ.

٤٥٣. عن معاوية بن عمّار، عن أبي عبد الله عليه السلام، قال: قلتُ: ﴿مَن ذَا الَّذِي يَشْفَعُ عِندَهُ إِلَّا بِإِذْنِهِ﴾؟ قال عليه السلام: نحنُ أُولئك الشافِعون.

٤٥٤. عن عبد الله بن سِنان، عن أبي عبد الله عليه السلام، أنّه قال: إنّ الشياطين يقولون: لكلّ شيءٍ ذُروة، وذُروة القرآن آية الكرسي، من قرأ آية الكرسيّ مرّةً صرَفَ الله عنه ألف مَكْروهٍ من مكاره الدنيا، وألف مَكْروهٍ من مكاره الآخرة، أيسر مكروه الدنيا الفقْر، وأيسر مَكْروه الآخرة عذاب القبر، وإنّي لأستعين بها على صُعُود الدَّرَجَة.

٤٥٥. عن حمّاد، عنه عليه السلام، قال: رأيتُه جالسًا مُتورّكًا برجله على فَخِذِه، فقال له رجل عنده: جُعلت فِداك، هذه جِلسةٌ مكروهة؟ فقال: لا، إنّ اليهود قالت: إنّ الربّ لمّا فَرَغ من خلق السماوات والأرض جَلس على الكُرسّي هذه الجلسة ليستريح، فأنزل الله: ﴿اللَّهُ لَا إِلَٰهَ إِلَّا هُوَ الْحَيُّ الْقَيُّومُ لَا تَأْخُذُهُ سِنَةٌ وَلَا نَوْمٌ﴾ لم يَكُن مُتوركًا كما كان.

456. From Zurāra, from Abū ʿAbd Allāh عليه السلام regarding the verse: ﴾*His throne extends over the heavens and the earth*﴿. Abū ʿAbd Allāh said, 'The heavens, the earth and everything that God has created is encompassed by the Throne.' [2:255]

457. From Zurāra who narrated, 'I asked Abū ʿAbd Allāh عليه السلام about God's verse: ﴾*His throne extends over the heavens and the earth*﴿, is it the Throne that extends over the heavens and the earth or the heavens and the earth that extend over the Throne? He replied, "Everything is encompassed by the Throne."' [2:255]

458. From Muḥsin al-Muthannā,[142] from whoever narrated it from Abū ʿAbd Allāh عليه السلام who narrated, 'Abū Dharr asked, "O Messenger of God, what is the best thing to have been revealed to you?" He replied, "The Verse of the Throne. The seven heavens and the earth compared to the Throne are only as the likeness of a ring thrown onto a wasteland, and their value relative to the value of the Throne is as the value of the wasteland to the ring."' [2:255]

459. From Zurāra who narrated, 'I asked one of the two [Imam al-Bāqir or Imam al-Ṣādiq] about the verse: ﴾*His Throne extends over the heavens and the earth*﴿, which of the two extends over the other? He replied, "All of the earth, all of the heavens and everything that God has created is within the Throne."' [2:255]

460. From Zurāra who narrated, 'I asked Abū ʿAbd Allāh عليه السلام about the verse: ﴾*His throne extends over the heavens and the earth*﴿, is it the heavens and the earth that extend over the Throne or is it the Throne that extends over the heavens and the earth? He replied, "No, it is the Throne that extends over the heavens and the earth; and the Seat of Divine Authority and everything that God has created is within the Throne."' [2:255]

142 This is probably Muḥsin al-Maythamī. See Khūʾī, *Muʿjam*, 14:196.

٤٥٦. عن زُرارة، عن أبي عبدالله عليه السلام، في قول الله تعالى: ﴿وَسِعَ كُرْسِيُّهُ السَّمَوَاتِ وَ الأَرْضِ﴾، قال أبوعبدالله عليه السلام: السماوات والأرض وجميع ما خلق الله في الكرسّي.

٤٥٧. عن زُرارة، قال: سألتُ أبا عبدالله عليه السلام عن قول الله: ﴿وَسِعَ كُرْسِيُّهُ السَّمَوَاتِ وَالأَرْضَ﴾ وَسع الكرسيُّ السماواتِ والأرض، أم السماواتُ والأرضُ وَسعْنَ الكرسيَّ؟ فقال عليه السلام: إنّ كلّ شيءٍ في الكُرسيّ.

٤٥٨. عن محسن المثنّى، عمّن ذكره، عن أبي عبدالله عليه السلام، قال: قال أبو ذَرّ: يا رسول الله، ما أفضل ما أُنزِل عليك؟ قال: آية الكرسيّ، ما السّماوات السبع والأرضون السبع في الكرسيّ إلاّ كحَلقةٍ مُلقاةٍ بأرض فَلاَةٍ، وإنّ فَضله على العَرش كفضل الفَلاة على الحَلقة.

٤٥٩. عن زُرارة، قال: سألتُ أحدهُما عليهما السلام عن قوله تعالى: ﴿وَسِعَ كُرْسِيُّهُ السَّمَوَاتِ وَالأَرْضَ﴾ أيّهُما وَسِع الآخر؟ قال عليه السلام: الأرضون كلّها، والسّماوات كلّها، وجميع ما خلق الله في الكُرسيّ.

٤٦٠. عن زُرارة، قال: سألتُ أبا عبدالله عليه السلام، عن قول الله ﴿وَسِعَ كُرْسِيُّهُ﴾ السّماواتُ والأرضُ وَسِعْنَ الكرسيّ، أو الكرسّي وَسِع السّماوات والأرض؟ قال: لا، بل الكُرسيّ وَسِع السّماواتِ والأرضَ، والعرش وكلّ شيءٍ خَلَق الله في الكُرسيّ.

461. From al-Aṣbagh b. Nubāta who narrated, 'The Commander of the Faithful عليه السلام was once asked about the verse: ﴾*His throne extends over the heavens and the earth*﴿ so he said, "The sky and the earth, and all the creatures that they contain were created within the enclosure of the Throne. It has four angels that carry it with God's permission."' [2:255]

462. From Zurāra, Ḥumrān and Muḥammad b. Muslim, from Abū Jaʿfar عليه السلام and Abū ʿAbd Allāh عليه السلام regarding the phrase: ﴾*the firmest hand-hold*﴿, that it is to have faith in God and to believe in Him alone. [2:256]

463. From ʿAbd Allāh b. Abī Yaʿfūr who narrated, 'I said to Abū ʿAbd Allāh عليه السلام, "I mingle with people and am very surprised to see people who do not accept your authority over them, and rather accept the authority of those other two, persons in whom there is trustworthiness, honesty, loyalty. Whereas there are others who do accept your authority over them but do not have this trustworthiness, nor loyalty nor honesty about them?"

He continued, 'So he stood up,' or ʿAbd Allāh عليه السلام was seated, and he came towards me angrily saying, "The one who adheres to the authority of an unjust Imam unauthorized by God has no religion. And the one who adheres to the authority of a just Imam [appointed] by God bears no blame."

So I exclaimed, "Those people have no religion and these have no blame?"

He said, "Yes. Those have no religion, and these have no blame."

Then he continued, "Have you not heard the words of God, ﴾*God is the ally of those who believe: He brings them out of the depths of darkness and into the light*﴿. He brings them out of the depths of the darkness of sins and into the light of repentance and forgiveness, because of their adherence to every just Imam [appointed] by God. God says: ﴾*As for the disbelievers, their allies are false gods who take them from the light into the depths of darkness.*﴿.

I asked, "But does God not refer to the disbelievers here, when He says, ﴾*As for the disbelievers*﴿?"

He replied, "And which light do the disbelievers have amid their disbelief that He should take them out of, and into the darkness? By this, God means that they were in the light of Islam, but when they adhere to every unjust leader unauthorized by God, then they, through this adherence of theirs, leave the light of Islam and go into the darkness of disbelief, and as a result the Fire becomes incumbent upon them along with the disbelievers."

٤٦١ . عن الأصبغ بن نُباتة، قال: سُئل أمير المؤمنين عليه السلام عن قول الله تعالى: ﴿وَسِعَ كُرْسِيُّهُ السَّمَوَاتِ وَالأَرْضَ﴾، فقال: إنّ السّماء والأرض وما فيهما من خَلقٍ مَخلوقٍ في جوف الكُرسيّ، وله أربعة أملاكٍ يَحْمِلونه بإذن الله.

٤٦٢ . عن زُرارة، وحُمران، ومحمّد بن مُسلم، عن أبي جعفر وأبي عبد الله عليهما السلام، في قول الله تعالى: ﴿العُرْوَةِ الوُثْقَى﴾، قال: هي الإيمان بالله، يؤمن بالله وحده.

٤٦٣ . عن عبد الله بن أبي يَعفور، قال: قلتُ لأبي عبد الله عليه السلام: إنّي أخالِط الناس، فيَكثُر عَجَبي من أقوامٍ لا يتولّونكم، ويتولّون فُلانًا وفُلانًا، لهُم أمانة وصِدق ووفاء، وأقوامٌ يتولّونكم، ليس لهم تلك الأمانة، ولا الوفاء ولا الصدق!

قال: فاستوى أبو عبد الله عليه السلام جالسًا، وأقبل عليّ كالغضبان، ثم قال: لا دين لمن دان بولاية إمام جائرٍ ليس من الله، ولا عتب على من دان بولاية إمام عدلٍ من الله.

قال: قلتُ: لا دين لأُولئك، ولا عتب على هؤلاء؟

فقال: نعم لا دين لأُولئك، ولا عتب على هؤلاء.

ثمّ قال: أما تسمع لقول الله تعالى: ﴿اللهُ وَلِيُّ الَّذِينَ ءَامَنُوا يُخْرِجُهُم مِّنَ الظُّلُمَاتِ إِلَى النُّورِ﴾؟ يُخرجهم من ظُلمات الذنوب إلى نُور التوبة والمغفرة، لولا يتهم كلّ إمام عادلٍ من الله، وقال الله: ﴿وَالَّذِينَ كَفَرُوا أَوْلِيَاؤُهُمُ الطَّاغُوتُ يُخْرِجُونَهُم مِّنَ النُّورِ إِلَى الظُّلُمَاتِ﴾.

قال: قلتُ: أليس الله عنى بها الكفّار حين قال: ﴿وَالَّذِينَ كَفَرُوا﴾؟

Then he recited: ﴾*they are the inhabitants of the Fire, and there they will remain.*﴿.' [2:257]

464. From Mas'ada b. Ṣadaqa who said, 'Abū 'Abd Allāh ﷺ narrated to us the story of the two sides and the covenant they each made,[143] until he reached the point where God makes an exception in the case of both sides and said, "Good and evil are both creations that God has created, and He can do as He wills in transforming whatever He wishes from one state to the next in all that He has decreed. And the Divine Will regarding His creation is ultimately in line with the good and evil He had apportioned for them, and this is what God says in His Book: ﴾*God is the ally of those who believe: He brings them out of the depths of darkness and into the light. As for the disbelievers, their allies are false gods who take them from the light into the depths of darkness.*﴿. The light is the household of Muḥammad ﷺ, and the darkness is their opponents."' [2:257]

465. From Mihzam al-Asadī who narrated, 'I heard Abū 'Abd Allāh ﷺ say, "God, Blessed and most High, says: 'I will surely chastise every group of people that adheres to an imam who has not been authorized by God, even if that group is one which performs good and righteous deeds. And I will surely forgive every group of people who adheres to every Imam authorized by God, even if they commit misdeeds.'" I asked, "So He would pardon these and chastise those?" He replied, 'Yes. God says: ﴾*God is the ally of those who believe: He brings them out of the depths of darkness and into the light*﴿. Then he went on to quote the above narration from 'Alī b. Ya'fūr, narrated by Muḥammad b. al-Ḥusayn, and added the following to it: "So the enemies of 'Alī, the Commander of the Faithful, are the ones who will remain in the Fire forever, even if in their religious practice they were at the peak of piety, asceticism and worship. Those who believe in 'Alī ﷺ are the ones who will abide in the Garden forever, even if in their deeds they did [wrong]."' [2:257]

143 This refers to the creation of good and evil and their respective parties of adherents on two opposite sides.

قال: فقال ﷺ: وأيّ نورٍ للكافر وهو كافر، فأخرج منه إلى الظُلمات؟ إنّما عنى الله بهذا أنّهم كانوا على نُور الإسلام، فلمّا أن تولّوا كلّ إمامٍ جائرٍ ليس من الله، خرجوا بولا يتهم إيّاهم من نور الإسلام إلى ظُلمات الكُفر، فأوجب لهم النّار مع الكُفّار، فقال: ﴿أُولَئِكَ أَصْحَابُ النَّارِ هُمْ فِيهَا خَالِدُونَ﴾.

٤٦٤. عن مَسْعَدَة بن صَدَقَة، قال: قَصّ أبو عبدالله ﷺ قِصّة الفريقين جميعًا في المِيثاق، حتّى بلغ الاستثناء من الله في الفريقين، فقال: إنّ الخير والشرّ خَلقان من خَلق الله، له فيهما المشيئة في تحويل ما يشاء فيما قدّر فيها حال عن حالٍ، والمشيئة فيما خَلَق لها من خَلْقه في مُنتهى ما قسّم لهم من الخير والشرّ، وذلك أنّ الله تعالى قال في كتابه: ﴿اللَّهُ وَلِيُّ الَّذِينَ آمَنُوا يُخْرِجُهُمْ مِنَ الظُّلُمَاتِ إِلَى النُّورِ وَالَّذِينَ كَفَرُوا أَوْلِيَاؤُهُمُ الطَّاغُوتُ يُخْرِجُونَهُمْ مِنَ النُّورِ إِلَى الظُّلُمَاتِ﴾. فالنُور هُم آل محمّد ﷺ والظُلمات عدّوهم.

٤٦٥. عن مِهْزَم الأسديّ، قال: سَمِعتُ أبا عبدالله ﷺ يقول: قال الله تبارك وتعالى: لأُعذّبنّ كُلّ رعيّةٍ دانت بإمامٍ ليس من الله، وإن كانت الرَّعيّة في أعمالها بَرّةً تقيّةً، ولأَعْفونّ عن كُلّ رَعيّةٍ دانت بكُلّ إمام من الله وإن كانت الرَّعيّة في أعمالها سيّئة.

قلتُ: فيعفو عن هؤلاء، ويعذّب هؤلاء؟ قال: نعم، إنّ الله يقول: ﴿اللَّهُ وَلِيُّ الَّذِينَ آمَنُوا يُخْرِجُهُمْ مِنَ الظُّلُمَاتِ إِلَى النُّورِ﴾. ثمّ ذكر الحديث الأوّل حديث ابن أبي يعفور، رواية محمّد بن الحسين، وزاد فيه: فأعداء أمير المؤمنين ﷺ هُم الخالدون في النّار،

466. From Abū Baṣīr who said, 'When Yūsuf entered the presence of the king, the king said to him, "How are you, Ibrāhīm?" He replied, "I am not Ibrāhīm. I am Yūsuf, son of Ya'qūb, son of Isḥāq, son of Ibrāhīm عليه السلام." He continued, 'He had been the contemporary of Ibrāhīm who had disputed with him about his Lord, and he was still a young man at four hundred years of age.' [2:258]

467. From Abān, from Ḥujr, from Abū 'Abd Allāh عليه السلام who said, 'Ibrāhīm عليه السلام contradicted his community and denounced their false gods until he was brought before Nimrūd, so he contended with them saying: ﴿ *When Ibrāhīm said, 'It is my Lord who gives life and death,' he said, 'I too give life and death.' So Ibrāhīm said, 'God brings the sun from the east; so bring it from the west.' The disbeliever was dumbfounded: God does not guide those who do evil* ﴾.' [2:258]

468. From Ḥanān b. Sadīr, from a man from among the companions of Abū 'Abd Allāh عليه السلام who narrated, 'I heard him say, "The ones to undergo the worst punishment on the Day of Resurrection will be seven people: the first of them will be Ādam's son who killed his own brother, then Nimrūd b. Kan'ān who disputed with Ibrāhīm about his Lord."' [2:258]

469. From Abū Baṣīr, from Abū 'Abd Allāh عليه السلام regarding God's verse: ﴿ *Or take the one who passed by a ruined town. He said, 'How will God give this life when it has died?'* ﴾. He said, 'God sent a prophet to the Children of Israel called Irmiyā[144] and said to him, "Ask them which land I have selected from all the finest lands, and sowed therein the finest crop, weeding it of all foreign elements, then I withdrew and locust beans grew instead."'

144 Jeremiah in the Biblical and Hebrew traditions.

وإن كانوا في أديانهم على غاية الوَرَع والزهد والعبادة، والمؤمنون بعليّ عليه السلام هُم الخالدون في الجنّة وإن كانوا في أعمالهم على ضدّ ذلك.

٤٦٦. عن أبي بصير، قال: لمّا دخل يُوسُف عليه السلام على الملك، قال له: كيف أنت، يا إبراهيم؟ قال: إنّي لستُ بإبراهيم، أنا يُوسف بن يعقوب بن إسحاق بن إبراهيم. قال: وهو صاحب إبراهيم، الذي حاجّ إبراهيم في ربّه. قال: وكان أربعمائة سنة شابًّا.

٤٦٧. عن أبان، عن حُجر، عن أبي عبد الله عليه السلام، قال خالف إبراهيم عليه السلام قومه، وعاب آلهتهم حتّى أدخل على نمْرُود فخَاصَمَه، فقال إبراهيم عليه السلام: ﴿رَبِّيَ الَّذِي يُحْيِي وَيُمِيتُ قَالَ أَنَا أُحْيِي وَأُمِيتُ قَالَ إِبْرَاهِيمُ فَإِنَّ اللَّهَ يَأْتِي بِالشَّمْسِ مِنَ الْمَشْرِقِ فَأْتِ بِهَا مِنَ الْمَغْرِبِ فَبُهِتَ الَّذِي كَفَرَ وَاللَّهُ لَا يَهْدِي الْقَوْمَ الظَّالِمِينَ﴾.

٤٦٨. وعن حَنان بن سَدِير، عن رجلٍ من أصحاب أبي عبد الله عليه السلام، قال: سمِعتُه يقول: إنّ أشدّ الناس عذابًا يوم القيامة لسبعة نَفَر: أوّلهم ابن آدم الذي قتل أخاه، ونمْرُود بن كَنْعان الّذي حاجّ إبراهيم في ربّه.

٤٦٩. عن أبي بصير، عن أبي عبد الله عليه السلام، في قول الله تعالى: ﴿أَوْ كَالَّذِي مَرَّ عَلَىٰ قَرْيَةٍ وَهِيَ خَاوِيَةٌ عَلَىٰ عُرُوشِهَا قَالَ أَنَّىٰ يُحْيِي هَٰذِهِ اللَّهُ بَعْدَ مَوْتِهَا﴾. فقال عليه السلام: إنّ الله بعث إلى بني إسرائيل نبيًّا يقال له إرميا، فقال الله تعالى: قل لهم: ما بلد تنَقّيتُهُ من كرائم البُلدان، وغَرستُ فيه من كرائم الغَرْس، ونَقّيتُه من كل غريبةٍ، فأخلف فأنبت خُرْنُوبًا.

He continued, 'They laughed and scorned. So he complained about them to God, and God revealed to him saying, "Tell them that the land is Jerusalem, and the crop is the Children of Israel whom I have cleansed of all impurity and from whom I have kept all tyrants away. When left to themselves, however, they committed acts of disobedience to God. So now I will impose over them in their land someone who will shed their blood and usurp their wealth. Even if they come crying to Me, I will not have mercy on their tears, and if they call out to Me, I will not answer their plea. [I will make them fail, and it will fail too], then I will destroy it for a hundred years, after which I will revive it again."

When he told them of this, the scholars from among them were grief stricken and exclaimed, "O prophet of God, but what have we done wrong? We never committed the same acts as them. Go back to your Lord on our behalf."

So he fasted for seven consecutive days, but no revelation came to him. Then he ate something light and fasted again for seven days, but again nothing was revealed to him. So he again ate something light and fasted another seven days, and on the twenty-first day, God revealed to him saying, "Stop whatever you are doing. Do you dare to negotiate with Me in a matter that I have decreed, or shall I send you back to where you came from?"

Then He revealed to him to tell them, "It is because you saw wrong being done but you did not prohibit it." Then God imposed Nebuchadnezzar's rule over them, and he did to them what you already know. Then he sent Nebuchadnezzar to the prophet saying, "You have told us about your Lord, and you have told them about what I will do to them. So now you are free to stay here, if you please, or leave, if you wish."

Then he said, "I will leave." Thereupon he packed provisions of juice and figs for himself and left. When he had reached a distance where the town was just out of sight, he turned towards it and said: ﴾*'How will God give this life when it has died?' So God made him die for a hundred years*﴿. He made him die in the morning, and when He raised him up again it was evening, just before the sun had disappeared. The first thing He resurrected were his eyes, which were as white as the whites of eggs.

Then he was asked: ﴾*'How long did you stay like that?' He answered, 'A day'*﴿, but when he saw that the sun had not even fully set yet he said: ﴾*or part of a day. God said, 'No, you stayed like that for a hundred years. Look at*

قال: فَضَحِكُوا واسْتَهْزَءُوا به، فشكاهم إلى الله، قال: فأوحى الله إليه: أن قل لهم: إنّ البلد بيت المَقدِس، والغَرْس بنو إسرائيل، تنقّيتُه من كلّ غريبةٍ، ونحيّت عنهم كلّ جبّارٍ، فأخلفوا فعَمِلُوا بمعاصي الله، فلأُسلّطنّ عليهم في بلدهم من يَسفِك دماءَهُم، ويأخُذ أموالهم، فإن بَكَوا إليَّ فلم أرْحَم بُكاءَهُم، وإن دَعَوا لم أسْتَجِبْ دُعاءهم، ثمّ لأُخرِبَنّها مائة عامٍ، ثمّ لأُعمِّرنّها.

فلمّا حدّثهم جزِعت العُلماء فقالوا: يارسول الله، ما ذنْبُنا نحنُ ولم نكن نعمل بعملهم؟ فَعَاوِد لنا ربّك، فصام سبعاً ، فلم يُوح إليه شيءُ، فأكَلَ أكلةً ثمّ صام سبعًا فلم يُوح إليه شيءُ. فأكل أكلةً ثمّ صام سبعًا، فلمّا أن كان يوم الواحد والعشرين أوحى الله إليه: لتَرجِعنّ عمّا تصنع، أتُراجعني في أمرٍ قضيتُه؟ أولأُ رُدّنّ وجهك على دُبُرك.

ثم أوحى إليه: قُلْ لهم: لأنّكم رأيتُم المُنكر فلم تُنكروه، فسلّط الله عليهم بُختَ نَصَّر، فصنع بهم ما قد بلغك، ثم بَعث بُخت نَصَّر إلى النبيّ فقال: إنّك قد نُبِّئت عن ربّك وحدّثتهم بما أصنع بهم، فإن شِئت فأقِمْ عندي فيمن شِئت، وإن شِئْتَ فاخْرج.

فقال: لا، بل أخْرج، فتزوّد عصيرًا وتِينًا وخَرَج، فلمّا أن غاب مدّ البَصَر التفت إليها، فقال: ﴿أَنَّىٰ يُحْيِي هَٰذِهِ اللَّهُ بَعْدَ مَوْتِهَا فَأَمَاتَهُ اللَّهُ مِائَةَ عَامٍ﴾ أماته غُدوةً، وبَعَثه عَشيّةً قبل أن تغيب الشمس، وكان أوّل شيءٍ خُلق منه عيناه في مثل غِرقئ البيض، ثمّ قيل له: ﴿كَمْ لَبِثْتَ قَالَ لَبِثْتُ يَوْمًا﴾ فلمّا نظر إلى الشمس لم تَغِب، قال: ﴿أَوْ بَعْضَ يَوْمٍ قَالَ بَل لَّبِثْتَ مِائَةَ عَامٍ فَانظُرْ إِلَىٰ طَعَامِكَ وَشَرَابِكَ لَمْ يَتَسَنَّهْ وَانظُرْ إِلَىٰ حِمَارِكَ وَلِنَجْعَلَكَ آيَةً لِّلنَّاسِ وَانظُرْ إِلَى الْعِظَامِ كَيْفَ نُنشِزُهَا ثُمَّ نَكْسُوهَا لَحْمًا﴾ .

your food and drink: they have not gone bad. Look at your donkey – We will make you a sign for the people – look at the bones: see how We bring them together and clothe them with flesh!﴾.

He عليه السلام continued, 'So he began to look at his bones, how each one connected to the next and the way the veins were flowing. When he stood up straight he said, ﴿*When all became clear to him, he said, 'Now I know that God has power over everything*﴾."'

In Hārūn's narration, he prepared juice and milk as provisions for himself. [2:259]

470. From Jābir, from Abū Ja'far عليه السلام who said, 'This verse was revealed to the Messenger of God like this: ﴿*look at the bones: see how We bring them together and clothe them with flesh! For it had not yet become clear to him.*﴾.' He said, 'It had not yet become clear to the Messenger of God that it was in the heavens; the Messenger of God said: ﴿*Now I know that God has power over everything*﴾. The Messenger of God submitted to his Lord and [already] believed in God's statement, and when it became apparent to him, he said: ﴿*Now I know that God has power over everything*﴾.' [2:259]

471. From Abū Ṭāhir al-'Alawī, from 'Alī b. Muḥammad al-'Alawī, from 'Alī b. Marzūq, from Ibrāhīm b. Muḥammad who said, 'A group of scholars narrated once that Ibn al-Kawwā asked 'Alī عليه السلام, "O Commander of the Faithful, have there never been children older than their fathers in this world?" He replied, "Yes, they were the children of 'Uzayr. When he passed by a ruined village, and he came across a corpse with a donkey under it, and a bag of figs and a waterskin filled with juice. So he passed by this ruined village saying: 'How will God give life to this when it has died?' So God made him die for a hundred years, and his son had children in the meantime. Then God resurrected him, and revived him to the same age as when he had died. So his offspring were older than their father."'

472. From Abū Baṣīr, from Abū 'Abd Allāh عليه السلام regarding Ibrāhīm's statement: ﴿*My Lord, show me how You give life to the dead*﴾. Abū 'Abd Allāh عليه السلام said, 'When the dominion of the heavens and the earth was shown to Ibrāhīm he witnessed a man fornicating, so he invoked God's wrath on him causing him to die. Then he saw another man [doing the same], so he did as before and

قال: فجعل يَنْظُر إلى عِظامه، كيف يَصِلُ بعضُها إلى بعض، ويرى العُروق كيف تجري، فلمّا استوى قائمًا، قال: ﴿أَعْلَمُ أَنَّ اللهَ عَلَىٰ كُلِّ شَيْءٍ قَدِيرٌ﴾.

وفي رواية هارون: فتزوّد عصيرًا ولبنًا.

٤٧٠. عن جابر، عن أبي جعفر عليه السلام، قال: نزلت هذه الآية على رسول الله صلى الله عليه وآله هكذا: ﴿أَلَمْ تَرَ إِلَى الْعِظَامِ كَيْفَ نُنْشِزُهَا ثُمَّ نَكْسُوهَا لَحْمًا فَلَمَّا تَبَيَّنَ لَهُ﴾ قال: ما تبيّن لرسول الله أنّها في السماوات. قال رسول الله: أعلم أنّ الله على كلّ شيءٍ قدير. سلّم رسول الله صلى الله عليه وآله وسلم للربّ، وآمن بقول الله: ﴿فَلَمَّا تَبَيَّنَ لَهُ قَالَ أَعْلَمُ أَنَّ اللهَ عَلَىٰ كُلِّ شَيْءٍ قَدِيرٌ﴾.

٤٧١. أبو طاهِر العَلَوي، عن عليّ بن محمّد العلوي، عن عليّ بن مَرزوق، عن إبراهيم بن محمّد، قال: ذكر جماعةٌ من أهل العلم أنّ ابن الكوّاء قال لعليّ عليه السلام: يا أمير المؤمنين، ما وَلَدٌ أكبر من أبيه من أهل الدنيا؟ قال: نعم، أولئك وُلد عُزير، حيث مرّ على قريةٍ خَرِبةٍ، وقد جاء من ضَيعةٍ له تحته حمار، ومعه شَنّة فيها تينٌ، وكُوز فيه عصيرٌ، فمرّ على قريةٍ خَرِبةٍ فقال: ﴿أَنَّىٰ يُحْيِي هَٰذِهِ اللهُ بَعْدَ مَوْتِهَا فَأَمَاتَهُ اللهُ مِائَةَ عَامٍ﴾ فتوالد وُلده وتَنَاسَلُوا، ثمّ بعث الله إليه فأحياه في المَوْلِد الذي أماته فيه، فأُولئك وُلده أكبر من أبيهم.

٤٧٢. عن أبي بصير، عن أبي عبد الله عليه السلام، في قول إبراهيم عليه السلام: ﴿رَبِّ أَرِنِي كَيْفَ تُحْيِي الْمَوْتَىٰ﴾. قال: أبو عبد الله عليه السلام: لمّا أُري إبراهيم مَلَكُوت السماوات والأرض، رأى رجُلاً يزني، فدعا عليه فمات، ثمّ رأى آخر، فدعا عليه فمات، حتّى رأى ثلاثةً، فدعا عليهم فماتوا، فأوحى الله إليه: أن يا إبراهيم، إنّ دَعْوَتَكَ مُجابةٌ، فلا تَدْعُ على عبادي، فإنّي

he too died, until he had seen three such men and invoked God's wrath on them all and they all died. So God revealed to him saying, "O Ibrāhīm, your invocation gets a response, so do not use it against My servants, for indeed had I wanted I would not have created them. I have created people in three categories: a servant who will worship Me and not associate any other with Me, and I reward Him; a servant who worships other than Me, and he will not escape Me; and a servant who worships other than Me, but I will bring forth from his progeny someone who will worship Me."

Then he turned around and saw a dead animal on the seashore, half of which was in the water and the other half on land. The creatures of the sea were coming and eating it, then returning and being eaten by other aquatic creatures in turn. The scavengers on land too were coming and eating it, and being eaten by other predators themselves in turn. When Ibrāhīm saw that he was taken aback and said, "﴾*My Lord, show me how You give life to the dead*﴿, how can something that has assimilated with something else come back? These are species that have eaten each other." ﴾*He said, 'Do you not believe, then?' 'Yes,' said Ibrāhīm, 'but just to put my heart at rest*﴿, meaning until I see this as God sees all things. ﴾*So God said, 'Take four birds and train them to come back to you. Then place a part of them on separate hilltops'*﴿, mincing them up and mixing them just as this corpse became mixed up among the animals that ate it and were eaten in turn. ﴾*Then place a part of them on separate hilltops, call them back, and they will come flying to you*﴿. So when he called them back, they responded. There were ten hilltops in total.' [2:260]

473. Abū Baṣīr narrated from Abū ʿAbd Allāh عليه السلام that there were ten hilltops, and the birds were a cockerel, a dove, a peacock and a crow. He [God] said, 'Take four birds and cut them up together with their flesh, bones and feathers. Then retain their heads and distribute the rest of their parts across ten hilltops, a part on each hilltop.' So whatever feathers, flesh, and blood were on one hilltop began to go towards another hilltop to combine with the rest of it, and so on until it came back to him and he placed its head back onto its neck until he had finished with all four birds. [2:260]

لو شِئتُ لم أخْلُقهم، إنّي خَلَقتُ خَلْقي على ثَلاثة أصنافٍ: عبدٌ يَعْبُدني لا يُشْرِك بي شيئًا فأُثيبه، وعبد يَعْبُدُ غيري فلن يفوتني، وعبدٌ يَعبُدُ غيري فأُخرجُ من صُلبه من يَعْبُدني.

ثمّ التفت إبراهيم ﵇ فرأى جِيفةً على ساحلٍ، بعضها في الماء وبعضها في البرّ، تجيء سِباعُ البرّ فتأكُل بعضها بعضًا، فَيشِدّ بعضها على بعضٍ، فيأكُل بعضها بعضًا. فعند ذلك تَعَجّب إبراهيم ﵇ ممّا رأى، وقال: ﴿رَبِّ أَرِنِي كَيْفَ تُحْيِي الْمَوْتَىٰ﴾ كيف تُخرج ما تَنَاسَخ، هذه أممٌ أكَل بعضها بعضًا ﴿قَالَ أَوَلَمْ تُؤْمِن قَالَ بَلَىٰ وَلَٰكِن لِّيَطْمَئِنَّ قَلْبِي﴾ يعني حتّى أرى هذا كما أراني الله الأشياء كلّها، قال: ﴿خُذْ أَرْبَعَةً مِّنَ الطَّيْرِ فَصُرْهُنَّ إِلَيْكَ﴾ ثمّ أجعل على كلّ جبلٍ منهنّ جُزءًا وتقطّعهنّ وتخلطهنّ كما اختلطت هذه الجيفة في هذه السباع التي أكلت بعضها بعضًا ﴿ثُمَّ اجْعَلْ عَلَىٰ كُلِّ جَبَلٍ مِّنْهُنَّ جُزْءًا ثُمَّ ادْعُهُنَّ يَأْتِينَكَ سَعْيًا﴾ فلمّا دعاهنّ أجبنه، وكانت الجبال عَشَرة.

٤٧٣. وروى أبو بصير، عن أبي عبد الله ﵇: وكانت الجبال عَشَرة، وكانت الطيور: الدِيك، والحَمامة، والطاوُوس، والغُراب. وقال: فخُذ أربعةً من الطير فقطّعهنّ بلَحمهنّ وعِظامهنّ وريشهنّ، ثمّ أمسِكْ رؤوسهنّ، ثمّ فرِّقهنّ على عَشَرة جبال على كلّ جَبلٍ مِنهنّ جزءٌ، فجعل ما كان في هذا الجبل يذهب إلى هذا الجبل بريشه ولحمه ودمه، ثمّ يأتيه حتّى يَضَع رأسه في عُنُقه حتّى فَرَغ من أربعتِهنّ.

474. From Maʿrūf b. Kharrabūdh[145] who said, 'I heard Abū Jaʿfar عليه السلام say, "When God revealed to Ibrāhīm عليه السلام saying, ﴾ *Take four birds* ﴿, Ibrāhīm set about taking an ostrich, a peacock, a goose and a cockerel. He feathered them after slaughtering them, then placed them in a mortar and chopped them up, and then distributed them on the hilltops of Jordan. In those days there were ten hilltops in total. So he placed a part of them on each hilltop, then called them by their names, and they came back to him swiftly, meaning immediately. At that point Ibrāhīm said, 'I know that God has power over all things.'" [2:260]

475. From ʿAlī b. Asbāṭ, that Abū al-Ḥasan al-Riḍā عليه السلام was once asked about God's verse: ﴾ *'Yes,' he said, 'but just to put my heart at rest'* ﴿, and whether there was any doubt in his heart. He replied, 'No, but he wanted for God to increase his conviction.' He continued, 'A 'part'[146] equals one tenth.' [2:260]

476. From ʿAbd al-Ṣamad b. Bashīr[147] who narrated, 'Abū Jaʿfar al-Manṣūr gathered the judges together and posed to them, "A man has bequeathed one part of his wealth, so how much is one part?" They did not know what one part amounted to exactly and complained to him about it.

Thereupon he sent a courier to the governor of Medina to get him to ask Jaʿfar b. Muḥammad عليه السلام: "A man has bequeathed one part of his wealth; how much does that amount to, as it has been too difficult for the judges to solve and they do not know how much one part is? He can either tell you the answer [i.e. the governor of Medina] or else have him brought to me with the courier."

So the governor of Medina came to Abū ʿAbd Allāh عليه السلام and said to him, "Abū Jaʿfar has sent me to you to ask you about a man who has bequeathed one part of his wealth. He has asked the judges, but they were unable to tell

---

145 Maʿrūf b. Kharrabūdh (d. *ca.* 160/777), one of the leading narrators of traditions from Imam Muḥammad al-Bāqir and Jaʿfar al-Ṣādiq; he is considered one of the six People of Consensus (*aṣḥāb al-ijmāʿ*).

146 This refers to the verse: ﴾ *Then place a part of them on separate hilltops* ﴿ (Q. 2:260).

147 ʿAbd al-Ṣamad b. Bashīr al-ʿUrāmī al-ʿAbdī, Kufan client of the Banū ʿAbd al-Qays, was a very reliable companion of Imam Jaʿfar al-Ṣādiq. See Ḥillī, *Khulāṣat al-aqwāl*, 226 (nr. 756); Khūʾī, *Muʿjam*, 11: 25–6 (nr. 6528); Modarressi, *Tradition and Survival*, 176–7 (nr. 26).

٤٧٤. عن مَعْرُوف بن خَرَّبُوذ، قال: سَمِعتُ أبا جعفر عليه السلام يقول: إنَّ الله لمّا أوحى إلى إبراهيم عليه السلام أن خُذ أربعة من الطير، عَمَد إبراهيم عليه السلام فأخذ النَّعامة والطاوُوس والوَزَّة والدِّيك، فنَتَف ريشُهنَّ بعد الذّبح، ثمّ جعلهنّ في مِهراسةٍ فَهَرَسَهُنّ، ثمّ فرّقهنّ على جبال الأردُنّ، وكانت يومئذٍ عشرة أجبال، فوضع على كلّ جبلٍ منهنّ جُزءًا، ثمّ دعاهنّ بأسمائِهنّ، فأقبلن إليه سَعْيًا –يعني مسرعات– فقال إبراهيم عليه السلام عند ذلك: أعلم أنّ الله على كُلّ شيءٍ قدير.

٤٧٥. عن عليّ بن أسباط: أنَّ أبا الحسن الرضا عليه السلام سُئِل عن قوله الله تعالى: ﴿قَالَ بَلَىٰ وَلَٰكِن لِّيَطْمَئِنَّ قَلْبِي﴾ أكان في قلبِه شكّ؟ قال: لا، ولكنّه أراد من الله الزيادة في يقينه، قال: والجُزء واحدٌ من عَشَرة.

٤٧٦. عن عبد الصَّمَد بن بَشير، قال: جُمِعَ لأبي جعفر المنصور القُضاة، فقال لهم: رجُلٌ أوصى بجُزءٍ من ماله، فكم الجُزء؟ فلم يعلموا كم الجُزء، أشكلوه فيه.

فأبرد بريدًا إلى صاحب المدينة أن يسأل جعفر بن محمّد عليه السلام: رجُلٌ أوصى بجزءٍ من ماله، فكم الجُزء؟ فقد أشكل ذلك على القُضاة، فلم يعلموا كم الجُزء، فإن هو أخبرك به، وإلاّ فاحمله على البريد ووجّهه إليّ.

فأتى صاحب المدينة أبا عبدالله عليه السلام، فقال له: إنّ أبا جعفر بَعَثَ إليّ أن أسألك عن رجلٍ أوصى بجُزءٍ من ماله، وسأل مَن قبلَه مِن القُضاة فلم يُخبروه ما هو، وقد كَتَبَ إليّ: أن إنْ فسّرت ذلك له وإلاّ حملتك على البريد إليه.

him how much that is. He wrote to me saying you can either explain this for him or that I should have you brought to him with the courier."

So Abū ʿAbd Allāh said, "This is evident in God's Book. God says: ﴾*And when Ibrāhīm said, 'My Lord, show me how You give life to the dead,' He said, 'Do you not believe, then?' 'Yes,' said Ibrāhīm, 'but just to put my heart at rest.' So God said, 'Take four birds and train them to come back to you. Then place a* part *of them on separate hilltops*﴿. There were four birds and ten hilltops, so the man should take out one part out of ten [of his wealth]. Ibrāhīm then called for a mortar, and minced up all the birds together, keeping the heads with him. Then he called out to them as he had been commanded, and began to watch as the feathers came out, the veins one by one until a wing had been formed and was flying towards Ibrāhīm. So Ibrāhīm reached over and took one of the heads, holding it forth. The head he was holding out, however, did not belong to the body before him, until another one came forth to join that head, and so on until they were all completed and fully formed."' [2:260]

477. From ʿAbd al-Raḥmān b. Sayāba[148] who narrated, 'There was a woman who made a bequest to me and told me, "Use two-thirds [of my estate after my death] to pay off my nephew's debt, and give one part to such and such a lady." So I asked Ibn Abī Laylā about it, and he said, "I do not think she gets anything, and I do not know what one part is." Then I asked Abū ʿAbd Allāh عليه السلام, telling him about what the woman had said and what Ibn Abī Laylā had said about it. So he responded, "Ibn Abī Laylā is wrong. She gets one-tenth of the remaining third, for God commanded Ibrāhīm عليه السلام: ﴾*Then place a part of them on separate hilltops*﴿, and in those days there were ten hilltops, so one part is equivalent to one-tenth of something."' [2:260]

478. From Abū Baṣīr, from Abū ʿAbd Allāh عليه السلام who said regarding a man who bequeathed one part of his wealth, 'One part is equivalent to one-tenth because there were ten hilltops. The birds were a peacock, a dove, a cockerel and a hoopoe bird. God commanded him to chop them into pieces, mix them altogether and place a part of the mixture on each of ten hilltops, then

148 ʿAbd al-Raḥmān b. Sayāba al-Kūfī al-Balkhī al-Bazzāz, a companion of Imam Jaʿfar al-Ṣādiq about whom there is scant information. See Khūʾī, *Muʿjam*, 10: 360–1 (nr. 6396).

فقال أبو عبد الله عليه السلام: هذا في كتاب الله بيّن، إنّ الله تعالى يقول: لمّا قال إبراهيم عليه السلام: ﴿رَبِّ أَرِنِي كَيْفَ تُحْيِ الْمَوْتَىٰ﴾ إلى قوله: ﴿كُلِّ جَبَلٍ مِّنْهُنَّ جُزْءًا﴾ فكانت الطير أربعة، والجبال عَشَرَة، يُخرج الرجل من كلّ عَشَرَة أجزاءٍ جُزءًا واحدًا. وإنّ إبراهيم عليه السلام دعا بمِهْرَاسٍ فدقّ فيه الطيور جميعًا، وحَبَسَ الرؤوس عنده، ثمّ إنّه دعا بالذي أُمِر به، فجعل يَنْظُر إلى الرِّيش كيف يَخْرُج، وإلى العُرُوق عِرقًا عِرْقًا حتّى تَمّ جَنَاحه مُستويًا، فأهوى نحو إبراهيم عليه السلام فقال إبراهيم ببعض الرؤوس فاستقبله به، فلم يكن الرأس الذي استقبله به لذلك البَدَن حتّى انتقل إليه غيره، فكان موافقًا للرأس، فتمّت العِدّة وتمّت الأبدان.

٤٧٧. عن عبد الرّحمن بن سَيابة، قال إنّ امراةً أوصت إليّ، وقالت لي: ثُلُثي تقضي به دَين ابن أخي، وجُزء منه لفلانةٍ، فسألت عن ذلك ابن أبي ليلى، فقال: ما أرى لها شيئًا، وما أدري ما الجُزء.

فسألتُ أبا عبد الله عليه السلام، وأخبرتُه كيف قالت المرأة، وما قال ابن أبي ليلى، فقال: كَذَبَ ابن أبي ليلى، لها عُشر الثُلُث، إنّ الله أمر إبراهيم عليه السلام فقال: ﴿اجْعَلْ عَلَىٰ كُلِّ جَبَلٍ مِّنْهُنَّ جُزْءًا﴾ وكانت الجبال يومئذٍ عَشَرة، وهو العُشر من الشيء.

٤٧٨. عن أبي بصير، عن أبي عبد الله عليه السلام، في رجلٍ أوصى بجُزءٍ من ماله، فقال: جُزءٌ من عَشَرَةٍ، كانت الجبال عَشَرَةً، وكان الطير: الطاوُوس، والحمامة، والدِّيك، والهُدهُد، فأمره الله أن يُقطّعهنّ ويَخْلُطهُنّ، وأن يَضَعَ على كلّ جَبَلٍ منهنّ جُزءًا، وأن يأخُذَ رأس كُلّ طيرٍ منها بيده، قال: فكان إذا أخذ رأس الطير منها بيده، تَطَايَرَ إليه ما كان منه حتّى يَعود كما كان.

to hold up each head in turn. As he held up each head in his hand, the body that belonged to it flew towards it and was restored to its original state.' [2:260]

479. From Muḥammad b. Ismāʿīl, from ʿAbd Allāh b. ʿAbd Allāh who narrated, ʿAbū Jaʿfar b. Sulaymān al-Khurāsānī came to me saying, "A man from Khurasan from among the pilgrims going for Hajj came to stay at my house, so we were exchanging news, and he said, 'A brother of ours passed away in Marw and bequeathed a hundred thousand dirhams to me, and asked me to give one part of it to Abū Ḥanīfa. However, I did not know what portion of the bequest one part equalled. When I arrived in Kufa, I went to Abū Ḥanīfa and asked him about the one part, and he said it was a quarter. My heart did not agree with this, so I told him, "I will not [execute the will] until I have performed the Hajj and investigated the matter further." When I saw that all the people in Kufa were in unanimous agreement about it being a quarter, I said to Abū Ḥanīfa, "There is no problem, I will transfer it to you, Abū Ḥanīfa, but I must perform the Hajj and investigate it first." So Abū Ḥanīfa said, "I too am coming for Hajj."

When we arrived in Mecca and were circumambulating the Kaʿba we came upon an old man sitting down supplicating and glorifying God, having completed his circumambulation. When Abū Ḥanīfa turned and saw him, he said, "If you wanted to ask the most supreme of all people, then this is the man you should ask, as there is no one else like him." I asked, "Who is he?" He replied, "Jaʿfar b. Muḥammad عليه السلام."

So just as I had sat down and managed to find a spot, Abū Ḥanīfa went around from behind Jaʿfar b. Muḥammad عليه السلام and sat next to me. He greeted him and showed him great respect, whilst several people were coming up to him, greeting him, praising him and sitting down. When I saw this great show of respect towards him, I felt more emboldened, and Abū Ḥanīfa signalled to me to go ahead and speak, so I said, "May I be your ransom; I am a man from Khurasan. A man died there and made a bequest of a hundred thousand dirhams to me and asked me to give one part of it to someone whom he specified. May I be your ransom, but how much of it is one part?"

So Jaʿfar b. Muḥammad عليه السلام replied, "Abū Ḥanīfa, it is to you that he made this bequest, so you answer it." He replied, "A quarter." So he asked Ibn Abī Laylā, "What do you say?" He replied, "A quarter."

٤٧٩. عن محمّد بن إسماعيل، عن عبد الله بن عبد الله، قال: جاءني أبو جعفر بن سُليمان الخُراسانيّ، وقال: نَزَلَ بي رجلٌ من خُراسان من الحُجّاج، فتذاكرنا الحديث، فقال: مات لنا أخٌ بمَرو، وأوصى إليّ بمائة ألف دِرهم، وأمرني أن أُعطي أبا حنيفة منها جُزءًا، ولم أعرف الجُزء كَم هو مّما ترك؟ فلمّا قَدِمتُ الكوفة أتيتُ أبا حنيفة، فسألتُهُ عن الجُزء، فقال لي: الرُّبع، فأبى قلبي ذلك، فقلتُ: لا أفعل حتّى أَحُجّ وأستقصي المسألة، فلمّا رأيتُ أهل الكوفة قد أجمعوا على الرُّبع، قلتُ لأبي حنيفة: لا سَوءة بذلك، لك أوصى بها يا أبا حنيفة، ولكن أَحُجّ وأستقصي المسألة، فقال أبو حنيفة: وأنا أُريدُ الحَجّ.

فلمّا أتينا مكّة، وكنّا في الطّواف، فإذا نحن برجلٍ شيخ قاعِد، قد فَرَغ من طَوافه، وهو يَدْعُو ويُسبّح، إذ التفتَ أبو حنيفة، فلمّا رآه قال: إن أردتَ أن تسأل غاية الناس، فَسَلْ هذا، فلا أحد بعده. قلتُ: ومَن هذا؟ قال: جَعفر بن محمّد عليه السلام.

فلمّا قعدتُ واستمكنتُ، إذ استدار أبو حنيفة خلف ظَهر جعفر بن محمّد عليه السلام، فقعد قريبًا منّي، فسلّم عليه وعظّمه، وجاء غير واحد مُزْدَلِفين مُسلّمين عليه وقعدوا، فلمّا رأيتُ من تعظيمهم له اشتدّ ظهري، فغمزني أبو حنيفة أن تَكَلَّمْ. فقلتُ: جُعِلت فداك، إنّي رجلٌ من أهل خُراسان، وإنّ رجلاً مات وأوصى إليّ بمائة ألف دِرهم، وأمرني أن أُعطيَ منها جُزءًا، وسمىّ لي الرجل، فكم الجُزء، جُعِلتُ فداك؟

فقال جعفر بن محمّد عليه السلام: يا أبا حنيفة، لك أوصى، قُل فيها؟ فقال: الرُّبع. فقال لابن أبي ليلى: قُل فيها؟ فقال: الرُّبع.

So Ja'far عليه السلام asked, "And from where did you conclude a quarter?" They said, "From God's verse: ﴿ *Take four birds and train them to come back to you. Then place a part of them on separate hilltops* ﴾."

So Abū 'Abd Allāh عليه السلام said to them, and I heard this myself, "We know that there were four birds, but how many hilltops were there? The parts were divided according to the number of hilltops, not birds." So they said, "We thought there were four." So Abū 'Abd Allāh عليه السلام said, "There were actually ten hilltops."' [2:260]

480. From Ṣāliḥ b. Sahl al-Hamadānī[149], from Abū 'Abd Allāh عليه السلام who said regarding the verse: ﴿ *Take four birds and train them to come back to you. Then place a part of them on separate hilltops, call them back, and they will come flying to you: know that God is all powerful and wise* ﴾: 'He took a hoopoe bird, a sparrow-hawk, a peacock and a crow, then slaughtered them and kept their heads aside. Then he mashed up their feathers, their flesh and their bones with the beaks until they had mixed together. He then divided them into ten portions on each of ten hilltops. Then he kept some water and seed next to him, and held the beaks between his fingers, then called out, "Come to me swiftly by God's permission." So they all flew around with the flesh and bones and feathers until they had formed into the bodies in their original state, and each body came and joined with the neck that corresponded with its beak. Ibrāhīm let go of the beaks and they rose up and began to drink from the water and peck at the seed. Then they said, "O prophet of God, you have given us life, may God grant you life." So he replied, "Rather it is God who gives life and death."

This is its outward exegesis, but its exegesis according to the inward aspect of the Qur'an is: 'Take four of those who have the capacity to heed your speech and entrust them with your knowledge. Then despatch them to the corners of the earth as your proofs over people. And when you want them to come back to you, call them by the Greatest Name [of God], they will come swiftly back by God's permission.' [2:260]

---

149 Ṣāliḥ b. Sahl al-Hamadhānī, a well-known liar and fabricator of the Imams' traditions. He is reported to have believed in the Lordship of Imam Ja'far al-Ṣādiq and is condemned by all major scholars of Shī'ī *rijāl*. See Ḥillī, *Khulāṣat al-aqwāl*, 359 (nr. 1416).

فقال جعفر عليه السلام: ومِن أين قُلتُم الرُّبع؟ قالو: لقول الله: ﴿ فَخُذْ أَرْبَعَةً مِّنَ الطَّيْرِ فَصُرْهُنَّ إِلَيْكَ ثُمَّ اجْعَلْ عَلَىٰ كُلِّ جَبَلٍ مِّنْهُنَّ جُزْءًا ﴾.

فقال أبو عبدالله عليه السلام لهم — وأنا أسمع هذا —: قد عَلِمت الطير أربعة، فكم كانت الجبال؟ إنّما الأجزاء ليس للطير، فقالوا: ظننّا أنّها أربعة. فقال أبو عبدالله عليه السلام: ولكنّ الجبال عَشَرَة.

٤٨٠. عن صالح بن سَهْل الهَمَداني، عن أبي عبدالله عليه السلام، في قوله: ﴿ فَخُذْ أَرْبَعَةً مِّنَ الطَّيْرِ فَصُرْهُنَّ إِلَيْكَ ثُمَّ اجْعَلْ عَلَىٰ كُلِّ جَبَلٍ مِّنْهُنَّ جُزْءًا ﴾ الآية. فقال: أخذ الهُدهُد والصُّرَد والطاوُوس والغُراب، فَذَبحهنّ وعزل رُؤوسهنّ، ثم نَحَزَ أبدانهنّ بالمِنْحاز ولُحومهنّ وعِظامهنّ حتّى اختَلَط، ثمّ جزّأهنّ عَشَرَة أجزاءٍ على عَشَرَة جبالٍ، ثمّ وضع عنده حَبًّا وماءً، ثمّ جعل مناقيرهنّ بين أصابعه، ثمّ قال: سعيًا بإذن الله، فتطايرت بعضهنّ إلى بعض، اللُّحوم والرِّيش والعِظام حتّى استوت بالأبدان كما كانت، وجاء كلُّ بدنٍ حتّى التَزق برقبته الّتي فيها المِنقار، فخلّى إبراهيم عليه السلام عن مناقيرها فوقعنَ وشَرِبن من ذلك الماء، والتَقَطن من ذلك الحبّ، قُلن: يا نبيّ الله، أحييتنا أحياك الله، فقال: بل الله يُحيي ويميت.

فهذا تفسيره في الظاهر، وأمّا تفسيره في باطن القرآن، قال: خُذ أربعةً ممّن يحتمل الكلام فاستودعهم عِلمك، ثمّ ابْعثهم في أطراف الأرض حُججًا لك على الناس، فاذا أرَدْتَ أن يأتُوك دَعَوتهم بالاسم الأكبر، يأتونك سعيًا بإذن الله.

481. From ʿUmar b. Yazīd who narrated, ʿI heard Abū ʿAbd Allāh ﷺ say, "When a believer does his best in an action, God multiplies that action for him to seven hundred times its like, as per God's verse: ﴾ *God gives multiple increase to whoever He wishes* ﴿ . So do your best in whatever actions you do to earn God's reward." So I asked, "And what does doing one's best involve?" He replied, "When you pray, perfect your bowing and prostration. When you fast keep away from anything that may spoil your fast, and when you perform the Hajj, stay away from anything that is forbidden to you in the state of *iḥrām* during your Hajj and *ʿumra*." He continued, "Every action that you do should be cleansed of any contamination."ʾ [2:261]

482. From Ḥumrān, from Abū Jaʿfar ﷺ. He narrated, ʿI asked him, "Are you of the opinion that the believer (*mu'min*) has a certain superiority over the Muslim in matters of inheritance, legal decrees, and certain rulings whereby the believer receives more inheritance than the Muslim and other such things?" He replied, "No, the same thing applies to both when the imam passes a judgement in their case, but the believer does have superiority over the Muslim in their actions through which they seek proximity to God." I asked, "But does God not say: ﴾ *Whoever has done a good deed will have it ten times to his credit* ﴿(8:160)? I assumed that they all had the same reward for their prayer, charity, fasting, and pilgrimage as the believers." He replied, "Does God not say, ﴾ *God gives multiple increase to whoever He wishes* ﴿(2:261)? So believers are the ones for whom God increases their deeds by seventy times for each good deed, and this is His special favour on them. God increases the recompense of a believer's good deeds exponentially according to the quality of his faith, and He does whatever He wishes when it comes to the believers."ʾ

٤٨١. عن عُمر بن يزيد، قال: سَمِعتُ أبا عبد الله عليه السلام يقول: إذا أحسَنَ المؤمن عَمَله ضاعف الله له عَمَله بكلّ حسنةٍ سبعمائة ضِعف، فذلك قول الله: ﴿وَاللَّهُ يُضَاعِفُ لِمَن يَشَاءُ﴾ فأحْسِنُوا أعمالكم التي تعْمَلُونها لثواب الله. قلتُ: وما الإحسان؟ قال: إذا صَلّيتَ فأحْسِن رُكُوعك وسُجُودك، وإذا صُمْتَ فَتَوقّ كُلّ ما فيه فساد صَومك، وإذا حَجَجْتَ فَتَوقّ كلّ ما يَحْرُم عليك في حجّتك وعُمرتك. قال: وكُلّ عملٍ تعْمَله فليكن نقيًّا من الدَّنس.

٤٨٢. عن حُمران، عن أبي جعفر عليه السلام، قال: قُلتُ له: أرأيتَ المؤمن له فضلٌ على المُسلم في شيءٍ من المواريث والقضايا والأحكام حتىّ يكون للمؤمن أكثر ممّا يكون للمسلم في المواريث أو غير ذلك؟

قال: لا، هما يجريان في ذلك مَجرًى واحدًا، إذا حكم الإمام عليهما، ولكنّ للمؤمن فضلاً على المُسلم في أعمالهما، يتقرّبان به إلى الله.

قال: فقلتُ: أليس الله يقول: ﴿مَن جَاءَ بِالْحَسَنَةِ فَلَهُ عَشْرُ أَمْثَالِهَا﴾؟ وزعمت أنّهم مجتمعون على الصلاة والزكاة والصوم والحجّ مع المؤمن؟

قال: فقال: أليس الله قد قال: ﴿اللَّهُ يُضَاعِفُ لِمَن يَشَاءُ﴾ أضعافًا كثيرة؟ فالمؤمنون هم الذين يُضاعِفُ الله لهم الحسنات، لكُلّ حَسَنةٍ سبعين ضِعفًا، فهذا من فَضْلهم، ويَزيد الله المُؤمن في حسناته على قَدر صِحّة إيمانه أضعافًا مضاعفةً كثيرةً، ويَفْعل الله بالمؤمنين ما يشاء.

483. From Mufaḍḍal b. Muḥammad al-Juʿfī who narrated, 'I asked Abū ʿAbd Allāh عليه السلام about God's verse: ﴾*Those who spend their wealth in God's cause are like grains of corn that produce seven ears*﴿. He said, "The grain is Fāṭima, may God bless her, and the seven ears of corn are seven of her offspring, the seventh of whom will be the Avenger (*al-qā'im*)." I asked, "What about al-Ḥasan?" He replied, "Although al-Ḥasan is an Imam appointed by God, and obedience to him is mandatory, he is not one of the seven ears of corn. The first of them is al-Ḥusayn and the last of them is the Avenger." I then asked, "What about the phrase: ﴾*each bearing a hundred grains*﴿?" He replied, "Each of their descendants in Kufa will in turn have a hundred descendants, and this can be none other than these seven."' [2:261]

484. From Muḥammad al-Wābishī, from Abū ʿAbd Allāh عليه السلام who said, 'When a believing servant does his best, God multiplies the worth of his deeds for him to seven hundred times their like for every good deed, and this is as per the statement of God, Blessed and most High: ﴾*God gives multiple increase to whoever He wishes*﴿.' [2:261]

485. From al-Mufaḍḍal b. Ṣāliḥ, from one of his associates, from Jaʿfar b. Muḥammad عليه السلام and Abū Jaʿfar عليه السلام who said regarding the verse: ﴾*You who believe, do not cancel out your charitable deeds with reminders and hurtful words*﴿, 'It was revealed about ʿUthmān, and applied to Muʿāwiya and both of their followers.' [2:264]

486. From Sallām b. al-Mustanīr, from Abū Jaʿfar عليه السلام, who said about the verse: '﴾*You who believe, do not cancel out your charitable deeds with reminders and hurtful words*﴿ to Muḥammad ﷺ and the family of Muḥammad, this is the interpretation.' He continued, 'It was revealed about ʿUthmān.' [2:264]

٤٨٣. عن المُفَضَّل بن محمّد الجُعفي، قال: سألتُ أبا عبدالله عليه السلام عن قول الله تعالى: ﴿ كَمَثَلِ حَبَّةٍ أَنبَتَتْ سَبْعَ سَنَابِلَ ﴾ قال: الحبّة فاطمة (صلى الله عليها)، والسّبع السّنابل سبعةٌ من وُلدها سابِعُهم قائمُهم.

قلتُ: الحسن عليه السلام؟ قال: إنّ الحسن عليه السلام إمامٌ من الله مفترضٌ طاعتُه، ولكن ليس من السّنابل السّبعة، أوّلهم الحسين عليه السلام، وآخرهم القائم عليه السلام.

فقلتُ: قوله: ﴿فِي كُلِّ سُنبُلَةٍ مِّائَةُ حَبَّةٍ﴾؟ قال: يُولد للرجلُ منهم في الكرّة مائة من صُلبه، وليس ذلك إلاّ هؤلاء السبعة.

٤٨٤. عن محمّد الوابِشيّ، عن أبي عبدالله عليه السلام، قال: إذا أحسن العبد المؤمن، ضَاعَفَ الله له عمله، لكُلّ حسنةٍ سبعمائة ضِعْفٍ، وذلك قول الله تبارك وتعالى ﴿وَاللَّهُ يُضَاعِفُ لِمَن يَشَاءُ﴾.

٤٨٥. عن المُفَضَّل بن صالح، عن بعض أصحابه، عن جعفر بن محمّد، وأبي جعفر عليه السلام، في قول الله تعالى: ﴿يَا أَيُّهَا الَّذِينَ آمَنُوا لَا تُبْطِلُوا صَدَقَاتِكُم بِالْمَنِّ وَالْأَذَىٰ﴾ إلى آخر الآية، قال: نزلت في عثمان، وجرت في معاوية وأتباعهما.

٤٨٦. عن سلاّم بن المستنير، عن أبي جعفر عليه السلام في قوله تعالى: ﴿يَا أَيُّهَا الَّذِينَ آمَنُوا لَا تُبْطِلُوا صَدَقَاتِكُم بِالْمَنِّ وَالْأَذَىٰ﴾ لمحمّد وآل محمّد عليه الصلاة والسلام، هذا تأويل. قال: أُنزلت في عثمان.

487. From Abū Baṣīr, from Abū ʿAbd Allāh عليه السلام who said regarding the verse: ﴾*You who believe, do not cancel out your charitable deeds with reminders and hurtful words like someone who spends his wealth only to be seen by people, not believing in God and the Last Day. Such a person is like a rock with earth on it: heavy rain falls and leaves it completely bare. Such people get no rewards for their works,*﴿(2:264): '[The word] *ṣafwān* means 'a rock'; and ﴾*those who spend their wealth to show off*﴿(4:38) are [Abū Bakr, ʿUmar and ʿUthmān], and Muʿāwiya and their adherents.'

488. From Sallām b. al-Mustanīr, from Abū Jaʿfar عليه السلام who said regarding the verse: ﴾*But those who spend their wealth in order to gain God's approval*﴿, 'This was revealed about ʿAlī عليه السلام.' [2:265]

489. From Abū Baṣīr, from Abū ʿAbd Allāh عليه السلام who recited: ﴾*But those who spend their wealth in order to gain God's approval*﴿ and said, "Alī, the Commander of the Faithful, is the best of such people, who spend their wealth in order to gain God's approval.' [2:265]

490. From Abū Baṣīr, from Abū Jaʿfar عليه السلام who explained that the phrase ﴾*a fiery whirlwind*﴿ was a type of wind. [2:266]

491. From ʿAbd Allāh b. Sinān, from Abū ʿAbd Allāh عليه السلام who explained that the verse: ﴾*You who believe, give charitably from the good things you have acquired and that We have produced for you from the earth. Do not give away the bad things that you yourself would only accept with your eyes closed*﴿ was revealed about a group of people at the time of the Messenger of God صلى الله عليه وآله who used to give the worst of their produce away in charity, which were the dates with thin skins and large stones called *al-muʿāfāra*. This is when God revealed the verse: ﴾*Do not give away the bad things that you yourself would only accept with your eyes closed.*﴿. (2:267)

492. From Abū Baṣīr who narrated, 'I asked Abū ʿAbd Allāh عليه السلام about: ﴾*and that which We have produced for you from the earth*﴿. He said, "When the Messenger of God صلى الله عليه وآله used to command for date palms to be purified through giving them in charity, a group of people would bring bunches of dates that were the worst of their crop, which they would then offer as charity. They

٤٨٧. عن أبي بصير، عن أبي عبدالله عليه السلام في قوله تعالى: ﴿يَا أَيُّهَا الَّذِينَ آمَنُوا لَا تُبْطِلُوا صَدَقَاتِكُمْ بِالْمَنِّ وَالْأَذَى﴾ إلى قوله: ﴿لَا يَقْدِرُونَ عَلَى شَيْءٍ مِمَّا كَسَبُوا﴾ قال: صَفوان، أي حَجَر، ﴿وَالَّذِينَ يُنْفِقُونَ أَمْوَالَهُمْ رِئَاءَ النَّاسِ﴾ فلان وفلان، وفلان، ومُعاوية، وأشياعهم.

٤٨٨. عن سلاّم بن المُستنير، عن أبي جعفر عليه السلام قال: في قوله تعالى: ﴿الَّذِينَ يُنْفِقُونَ أَمْوَالَهُمُ ابْتِغَاءَ مَرْضَاةِ اللَّهِ﴾. قال: أُنزلت في عليّ عليه السلام.

٤٨٩. عن أبي بصير، عن أبي عبدالله عليه السلام، قال: ﴿الَّذِينَ يُنْفِقُونَ أَمْوَالَهُمُ ابْتِغَاءَ مَرْضَاةِ اللَّهِ﴾، قال: عليّ أمير المؤمنين عليه السلام أفضلُهم، وهو ممّن يُنفق ماله ابتغاء مرضات الله.

٤٩٠. عن أبي بصير، عن أبي جعفر عليه السلام: ﴿إِعْصَارٌ فِيهِ نَارٌ﴾، قال عليه السلام: ريحٌ.

٤٩١. عن عبدالله بن سِنان، عن أبي عبدالله عليه السلام، في قول الله تعالى: ﴿يَا أَيُّهَا الَّذِينَ آمَنُوا أَنْفِقُوا مِنْ طَيِّبَاتِ مَا كَسَبْتُمْ وَمِمَّا أَخْرَجْنَا لَكُمْ مِنَ الْأَرْضِ وَلَا تَيَمَّمُوا الْخَبِيثَ مِنْهُ تُنْفِقُونَ﴾. قال: كان أناس على عهد رسول الله صلى الله عليه وآله يتصدّقون بِشرّ ما عندهم من التّمر الرقيق القِشر، الكبير النّوى، يُقال له: المُعافارة، ففي ذلك أنزل الله: ﴿وَلَا تَيَمَّمُوا الْخَبِيثَ مِنْهُ تُنْفِقُونَ﴾.

٤٩٢. عن أبي بصير، قال سألتُ أبا عبدالله عليه السلام: ﴿وَمِمَّا أَخْرَجْنَا لَكُمْ مِنَ الْأَرْضِ﴾؟ قال: كان رسول الله صلى الله عليه وآله إذا أمر بالنخل أن يُزكّى، يجيء قومٌ بألوانٍ من التمر، هو من أردأ التمر

were dates known as *al-juʿrūr* and *al-muʿāfāra*, thin-skinned and with large stones. Some people used to bring these instead of the good dates, so the Messenger of God ﷺ said, 'Do not weigh up these two to be valued, and do not bring any more of these again.' This is when God revealed: ﴾ *You who believe, give charitably from the good things you have acquired and that We have produced for you from the earth. Do not give away the bad things that you yourself would only accept with your eyes closed* ﴿ , and closing one's eyes means to accept blindly these two types of dates as profitable."

He also said, "Charity given by the one who earns unlawfully does not even reach God."' [2:267]

493. From Rifāʿa, from Abū ʿAbd Allāh عليه السلام who said regarding the verse: ﴾ *that you yourself would only accept with your eyes closed* ﴿, 'The Messenger of God ﷺ sent ʿAbd Allāh b. Rawāḥa and said to him, "Do not value a single *juʿrūr* or *muʿāfāra* date," as people used to bring these bad dates and God, exalted be His mention, revealed: ﴾ *that you yourself would only accept with your eyes closed.* ﴿. He also mentioned that ʿAbd Allāh included some bad dates in his valuation of them, so the Prophet ﷺ said, "Do not value any *juʿrūr* and *muʿāfāra* dates, O ʿAbd Allāh ."' [2:267]

494. From Zurāra, from Abū Jaʿfar عليه السلام who said regarding the verse: ﴾ *Do not give away the bad things that you yourself would only accept with your eyes closed* ﴿: 'People used to have surplus in their wealth that they had previously gained through usury or fraudulent earnings, so someone from among them tried to give it away and spend it in charity, and God forbade them from doing so.' [2:267]

495. From Abū al-Ṣabbāḥ, from Abū Jaʿfar عليه السلام who said, 'I asked him about God's words: ﴾ *Do not give away the bad things that you yourself would only accept with your eyes closed* ﴿, so he said, "When people embraced Islam they used to have unlawful earnings from usury and fraud, and some would single that out from their wealth and give it to charity. So God forbade them from doing that, for charity only thrives [when given] out of wholesome earnings."' [2:267]

يؤدّونه عن زكاتهم تمرًا، يقال له: الجعرور والمُعافارة، قليلة اللحاء عظيمة النّوى، فكان بعضهم يجئ بها عن التمر الجيّد، فقال رسول الله ﷺ: لا تخْرصوا هاتين ولا تجيئوا منها بشيءٍ، وفي ذلك أنزل الله تعالى: ﴿يَا أَيُّهَا الَّذِينَ آمَنُوا أَنفِقُوا مِن طَيِّبَاتِ مَا كَسَبْتُمْ﴾ إلى قوله: ﴿إِلاَّ أَن تُغْمِضُوا فِيهِ﴾ والإغماض: أن يأخذ هاتين التّمرتين من التّمر.

وقال: لا يصل إلى الله صدقةٌ من كسبٍ حرام.

٤٩٣. عن رِفاعة عن أبي عبدالله، في قول الله: ﴿إِلاَّ أَن تُغْمِضُوا فِيهِ﴾، فقال: بعث رسول الله ﷺ عبدالله بن رَواحة، فقال: لا تخرِصوا جُعرُورًا ولا معافارةً؛ وكان أُناسٌ يَجيئون بتمر سوء، فأنزل الله جلّ ذكره: ﴿وَلَسْتُم بِآخِذِيهِ إِلاَّ أَن تُغْمِضُوا فِيهِ﴾ وذكر أنّ عبدالله خَرَص عليهم تَمر سوء، فقال النّبي ﷺ: يا عبدالله، لا تخرِص جُعرُورًا ولا مُعافارةً.

٤٩٤. عن زُرارة، عن أبي جعفر عليه السلام، في قول الله تعالى: ﴿وَلا تَيَمَّمُوا الْخَبِيثَ مِنْهُ تُنفِقُونَ﴾، قال: كانت بقايا في أموال النّاس أصابوها من الربا أو من [المكاسب] الخبيثة قبل ذلك، فكان أحدهم يتيمّمها فيُنفقها ويَتصدّق بها، فنهاهم الله عن ذلك.

٤٩٥. عن أبي الصّبّاح، عن أبي جعفر عليه السلام، قال: سألتُه عن قول الله تعالى: ﴿وَلا تَيَمَّمُوا الْخَبِيثَ مِنْهُ تُنفِقُونَ﴾ قال: كان النّاس حين أسلمُوا عندهم مكاسب من الرِّبا، ومن أموالٍ خبيثةٍ، فكان الرجُل يتعمّدها من بين ماله فيتصدّق بها، فنهاهم الله عن ذلك، وإنَّ الصَّدقة لا تصلُح إلاّ من كسبٍ طيّبٍ.

496. From Isḥāq b. ʿAmmār, from Jaʿfar b. Muḥammad عليه السلام who said, ‘The people of Medina used to bring their charity for ʿĪd al-Fiṭr to the Prophet’s mosque, and this included a cluster of dates known as *al-juʿrūr* and another known as *al-muʿāfāra*, which had large stones, thin skins, and a bitter taste. The Messenger of God ﷺ told the valuer, “Do not include these two types of dates in your valuation so that they are too embarrassed to bring them next time.” After this God revealed: ﴾*Do not give away the bad things that you yourself would only accept with your eyes closed*﴿.’ [2:267]

497. From Muḥammad b. Khālid al-Ḍabbī who narrated, ‘Ibrāhīm al-Nakhaʿī passed by a woman called Umm Bakr sitting on her doorstep early in the morning. In her hand was a spinning wheel that she was spinning on. He said, “Umm Bakr, are you not too old for this now? Is it not time for you to put your spinning wheel down?” She replied, “How can I put it down when I have heard ʿAlī b. Abī Ṭālib, the Commander of the Faithful عليه السلام say, ‘This is one of the wholesome means of earning a living.’”’ [2:267]

498. From Hārūn b. Khārija[150], from Abū ʿAbd Allāh عليه السلام. I asked him, ‘Why is it that I feel happy for no apparent reason, neither because of myself, nor to do with my wealth, nor my companion; and at other times I feel sad for no apparent reason to feel sad about, neither in myself nor my wealth.’ He replied, ‘Yes. Satan approaches the heart and says to it: “If God truly wished good for you, He would not have given your enemy superiority over you, and He would not have made you need him in any way. You are awaiting the same fate as those before you, and they did not say anything either.” This is the one who feels sad without reason. The one who feels happy, however, it is when an angel approaches the heart and says to it, “If God has shown you your enemy having more, and has made you need him, it is only for a few days. I am giving you glad tidings of forgiveness from God, and His abundance.” This is the purport of God’s verse: ﴾*Satan threatens you with the prospect of poverty and commands you to do foul deeds; God promises you His forgiveness and His abundance: God is limitless and all-knowing*﴿.’ [2:268]

150 Abū al-Ḥasan Hārūn b. Khārija, on whom there is scant information, is considered a reliable narrator in Shīʿī works of *rijāl*. See Ḥillī, *Khulāṣat al-aqwāl*, 290 (nr. 1070); Modarressi, *Tradition and Survival*, 249–50 (nr. 80).

٤٩٦. عن إسحاق بن عمّار، عن جعفر بن محمّد عليه السلام، قال: كان أهل المدينة يأتون بِصَدقة الفِطر إلى مسجِد رسول الله صلى الله عليه وآله وفيه عِذق يُسمّى الجُعرُور، وعِذق يُسمّى مُعافارة، كانا عظيماً نواهما، رقيقاً لحاؤهما، في طعمهما مرارة، فقال رسول الله صلى الله عليه وآله للخارص: لا تَخرِص عليهم هذين اللّونَين، لعلّهم يستحيُون لا يأتون بهما، فأنزل الله تعالى: ﴿يَا أَيُّهَا الَّذِينَ آمَنُوا أَنْفِقُوا مِنْ طَيِّبَاتِ مَا كَسَبْتُمْ﴾ إلى قوله: ﴿تُنْفِقُونَ﴾.

٤٩٧. عن محمّد بن خالد الضَّبِّي، قال: مرّ إبراهيم النَّخَعيّ على امرأةٍ وهي جالسة على باب دارها بُكرةً، وكان يقال لها: أُمّ بكر، وفي يدها مِغزَل تَغزِل به، فقال: يا أُمّ بكر، أما كَبِرت، ألم يأن لكِ أن تَضَعي هذا المِغزَل؟ فقالت: وكيف أضعه وَسَمِعتُ عليّ بن أبي طالب أمير المؤمنين عليه السلام يقول: هو من طيّبات الكَسْب.

٤٩٨. عن هارون بن خارجة، عن أبي عبدالله عليه السلام، قال: قلتُ له: إنّي أفْرَحُ من غير فَرَح أراه في نفسي، ولا في مالي، ولا في صديقي، وأحْزَنُ من غير حُزنٍ أراه في نفسي ولا في مالي، ولا في صديقي.

قال: نعم، إنّ الشيطان يُلِمُّ بالقلب، فيقول لو كان لك عند الله خير، ما أدالَ عليك عدوّك، ولا جعل بك إليه حاجة، هل تنتظر إلاّ مثل الذي انتظر الذين من قبلك، فهل قالوا شيئًا؟ فذاك الذي يُحزِن من غير حُزن.

وأمّا الفرح، فإنّ المَلَك يُلِمُّ بالقلب فيقول: إن كان الله أدالَ عليك عدوَّك وجعل بك إليه حاجةً، فإنّما هي أيّامٌ قلائل، أبْشِر بمَغفِرةٍ من الله وفَضْلٍ، وهو قول الله تعالى:

499. From Abū Baṣīr who narrated, 'I asked him about the verse: ﴾*Whoever is given wisdom has truly been given much good*﴿. He replied, "It is obedience to God and recognition of the Imam."' [2:269]

500. From Abū Baṣīr who narrated, 'I heard Abū Ja'far عليه السلام say: ﴾*Whoever is given wisdom has truly been given much good*﴿, "It is the recognition [of the Imam]."' [2:269]

501. From Abū Baṣīr, who narrated, 'I heard Abū Ja'far عليه السلام say: ﴾*Whoever is given wisdom has truly been given much good*﴿, "It is the recognition [of the Imam], and [the capacity] to refrain from the grave sins for which God has made chastisement in Hellfire obligatory."' [2:269]

502. From Sulaymān b. Khālid[151] who narrated, 'I asked Abū 'Abd Allāh عليه السلام about God's verse: ﴾*Whoever is given wisdom has truly been given much good*﴿, so he replied, "Wisdom is a thorough understanding and comprehensive knowledge of religion; whoever from among you knows his religion is a wise man. There is no believer's death more beloved to Iblīs than the death of a scholar."' [2:269]

503. From al-Ḥalabī, from Abū 'Abd Allāh عليه السلام. 'I asked him about the verse: ﴾*If you give charity openly, it is good, but if you keep it secret and give to the needy in private, that is better for you*﴿. He replied, "It does not refer to the obligatory alms tax (*zakāt*), but that a man should give charity privately out of his own accord. The alms tax is given openly, not in secret."' [2:271]

504. From Jābir al-Ju'fī, from Abū Ja'far عليه السلام who said, 'God despises the importunate beggar.' [2:273]

---

151 Abū al-Rabī' Sulaymān b. Khālid b. Dihqān Nāfila al-Aqta', who originally accompanied Zayd b. 'Alī in his revolt, later became a trustworthy and reliable companion of Imam Muḥammad al-Bāqir and Imam Ja'far al-Ṣādiq. See Ḥillī, *Khulāṣat al-aqwāl*, 153–4 (nr. 445); Modarressi, *Tradition and Survival*, 374–5 (nr. 197).

﴿الشَّيْطَانُ يَعِدُكُمُ الْفَقْرَ وَيَأْمُرُكُم بِالْفَحْشَاءِ وَاللَّهُ يَعِدُكُم مَّغْفِرَةً مِّنْهُ وَفَضْلًا﴾.

٤٩٩. عن أبي بصير، قال: سألتُهُ عن قول الله عزّ وجلّ: ﴿وَمَن يُؤْتَ الْحِكْمَةَ فَقَدْ أُوتِيَ خَيْرًا كَثِيرًا﴾، قال: هي طاعة الله، ومعرفة الإمام.

٥٠٠. عن أبي بصير، قال: سَمِعتُ أبا جعفر عليه السلام يقول: ﴿وَمَن يُؤْتَ الْحِكْمَةَ فَقَدْ أُوتِيَ خَيْرًا كَثِيرًا﴾، قال: المعرِفة.

٥٠١. عن أبي بصير، قال سَمِعتُ أبا جعفر عليه السلام يقول: ﴿وَمَن يُؤْتَ الْحِكْمَةَ فَقَدْ أُوتِيَ خَيْرًا كَثِيرًا﴾، قال: معرفة الإمام، واجتناب الكبائر الّتي أوجَبَ الله عليها النّار.

٥٠٢. عن سُليمان بن خالد، قال: سألتُ أبا عبدالله عليه السلام عن قول الله تعالى: ﴿وَمَن يُؤْتَ الْحِكْمَةَ فَقَدْ أُوتِيَ خَيْرًا كَثِيرًا﴾. فقال عليه السلام: إنّ الحكمة: المعرفة والتفقُّه في الدين، فمَن فَقِهَ منكم فهو حكيمٌ، وما من أحدٍ يموت من المؤمنين أحبُّ إلى إبليس من فقيه.

٥٠٣. عن الحلَبيّ، عن أبي عبدالله عليه السلام قال: سألتُهُ عن قول الله تعالى: ﴿وَإِن تُخْفُوهَا وَتُؤْتُوهَا الْفُقَرَاءَ فَهُوَ خَيْرٌ لَّكُمْ﴾، قال: ليس تلك الزكاة، ولكنّه الرجل يَتصدّق لنفسه، الزكاة علانيةً ليس بسِرّ.

٥٠٤. عن جابر الجُعفي، عن أبي جعفر عليه السلام، قال: إنّ الله يبغُض المُلْحِف.

505. From Abū Baṣīr who narrated, 'I asked Abū 'Abd Allāh عليه السلام about the verse: ﴿ *Those who give, out of their own possessions, by night and by day, in private and in public, will have their reward with their Lord: no fear for them, nor will they grieve* ﴾ . He said, "This does not refer to the alms tax."' [2:274]

506. From Abū Isḥāq who said, "'Alī b. Abī Ṭālib عليه السلام had four dirhams and nothing else; so he would give away in charity one dirham at night, one dirham in the daytime, one in secret and one in public. When the Prophet ﷺ heard about this, he asked him, "'Alī, what prompted you to do this?" He replied, "The fulfilment of God's promise." So God revealed: ﴿ *Those who give, out of their own possessions, by night and by day, in private and in public, will have their reward with their Lord: no fear for them, nor will they grieve* ﴾.' [2:274]

507. From Shihāb b. 'Abd Rabbih who narrated, 'I heard Abū 'Abd Allāh عليه السلام say, "The one who takes usury will not depart from this world without first having been tormented by Satan's touch."' [2:275]

508. From Zurāra who narrated, 'Abū 'Abd Allāh عليه السلام said, "Usury is only applicable to those commodities that can be weighed and measured."' [2:275]

509. From Muḥammad b. Muslim, from Abū 'Abd Allāh عليه السلام regarding the verse: ﴿ *Whoever, on receiving God's warning, stops taking usury may keep his past gains God will be his judge* ﴾. He said, 'The warning is repentance.' [2:275]

510. From Muḥammad b. Muslim, that a man went to Abū Ja'far عليه السلام who he had previously dealt in usury to increase his wealth, and after having asked various other scholars who had told him, 'Nothing can avail you now unless you return it all to its rightful owners.' So when he related all this to Abū Ja'far عليه السلام, Abū Ja'far said to him, "Your way out is in God's Book wherein is found His statement: ﴿ *Whoever, on receiving God's warning, stops taking usury may keep his past gains – God will be his judge* ﴾. The warning is repentance." [2:275]

٥٠٥. عن أبي بَصير، قال: قلتُ لأبي عبدالله عليه السلام، قوله تعالى: ﴿الَّذِينَ يُنْفِقُونَ أَمْوَالَهُمْ بِاللَّيْلِ وَالنَّهَارِ سِرًّا وَعَلَانِيَةً﴾؟ قال: ليس من الزكاة.

٥٠٦. عن أبي إسحاق، قال: كان لعليّ بن أبي طالب عليه السلام أربعة دراهم، لم يَمْلِك غيرها، فتصدَّق بدرهم ليلاً، وبدرهم نهارًا، وبدرهم سرًّا، وبدرهم علانيةً، فبَلَغَ ذلك النبيّ ﷺ فقال: يا عليّ، ما حَمَلك على ما صنعت؟ قال: إنجاز موعود الله، فأنزل الله تعالى: ﴿الَّذِينَ يُنْفِقُونَ أَمْوَالَهُمْ بِاللَّيْلِ وَالنَّهَارِ سِرًّا وَعَلَانِيَةً﴾ الآية.

٥٠٧. عن شهاب بن عبد ربّه، قال: سَمِعتُ أبا عبدالله عليه السلام يقول: آكِلُ الرِّبا لا يَخرُج من الدنيا حتى يَتَخبَّطه الشيطان.

٥٠٨. عن زُرارة، قال: أبو عبدالله عليه السلام، لا يكون الرِّبا إلاّ فيما يُوزَن ويُكال.

٥٠٩. عن محمّد بن مُسلم، عن أبي عبدالله عليه السلام، في قول الله تعالى: ﴿فَمَنْ جَاءَهُ مَوْعِظَةٌ مِنْ رَبِّهِ فَانْتَهَى فَلَهُ مَا سَلَفَ وَأَمْرُهُ إِلَى اللَّهِ﴾، قال: المَوعظة: التَّوبة.

٥١٠. عن محمّد بن مُسلم: إنّ رجلاً سأل أبا جعفر عليه السلام، وقد عَمِل بالرِّبا حتّى كَثُر ماله، بعد أن سأل غيره من الفُقهاء، فقالوا له: ليس يُقْبَل منك شيءٌ إلاّ أن تَرُدّه إلى أصحابه، فلمّا قصّ على أبي جعفر عليه السلام، قال له أبو جعفر عليه السلام: مَخرجك في كتاب الله قوله: ﴿فَمَنْ جَاءَهُ مَوْعِظَةٌ مِنْ رَبِّهِ فَانْتَهَى فَلَهُ مَا سَلَفَ وَأَمْرُهُ إِلَى اللَّهِ﴾ والمَوعظة: التَّوبة.

511. From Sālim b. Abī Ḥafṣa[152], from Abū ʿAbd Allāh عليه السلام who narrated, 'God says: "Every single thing that you give in the possession of someone else, other than Me, is kept by them, except for charity. That I snatch up in My own Hand, so much so that even when a man or a woman gives as little as a single date in charity, or even a piece of a date, I make it thrive for them, just like a man nurtures a foal or a young camel and makes it thrive. Moreover, it [the charity] will meet Me on the Day of Resurrection as large as Uḥud, or even larger than Uḥud."' [2:276]

512. From Muḥammad al-Qimām, from ʿAlī b. al-Ḥusayn عليه السلام, from the Prophet صلى الله عليه وآله who said, 'God makes the charity given by each of you flourish for you, just as you make your children flourish, such that you will find it on the Day of Resurrection as large as Uḥud.' [2:276]

513. From Abū Ḥamza, from Abū Jaʿfar عليه السلام who said, 'God, Blessed and most High, has said, "I am the Creator of everything, and let others keep things in their possession except for charity. That I snatch up with My own Hand, such that when a man or a woman gives even a morsel of a date in charity, I make it thrive for him, just like you make your foal or young camel thrive. Then I release it on the Day of Resurrection, larger than Uḥud."' [2:276]

514. From ʿAlī b. Jaʿfar, from his brother Mūsā, from Abū ʿAbd Allāh عليه السلام who narrated, 'The Messenger of God صلى الله عليه وآله said, "Everything has been assigned a proprietor except for charity, for God takes that up in His own Hand and makes it flourish just like you make your children flourish, until it meets Him on the Day of Resurrection as large as Uḥud."' [2:276]

515. From al-Ḥalabī, from Abū ʿAbd Allāh عليه السلام, who was asked about a man who owed a debt due at a given time and went to the lender saying, "Give me relief." So he عليه السلام said, "I do not see a problem with that since there is no

152 Abū Yūnus Sālim b. Abī Ḥafṣa (d. 137/754–5), a client of the Banū ʿIjl and a Zaydī narrator of the traditions of Imam Muḥammad al-Bāqir. Shīʿī biographers note that he did not agree with Imam Jaʿfar al-Ṣādiq on certain points and was not on good terms with his followers. See Modarressi, *Tradition and Survival*, 105–7 (nr. 9).

٥١١. عن سالم بن أبي حَفْصَة، عن أبي عبدالله عليه السلام، قال: إنّ الله يقول: ليس من شيء إلاّ وكّلتُ به من يَقْبِضُه غيري، إلاّ الصّدقة فإنّي أتلقّفُها بيدي تلقّفًا، حتّى إنّ الرجل والمرأة يَتَصَدّق بالتّمرة وبشقّ تمرة، فأُربيها له كما يُربي الرجل فِلْوَه وفَصِيلَه، فيلقاني يوم القيامة وهي مثل أُحُد وأعظم من أُحُد.

٥١٢. عن محمّد القمّام، عن عليّ بن الحسين عليه السلام، عن النبي صلى الله عليه وآله، قال: إنّ الله لَيُربي لأحدكم الصَّدقة كما يُربي أحدكم ولده، حتّى يَلْقاهُ يوم القيامة وهو مثل أُحُد.

٥١٣. عن أبي حمزة، عن أبي جعفر عليه السلام، قال: قال الله تبارك وتعالى: أنا خالق كلّ شيء، وكّلت بالأشياء غيري إلاّ الصّدقة، فإنّي أَقْبِضُها بيدي، حتّى إنّ الرجُل أو المرأة يصدّق بشقّة التمرة فأُربيها له كما يُربي الرجل منكم فَصِيله وفِلْوَه، حتّى أَتْرُكُه يوم القيامة أعظم من أُحُد.

٥١٤. عن عليّ بن جعفر، عن أخيه موسى، عن أبي عبدالله عليه السلام، قال: قال رسول الله صلى الله عليه وآله: إنّه ليس شيءٌ إلاّ وقد وُكِّلَ به مَلَكٌ غير الصّدقة، فإنّ الله يأخُذه بيده ويُربيه كما يُربي أحدكم ولده، حتّى يلقاه يوم القيامة وهو مثل أُحُد.

٥١٥. عن الحَلَبيّ، عن أبي عبدالله عليه السلام، عن الرجل يكونُ عليه الدَّين إلى أجل مُسمّى، فيأتيه غَريمُه فيقول: أنْقِد لي. فقال: لا أرى به بأسًا، لأنّه لم يَزِد على رأس ماله، وقال الله تعالى: ﴿فَلَكُمْ رُءُوسُ أَمْوَالِكُمْ لَا تَظْلِمُونَ وَلَا تُظْلَمُونَ﴾.

increase in the capital sum. God says: ﴾*You shall have your capital if you repent, and without suffering loss or causing others to suffer loss*﴿." [2:279]

516. From Abū ʿAmr al-Zubayrī, from Abū ʿAbd Allāh عليه السلام who said, 'Repentance purifies one from the filth of wrongdoing. He says: ﴾*You who believe, beware of God: give up any outstanding dues from usury, if you are true believers. If you do not, then be warned of war from God and His Messenger. You shall have your capital if you repent, and without suffering loss or causing others to suffer loss. If the debtor is in difficulty, then delay things until matters become easier for him; still, if you were to write it off as an act of charity; that would be better for you, if only you knew. Beware of a Day when you will be returned to God: every soul will be paid in full for what it has earned, and no one will be wronged*﴿. This is the repentance that God urges from His servants, and has promised a reward for it too. Wherefore whoever opposes the repentance that God has commanded him to do earns God's displeasure, and the Fire becomes a better and more befitting place for him to be in.' [2:278–9]

517. From Muʿāwiya b. ʿAmmār who narrated, 'I heard Abū ʿAbd Allāh عليه السلام say, "The Messenger of God صلى الله عليه وآله said, 'Whoever wants God to shelter him under the shade of His Throne on the day when there will be no shade except His, should give respite to one who is in financial difficulty or write off his dues towards him.'" [2:280]

518. From Abū al-Jārūd, from Abū Jaʿfar عليه السلام, who narrated, 'The Messenger of God صلى الله عليه وآله has said, "Whoever would like God to protect him from the gusts of Hell should grant respite to one who is financially constrained, or write off his dues towards him."' [2:280]

٥١٦. عن أبي عَمرو الزُّبيري، عن أبي عبدالله عليه السلام، قال: إنّ التَّوبة مُطهّرة من دَنَس الخَطِيئة، قال: ﴿يَا أَيُّهَا الَّذِينَ آمَنُوا اتَّقُوا اللَّهَ وَذَرُوا مَا بَقِيَ مِنَ الرِّبَا إِنْ كُنْتُمْ مُؤْمِنِينَ﴾ إلى قوله: ﴿لَا تُظْلَمُونَ﴾، فهذا ما دَعا الله إليه عباده من التَّوبة، ووعَدَ عليها من ثوابه، فمَن خالف ما أمر الله به من التَّوبة سَخِط الله عليه، وكانت النّار أولى به وأحقّ.

٥١٧. عن معُاوية بن عمّار الدُّهنيّ، قال: سَمِعتُ أبا عبدالله عليه السلام يقول: قال رسول الله صلى الله عليه وآله: من أراد أن يُظِلَّه في ظلّ عرشه يوم لا ظِلَّ إلاّ ظِلُّه، فليُنْظِر مُعسِرًا، أو لِيَدَع له من حَقِّه.

٥١٨. عن أبي الجارود، عن أبي جعفر عليه السلام، قال: قال رسول الله صلى الله عليه وآله: من سَرَّه أن يَقِيَهُ الله من نَفَحاتِ جَهَنَّم، فليُنْظِر مُعسِرًا، أو لِيَدَعَ له من حَقِّه.

519. From al-Qāsim b. Sulaymān, from Abū ʿAbd Allāh عليه السلام that Abū al-Yasar[153] was a man from the *anṣār* from the tribe of Banū Salama.[154] The Messenger of God صلى الله عليه وآله said, 'Who from among you all would like to be distanced from the eruption of the Hellfire?' So the people said, 'Us, O Messenger of God.' So he said, 'Whoever grants respite to a debtor or absolves one who is financially constrained.' [2:280]

520. From Isḥāq b. ʿAmmār who said, 'I asked Abū ʿAbd Allāh عليه السلام, "Does a man not have to give his debtor a deadline?" He replied, "No, he does not give him a deadline; God gives him respite."' [2:280]

521. From Abān, from whoever related it to him, from Abū ʿAbd Allāh عليه السلام who said, 'The Messenger of God صلى الله عليه وآله said on a hot day, "Whoever would like God to shade him under the shade of His Throne on the day when there will be no shade except His, should give respite to a debtor or absolve one who is financially constrained."' [2:280]

522. From Ḥanān b. Sadīr, on his father's authority, from Abū Jaʿfar عليه السلام who said, 'God will bring out a group of people from under His Throne on the Day of Resurrection whose faces will be illuminated, whose clothes will be illuminated, whose accessories will be illuminated as well as the chairs that they will be seated on. God will display them before everyone, and they will

153 Abū al-Yasar was a companion of the Prophet whose original name was Kaʿb b. ʿAmr al-Anṣārī al-Salamī, hailing from the Medinan tribe of Banū Salama, who converted to Islam after the Prophet's migration there. He is the one who, according to the books of *tārīkh*, captured ʿAbbās b. ʿAbd al-Muṭṭalib in the Battle of Badr, and fought alongside ʿAlī in the Battle of Ṣiffīn. It has been narrated that he once absolved a man from repaying a loan that he had given him due to his pity for the poverty and hardship that the man was undergoing. This *ḥadīth* probably related to that generosity of his. See his biographical entry in al-Hākim al-Naysābūrī, *al-Mustadrak ʿalā al-ṣaḥīḥayn* (Beirut: Dār al-kut ub al-ʿilmiyya, 2002), 3:577 (*Kitāb maʿrifat al-ṣaḥāba*, nr. 1731–1735) and Muḥammad b. Aḥmad Shams al-Dīn al-Dhahabī, *Siyar aʿlām al-nubalā'*, (Beirut: Mu'assasat al-Risāla, 1985), 2:537 (*Faṣl fī baqiyyat kubarā' al-ṣaḥābā*, nr. 109).

154 Something is clearly missing here, but it can be found in full in Mufīd, *al-Amālī*, 315 (no. 7) where it has been quoted as follows: 'Abū Lubāba b. ʿAbd al-Mundhir came to him to dispute about a loan that he owed him. He heard him say, however, "Tell him that he is not at home." So Abū Lubāba shouted out, "Abū al-Yasar! Come out to see me, now!" So he asked, "What led you to do that?!" So he replied, "Financial constraint, O Abū Lubāba." So he said, "[By] God?" He replied, "God." So Abū Lubāba said [...].'

٥١٩. عن القاسم بن سُليمان، عن أبي عبدالله عليه السلام: إنّ أبا اليَسَر رجلٌ من الأنصار من بني سَلِمَة، قال رسول الله صلى الله عليه وآله: أيُّكم يُحِبّ أن يستظلّ من فَور جهنّمَ؟ فقال القوم: نحنُ يا رسول الله. فقال: من أنظر غريمًا، أو وضع لمُعْسِر.

٥٢٠. عن إسحاق بن عمّار، قلتُ لأبي عبدالله عليه السلام، ما للرّجل أن يَبلُغَ من غريمه؟ قال: لاَ يبْلغُ به شيئًا، الله أنْظَره.

٥٢١. عن أبان، عمّن أخبره، عن أبي عبدالله عليه السلام، قال: قال رسول الله صلى الله عليه وآله في يومٍ حارّ: من سَرَّه أن يُظِلَّه الله يوم لا ظِلَّ إلاّ ظلّه، فليُنْظِر غَريمًا أو ليَدَع لِمُعسِر.

٥٢٢. عن حَنان بن سَدير، عن أبيه، عن أبي جعفر عليه السلام، قال: يَبْعَثُ الله قومًا من تحت العرش يوم القيامة، وُجُوهُهم من نُورٍ، ولِباسُهم من نُورٍ، ورياشُهم من نُورٍ، جُلوسًا على كراسيّ من نُور.

قال: فيُشرِف الله لهم الخَلْقَ فيقولون: هؤلاء الأنبياء؟ فينادي مُنادٍ من تحت العرش: ليسوا بأنبياء. قال: فيقولون: هؤلاء شهداء؟ قال: فينادي منادٍ من تحت العرش: ليس هؤلاء شهداء، ولكن هؤلاء قومٌ يُيَسّرون على المؤمنين، ويُنظِرُون المُعْسِر حتّى يَيْسِر.

exclaim: "These are the prophets!" A voice will call out from beneath the Throne, "No, these are not prophets." So they will ask, "Are they the martyrs, then?" The voice from beneath the Throne will call out, "No, these are not martyrs. They are people who provided financial help to the believers and gave respite to those who were constrained to afford them ease."' [2:280]

523. From Ibn Sinān, from Abū Ḥamza who said, 'There are three types of people whom God will shade on the Day of Resurrection when no shade shall avail except His: (1) a man who was being seduced by a beautiful woman but left her saying, "I fear God, the Lord of the universe"; (2) a man who gave respite to one who was in financial constraint or absolved him of his dues to him; (3) and a man whose heart was attached to the love of mosques. ﴾*If you were to write it off as an act of charity, that would be better for you*﴿: this means that if you were to donate to him the wealth that he owes you as an act of charity towards him, it would be better for you, so one can either write off the debt of one who is in financial difficulty or give him respite therein.' Abū 'Abd Allāh عليه السلام narrated that the Messenger of God ﷺ said, 'For each day that one grants respite to a debtor who is financially constrained, God counts it as charity on his part equivalent to his due, until it is paid off.' [2:280]

524. From 'Umar b. Sulaymān, from a man from al-Jazīra [North Western Mesopotamia] who narrated, 'A man came and asked al-Riḍā عليه السلام, "May I be your ransom; God, Blessed and most High, says: ﴾*then delay things until matters become easier*﴿. So tell me about this delay which God mentions, does it have a defined limit whereby the debtor must necessarily be given respite, if, for example, he has borrowed money from someone and spent it on his dependants and has no crops whose harvest he is anticipating, nor dues that he is awaiting repayment for, nor profits still to be remitted to him?" He replied, "Yes. He should wait until the case can finally reach the imam who can then settle the debt that he is due from the public debt fund if the debtor had spent it in obedience to God. If, however, he had spent it in transgression against God, then the imam cannot bail him out." I asked, "So what about a man in whom one has confidence [of repayment], but it is not known whether he has spent it in obedience or transgression to God?" He replied, "He [i.e. the imam] should endeavour to get his money back for him, then he [i.e. the debtor] must pay it back even while being subdued."' [2:280]

٥٢٣ . عن ابن سِنان، عن أبي حمزة، قال: ثلاثة يُظِلّهم الله يوم القيامة يوم لا ظِلّ إلاّ ظِلُّه: رجُلٌ دَعَته امرأةٌ ذاتُ حُسنٍ إلى نفسها فتركها، وقال: إنّي أخافُ الله ربَّ العالمين، ورجُلٌ أَنْظَر مُعسِرًا أو ترك له من حقِه، ورجُلٌ مُعلَّقٌ قلبُهُ بحُبِّ المَساجد ﴿وَأَنْ تَصَدَّقُوا خَيْرٌ لَكُمْ﴾ يعني أن تَصَدّقوا بمالكم عليه فهو خيرٌ لكم، فَلْيَدَع مُعْسِرًا أو لِيَدَع لهُ من حَقِه نَظرًا.

قال أبو عبد الله عليه السلام: قال رسول الله صلى الله عليه وآله: من أنظر مُعسِرًا كان له على الله في كلّ يوم صَدَقةٌ بمثل ما له عليه، حتّى يستوفي حقَّه.

٥٢٤ . عن عُمر بن سُليمان، عن رجُلٍ من أهل الجزيرة، قال: سأل الرضا عليه السلام، رجُلٌ، فقال له: جُعِلتُ فداك: إنّ الله تبارك وتعالى يقول: ﴿فَنَظِرَةٌ إِلَى مَيْسَرَةٍ﴾ فأخبرني عن هذه النَّظِرة الّتي ذكرها الله، لها حَدّ يُعرَف إذا صار هذا المُعسِر لا بُدّ له من أن يُنْظَرَ، وقد أخذ مال هذا الرجُل، وأنفق على عياله، وليس له غلّة ينتَظِر إدراكها، ولا دَين ينتَظِر محلّه، ولا مال غائب ينتَظِر قُدومه؟

قال: نعم، يُنْتَظَر بقَدر ما ينتهي خبره إلى الإمام، فيقضي عنه ما عليه من سَهم الغارمين، إذا كان أنفقه في طاعة الله، فإن كان أنفقه في معصية الله فلا شيء له على الإمام.

قلتُ: فما لهذا الرجُل الذي ائتمَنه، وهو لا يعلم فيم أَنْفَقَهُ في طاعة الله، أو مَعْصِيَته؟ قال: يَسْعى له في ماله فيَرُدّه وهو صاغر.

525. From Ibn Sinān who narrated, 'I asked Abū 'Abd Allāh عليه السلام, "When should a boy be handed responsibility for his wealth?" He replied, "When he reaches maturity and is perceived to be responsible, and is neither feeble-minded nor weak." I asked, "But there are those who reach fifteen or sixteen years of age and are still immature." He replied, "Even a thirteen-year-old can be granted this as long as he is neither feeble-minded nor weak." I asked, "And what does it mean to be feeble-minded and weak?" He replied, "The feeble-minded one is he who drinks alcohol, and the weak one is he who mistakes one for two."' [2:280]

526. From Yazīd, Abū Usāma[155] from Abū 'Abd Allāh عليه السلام; he said, 'I asked him about God's verse: ﴾*Let the witnesses not refuse when they are summoned*﴿. He replied, "It is not allowed for someone when summoned to give evidence to refuse to do so saying, 'I will not give evidence for you.'" [2:282]

527. From Muḥammad b. al-Fuḍayl, from Abū al-Ḥasan Mūsā عليه السلام who said, regarding the verse: ﴾*Let the witnesses not refuse when they are summoned*﴿, 'When someone asks you to witness a debt or dues, it is not allowed for anyone to shirk away from doing so.' [2:282]

528. From Abū al-Ṣabbāḥ, from Abū 'Abd Allāh عليه السلام regarding the verse: ﴾*Let the witnesses not refuse when they are summoned*﴿. He said, 'Before the summons.' He continued, 'No one can refuse when he is summoned to give evidence for something that he has witnessed by saying, "I will not witness this for you," and this is before writing it down.' [2:282]

529. From Muḥammad b. 'Īsā, from Abū Ja'far عليه السلام who said, 'There is no such thing as a pawn, except a deposit retained in security.' [2:282]

---

155 Although the sources cite Yazīd b. Usāma, the correct version is as above, as Abū Usāma was the agnomen for Zayd b. Yūnus al-Shaḥḥām, known as Abū Usāma, and better known as Zayd al-Shaḥḥām. He narrated from Abū 'Abd Allāh and Abū al-Ḥasan. See Khū'ī, *Mu'jam*, 8:379 (nr. 4904).

٥٢٥. عن ابن سِنان، قال: قلتُ لأبي عبد الله عليه السلام: متى يُدفع إلى الغُلام ماله؟ قال: إذا بلغ وأُونِس منه رُشد، ولم يكن سفيهًا أو ضعيفًا.

قال: قلتُ: فإنّ منهم من يَبْلُغ خمس عشرة سنة وستّ عشرة سنة، ولم يبلُغ؟ قال: إذا بلغ ثَلاث عشرة سنة جاز أمره، إلاّ أن يكون سفيهًا أو ضعيفًا.

قال: قلتُ: وما السّفيه والضّعيف؟ قال: السّفيه: شارب الخمر، والضّعيف: الذي يأخُذ واحدًا باثنين.

٥٢٦. عن يزيد أبي أُسامة، عن أبي عبد الله عليه السلام، قال: سألتُهُ عن قول الله عزّ وجلّ: ﴿وَلَا يَأْبَ الشُّهَدَاءُ إِذَا مَا دُعُوا﴾، قال عليه السلام: لا ينبغي لأحد إذا ما دُعي إلى الشهادة ليشهد عليها، أن يقول: لا أشهد لكم.

٥٢٧. عن محمّد بن الفُضيل، عن أبي الحسن موسى عليه السلام، في قول الله تعالى: ﴿وَلَا يَأْبَ الشُّهَدَاءُ إِذَا مَا دُعُوا﴾، قال عليه السلام: إذا دعاك الرجُل لتشهد على دَين أو حقّ لا ينبغي لأحدٍ أن يتقاعس عنه.

٥٢٨. عن أبي الصَّبّاح، عن أبي عبد الله عليه السلام، في قوله تعالى: ﴿وَلَا يَأْبَ الشُّهَدَاءُ إِذَا مَا دُعُوا﴾، قال: قبل الشهادة، قال: لا ينبغي لأحدٍ إذا ما دُعِي للشهادة أن يَشْهَد عليها، أن يقول: لا أشْهَد لكم، وذلك قبل الكتاب.

٥٢٩. عن محمّد بن عيسى، عن أبي جعفر عليه السلام، قال: لا رَهْنَ إلاّ مقبوض.

530. From Hishām b. Sālim, from Abū ʿAbd Allāh عليه السلام; he said, 'I asked him, "[When does] ﴾*Do not conceal evidence*﴿ refer to?" He replied, "After having witnessed it."' [2:283]

531. From Hishām, from Abū ʿAbd Allāh عليه السلام regarding to the verse: ﴾*Let the witnesses not refuse*﴿. He said, 'Before giving witness.' [2:282]

532. From Saʿdān, from a man, from Abū ʿAbd Allāh عليه السلام who said regarding the verse: ﴾*whether you reveal or conceal your thoughts, God will call you to account for them. He will forgive whoever He will and punish whoever He will*﴿: 'God is entitled not to admit into the Garden whosoever has even an atom's worth of love for these two in his heart.' [2:284]

533. From Abū ʿAmr al-Zubayrī, from Abū ʿAbd Allāh عليه السلام who said, 'God has made faith incumbent upon every part of man's body, and apportioned it between his body parts, such that each part has been entrusted with an exclusive portion of faith not possessed by an adjacent part. Among these is his heart with which he reasons, thinks and understands things, and which governs his body to the extent that none of his limbs advance or retract without prior thought and command from it. The portion of faith that has been made incumbent upon the heart is for it to attest, acknowledge, affirm, approve and submit to the fact that there is no god but He alone, without a partner; one God, who has taken neither spouse nor offspring and that Muḥammad ﷺ is His servant and His messenger. It is also to attest to whatever has come from God by way of a messenger or scripture. This is what God has made incumbent upon the heart to attest to and acknowledge, and this is its sphere of action, as per the verses: ﴾*With the exception of those who are forced to say they do not believe, although their hearts remain firm in faith, those who reject God after believing in Him and open their hearts to disbelief will have the wrath of God upon them and a grievous punishment awaiting them*﴿ (16:107); ﴾*Truly it is in the remembrance of God that hearts find peace*﴿ (13:28); ﴾*Those who say with their mouths, 'We believe,' but have no faith in their hearts*﴿ (5:41); and ﴾*Whether you reveal or conceal your thoughts, God will call you to account for them. He will forgive whoever He will and punish whoever He will*﴿ (2:284). So that is the attestation and acknowledgement

٥٣٠ . عن هِشام بن سالم، عن أبي عبد الله عليه السلام، قال: قلتُ: ﴿وَلَا تَكْتُمُوا الشَّهَادَةَ﴾، قال: بعد الشهادة.

٥٣١ . عن هِشام، عن أبي عبد الله عليه السلام، في قوله تعالى: ﴿وَلَا يَأْبَ الشُّهَدَاءُ﴾، قال: قبل الشّهادة.

٥٣٢ . عن سَعدان، عن رجُلٍ، عن أبي عبد الله عليه السلام، في قوله تعالى: ﴿وَإِنْ تُبْدُوا مَا فِي أَنْفُسِكُمْ أَوْ تُخْفُوهُ يُحَاسِبْكُمْ بِهِ اللَّهُ فَيَغْفِرُ لِمَنْ يَشَاءُ وَيُعَذِّبُ مَنْ يَشَاءُ﴾، قال عليه السلام: حقيقٌ على الله تعالى أن لا يُدخِل الجنّة من كان في قلبه مِثقال حَبّةٍ من خَرْدَلٍ من حُبّهما.

٥٣٣ . عن أبي عَمرو الزُّبَيريّ، عن أبي عبد الله عليه السلام، قال: إنّ الله فرض الإيمان على جَوارح بني آدم وقسّمه عليها وفرّقه فيها، فليس من جوارحه جارحةٌ إلاّ وقد وُكّلت من الإيمان بغير ما وُكّلت به أُختها، فمنها قَلْبُهُ الذي به يَعْقِل ويَفْقَه وَيَفْهَم، وهو أمير بَدَنِهِ الذي لا تَرِدُ الجوارح ولا تَصْدُر إلاّ عن رأيه وأمره.

فأمّا ما فرضَ على القلب من الإيمان: فالإقرار والمعرفة، والعقد، والرضا، والتسليم بأن لا إله إلاّ هو وحده لا شريك له إلهًا واحدًا، لم يتّخِذ صاحبةً ولا ولدًا، وأنّ محمّدًا عبده ورسوله، والإقرار بما جاء من عند الله من نبيّ أو كتاب، فذلك ما فرض الله على القلب من الإقرار والمعرفةِ وهو عَمَلُه، وهو قول الله تعالى: ﴿إِلَّا مَنْ أُكْرِهَ وَقَلْبُهُ مُطْمَئِنٌّ بِالْإِيمَانِ وَلَكِنْ مَنْ شَرَحَ بِالْكُفْرِ صَدْرًا﴾، وقال ﴿أَلَا بِذِكْرِ اللَّهِ تَطْمَئِنُّ الْقُلُوبُ﴾، وقال: ﴿الَّذِينَ قَالُوا آمَنَّا بِأَفْوَاهِهِمْ وَلَمْ تُؤْمِنْ قُلُوبُهُمْ﴾، وقال: ﴿وَإِنْ تُبْدُوا مَا فِي أَنْفُسِكُمْ أَوْ

that God has made incumbent upon the heart, and that is its sphere of action and the fountainhead of faith.'

534. From 'Abd al-Ṣamad b. Bashīr who narrated, 'A story about the origin of the *adhān* (ritual call to prayer) was mentioned in Abū 'Abd Allāh 's presence, that a man from the *anṣār* saw the *adhān* in his dream, so he told the Messenger of God ﷺ about it, who then commanded him to make Bilāl perform it.

So Abū 'Abd Allāh said, "They are lying. The Messenger of God ﷺ was sleeping in the shade of the Ka'ba when Jibrīl عليه السلام came to him with a metal bowl filled with water from Paradise. He woke him up and asked him to wash with it, then placed him on a palanquin of thousands of luminescent colours. Then he ascended with him until they reached the gates of the heavens. When the angels saw him, they retreated away from the gates exclaiming: 'Two gods! One on the earth and one in the heavens!'

Muḥammad b. al-Ḥasan mentioned the following in his narration: 'They retreated away from the gates of heaven, exclaiming: Our God!' God commanded Jibrīl to say, '*Allāhu Akbar, Allāhu Akbar* (God is greater!)' So the angels came back towards the gates and realized that this was a human, and opened the gates. The Messenger of God ﷺ entered until he reached the second heaven. Again the angels retreated away from the gates of heaven exclaiming: 'Two gods! One on the earth and one in the heavens!' So Jibrīl said, '*Ashhadu an lā ilāha illa Llāh, Ashhadu an lā ilāha illa Llāh* (I bear witness that there is no god but God).' So the angels returned and realized that this was a created being, so they opened the gates, and he ﷺ entered and continued until he reached the third heaven. The angels retreated from its gates, and Jibrīl said: '*Ashhadu anna Muḥammadan rasūl Allāh, Ashhadu anna Muḥammadan rasūl Allāh* (I bear witness that Muḥammad is the Messenger of God).' So the angels returned and opened the gate.

تُخْفُوهُ يُحَاسِبْكُمْ بِهِ اللهُ فَيَغْفِرُ لِمَنْ يَشَاءُ وَيُعَذِّبُ مَنْ يَشَاءُ﴾، فذلك ما فرض الله على القلب من الإقرار والمعرفة، وهو عَمَلُه، وهو رأس الإيمان.

٥٣٤. عن عبد الصّمد بن بشير، قال: ذُكر عند أبي عبدالله عليه السلام بَدْء الأذان، فقال: إنّ رجلاً من الأنصار رأى في منامه الأذان، فَقَصّه على رسول الله صلى الله عليه وآله، وأمره رسول الله صلى الله عليه وآله أن يُعلّمه بِلالاً.

فقال أبو عبدالله عليه السلام: كَذَبوا، إنّ رسول الله صلى الله عليه وآله كان نائمًا في ظِلّ الكعبة، فأتاه جَبْرَئيل عليه السلام ومعه طاسٌ فيه ماءٌ من الجنّة، فأيقظه وأمره أن يغتسل به، ثمّ وضعه في مَحْمِل له ألف ألف لون من نُورٍ، ثمّ صَعِد به حتّى انتهى إلى أبواب السّماء، فلمّا رأته الملائكة نَفَرت عن أبواب السّماء، وقالت: إلهين: إله في الأرض، وإله في السماء؟!

قال محمّد بن الحسن في حديثه: نَفَرت عن أبواب السماء، فقالت: إلهنا.

فأمر الله تعالى جبرئيل عليه السلام، فقال: الله أكبر، الله أكبر، فتراجعت الملائكة نحو أبواب السّماء وعَلِمت أنّه مَخْلُوقٌ، ففتحت الباب، فدخل صلى الله عليه وآله حتّى انتهى إلى السّماء الثانية، فنفَرَت الملائكة عن أبواب السّماء، فقالت: إلهين: إله في الأرض، وإله في السّماء؟! فقال جبْرَيل عليه السلام: أشهد أن لا إله إلاّ الله، أشهد أن لا إله إلاّ الله، فتراجعت الملائكة وعَلِمَت أنّه مَخْلُوق.

ثم فُتِحَ الباب، فدخل صلى الله عليه وآله، ومرّ حتّى انتهى إلى السّماء الثالثة، فنَفَرت الملائكة عن أبواب السماء، فقال جبْرَئيل عليه السلام: أشهد أنّ محمّدًا رسول الله، أشهد أنّ محمّدًا رسول الله، فتراجعت الملائكة وفتح الباب.

The Prophet ﷺ passed through until he reached the fourth heaven, and there was an angel sitting on an elevated seat with three hundred thousand angels under his authority and three hundred thousand more under each one of them. [So the Prophet ﷺ considered going into prostration, assuming that this was Him], when a voice called out saying: 'Stand up.' So the angel stood up immediately, [and the Prophet ﷺ realized that this was a mere servant of God]. He continues to stand in this manner until the Day of Resurrection."

He continued, "The gate was opened, and the Prophet ﷺ passed through until he reached the seventh heaven, and ended up at the lote-tree (*sidrat al-muntahā*)." He continued, "So the lote-tree said, 'No creature before you has ever gone past me.' Then he moved closer, then even closer still, coming down further until he was two bow-lengths away or even nearer. God revealed to His servant what He revealed." He continued, "Then he handed him two books, the record of the People on the Right in his right hand and the record of the People on the Left in his left hand. So he took the record of the People on the Right in his right hand, looked at it and found therein all the names of the inhabitants of Paradise, with their ancestry and their tribes."

He continued, "Then God said: ﴾*The Messenger believes in what has been sent down to him from his Lord*﴿, so the Messenger of God ﷺ said: ﴾*They all believe in God, His angels, His scriptures, and His messengers. 'We make no distinction between any of His messengers.'*﴿. So God said: ﴾*And they say, 'We hear and obey'*﴿, and the Prophet ﷺ exclaimed: ﴾*'Grant us Your forgiveness, our Lord. To You we all return!'*﴿ Then God said: ﴾*God does not burden any soul with more than it can bear: each gains whatever good it has done, and suffers its bad*﴿ , and the Prophet ﷺ beseeched: ﴾*Lord, do not take us to task if we forget or make mistakes*﴿. So God replied, 'Of course.'

Then the Prophet ﷺ asked: ﴾*Lord, do not burden us as You burdened those before us*﴿. So God replied, 'Of course.'

ومرّ النبيّ ﷺ حتّى انتهى إلى السّماء الرابعة، فإذا هو بملَك مُتّكئٍ على سرير، تحت يده ثلاثمائة ألف مَلَك، تحت كلّ مَلَك ثلاثمائة ألف مَلَك، فهَمَّ النبي ﷺ بالسُّجُود، ظنّ أنّه، فنُودي: أن قُم، قال: فقام الملَك على رِجليه، قال: فعلِم النبيّ ﷺ أنّه عبدٌ مخلوقٌ، قال: فلا يزال قائمًا إلى يوم القيامة.

قال: وفُتِح الباب، ومرّ النّبي ﷺ حتّى انتهى إلى السماء السابعة، قال: وانتهى إلى سدرة المنتهى، قال: فقالت السِّدرة: ما جاوزني مَخْلُوقٌ قبلك، قال: ثمّ مضى فدنا فتدلّى، فكان قاب قوسين أو أدنى، فأوحى إلى عبده ما أوحى، قال: فدفع إليه كتابين، كتاب أصحاب اليمين بيمينه، وكتاب أصحاب الشّمال بشماله، فأخذ كتاب أصحاب اليمين بيمينه، وفَتَحَه فنَظَر فيه، فإذا فيه أسماء أهل الجنّة وأسماء آبائهم وقبائلهم.

قال: فقال الله تعالى: ﴿آمَنَ الرَّسُولُ بِمَا أُنزِلَ إِلَيْهِ مِن رَّبِّهِ﴾ فقال رسول الله ﷺ: ﴿كُلٌّ آمَنَ بِاللَّهِ وَمَلَائِكَتِهِ وَكُتُبِهِ وَرُسُلِهِ لَا نُفَرِّقُ بَيْنَ أَحَدٍ مِّن رُّسُلِهِ﴾ فقال الله: ﴿وَقَالُوا سَمِعْنَا وَأَطَعْنَا﴾، فقال النبيّ ﷺ: ﴿غُفْرَانَكَ رَبَّنَا وَإِلَيْكَ الْمَصِيرُ﴾، قال الله: ﴿لَا يُكَلِّفُ اللَّهُ نَفْسًا إِلَّا وُسْعَهَا لَهَا مَا كَسَبَتْ وَعَلَيْهَا مَا اكْتَسَبَتْ﴾.

قال النّبي ﷺ: ﴿رَبَّنَا لَا تُؤَاخِذْنَا إِن نَّسِينَا أَوْ أَخْطَأْنَا﴾، قال: فقال الله تعالى: قد فعلت. فقال النّبي ﷺ: ﴿رَبَّنَا وَلَا تَحْمِلْ عَلَيْنَا إِصْرًا كَمَا حَمَلْتَهُ عَلَى الَّذِينَ مِن قَبْلِنَا﴾، فقال: قد فعلت.

The Prophet ﷺ then beseeched: ﴾*Lord, do not burden us with more than we have strength to bear. Pardon us, forgive us, and have mercy on us. You are our Protector, so help us against the disbelievers*﴿. God replied in the affirmative to all of this, then he folded up the book and kept it in his hand. Then he opened the other record of the People on the Left and found the names of the inmates of the Hellfire, with their ancestors and tribes therein. The Messenger of God ﷺ said, 'These are the people who do not believe', and God replied, ﴾*'Then rescue them, saying peace, and they will come to know.'*﴿(43:89)"

He continued, "So when he had finished conversing with his Lord, he returned to *al-bayt al-maʿmūr* (the Oft-Visited House), which is in the seventh heaven directly above the Kaʿba. All the prophets, messengers, and angels gathered around him, then he commanded Jibrīl to perform the *adhān*. Then he established the prayer, with the Messenger of God ﷺ leading them all. When he had completed it, he turned towards them, and God said to him, ﴾*'Ask those who were given charge of the Scripture before you, that the truth has indeed come to you from your Lord, so do not be one of those who doubt.'*﴿(10:94) So the Prophet ﷺ asked them on that day. Then he descended back down with the two records, and handed them to the Commander of the Faithful عليه السلام."

Abū ʿAbd Allāh عليه السلام concluded, "And that was the origin of the *adhān*."' [2:285–6]

535. From ʿAbd al-Ṣamad b. Bashīr who narrated, 'I heard Abū ʿAbd Allāh عليه السلام say, "Jibrīl عليه السلام came to the Messenger of God ﷺ once when he was in the valley (of Mecca) with Burāq, who was smaller than a mule but larger than a donkey, adorned with a palanquin with a million illuminated colours. When he approached it to mount it, it balked, so Jibrīl struck it hard enough for Burāq to sweat. Then he said to it, 'Calm down, for this is Muḥammad.' Then it sped off with him from Jerusalem to the heavens, where the angels flew away from the gates of the heavens [upon seeing him]. So Jibrīl said, '*Allāhu Akbar, Allāhu Akbar*' and the angels realized that it was a servant created [by God]. Then they met Jibrīl and asked him, 'Who is this, Jibrīl?' He replied, 'This is Muḥammad.'

So they greeted him, and then he sped off with him to the second heaven. Again the angels flew back from the gates, and Jibrīl said: '*Ashhadu an lā*

فقال النبي ﷺ: ﴿رَبَّنَا وَلَا تَحْمِلْ عَلَيْنَا إِصْرًا كَمَا حَمَلْتَهُ عَلَى الَّذِينَ مِن قَبْلِنَا رَبَّنَا وَلَا تُحَمِّلْنَا مَا لَا طَاقَةَ لَنَا بِهِ وَاعْفُ عَنَّا وَاغْفِرْ لَنَا وَارْحَمْنَا أَنتَ مَوْلَانَا فَانصُرْنَا عَلَى الْقَوْمِ الْكَافِرِينَ﴾ كلّ ذلك يقول الله: قد فعلت.

ثمّ طوى الصّحيفة فأمسكها بيمينه، وفتح الأُخرى، صحيفة أصحاب الشِمال، فإذا فيها أسماء أهل النار، وأسماء آبائهم وقبائلهم، قال: فقال رسول الله ﷺ: إنّ هؤلاء قومٌ لا يؤمنون. فقال الله تعالى: يا محمّد ﴿فَاصْفَحْ عَنْهُمْ وَقُلْ سَلَامٌ فَسَوْفَ يَعْلَمُونَ﴾.

قال: فلمّا فرغ من مُناجاة ربّه، رُدّ إلى البيت المَعْمُور، وهو في السّماء السابعة بحذاء الكعبة، قال: فجمع له النبيّين والمُرسلين والملائكة، ثمّ أمر جبَرْئيل عليه السلام فأتمّ الأذان، وأقام الصلاة، وتقدّم رسول الله ﷺ فصلّى بهم، فلمّا فرَغ التفت إليهم، فقال الله تعالى له: ﴿فَاسْأَلِ الَّذِينَ يَقْرَءُونَ الْكِتَابَ مِن قَبْلِكَ لَقَدْ جَاءَكَ الْحَقُّ مِن رَّبِّكَ فَلَا تَكُونَنَّ مِنَ الْمُمْتَرِينَ﴾. فسألهم يومئذ النبيّ ﷺ، ثمّ نزل ومعه صحيفتان، فدفعهما إلى أمير المؤمنين عليه السلام.

فقال أبو عبدالله عليه السلام: فهذا كان بَدْء الأذان.

٥٣٥. عن عبد الصّمد بن بشير، قال: سِمعتُ أبا عبدالله عليه السلام يقول: أتى جبَرْئيل عليه السلام رسول الله ﷺ وهو بالأبْطح بالبُراق، أصغر من البَغل، وأكبر من الحِمار، عليه ألف ألف مِحفّةٍ من نُور فشَمَسَ البرُاق حين أدناه منه لِيركَبَه، فلَطَمه جبَرْئيل عليه السلام لَطْمَة عَرِق البُراق منها، ثمّ قال: اسكُنْ، فإنّه محمّدٌ، ثمّ زَفّ به من بيت المَقْدِس إلى السّماء، فتطايرت الملائكة

ilāha illa Llāh, Ashhadu an lā ilāha illa Llāh.' The angels realised and said, 'It is a servant created [by God].' Then they met Jibrīl and asked him who this was, to which he replied, 'Muḥammad', so they greeted him.

This continued, heaven after heaven until the *adhān* was complete. Then the Messenger of God ﷺ prayed with them in the seventh heaven, leading them all. Then Jibrīl took him along again, until they ended up at a place where he placed his finger in his side, then raised him up high saying, 'Go forth, Muḥammad.' So he replied, 'Are you leaving me in this place, Jibrīl?' He replied, 'I am not allowed to go beyond this point, Muḥammad. You are stepping into a place where nobody before you has ever trod, nor will ever tread after you.'"

He continued, "Then God opened him up to whatever great things He willed; and then addressed him saying: ﴾*The Messenger believes in what has been sent down to him from his Lord*﴿, so he replied, 'Yes, my Lord, ﴾*and the believers all believe in God, His angels, His scriptures, and His messengers. We make no distinction between any of His messengers. And they say,* ﴾*We hear and obey. Grant us Your forgiveness, our Lord. To You we all return!*﴿.'

So God, Blessed and most High, said: ﴾*God does not burden any soul with more than it can bear: each gains whatever good it has done, and suffers its bad*﴿, and Muḥammad ﷺ said: ﴾*Lord, do not take us to task if we forget or make mistakes. Lord, do not burden us as You burdened those before us. Lord, do not burden us with more than we have strength to bear. Pardon us, forgive us, and have mercy on us. You are our Protector, so help us against the disbelievers*﴿.

God asked, 'O Muḥammad ﷺ, who from among your community will succeed you after you?' He replied, 'God knows better.' So He said, "Alī is the Commander of the Faithful.'"

Abū 'Abd Allāh said, "By God, his vicegerency was authorised by none other than God, orally to Muḥammad ﷺ."' [2:285–6]

من أبواب السماء، فقال جبْرَئيل: الله أكبر، الله أكبر، فقالت الملائكة: عبدٌ مخلوقٌ. قال: ثمّ لَقُوا جبْرَئيل، فقالوا: يا جبْرَئيل، من هذا؟ قال: هذا محمّد، فسلّموا عليه.

ثمّ زَفّ به إلى السّماء الثانية، فتطايرت الملائكة، فقال جبْرَئيل: أشهد أن لا إله إلا الله، أشهد أن لا إله إلا الله، فقالت الملائكة: عَبدٌ مخلوقٌ، فَلَقُوا جبْرَئيل، فقالوا: من هذا؟ فقال: محمّد، فسلّموا عليه.

فلم يَزَل كذلك في سَماء سَماء، ثمّ أتمّ الأذان، ثمّ صلّى بهم رسول الله ﷺ في السماء السابعة، وأمّهم رسول الله ﷺ، ثمّ مضى به جبْرَئيل عليه السلام حتّى انتهى به إلى موضع، فوضع إصْبَعَهُ على مَنكِبه ثمّ رفعه، فقال له: امضِ، يا محمّد، فقال له: يا جبْرَئيل، تدعني في هذا الموضع؟ قال: فقال له: يا محمّد، ليس لي أن أجوز هذا المقام، ولقد وَطِئتَ مَوضعًا ما وَطِئه أحَدٌ قبلك، ولا يَطَؤهُ أحدٌ بعدك.

قال: ففتح الله له من العظيم ما شاء الله، قال: فكلّمه الله تعالى: ﴿آمَنَ الرَّسُولُ بِمَا أُنزِلَ إِلَيْهِ مِن رَّبِّهِ﴾. قال: نعم يا ربّ ﴿وَالْمُؤْمِنُونَ كُلٌّ آمَنَ بِاللَّهِ وَمَلَائِكَتِهِ وَكُتُبِهِ وَرُسُلِهِ لَا نُفَرِّقُ بَيْنَ أَحَدٍ مِّن رُّسُلِهِ وَقَالُوا سَمِعْنَا وَأَطَعْنَا غُفْرَانَكَ رَبَّنَا وَإِلَيْكَ الْمَصِيرُ﴾.

قال الله تبارك وتعالى: ﴿لَا يُكَلِّفُ اللَّهُ نَفْسًا إِلَّا وُسْعَهَا لَهَا مَا كَسَبَتْ وَعَلَيْهَا مَا اكْتَسَبَتْ﴾ قال محمد ﷺ: ﴿رَبَّنَا لَا تُؤَاخِذْنَا إِن نَّسِينَا أَوْ أَخْطَأْنَا رَبَّنَا وَلَا تَحْمِلْ عَلَيْنَا إِصْرًا كَمَا حَمَلْتَهُ عَلَى الَّذِينَ مِن قَبْلِنَا رَبَّنَا وَلَا تُحَمِّلْنَا مَا لَا طَاقَةَ لَنَا بِهِ وَاعْفُ عَنَّا وَاغْفِرْ لَنَا وَارْحَمْنَا أَنتَ مَوْلَانَا فَانصُرْنَا عَلَى الْقَوْمِ الْكَافِرِينَ﴾.

536. From Qatāda who narrated, 'When the Messenger of God ﷺ used to recite these verses: ﴾*The Messenger believes in what has been sent down to him from his Lord, as do the faithful. They all believe in God, His angels, His scriptures, and His messengers. 'We make no distinction between any of His messengers,' they say, 'We hear and obey. Grant us Your forgiveness, our Lord. To You we all return!' God does not burden any soul with more than it can bear: each gains whatever good it has done, and suffers its bad—'Lord, do not take us to task if we forget or make mistakes. Lord, do not burden us as You burdened those before us. Lord, do not burden us with more than we have strength to bear. Pardon us, forgive us, and have mercy on us. You are our Protector, so help us against the disbelievers'*﴿, he would say, "One of God's truths is that He had an inscription above His Throne two thousand years before He created the heavens and the earth. Then He sent down two of its verses, using them to conclude The Cow (*sūrat al-baqara*). So any house in which these are recited will not be entered by Satan." [2:285]

537. From Zurāra, Ḥumrān and Muḥammad b. Muslim, from one of two Imams [al-Ṣādiq or al-Bāqir], that he said, 'Whenever they beseech Him, they are responded to, for ﴾*God does not burden any soul with more than it can bear*﴿. Whatever God has made incumbent upon it, ﴾*each gains whatever good it has done, and suffers its bad*﴿ and His statement: ﴾*do not burden us as You burdened those before us*﴿.' [2:286]

538. From 'Amr b. Marwān al-Khazzāz who narrated, 'I heard Abū 'Abd Allāh عليه السلام narrate, "The Messenger of God ﷺ said, 'My community have been absolved of four things: (1) that which they commit mistakenly, (2) that which they forget, (3) that which they are compelled to do, and (4) that which is beyond their capacity to bear; and this is in God's Book, Blessed and most High: ﴾*Lord, do not take us to task if we forget or make mistakes. Lord, do not burden us as You burdened those before us. Lord, do not burden us with more than we have strength to bear*﴿(2:285) and: ﴾*With the exception of those who are forced to say they do not believe, although their hearts remain firm in faith*﴿(16:106).'"'

قال: قال الله: يا محمّد، من لأمّتك بعدك؟ فقال: الله أعلم، قال: عليّ أمير المؤمنين.

قال: قال أبو عبدالله عليه السلام: والله: ما كانت ولايته إلاّ من الله تعالى مُشافهةً لمحمد صلى الله عليه وآله وسلم.

٥٣٦. عن قَتادة، قال: كان رسول الله صلى الله عليه وآله وسلم إذا قرأ هذه الآية: ﴿آمَنَ الرَّسُولُ بِمَا أُنزِلَ إِلَيْهِ مِن رَّبِّهِ﴾ حتّى يختِمها، قال: وحقّ الله، إنّ لله كتابًا قبل أن يخلُق السماوات والأرض بألفي سنة، فوضعه عنده فوق العَرش، فأنزل آيتين خَتَم بهما البقرة، فأيّما بيت قُرِئتا فيه لم يَدخُلهُ شيطان.

٥٣٧. عن زُرارة وحُمران ومحمّد بن مسلم، عن أحدهما عليه السلام، قال: في آخر البقرة لمّا دَعَوا أُجيبوا: ﴿لاَ يُكَلِّفُ اللّهُ نَفْسًا إِلاَّ وُسْعَهَا﴾، قال: ما افترض الله عليها ﴿لَهَا مَا كَسَبَتْ وَعَلَيْهَا مَا اكْتَسَبَتْ﴾، وقوله: ﴿وَلاَ تَحْمِلْ عَلَيْنَا إِصْرًا كَمَا حَمَلْتَهُ عَلَى الَّذِينَ مِن قَبْلِنَا﴾.

٥٣٨. عن عَمرو بن مَروان الخزّاز، قال: سَمِعتُ أبا عبدالله عليه السلام قال: قال رسول الله صلى الله عليه وآله وسلم: رُفعت عن أُمّتي أربع خصال: ما أخطأُوا، وما نَسوا، وما أُكرِهُوا عليه، وما لم يُطيقوا، وذلك في كتاب الله، قول الله تبارك وتعالى: ﴿رَبَّنَا لاَ تُؤَاخِذْنَا إِن نَّسِينَا أَوْ أَخْطَأْنَا رَبَّنَا وَلاَ تَحْمِلْ عَلَيْنَا إِصْرًا كَمَا حَمَلْتَهُ عَلَى الَّذِينَ مِن قَبْلِنَا رَبَّنَا وَلاَ تُحَمِّلْنَا مَا لاَ طَاقَةَ لَنَا بِهِ﴾ وقول الله تعالى: ﴿إِلاَّ مَنْ أُكْرِهَ وَقَلْبُهُ مُطْمَئِنٌّ بِالإِيمَانِ﴾.

The Family of ʿImrān

3. The Family of ʿImrān

1. From Abū Baṣīr, from Abū ʿAbd Allāh عليه السلام that he heard him say, ʻWhoever recites the Chapter of the Cow (*sūrat al-baqara*) and the Chapter of the Family of ʿImrān (*sūrat āl ʿImrān*) shall arrive on the Day of Resurrection being shaded by them both like two clouds or canopies over his head.'

2. From ʿAbd Allāh b. Sinān, from Abū ʿAbd Allāh عليه السلام who said about the verse: ﴾*Alif Lām Mīm. God: there is no god but Him, the Ever-Living, the Ever-Watchful. Step by step, He has sent the Scripture down to you* [*Prophet*] *with the Truth, confirming what went before: He sent down the Torah and the Gospel earlier as a guide for people and He has sent down the distinction* [*between right and wrong*]﴿: ʻThis refers to every decisive command, and the Scripture is the Qur'an as a whole in which the prophets that came before him are corroborated.' [3:1–3]

3. From ʿAbd al-Raḥmān b. Kathīr al-Hāshimī, from Abū ʿAbd Allāh عليه السلام regarding the verse: ﴾*It is He who has sent this Scripture down to you* [*Prophet*]. *Some of its verses are definite in meaning.*﴿ He said, ʻThey are the Commander of the Faithful (*amīr al-mu'minīn*) and the Imams, peace be upon them; ﴾*and others are indefinite*﴿ – this is *x*, *y*, and *z*.[1] ﴾*The perverse at heart*﴿ – these are their companions and those who adhere to their authority, ﴾*eagerly pursue the ambiguities in their attempt to make trouble and to pin down a specific meaning of their own.*﴿' [3:7]

---

1 A reference to Abū Bakr, ʿUmar b. al-Khaṭṭab and ʿUthmān b. ʿAffān – the first three caliphs of Islam.

بسم الله الرحمن الرحيم

من سورة آل عمران

١. عن أبي بَصير، عن أبي عبد الله عليه السلام، قال: سَمِعتُه يقول: من قرأ سورة البقرة وآل عمران، جاء يوم القيامة تُظِلاّنه على رأسه، مثل الغَمامَتَين، أو الغَيابَتَين.

٢. عن عبد الله بن سِنان، عن أبي عبد الله عليه السلام، في قول الله تعالى: ﴿الٓمٓ ۞ اللَّهُ لَآ إِلَٰهَ إِلَّا هُوَ الْحَيُّ الْقَيُّومُ ۞ نَزَّلَ عَلَيْكَ الْكِتَابَ بِالْحَقِّ مُصَدِّقًا لِّمَا بَيْنَ يَدَيْهِ وَأَنزَلَ التَّوْرَاةَ وَالْإِنجِيلَ ۞ مِن قَبْلُ هُدًى لِّلنَّاسِ وَأَنزَلَ الْفُرْقَانَ﴾. قال: هو كُلّ أمرٍ محكمٍ، والكتاب هو جُملة القُرآن الذي يُصدّق فيه مَن كان قَبْله من الأنبياء.

٣. عن عبد الرّحمن بن كَثير الهاشميّ، عن أبي عبد الله عليه السلام، في قول الله: ﴿هُوَ الَّذِي أَنزَلَ عَلَيْكَ الْكِتَابَ مِنْهُ آيَاتٌ مُّحْكَمَاتٌ﴾، قال: أمير المؤمنين والأئمة عليهم السلام، ﴿وَأُخَرُ مُتَشَابِهَاتٌ﴾ فُلان وفُلان، ﴿فَأَمَّا الَّذِينَ فِي قُلُوبِهِمْ زَيْغٌ﴾ أصحابهم وأهل ولايتهم ﴿فَيَتَّبِعُونَ مَا تَشَابَهَ مِنْهُ ابْتِغَاءَ الْفِتْنَةِ وَابْتِغَاءَ تَأْوِيلِهِ﴾.

4. Abū 'Abd Allāh عليه السلام was asked about the definite and indefinite verses and he said, 'The definite verses are those which call for action, while the indefinite are those which can appear ambiguous to one who is ignorant of them.' [3:7]

5. From Abū Baṣīr, from Abū 'Abd Allāh عليه السلام who said, 'The Qur'an consists of definite and indefinite verses. As for those which are definite, we have faith in them and act upon them and base our practices on them. As for those which are indefinite, we need only have faith in them but need not act upon them, as per God's statement: ﴾*The perverse at heart eagerly pursue the ambiguities in their attempt to make trouble and to pin down a specific meaning of their own: only God knows the true meaning, and those firmly grounded in knowledge say, 'We believe in it: it is all from our Lord.'*﴿ Those who are firmly grounded in knowledge are the Household of Muḥammad.' [3:7]

6. From Mas'ada b. Ṣadaqa, from Ja'far b. Muḥammad عليه السلام, on his father's authority, that a man once said to the Commander of the Faithful عليه السلام, 'Would you describe our Lord for us so that our love for Him and our knowledge of Him may increase.' So he was angered and addressed the people, saying, 'O servant of God, why do you not take the description of Him that the Qur'an gives you seriously, a description which the Messenger صلى الله عليه وآله had himself adopted well before you? Follow its example and enlighten yourself through its guidance, for it is a bounty and a source of wisdom that you have been given; so utilise it and be among those who are grateful. The things that Shayṭān urges you to delve into, things that have neither been prescribed in the Qur'an and concerning which there is no precedent within the practice of the Prophet or the Imams of guidance, relinquish the knowledge of it to God. Do not measure God's grandeur in proportion to your intellect lest you be of the wretched ones.

Know, O servant of God, that ﴾*those who are firmly grounded in knowledge*﴿ are the ones whom God has freed from the desire to barge in on the locked doors that guard the unseen, readily admitting their lack of knowledge of the inner meanings of the transcendental and hidden. They say, ﴾*We believe in it – everything is from our Lord*﴿ and God praises their acknowledgement of their own incapacity to grasp that about which they have no idea. This relinquishment of theirs, of delving into that which He has not tasked them to dig into, is what He calls "firm grounding."' [3:7]

٤ . وسُئل أبو عبد الله ﵇، عن المُحكم والمُتَشابه، قال: المُحكم ما يُعمل به، والمُتشابه ما اشْتبه على جاهِلِه.

٥ . عن أبي بصير، عن أبي عبد الله ﵇، يقول: إنّ القرآن مُحكم ومُتشابه، فأمّا المُحكم فنؤمن به ونعمل به ونَدين به، وأمّا المُتشابه فنؤمن به ولا نعمل به، وهو قول الله: ﴿فَأَمَّا الَّذِينَ فِي قُلُوبِهِمْ زَيْغٌ فَيَتَّبِعُونَ مَا تَشَابَهَ مِنْهُ ابْتِغَاءَ الْفِتْنَةِ وَابْتِغَاءَ تَأْوِيلِهِ وَمَا يَعْلَمُ تَأْوِيلَهُ إِلَّا اللَّهُ وَالرَّاسِخُونَ فِي الْعِلْمِ يَقُولُونَ آمَنَّا بِهِ كُلٌّ مِنْ عِنْدِ رَبِّنَا﴾ والراسخون في العلم هم آل محمد عليهم السلام.

٦ . عن مَسْعَدَة بن صَدَقة، عن جعفر بن محمّد، عن أبيه عليهم السلام، أنّ رجلاً قال لأمير المؤمنين ﵇: هل تَصِف لنا ربّنا نزداد له حُبًّا وبه معرفةً؟ فغَضِب ﵇ وخطب الناسَ، فقال فيما قال: عليك — يا عبد الله — بما دَلّك عليه القُرآن من صِفته، وتَقدّمَك فيه الرسول من مَعْرِفَتِه، فأْتَمّ به واستَضِيء بنُور هدايته، فإنّما هي نعمةٌ وحكمةٌ أوتيتها، فخُذ ما أُوتيت وكُن من الشاكرين، وما كلّفك الشيطان عليه. ممّا ليس عليك في الكتاب فَرْضُه، ولا في سنّة الرسول وأئمّة الهداة أثره، فَكِلْ عِلْمَهُ إلى الله، ولا تُقدّر عَظَمَة الله.

واعلم — يا عبد الله — أنّ الرّاسخين في العلم هم الذين أغناهُم الله عن الاقتِحام على السُّدد المَضروبة دون الغُيوب، إقرارًا بجَهْل ما جهلوا تفسيره من الغَيب المَحجوب، فقالوا: آمنّا به كلٌّ من عند ربّنا، وقد مَدحَ الله اعترافهم بالعَجْز عن تناوُل ما لم يُحيطوا به عِلمًا، وسمّى تَرْكَهم التَعمُّق فيما لم يُكلّفهم البحث عنه رُسُوخًا.

7. From Burayd b. Muʿāwiya who narrated, 'I asked Abū Jaʿfar ﵇ about God's verse: ﴾*only God knows the true meaning, and those firmly grounded in knowledge.*﴿ He replied, "It refers to the true meaning of the entirety of the Qur'an known only to God and those who are firmly grounded in knowledge. The Messenger of God is the best of those who are firmly grounded, whom God Himself has taught the interpretation and the instances of the revelation of everything that He has revealed to him [i.e. the Prophet]. God would not reveal anything to him without teaching him its true meaning, and his successors after him know it all as well. Those who do not have knowledge of it ask: 'What do we do when we do not know the true meaning of it?' So God answered them: ﴾*Say, 'We believe in it: it is all from our Lord.'*﴿ The Qur'an has specific and general verses, verses which abrogate and others which are abrogated, and definite and indefinite ones; and those who are firmly grounded in knowledge are conversant with all this."' [3:7]

8. From al-Fuḍayl b. Yasār, from Abū Jaʿfar ﵇ who said: '﴾*only God knows the true meaning, and those firmly grounded in knowledge*﴿ – we have knowledge of it.' [3:7]

9. From Abū Baṣīr, from Abū ʿAbd Allāh ﵇ who said, 'We are the ones who are firmly grounded in knowledge, and thus we are the ones to know the true meaning of it.' [3:7]

10. From Samāʿa b. Mihrān who narrated, 'Abū ʿAbd Allāh ﵇ said, "Frequently and repeatedly say: ﴾*Our Lord, do not let our hearts deviate after You have guided us*﴿ and never consider yourselves immune from deviation."' [3:8]

11. From Jamīl b. Darrāj who narrated, 'Abū ʿAbd Allāh ﵇ said, "There is nothing more pleasurable to the people of this world and the next than the enjoyment of women, for in His verse God states: ﴾*The love of desirable things is made alluring for men – women, children, gold and silver treasures piled up high, horses with fine markings, livestock, and farmland – these may be the joys of this life, but God has the best place to return to.*﴿" He then continued, "The people of Paradise too will not find anything more pleasurable and more enjoyable in Paradise than marriage – not food, nor drink."' [3:14]

٧. عن بُريد بن مُعاوية، قال: قلتُ لأبي جعفر عليه السلام: قول الله تعالى: ﴿وَمَا يَعْلَمُ تَأْوِيلَهُ إِلاَّ اللهُ وَالرَّاسِخُونَ فِي الْعِلْمِ﴾. قال: يعني تأويل القرآن كلّه، إلاّ الله والراسخون في العلم، فرسول الله صلى الله عليه وآله وسلم أفضلَ الراسخين، قد علّمه الله جميع ما أنزل عليه من التنزيل والتأويل، وماكان الله مُنزلاً عليه شيئاً لم يُعلّمه تأويله، وأوصياؤه من بعده يَعْلَمُونه كُلَّه. فقال الذين لا يعلمون: ما نقول إذا لم نعلم تأويله؟ فأجابهم الله: ﴿يَقُولُونَ آمَنَّا بِهِ كُلٌّ مِنْ عِنْدِ رَبِّنَا﴾، والقرآن له خاصٌّ وعامٌّ، وناسخٌ ومنسوخٌ، ومُحكمٌ ومُتشابهٌ، فالراسخون في العلم يعلمونه.

٨. عن الفُضيل بن يَسار، عن أبي جعفر عليه السلام، قال: ﴿وَمَا يَعْلَمُ تَأْوِيلَهُ إِلاَّ اللهُ وَالرَّاسِخُونَ فِي الْعِلْمِ﴾ نحنُ نَعْلَمُه.

٩. عن أبي بَصير، عن أبي عبدالله عليه السلام، قال: نحنُ الراسخون في العلم، فنحنُ نعلم تأويله.

١٠. عن سَماعة بن مِهران، قال: قال: أبو عبدالله عليه السلام: أَكْثِرُوا من أن تقولوا: ﴿رَبَّنَا لاَ تُزِغْ قُلُوبَنَا بَعْدَ إِذْ هَدَيْتَنَا﴾. ولا تأمَنُوا الزَّيْغ.

١١. عن جميل بن درّاج، قال: قال أبو عبدالله عليه السلام: ما يَتلذّذ الناس في الدُنيا والآخرة بلذّة أكثرلهم من لذّة النساء، وهوقول الله تبارك وتعالى: ﴿زُيِّنَ لِلنَّاسِ حُبُّ الشَّهَوَاتِ مِنَ النِّسَاءِ وَالْبَنِينَ وَالْقَنَاطِيرِ الْمُقَنْطَرَةِ مِنَ الذَّهَبِ وَالْفِضَّةِ﴾ إلى آخر الآية، ثمّ قال: إنّ أهل الجنّة ما يتلذّذون بشيء في الجنّة أشهى عندهم من النِكاح، لا طعام ولا شراب.

12. From Abū Baṣīr, from Abū ʿAbd Allāh عليه السلام who said regarding God's words: ﴾*where they will stay with pure spouses*﴿, 'They will neither menstruate nor need to relieve themselves.' [3:15]

13. From Zurāra who narrated, 'Abū Jaʿfar عليه السلام said, "Whoever diligently perseveres with the night prayer and the single unit of prayer (*al-witr*), seeking forgiveness therein seventy times, and maintains this as a regular practice will be registered among those who seek forgiveness in the early hours before dawn."' [3:17]

14. From Abū Baṣīr who said, 'I asked Abū ʿAbd Allāh عليه السلام about the verse of God, Blessed and most High: ﴾*those who pray for forgiveness before dawn.*﴿ He replied, "The Messenger of God ﷺ would pray for forgiveness seventy times in his *witr* prayer before dawn."' [3:17]

15. From ʿUmar, from Abū ʿAbd Allāh عليه السلام who said, 'Whoever says: "I seek God's forgiveness and turn to him in repentance" seventy times at the end of his *witr* prayer and maintains this regularly for a year, he is registered by God to be among those who seek forgiveness in the early hours.' [3:17]

16. In another narration on his authority: 'He is bound to be forgiven.' [3:17]

17. From ʿUmar b. Yazīd who narrated, 'I heard Abū ʿAbd Allāh عليه السلام say, "Whoever seeks God's forgiveness seventy times in his *witr* prayer after bowing down in *rukūʿ* and maintains this regularly for a year is counted among those who seek forgiveness in the early hours."' [3:17]

18. From Mufaḍḍal b. ʿUmar who said, 'I asked Abū ʿAbd Allāh عليه السلام, "May I be your ransom – I end up missing the night prayer, so can I pray the one that I missed straight after the dawn (*fajr*) prayer but before sunrise?" He replied, "Yes, but do not instruct your family members to do the same lest they make it into a habit and thus by so doing defeat the purpose of God's statement, Mighty and Exalted: ﴾*those who pray for forgiveness before dawn.*﴿"' [3:17]

١٢. عن أبي بَصير، عن أبي عبدالله عليه السلام، في قول الله عزّ وجلّ: ﴿فِيهَا أَزْوَاجٌ مُطَهَّرَةٌ﴾، قال: لا يَحِضن ولا يُحدِثن.

١٣. عن زُرارة، قال: قال أبو جعفر عليه السلام: من داوم على صلاة الليل والوِتر، واستغفر الله في كلّ وترٍ سبعين مرّةً، ثمّ وَاظَبَ على ذلك سَنةً، كُتِب من المُستغفرين بالأسحار.

١٤. عن أبي بَصير، قال: قلتُ لأبي عبدالله عليه السلام: قول الله تبارك وتعالى: ﴿وَالْمُسْتَغْفِرِينَ بِالأَسْحَارِ﴾: استغفَرَ رسول الله صلى الله عليه وآله وسلم في وِتْرِه سبعين مرّةً.

١٥. عن عمر، عن أبي عبدالله عليه السلام، قال: من قال في آخر الوتر في السَّحر: أستغفر الله وأتوب إليه، سبعين مرّةً، ودام على ذلك سنةً، كَتَبه الله من المستغفرين بالأسحار.

١٦. وفي رواية أخرى عنه عليه السلام: وجَبَت له المَغْفِرَة.

١٧. عن عُمر بن يزيد، قال: سَمِعتُ أبا عبدالله عليه السلام يقول: من استغفرَ الله سبعين مرّةً في الوِتْرِ بعد الركُوع، فدام على ذلك سنةً، كان من المستَغْفِرِينَ بالأسحار.

١٨. عن مُفَضّل بن عُمر، قال: قلتُ لأبي عبدالله عليه السلام: جُعِلتُ فداك، تفوتني صلاةُ الليل فأُصلّي الفجر، فلِيَ أن أُصلّي بعد صلاة الفجر ما فاتني من صلاة وأنا في صلاةٍ قبل طُلوع الشمس؟ فقال: نعم، ولكن لا تُعلّم به أهلك فيتّخذونه سُنّة، فيُبْطل قول الله جلّ وعزّ: ﴿وَالْمُسْتَغْفِرِينَ بِالأَسْحَارِ﴾.

19. From Jābir who narrated, 'I asked Abū Jaʿfar عليه السلام about this verse: ﴾*God bears witness that there is no god but Him, as do the angels and those who have knowledge. He upholds justice. There is no god but Him, the Almighty, the All-Wise.*﴿ Abū Jaʿfar عليه السلام said, ﴾*God bears witness that there is no god but He*﴿, so God, Blessed and most High, Himself is bearing witness to this fact.

As for the words: ﴾*as do the angels*﴿, He honoured the angels through their submission to their Lord, so they confirm and testify to it just as He did.

As for the phrase: ﴾*and those who have knowledge. He upholds justice*﴿ – those who have knowledge are the prophets and their successors, and they are upholders of justice. Justice is the maintenance of outward equity, whereas the Commander of the Faithful عليه السلام himself is inward equity."' [3:18]

20. From Marzabān al-Qummī[2] who narrated, 'I asked Abū al-Ḥasan عليه السلام about God's verse: ﴾*God bears witness that there is no god but Him, as do the angels and those who have knowledge. He upholds justice.*﴿ He replied, "This is the Imam."' [3:18]

21. From Ismāʿīl who, without mentioning his source, cited Saʿīd b. Jubayr[3] as having said, 'The Kaʿba used to have three hundred and sixty idols in it, one or two representing each Arab locality. So when this verse: ﴾*God bears witness that there is no god but Him*﴿ until ﴾*the Almighty, the All-Wise*﴿ was revealed, the idols of the Kaʿba fell into prostration.' [3:18]

22. From Muḥammad b. Muslim who narrated, 'I asked him about the verse: ﴾*True Religion, in God's eyes, is Islam:* [*devotion to Him alone*]﴿, and he said, "True religion constitutes faith."' [3:19]

---

2 Marzabān b. ʿImrān al-Qummī al-Ashʿarī, about whom there is scant information. See Ḥillī, *Khulāṣat al-aqwāl*, 280–1 (nr. 1027).

3 Abū ʿAbd Allāh Saʿīd b. Jubayr b. Hishām al-Asadī al-Kūfī (d. 95/714), a prominent member of the generation of successors (*tābiʿīn*) and one of the earliest supporters and allies of Imam Zayn al-ʿĀbidīn who would frequently praise ʿAlī b. Abī Ṭālib openly in public. He joined the revolt instigated by ʿAbd al-Raḥmān b. al-Ashʿath against the Umayyads and as a result was killed by al-Ḥajjāj b. Yūsuf al-Thaqafī. He is held in high esteem by Sunnī and Shīʿa historians alike. See Ḥillī, *Khulāṣat al-aqwāl*, 157 (nr. 545).

١٩. عن جابر، قال: سألتُ أبا جعفر عليه السلام عن هذه الآية: ﴿شَهِدَ اللهُ أَنَّهُ لاَ إِلَهَ إِلاَّ هُوَ وَالْمَلاَئِكَةُ وَأُولُو الْعِلْمِ قَائِمًا بِالْقِسْطِ لاَ إِلَهَ إِلاَّ هُوَ الْعَزِيزُ الْحَكِيمُ﴾. قال أبو جعفر عليه السلام: ﴿شَهِدَ اللهُ أَنَّهُ لاَ إِلَهَ إِلاَّ هُوَ﴾ فإنّ الله تبارك وتعالى يَشْهَد بها لنفسه، وهو كما قال.

فأمّا قوله: ﴿وَالْمَلاَئِكَةُ﴾ فإنّه أكرم الملائكة بالتسليم لربّهم، وصدّقوا وشَهِدُوا كما شَهِدَ لنفسه.

وأمّا قوله: ﴿وَأُولُو الْعِلْمِ قَائِمًا بِالْقِسْطِ﴾ فإنّ أُولي العلم الأنبياء والأوصياء، وهم قيام بالقِسط، والقِسط: هو العَدْل في الظاهر، والعَدْل في الباطن: أمير المؤمنين عليه السلام.

٢٠. عن مَرْزُبان القُميّ، قال: سألتُ أبا الحسن عليه السلام عن قول الله عزّ وجلّ: ﴿شَهِدَ اللهُ أَنَّهُ لاَ إِلَهَ إِلاَّ هُوَ وَالْمَلاَئِكَةُ وَأُولُو الْعِلْمِ قَائِمًا بِالْقِسْطِ﴾، قال: هو الإمام.

٢١. عن إسماعيل، رفعه إلى سعيد بن جُبَير، قال: كان على الكعبة ثلاثمائة وستّون صنمًا، لكلّ حيّ من أحياء العرب الواحد والاثنان، فلمّا نزلت هذه الآية: ﴿شَهِدَ اللهُ أَنَّهُ لاَ إِلَهَ إِلاَّ هُوَ﴾ إلى قوله: ﴿الْعَزِيزُ الْحَكِيمُ﴾ خرّت الأصنامُ في الكعبة سُجّدًا.

٢٢. عن محمّد بن مُسلم، قال: سألتُه عن قوله تعالى: ﴿إِنَّ الدِّينَ عِندَ اللهِ الإِسْلاَمُ﴾، فقال: الدين فيه الإيمان.

23. From Muḥammad b. Muslim, from Abū Jaʿfar عليه السلام who said regarding the verse: ﴿*True Religion, in God's eyes, is Islam:* [*devotion to Him alone*]﴾, 'This means that true religion constitutes faith.' [3:19]

24. From Dāwūd b. Farqad who narrated, 'I asked Abū ʿAbd Allāh عليه السلام about God's verse: ﴿*Say, 'God, holder of all sovereignty, You give sovereignty to whoever You will and remove it from whoever You will* [...]*'*﴾, "So did God grant the Umayyads their sovereignty?" He replied, "No, it is not how people believe it to be. God has granted us the sovereignty, but the Umayyads have taken it for themselves. It is as if a man was to possess a garment and someone else took it from him; it does not actually belong to the one who took it."' [3:26]

25. From al-Ḥusayn b. Zayd b. ʿAlī[4], from Jaʿfar b. Muḥammad, on his father's authority عليه السلام who narrated, 'The Messenger of God صلى الله عليه وآله used to say, "The one who does not dissimulate his faith [under duress] has no faith." He continued, "God says: ﴿*except when you need to protect yourselves from them.*﴾"' [3:28]

26. From Abū ʿUbayda Ziyād al-Hadhdhāʾ who narrated, 'I went to Abū Jaʿfar عليه السلام and said to him, "May I be your ransom – sometimes Shayṭān gets the better of me and my soul becomes wretched. Then I remember my love for you and my devotion to you and my soul becomes better again." So he replied, "Dear Ziyād! Is religion anything but love? Have you not read God's verse: ﴿*Say, 'If you love God, follow me, and God will love you and forgive you your sins*﴾?"' [3:31]

27. From Bashīr al-Dahhān, from Abū ʿAbd Allāh عليه السلام who said, 'You have acknowledged [true faith] in the midst of many rejecters and you demonstrate love in the midst of many haters. This love may either be for the sake of God and His Messenger or for the sake of this world. Whatever is for God and His Messenger, He is the one to reward it. Whoever loves for [gain in] this world,

4 Abū ʿAbd Allāh al-Ḥusayn b. Zayd b. ʿAlī b. al-Ḥusayn b. ʿAlī b. Abī Ṭālib, a companion of the sixth and seventh Imams. He was brought up by Imam Jaʿfar al-Ṣādiq and was married to his own niece, the daughter of Muḥammad b. ʿAbd Allāh al-Arqaṭ. See Ḥillī, *Khulāṣat al-aqwāl*, 118 (nr. 290); Modarressi, *Tradition and Survival*, 280–83 (nr. 100).

٢٣. عن محمّد بن مُسلم، عن أبي جعفر عليه السلام، قال: ﴿إِنَّ الدِّينَ عِنْدَ اللهِ الإِسْلَامُ﴾، قال: يعني الدين فيه الإيمان.

٢٤. عن داود بن فَرْقَد، قال: قلتُ لأبي عبدالله عليه السلام: قول الله سبحانه وتعالى: ﴿قُلِ اللَّهُمَّ مَالِكَ الْمُلْكِ تُؤْتِي الْمُلْكَ مَنْ تَشَاءُ وَتَنْزِعُ الْمُلْكَ مِمَّنْ تَشَاءُ﴾ فقد آتى الله بني أُميّة المُلك! فقال عليه السلام: ليس حيث يذهب الناس إليه، إنّ الله آتانا المُلك وأخذه بنو أُميّة بمنزلة الرجل يكون له الثوب ويأخُذُهُ الآخر، فليس هو للّذي أخذه.

٢٥. عن الحسين بن زَيد بن عليّ، عن جعفر بن محمّد، عن أبيه عليهما السلام، قال: كان رسول الله صلى الله عليه وآله يقول: لا إيمان لمن لا تقيّة له، ويقول: قال الله تعالى: ﴿إِلَّا أَنْ تَتَّقُوا مِنْهُمْ تُقَاةً﴾.

٢٦. عن زياد أبي عُبيدة الحَذّاء، قال: دخلتُ على أبي جعفر عليه السلام، فقلتُ: بأبي أنت وأُمّي، رُبّما خلا بي الشيطان فخُبُثَت نفسي، ثمّ ذكرتُ حبّي إيّاكم، وانقطاعي إليكم فطابت نفسي؟

فقال: يا زياد، ويحك وما الدين إلاّ الحُبّ، ألا ترى إلى قول الله تعالى: ﴿إِنْ كُنْتُمْ تُحِبُّونَ اللهَ فَاتَّبِعُونِي يُحْبِبْكُمُ اللهُ﴾.

٢٧. عن بَشير الدّهان، عن أبي عبدالله عليه السلام، قال: قد عرفتم فيَّ منكرين كثيرًا، وأحببتم فيَّ مبغضين كثيرًا، وقد يكون حُبًّا لله في الله ورسوله، وحُبًّا في الدنيا، فما كان في الله ورسوله فثوابه على الله، وما كان في الدنيا فليس في شيءٍ، ثمّ نفض يده، ثمّ قال: إنّ هذه المُرجِئة،

however, ends up with nothing.' Then he motioned with his hand, saying, 'Every single one of these Murji'ites, Qadarites and Kharijites believes that he is on the right path, but you all are the ones who have demonstrated love for us for the sake of God.' Then he recited: ﴾*Obey God and the Messenger, and those in authority among you*﴿(4:59); ﴾*So accept whatever the Messenger gives you, and abstain from whatever he forbids you*﴿(59:7); ﴾*Whoever obeys the Messenger obeys God*﴿(4:80); ﴾*Say, 'If you love God, follow me, and God will love you and forgive you your sins.'*﴿ [3:31]

28. From Burayd b. Muʿāwiya al-ʿIjlī who narrated, 'I was with Abū Jaʿfar عليه السلام when a traveller from Khurasan arrived on foot. He uncovered his legs, which had swelled up. He said, "By God, I have gone through everything just for my love for you, the Ahl al-Bayt." So Abū Jaʿfar عليه السلام said, "By God, even if a rock were to express its love for us, God would resurrect it with us. Is religion anything but love? God says: ﴾*Say, 'If you love God, follow me, and God will love you'*﴿ and ﴾*they show love for those who migrated to them*﴿ (59:9) – is religion anything but love?"' [3:31]

29. From Ribʿī b. ʿAbd Allāh who narrated, 'May I be your ransom – We name ourselves after your names and the names of your forefathers – will that be beneficial to us?' He replied, 'Of course, by God. Is religion anything but love? God says: ﴾*Say, 'If you love God, follow me, and God will love you and forgive you your sins.'*﴿ [3:31]

30. From Ḥanān b. Sadīr, on his father's authority, from Abū Jaʿfar عليه السلام who recited the verse: ﴾*God chose Ādam, Nūḥ, Ibrāhīm's family, and the family of ʿImrān, over all other people, in one line of descent*﴿ and said, 'We are from them and we are the only ones remaining of that progeny.' [3:33–34]

وهذه القَدَريَة، وهذه الخوارج ليس منهم أحدٌ إلاّ يرى أنه على الحق، وإنّكم إنّما أحببتمونا في الله، ثمّ تلا: ﴿أَطِيعُوا اللَّهَ وَأَطِيعُوا الرَّسُولَ وَأُولِي الْأَمْرِ مِنكُمْ﴾، ﴿وَمَا آتَاكُمُ الرَّسُولُ فَخُذُوهُ وَمَا نَهَاكُمْ عَنْهُ فَانتَهُوا﴾، و﴿مَّن يُطِعِ الرَّسُولَ فَقَدْ أَطَاعَ اللَّهَ﴾، ﴿إِن كُنتُمْ تُحِبُّونَ اللَّهَ فَاتَّبِعُونِي يُحْبِبْكُمُ اللَّهُ﴾.

٢٨. عن بُريد مُعاوية العِجليّ، قال: كنتُ عند أبي جعفر عليه السلام إذ دخل عليه قادمٌ من خُراسان ماشيًا، فأخرج رجليه وقد تورّمتا، وقال: أما والله ما جاءني من حيث جئتُ إلاّ حُبّكم أهل البيت. فقال أبو جعفر عليه السلام: والله لو أحبّنا حجرٌ حشره الله معنا، وهل الدِّين إلاّ الحُبّ، إنّ الله تعالى يقول: ﴿قُلْ إِن كُنتُمْ تُحِبُّونَ اللَّهَ فَاتَّبِعُونِي يُحْبِبْكُمُ اللَّهُ﴾، وقال: ﴿يُحِبُّونَ مَنْ هَاجَرَ إِلَيْهِمْ﴾ وهل الدِّين إلاّ الحُبّ.

٢٩. عن رِبعي بن عبدالله، قال: قيل لأبي عبدالله عليه السلام: جُعِلتُ فِداك: إنّا نُسمّي بأسمائكم، وأسماء آبائكم، فينفعنا ذلك؟ فقال: إي والله، وهل الدِّين إلاّ الحُبّ، قال الله تعالى: ﴿إِن كُنتُمْ تُحِبُّونَ اللَّهَ فَاتَّبِعُونِي يُحْبِبْكُمُ اللَّهُ وَيَغْفِرْ لَكُمْ ذُنُوبَكُمْ﴾.

٣٠. عن حَنان بن سَدير، عن أبيه، عن أبي جعفر عليه السلام، قال: ﴿إِنَّ اللَّهَ اصْطَفَىٰ آدَمَ وَنُوحًا وَآلَ إِبْرَاهِيمَ وَآلَ عِمْرَانَ عَلَى الْعَالَمِينَ ۞ ذُرِّيَّةً بَعْضُهَا مِن بَعْضٍ﴾، قال عليه السلام: نحنُ منهم، ونحنُ بقية تلك العِترة.

31. From Hishām b. Sālim who narrated, 'I asked Abū 'Abd Allāh ﷺ about God's verse: ﴾*God chose Ādam, Nūḥ, Ibrāhīm's family, and the family of 'Imrān, over all other people, in one line of descent.*﴿ He said, "It is [supposed to be]: ﴾*Ibrāhīm's family **and Muḥammad's family over all people***﴿, but they have replaced one name instead of the other."' [3:33–34*]

32. From Abū Ḥamza, from Abū Ja'far ﷺ who narrated, 'When Muḥammad ﷺ had fulfilled the term of his prophethood and had come to the end of his days, God revealed to him, saying: "O Muḥammad, you have fulfilled the term of your prophethood and come to the end of your days now, so deposit all the knowledge that you have about faith, the Greatest Name [of God], the heritage and legacy of the knowledge of the prophets in your progeny, for I have not impeded your progeny from possessing knowledge of the faith, the Greatest Name, the heritage and legacy of prophets, just as I did not impede the households of the prophets that came between you and your forefather Ādam from that knowledge." This is what God means by: ﴾*God chose Ādam, Nūḥ, Ibrāhīm's family, and the family of 'Imrān, over all other people, in one line of descent – God hears and knows all.*﴿

God, Mighty and most High, did not deposit knowledge haphazardly nor did he place any of His creatures in charge of it, neither a favoured angel nor a prophetic messenger. Rather He sent messengers from among his angels with strict instructions to enjoin upon them what He likes and forbid them from what He dislikes. He expounded to him all the facts about His human creation until he knew them thoroughly, and in turn taught the prophets and their vicegerents, their supporters and progeny in the one line of descent, as per the verse: ﴾*We gave the descendants of Ibrāhīm the Scripture and wisdom – and We gave them a great kingdom.*﴿(4:54) The scripture is prophethood itself; wisdom refers to the wisest men from among the elite prophets, and the great kingdom are the Imams of guidance selected exclusively. These are all from that progeny in one single line of descent, and in which He has placed the last of them. They are tasked with the last days and the preservation of the covenant until the world ends, and the scholars and men of authority from among them are responsible for extracting that knowledge and guidance.' [3:33–34]

٣١. عن هشام بن سالم، قال: سألتُ أبا عبد الله عليه السلام عن قول الله تعالى: ﴿إِنَّ اللَّهَ اصْطَفَى آدَمَ وَنُوحًا﴾، قال عليه السلام: هو آل إبراهيم وآل محمّدٍ على العالمين، فَوَضَعُوا اسماً مكان اسم.

٣٢. عن أبي حمزة، عن أبي جعفر عليه السلام، قال: لمّا قضى محمد صلى الله عليه وآله نبُوّته، واستُكملت أيّامه، أوحى الله: يا محمّد، قد قُضيت نبوّتك، واستكملت أيّامك، فاجعل العلم الذي عندك من الإيمان، والاسم الأكبر، وميراث العلم وآثار علم النُبوّة في العَقِب في ذُرّيّتك، فإنّي لم أقطع العلم والإيمان والاسم الأكبر وميراث العلم وآثار علم النُبوّة من العقِب من ذُرّيّتك، كما لم أقطعها من بيوتات الأنبياء الذين كانوا بينك وبين أبيك آدم، وذلك قول الله تعالى: ﴿إِنَّ اللَّهَ اصْطَفَى آدَمَ وَنُوحًا وَآلَ إِبْرَاهِيمَ وَآلَ عِمْرَانَ عَلَى الْعَالَمِينَ ۝ ذُرِّيَّةً بَعْضُهَا مِنْ بَعْضٍ وَاللَّهُ سَمِيعٌ عَلِيمٌ﴾.

وإنّ الله جلّ وتعالى لم يجعل العِلم جهْلاً، ولم يَكِل أمْرَه إلى أحدٍ من خلقه، لا إلى مَلَكٍ مُقرّبٍ، ولا إلى نبيّ مُرسل، ولكنّه أرسل رُسُلاً من ملائكته، فقال لهم: كذا وكذا، فأمرهم بما يُحِبّ، ونهاهم عمّا يكره، فقصّ عليه أمر خلْقِهِ بعلمٍ، فَعلم ذلك العِلم، وعلّم أنبياءه، وأصفياءه من الأنبياء والأعوان والذُريّة الّتي بعضها من بعضٍ، فذلك قوله تعالى: ﴿فَقَدْ آتَيْنَا آلَ إِبْرَاهِيمَ الْكِتَابَ وَالْحِكْمَةَ وَآتَيْنَاهُمْ مُلْكًا عَظِيمًا﴾.

فأمّا الكتاب فهو النُبوّة وأمّا الحكمة فهم الحكماء من الأنبياء في الصّفوة، وأمّا المُلك العظيم فهُم الأئمّة الهُداة في الصّفوة، وكلّ هؤلاء من الذُّرّيّة الّتي بعضها من بعضٍ الّتي جعل فيهم البقيّة، وفيهم العاقبة، وحِفظ المِيثاق حتّى تنقضي الدنيا، وللعُلماء ولولاة الأمر الاستنباط للعِلم والهداية.

33. From Aḥmad b. Muḥammad, from al-Riḍā, from Abū Ja'far عليه السلام who said, 'Whoever presumes that he is immune from the [Divine] decree is wrong, for it is only God's will that prevails over His creatures. He wills whatever He wishes and does whatever He wills. God says: ﴾ *a progeny, in one line of descent – God hears and knows all.* ﴿ The descendants are from the ancestors and vice versa, so when you know something about it [the progeny] as an actual fact, even if it applied to someone else before them, then the narrative now applies to this situation that you have come to know about.' [3:34]

34. From Abū 'Abd al-Raḥmān[5], from Abū Kalada, from Abū Ja'far عليه السلام who narrated, 'The Messenger of God صلى الله عليه وآله said, "Comfort, tranquillity, mercy, assistance, ease, prosperity, contentment, pleasure, relief, victory, proximity and love from God and His Messenger are all reserved for those who love 'Alī and accept the Imamate of the vicegerents after him. It becomes their right upon me to facilitate their entry into Paradise through my intercession, and it is my right upon my Lord that He grants me that regarding them because they are my followers; and whoever follows me is a part of me, just like the example of Ibrāhīm regarding me. He is a part of me and I am a part of him; his religion is my religion and mine his; his practice is my practice and mine is his; my virtue is his virtue, and even though I have been favoured above him, this favour is actually a favour to him. This confirms God's statement: ﴾ *a progeny, in one line of descent – God hears and knows all* ﴿."' [3:34]

35. From Ayyūb, who narrated, 'Abū 'Abd Allāh عليه السلام heard me reciting: ﴾ *God chose Ādam, Nūḥ, Ibrāhīm's family, and the family of 'Imrān, over all other people* ﴿, so he said to me, "And 'the family of Muḥammad' was there too, but they effaced it, leaving 'the family of Ibrāhīm and the family of 'Imrān'."' [3:33–34*]

5 Referring most likely to Abū 'Abd al-Raḥmān al-Kindī, a known liar and exaggerator (*ghālī*) about the status of the Imams who was cursed by them. See Ḥillī, *Khulāṣat al-aqwāl*, 423 (nr. 1726).

٣٣. عن أحمد بن محمّد، عن الرضا، عن أبي جعفر عليه السلام، قال: من زعم أنّه قد فرَغ من الأمر فقد كَذَب، لأنّ المشيئة لله في خلقه، يُريدُ ما يشاءُ، ويفعلُ ما يُريد، قال الله: ﴿ذُرِّيَّةً بَعْضُهَا مِنْ بَعْضٍ وَاللَّهُ سَمِيعٌ عَلِيمٌ﴾ آخرها من أوّلها، وأوّلها من آخرها، فإذا أُخبرتم بشيء منها بعينه أنّه كائنٌ وكان في غيره منه، فقد وقع الخبر على ما أُخبِرتم عنه.

٣٤. عن أبي عبد الرحمن، عن أبي كَلَدَة، عن أبي جعفر عليه السلام، قال: قال رسول الله صلى الله عليه وآله وسلم: الرُّوح والراحة، والرَّحمة والنُّصرة، واليُسر واليسار، والرِّضا والرِّضوان، والمَخْرَج والفَلْج، والقُرب والمَحَبَة من الله ومن رسوله لمن أحبَّ عليّاً وائتمّ بالأوصياء من بعده، حقٌّ عليَّ أن أُدخِلهم في شَفَاعتي، وحقّ على ربّي أن يستجيب لي فيهم، لأنّهم أتباعي، ومن تَبِعني فإنّه منّي، مَثَلُ إبراهيم جَرى فيَّ، ولايته منّي، وأنا منه، دينه ديني، وديني دينه، وسُنّته سُنّتي، وسُنّتي سُنّته، وفضلي فضله، وأنا أفضل منه؟ وفضلي له فضل، وذلك تصديق قول ربّي: ﴿ذُرِّيَّةً بَعْضُهَا مِنْ بَعْضٍ وَاللَّهُ سَمِيعٌ عَلِيمٌ﴾.

٣٥. عن أيّوب، قال: سَمِعني أبو عبد الله عليه السلام، وأنا أقرأ: ﴿إِنَّ اللَّهَ اصْطَفَى آدَمَ وَنُوحًا وَآلَ إِبْرَاهِيمَ وَآلَ عِمْرَانَ عَلَى الْعَالَمِينَ﴾، فقال لي: وآل محمدٍ كانت فمَحوها، وتَركُوا آل إبراهيم وآل عمران.

36. From Abū ʿAmr al-Zubayrī, from Abū ʿAbd Allāh عليه السلام. ʿI asked him, "What is the evidence in God's Book that the family of Muḥammad are the ones being referred to as the People of his Household' (*ahl al-bayt*)?" He replied, "The statement of God, Blessed and most High: ﴾*God chose Ādam, Nūḥ, Ibrāhīm's family, and the family of ʿImrān,* ***and the family of Muḥammad***﴿ – that is how it was revealed – ﴾*over all other people, in one line of descent – God hears and knows all.*﴿ People's progenies can only come from their lineage and their own loins."' [3:33–34*]

God, most High, said, ﴾*Work thankfully, family of David, for few of my servants are truly thankful.*﴿ (34:13) and the family of ʿImrān and the family of Muḥammad, as mentioned in the narration of Abū Khālid al-Qammāṭ from him عليه السلام.

37. From Ismāʿīl al-Juʿfī[6], from Abū Jaʿfar عليه السلام who narrated, 'When the wife of ʿImrān dedicated what was growing in her womb [in devotion to God], [she knew that] the devotee of the mosque, once she had given birth to him and submitted him to the mosque, could never again leave it. So when she gave birth to Maryam, ﴾*she said, 'My Lord! I have given birth to a girl' – God knew best what she had given birth to: the male is not like the female – 'I name her Maryam and I commend her and her offspring to Your protection from the rejected Satan.'*﴿ The prophets drew lots against her, and Zakariyyā drew the short straw. He was her sister's husband, so she entrusted her in his charge and submitted her to the mosque. When she reached the age of maturity she was the most beautiful of all women; and when she would pray, the whole prayer niche would be illuminated by her light. Zakariyyā once visited her and found her with winter fruits in summer, and summer fruits in winter, and exclaimed: "Maryam, how is it you have these provisions?" and she said, "They are from God." ﴾*There and then Zakariyyā prayed to his Lord, saying,*[7] *"I fear* [*what*] *my kinsmen* [*will do*] *when I am gone, for my wife is barren, so grant me a successor – a gift from You*﴿ and the rest of the story that God mentions about Zakariyyā and Yaḥyā.' [3:35–38]

---

6 Referring most likely to Ismāʿīl b. Jābir al-Juʿfī al-Kūfī, a praiseworthy and reliable companion of Muḥammad al-Bāqir. See Ḥillī, *Khulāṣat al-aqwāl*, 54 (nr. 30).

7 The complete verse (Q. 3:38) is as follows: ﴾*There and then Zakariyyā prayed to his Lord, saying, 'Lord, from Your grace grant me virtuous offspring: You hear every prayer*﴿, though in ʿAyyāshī's text Zakariyyā's prayer is different according to the wording found in Q. 19:5.

٣٦. عن أبي عَمرو الزُّبَيْري، عن أبي عبد الله عليه السلام قال: قلتُ له: ما الحُجّة في كتاب الله أنّ آل محمّد هم أهل بيته؟ قال: قول الله تبارك وتعالى: ﴿إِنَّ اللَّهَ اصْطَفَىٰ آدَمَ وَنُوحًا وَآلَ إِبْرَاهِيمَ وَآلَ عِمْرَانَ﴾ وآل محمّدٍ، هكذا نزلت ﴿عَلَى الْعَالَمِينَ ۝ ذُرِّيَّةً بَعْضُهَا مِنْ بَعْضٍ وَاللَّهُ سَمِيعٌ عَلِيمٌ﴾ ولا تكون الذُرّيّة من القوم إلاّ نسلهم من أصلابهم.

وقال تعالى: ﴿اعْمَلُوا آلَ دَاوُودَ شُكْرًا وَقَلِيلٌ مِنْ عِبَادِيَ الشَّكُورُ﴾ وآل عِمران وآل محمّدٍ في رواية أبي خالد القمّاط عنه عليه السلام.

٣٧. عن إسماعيل الجُعفي، عن أبي جعفر عليه السلام، قال: إنّ امرأة عِمران لمّا نذرَت ما في بطنها مُحرّرًا، قال: والمُحَرّر للمسجد إذا وضعته أو دخل المسجد، فلم يَخرُج من المسجد أبدًا، فلمّا وَلَدت مريم ﴿قَالَتْ رَبِّ إِنِّي وَضَعْتُهَا أُنْثَىٰ وَاللَّهُ أَعْلَمُ بِمَا وَضَعَتْ وَلَيْسَ الذَّكَرُ كَالْأُنْثَىٰ وَإِنِّي سَمَّيْتُهَا مَرْيَمَ وَإِنِّي أُعِيذُهَا بِكَ وَذُرِّيَّتَهَا مِنَ الشَّيْطَانِ الرَّجِيمِ﴾ فَسَاهَمَ عليها النبيّون، فأصابت القُرعة زكريّا عليه السلام وهو زوج أُختها، وكَفَّلَهَا وأدخلها المسجد، فلمّا بَلَغَتْ ما تَبلُغ النساء من الطَمث وكانت أجمل النساء، وكانت تُصلّي فيضيء المِحراب لنُورها، فدخل عليها زكريّا، فإذا عندها فاكهةُ الشتاء في الصيف، وفاكهة الصيف في الشّتاء، فقال: ﴿أَنَّىٰ لَكِ هَٰذَا قَالَتْ هُوَ مِنْ عِنْدِ اللَّهِ﴾ فهُنالك دعا زكريّا ربّه قال: ﴿وَإِنِّي خِفْتُ الْمَوَالِيَ مِنْ وَرَائِي﴾ إلى ما ذَكَر الله من قِصّة زكريّا ويحيى.

38. From Ḥafṣ b. al-Bakhtarī, from Abū ʿAbd Allāh عليه السلام regarding the verse: ﴾*Lord, I have dedicated what is growing in my womb entirely to You*﴿, 'The devotee would live in the temple and never leave again. When she had given birth to a girl, ﴾*she said, 'My Lord! I have given birth to a girl' – God knew best what she had given birth to: the male is not like the female*﴿, since the female menstruates and has to come out of the mosque, whereas the devotee never leaves the mosque.' [3:36]

39. In a narration by Ḥarīz, from one of the two Imams who said, 'She dedicated that which was growing in her womb to the temple to serve the worshippers, and the male is not like the female in service.' He continued, 'While she was young, she would serve them and distribute offerings to them until she reached maturity. Then Zakariyyā was commanded to seclude her from the worshippers. Whenever he would visit her, he would find her with winter fruits in the summer months and summer fruits in the winter. So there and then he supplicated his Lord to grant him a son, so He granted him Yaḥyā.' [3:35–37]

40. From Jābir, from Abū Jaʿfar عليه السلام. 'I heard him say, "God revealed to ʿImrān: 'I am going to grant you a son who will cure the blind and the leper, give life to the dead with the permission of God, and be a messenger to the Children of Israel.'

So he informed his wife Ḥanna of this, and she became pregnant and gave birth to Maryam, saying: 'My Lord, I have given birth to a girl, and a girl cannot be a prophet!'

So ʿImrān said to her, 'A son of hers will be a prophet.'

So when she realized that, she said what she is quoted to have said, and God said, and His word is the truth: ﴾*God knew best what she had given birth to.*﴿"

Then Abū Jaʿfar عليه السلام said, "And that was ʿĪsā, son of Maryam. So when we foretell you something about one of us and it ends up being actualized by his son or grandson or great-grandson, do not dispute that for it was still about him."' [3:35–37]

٣٨. عن حَفص بن البَخْتَري، عن أبي عبدالله عليه السلام، في قول الله تبارك وتعالى: ﴿إِنِّي نَذَرْتُ لَكَ مَا فِي بَطْنِي مُحَرَّرًا﴾ المُحرَّر: يكون في الكنيسة، لا يخرج منها، فلمّا وضعتها أُنثى ﴿قَالَتْ رَبِّ إِنِّي وَضَعْتُهَا أُنْثَى وَاللهُ أَعْلَمُ بِمَا وَضَعَتْ وَلَيْسَ الذَّكَرُ كَالأُنْثَى﴾ إنّ الأُنثى تحيض فتخرج من المسجد، والمُحرّر لا يخرج من المسجد.

٣٩. وفي رواية حَريز، عن أحدهما عليهما السلام، قال: نَذَرت ما في بطنها للكَنيسة أن تَخْدُم العُبّاد، وليس الذّكر كالأُنثى في الخِدمة، قال: فشَبَّت وكانت تَخْدُمهم وتُناولهم حتّى بَلَغَت، فأمر زكريّا أن يتّخذ لها حِجابًا، دون العُبّاد، فكان يَدْخُل عليها فيرى عندها ثَمَرة الشتاء في الصّيف، وثمرة الصّيف في الشِتاء، فُهنالك دعا وسأل ربّه أن يَهَبَ له ذَكَرًا، فَوَهب له يحيى عليه السلام.

٤٠. عن جابر، عن أبي جعفر عليه السلام، قال سَمِعتُه يقول: أوحى الله تعالى إلى عِمران: أنّي واحبٌ لك ذَكَرًا، يُبرئُ الأكمه والأبرص، ويُحيي الموتى بإذن الله، ورسولاً إلى بني إسرائيل.

قال: فأخبر بذلك امرأته حَنّة، فَحَمَلت فَوَضَعت مريم؛ فقالت: ربّ إنّي وضعتها أُنثى، والأُنثى لا تكون رسولاً.

وقال لها عِمران: إنّه ذكر يكون منهما نبيًّا، فلمّا رأت ذلك قالت ما قالت، فقال الله وقوله الحقّ: ﴿وَاللهُ أَعْلَمُ بِمَا وَضَعَتْ﴾.

فقال أبو جعفر عليه السلام: فكان ذلك عيسى بن مريم عليه السلام، فإن قلنا لكم: إنّ الأمر يكون في أحدِنا، فكان في ابنه وابن ابنه، أو ابن ابنه، فقد كان فيه، فلا تُنكِروا ذلك.

41. From Saʿd al-Iskāf, from Abū Jaʿfar ﷺ who said, "ʿĪsā, son of Maryam, once met Iblīs and asked him, "Have any of your stratagems against me been effective?" He replied, "[No, because of] Your grandmother who said: ﴿ *'My Lord! I have given birth to a girl' – God knew best what she had given birth to: the male is not like the female – 'I name her Maryam and I commend her and her offspring to Your protection from the rejected Satan.'* ﴾' [3:36]

42. From Sayf, from Najm, from Abū Jaʿfar ﷺ who narrated, 'Fāṭima, peace be upon her, undertook the housework, kneading the dough, baking the bread and sweeping the house for ʿAlī, whilst ʿAlī ﷺ undertook for her all the jobs outside of the house, such as carrying the firewood and bringing the food. One day he asked her, "Fāṭima, do you have anything to eat?" She replied, "No. By the One Who has augmented your right, we have not had anything for three days of which I can offer you anything to eat." He replied, "Then why did you not you tell me?" She replied, "The Messenger of God ﷺ has forbidden me from ever asking you for anything, saying: 'Do not ask your cousin for anything. If he brings you something, well and good; but if not, do not ask him for it.'" He [the Imam] continued, "So the Imam ﷺ went out and met a man from whom he borrowed a dinar. Then, as he was returning with it after nightfall, he met Miqdād b. al-Aswad[8]. He asked Miqdād, 'What brings you out at this time of night?' He replied, 'Hunger, by the One Who has augmented your right, O Commander of the Faithful.'"

I interrupted Abū Jaʿfar, "Was the Messenger of God ﷺ still alive?"

He replied, "Yes, the Messenger of God ﷺ was still alive."

He ﷺ continued, "He [Miqdād] said, 'It has made me come out and borrow a dinar from you for which I will be most obliged to you.' So he gave it to him and came back to find the Messenger of God seated whilst Fāṭima was praying, and between them something covered. When she finished, she brought that thing, and lo and behold it was a bowl with bread and meat. He exclaimed, 'Fāṭima, how did you get this?' She replied, ﴿ *It is from God: God provides limitlessly for whoever He wills.* ﴾

Then the Messenger of God ﷺ said, 'Shall I narrate to you about someone like you and someone like her?' He replied, 'Of course.'

8 Abū Muḥammad al-Miqdād b. al-Aswad, one of the most loyal and trustworthy companions of ʿAlī b. Abī Ṭālib. See Ḥillī, *Khulāṣat al-aqwāl*, 277 (nr. 1012).

٤١. عن سَعْد الإسكاف، عن أبي جعفر عليه السلام، قال: لقي إبليس عيسى ابن مريم عليه السلام، فقال: هل نالني من حَبائلك شيء؟ قال: جَدّتُك التي قالت: ﴿رَبِّ إِنِّي وَضَعْتُهَا أُنثَىٰ﴾ إلى ﴿الشَّيْطَانِ الرَّجِيمِ﴾.

٤٢. عن سَيف، عن نَجم، عن أبي جعفر عليه السلام، قال: إنّ فاطمة عليها السلام ضمِنَت لعليّ عليه السلام عَمَل البيت والعَجين والخُبز وقَمّ البيت، وضمِنَ لها عليّ عليه السلام ما كان خلف الباب من نَقل الحَطب، وأن يجيء بالطعام، فقال لها يومًا: يا فاطمة، هل عندك شيء؟ قالت: لا، والذي عظّم حقّك، ما كان عندنا منذ ثَلاثة أيّام شيءٌ نُقريك به. قال: أفلا أخبرتني؟ قالت: كان رسول الله صلى الله عليه وآله نَهاني أن أسألك شيئًا، فقال: لا، تسألي ابن عمّك شيئًا، إن جاءك بشيء عفوًا، وإلاّ فلا تسأليه.

قال: فخَرَج الإمام عليه السلام فلقيَ رجُلاً فاستقرض منه دينارًا، ثمّ أقبل به وقد أمسى، فلقي المِقداد بن الأسود، فقال للمِقداد، ما أخرجك في هذه الساعة؟ قال: الجُوع، والذي عظّم حقّك يا أمير المؤمنين.

قال: قلت لأبي جعفر عليه السلام: ورسول الله صلى الله عليه وآله حيّ؟ قال: ورسول الله صلى الله عليه وآله حيّ.

قال: فهو أخرجني، وقد استقرضتُ دينارًا، وسأوثِرك به؛ فدفعه إليه، فأقبل فوجد رسول الله صلى الله عليه وآله جالسًا، وفاطمة تُصلّي، وبينهما شيءٌ مُغطّى، فلمّا فرَغت أجترّت ذلك الشيء، فإذا جَفْنَة من خُبزٍ ولَحم، قال: يا فاطمة، أنّى لك هذا؟ قالت: ﴿هُوَ مِنْ عِندِ اللَّهِ إِنَّ اللَّهَ يَرْزُقُ مَن يَشَاءُ بِغَيْرِ حِسَابٍ﴾.

So he said, 'It is the similitude of Zakariyyā: when he entered Maryam's sanctuary and found provisions with her. He asked, ﴾*'Maryam, how is it you have these provisions?' and she said, 'They are from God: God provides limitlessly for whoever He wills.'*﴿ They ate from that for a whole month, and this is the same bowl that the Qā'im عليه السلام will eat from and we have it in our possession.'" [3:37]

43. From Ismā'īl b. 'Abd al-Raḥmān al-Ju'fī[9] who narrated, 'I said to Abū 'Abd Allāh عليه السلام, "Mughīra b. Sa'īd[10] claims that the menstruating woman has to make up her missed prayers just as she does her fasts – [is this true]?" He replied, "What is wrong with him; may God not make him succeed. The wife of 'Imrān dedicated what was in her womb to God, and one who is dedicated to the mosque never leaves it. So when she gave birth to Maryam ﴾*she said, 'My Lord! I have given birth to a girl, and the male is not like the female.'*﴿ So she entrusted her to the mosque after she had given birth to her. When she reached maturity as a woman, she was made to leave the mosque. You do not find there having been days that she would have had to make up when she was on it [i.e. her menses] during the time that she was in the mosque."' [3:36]

44. From Abū Baṣīr, from Abū 'Abd Allāh عليه السلام who said, 'When Zakariyyā supplicated his Lord to grant him a son and the angels called out to him delivering the news thereof, he wished to know whether the voice [he had heard] was indeed from God. So He [God] revealed to him that the sign of that would be that his tongue would no longer be capable of uttering any speech for three days. When this happened and he was unable to speak, he knew that no one had the power to do that except God, and that is God's verse: ﴾*He said, 'My Lord, give me a sign.' 'Your sign,'* [*the angel*] *said, 'is that you will not communicate with anyone for three days, except by gestures.'*﴿ [3:41]

9 Ismā'īl b. 'Abd al-Raḥmān al-Ju'fī al-Kūfī (d. before 148/765), a *tābi'ī* and companion of Imam Ja'far al-Ṣādiq. See Ḥillī, *Khulāṣat al-aqwāl*, 54 (nr. 31).

10 Mughīra b. Sa'īd, a liar and fabricator of the Imams' traditions. See Ḥillī, *Khulāṣat al-aqwāl*, 411 (nr. 1667).

فقال رسول الله ﷺ: ألا أُحدّثك بمثلك ومثلها؟ قال: بلى، قال: مثل زكريّا إذ دخل على مريم المِحرَاب، فوجد عندها رزقًا، قال: ﴿يَا مَرْيَمُ أَنَّى لَكِ هَذَا قَالَتْ هُوَ مِنْ عِنْدِ اللَّهِ إِنَّ اللَّهَ يَرْزُقُ مَنْ يَشَاءُ بِغَيْرِ حِسَابٍ﴾ فأكلوا منها شهرًا، وهي الجَفْنَة التي يأكُل منها القائم ؑ، وهي عندنا.

٤٣. عن إسماعيل بن عبد الرّحمن الجُعفي، قال: قلتُ لأبي عبدالله ؑ: يقول المُغيرة بن سعيد: إنّ الحائض تقضي الصّوم؟ فقال: ما لَهُ! لا وفّقه الله، إنّ امرأة عِمران نَذَرت ما في بطنها مُحرّرًا، والمُحرّر للمسجد لا يخرج منه أبدًا، فلمّا وَضَعَت مريم قالتْ: ربّ إنّي وَضعتها أُنثى وليس الذكر كالأُنثى. فلمّا وضعتها أُدْخِلت المسجد، فلمّا بَلَغَت مَبْلَغ النساء أُخرجت من المسجد، فما تَجِد أيّامًا تقضيه، وهي عليها أن تكون الدّهر في المسجد.

٤٤. عن أبي بصير، عن أبي عبدالله ؑ، قال: إنّ زكريّا لمّا دعا ربّه أن يَهَب له ذَكَرًا، فنادتْه الملائكة بما نادَتْهُ به، أحبّ أن يعلم أنّ ذلك الصوت من الله، أوحى إليه: أنّ آية ذلك أن يُمسِك لسانه عن الكلام ثلاثة أيّام. قال: فلمّا أَمسَك لسانه، ولم يتكلّم، علِم أنّه لا يَقْدِر على ذلك إلاّ الله، وذلك قول الله: ﴿رَبِّ اجْعَلْ لِي آيَةً قَالَ آيَتُكَ أَلَّا تُكَلِّمَ النَّاسَ ثَلَاثَةَ أَيَّامٍ إِلَّا رَمْزًا﴾.

45. From Ḥammād, from whoever narrated it to him, from one of the two [Muḥammad al-Bāqir or Jaʿfar al-Ṣādiq] that he said, 'When Zakariyyā asked his Lord to grant him a son, God granted him Yaḥyā, [the news of which] astonished him, so he said, ﴾ *'My Lord, give me a sign.' 'Your sign,'* [*the angel said,*] *'is that you will not communicate with anyone for three days, except by gestures.'* ﴿ So he used to motion with his head, and that is gesturing.' [3:41]

46. From Ismāʿīl al-Juʿfī, from Abū Jaʿfar عليه السلام: ﴾ *He will be noble and chaste* ﴿ – chaste meaning abstaining from women, ﴾ *and a prophet, one of the righteous.* ﴿ [3:39]

47. From Ḥusayn b. Aḥmad[11], on his father's authority, from Abū ʿAbd Allāh عليه السلام. He said, 'I heard him say, "Obedience to God is to serve Him on the earth, and of this service there is nothing equivalent to prayer; hence the reason why the angels called out to Zakariyyā while he was engaged in prayer in the sanctuary."' [3:39]

48. From al-Ḥakam b. ʿUtayba who narrated, 'I asked Abū Jaʿfar عليه السلام about God's verse in the Book: ﴾ *The angels said to Maryam: 'Maryam, God has chosen you and made you pure: He has truly chosen you above all women'* ﴿ and why He has chosen her twice, when a choice is in fact only the once.

So he said to me, "Ḥakam, this has both an interpretation as well as an inner meaning." So I said, "Then please interpret it for us – may God make you prosper."

He replied, "It means that He chose her specifically from the entire progeny of the chosen prophets and messengers; then He purified her birth inasmuch as her maternal and paternal ancestors were free from debauchery; and then he singled her out for what He mentions in the Qur'an: ﴾ *'Maryam, be devout to your Lord, prostrate yourself in worship, bow down with those who pray,'* ﴿ in gratitude to God. Then He tells His messenger Muḥammad ﷺ about this, informing him of what was unknown to him about the story of

11 Probably referring to Abū ʿAbd Allāh al-Ḥusayn b. Aḥmad al-Manqarī al-Tamīmī, an associate of Imam Mūsā al-Kāẓim. He is noted in the books of *rijāl* as someone who transmitted obscure traditions and is also described as weak (*ḍaʿīf*). See Ḥillī, *Khulāṣat al-aqwāl*, 338 (nr. 1333).

٤٥. عن حمّاد، عمَّن حدَّثه، عن أحدهما عليه السلام، قال: لمّا سأل زكريّا ربّه أن يَهبَ له ذَكَرًا، فوهب الله له يحيى، فدخله من ذلك، فقال: ﴿قَالَ رَبِّ اجْعَل لِّي آيَةً قَالَ آيَتُكَ أَلَّا تُكَلِّمَ النَّاسَ ثَلَاثَةَ أَيَّامٍ إِلَّا رَمْزًا﴾ فكان يُومئ برأسه، وهو الرَّمز.

٤٦. عن إسماعيل الجُعفي، عن أبي جعفر عليه السلام ﴿وَسَيِّدًا وَحَصُورًا﴾ والحَصُور: الذي يأبى النساء ﴿وَنَبِيًّا مِّنَ الصَّالِحِينَ﴾.

٤٧. عن حسين بن أحمد، عن أبيه، عن أبي عبد الله عليه السلام، قال: سَمِعتُه يقول: إنَّ طاعة الله خِدمته في الأرض، فليس شيءٌ من خدمته تَعْدِل الصلاة، فمن ثمَّ نادت الملائكة زكريا وهو قائم يصلّي في المحراب.

٤٨. عن الحَكَم بن عُتيبة، قال: سألتُ أبا جعفر عليه السلام عن قول الله في الكتاب: ﴿وَإِذْ قَالَتِ الْمَلَائِكَةُ يَا مَرْيَمُ إِنَّ اللَّهَ اصْطَفَاكِ وَطَهَّرَكِ وَاصْطَفَاكِ عَلَىٰ نِسَاءِ الْعَالَمِينَ﴾ اصطفاها مرّتين، والاصطفاء إنّما هو مرّةً واحدةً.

قال: فقال لي: يا حَكَم، إنّ لهذا تأويلاً وتفسيرًا. فقلت له: ففسّره لنا أبقاك الله. قال: يعني اصطفاه إيّاها أوّلاً من ذُريّة الأنبياء المُصْطَفين المرسلين، وطهّرها من أن يكون في ولادتها من آبائها وأُمّهاتها سِفاحُ، واصطفاها بهذا في القرآن ﴿يَا مَرْيَمُ اقْنُتِي لِرَبِّكِ وَاسْجُدِي وَارْكَعِي مَعَ الرَّاكِعِينَ﴾ شكرًا لله. ثمّ قال لنبيّه محمّد صلى الله عليه وآله يُخْبِره بما غاب عنه من خبَر مريم وعيسى عليهما السلام: يا محمّد ﴿ذَٰلِكَ مِنْ أَنبَاءِ الْغَيْبِ نُوحِيهِ إِلَيْكَ﴾ في مريم وابنها، وبما خصّهما الله به وفضّلهما وأكْرَمهما حيث قال: ﴿وَمَا كُنتَ

Maryam and 'Īsā, saying, ﴾*This is an account of things beyond your knowledge that We reveal to you* [*Muhammad*]﴿ about Maryam and her son, the disputes that involved them and how He distinguished them and honoured them, when He says: ﴾*you were not present among them*﴿ O Muḥammad – as in coming from the Lord of the angels – ﴾*when they cast lots to see which of them should take charge of Maryam*﴿ when she was taken from her father.' [3:42–44]

[In another narration from Ibn Khurrazād, [it says]: ﴾*which of them should take charge of Maryam*﴿ when she was taken from her parents, ﴾*you were not present with them*﴿ – O Muḥammad – ﴾*when they argued*﴿ about Maryam and the birth of her son 'Īsā, as to who would take charge of her and her son.

He narrated, 'I asked him, "May God make you prosper, who took charge of her then?"

He replied, "Have you not heard God's statement?" and quoted the verse.'

'Alī b. Mahziyār[12] in his narration added the following: ﴾*but when she gave birth, she said, 'My Lord! I have given birth to a girl' – God knew best what she had given birth to: the male is not like the female – 'I name her Maryam and I commend her and her offspring to Your protection from the rejected Satan'*﴿ – He narrated, 'I asked him, "Did Maryam menstruate like other women?" He replied, "Yes, she was a woman like any other."'

[In another narration with reference to: ﴾*When they cast lots to see which of them should take charge of Maryam*﴿, he said, 'They cast lots regarding her, and Zakariyyā drew the short straw and was given charge of her.'

Yazīd b. Rukāna[13] said that they drew lots concerning Ḥamza's daughter too, just as they had done in Maryam's case. He asked, 'May I be your ransom – did Ḥamza follow these practices and examples when they disputed about his daughter as they did with Maryam?' He replied, 'Yes.' Regarding: ﴾*He has truly chosen you above all women*﴿, he said, '[Above] the women of her day and age. Fāṭima, however – may peace be upon her – was the chief of all women of all time.'] [3:44–45]

---

12 Abū al-Ḥasan 'Alī b. Mahziyār al-Ahwāzī, a convert to Islam in his early youth and a reliable companion and narrator of the eighth, ninth and tenth Imams' traditions. See Ḥillī, *Khulāṣat al-aqwāl*, 175–6 (nr. 517); Khū'ī, *Mu'jam*, 13: 206–19 (nr. 8553)

13 We could not find any individual by this name in the major works of Shī'ī *rijāl*.

لَدَيْهِمْ ﴾ يا محمّد، يعني بذلك الربُّ الملائكة ﴿ إِذْ يُلْقُونَ أَقْلَامَهُمْ أَيُّهُمْ يَكْفُلُ مَرْيَمَ ﴾ حين أُيْتِمَت من أبيها.

وفي رواية أُخرى، عن ابن خُرّزاد ﴿ أَيُّهُمْ يَكْفُلُ مَرْيَمَ ﴾ حين أُيْتِمت من أبويها ﴿ وَمَا كُنْتَ لَدَيْهِمْ ﴾ يا محمّد ﴿ إِذْ يَخْتَصِمُونَ ﴾ في مريم عند ولادتها بعيسى عليه السلام أيّهم يَكْفُلها ويكفل ولدها.

قال: فقلتُ له: أبقاك الله، فمن كَفَّلها؟ فقال: أما تَسْمَع لقوله تعالى؟ الآية.

وزاد علي بن مهْزيار في حديثه ﴿ فَلَمَّا وَضَعَتْهَا قَالَتْ رَبِّ إِنِّي وَضَعْتُهَا أُنْثَى وَاللَّهُ أَعْلَمُ بِمَا وَضَعَتْ وَلَيْسَ الذَّكَرُ كَالْأُنْثَى وَإِنِّي سَمَّيْتُهَا مَرْيَمَ وَإِنِّي أُعِيذُهَا بِكَ وَذُرِّيَّتَهَا مِنَ الشَّيْطَانِ الرَّجِيمِ ﴾، قال: قلتُ: أكان يُصيب مريم ما يصيب النساء من الطَّمث؟ قال: نعم، ماكانت إلاّ امرأة من النساء.

وفي رواية أُخرى ﴿ إِذْ يُلْقُونَ أَقْلَامَهُمْ أَيُّهُمْ يَكْفُلُ مَرْيَمَ ﴾، قال: اسْتَهَمُوا عليها، فخرج سَهم زكريا، فكَفَّل بها.

وقال يزيد بن رُكانة: اخْتَصَمُوا في بنت حمزة، كما اخْتَصَمُوا في مريم. قال: قلتُ له: جُعِلت فداك، حمزة استنّ السُّنن والأمثال، كما اخْتَصَمُوا في مريم اخْتَصَمُوا في بنت حمزة؟ قال: نعم. ﴿ وَاصْطَفَاكِ عَلَى نِسَاءِ الْعَالَمِينَ ﴾، قال: نساء عالَمِيها.

49. From al-Hudhalī, from a man who said, "Īsā grew up and when he reached seven or eight years of age, he began to inform them about what they had been eating and what they were storing in their houses. He brought the dead back to life in front of their very eyes and cured the blind and the leper. He taught them the Torah, and God revealed the Injīl (Gospel) to him when He wanted to establish the proof against them.' [3:48]

50. From Muḥammad b. Abī 'Umayr, from whoever mentioned it without giving his source, citing one of the infallibles as having said, 'Some companions of 'Īsā عليه السلام asked him to bring a dead man back to life for them, so he took them to the grave of Sām, son of Nūḥ, and addressed him saying, "Rise, by the permission of God, O Sām, son of Nūḥ." Thereupon the grave split open. Then he repeated the words and it shook. He repeated the words yet again and Sām, son of Nūḥ, emerged from his grave. 'Īsā asked him, "Which would you prefer: to stay in there or to come back here?" He replied, "O Spirit of God, I would rather come back, for I have been experiencing the torture of death – or he might have said the burning pangs of death – in my body up until now."' [3:49]

51. From Abān b. Taghlib[14] who narrated, 'Abū 'Abd Allāh عليه السلام was asked, "Did 'Īsā, son of Maryam, ever bring anyone back to life after death long enough to be able to eat, earn, subsist and procreate again?"

He replied, "Yes. He once had a friend who was as close to him as a brother in faith, and 'Īsā would frequent him and stay with him. 'Īsā had been away from him for some time and went to pay him a visit and greet him. So his mother came out instead, and he inquired about him. She said to him, 'He has passed away, O Messenger of God.'

He asked her if she would like to see him, and she replied yes, so he said, 'Tomorrow, I will come back and bring him back to life for you, with God's permission.'

---

14 Abū Sa'īd Abān b. Taghlib b. Rabāḥ al-Raba'ī al-Bakrī al-Jurayrī (d. 141/758–9) was a leading figure of the Imāmī community in Medina and a high-ranking companion of the fourth, fifth and sixth Imams. He was instructed by the fifth Imam to preach and give legal verdicts (*fatwā*) in the Prophet's mosque at Medina. He was also an authority on the different recitations (*qirā'āt*) of the Qur'an. See Ḥillī, *Khulāṣat al-aqwāl*, 73–4 (nr. 119); Modarressi, *Tradition and Survival*, 107–116 (nr. 10).

٤٩. قال عليه السلام: وكانت فاطمة عليها السلام سيّدة نساء العالمين. عن الهُذَلي، عن رجل، قال: مَكَث عيسى عليه السلام حتّى بلغ سبع سنين، أو ثمان سنين، فجعل يُخْبِرهم بما يأْكُلُون وما يَدَّخِرون في بيوتهم، فأقام بين أظهرهم يُحيي الموتى، ويبرئ الأكمه والأبرص، ويُعَلِّمهم التوراة، وأنزل الله عليه الإنجيل، لما أراد الله عليهم حُجَّة.

٥٠. عن محمّد بن أبي عمير، عمّن ذكره، عمّن رَفَعه، قال: إنَّ أصحاب عيسى عليه السلام سألوه أن يُحيي لهم ميتًا، قال: فأتى بهم إلى قبر سام بن نُوح، فقال له: قُم بإذن الله يا سام بن نُوح. قال: فانشقَّ القبر، ثمّ أعاد الكلام فتحرَّك، ثمّ أعاد الكلام فخرج سام بن نُوح.

فقال له عيسى عليه السلام: أيُّهما أحبُّ إليك، تبقى أو تعود؟ قال: فقال: يا رُوح الله، بل أعود، إنّي لأجد حُرْقة الموت — أو قال: لَذْعَة الموت — في جوفي إلى يومي هذا.

٥١. عن أبان بن تَغْلِب قال: سُئِل أبوعبدالله عليه السلام: هل كان عيسى بن مريم أحيا أحدًا بعد موته حتّى كان له أُكُلٌ ورِزقٌ ومُدَّةٌ وولد؟

قال: فقال: نعم، إنّه كان له صديقٌ مؤاخٍ له في الله، كان عيسى عليه السلام يمُرّ به فينْزِل عليه، وإنَّ عيسى عليه السلام غاب عنه حينًا، ثمّ مرّ به ليُسلم عليه، فخَرَجَتْ إليه أُمّه لتُسَلّم، فسألها عنه، فقالت أُمُّه: مات يا رسول الله.

فقال لها: أتحبّين أن تريه؟ قالت: نعم. قال لها: إذا كان غدًا أتيتك حتّى أُحييه لكِ بإذن الله.

On the morrow, he came and said to her, 'Come with me to his grave.' So they set off together until they reached his grave. Īsā ﷺ stood and supplicated God and the grave burst open, and her son came out alive. When his mother saw him and he saw her, they wept together, and 'Īsā ﷺ was moved with compassion towards them, so he asked him, 'Would you like to stay with your mother in this world?'

He replied, 'O Messenger of God, to live here for a lifetime with food and sustenance, or without sufficient time, food or sustenance?'

So 'Īsā replied, 'Yes, with food and sustenance, and a lifespan of twenty years during which you will get married and have children.'

He said, 'In that case, yes.'

So 'Īsā ﷺ sent him with his mother, and he lived for twenty years and had children."' [3:49]

52. From Muḥammad al-Ḥalabī, from Abū 'Abd Allāh ﷺ who narrated, 'There was a span of four hundred years between Dāwūd and 'Īsā b. Maryam, and 'Īsā's Law (*sharī'a*) was naught except that he too had been sent to proclaim the unity and pure worship of the One God – the same as what Nūḥ, Ibrāhīm and Mūsā had been entrusted with. God revealed the Gospel to him and took the covenant from him just as he had done with the rest of the prophets before him. He made it a law within the scripture that he ought to establish the prayer and the religion, to enjoin good and forbid evil, to prohibit the forbidden and allow what was lawful. He also revealed in the Gospel warnings, parables and generic penalties, without stipulating laws of retribution, legal boundaries, and laws of inheritance therein. He also revealed to him a dispensation which was lighter than that which He had previously revealed to Mūsā ﷺ in the Torah, and this is the significance of God's verse when 'Īsā b. Maryam addresses the Children of Israel, saying: ﴿ *and to make some things lawful to you which used to be forbidden.* ﴾ 'Īsā also commanded the believers who were with him and who followed him to believe in both the constitution of the Torah as well as the Gospel.' [3:50]

53. From Abū 'Umayr, from one of our associates, from a man who narrated it from Abū 'Abd Allāh ﷺ who said, 'He [i.e. God] raised 'Īsā b. Maryam up to Himself wearing a heavy cloak made of wool spun, knitted and woven by

فلمّا كان من الغد أتاها، فقال لها: انطلقي معي إلى قبره، فانطلقا حتّى أتيا قبره، فوقف عيسى عليه السلام، ثمّ دعا الله، فانفرج القبر، وخرج ابنها حيًّا، فلمّا رأته أمّه ورآها بكيا، فرحمهما عيسى عليه السلام. فقال له: أتُحِبّ أن تبقى مع أُمّك في الدنيا؟ قال: يا رسول الله، بأكل وبرِزْقٍ ومُدّة، أو بغير مدّةٍ ولا رِزْقٍ ولا أكل؟ فقال له عيسى عليه السلام: بل برِزْقٍ وأكل ومُدّة، تُعمّر عشرين سنة، وتُزوّج ويُولَد لك، قال: فنعم إذاً، قال: فدفعه عيسى عليه السلام إلى أُمّه، فعاش عشرين سنة، وولد له.

٥٢. عن محمّد الحلبيّ، عن أبي عبدالله عليه السلام، قال: كان بين داود وعيسى بن مريم عليه السلام أربعمائة سنة، وكان شريعة عيسى عليه السلام أنّه بُعِث بالتوحيد والإخلاص، وبما أوصى به نوح وإبراهيم وموسى عليهما السلام، وأُنزِل عليه الإنجيل، وأُخِذ عليه الميثاق الذي أُخِذ على النبيّين، وشُرّع له في الكتاب إقام الصلاة مع الدين، والأمر بالمعروف، والنهي عن المنكر، وتحريم الحرام، وتحليل الحلال، وأُنزِل عليه في الإنجيل مواعظ وأمثال وحدود، ليس فيها قِصاص، ولا أحكام حُدود، ولا فرض مواريث، وأُنزل عليه تخفيف ما كان نزل على موسى عليه السلام في التوراة، وهو قول الله تعالى في الذي قال عيسى بن مريم لبني إسرائيل: ﴿وَلِأُحِلَّ لَكُم بَعْضَ الَّذِي حُرِّمَ عَلَيْكُمْ﴾ وأمر عيسى عليه السلام مَن معه ممّن اتّبعه من المؤمنين أن يُؤمنوا بشريعة التوراة والإنجيل.

Maryam. When he reached the heavens he was told: "O ʿĪsā, cast the adornment of this world away from yourself."' [3:55]

54. From Ḥarīz, from Abū ʿAbd Allāh عليه السلام who narrated, 'The Commander of the Faithful عليه السلام was once asked about his [i.e. Prophet ʿĪsā's] virtues, so he mentioned some of them. Then they asked him to continue, so he said, "Once, two of the priests among the Christians of Najrān came to the Messenger of God صلى الله عليه وآله and were talking to him about ʿĪsā; so God revealed the verse: ﴾*In God's eyes ʿĪsā is just like Ādam: He created him from dust, said to him, 'Be', and he was.*﴿ Then the Prophet صلى الله عليه وآله entered [the designated area] holding ʿAlī by the hand, and al-Ḥasan, al-Ḥusayn and Fāṭima. Then he went outside and lifted his hands up to the sky, fingers spread, and called them to invoke God's rejection on the liars."

Abū Jaʿfar عليه السلام continued, "This is the way he invokes God's rejection – by interlacing one hand with the other, and raising them both to the sky. When the two priests saw him doing that, one said to the other: 'By God, if he is indeed a prophet then we will most definitely perish. If he is not, however, then his people will suffice against us; so they desisted from the contest and left.'"' [3:59]

55. From Muḥammad b. Saʿīd al-Azdī,[15] from Mūsā b. Muḥammad b. Riḍā, from his brother, from Abū al-Ḥasan عليه السلام that he said regarding the verse: ﴾*say, 'Come, let us gather our sons and your sons, our women and your women, ourselves and yourselves, and let us pray earnestly and invoke God's rejection on those of us who are lying'*﴿ – 'Were he to have himself said, "Come, let us invoke God's rejection on you," they would not have agreed to the contest of invoking God's rejection on the liars; but because they knew that His Messenger was only relaying the message from Him, he could not possibly be lying.' [3:61]

56. From Abū Jaʿfar al-Aḥwal[16] who narrated, 'Abū ʿAbd Allāh عليه السلام asked, "What do the Quraysh say regarding the *khums* [income tax prescribed in the

---

15 Some sources quote it as al-Urdunī.

16 Abū Jaʿfar al-Aḥwal, whose reliability has not been conclusively established in the works of Shīʿī *rijāl*. See Khūʾī, *Muʿjam*, 22:95 (nr. 14046).

٥٣. عن أبي عمير، عن بعض أصحابنا، عن رجل حدّثه عن أبي عبد الله عليه السلام، قال: رُفِع عيسى بن مريم عليه السلام بِمِدْرَعة صُوفٍ من غزل مريم عليها السلام، ومن نَسْج مريم، ومن خياطة مريم، فلمّا انتهى إلى السماء نُودي: يا عيسى، ألق عنك زينة الدُّنيا.

٥٤. عن حَرِيز، عن أبي عبد الله عليه السلام، قال: إنّ أمير المؤمنين عليه السلام سُئِل عن فضائله، فذكر بعضها، ثمّ قالوا له، زِدنا. فقال: إنّ رسول الله صلى الله عليه وآله أتاه حَبْران من أحبار النصارى، من أهل نجران، فتكلّما في أمر عيسى عليه السلام، فأنزل الله تعالى هذه الآية ﴿إِنَّ مَثَلَ عِيسَىٰ عِندَ اللَّهِ كَمَثَلِ آدَمَ﴾ إلى آخر الآية، فدخل رسول الله صلى الله عليه وآله فأخذ بيد عليّ والحسن والحسين وفاطمة عليهم السلام، ثمّ خرج ورفع كفّه إلى السماء، وفرّج بين أصابعه، ودعاهم إلى المُبَاهَلة.

قال: وقال أبو جعفر عليه السلام، وكذلك المُبَاهَلة، يُشَبّك يده في يده يرفعهما إلى السماء، فلمّا رآه الحَبْران قال أحدهما لصاحبه: والله لئن كان نبيًا لنهلِكنّ، وإن كان غير نبيّ كَفَانا قومه، فكفّا وانْصَرَفا.

٥٥. عن محمّد بن سعيد الأزدي، عن موسى بن محمّد بن الرضا، عن أخيه أبي الحسن عليه السلام، أنّه قال في هذه الآية ﴿فَقُلْ تَعَالَوْا نَدْعُ أَبْنَاءَنَا وَأَبْنَاءَكُمْ وَنِسَاءَنَا وَنِسَاءَكُمْ وَأَنفُسَنَا وَأَنفُسَكُمْ ثُمَّ نَبْتَهِلْ فَنَجْعَل لَّعْنَتَ اللَّهِ عَلَى الْكَاذِبِينَ﴾ ولو قال: تَعَالَوا نَبْتَهِل فَنَجْعَل لَعْنَةَ الله عليكم، لم يَكُونوا يُجيبون للمُبَاهَلَة، وقد علِم أنّ نبيّه مُؤدٍّ عنه رسالته، وما هو من الكاذبين.

Qurʾan)]?" I replied, "They allege that it belongs to them." He said, "By God, they have not been just to us. If there were to be a mutual invocation of God's rejection they would use us for their own gain, and if there is a contest they use us to win it, and yet they deem themselves to be equal to us."' [3:61]

57. From al-Aḥwal, from Abū ʿAbd Allāh عليه السلام. He narrated, 'I told him about something that people were querying, so he said, "Tell them: the Quraysh claim that they are the close relatives who are entitled to the battle gains (*al-anfāl*), so we say to them, 'The Messenger of God ﷺ did not call anyone to contend with the enemy on the day of Badr save for the People of his Household; and in the invocation of God's rejection upon the liars he brought ʿAlī, al-Ḥasan, al-Ḥusayn and Fāṭima, upon whom be peace. So they want us to do the hard work and reap the benefits for themselves?!'"' [3:61]

58. From al-Mundhir who said, "Alī عليه السلام narrated, "When this verse was revealed: ﴾*Come, let us gather our sons and your sons, our women and your women, ourselves and yourselves, and let us pray earnestly and invoke God's rejection on those of us who are lying*﴿, he [i.e. the Messenger of God] took ʿAlī, Fāṭima and their two sons, upon them be peace, by the hand. On seeing this a man from among the Jews exclaimed, 'Do not do it, otherwise a grave calamity will befall you.' However, they did not pay heed to him."' [3:61]

59. From ʿĀmir b. Saʿd[17] who said, 'Muʿāwiya once asked my father [Saʿd b. Abī Waqqāṣ], "What is stopping you from cursing Abū Turāb [i.e. ʿAlī b. Abī Ṭālib]?" He replied, "Three things that I have narrated[18] from the Prophet ﷺ – when the verse of mutual-cursing (*mubāhila*) was revealed: ﴾*Come, let us gather our sons and your sons, our women and your women, ourselves and yourselves, and let us pray earnestly and invoke God's rejection on those of us who are lying*﴿ – the Messenger of God ﷺ took ʿAlī by the hand, along with Fāṭima, al-Ḥasan and al-Ḥusayn, peace be upon them, and said, 'These are my family.'"' [3:61]

---

17 ʿĀmir b. Saʿd b. Abī Waqqāṣ (d. 96/714–15), a member of the generation of successors (*tābiʿī*) and prominent narrator of the Prophet's traditions in Sunnī *ḥadīth* collections.

18 ʿAllāma al-Majlisī in his *Biḥār al-anwār* quotes this as 'I have seen', which is probably the more accurate version.

٥٦. عن أبي جعفر الأحول، قال: قال أبو عبد الله عليه السلام: ما تقول قريش في الخُمس؟ قال: قلت: تَزْعُم أنَّه لها. قال: ما أنصفونا، والله لو كان مُبَاهَلَةً ليُبَاهلنّ بنا، ولئن كان مُبارزةً ليُبَارِزنّ بنا، ثمّ نكون وهم على سَواء؟!

٥٧. عن الأحول، عن أبي عبد الله عليه السلام، قال: قلتُ له عليه السلام شيئًا ممّا أنكرته الناس، فقال: قل لهم: إنّ قُريشًا قالوا: نحنُ أُولوا القُربى الذين هم لهم الغَنِيمة. فقل لهم: كان رسول الله صلى الله عليه وآله لم يَدْعُ للبِراز يوم بدرٍ غير أهل بيته، وعند المُبَاهلَة جاء بعلي والحسن والحسين وفاطمة عليهم السلام، أفيكون لنا المُرّ، ولهم الحُلو؟!

٥٨. عن المُنْذِر، قال: حدّثنا عليّ عليه السلام، قال: لمّا نزلت هذه الآية ﴿فَقُلْ تَعَالَوْا نَدْعُ أَبْنَاءَنَا وَأَبْنَاءَكُمْ﴾ الآية، قال: أخذ بيد عليّ وفاطمة وابنيهما عليهم السلام، فقال رجل من اليهود: لا تَفْعَلُوا فيُصيبكم عَنَت فلم يراعوه.

٥٩. عن عامر بن سعد، قال: قال معاوية لأبي: ما يمنعك أن تَسُبَّ أبا تراب؟ قال: لِثَلاثٍ رويتهنّ عن النبي صلى الله عليه وآله، لمّا نزلت آية المُبَاهلة ﴿تَعَالَوْا نَدْعُ أَبْنَاءَنَا وَأَبْنَاءَكُمْ﴾ الآية، أخذ رسول الله صلى الله عليه وآله بيد عليّ وفاطمة والحسن والحسين عليهم السلام قال: هؤلاء أهلي.

60. From ʿUbayd Allāh al-Ḥalabī[19], from Abū ʿAbd Allāh عليه السلام who narrated, ʻThe Commander of the Faithful عليه السلام said, "﴾*Ibrāhīm was neither a Jew nor a Christian.*﴿ He was neither a Jew praying towards the west, nor a Christian praying towards the east. Rather he was an upright Muslim, and he was on the same creed as Muḥammad صلى الله عليه وآله."' [3:67]

61. From ʿUmar b. Yazīd, from Abū ʿAbd Allāh عليه السلام. He narrated, ʻI asked him, "By God, are you really from the family of Muḥammad?"'

He said, ʻI asked him again, "May I be your ransom – from their very selves?"

He replied, "Yes, by God, from their very own selves" – and he repeated this three times. Then he turned to look at me and said to me, "O ʿUmar, God says: ﴾*The people who are closest to Ibrāhīm are those who truly follow his ways, this Prophet, and* [*true*] *believers – God is close to* [*true*] *believers.*﴿' [3:68]

62. From ʿAlī b. al-Nuʿmān[20], from Abū ʿAbd Allāh عليه السلام who said regarding the verse: ﴾*The people who are closest to Ibrāhīm are those who truly follow his ways, this Prophet, and* [*true*] *believers – God is close to* [*true*] *believers*﴿, ʻThese are the Imams and their followers.' [3:68]

63. From Abū al-Ṣabbāḥ al-Kinānī who narrated, ʻI heard Abū ʿAbd Allāh عليه السلام say regarding God's verse: ﴾*The people who are closest to Ibrāhīm are those who truly follow his ways, this Prophet, and* [*true*] *believers – God is close to* [*true*] *believers*﴿, "By God, ʿAlī is on the creed and path of Ibrāhīm, and you are the closest of people to him."' [3:68]

---

19 Abū ʿAlī ʿUbayd Allāh b. ʿAlī b. Abī Shuʿba al-Ḥalabī, along with his brothers and his father ʿAlī b. Abī Shuʿba, belonged to a noble family of loyalists renowned for their support and fidelity toward the Imams of the Ahl al-Bayt all the way back to their grandfather Abū Shuʿba, who narrated the traditions of Imams al-Ḥasan and al-Ḥusayn. ʿUbayd Allāh in particular is credited with the accolade of having been the first historical personage to author a book in the Shīʿī school of thought. This book is claimed to have been read out aloud in the presence of the sixth Imam Jaʿfar al-Ṣādiq, who praised it highly and approved of its narrations with some corrections. See Ḥillī, *Khulāṣat al-aqwāl*, 203 (nr. 644); Modarressi, *Tradition and Survival*, 380–2 (nr. 204).

20 Abū al-Ḥasan ʿAlī b. al-Nuʿmān al-Aʿlam al-Nakhaʿī, a reliable narrator of the eighth Imam's traditions and a leading scholar of his day. See Ḥillī, *Khulāṣat al-aqwāl*, 180 (nr. 536).

٦٠. عن عبيد الله الحلبي، عن أبي عبدالله عليه السلام، قال: قال أمير المؤمنين عليه السلام: ﴿مَا كَانَ إِبْرَاهِيمُ يَهُودِيًّا وَلَا نَصْرَانِيًّا﴾ لا يهوديًا يُصلّي إلى المغرب، ولا نصرانيًا يُصلّي إلى المشرق ﴿وَلَٰكِن كَانَ حَنِيفًا مُّسْلِمًا﴾ يقول: كان على دين محمّد صلى الله عليه وآله وسلم.

٦١. عن عمر بن يزيد، عن أبي عبدالله عليه السلام، قال: قال: أنتم والله من آل محمّد.

قال: فقلت: جُعلت فداك، من أنفسهم؟

قال: من أنفسهم والله - قالها ثلاثًا - ثمّ نظر إليّ فقال لي: يا عمر، إنّ الله يقول: ﴿إِنَّ أَوْلَى النَّاسِ بِإِبْرَاهِيمَ لَلَّذِينَ اتَّبَعُوهُ وَهَٰذَا النَّبِيُّ وَالَّذِينَ آمَنُوا وَاللَّهُ وَلِيُّ الْمُؤْمِنِينَ﴾.

٦٢. عن عليّ بن النُّعمان، عن أبي عبدالله عليه السلام، في قوله تعالى: ﴿إِنَّ أَوْلَى النَّاسِ بِإِبْرَاهِيمَ لَلَّذِينَ اتَّبَعُوهُ وَهَٰذَا النَّبِيُّ وَالَّذِينَ آمَنُوا وَاللَّهُ وَلِيُّ الْمُؤْمِنِينَ﴾، قال: هم الأئمّة وأتباعهم.

٦٣. عن أبي الصبّاح الكِناني، قال: سَمِعتُ أبا عبدالله عليه السلام يقول في قول الله تعالى: ﴿إِنَّ أَوْلَى النَّاسِ بِإِبْرَاهِيمَ لَلَّذِينَ اتَّبَعُوهُ وَهَٰذَا النَّبِيُّ وَالَّذِينَ آمَنُوا وَاللَّهُ وَلِيُّ الْمُؤْمِنِينَ﴾، ثمّ قال: عليّ والله على دين إبراهيم ومِنهاجه، وأنتم أولى الناس به.

64. From 'Alī b. Maymūn al-Ṣā'igh Abū al-Akrād[21], from 'Abd Allāh b. Abī Ya'fūr who narrated, 'I heard Abū 'Abd Allāh عليه السلام say, "There are three types of people to whom God will neither look on the Day of Resurrection nor cleanse, and they shall have an agonizing torment: one who wrongfully claims the Imamate designated by God; one who rebels against an Imam designated by God; and one who declares that so and so can be counted within the fold of Islam."' [3:77]

65. From Abū Ḥamza al-Thumālī, from 'Alī b. al-Ḥusayn عليه السلام who said, 'There are three types of people to whom God will neither speak nor look at nor cleanse of their sins on the Day of Resurrection, and they shall have an agonizing torment: the one who rebels against an Imam designated by God; the one who alleges to be an Imam without designation from God; and the one who wrongfully declares that so and so can be counted within the fold of Islam.' [3:77]

66. From Isḥāq b. Abī Hilāl[22] who narrated, "Alī عليه السلام said, "Shall I tell you of the worst type of fornication?" They replied, "Yes, O Commander of the Faithful." He said, "It is the married woman who cheats on her husband, then imposes the child [resulting from her fornication] on her husband. God will neither speak to, nor look at, nor cleanse such a woman, and she will have an agonizing torment."' [3:77]

67. From Muḥammad al-Ḥalabī who narrated, 'Abū 'Abd Allāh عليه السلام said, "There are three types of people whom God will neither look at on the Day of Resurrection nor cleanse of their sins, and they will have an agonizing torment: the man whose wife fornicates with his knowledge of it; the man of obscene and vulgar speech and character who encourages the same; and the man who begs from people whilst hoarding riches."' [3:77]

---

21 Abū al-Ḥasan (=Abū al-Akrād) 'Alī b. Maymūn al-Ṣā'igh, originally of Kufa, narrated traditions from the sixth and seventh Imams. His reliability however is uncertain among the authors of Shī'a *rijāl*. See Ḥillī, *Khulāṣat al-aqwāl*, 180–81 (nr. 538).

22 Isḥāq b. Abī Hilāl al-Madā'inī, about whom there is scant information. See Khū'ī, *Mu'jam*, 3:196 (nr. 1121).

٦٤. عن عليّ بن ميمون الصائغ أبي الأكراد، عن عبد الله بن أبي يَعْفُور، قال: سَمِعتُ أبا عبد الله ﵇ يقول: ثلاثة لا يَنْظُر الله إليهم يوم القيامة، ولا يُزكّيهم، ولهم عذاب أليم: من ادَّعي إمامةً من الله ليست له، ومن جَحَد إماماً من الله، ومن قال: إنَّ لفلان وفلان في الإسلام نصيباً.

٦٥. عن أبي حمزة الثُّمالي، عن عليّ بن الحسين عليهما السلام، قال: ثلاثة لا يُكلّمهم الله يوم القيامة، ولا يَنْظُر إليهم، ولا يُزكّيهم ولهم عذاب أليم: من جَحد إماماً من الله، أو ادّعى إماماً من غير الله، أو زَعَم أنَّ لفلان وفلان في الإسلام نصيباً.

٦٦. عن إسحاق بن أبي هلال، قال: قال عليّ ﵇: ألا أُخبركم بأكبر الزِّنا؟ قالوا: بلى يا أمير المؤمنين. قال: هي المرأة تَفْجُر ولها زوج، فتأتي بولد فتُلْزِمه زوجها، فتلك التي لا يُكَلّمها الله، ولا يَنْظُر إليها، ولا يُزكّيها، ولها عذاب أليم.

٦٧. عن محمّد الحلبي، قال: قال أبو عبد الله ﵇: ثلاثة لا يَنْظُر الله إليهم يوم القيامة، ولا يزكّيهم ولهم عذابٌ أليم: الدَّيُّوث من الرجال والفاحش المتُفَحّش، والذي يسأل الناس وفي يَدِه ظَهْر غِنى.

68. From Abū Ḥamza, from Abū Jaʿfar عليه السلام who said, 'There are three types of people to whom God will neither speak nor look at nor cleanse on the Day of Resurrection, and they shall have an agonizing torment: the fornicating old man; the haughty beggar and the overbearing king.' [3:77]

69. From al-Sakūnī, from Jaʿfar b. Muḥammad عليه السلام, on authority of his father عليه السلام who narrated, 'The Messenger of God ﷺ said, "There are three types of people whom God will neither look at nor cleanse on the Day of Resurrection, and they shall have an agonizing torment: the one who trails his garment on the floor in pompousness; the trader who falsely embellishes his wares by lying; and the man who comes to you pretending to bare his soul while his heart is full of deceit."' [3:77]

70. From Abū Dharr, from the Prophet ﷺ that he said, 'There will be three types of people on the Day of Resurrection whom God will neither speak to nor cleanse of their sins, and they will have an agonizing torment.' I asked, 'Who are these failed losers?' He replied, 'The one who trails his garment pompously, the one who makes others feel obliged to him, and the one who only sells his wares through lies and false claims' – he repeated these three times. [3:77]

71. From Salmān who said, 'Three types of people will not be looked at by God on the Day of Resurrection: the fornicating old man; the haughty and pompous beggar; and the man who swears false oaths over his wares [to sell them] – he never makes a single transaction without a false claim.' [3:77]

72. From Abū Maʿmar al-Saʿdī[23] who narrated, "ʿAlī b. Abī Ṭālib عليه السلام said regarding the verse: ﴾*God will neither speak to them nor look at them on the Day of Resurrection*﴿, "It means He will not look at them compassionately, i.e. He will not have mercy on them. An Arab man would say to a chief or a king: you do not look at us, and that would mean you do not treat us well. This is the kind of look which God has towards His creatures."' [3:77]

23 We were unable to identify this individual in the books of Shīʿa *rijāl*.

٦٨. عن أبي حمزة، عن أبي جعفر عليه السلام، قال: ثَلاثة لا يُكلّمهم الله يوم القيامة، ولا يَنْظُر إليهم، ولا يُزَكّيهم، ولهم عذابٌ أليم: شيخٌ زانٍ، ومُقِلٌّ مُختَالٌ، ومَلِكٌ جبّار.

٦٩. عن السّكوني، عن جعفر بن محمّد، عن أبيه عليهما السلام، قال: قال رسول الله صلى الله عليه وآله وسلم: ثَلاثة لا يَنْظُر إليهم يوم القيامة، ولا يُزكّيهم، ولهم عذابٌ أليم: المُرخي ذَيْلَه من العَظَمة، والمُزَكّي سِلعَتَه بالكَذِب، ورجلٌ استقبلك بودِّ صدره، فيُواري قلبه مُمتلئ غِشّاً.

٧٠. عن أبي ذرّ رحمه الله، عن النبي صلى الله عليه وآله وسلم أنّه قال: ثَلاثة لا يُكلّمهم الله يوم القيامة، ولا يُزكّيهم، ولهم عذابٌ أليم. قلت: مَن هم، خابوا وخَسِروا؟ قال: المُسْبِل والمَنّان، والمُنْفِق سِلعَتَه بالحَلْف الكاذب، أعادها ثَلاثاً.

٧١. عن سلمان رحمه الله، قال: ثَلاثة لا يَنْظُر الله إليهم يوم القيامة: الأَشْمط الزّان، ورجُل مُفْلِسٌ مَرِحٌ مُخْتَالٌ، ورجل اتَّخذ يمينه بِضاعةً، فلا يشتري إلاّ بيمين، ولا يبيع إلاّ بيمين.

٧٢. عن أبي مَعْمَر السَّعدي، قال: قال عليّ بن أبي طالب عليه السلام، في قوله تعالى: ﴿وَلَا يَنظُرُ إِلَيْهِمْ يَوْمَ الْقِيَامَةِ﴾ يعني لا يَنْظُر إليهم بخيرٍ، لمن لا يَرْحمهم، وقد يقول العرب للرجل السيّد أو للمَلِك، لا تَنْظُر إلينا، يعني أنّك لا تُصيبنا بخَير، وذلك النَّظَر من الله إلى خَلقِهِ.

73. From Ḥabīb al-Sijistānī[24] who narrated, 'I asked Abū Ja'far عليه السلام about God's verse: ﴿*God took a pledge from the prophets, saying, 'If, after I have bestowed Scripture and wisdom upon you, a messenger comes confirming what you have been given, you must believe in him and support him'*﴾ – how could Mūsā believe in 'Īsā and support him without even knowing him? And how would 'Īsā believe in Muḥammad ﷺ and support him without ever having met him?

So he replied, "Ḥabīb, indeed many verses of the Qur'an have been cast out of it – and only a few letters have been added to it by scribes who made mistakes or men who misunderstood; so this is one such misunderstanding.

Now read it: ﴿*God took a pledge from **the communities of** the prophets, saying, 'If, after I have bestowed Scripture and wisdom upon you, a messenger comes confirming what you have been given, you must believe in him and support him'*﴾ – this is how God revealed it, Ḥabīb.

By God, not a single community from the communities before Mūsā upheld their covenant with God towards any prophet that God sent down after their own. In fact, the community to which Mūsā was sent belied him when he came to them. Neither did they believe him nor did they support him, except for a few of them. The community of 'Īsā belied Muḥammad ﷺ and refused to believe in him or support him when he came to them, except a few of them. This very community rebelled against the pledge that the Messenger of God ﷺ made with them with regard to 'Alī b. Abī Ṭālib عليه السلام on the day that he appointed him over the people, established him and invited them to his authority (*walāya*) and his obedience during his lifetime. He personally made them bear witness to it despite themselves when there is no pledge more binding than the Messenger of God's statement concerning 'Alī b. Abī Ṭālib – but by God, they did not fulfil it; rather they defied and belied."' [3:81*]

74. From Bukayr who narrated, 'Abū Ja'far عليه السلام said, "When God took the pledge from our followers to adhere to our guardianship (*walāya*) whilst they were still in the sub-atomic realm and they made pledges attesting to His Lordship and Muḥammad's prophethood, God displayed His Imams to

24 Ḥabīb al-Sijistānī is said to have been a Khārijite originally, but later converted to Shī'ism. He was a companion of the fifth and sixth Imams. See Ḥillī, *Khulāṣat al-aqwāl*, 132 (nr. 351)

٧٣. عن حبيب السِّجستاني، قال: سألتُ أبا جعفر عليه السلام عن قول الله تعالى: ﴿وَإِذْ أَخَذَ اللَّهُ مِيثَاقَ النَّبِيِّينَ لَمَا آتَيْتُكُم مِّن كِتَابٍ وَحِكْمَةٍ ثُمَّ جَاءَكُمْ رَسُولٌ مُّصَدِّقٌ لِّمَا مَعَكُمْ لَتُؤْمِنُنَّ بِهِ وَلَتَنصُرُنَّهُ﴾ فكيف يُؤمِن موسى بعيسى ويَنْصُره ولم يُدرِكه، وكيف يُؤمِن عيسى بمحمّد صلى الله عليه وآله وسلم ويَنْصُره ولم يُدرِكه؟

فقال: يا حبيب، إنّ القرآن قد طُرح منه آي كثيرة، ولم يُزَد فيه إلا حُرُوف أخطأت بها الكَتَبة وتوَهَّمَتها الرجال، وهذا وَهْمٌ، فاقرأها ﴿وَإِذْ أَخَذَ اللَّهُ مِيثَاقَ ــ أُمَم ــ النَّبِيِّينَ لَمَا آتَيْتُكُم مِّن كِتَابٍ وَحِكْمَةٍ ثُمَّ جَاءَكُمْ رَسُولٌ مُّصَدِّقٌ لِّمَا مَعَكُمْ لَتُؤْمِنُنَّ بِهِ وَلَتَنصُرُنَّهُ﴾ هكذا أنزلها الله يا حبيب.

فوالله ما وفَتْ أُمّةٌ من الأمم التي كانت قبل موسى بما أخذ الله عليها من الميثاق لكُلّ نبيٍّ بعثه الله بعد نبيّها، ولقد كذّبت الأمّة الّتي جاءها موسى لمّا جاءها موسى، ولم يؤمنوا به، ولا نَصَرُوه، إلاّ القليل منهم، ولقد كذّبت أُمّة عيسى بمحمّد صلى الله عليه وآله وسلم، ولم يُؤمنوا به، ولا نصروه لمّا جاءها، إلاّ القليل منهم.

ولقد جَحَدت هذه الأُمّة بما أخَذَ عليها رسول الله صلى الله عليه وآله وسلم من المِيثاق لعليّ ابن أبي طالب عليه السلام يوم أقامه للناس ونَصَبه لهم ودعاهم إلى ولايته وطاعته في حياته وأشهدهم بذلك على أنفسهم، فأيّ ميثاق أوكد من قول رسول الله صلى الله عليه وآله وسلم في عليّ بن أبي طالب عليه السلام؟ فوالله ما وَفَوا به، بل جَحَدوا وكذّبوا.

٧٤. عن بُكَير، قال: قال: أبو جعفر عليه السلام: إنّ الله أخذ مِيثاق شيعتنا بالولاية لنا وهم ذَرٌّ، يوم أخذ الميثاق على الذّرّ بالإقرار له بالرّبوبية، ولمحمّد صلى الله عليه وآله وسلم بالنبوّة، وعَرَض الله على محمّد وآله

Muḥammad while they were still [in the form of shadowy] outlines, peace be upon him and his family." He continued, "He created them from the same clay as He created Ādam. He created the souls of our followers two thousand years before their bodies, when He showed them and the Messenger of God ﷺ introduced them to ʿAlī عليه السلام. And we can distinguish them from the tone of their speech." [3:81]

75. From Zurāra who narrated, 'I asked Abū Jaʿfar عليه السلام: "When God took pledges from humans in the sub-atomic realm and showed Himself to them, did they actually see Him?" He replied, "Yes, Zurāra. When they were particles before Him, He took pledges from them attesting to His Lordship over them and to Muḥammad's prophethood. Then He apportioned their decreed sustenance in the world and made them forget ever having seen Him while installing knowledge of Him in their hearts. So God must necessarily bring into this world whoever made the pledge with Him; and whoever then defies the pledge that he made attesting to Muḥammad, peace be upon him and his family, is not availed by his pledge attesting to God's Lordship. Whoever maintains his pledge attesting to Muḥammad عليه السلام is benefitted by his pledge to His Lord."' [3:81]

76. From Fayḍ b. Abī Shayba[25] who narrated, 'I heard Abū ʿAbd Allāh عليه السلام say after reciting this verse: ﴾ *God took a pledge from the prophets, saying, 'If, after I have bestowed Scripture and wisdom* [...] ﴿, [It was to the effect of]: "You must believe in the Messenger of God and you must support the Commander of the Faithful [ʿAlī b. Abī Ṭālib] عليه السلام." I exclaimed, "You must support the Commander of the Faithful?" He replied, "Yes, right from Ādam onwards. Every single prophet or messenger sent by God will be returned to the life of this world in order to fight with the Commander of the Faithful عليه السلام."' [3:81]

77. From Sallām b. al-Mustanīr, from Abū ʿAbd Allāh عليه السلام who said, 'You call yourselves by a title [i.e. "Commander of the Faithful"] which God did not designate for anyone except ʿAlī b. Abī Ṭālib, and whose true meaning has not even manifested itself yet.'

I asked, 'May I be your ransom, when will its true meaning be manifest?'

---

25 We could not find any individual by this name in the *rijāl* works.

السلام أئمّتَه الطّيبين وهم أظلّة، قال: وخلقهم من الطينة التي خَلَق منها آدم، قال: وخَلَق أرواح شيعتنا قبل أبدانهم بألفي عام، وعرض عليهم، وعرّفهم رسول الله ﷺ عليّاً عليه السلام، ونحن نَعْرِفهم في لَحْن القول.

٧٥. عن زُرارة، قال: قلتُ لأبي جعفر عليه السلام: أرأيت حين أخذ الله المِيثاق على الذَّرّ في صُلْب آدم فعرضهم على نفسهم، كانت مُعاينةً منهم له؟ قال: نعم يا زُرارة وهم ذَرٌّ بين يديه، وأخذ عليهم بذلك الميثاق بالربوبيّة له، ولمحمّد ﷺ بالنبوّة، ثمّ كَفَل لهم بالأرزاق، وأنساهم رؤيته، وأثبت في قلوبهم معرفته، فلابدّ من أن يُخْرِج الله إلى الدنيا كلّ مَن أخَذَ عليه المِيثاق، فمن جَحَد ممّا أخذ عليه المِيثاق لمحمّد عليه السلام وآله، لم يَنْفَعْه إقراره لربّه بالمِيثاق، ومَن لم يَجْحَد ميثاق محمّد وآله عليهم السلام نَفَعَه المِيثاق لربّه.

٧٦. عن فيض بن أبي شيبة، قال: سَمِعتُ أبا عبد الله عليه السلام يقول: وتلا هذه الآية ﴿وَإِذْ أَخَذَ اللهُ مِيثَاقَ النَّبِيِّينَ لَمَا آتَيْتُكُمْ مِنْ كِتَابٍ وَحِكْمَةٍ﴾ إلى آخر الآية، قال: لتُؤمنَنّ برسول الله ﷺ، ولتَنْصُرنّ أمير المؤمنين عليه السلام.

قلت: ولتَنْصُرنّ أمير المؤمنين! قال: نعم، من آدم فَهَلُمّ جرّاً، ولا يبعث الله نبيّاً ولا رسولاً إلاّ رُدّ إلى الدنيا حتّى يُقاتل بين يدَي أمير المؤمنين عليه السلام.

٧٧. عن سلاّم بن المُستنير، عن أبي عبد الله عليه السلام، لقد تَسَمّوا باسم ما سمّى الله به أحداً، إلاّ عليّ بن أبي طالب، وما جاء تأويله.

قلت: جُعِلت فداك، متى يجيئ تأويله؟

He replied, 'When he comes [back to life] God will gather all the prophets and believers before him so that they may support him as per the verse: ﴾*God took a pledge from the prophets, saying, 'If, after I have bestowed Scripture and wisdom upon you, a messenger comes confirming what you have been given, you must believe in him and support him. Do you affirm this and accept My pledge as binding on you?' They said, 'We do.' He said, 'Then bear witness and I too will bear witness.*﴿ On that day, the banner of the Messenger of God will be passed on to 'Alī b. Abī Ṭālib and he will be the Commander of all creation. All of creation will gather under his banner alone and he will be their chief, and that is the true meaning of it.' [3:81]

78. From 'Ammār b. Abī al-Aḥwaṣ[26], from Abū 'Abd Allāh عليه السلام, 'God, Blessed and most High, created two seas at the onset of creation: one sweet and fresh, and the other bitterly salty.

Then He took the clay intended for Ādam's creation from the sweet freshwater and dipped it in the briny water, making a shape out of dark mud resulting in the creation of Ādam. Then he took a lump of clay from Ādam's right shoulder and planted it in Ādam's loins, saying: "These will certainly go to Paradise."

Then He took a lump of clay from Ādam's left shoulder and planted it in Ādam's loins, saying, "These will certainly enter the Fire, and I cannot be taken to task nor questioned about what I do, but I reserve the right to alter My decree regarding them for any enmity towards these people, and they will be tested."'

Abū 'Abd Allāh continued, 'The people of the left protested against their Lord on that day while they were yet mere particles, saying, "Our Lord, why have You decreed our fate in the Fire, being the Equitable Judge that You are, before even having tested us and tried us with messengers, and before having ascertained our obedience or rebellion?"

God, Blessed and most High, replied, "I will inform you of the proof against you right now as regards obedience and rebellion, then see if you can still make excuses after you have been informed."'

---

26 Abū al-Yaqẓān 'Ammār b. Abī al-Aḥwaṣ al-Bakrī, a narrator of the fifth and sixth Imams' traditions. See Khū'ī, *Mu'jam*, 13:264–5 (nr. 8632).

قال: إذا جاء جمع الله أمامه النبيّين والمؤمنين حتّى يَنْصُروه، وهو قول الله تعالى: ﴿وَإِذْ أَخَذَ اللَّهُ مِيثَاقَ النَّبِيِّينَ لَمَا آتَيْتُكُم مِّن كِتَابٍ وَحِكْمَةٍ﴾ إلى قوله: ﴿وَأَنَا مَعَكُم مِّنَ الشَّاهِدِينَ﴾ فيومئذ تُدْفَع راية رسول الله ﷺ اللِّواء إلى عليّ ابن أبي طالب عليه السلام، فيكون أمير الخلائق كلِّهم أجمعين، يكون الخلائق كُلّهم تحت لوائه، ويكون هو أميرهم، فهذا تأويله.

٧٨. عن عمّار بن أبي الأحوص، عن أبي عبد الله عليه السلام، قال: أنّ الله تبارك وتعالى خَلَق في مُبتدأ الخَلْق بَحْرين، أحدهما عَذْب فُرات، والآخر مِلح أُجاج، ثمّ خَلَق تُربة آدم من البحر العَذْب الفُرات، ثمّ أجراه على البحر الأُجاج، فجعله حَمَأً مَسْنُونًا وهو خَلَق آدم.

ثمّ قَبَض قَبْضَةً من كَتِف آدم الأيمن، فَذَرأها في صُلب آدم، فقال: هؤلاء في الجنّة ولا أُبالي، ثمّ قَبَض قَبْضَةً من كَتِف آدم الأيسر، فَذَرأها في صُلب آدم، فقال: هؤلاء في النار ولا أُبالي، ولا أُسأل عمّا أفعل، ولي في هؤلاء البَدَاء بعد وفي هؤلاء، وهؤلاء سَيُبْتَلُون.

قال: أبو عبد الله عليه السلام: فاحتجّ يومئذ أصحاب الشمال وهم ذَرّ على خالقهم، فقالوا: يا ربّنا، لِمَ أوجبت لنا النار وأنت الحَكَم العَدْل من قبل أن تحتجّ علينا وتَبْلُونا بالرُّسل وتَعلَم طاعتنا لك ومَعْصِيتنا؟

فقال الله تبارك وتعالى: فأنا أُخبركم بالحُجَّة عليكم الآن في الطاعة والمعصية، والإعذار بعد الإخبار.

قال أبو عبد الله عليه السلام: فأوحى الله إلى مالك خازن النّار: أنْ مُر النّار تَشْهَق ثمّ تُخْرِج عُنُقًا منها، فَخَرَجت لهم، ثمّ قال الله لهم: ادْخُلوها طائعين، فقالوا: لا نَدْخلها طائعين.

Abū ʿAbd Allāh continued, ʿSo God commanded the gatekeeper of Hell to stoke the fire high and bring forth some of it, so it came forth. Then He told them to enter into it willingly, but they retorted, "We will not enter it willingly." So He said, "Enter it willingly or I will punish you by making you enter it forcefully." They said, "We would rather escape to You and discuss with You about why You have decreed it upon us, why You have made us the people of the left and how You expect us to enter it willingly. Why do You not start by making the people of the right enter it first so that You have treated us all equally."'

Abū ʿAbd Allāh عليه السلام continued, 'So He commanded the people of the right, still only particles before Him, saying, "Enter this Fire willingly." So they promptly rushed towards it and all entered into it, and God rendered it cold and safe for them, and took them out of it. Then God, Blessed and most High, called out to both the people of the right as well as the left: "Am I not your Lord?" The people of the right replied, "Of course, our Lord. We are Your inception and creation, and we willingly attest to You." The people of the left said, "Of course, our Lord. We are your inception and creation, reluctantly."

This is the meaning of God's verse: ﴾*Everyone in the heavens and earth submits to Him, willingly or unwillingly; they will all be returned to Him*﴿ – It is their attestation to God's Oneness.' [3:83]

79. From ʿUbāya al-Asadī[27] that he heard the Commander of the Faithful عليه السلام say: ﴾*Everyone in the heavens and earth submits to Him, willingly or unwillingly; they will all be returned to Him*﴿ – 'Has this happened yet?'

I replied, 'Yes, Commander of the Faithful.'

He retorted, 'No! By the One who holds my soul in His Hand, not until a woman can face an impediment and remain completely safe, neither fearing snake nor scorpion, nor anything else besides.' [3:83]

---

27 ʿUbāya b. Ribʿī al-Asadī, a companion and supporter of ʿAlī b. Abī Ṭālib about whom there is scant information. See Ḥillī, *Khulāṣat al-aqwāl*, 307 (nr. 1183).

ثمّ قال: ادْخُلوها طائعين أولأُعذّبنّكم بها كارهين. قالوا: إنّما هَرَبنا إليك منها، وحَاجَجْنَاك فيها حيث أوْجَبْتَها علينا، وصَيّرتنا من أصحاب الشمال، فكيف نَدْخُلها طائعين؟ ولكن ابدأ بأصحاب اليمين في دخولها كي تكون قد عَدَلْتَ فينا وفيهم.

قال أبو عبد الله عليه السلام: فأمَرَ أصحاب اليمين وهم ذَرّ بين يديه، فقال: ادْخُلوا هذه النار طائعين. قال: فطَفِقُوا يَتَبادَرُون في دُخُولها، فَوَلَجُوا فيها جميعًا، فصيّرها الله عليهم بَرْدًا وَسَلامًا، ثُمّ أخرجهم منها، ثُمّ إنّ الله تبارك وتعالى نادى في أصحاب اليمين وأصحاب الشمال: ألستُ بربّكم؟ فقال أصحاب اليمين: بلى يا ربَّنا، نحن بَريّتُك وخَلْقُك مُقِرّين طائعين، وقال أصحاب الشمال: بلى يا ربّنا، نحن بَريّتك وخَلْقُك كارهين.

وذلك قول الله تعالى: ﴿وَلَهُ أَسْلَمَ مَنْ فِي السَّمَاوَاتِ وَالأَرْضِ طَوْعًا وَكَرْهًا وَإِلَيْهِ يُرْجَعُونَ﴾، قال: تَوحيدهم لله تعالى.

٧٩. عن عباية الأسدي، أنّه سَمِع أمير المؤمنين عليه السلام يقول: ﴿وَلَهُ أَسْلَمَ مَنْ فِي السَّمَاوَاتِ وَالأَرْضِ طَوْعًا وَكَرْهًا وَإِلَيْهِ يُرْجَعُونَ﴾ أكان ذلك بعد؟

قلتُ: نعم يا أمير المؤمنين.

قال: كلاّ والّذي نفسي بيده حتّى تَدخُل المرأة بمن عذب آمنين لا يَخاف حيّةً ولا عقربًا فما سِوى ذلك.

80. From Ṣāliḥ b. Maytham[28] who narrated, 'I asked Abū Jaʿfar عليه السلام about God's verse: ﴿*Everyone in the heavens and earth submits to Him, willingly or unwillingly; they will all be returned to Him.*﴾ He said, "This is in response to when 'Alī عليه السلام said, 'I am the most justified of all people with respect to the verse: ﴿*They have sworn by God with their strongest oaths that He will not raise the dead to life. But He will – it is His binding promise, though most people do not realize it; in order to make clear for them what they have differed about and so that the disbelievers may realize that what they said was false.*﴾ (16:38–9)'"' [3:83]

81. From Rifāʿa b. Mūsā[29] who narrated, 'I heard Abū 'Abd Allāh عليه السلام recite: ﴿*Everyone in the heavens and earth submits to Him, willingly or unwillingly; they will all be returned to Him*﴾ and say, "When the Qā'im عليه السلام rises no spot on the earth will remain without the call, "There is no god but God and Muḥammad is the Messenger of God" therein."' [3:83]

82. From Ibn Bukayr who narrated, 'I asked Abū al-Ḥasan عليه السلام about His verse: ﴿*Everyone in the heavens and earth submits to Him, willingly or unwillingly; they will all be returned to Him.*﴾ He replied, "It has been revealed about the Qā'im عليه السلام who, when he will rise against the Jews, the Christians, the Sabians, the atheists, the apostates and the disbelievers in the far off corners of the Earth, he will show Islam to them. Those who submit willingly he will command to pray and give the alms, and all that is incumbent upon a Muslim as a duty towards God. As for those who refuse to submit he will behead them until none but monotheists will remain throughout the whole world."

I asked him, "May I be your ransom, surely there are too many people out there [to do that]." He replied, "When God wills something, He can make the many seem few, and the few numerous."' [3:83]

83. From Ḥanān b. Sadīr, on his father's authority who narrated, 'I asked Abū Jaʿfar عليه السلام, "Were the sons of Yaʿqūb prophets?" He replied, "No, they were

28 Ṣāliḥ b. Maytham, about whom there is scant information. See Ḥillī, *Khulāṣat al-aqwāl*, 169 (nr. 497).

29 Rifāʿa b. Mūsā al-Nakhkhās was a righteous and reliable transmitter of the sixth and seventh Imams' traditions. See Ḥillī, *Khulāṣat al-aqwāl*, 146 (nr. 408); Modarressi, *Tradition and Survival*, 360–1 (nr. 174).

٨٠. عن صالح بن مِيثم، قال: سألتُ أبا جعفر عليه السلام عن قول الله عزّ وجلّ: ﴿وَلَهُ أَسْلَمَ مَن فِي السَّمَاوَاتِ وَالأَرْضِ طَوْعًا وَكَرْهًا﴾، قال: ذلك حين يقول عليّ عليه السلام: أنا أولى الناس بهذه الآية ﴿وَأَقْسَمُوا بِاللهِ جَهْدَ أَيْمَانِهِمْ لاَ يَبْعَثُ اللهُ مَن يَمُوتُ بَلَى وَعْدًا عَلَيْهِ حَقًّا وَلَكِنَّ أَكْثَرَ النَّاسِ لاَ يَعْلَمُونَ﴾ إلى قوله: ﴿كَاذِبِينَ﴾.

٨١. عن رِفاعة بن موسى، قال: سَمِعتُ أبا عبد الله عليه السلام يقول: ﴿وَلَهُ أَسْلَمَ مَن فِي السَّمَاوَاتِ وَالأَرْضِ طَوْعًا وَكَرْهًا﴾، قال: إذا قام القائم عليه السلام لا تبقى أرض إلاّ نودي فيها بشهادة أن لا إله إلا الله، وأن محمّدًا رسول الله.

٨٢. عن ابن بُكير، قال: سألتُ أبا الحسن عليه السلام عن قوله تعالى: ﴿وَلَهُ أَسْلَمَ مَن فِي السَّمَاوَاتِ وَالأَرْضِ طَوْعًا وَكَرْهًا﴾. قال: أُنزِلت في القائم عليه السلام إذا خرج باليهود والنَّصارى والصَّابئين والزَّنادِقة وأهل الرِدَّة والكُفّار في شرق الأرض وغربها، فعَرَض عليهم الإسلام، فمن أسلم طوعًا أمره بالصلاة والزكاة، وما يُؤمر به المسلم ويجب لله عليه، ومَنْ لم يُسلم ضَرَب عُنُقَه حتى لا يبقى في المشارق والمغاب أحدٌ إلاّ وحّد الله تعالى.

قلت له: جُعِلت فداك، إنَّ الخلق أكثر من ذلك؟ فقال: إنّ الله إذا أراد أمرًا قلَّل الكثير، وكثَّر القليل.

٨٣. عن حَنَان بن سدير، عن أبيه، قال: قلت لأبي جعفر عليه السلام: هل كان وُلد يعقوب أنبياء؟ قال: لا، ولكنّهم كانوا أسباطًا، أولاد الأنبياء، لم يَكونوا يُفارقون الدُنيا إلا سُعَداء، تَابُوا وتَذَكَّروا ما صَنَعُوا.

tribes descended from the prophets. They left this world in a good state having repented and confessed to what they had done."' [3:84]

84. From Yūnus b. Ẓibyān, from Abū ʿAbd Allāh ﷺ who said, ﴾*None of you* ***believers will attain true piety unless you give away that which you cherish***﴿ – 'This is how he read it.' [3:92*]

85. From Mufaḍḍal b. ʿUmar who narrated, 'I entered the presence of Abū ʿAbd Allāh ﷺ one day with something that I placed before him. He asked, "What is this?" So I replied, "This is a gift from your adherents and your servants."

He said to me, "O Mufaḍḍal, I would not accept it for my own needs, but I only do so in order that they may be purified thereby." Then he added, "I have heard my father say, 'Whoever goes a whole year without gifting some of his wealth to us, however much or little it may be, God will not look at him on the Day of Resurrection unless God decides to pardon him for it.'"

Then he continued, "Mufaḍḍal, this is a duty that God has made incumbent upon our followers (*shīʿa*) in His Book when He says: ﴾*None of you* [*believers*] *will attain true piety unless you give out of what you cherish.*﴿ We are the piety, the righteousness, the path to guidance and the door of righteousness, and our supplication is never barred from God. Stick to that which has been made lawful to you and refrain from whatever is prohibited to you. Beware of asking any of the jurists about matters that do not concern you and anything which God has chosen to keep hidden from you."' [3:92]

86. From ʿAbd Allāh b. Abī Yaʿfūr who narrated, 'I asked Abū ʿAbd Allāh ﷺ about God's verse: ﴾*Except for what Isrāʾīl made unlawful for himself, all food was lawful to the Children of Isrāʾīl.*﴿ He replied, "Whenever Isrāʾīl[30] used to eat camel meat he would be gripped by pain in his side, so he forbade himself from consuming camel meat. This was before the revelation of the Torah. When the Torah was revealed he did not prohibit it, but he continued to refrain from eating it."' [3:93]

30 Isrāʾīl is another name for Prophet Yaʿqūb.

٨٤ . عن يُونس بن ظِبيان، عن أبي عبدالله عليه السلام، قال: ﴿لَن تَنَالُوا الْبِرَّ حَتَّىٰ تُنفِقُوا مِمَّا تُحِبُّونَ﴾ هكذا قرأها.

٨٥ . عن مُفضَّل بن عمر، دخلتُ على أبي عبدالله عليه السلام يومًا ومعي شيءٌ فَوَضَعْتُهُ بين يديه، فقال: ما هذا؟ فقلتُ: هذه صِلَة مواليك وعبيدك.

قال: فقال لي: يا مُفَضَّل، إنّي لأقبل ذلك، وما أقبله من حاجتي إليه، وما أقبله إلاّ ليزّكوا به. ثمّ قال: سَمِعتُ أبي يقول: مَن مَضَت له سنة لم يَصِلْنا من ماله، قَلَّ أو كثُر، لم يَنْظُر الله إليه يوم القيامة، إلاّ أن يعفو الله عنه.

ثمّ قال: يا مُفضَّل، إنّها فريضةٌ فرضها الله على شيعتنا في كتابه، إذ يقول: ﴿لَن تَنَالُوا الْبِرَّ حَتَّىٰ تُنفِقُوا مِمَّا تُحِبُّونَ﴾ فنحن البِرّ والتقوى، وسبيل الهدى، وباب التقوى، لا يُحجَب دعاؤنا عن الله، اقْتَصِرُوا على حَلاَلكم وحَرَامكم فاسألوا عنه، وإيّاكم أن تسألوا أحدًا من الفُقهاء عمّا لا يَعْنيكم وعمّا سَتَر الله عنكم.

٨٦ . عن عبدالله بن أبي يَعْفُور، قال: سألتُ أبا عبدالله عليه السلام عن قول الله تعالى: ﴿كُلُّ الطَّعَامِ كَانَ حِلًّا لِّبَنِي إِسْرَائِيلَ إِلَّا مَا حَرَّمَ إِسْرَائِيلُ عَلَىٰ نَفْسِهِ﴾.

قال: إنّ إسرائيل كان إذا أكَل لُحوم الإبل هيَّج عليه وَجَع الخَاصِرة، فحَرَّم على نفسه لَحم الإبل، وذلك من قَبْل أن تَنْزِل التوراة، فلمّا أُنزلت التوراة لم يُحَرّمه، ولم يأكُله.

87. From ʿUmar b. Yazīd who narrated, 'I wrote to Abū al-Ḥasan عليه السلام asking him about a man who wanted his slave to be emancipated after his death – does he have to sell him to do so? He wrote back, saying: ﴾*Except for what Isrāʾīl made unlawful for himself, all food was lawful to the Children of Isrāʾīl.*﴿' [3:93]

88. From Ḥabbāba al-Wālibiyya[31] who narrated, 'I heard al-Ḥusayn b. ʿAlī عليه السلام say, "I do not know of anyone else adhering to the religion of Ibrāhīm other than us and our followers (*shīʿa*)."' Ṣāliḥ narrated it as being, 'There is no one adhering to Ibrāhīm's religion,' and Jābir narrated it as, 'I do not know of anyone adhering to Ibrāhīm's religion.' [3:95]

89. From ʿAbd al-Ṣamad b. Saʿd[32] who narrated, 'Abū Jaʿfar[33] wanted to buy the houses belonging the people of Mecca in order to extend the mosque, but they refused. He tried persuading them but they declined, which upset him. So he went to Abū ʿAbd Allāh عليه السلام and said to him, "I asked these people for a small part of their dwellings and courtyards so that we can extend the mosque but they refused, and it has upset me greatly."

Abū ʿAbd Allāh replied, "How can it upset you when you have a clear proof against them in this regard?"

So he asked, "What proof do I use against them?"

He replied, "God's Book."

He asked, "Where exactly?"

He replied, "God's verse: ﴾*The first House* [*of worship*] *to be established for people was the one at Bakka* [*Mecca*]﴿' – God has told you that the first house to be established for people was the one at Mecca; so if they occupied the premises before the House, then they have a right over their courtyards, but if the House preceded them then the courtyard belongs there."

So Abū Jaʿfar called them and used this proof to convince them, to which they conceded: 'Do whatever you want.'' [3:96]

---

31 Ḥabbāba al-Wālibiyya, a narrator of the first, third and fifth Imams' traditions. See Khūʾī, *Muʿjam*, 24:211–3 (nr. 15636).

32 There is no mention of any individual by this name in either Ḥillī's *Khulāṣat al-aqwāl* or Khūʾī's *Muʿjam*.

33 This is Abū Jaʿfar al-Manṣūr, the Abbasid caliph and the brother of al-ʿAbbās al-Saffāḥ.

٨٧. عن عمر بن يزيد، قال: كَتُبت إلى أبي الحسن ﵇ أسأله عن رجلٍ دبَّر مَمْلُوكه، هل له أن يبيع عِتقه؟ قال: كتب ﵇ ﴿كُلُّ الطَّعَامِ كَانَ حِلاًّ لِبَنِي إِسْرَائِيلَ إِلاَّ مَا حَرَّمَ إِسْرَائِيلُ عَلَى نَفْسِهِ﴾.

٨٨. عن حَبَابة الوَالبِيّة، قال: سَمِعتُ الحسين بن علي عليهم السلام يقول: ما أعلم أحدًا على مِلَّة إبراهيم إلاّ نحن وشيعتنا. قال صالح: ما أحد على مِلَّة إبراهيم... قال جابر: ما أعلم أحدًا على مِلَّة إبراهيم...

٨٩. عن عبد الصمد بن سعد، قال: طلب أبو جعفر أن يشترى من أهل مكَّة بُيُوتهم ليَزيد في المسجد فأبوا، فأرْغَبَهم فامْتَنَعُوا، فضاق بذلك، فأتى أبا عبد الله ﵇، فقال: له: إنّي سألتُ هؤلاء شيئًا من منازلهم وأفنيتهم لنَزِيد في المسجد، وقد مَنَعُوني ذلك، فقد غَمَّني غَمًّا شديدًا.

فقال أبو عبد الله ﵇. لم يَغُمّك ذلك، وحُجّتك عليهم فيه ظاهرة؟

فقال: وبما احتجُّ عليهم؟

فقال: بكتاب الله.

فقال: في أيّ موضع؟

فقال: قول الله تعالى: ﴿إِنَّ أَوَّلَ بَيْتٍ وُضِعَ لِلنَّاسِ لَلَّذِي بِبَكَّةَ﴾ قد أخبَرك الله أن أوّل بيت وُضِع للناس لَلَّذي

بِبَكَّة، فإن كانوا هم نَزَلوا قبل البيت فَلَهُم أفْنِيَتُهم، وإن كان البيت قديمًا قَبْلَهم فَلَه فِناؤه.

فَدَعَاهم أبو جعفر، فاحتجَّ عليهم بهذا، فقالوا له: اصْنَع ما أحْبَبْت.

90. From al-Ḥasan b. ʿAlī b. al-Nuʿmān[34] who said, 'When al-Mahdī[35] was building the Sacred Mosque there was a house which remained within the mosque's quarters, so he requested it from its owners but they refused. So he asked the jurists about it and they all said to him, "Something belonging to someone else must never be included as part of the Sacred Mosque."

So ʿAlī b. Yaqṭīn[36] said to him, "O commander of the faithful, if you were to write to Mūsā b. Jaʿfar عليه السلام he would inform you of what to do in this situation."

So he wrote to the governor of Medina: "Go and ask Mūsā b. Jaʿfar about a house that we wish to include within the Sacred Mosque but whose owner is refusing – how do we resolve this?"

He continued, 'This was addressed to Abū al-Ḥasan عليه السلام, so Abū al-Ḥasan asked, "Does this have to be answered immediately?"

So he replied, "It is an urgent matter."

So he told him: "Write: 'In the Name of God, the Beneficent, the Merciful. If the Kaʿba settled there after the people, then the people have a greater right to its courtyard, and if the people came to settle in the vicinity of the Kaʿba, then the Kaʿba has a greater right over the courtyard.'"

When the letter reached al-Mahdī he took the letter, kissed it, then commanded for the house to be demolished. So the owners of the house went to Abū al-Ḥasan عليه السلام and asked him to write to al-Mahdī on their behalf for compensation in return for their house. So he wrote to him saying, "Give them some compensation at least," so he satisfied them thereby.' [3:96]

91. From Muḥammad b. Muslim, from Abū Jaʿfar عليه السلام who said, 'God, Blessed and most High, is just as He has described Himself. His Throne was on water, the water was in the air, and the air did not move; and there was nothing but water then. When He created, the water was sweet and fresh. So when God

---

34 Al-Ḥasan b. ʿAlī b. al-Nuʿmān, about whom there is scant information, is deemed to have been a reliable narrator of traditions. See Ḥillī, *Khulāṣat al-aqwāl*, 104 (nr. 238).

35 Al-Mahdī here refers to Muḥammad b. al-Manṣūr, the Abbasid caliph.

36 Abū al-Ḥasan ʿAlī b. Yaqṭīn b. Mūsā al-Baghdādī (d. 182/798), originally of Kufa, was a high ranking companion of the seventh Imam and a prominent narrator of the Imams' traditions. He was appointed to the court of the Abbasid caliph al-Mahdī in year 168/784 and also served his successor al-Hādī. See Ḥillī, *Khulāṣat al-aqwāl*, 174–75 (nr. 514); Modarressi, *Tradition and Survival*, 194–98 (nr. 38).

٩٠. عن الحسن بن عليّ بن النُعمان، قال: لمّا بنى المهديّ في المسجد الحرام، بقيت دار في تَربيع المسجد، فَطَلَبها من أربابها فامْتَنَعُوا، فسأل عن ذلك الفُقَهاء، فكُلٌّ قال له: إنّه لا يَنْبَغي أن يُدْخِل شيئًا في المسجد الحرام غَصبًا.

فقال له عليّ بن يَقْطِين: يا أمير المؤمنين، لوكَتَبتَ إلى موسى بن جعفر عليهما السلام لأخبرك بوجه الأمر في ذلك؟

فكتب إلى والي المدينة أن يسأل موسى بن جعفر عن دارٍ أردنا أن نُدْخِلها في المسجد الحرام، فامتنع علينا صاحِبُها، فكيف المَخْرَج من ذلك؟

فقال ذلك لأبي الحسن عليه السلام، فقال أبو الحسن عليه السلام: ولا بُدّ من الجواب في هذا؟

فقال له: الأمر لا بُدَّ منه.

فقال له: اكْتُب (بسم الله الرحمن الرحيم: إنْ كانت الكعبة هي النازلة بالناس، فالناس أولى بفِنائها، وإن كان الناس هم النازلون بِفناء الكعبة، فالكعبة أولى بِفنائها) فلمّا أتى الكتاب إلى المهديّ أخذ الكتاب فَقبّله، ثمّ أمر بِهَدْم الدار، فأتى أهل الدّار أبا الحسن عليه السلام، فسألوه أن يَكْتُب لهم إلى المهديّ كتابًا في ثَمَن دارِهم، فكتب عليه السلام إليه: أن ارْضَخ لهم شيئًا، فأرضاهم.

٩١. عن محمّد بن مسلم، عن أبي جعفر عليه السلام، قال: كان الله تبارك وتعالى كما وصف نفسه، ﴿وَكَانَ عَرْشُهُ عَلَى ٱلْمَآءِ﴾، والماء على الهواء، والهواء لا يجري، ولم يَكُن غير الماء خَلَق، والماء يومئذ عَذْبٌ فُرات، فلمّا أراد الله أن يَخْلُق الأرض أمَرَ الرياح الأربع، فضربن

wished to create the earth, He commanded the four winds to blow the water until a wave formed. Then a single line of foam formed on top, so he gathered it together in the location of the House. Then God gave a command and the foam became a mountain. Then He levelled the earth beneath it.' Then he recited: ﴾ *The first House [of worship] to be established for people was the one at Mecca. It is a blessed place; a source of guidance for all people.* ﴿ [3:96]

92. From Zurāra who narrated, 'Abū Jaʿfar عليه السلام was asked about the House and whether people used to come to it for pilgrimage before the advent of the Prophet صلى الله عليه وآله. He replied, "Yes. They do not know that people used to come for pilgrimage, and we will tell you that Ādam, Nūḥ, and Sulaymān went to the House for pilgrimage with Jinn, people and birds. Mūsā too went to it for pilgrimage on a red camel, saying, '*Labbayk labbayk*' for it is as God most High states: ﴾ *The first House [of worship] to be established for people.* ﴿"' [3:96]

93. From ʿAbd Allāh b. Sinān, from Abū ʿAbd Allāh عليه السلام who said, 'Mecca is the whole village, whereas Bakka is the place where the [black] stone is and where the people crowd around and push each other.' [3:96]

94. From Jābir, from Abū Jaʿfar عليه السلام that Bakka is the location of the House whereas Mecca is the sanctuary, which is in accordance with the verse: ﴾ *whoever enters it is safe.* ﴿' [3:97]

95. From al-Ḥalabī, from Abū ʿAbd Allāh عليه السلام saying, 'I asked him: Why was Mecca called Bakka? He replied, "Because people crowd around and push each other with their hands [therein]."' [3:96]

96. From Jābir, from Abū Jaʿfar عليه السلام that 'Bakka is the location of the House whereas Mecca refers to the whole area that is encompassed by the sanctuary.' [3:96]

الماء حتّى صار موجاً، ثمّ أزبد زَبْدَةً واحدةً، فجمعه في موضع البيت، فأمر الله فصار جبلاً من زَبَدٍ، ثمّ دحا الأرض من تحته، ثمّ قال: ﴿ إِنَّ أَوَّلَ بَيْتٍ وُضِعَ لِلنَّاسِ لَلَّذِي بِبَكَّةَ مُبَارَكًا وَهُدًى لِلْعَالَمِينَ ﴾ .

٩٢. عن زُرارة، قال: سُئِل أبو جعفر عليه السلام عن البيت، أكان يُحَجُّ إليه قبل أن يُبْعَث النبيّ صلى الله عليه وآله وسلم؟ قال: نعم، لا يَعْلَمُون أنّ الناس قد كانوا يَحُجُّون، ونُخْبِرُكم أنّ آدم ونُوحاً وسُليمان قد حَجُّوا البيت بالجِنّ والإنس والطَّير، ولقد حَجَّه موسى عليه السلام على جملٍ أحمر، يقول: لبّيك لبّيك، فإنّه كما قال الله تعالى: ﴿ إِنَّ أَوَّلَ بَيْتٍ وُضِعَ لِلنَّاسِ لَلَّذِي بِبَكَّةَ مُبَارَكًا وَهُدًى لِّلْعَالَمِينَ ﴾ .

٩٣. عن عبد الله بن سِنان، عن أبي عبد الله عليه السلام، قال: مَكّة: جُملة القَرية، وبَكّة: مَوضِع الحَجر الذي يَبُكُّ الناس بعضهم بعضاً.

٩٤. عن جابر، عن أبي جعفر عليه السلام، قال: إنّ بَكَّة موضع البيت، وإنّ مَكَّة الحَرَم، وذلك قوله تعالى: ﴿ فَمَن دَخَلَهُ كَانَ آمِنًا ﴾ .

٩٥. عن الحَلَبي، عن أبي عبد الله عليه السلام، قال: سألتُهُ لِمَ سُمّيَت مَكَّة بَكَّة؟ قال: لأنّ الناس يَبُكُّ بعضُهم بعضاً بالأيدي.

٩٦. عن جابر، عن أبي جعفر عليه السلام، قال: إنّ بَكَّة موضع البيت، وإنّ مَكَّة جميع ما اكْتَنَفَهُ الحَرَم.

97. From al-Ḥalabī, from Abū ʿAbd Allāh عليه السلام who said, ‘It was found written on two of the stones of the House that: “Indeed, I am God, owner of Bakka, which I created on the day that I created the heavens and the earth, and on the day that I created the sun and the moon, and I created the two mountains and encircled them with seven angels.”

On another stone: “This is God’s sacred House at Bakka whose inhabitants God provided with sustenance through three sources, and blessed them with meat and water, which was first gifted to Ibrāhīm.”’ [3:96]

98. From ʿAlī b. Jaʿfar b. Muḥammad, from his brother Mūsā [al-Kāẓim] عليه السلام. He narrated, ‘I asked him about Mecca and why it had been named Bakka? He replied, “Because the people crowd around and bump into each other with their hands, meaning that they push each other with their hands in the mosque around the Kaʿba.”’ [3:96]

99. From Ibn Sinān who narrated, ‘I asked Abū ʿAbd Allāh عليه السلام about God’s verse: ﴾*there are clear signs in it*﴿ – what are these clear signs? He replied, “The Station of Ibrāhīm which he was standing on and the ground upon which his feet left an imprint, the [Black] Stone and the site of Ismāʿīl.”’ [3:97]

100. From Muḥammad b. Muslim, from Abū Jaʿfar عليه السلام. ‘I asked him about the verse: ﴾*whoever enters it is safe.*﴿

He replied, “Anyone fearing for his life is safe here as long as he is not being prosecuted for transgressing God’s laws, for which he must be arrested.”

I asked, “So someone who fights God and His Messenger and spreads corruption in the land can be safe here too?”

He replied, “This is the same as someone who rejects the path,[37] so his mount should be taken away from him and the imam can do whatever he wills with him.”

Then I asked him about the carrier-pigeon,[38] and whether it can enter the sanctuary.

37 According to al-Ḥurr al-ʿĀmilī, *Wasāʾil al-shīʿa*, 13:229 (nr. 11) the tradition should read: ‘This is like someone who is cheating’, whereas according to Baḥrānī, *Burhān*, 1:660 (nr. 1865) it should read: ‘This is like someone lying in ambush on the path.’

38 In other sources the words mentioned are ‘traitor’ and ‘rebel’ rather than ‘carrier-pigeon,’ so this is perhaps a transcription error.

٩٧. عن الحلبي، عن أبي عبدالله ﷺ، قال: إنّه وُجِد في حَجَر من حَجَرات البيت مكتوبًا: إنّي أنا الله ذو مكّة، خلقتُها يوم خَلَقْتُ السماوات والأرض، ويوم خَلَقْتُ الشمس والقمر، وخلقتُ الجبلين، وحَفَفْتُها بسبعة أملاك حفًّا.

وفي حَجَر آخر: هذا بيتُ الله الحرام ببَكَّة، تَكَفَّل الله برِزْق أهله من ثلاثة سُبُل، مبارك لهم في اللَّحم والماء، أوّل من نُحِلَه إبراهيم.

٩٨. عن عليّ بن جعفر بن محمّد، عن أخيه موسى ﷺ: قال سألْتُه عن مَكَّة، لِمَ سُمِّيَت بَكَّة؟ قال: لأنَّ الناس يَبُكُّ بعضهم بعضًا بالأيدي، يعني يَدْفَعُ بعضهم بعضًا بالأيدي في المسجد حول الكَعْبة.

٩٩. عن ابن سِنان، قال: سألتُ أبا عبدالله ﷺ عن قول الله عزّ وجلّ: ﴿فِيهِ آيَاتٌ بَيِّنَاتٌ﴾ فما هذه الآيات البيّنات؟ قال: مقام إبراهيم، حين قام عليه فأثّرت قدماه فيه، والحَجَر ومنزل إسماعيل ﷺ.

١٠٠. عن محمّد بن مسلم، عن أبي جعفر ﷺ، قال: سألْتُهُ عن قوله سبحانه ﴿وَمَن دَخَلَهُ كَانَ آمِنًا﴾، قال: يأمَنُ فيه كلُّ خائفٍ، ما لم يكُن عليه حدٌّ من حُدود الله ينبغي أن يُؤخَذَ به.

قلت: فيأمَنُ فيه من حاربَ الله ورسوله، وسعى في الأرض فسادًا؟ قال: هو مثل الذي يكْمَن بالطريق، فيأخُذ الشاة أو الشيء، فيصنع به الإمام ما شاء.

قال: وسألْتُهُ عن طائرٍ يَدْخُل الحَرَم؟ قال: لا يُؤخَذُ ولا يُمَسُّ، لأنّ الله يقول ﴿وَمَن دَخَلَهُ كَانَ آمِنًا﴾.

He replied, "It/he can neither be captured nor harmed, because God says: ﴾*whoever enters it is safe.*﴿"' [3:97]

101. From 'Abd Allāh b. Sinān, from Abū 'Abd Allāh ﷺ. 'I asked him, "Regarding the verse: ﴾*whoever enters it is safe*﴿, does He mean the House or the sanctuary?" He replied, "Whoever from among the people in general enters the sanctuary seeking refuge therein is safe. Whoever from among the believers enters the House seeking refuge therein is safe from God's wrath. Any beast, predator or bird too that enters it is safe from being hunted or harmed until it leaves the sanctuary."' [3:97]

102. From Hishām b. Sālim, from Abū 'Abd Allāh ﷺ who said, 'Whoever enters Mecca – the Sacred Mosque – acknowledging our right and our sanctity the way He acknowledges its right and its sanctity, God forgives him his sins and suffices him in all the problems of this world that trouble him. This is the meaning of the verse: ﴾*whoever enters it is safe.*﴿' [3:97]

103. From [Muḥsin] al-Muthannā, from Abū 'Abd Allāh ﷺ who, when I asked him about God's verse: ﴾*whoever enters it is safe*﴿ said, 'When a thief commits a crime outside the sanctuary then enters it, no one is allowed to arrest him. However, he can be denied access to the market and no one should transact with him or talk to him such that he is compelled to leave, after which he can be arrested. When he is arrested, he must be prosecuted. If he committed the crime within the sanctuary then he is arrested and prosecuted within the sanctuary itself, for whoever transgresses in the sanctuary must be prosecuted in the sanctuary.' [3:97]

104. 'Abd Allāh b. Sinān also narrated, 'I heard him say, "As regards an animal that is brought into the sanctuary and is normally allowed to be hunted, when it enters the sanctuary it must not be killed, for God says: ﴾*whoever enters it is safe.*﴿"' [3:97]

١٠١. عن عبدالله بن سِنان، عن أبي عبدالله ﴿عليه السلام﴾، قال: قلتُ: أرأيت قوله تعالى: ﴿فَمَن دَخَلَهُ كَانَ آمِنًا﴾ البيت عنى، أو الحَرَم؟ قال: مَن دَخَل الحَرَم من الناس مُستجيرًا به فهو آمِنٌ، ومَن دَخَل البيت من المؤمنين مُستجيرًا به فهو آمنٌ من سَخَط الله ومن دَخَل الحَرَم من الوَحْش والسِّباع والطَّير فهو آمنٌ من أن يُهَاج أو يُؤذى حتّى يَخْرُج من الحَرَم.

١٠٢. عن هِشام بن سالم، عن أبي عبدالله ﴿عليه السلام﴾، قال: مَن دَخَل مكّة المسجد الحرام، يَعْرف من حقّنا وحرمتنا ما عَرَف من حَقّها وحُرمتها، غَفَر الله له ذَنْبَهُ وكَفَاهُ ما أَهَمَّه من أمر الدنيا والآخرة، وهو قوله تعالى ﴿وَمَن دَخَلَهُ كَانَ آمِنًا﴾.

١٠٣. عن المُثنّى، عن أبي عبدالله ﴿عليه السلام﴾، وسألتُهُ عن قول الله عزّ وجلّ: ﴿وَمَن دَخَلَهُ كَانَ آمِنًا﴾، قال: إذا أحدث السارق في غير الحَرَم، ثمّ دخل الحَرَم، لم يَنْبَغِ لأحدٍ أن يأخُذه، ولكن يُمْنَع من السُّوق، ولا يُبَايع ولا يُكلّم، فإنّه إذا فُعِل ذلك به، أوشك أن يَخْرُج فيُؤخَذ، لأنّه من جَنَى في الحَرَم أُقيم عليه الحَدُّ في الحَرَم.

١٠٤. وقال عبدالله بن سِنان: سَمِعتُهُ يقول فيما أُدخل الحرم ممّا صِيد في الحِلّ، قال: إذا دَخَل الحَرَم فلا يُذْبَح، إنّ الله يقول ﴿وَمَن دَخَلَهُ كَانَ آمِنًا﴾.

105. From 'Imrān al-Ḥalabī[39], from Abū 'Abd Allāh ﷺ regarding His verse: ﴿*whoever enters it is safe*﴾. He [the Imam] said, 'When the servant commits a crime outside the sanctuary then flees therein, he cannot be arrested. However, he can be denied access to the market and no one is allowed to transact with him, feed him, quench his thirst or speak to him. If he is treated in this way then he will be compelled to leave, after which he can be arrested. If his crime was committed within the sanctuary, then he is arrested therein.' [3:97]

106. From 'Abd al-Khāliq al-Ṣayqal[40] who narrated, 'I asked Abū 'Abd Allāh ﷺ about God's verse: ﴿*whoever enters it is safe*﴾, so he replied, "Indeed, you have asked me about something that no one has ever asked me before, except for what God wills." Then he continued, "Whoever comes to this House acknowledging that it is the House which God has commanded [mankind] to visit, and truly acknowledging us, the Ahl al-Bayt, then he will remain safe in this world and the Hereafter."' [3:97]

107. From 'Alī b. 'Abd al-'Azīz[41] who narrated, 'I asked Abū 'Abd Allāh ﷺ, "May I be your ransom – God's verse: ﴿*there are clear signs in it; it is the place where Ibrāhīm stood to pray; whoever enters it is safe*﴾ – so even a Murji'ite, a Qadarite, a Ḥarūrī[42] and an atheist who does not believe in God may enter it?" He replied, "No, by no means."

I asked, "Then who can - may I be your ransom?" He replied, "Whoever enters it, acknowledging our right in the same way that he acknowledges it [i.e. the House], he is taken out of sin, and he is sufficed against his troubles in this world and the Hereafter."' [3:97]

---

39 Abū al-Faḍl 'Imrān b. 'Alī b. Abī Shu'ba, a reliable narrator of traditions. See Ḥillī, *Khulāṣat al-aqwāl*, 219 (nr. 725).

40 'Abd al-Khāliq al-Ṣayqal, about whom there is scant information, was a narrator of the sixth Imam's traditions. His reliability as a narrator is unconfirmed in the sources. See Khū'ī, *Mu'jam*, 10:310 (nr. 6313).

41 There are several individuals bearing this name in the works of Shī'a *rijāl*. See Modarressi, *Tradition and Survival*, 181–3 (nr. 31).

42 The Ḥarūriyya were a Khārijite sect originating from Ḥarūrā, a place near Kufa, and named thus after their leader Ḥabīb b. Yazīd al-Ḥarūrī. See Amīn, *Mu'jam al-firaq al-islāmiyya*, 94.

١٠٥. عن عِمران الحلبي، عن أبي عبدالله عليه السلام، في قوله: ﴿وَمَن دَخَلَهُ كَانَ آمِنًا﴾. قال عليه السلام: إذا أحدث العبد في غير الحَرَم ثمّ فَرَّ إلى الحَرَم، لم يَنْبَغِ أن يُؤخَذ، ولكن يمنَع منه السُّوق، ولا يبايع ولا يُطْعَم، ولا يُسقى ولا يُكلَّم، فإنّه إذا فُعِل ذلك به يُوشِك أن يَخرُج فيُؤخَذ، وإن كان إحداثه في الحَرَم أُخِذ في الحَرَم.

١٠٦. عن عبد الخالق الصَّيقل، قال: سألتُ أبا عبدالله عليه السلام عن قول الله تعالى ﴿وَمَن دَخَلَهُ كَانَ آمِنًا﴾. فقال: لَقَد سألتني عن شيءٍ ما سألني عنه إلاّ ما شاء الله، ثمّ قال: إنّ مَن أَمَّ هذا البيت وهو يَعْلَمُ أنه البيت الذي أمَرَ الله به، وعَرَفنا أهل البيت حَقَّ مَعْرِفتنا، كان آمنًا في الدُّنيا والآخِرة.

١٠٧. عن عليّ بن عبد العزيز، قال: قلتُ لأبي عبدالله عليه السلام: جُعِلتُ فِداك، قول الله تعالى: ﴿آيَاتٌ بَيِّنَاتٌ مَقَامُ إِبْرَاهِيمَ وَمَنْ دَخَلَهُ كَانَ آمِنًا﴾ وقد يَدْخُلُه المُرجئ والقَدَري والحَروري والزِّنديق الذي لا يُؤمِن بالله؟ قال: لا ولا كرامة.

قلت: فمَن جُعِلت فِداك؟ قال: ومَنَ دَخَلَهُ وهو عارِفٌ بحَقِّنا كما هو عارِفٌ له، خَرَج من ذُنُوبه، وكُفِي همّ الدّنيا والآخِرة.

108. From Ibrāhīm b. 'Alī[43], from 'Abd al-'Aẓīm b. 'Abd Allāh b. 'Alī b. al-Ḥasan b. Zayd b. al-Ḥasan b. 'Alī b. Abī Ṭālib ﵇ from al-Ḥasan b. Maḥbūb, from Mu'āwiya b. 'Ammār, from Abū 'Abd Allāh ﵇ who said regarding God's statement: ﴿*Pilgrimage to the House is a duty owed to God by people who are able to undertake it*﴾: 'This is for one who can afford it and is healthy enough. If he puts it off due to business, then he is not allowed to do that; and if he dies as such, he will have neglected one of the laws of Islam – having abandoned the Hajj while having the means to perform it. And if someone asks him to transport him there but he declines out of embarrassment, he cannot do that and he must go, even if it is on a lame, three-legged donkey; and this is as per God's words: ﴿*Those who reject this* [*should know that*] *God has no need of anyone.*﴾'

He continued, 'Whoever rejects this has disbelieved.' He said, 'And he can only be a disbeliever if he abandons one of the laws of Islam. God says: ﴿*The pilgrimage takes place during the prescribed months. There should be no indecent speech, misbehaviour, or quarrelling for anyone undertaking the pilgrimage.*﴾ 2:197 The duties incumbent [on him] are the *talbiya,* the *ish'ār* and garlanding the animal. Whichever of these he performs, he has undertaken the Hajj. Hajj is only incumbent in these months, which God has designated saying: ﴿*The pilgrimage takes place during the prescribed months.*﴾' [3:97]

109. From Zurāra who narrated, 'Abū Ja'far ﵇ said, "Islam is founded on five things: (1) the daily prayer, (2) charity, (3) fasting, (4) pilgrimage and (5) authority (*walāya*)."

He said, 'I asked him, "Which of these is the best?"

He replied, "Divine authority is the best of all because it is the key to the rest of them. The one vested with divinely-mandated authority is the one who leads them to the rest of them."

I asked, "Then which one is the best after that?"

He replied, "The daily prayer. The Messenger of God ﷺ has said, 'The daily prayer is the pillar of your religion.'"

43 Ibrāhīm b. 'Alī al-Kūfī, about whom there is scant information, is mentioned by al-'Allāma al-Ḥillī as someone who never narrated a single tradition of the Imams but who nevertheless appears in the *isnād* of a number of Shī'ī traditions. See Ḥillī, *Khulāṣat al-aqwāl*, 53 (nr. 26).

١٠٨. عن إبراهيم بن علي، عن عبد العظيم بن عبدالله بن علي بن الحسن بن زيد بن الحسن بن علي بن أبي طالب عليه السلام، عن الحسن بن محبوب، عن معاوية بن عمّار، عن أبي عبدالله عليه السلام، في قول الله عزّ وجلّ: ﴿وَلِلَّهِ عَلَى النَّاسِ حِجُّ الْبَيْتِ مَنِ اسْتَطَاعَ إِلَيْهِ سَبِيلًا﴾.

قال: هذا لِمن كان عِنده مالٌ وصِحّة، فإن سَوّفَهُ للتِّجارة فلا يَسَعه ذلك، وإن مات على ذلك فقد تَرَكَ شريعةً من شرائع الإسلام، إذا تَرَكَ الحجَّ وهو يَجِدُ ما يَحُجُّ به، وإن دعاه أحدٌ، إلى أن يَحمِله فاستحيى فلا يفعل، فإنّه لا يَسَعه إلاّ أن يَخرُج ولو على حِمارٍ أجْدَع أبتَر، وهو قول الله: ﴿وَمَنْ كَفَرَ فَإِنَّ اللَّهَ غَنِيٌّ عَنِ الْعَالَمِينَ﴾.

قال: ومَن تَرَكَ. قلت: كَفَر؟ قال: ولِمَ لا يَكْفُر وقد تَرَكَ شريعةً من شرائع الإسلام؟ يقول الله: ﴿الْحَجُّ أَشْهُرٌ مَعْلُومَاتٌ فَمَنْ فَرَضَ فِيهِنَّ الْحَجَّ فَلَا رَفَثَ وَلَا فُسُوقَ وَلَا جِدَالَ فِي الْحَجِّ﴾ فالفريضة التلبية والإشعار والتقليد، فأيّ ذلك فَعَل فقد فَرَض الحجّ، ولا فَرْض إلاّ في هذه الشُّهور التي قال الله: ﴿الْحَجُّ أَشْهُرٌ مَعْلُومَاتٌ﴾.

١٠٩. عن زُرارة، قال: قال أبو جعفر عليه السلام: بُني الإسلام على خمسة أشياء: على الصلاة والزكاة والصوم والحجّ والولاية.

قال: قلتُ: فأيّ ذلك أفضل؟

قال: الولاية أفضلهنّ، لأنّها مِفْتاحُهنّ، والوالي هو الدليل عليهنّ.

قال: قلتُ: ثمّ الذي يلي من الفَضْل؟

قال: الصلاة، إنّ رسول الله صلى الله عليه وآله قال: الصلاة عَمُودُ دِينكم.

I asked, "And the next best after that?"

He replied, "Charity, for it is closely linked to it and its mention is preceded only by the prayer. The Messenger of God ﷺ has said, 'Charity does away with sins.'"

I asked, "What is next after that?"

He replied, "Pilgrimage, because God says: ﴾*Pilgrimage to the House is a duty owed to God by people who are able to undertake it. Those who reject this* [*should know that*] *God has no need of anyone.*﴿ The Messenger of God ﷺ has said, 'A pilgrimage which is accepted is better than twenty supererogatory prayers, and whoever circumambulates this House seven times and follows it with an excellent two-unit prayer, he is forgiven.' He has said what He has said regarding the days of 'Arafa and Muzdalifa."

I asked, "Then what comes next?"

He replied, "Then fasting."

So I asked, "Why is it that fasting comes last of all?"

He replied, "The Messenger of God ﷺ said, 'Fasting is a shield [protecting] from the Fire.'" Then he continued, "The best of all things are those that when you fail to perform them, they cannot be pardoned except that you must go back and perform them exactly as they are. Prayer, charity, pilgrimage and adherence to the divinely-mandated authority are such that nothing else can substitute their place in one's fulfilment of them. The fast, however, is such that if you miss it or cannot fast or are travelling during it, can be made up on other days. You can even atone for that sin by giving compensation, and you would not have to make it up. It is not like the other four, which cannot be compensated by anything [other than the act itself]."' [3:97]

قال: قلتُ: الذي يليها في الفَضْل؟

قال: الزكاة، لأنّه قَرَنها بها، وبدأ بالصلاة قبلها وقال رسول الله ﷺ: الزكاة تُذهِبُ الذُّنوب.

قال: قلتُ: فالّذي يليها في الفَضْل؟

قال: الحجّ، لأنّ الله يقول: ﴿وَلِلَّهِ عَلَى النَّاسِ حِجُّ الْبَيْتِ مَنِ اسْتَطَاعَ إِلَيْهِ سَبِيلًا وَمَن كَفَرَ فَإِنَّ اللَّهَ غَنِيٌّ عَنِ الْعَالَمِينَ﴾. وقال رسول الله عليه الصلاة والسلام لَحَجَّةٌ متقبَّلةٌ خيرٌ من عشرين صلاة نافلة، ومَن طاف بهذا البيت طَوَافًا أحصى فيه سُبُوعه وأحسن رَكْعتيه غُفِر له، وقال يوم عَرَفة ويوم المُزْدَلِفة ما قال.

قال: قلتُ: ثمّ ماذا يَتْبَعُه؟

قال: ثمّ الصَّوم.

قال: قلت: ما بال الصوم آخر ذلك أجمع؟

فقال: قال رسول ﷺ: الصَّومُ جُنَّة من النار.

قال: ثمّ قال عليه السلام: إنّ أفضلَ الأشياءِ ما إذا كان فاتك لم يَكُن لك منه التَّوبة دون أن تَرْجِع إليه فتؤدّيه بعينه، إنّ الصلاة والزكاة والحَجّ والولاية ليس ينفع شيءٌ مكانها دون أدائها، وإنّ الصَّوم إذا فاتك أو أفْطَرْت أو سافرت فيه أدَّيت مكانه أيّامًا غيرها، وفَدَيت ذلك الذَّنب بِفدية، ولا قضاء عليك، وليس مثل تلك الأربعة شيءٌ يُجزيك مكانها غيرها.

110. From ʿUmar b. [Muḥammad b. ʿAbd al-Raḥmān b.] Udhayna[44] who narrated, ʿI asked Abū ʿAbd Allāh ﷺ about the verse: ﴾*Pilgrimage to the House is a duty owed to God by people who are able to undertake it*﴿ and whether it refers specifically to Hajj and not *ʿumra*? He replied, "It refers to both Hajj and *ʿumra* because they have both been made incumbent."' [3:97]

111. From ʿAbd al-Raḥmān b. Sayāba, from Abū ʿAbd Allāh ﷺ who said regarding God's verse: ﴾*Pilgrimage to the House is a duty owed to God by people who are able to undertake it*﴿, 'Whoever is able-bodied, with the means to travel and has enough provision and a mount can undertake the pilgrimage.' [3:97]

112. In al-Kanānī's narration, from Abū ʿAbd Allāh, it says, 'If he can walk for part of the journey and ride for part, then he should do so. ﴾*Those who reject this*﴿ means: [those who] abandon it.' [3:97]

113. From Abū al-Rabīʿ al-Shāmī who narrated, 'Abū ʿAbd Allāh ﷺ was asked about God's verse: ﴾*Pilgrimage to the House is a duty owed to God by people who are able to undertake it*﴿, so he asked [in turn], "What do the people [i.e. the majority] say?" He was told, "Provision and a mount."' He continued, 'So Abū ʿAbd Allāh ﷺ said, "Abū Jaʿfar ﷺ was asked about this and he said, 'People would perish if the verse meant that someone should have a mount and the same provision that would otherwise sustain his dependants in his absence, such that they would be needless of having to resort to others. If he used that money for his pilgrimage, and set about asking people to provide for his family in his absence instead they would certainly be ruined then.' So he was asked, 'What is the solution then?' He replied, 'Sufficient financial means to be able to use some for the pilgrimage and leave some behind for his family to sustain themselves. Has God not made charity incumbent, and binding only on the one who possesses more than two hundred dirhams?'"' [3:97]

44 ʿUmar b. Muḥammad b. ʿAbd al-Raḥmān b. Udhayna, a trustworthy narrator of the fifth and sixth Imams and a leading figure of the Shīʿī community in Basra. See Ḥillī, *Khulāṣat al-aqwāl*, 211 (nr. 687); Khūʾī, *Muʿjam*, 14:21–25 (nr. 8714).

١١٠. عن عمر بن أُذينة، قال: قلتُ لأبي عبد الله عليه السلام، في قوله تعالى: ﴿وَلِلَّهِ عَلَى النَّاسِ حِجُّ الْبَيْتِ مَنِ اسْتَطَاعَ إِلَيْهِ سَبِيلًا﴾ يعني به الحجّ دون العُمرة؟ قال: لا ولكنّه الحجّ والعُمرة جميعًا، لأنّهما مفروضان.

١١١. عن عبد الرّحمن بن سَيَابة، عن أبي عبد الله عليه السلام، في قول الله تعالى: ﴿وَلِلَّهِ عَلَى النَّاسِ حِجُّ الْبَيْتِ مَنِ اسْتَطَاعَ إِلَيْهِ سَبِيلًا﴾، قال: مَن كان صَحِيحًا في بَدَنه، مُخلّى سَرْبه، له زادٌ وَرَاحِلةٌ، فهو مُستطيعٌ للحجّ.

١١٢. وفي حديث الكِناني، عن أبي عبد الله عليه السلام، قال: وإن كان يَقْدِر أن يمشي بعضًا ويركَب بعضًا فليفعل ﴿وَمَن كَفَرَ﴾ قال: تَرَك.

١١٣. عن أبي الربيع الشامي، قال: سُئِل أبو عبدالله عليه السلام عن قول الله تعالى ﴿وَلِلَّهِ عَلَى النَّاسِ حِجُّ الْبَيْتِ مَنِ اسْتَطَاعَ إِلَيْهِ سَبِيلًا﴾، فقال: ما يقول الناس؟ فقيل له: الزاد والرّاحلة.

قال: فقال أبو عبد الله عليه السلام: سُئِل أبو جعفر عليه السلام عن هذا؟ فقال: لقد هَلَك الناسُ إذًا، لئن كان مَن كان له زادٌ وراحِلةٌ قَدر ما يَقُوت به عِياله، ويستغني به عن الناس، يَنْطَلِق إليهم فيسألهم إيّاه، ويَحُجّ به، لقد هَلَكُوا إذًا.

فقيل له: فما السبيل؟ قال: فقال: السَّعَة في المال، إذا كان يَحُجّ ببعضٍ ويُبقي ببعضٍ يَقُوتُ به عِياله، أليس الله قد فَرَض الزكاة، فلم يجعلها إلاّ على من يَمْلِك مائتي دِرْهَم؟

114. From Abū Baṣīr, from Abū Jaʿfar عليه السلام. He [Abū Baṣīr] said, 'I asked him, "A man has been offered the opportunity to go for pilgrimage [through a donation], but he is embarrassed to accept it – does he qualify as one who can undertake the pilgrimage?" He replied, "Yes, command him[45] [to accept], and he must not be embarrassed, even if he has to go on a three-legged donkey. If he can walk for part of the journey and ride the rest, then he must do so."' [3:97]

115. From Abū Usāma Zayd al-Shaḥḥām, from Abū ʿAbd Allāh عليه السلام regarding the verse: ﴾*Pilgrimage to the House is a duty owed to God by people who are able to undertake it*﴿ – I asked him, "What does 'ability' signify here?"

He replied, "He should have enough financial means to be able to undertake the pilgrimage."

I asked, "What if some money is donated to him to enable him to go for pilgrimage but he is embarrassed to accept it?"

He replied, "He qualifies as one who can undertake it. If he is capable of walking part of the way and riding the rest, then he must do so."

I asked, "What about God's statement: ﴾*Those who reject this [should know that] God has no need of anyone*﴿ – is this in reference to the pilgrimage?"

He replied, "Yes. It is a rejection of the bounty."

He [the narrator] continued, "It says 'Whoever neglects' in another report."' [3:97]

116. From Abū Baṣīr, from Abū ʿAbd Allāh عليه السلام. 'I [i.e. Abū Baṣīr] asked Abū ʿAbd Allāh about God's words: ﴾*who are able to undertake it.*﴿

He replied, "Just leave [for pilgrimage], and if you do not have one [i.e. a mount] you can walk."

I asked, "And if he is not able to do that?"

He replied, "He can walk and then ride for some of it."

I asked, "And if he is not able to do that either?"

He replied, "Then he can place himself at the service of a group of pilgrims and go with them."' [3:97]

45 This appears to be correct and corresponds to what is quoted in other later sources. However, a number of works cite it as: 'Yes, once', which may refer to the first time one goes for Hajj.

١١٤. عن أبي بصير، عن أبي جعفر ﵇، قال: قلتُ له: رجلٌ عُرِض عليه الحجّ فاستحيى أن يَقْبَله، أهو ممَّن يستطيع الحجّ؟ قال: نعم، مُره فلا يستحيي، ولو على حمارٍ أبتر، وإن كان يستطيع أن يمشي بعضًا ويَرْكَب بعضًا فليفعل.

١١٥. عن أبي أُسامة زيد الشحّام، عن أبي عبد الله ﵇، في قوله تعالى: ﴿وَلِلَّهِ عَلَى النَّاسِ حِجُّ الْبَيْتِ مَنِ اسْتَطَاعَ إِلَيْهِ سَبِيلًا﴾، قال: سألته ما السبيل؟ قال: يكُونُ له ما يَحُجّ به.

قلت: أرأيت إن عُرِض عليه مال يَحُجّ به فاستحيى من ذلك؟ قال: هو مِمّن استطاع إليه سبيلاً، قال ﵇: وإن كان يُطِيقُ المشي بعضًا والرُّكُوب بعضًا فليفعل.

قلت: أرأيت قول الله، ﴿وَمَن كَفَرَ﴾ أهو في الحَجّ؟ قال: نعم. قال: هو كُفْر النِّعَم. وقال: تَرْك، في خبرٍ آخر.

١١٦. عن أبي بصير، عن أبي عبد الله ﵇، قال: قلتُ لأبي عبد الله ﵇: قول الله تعالى: ﴿مَنِ اسْتَطَاعَ إِلَيْهِ سَبِيلًا﴾؟ قال: تَخْرُج، إذا لم يكن عندك تمشي.

قال: قلت: لا يَقْدِر على ذلك؟

قال: يمشي ويركب أحيانًا.

قلت: لا يقدر على ذلك؟

قال: يَخْدِمُ قومًا، ويَخْرُج معهم.

117. From ʿAbd al-Raḥmān b. al-Ḥajjāj who narrated, 'I asked Abū ʿAbd Allāh عليه السلام about God's verse: ﴾*Pilgrimage to the House is a duty owed to God by people who are able to undertake it.*﴿ He said, "To have a healthy body and financial means."' [3:97]

118. In Ḥafṣ al-Aʿwar's report on his authority عليه السلام too, it says, 'To have a healthy body and financial prosperity.' [3:97]

119. From al-Ḥusayn b. Khālid[46] who narrated, 'The first Abū al-Ḥasan عليه السلام asked: "How would you read this verse: ﴾*You who believe, be mindful of God, as is His due, and do not die except as muslims*﴿?"

I replied, "Muslims." He exclaimed, "Glory be to God – So He declares their faith first by calling them 'believers' and then asks them to be devoted Muslims; so does that mean that faith (*īmān*) precedes Islam?"

I replied, "That is how it is read in Zayd's reading."

He replied, "'Alī [b. Abī Ṭālib]'s reading of it, however, which is the exact revelation that Jibrīl brought down to Muḥammad – peace and blessings upon them both – is as follows: ﴾***except as devotees***﴿ to the Messenger of God and then the Imam after him.' [3:102*]

120. From Abū Baṣīr who narrated, 'I asked Abū ʿAbd Allāh عليه السلام about God's verse: ﴾*You who believe, be mindful of God, as is His due.*﴿ He replied, "He must be obeyed and not disobeyed, remembered and not forgotten, thanked and not spurned."' [3:102]

121. From Abū Baṣīr who narrated, 'I asked Abū ʿAbd Allāh عليه السلام about God's verse: ﴾*You who believe, be mindful of God, as is His due*﴿. He replied, "It has been abrogated." I asked, "What has it been abrogated by?" He replied, "God's verse: ﴾*Be mindful of God as much as you can.*﴿ (64:16)"' [3:102]

46 Al-Ḥusayn b. Khālid, a companion of the seventh Imam whose reliability is uncertain. See Khū'ī, *Mu'jam*, 6: 247–9 (nr. 3388).

١١٧. عن عبد الرّحمن بن الحَجّاج، قال: سألتُ أبا عبد الله عليه السلام عن قوله تعالى: ﴿وَلِلَّهِ عَلَى النَّاسِ حِجُّ الْبَيْتِ مَنِ اسْتَطَاعَ إِلَيْهِ سَبِيلًا﴾، قال: الصِّحّة في بَدَنه، والقُدرة في ماله.

١١٨. وفي رواية حَفص الأعور، عنه عليه السلام، قال: القُوّة في البَدَن، واليَسَار في المال.

١١٩. عن الحسين بن خالد، قال: قال أبو الحسن الأوّل عليه السلام: كيف تقرأ هذه الآية ﴿يَا أَيُّهَا الَّذِينَ آمَنُوا اتَّقُوا اللَّهَ حَقَّ تُقَاتِهِ وَلَا تَمُوتُنَّ إِلَّا وَأَنْتُمْ مُسْلِمُونَ﴾ ماذا؟ قلت: مُسْلِمُون.

فقال: سُبحان الله! يُوقع عليهم الإيمان، فيُسَمِّيهم مؤمنين، ثمّ يسألهم الإسلام، والإيمان فوق الإسلام!

قلت: هكذا تُقرأ في قراءة زيد، إنّما هي في قراءة عليّ عليه السلام وهو التنزيل الذي نَزَل به جبْرَئيل على محمّد صلى الله عليه وآله ﴿إِلَّا وَأَنْتُمْ مُسْلِمُونَ﴾ لرسول الله صلى الله عليه وآله ثمّ الإمام من بعده.

١٢٠. عن أبي بصير، قال سألتُ أبا عبد الله عليه السلام عن قول الله تعالى: ﴿اتَّقُوا اللَّهَ حَقَّ تُقَاتِهِ﴾، قال: يُطَاع فلا يُعصى، ويُذكَر فلا يُنسى، ويُشْكَر فلا يُكْفَر.

١٢١. عن أبي بصير، قال: سألتُ أبا عبدالله عليه السلام عن قول الله تعالى: ﴿اتَّقُوا اللَّهَ حَقَّ تُقَاتِهِ﴾، قال: منسوخةٌ. قلت، وما نسختها؟ قال: قول الله تعالى: ﴿اتَّقُوا اللَّهَ مَا اسْتَطَعْتُمْ﴾.

122. From Ibn Yazīd who narrated, 'I asked Abū al-Ḥasan عليه السلام about His verse: ﴿*Hold fast to God's rope all together.*﴾ He replied, "ʿAlī b. Abī Ṭālib عليه السلام is God's firm rope."' [3:103]

123. From Jābir, from Abū Jaʿfar عليه السلام who said, 'The progeny of Muḥammad, peace be upon him, is God's rope who He has commanded us to hold fast to, saying: ﴿*Hold fast to God's rope all together; do not split into factions.*﴾' [3:103]

124. From Muḥammad b. Sulaymān al-Baṣrī al-Daylamī[47], on his father's authority, from Abū ʿAbd Allāh عليه السلام who said about to the verse: ﴿*you were about to fall into a pit of Fire and He saved you from it*﴾, 'Muḥammad صلى الله عليه وآله.' [3:103]

125. From Abū al-Ḥasan ʿAlī b. Muḥammad b. Maytham[48], from Abū ʿAbd Allāh عليه السلام who said, 'Rejoice in the greatest of God's bounties upon you – God's statement: ﴿*you were about to fall into a pit of Fire and He saved you from it*﴾, for salvation is a gift, and God never retracts His gift.' [3:103]

126. From Ibn Hārūn who narrated, 'When Abū ʿAbd Allāh عليه السلام used to mention the Prophet صلى الله عليه وآله he would say, "May my father, my mother, my soul, my community and my family be ransomed in astonishment at the Arabs and why they do not carry us on their heads [in esteem] when God has said in His Book: ﴿*you were about to fall into a pit of Fire and He saved you from it*﴾ – by God, it is through God's Messenger that they have been saved."' [3:103]

127. From Abū ʿAmr al-Zubayrī, from Abū ʿAbd Allāh عليه السلام who said with regard to His verse: ﴿*Be a community that calls for what is good, urges what is right, and forbids what is wrong*﴾: 'Within this verse is a repudiation of the People of the Kaʿba (*ahl al-qibla*) for their misdeeds, for whosoever among the Muslims does not call for what is good, urge what is right and forbid

47 Muḥammad b. Sulaymān al-Baṣrī al-Daylāmī is an extremely weak and unreliable narrator of Imam Mūsā al-Kāẓim (and possibly also of Imam Jaʿfar al-Ṣādiq). He is also described as an exaggerator (*ghālī*) of the status of the Imams. See Ḥillī, *Khulāṣat al-aqwāl*, 402 (nr. 1624); Khūʾī, *Muʿjam*, 17: 135–9 (nr. 10900).

48 Despite many near equivalents, we could not find any individual with this exact name in Ḥillī's *Khulāṣat al-aqwāl* nor Khūʾī's *Muʿjam*.

١٢٢. عن ابن يزيد، قال: سألتُ أبا الحسن عليه السلام عن قوله تعالى: ﴿وَاعْتَصِمُوا بِحَبْلِ اللهِ جَمِيعًا﴾، قال: عليّ بن أبي طالب عليه السلام حَبْلُ الله المتين.

١٢٣. عن جابر، عن أبي جعفر عليه السلام، قال: آل محمّد عليهم السلام هم حَبْل الله الذي أمر بالاعتصام به، فقال: ﴿وَاعْتَصِمُوا بِحَبْلِ اللهِ جَمِيعًا وَلَا تَفَرَّقُوا﴾.

١٢٤. عن محمّد بن سُليمان البصري الدَّيلمي، عن أبيه، عن أبي عبد الله عليه السلام، ﴿وَكُنتُمْ عَلَىٰ شَفَا حُفْرَةٍ مِّنَ النَّارِ فَأَنقَذَكُم مِّنْهَا﴾ محمّد صلى الله عليه وآله وسلم.

١٢٥. عن أبي الحسن علي بن محمّد بن مِيثم، عن أبي عبد الله عليه السلام، قال: أبْشِرُوا بأعظم المِنَن عليكم، قول الله: ﴿وَكُنتُمْ عَلَىٰ شَفَا حُفْرَةٍ مِّنَ النَّارِ فَأَنقَذَكُم مِّنْهَا﴾ فالإنقاذ من الله هِبةٌ، والله لا يَرْجع من هِبَتِه.

١٢٦. عن ابن هارون، قال: كان أبو عبد الله عليه السلام إذا ذكر النبيّ صلى الله عليه وآله وسلم، قال: بأبي وأُمّي ونفسي وقومي وعِترتي، عَجَبٌ للعرب كيف لا تَحْمِلنا على رُؤوسها، والله يقول في كتابه: ﴿وَكُنتُمْ عَلَىٰ شَفَا حُفْرَةٍ مِّنَ النَّارِ فَأَنقَذَكُم مِّنْهَا﴾ فبرسول الله صلى الله عليه وآله وسلم والله أُنْقِذُوا.

١٢٧. عن أبي عمرو الزُّبيري، عن أبي عبد الله عليه السلام، قال في قوله تعالى: ﴿وَلْتَكُن مِّنكُمْ أُمَّةٌ يَدْعُونَ إِلَى الْخَيْرِ وَيَأْمُرُونَ بِالْمَعْرُوفِ وَيَنْهَوْنَ عَنِ الْمُنكَرِ﴾ قال: في هذه الآية تَكْفيرُ أهلِ القِبلة بالمعاصي، لأنّه من لم يكُن يَدْعو إلى الخَيرات، ويأمُر بالمعروف، ويَنْهى عن المنكر من المسلمين، فليس من الأُمّة التي وَصَفها الله، لأنّكم تزْعُمون أنّ جميع المُسلمين من

wrongdoing is not part of the community that God describes here. You assume that all Muslims are part of the community of Muḥammad, even though this verse describes the community of Muḥammad as being one that calls for what is good, urges what is right and forbids wrongdoing. So how can one who lacks these credentials be considered a part of the community, when he goes against God's requirements and descriptions of that community?' [3:104]

128. From Ḥammād b. ʿĪsā, from one of his associates, from Abū ʿAbd Allāh عليه السلام who said, 'In ʿAlī's عليه السلام recitation of: ﴾*[Believers], you are the best community singled out for people*﴿ he said, "They are the progeny of Muḥammad صلى الله عليه وآله."' [3:110]

129. And Abū Baṣīr, who said on his authority, 'He said, "Indeed this verse has been revealed especially about Muḥammad صلى الله عليه وآله and the vicegerents, for He has said: ﴾*[Believers],* ***you are the best community*** *singled out for people: you order what is right, forbid what is wrong*﴿ – this is exactly how Jibrīl brought it down, and He only meant by it Muḥammad and his vicegerents, God's blessings be upon them."' [3:110*]

130. From Abū ʿAmr al-Zubayrī, from Abū ʿAbd Allāh عليه السلام who said regarding God's verse: ﴾*[Believers], you are the best community singled out for people: you order what is right, forbid what is wrong*﴿, 'He means the community charged with answering the call of Ibrāhīm,[49] so they are the community that God sent guidance to; they are the middle community and the best community singled out for people.' [3:110]

131. From Yūnus b. ʿAbd al-Raḥmān, from a number of our associates, who traced it back to Abū ʿAbd Allāh عليه السلام who said about the verse: ﴾*unless they hold fast to a lifeline from God and a lifeline from mankind*﴿, 'The lifeline from God is God's Book and the lifeline from mankind is Alī b. Abī Ṭālib عليه السلام.' [3:112]

---

49 A reference to Q. 2:128 in which Prophet Ibrāhīm supplicates God, saying: ﴾*Our Lord, make us devoted to You; make our descendants into a community devoted to You. Show us how to worship and accept our repentance, for You are the Ever Relenting, the Most Merciful.*﴿

أُمَّة محمّد صلى الله عليه وآله، وقد بَدَت هذه الآية، وقد وَصَفتْ أُمَّة محمد بالدّعاء إلى الخير، والأمر بالمعروف، والنهي عن المنكر، ومن لم يُوجَد فيه الصِّفة التي وصفت بها، فكيف يكون من الأمَّة، وهو على خِلاف ما شَرَطه الله على الأُمَّة ووصفها به؟!

١٢٨. عن حمّاد بن عيسى، عن بعض أصحابه، عن أبي عبد الله عليه السلام، قال: في قراءة عليّ عليه السلام ﴿كُنتُمْ خَيْرَ أُمَّةٍ أُخْرِجَتْ لِلنَّاسِ﴾، قال: هم آل محمّد صلى الله عليه وآله.

١٢٩. وأبو بصير، عنه، قال: قال عليه السلام: إنّما أُنزلت هذه الآية على محمّد صلى الله عليه وآله فيه وفي الأوصياءِ خاصّة، فقال: ﴿أَنتُمْ خَيْرَ أُمَّةٍ أُخْرِجَتْ لِلنَّاسِ تَأْمُرُونَ بِالْمَعْرُوفِ وَتَنْهَوْنَ عَنِ الْمُنكَرِ﴾ هكذا والله نَزَل بها جبْرَئيل عليه السلام، وما عنى بها إلا محمّدًا وأوصياءه (صلوات الله عليهم).

١٣٠. عن أبي عمرو الزّبيري، عن أبي عبد الله عليه السلام، في قول الله تعالى: ﴿كُنتُمْ خَيْرَ أُمَّةٍ أُخْرِجَتْ لِلنَّاسِ تَأْمُرُونَ بِالْمَعْرُوفِ وَتَنْهَوْنَ عَنِ الْمُنكَرِ﴾، قال: يعني الأُمَّة التي وَجَبت لها دَعْوَة إبراهيم عليه السلام، فهم الأُمَّة التي بَعَث الله فيها ومنها وإليها، وهم الأُمَّة الوسطى، وهم خير أُمَّةٍ أُخْرِجت للنّاس.

١٣١. عن يُونس بن عبد الرّحمن، عن عِدَّة من أصحابنا، ورفعوه إلى أبي عبد الله عليه السلام، في قول تعالى: ﴿إِلاَّ بِحَبْلٍ مِنَ اللهِ وَحَبْلٍ مِنَ النَّاسِ﴾، قال: الحَبْلُ من الله كتاب الله، والحَبْل من الناس هو علي بن أبي طالب عليه السلام.

132. From Isḥāq b. ʿAmmār, from Abū ʿAbd Allāh عليه السلام who said after reciting the verse: ﴾*because they have persistently disbelieved in God's revelation and killed prophets without any right, all because of their disobedience and boundless transgression*﴿: 'By God, they did not physically strike them with their hands nor kill them with their swords, but they heard their narratives and their secrets then divulged them. So because of them they were arrested and killed, and this came to be counted as murder, assault, and a sin.' [3:112]

133. From Abū Baṣīr who narrated, 'I was reciting: ﴾*God helped you at Badr when you were very weak*﴿ in the presence of Abū ʿAbd Allāh when he said, "No, that is not how God has revealed it. Rather it was revealed as: ﴾***when you were few in number.***﴿"' [3:123*]

134. From ʿAbd Allāh b. Sinān, from Abū ʿAbd Allāh عليه السلام. He narrated, 'My father asked him about this verse: ﴾*God helped you at Badr when you were very weak.*﴿ He replied, "That is not how God revealed it – God would never disgrace His messenger. Rather it was revealed: ﴾***when you were few in number.***﴿"' The same narration is also reported from ʿĪsā, from Ṣafwān, from Ibn Sinān. [3:123*]

135. From Ribʿī b. Ḥarīz[50], from Abū ʿAbd Allāh عليه السلام that he recited it as: ﴾*God helped you at Badr when you were **very feeble***﴿, saying, 'They would not have been abased whilst the Messenger of God was among them, peace be upon him and his family.' [3:123*]

136. From Jābir, from Abū Jaʿfar عليه السلام who said, 'The angels were wearing white, flowing turbans on the Day of Badr.' [3:123]

137. From Ismāʿīl b. Hammām[51], from Abū al-Ḥasan عليه السلام who said regarding God's words: ﴾*swooping* [angels]﴿: 'Their turbans swathed around the Messenger of God, their trains flowing in front of him and behind him.' [3:124–125]

---

50 We have not been able to identify this individual.

51 We have not been able to identify this individual.

١٣٢. عن إسحاق بن عمّار، عن أبي عبد الله عليه السلام، وتلا هذه الآية ﴿ذَٰلِكَ بِأَنَّهُمْ كَانُوا يَكْفُرُونَ بِآيَاتِ اللَّهِ وَيَقْتُلُونَ الْأَنبِيَاءَ بِغَيْرِ حَقٍّ ذَٰلِكَ بِمَا عَصَوا وَكَانُوا يَعْتَدُونَ﴾، قال عليه السلام، والله ما ضَرَبُوهم بأيديهم، ولا قتلوهم بأسيافهم، ولكن سَمِعُوا أحاديثهم وأسرارهم فأذاعوها، فأُخِذُوا عليها فقُتِلُوا، فصار قَتْلاً واعتِداءً ومَعْصيةً.

١٣٣. عن أبي بصير، قال: قرأتُ عند أبي عبد الله عليه السلام ﴿وَلَقَدْ نَصَرَكُمُ اللَّهُ بِبَدْرٍ وَأَنتُمْ أَذِلَّةٌ﴾، قال: مه، ليس هكذا أنزله الله، إنّما أُنزلت (وأنتم قليل).

١٣٤. عن عبد الله بن سِنان، عن أبي عبد الله عليه السلام، قال: سأله أبي عن هذه الآية ﴿لَقَدْ نَصَرَكُمُ اللَّهُ بِبَدْرٍ وَأَنتُمْ أَذِلَّةٌ﴾، قال: ليس هكذا أنزله الله، ما أذلَّ الله رَسُوله قطّ، إنّما أُنزلت (وأنتم قليل).

عن عيسى، عن صفوان، عن ابن سِنان، مثله.

١٣٥. عن رِبعي بن حَرِيز، عن أبي عبد الله عليه السلام، أنّه قرأ ﴿وَلَقَدْ نَصَرَكُمُ اللَّهُ بِبَدْرٍ وَأَنتُمْ ضُعَفَاءُ﴾ وماكانوا أذِلَّة ورسول الله فيهم عليه وعلى آله السلام.

١٣٦. عن جابر، عن أبي جعفر عليه السلام، قال: كانت على الملائكة العمائم البِيض المُرْسَلة يوم بَدْر.

١٣٧. عن إسماعيل بن همّام، عن أبي الحسن صلى الله عليه وآله وسلم، في قول الله: ﴿مُسَوِّمِينَ﴾، قال: العَمائم، اعتمّ رسول الله صلى الله عليه وآله وسلم فَسَدَلَها من بين يديه ومن خلفه.

138. From Ḍurays b. ʿAbd al-Malik[52], from Abū Jaʿfar عليه السلام who said, 'The angels who helped Muḥammad ﷺ on the Day of Badr on earth have not yet ascended back up, nor shall they do so until they help the Master of this authority [i.e. the Twelfth Imam] and they are five thousand in number.' [3:124–125]

139. From Jābir al-Juʿfī who narrated, 'I recited the words of God: ﴾*it is not for you [Prophet] to decide* [...]﴿ in the presence of Abū Jaʿfar عليه السلام, so he said, "By God, of course, it was up to him to decide on matters and cannot be as you believe it to be. I am telling you that God, Blessed and most High, when He commanded His Prophet ﷺ to make ʿAlī's vicegerency manifest, he contemplated his people's animosity towards him which he knew full well, and that is the fact that God had distinguished him from them in all his virtues: he was the first to believe in the Messenger of God ﷺ and in the One who sent him; he was the most supportive of all people towards God and His Messenger, the most combative against their enemies and the most hostile against those who opposed them. His knowledge was distinct and unparalleled to anyone else, and the worth of his virtues was immeasurable.

So when the Prophet ﷺ contemplated his people's animosity towards him regarding these virtues, and the jealousy that they harboured against him, it angered him as a result. So God told him that it was not for him to decide the matter and that it was for God to decide, and to make ʿAlī عليه السلام his successor and the one vested with authority after him. This is what God meant. How can it not be up to him to decide matters when God Himself had licensed him to effectively legalise and prohibit things, saying: ﴾*accept whatever the Messenger gives you, and abstain from whatever he forbids you*﴿ (59:7)?' [3:128]

140. From Jābir who narrated, 'I asked Abū Jaʿfar عليه السلام, "Explain to me His words to His Prophet ﷺ: ﴾*it is not for you [Prophet] to decide...*﴿" So Abū Jaʿfar عليه السلام said, "What God said is one thing and what He willed is another, Jābir. The Messenger of God ﷺ desperately wished for ʿAlī عليه السلام to be the one after

52 Abū Ammāra Ḍurays b. ʿAbd al-Malik b. Aʿyan al-Shaybānī, about whom there is scant information, is considered a reliable narrator. See Ḥillī, *Khulāṣat al-aqwāl*, 172 (nr. 505); Khūʾī, *Muʿjam*, 10:161–3 (nr. 5971).

١٣٨. عن ضُريس بن عبد الملك، عن أبي جعفر عليه السلام، قال: إنّ الملائكة الذين نَصَرُوا محمّدًا صلى الله عليه وآله يوم بدر في الأرض، ما صَعِدوا بعدُ، ولا يَصْعَدُون حتّى يَنْصُروا صاحب هذا الأمر، وهم خمسة آلاف.

١٣٩. عن جابر الجُعفي، قال: قرأتُ عند أبي جعفر عليه السلام قول الله عزّ وجلّ: ﴿لَيْسَ لَكَ مِنَ الْأَمْرِ شَيْءٌ﴾ . قال: بلى والله، إنّ له من الأمر شيئًا وشيئًا وشيئًا، وليس حيثُ ذهبت، ولكنّي أُخبرك أنّ الله تبارك وتعالى لمّا أمر نبيّه صلى الله عليه وآله أن يُظْهِر ولاية عليّ عليه السلام فكّر في عَداوة قومه له ومعرفته بهم، وذلك للّذي فَضّله الله به عليهم في جميع خصاله، كان أوّل من آمَن برسول الله صلى الله عليه وآله وبمن أرسله، وكان أَنْصَر الناس لله ولرسوله صلى الله عليه وآله، وأَقْتَلهم لعدوّهما، وأشَدَّهم بُغضًا لمن خالفهما، وفَضْل عِلمه الذي لم يُساوِه أحدٌ، ومناقبه التي لا تُحصى شَرَفًا.

فلما فكّر النبي صلى الله عليه وآله في عَداوة قومه له في هذه الخصال، وحَسَدهم له عليها، ضاق عن ذلك، فأخبر الله أنّه ليس له من هذا الأمر شيء، إنّما الأمر فيه إلى الله أن يُصيّر عليًّا عليه السلام وصيّه ووليّ الأمر بعده، فهذا عنى الله تعالى، وكيف لا يكون له من الأمر شيء، وقد فوّض الله إليه أن جعل ما أحلّ فهو حلال، وما حرّم فهو حرام؛ قوله: ﴿مَا آتَاكُمُ الرَّسُولُ فَخُذُوهُ وَمَا نَهَاكُمْ عَنْهُ فَانْتَهُوا﴾ ؟

١٤٠. عن جابر، قال: قلتُ لأبي جعفر عليه السلام: قوله لنبيّه صلى الله عليه وآله: ﴿لَيْسَ لَكَ مِنَ الْأَمْرِ شَيْءٌ﴾ فسِّره لي. قال: فقال أبو جعفر عليه السلام: لشيء قاله الله، ولشيء أراده الله. يا جابر، إنّ

him over the people, but God's will was different to what the Messenger of God ﷺ wished for."

I asked, "So what did He mean by that?"

He replied, "Yes, in God's telling His Messenger ﷺ thus, He meant: 'The matter of 'Alī is not for you to decide, O Muḥammad. It is up to Me to decide about 'Alī and others. Have I not recited to you, O Muḥammad, what I revealed to you previously from My Book: ﴾*Alif Lam Mim. Do people think they will be left alone after saying 'We believe' without being put to the test? We tested those who went before them: God will certainly mark out which ones are truthful and which are lying.*﴿ (29:1–3)'" He continued, "The Messenger of God ﷺ left the matter for God to decide."' [3:128]

141. From al-Jarmī, from Abū Ja'far (عليه السلام) that he recited it as: ﴾***Whether you pardon them or whether you punish them is not for you [Prophet] to decide: they are wrongdoers.***﴿ [3:128*]

142. From Dāwūd b. Sirḥān, from a man, from Abū 'Abd Allāh (عليه السلام) that he said about the verse: ﴾*Hurry towards your Lord's forgiveness and a Garden as wide as the heavens and earth*﴿, 'If they were to be spread thus', and he opened his hands, placing them next to each other. [3:133]

143. From Abū 'Amr al-Zubayrī, from Abū 'Abd Allāh (عليه السلام) who said, 'God is compassionate towards a servant who refuses to let Shayṭān compete for the attention that he gives to his religion. In God's Book is the salvation from ruin, insight in the face of blindness, the signpost to guidance and the cure for what is in the hearts, in which He commands you all to seek forgiveness alongside repentance, saying: ﴾*those who remember God and implore forgiveness for their sins if they do something shameful or wrong themselves – who forgives sins but God? – and who never knowingly persist in doing wrong.*﴿ He also says: ﴾*Yet anyone who does evil or wrongs his own soul and then asks God for forgiveness will find Him most forgiving and merciful.*﴿ (4:110) This is the forgiveness that God has commanded to be sought and made repentance a prerequisite of it, along with uprooting all that God has forbidden, for He says: ﴾*good words rise up to Him and He lifts up the righteous deed.*﴿ (35:10) This verse shows that the seeking of forgiveness can only be raised towards God by righteous deeds and repentance.' [3:135]

رسول الله صلى الله عليه وآله كان حَرِيصًا على أن يكون عليٌّ عليه السلام من بعده على النّاس، وكان عند الله خِلاف ما أراد رسول الله صلى الله عليه وآله.

قال: قلت: فما معنى ذلك؟

قال: نعم، عنى بذلك قول الله لرسوله صلى الله عليه وآله: ﴿لَيْسَ لَكَ مِنَ الأَمْرِ شَيْءٌ﴾ يا محمّد في عليّ، الأمر إليَّ في عليّ وفي غيره، ألم أتلُ عليك يا محمّد فيما أنزلت من كتابي إليك ﴿الٓمٓ ۞ أَحَسِبَ النَّاسُ أَنْ يُتْرَكُوا أَنْ يَقُولُوا آمَنَّا وَهُمْ لاَ يُفْتَنُونَ﴾ إلى قوله: ﴿فَلَيَعْلَمَنَّ﴾.

قال: فوّض رسول الله صلى الله عليه وآله الأمر إليه.

١٤١. عن الجرمي عن أبي جعفر عليه السلام، أنّه قرأ ﴿لَيْسَ لَكَ مِنَ الأَمْرِ شَيْءٌ أَوْ تَتُوبَ عَلَيْهِمْ أَوْ تُعَذِّبَهُمْ فَإِنَّهُمْ ظَالِمُونَ﴾.

١٤٢. عن داود بن سِرحان، عن رجل، عن أبي عبد الله عليه السلام، في قول الله تعالى: ﴿وَسَارِعُوا إِلَى مَغْفِرَةٍ مِنْ رَبِّكُمْ وَجَنَّةٍ عَرْضُهَا السَّمَوَاتُ وَالأَرْضُ﴾، قال عليه السلام، إذا وضعوها كذا، وبسط يديه إحداهما مع الأُخرى.

١٤٣. عن أبي عمر والزُّبيري، عن أبي عبد الله عليه السلام، قال: رَحِم الله عبدًا لم يرضَ من نفسه أن يكون إبليس نظيرًا له في دينه، وفي كتاب الله نجاةٌ من الرّدى، وبصيرةٌ من العَمَى، ودليلٌ إلى الهُدى، وشِفاءٌ لما في الصُّدور، فيما أمركم الله به من الاستغفار مع التّوبة، قال الله: ﴿وَالَّذِينَ إِذَا فَعَلُوا فَاحِشَةً أَوْ ظَلَمُوا أَنْفُسَهُمْ ذَكَرُوا اللهَ فَاسْتَغْفَرُوا لِذُنُوبِهِمْ وَمَنْ يَغْفِرُ الذُّنُوبَ إِلاَّ اللهُ وَلَمْ يُصِرُّوا عَلَى مَا فَعَلُوا وَهُمْ يَعْلَمُونَ﴾ وقال: ﴿وَمَنْ

144. From Jābir, from Abū Jaʿfar عليه السلام who said regarding God's verse: ﴾*who forgives sins but God? – and who never knowingly persist in doing wrong*﴿: 'Persistence means that the servant sins, but he neither seeks God's forgiveness for it and nor does it occur to him to mend his ways – that is persistence.' [3:135]

145. From Zurāra, from Abū ʿAbd Allāh عليه السلام who said regarding God's words: ﴾*We deal out such days among people in turn*﴿, 'Since God created Ādam, He deals one hand and Iblīs deals one – so where is God's Hand in all this? Indeed, is He not the only One standing [in control]?' [3:140]

146. From al-Ḥasan b. ʿAlī [b. Ziyād] al-Washshā'[53], with a disconnected chain of transmission and without mentioning his source, cited Abū ʿAbd Allāh عليه السلام as having said, 'By God, you will be thoroughly examined, differentiated and sifted out until only the staunchest from among you remain.' I asked, 'And what does the 'staunchest' mean?' He replied, 'It is like when someone takes some meal and passes it through a thresh, throwing out the dross when the wheat has been separated from the chaff. He continues purifying it thus and straining it three times until he is left with only that which will pose no detriment to him.' [3:141]

53 Abū Muḥammad al-Ḥasan b. ʿAlī b. Ziyād al-Washshā' al-Kūfī, a trustworthy companion of Imam ʿAlī b. Mūsā al-Riḍā. See Ḥillī, *Khulāṣat al-aqwāl*, 104 (nr. 237); Khū'ī, *Muʿjam*, 6: 77–80 (nr. 3040).

يَعْمَلْ سُوءًا أَوْ يَظْلِمْ نَفْسَهُ ثُمَّ يَسْتَغْفِرِ اللهَ يَجِدِ اللهَ غَفُورًا رَحِيمًا﴾ فهذا ما أمر الله به من الاستغفار، واشترط معه التّوبة، والإقلاع عمّا حرّم الله، فإنّه يقول: ﴿إِلَيْهِ يَصْعَدُ الْكَلِمُ الطَّيِّبُ وَالْعَمَلُ الصَّالِحُ يَرْفَعُهُ﴾ وهذه الآية تَدُلُّ على أنّ الاستغفار لا يَرْفَعه إلى الله، إلّا العمل الصالح والتّوبة.

١٤٤. عن جابر، عن أبي جعفر عليه السلام، في قول الله عزّ وجلّ: ﴿وَمَنْ يَغْفِرُ الذُّنُوبَ إِلَّا اللهُ وَلَمْ يُصِرُّوا عَلَى مَا فَعَلُوا وَهُمْ يَعْلَمُونَ﴾، قال: الإصرار أن يُذنب العبد ولا يستغفر، ولا يُحَدِّث نفسه بالتّوبة، فذلك الإصرار.

١٤٥. عن زُرارة، عن أبي عبدالله عليه السلام، في قول الله تعالى: ﴿وَتِلْكَ الْأَيَّامُ نُدَاوِلُهَا بَيْنَ النَّاسِ﴾، قال: ما زال مذ خَلَق الله آدم دَولة لله ودولة لإبليس، فأين دَولة الله، أما هو إلّا قائمٌ واحدٌ؟

١٤٦. عن الحسن بن عليٍّ الوشّاء، بإسنادٍ له يرسله إلى أبي عبدالله عليه السلام، قال: والله لَتُمَحَّصُنَّ والله لَتُمَيَّزُنَّ والله لَتُغَرْبَلُنَّ حتّى لا يبقى منكم إلّا الأنْدَر.

قلت: وما الأنْدَر؟ قال: البَيْدَر، وهو أن يُدْخِل الرّجل فيه الطّعام يُطيِّن عليه، ثمّ يُخْرِجه قد أكل بعضه بعضًا، فلا يزال يُنَقِّيه، ثمّ يَكُنّ عليه، ثمّ يُخْرِجه، حتّى يفعل ذلك ثلاث مرّات، حتّى يبقى ما لا يَضُرُّه شيء.

147. From Dāwūd al-Raqqī[54] who narrated, 'I asked Abū 'Abd Allāh عليه السلام about God's verse: ﴾*Did you think you would enter the Garden without God first proving which of you would struggle for His cause and remain steadfast?*﴿ He replied, "God is the One who knows best what He is bringing into existence before He even does so when they are mere particles. He can tell apart those who will strive from those who will not, just as He knows which of His creatures He has destined to die before He causes them to die, without showing them [the cause of] their death during their lifetime."' [3:142]

148. From Ḥanān b. Sadīr, on his father's authority, from Abū Ja'far عليه السلام who said, 'People regressed to apostasy after the Prophet ﷺ except for three people.' I asked, 'And who are those three?' He replied, 'Al-Miqdād, Abū Dharr, and Salmān al-Fārsī. Then other people came to be known after a little while.' Then he continued, 'Those people who broke away and who refused to give allegiance until they themselves came to the Commander of the Faithful عليه السلام and forced him to give allegiance. This is the purport of God's verse: ﴾*Muḥammad is only a messenger before whom many messengers have been and gone. If he died or was killed, would you revert to your old ways? If anyone did so, he would not harm God in the least. God will reward the grateful.*﴿' [3:144]

149. From al-Fuḍayl b. Yasār, from Abū Ja'far عليه السلام who said, 'When the Messenger of God ﷺ passed away all of the people regressed to their pagan ways except for four: 'Alī, al-Miqdād, Salmān and Abū Dharr.' I asked, 'What about 'Ammār?' He replied, 'If you mean those who were not affected by anything at all, then it was these three.' [3:144]

150. From al-Aṣbagh b. Nubāta who narrated, 'I heard the Commander of the Faithful عليه السلام say in one of his addresses on the day of the Battle of the Camel: "O people! God - hallowed be His Name and mighty His force - has never

54 Abū Sulaymān Dāwūd b. Kathīr al-Raqqī, a client of the Banū Asad, was a companion of the fifth and sixth Imams who lived up until the lifetime of the eighth Imam. Shaykh al-Ṭūsī and al-Mufīd consider him to be a reliable and trustworthy narrator, but according to Najāshī and Ibn al-Ghaḍā'irī he is extremely weak and unreliable, both of whom regard him to have belonged to one of the heterodox movements exaggerating the status of the Imams. See Ḥillī, *Khulāṣat al-aqwāl*, 140–1 (nr. 388); Khū'ī, *Mu'jam*, 8: 139–40 (nr. 4451).

١٤٧. عن داود الرقّي، قال: سألتُ أبا عبدالله عليه السلام عن قول الله عزّ وجلّ ﴿أَمْ حَسِبْتُمْ أَنْ تَدْخُلُوا الْجَنَّةَ وَلَمَّا يَعْلَمِ اللَّهُ الَّذِينَ جَاهَدُوا مِنْكُمْ﴾. قال: إنّ الله هو أعلم بما هو مُكوّنه قبل أن يُكوّنه، وهم ذرّ، وعلِم من يُجاهد ممّن لا يُجاهد، كما علِم أنه يُميت خَلْقَه قبل أن يُميتهم، ولم يُرِهم موْتَهم وهم أحياء.

١٤٨. عن حَنان بن سَدير، عن أبيه، عن أبي جعفر عليه السلام، قال: كان الناسُ أهلَ رِدَّةٍ بعد النبيّ صلى الله عليه وآله إلاّ ثلاثة. فقلت: ومن الثلاثة؟ قال: المِقْداد، وأبو ذرّ، وسلمان الفارسي، ثمّ عَرَف أُناس بعد يسير. فقال: هؤلاء الذين دارت عليهم الرّحا، وأبوا أن يُبايعوا حتّى جاءوا بأمير المؤمنين عليه السلام مُكرَهًا فبايَع، وذلك قول الله: ﴿وَمَا مُحَمَّدٌ إِلَّا رَسُولٌ قَدْ خَلَتْ مِنْ قَبْلِهِ الرُّسُلُ أَفَإِنْ مَاتَ أَوْ قُتِلَ انْقَلَبْتُمْ عَلَى أَعْقَابِكُمْ وَمَنْ يَنْقَلِبْ عَلَى عَقِبَيْهِ فَلَنْ يَضُرَّ اللَّهَ شَيْئًا وَسَيَجْزِي اللَّهُ الشَّاكِرِينَ﴾.

١٤٩. عن الفُضيل بن يَسار، عن أبي جعفر عليه السلام، قال: إنّ رسول الله صلى الله عليه وآله لمّا قُبِض، صار الناس كُلُّهم أهل جاهلية إلاّ أربعة: عليّ، والمِقداد، وسلمان، وأبو ذرّ. فقلت: فعمّار؟ فقال: إن كنت تُريد الذين لم يُدخِلهم شيء فهؤلاء الثلاثة.

١٥٠. عن الأصبغ بن نُباتة، قال: سَمِعتُ أمير المؤمنين عليه السلام يقول في كلامٍ له يوم الجَمَل: يا أيُّها النّاس، إنّ الله (تبارك اسمُه وعزّ جُنده)، لم يَقْبِض نبيًّا قطّ حتّى يكون له في أُمّته من يهدي بهداه ويَقْصِد سيرته ويَدُلُّ على مَعالِم سَبيل الحقّ الذي فَرَض الله على عِباده، ثمّ قرأ ﴿وَمَا مُحَمَّدٌ إِلَّا رَسُولٌ قَدْ خَلَتْ﴾ الآية.

taken the life of a prophet without him first leaving behind in his community someone who will guide others with the same guidance, emulate his practice, and escort people towards the beacons on the path of truth that God has charged all His servants to tread. Then he recited: ﴾*Muḥammad is only a messenger before whom many messengers have been and gone...*﴿"' [3:144]

151. From 'Amr b. Abī al-Miqdām[55], on his father's authority who narrated, 'I asked Abū Ja'far عليه السلام, "The majority claim that the allegiance given to Abū Bakr when people gathered around him was approved by God and that God would not subject Muḥammad's community to trials after him."

So Abū Ja'far عليه السلام replied, "Well, they do not read God's Book – does He not say: ﴾*Muḥammad is only a messenger before whom many messengers have been and gone. If he died or was killed, would you revert to your old ways? If anyone did so, he would not harm God in the least. God will reward the grateful.*﴿

So I said to him, "But they interpret this verse in a different way."

He replied, "Did God not inform them of communities who preceded them, who disputed amongst themselves after clear signs had been brought to them, where He says: ﴾*We gave 'Īsā, son of Maryam, Our clear signs and strengthened him with the holy spirit. If God had so willed, their successors would not have fought each other after they had been brought clear signs. But they disagreed: some believed and some disbelieved. If God had so willed, they would not have fought each other, but God does what He will*﴿ (2:253)? From this, it can be gathered that the companions of Muḥammad, upon him be peace and blessings, fought each other too, and some of them believed and some disbelieved."' [3:144]

152. From 'Abd al-Ṣamad b. Bashīr, from Abū 'Abd Allāh عليه السلام who said, 'Have you considered that the Prophet ﷺ could have died or been killed, for God says: ﴾*If he died or was killed, would you revert to your old ways?*﴿ So he was poisoned before death – the two [women] made him drink it.[56] We say

55 Abū Muḥammad 'Amr b. Abī al-Miqdām Thābit b. Hurmuz, a Kufan client of Banū 'Ijl and a transmitter of Sunnī and Shī'ī *ḥadīth*. He narrated the traditions of Imam Muḥammad al-Bāqir and Imam Ja'far al-Ṣādiq. See Modarressi, *Tradition and Survival*, 205–6 (nr. 44).

56 The two women being referred to in this narration are Ḥafṣa bt. 'Umar b. al-Khaṭṭāb and 'Ā'isha bt. Abī Bakr.

١٥١. عن عمرو بن أبي المِقدام، عن أبيه، قال: قلتُ لأبي جعفر عليه السلام: إنّ العامّة تزعُم أنّ بيعة أبي بكر حيث اجتمع لها الناس كانت رضًا لله، وما كان الله ليَفْتِن أُمّة محمّد من بعده.

فقال أبو جعفر عليه السلام: وما يقرءون كتاب الله؟ أليس الله يقول: ﴿وَمَا مُحَمَّدٌ إِلَّا رَسُولٌ قَدْ خَلَتْ مِن قَبْلِهِ الرُّسُلُ أَفَإِنْ مَاتَ أَوْ قُتِلَ انقَلَبْتُمْ عَلَى أَعْقَابِكُمْ﴾ الآية؟

قال: فقلت له: إنّهم يُفسِّرون هذا على وجهٍ آخر. قال: فقال: أو ليس قد أخبر الله عن الذين من قبلهم من الأُمم أنّهم اختلفوا من بعد ما جاءتهم البيّنات حين قال: ﴿وَآتَيْنَا عِيسَى ابْنَ مَرْيَمَ الْبَيِّنَاتِ وَأَيَّدْنَاهُ بِرُوحِ الْقُدُسِ﴾ إلى قوله: ﴿فَمِنْهُم مَّنْ آمَنَ وَمِنْهُم مَّن كَفَرَ﴾ الآية؟ ففي هذا ما يُسْتَدَلُّ به على أنّ أصحاب محمّد عليه الصلاة والسلام قد اختلفوا من بعده، فمنهم من آمن، ومنهم من كَفَر.

١٥٢. عن عبد الصمد بن بشير، عن أبي عبد الله عليه السلام، قال: أتدرُون مات النبيّ صلى الله عليه وآله وسلم أو قُتِل، إنّ الله يقول: ﴿أَفَإِنْ مَاتَ أَوْ قُتِلَ انقَلَبْتُمْ عَلَى أَعْقَابِكُمْ﴾ فَسُمّ قبل الموت، إنّهما سَقَتَاه، فقلنا إنّهما وأبوهما شرّ من خلَق الله.

that they and their fathers [Abū Bakr and ʿUmar] are the worst of all God's creatures.' [3:144]

153. From al-Ḥusayn b. al-Mundhir[57] who narrated, 'I asked Abū ʿAbd Allāh عليه السلام about God's verse: ﴾*If he died or was killed, would you revert to your old ways?*﴿ – Murder or [natural] death? He replied, "It refers to those of his companions who did what they did."' [3:144]

154. From Manṣūr b. al-Walīd al-Ṣayqal[58] that he heard Abū ʿAbd Allāh Jaʿfar b. Muḥammad عليه السلام reciting: ﴾*Many prophets were killed, with large bands of godly men alongside them.*﴿ He said, 'Thousands and thousands.' Then he added, 'Indeed, by God, they were killed.' [3:146]

155. From al-Ḥasan b. Abī al-ʿAlā[59], from Abū ʿAbd Allāh عليه السلام when mentioning the Day of Uḥud and the moment when the Messenger of God's front teeth were broken and the people fled, climbing back up over the slopes while the Messenger was calling out to them from behind.

So God requited them with sorrow for sorrow, and after that they were overtaken by drowsiness. So I asked, 'What was [the cause of] this drowsiness?'

He replied, '[Due to] anxiety, for when they awoke, they exclaimed, "We have disbelieved." Abū Sufyān then came and stood atop the mountain with his idol Hubal, and said, "Hubal is high!" So the Messenger of God ﷺ retorted on that day, "God is higher and more exalted!"

Then the Messenger of God's teeth were broken and his gums began to bleed, so he said, "My Lord, I implore you to fulfil Your promise to me, for it truly only takes Your will for these not to be worshipped."

The Messenger of God ﷺ then said, "O ʿAlī, where were you?"

---

57 Al-Ḥusayn b. al-Mundhir, concerning whom there is scant information, is generally considered a reliable narrator. See Ḥillī, *Khulāṣat al-aqwāl*, 116 (nr. 286); Khūʾī, *Muʿjam*, 7: 102 (nr. 3669).

58 Abū Muḥammad Manṣūr b. al-Walīd b. al-Ṣayqal, a companion of either Muḥammad al-Bāqir or Jaʿfar al-Ṣādiq. See Khūʾī, *Muʿjam*, 19: 380–1 (nr. 12714).

59 This is probably a transcription or editorial mistake, and should in more likelihood be a reference to Abū ʿAlī al-Ḥusayn b. Abī al-ʿAlā al-Aʿwar, a reliable and trustworthy companion of Imam Jaʿfar al-Ṣādiq. See Khūʾī, *Muʿjam*, 6: 198–202 (nr. 3276).

١٥٣. عن الحسين بن المنذر، قال: سألتُ أبا عبدالله عليه السلام عن قوله تعالى: ﴿أَفَإِنْ مَاتَ أَوْ قُتِلَ انْقَلَبْتُمْ عَلَىٰٓ أَعْقَابِكُمْ﴾ القتل، أم الموت؟ قال: يعني أصحابه الذين فَعَلوا ما فعَلوا.

١٥٤. عن مَنْصُور بن الوليد الصَّيقل، أنّه سَمِع أبا عبدالله جعفر بن محمّد عليه السلام قرأ: ﴿وَكَأَيِّن مِّن نَّبِيٍّ قَاتَلَ مَعَهُۥ رِبِّيُّونَ كَثِيرٌ﴾، قال: ألوف وألوف، ثمّ قال: إي والله يُقتَلون.

١٥٥. عن الحسين بن أبي العلاء، عن أبي عبدالله عليه السلام، وذَكَر يوم أحد قال: إنّ رَسُول الله صلى الله عليه وآله وسلم كُسِرت رَبَاعِيته، وإنّ الناس وَلّوا مُصْعِدين في الوادي، والرسّول صلى الله عليه وآله وسلم يَدْعُوهم في أُخراهم، فأثابهم غمّاً بغَمٍ، ثمّ أنزل عليهم النُّعاس.

فقلت: النُّعاس ما هو؟ قال: الهَمّ، فلمّا اسْتَيقَظُوا قالوا: كَفَرنا، وجاء أبو سفيان فَعَلا فوق الجَبَل بإلهه هُبَل فقال: أُعْلُ هُبَل، فقال رسول الله صلى الله عليه وآله وسلم يومئذٍ: الله أعلى وأجلّ، فَكُسِرت رَبَاعِية رسول الله صلى الله عليه وآله وسلم، واشْتَكَت لَثّته، وقال: نَشَدْتُك يا ربّ ما وعدتني، فإنّك إن شئت لم تُعْبَد.

وقال رسول الله صلى الله عليه وآله وسلم: يا علي، أين كنت؟ فقال: يا رسول الله، لَزِقتُ بالأرض، فقال: ذاك الظنّ بك. فقال: يا عليّ، ائتني بماءٍ أغسل فمي، فأتاهُ في صَحَفَةٍ، فإذا رسول الله صلى الله عليه وآله وسلم قد عافَهُ، وقال: ائتني في يدك؛ فأتاه بماءٍ في كَفّه، فَغَسَل رسول الله صلى الله عليه وآله وسلم عن لِحيته.

He replied, "O Messenger of God, I was stuck on the battlefield."

He replied, "I thought as much." Then he continued, "ʿAlī, bring me some water so I can wash. So he brought some in a large vessel, which the Messenger of God disliked; so he said, "Bring it to me in your hand, so he brought him water in his cupped palm, and the Messenger of God washed his beard."' [3:154]

156. From Zurāra, Ḥumrān and Muḥammad b. Muslim, from one of the two [Imams al-Ṣādiq or al-Bāqir] regarding His verse: ﴾*it was Satan who caused them to slip, through some of their actions*﴿ – 'It was revealed about ʿUqba b. ʿUthmān and Saʿd b. ʿUthmān.' [3:154]

157. From Hishām b. Sālim, from Abū ʿAbd Allāh ﷺ who said, 'When the people turned back on their heels from the Prophet's side on the Day of Uḥud, the Messenger of God ﷺ called out, "God has indeed promised to make me victorious over the whole religion." So some of the hypocrites – and he mentioned them both by name – said, "We have been defeated and now you are taunting us?"' [3:154]

158. From ʿAbd al-Raḥmān b. Kathīr, from Abū ʿAbd Allāh ﷺ who said about His verse: ﴾*it was Satan who caused them to slip, through some of their actions*﴿, 'They are the companions of al-ʿAqaba.' [3:154]

159. From Jābir, from Abū Jaʿfar ﷺ; he narrated, 'I asked him about God's verse: ﴾*Whether you are killed for God's cause or die, God's forgiveness and mercy are better than anything people amass.*﴿ He said to me, "Jābir, do you know what God's cause is?" He replied, "I have no knowledge except that which I hear from you." So He said, "God's cause is ʿAlī and his progeny, peace be upon them; and whoever is killed upon adherence to their authority is killed for God's cause; and whoever dies while adhering to their authority dies for God's cause."' [3:157]

١٥٦. عن زُرارة، وحُمران، ومحمّد بن مسلم، عن أحدهما ﷺ، في قوله تعالى: ﴿إِنَّمَا اسْتَزَلَّهُمُ الشَّيْطَانُ بِبَعْضِ مَا كَسَبُوا﴾ فهو في عُقبة بن عثمان، وسعد بن عُثمان.

١٥٧. عن هِشام بن سالم، عن أبي عبدالله عليه السلام، قال: لمّا انْهَزَم الناس عن النبيّ ﷺ يوم أُحُد، نادى رسول الله ﷺ: إنّ الله قد وَعَدني أن يُظْهِرَني على الدين كلّه، فقال له بعض المنافقين وسمّاهما: فقد هُزِمنا وتَسْخَر بنا.

١٥٨. عن عبد الرّحمن بن كثير، عن أبي عبدالله عليه السلام، في قوله تعالى: ﴿إِنَّمَا اسْتَزَلَّهُمُ الشَّيْطَانُ بِبَعْضِ مَا كَسَبُوا﴾، قال: هم أصحاب العقَبة.

١٥٩. عن جابر، عن أبي جعفر عليه السلام، قال: سألتُهُ عن قول الله عزّ وجلّ: ﴿وَلَئِنْ قُتِلْتُمْ فِي سَبِيلِ اللَّهِ أَوْ مُتُّمْ﴾، قال عليه السلام لي: يا جابر، أتدري ما سبيل الله؟ قُلت: لا أعلم إلاّ أن أسمعه منك. فقال عليه السلام: سبيل الله عليّ وذريّته عليهم السلام، ومَن قُتِل في ولايتهم قُتِل في سبيل الله، ومَن مات في ولايتهم مات في سبيل الله.

160. From Zurāra who narrated, 'I did not like to ask Abū Jaʿfar directly ﷺ about the *rajʿa*,[60] and I sought to conceal that fact. So I said [to myself], "I am going to ask a subtle question through which I will get my answer." So I said, "Tell me about someone who is killed – can he [be said to] have died?"

He replied, "No. [Natural] Death is death, and killing is murder."

I asked, "Can anyone be killed and be said to have died?"

He replied, "God's words are truer than yours, for He has distinguished between them in the Qur'an saying: ﴿*Whether you are killed for God's cause or die*﴾ and: ﴿*Whether you die or are killed, it is to God that you will be gathered.*﴾ It is not as you are saying, Zurāra. Death is death, and killing is murder."

I asked, "But God says: ﴿*Every soul will taste death.*﴾ (3:185)"

He replied, "The one who is killed does not taste death." He continued, "He must be returned to life so that he may taste death."' [3:157–158]

161. From Zurāra, from Abū Jaʿfar ﷺ regarding God's verse: ﴿*Whether you die or are killed, it is to God that you will be gathered*﴾, in relation to which God has also said: ﴿*Every soul will taste death.*﴾ So Abū Jaʿfar ﷺ said, 'God has distinguished between them both.' Then he asked, 'Would you [be allowed to] kill a man if he killed your brother?'

I replied, 'Yes.'

He asked, 'And if he died a natural death, would you [be allowed to] kill anyone in his place?'

I replied, 'No.'

He said, 'See how God distinguishes between them both.' [3:158]

60 *Rajʿa*, meaning 'return,' refers to the Shīʿī–Imāmī belief that human beings eventually return back to life in this world after death in order for them to witness God's justice prevail on earth. In a more acute sense it refers to the notion that all of the Imams shall be resurrected for the aim and purpose of enacting revenge on their killers and oppressors, thereby gaining final victory at the end of times and enabling in the process God's justice to prevail throughout the lands of the earth under the guidance and leadership of the awaited Twelfth Imam. See s.v. "Radjʿa," *Encyclopaedia of Islam*, Second Edition, viii, 371b (E. Kohlberg).

١٦٠. عن زُرارة، قال: كَرِهت أن أسأل أبا جعفر عليه السلام عن الرَّجعة واسْتَخْفَيتُ ذلك. قلت: لأسألنّ مسألة لَطيفةً أبلُغُ فيها حاجتي. فقلت: أخبرني عمَّن قُتِل أمات؟ قال: لا، الموْت موتٌ، والقَتْل قتلٌ.

قلت: ما أحد يُقْتَل إلاّ وقد مات؟ فقال: قولُ الله أصدقُ من قولك، فرّق بينهما في القرآن فقال: ﴿أَفَإِنْ مَاتَ أَوْ قُتِلَ﴾ وقال: ﴿لَئِن مُّتُّمْ أَوْ قُتِلْتُمْ لَإِلَى اللهِ تُحْشَرُونَ﴾ وليس كما قُلتَ يا زُرارة، الموْت مَوْت، والقَتْل قَتْل.

قلت فإنّ الله يقول: ﴿كُلُّ نَفْسٍ ذَائِقَةُ الْمَوْتِ﴾ ؟ قال عليه السلام: مَن قُتِل لم يُذِق الموت، ثمّ قال: لابُدَّ من أن يَرْجِع حتّى يَذُوقَ الموت.

١٦١. عن زُرارة، عن أبي جعفر عليه السلام، في قول الله: ﴿وَلَئِنْ مُتُّمْ أَوْ قُتِلْتُمْ لَإِلَى اللهِ تُحْشَرُونَ﴾ وقد قال الله: ﴿كُلُّ نَفْسٍ ذَائِقَةُ الْمَوْتِ﴾ ؟ فقال أبو جعفر عليه السلام: قد فَرّق اللهُ بينهما.

ثم قال عليه السلام: أكُنتَ قاتلاً رجلاً لو قَتَل أخاك؟ قلت: نعم، قال عليه السلام: فلو مات موتًا، أكُنت قاتلاً به أحدًا؟ قلت: لا. قال: ألا ترى كيف فَرّق الله بينهما.

162. From 'Abd Allāh b. al-Mughīra[61], from whoever narrated it from Jābir, from Abū Ja'far ﵇. He narrated, 'He was asked about God's verse: ﴿ *Whether you are killed for God's cause or die.* ﴾ He said, "Jābir, do you know what God's cause is?" He replied, "I have no knowledge except that which I hear from you."

So He said, "God's cause is 'Alī and his progeny, peace be upon them; and whoever is killed upon adherence to their authority is killed for God's cause; and whoever dies while adhering to their authority dies for God's cause. There is no believer from this community who will not experience both [natural] death and murder." He continued, "Whoever is killed will be resurrected in order to experience [natural] death, and whoever dies will be resurrected so that he be killed."' [3:157]

163. From Ṣafwān who said, 'I sought permission for Muḥammad b. Khālid to come and meet Abū al-Ḥasan al-Riḍā ﵇, and I informed him that he does not adhere to the same school of thought [as us] and that he had said, "By God, I do not want to meet him only to be converted to his belief."

So he said, "Bring him in."

So he entered, and he said to him, "May I be your ransom – I have committed a sin and have transgressed against my soul." According to what they allege, [his sin was that] he had, in actual fact, been defaming him. He continued, "I seek God's forgiveness for what I have done, and would like for you to accept my apology and forgive me for what I have done too."

So he replied, "Yes, I accept it, for if I did not, it would only negate what this one and his companions believe to be true [about us] – pointing to me – and it would prove others, as in the opponents, right in what they believe. God has said to His Prophet, peace be upon him and his family: ﴿ *By an act of mercy from God, you [Prophet] were gentle in your dealings with them – had you been harsh, or hard-hearted, they would have dispersed and left you – so pardon them and ask forgiveness for them. Consult with them about matters.* ﴾"

61 Abū Muḥammad 'Abd Allāh b. al-Mughīra al-Bajalī, the client of Jundub b. 'Abd Allāh b. Sufyān al-'Alqī, was a close companion of Imam Mūsā al-Kāẓim and a trustworthy narrator of his traditions. See Ḥillī, *Khulāṣat al-aqwāl*, 199 (nr. 619); Khū'ī, *Mu'jam*, 11: 370–373 (nr. 7186).

١٦٢. عن عبدالله بن المُغيرة، عمَّن حدّثه، عن جابر عن أبي جعفر عليه السلام، قال: سُئِل عن قول الله: ﴿وَلَئِنْ قُتِلْتُمْ فِي سَبِيلِ اللَّهِ أَوْ مُتُّمْ﴾، قال: أتدري يا جابر ما سبيل الله؟ فقلت: لا والله إلاّ أن أسمعه منك.

قال: سبيل الله عليّ وذُريّته، فمن قُتِل في ولايته قُتِل في سبيل الله، ومن مات في ولايته مات في سبيل الله، ليس مَن يُؤمن مِن هذه الأمة إلاّ وله قَتْلةٌ ومِيتةٌ. قال: إنّه من قُتِل يُنْشَر حتّى يموت، ومن مات يُنْشَر حتّى يُقْتَل.

١٦٣. عن صَفوان، قال: استأذنتُ لمحمّد بن خالد على الرضا أبي الحسن عليه السلام، وأخبرته أنّه ليس يقول بهذا القول، وأنه قال: والله لا أريدُ بلقائه إلاّ لأنتهي إلى قوله.

فقال: أدْخِله فَدَخَل. فقال له: جُعِلتُ فِداك، إنّه كان فَرَط منّي شيءٌ، وأسْرفتُ على نفسي، وكان فيما يزْعُمون أنّه كان يُعيبه، فقال: وأنا أستغفرُ الله ممّا كان منّي، فاحبُّ أن تَقْبَل عُذري، وتغفر لي ماكان منّي.

فقال: نَعم أقبلُ، إن لم أقبل كان إبطال ما يقول هذا وأصحابه — وأشار إليّ بيده — ومصداق ما يقول الآخرون — يعني المخالفين — قال الله لنبيّه عليه وآله السلام: ﴿فَبِمَا رَحْمَةٍ مِنَ اللَّهِ لِنْتَ لَهُمْ وَلَوْ كُنْتَ فَظًّا غَلِيظَ الْقَلْبِ لَانْفَضُّوا مِنْ حَوْلِكَ فَاعْفُ عَنْهُمْ وَاسْتَغْفِرْ لَهُمْ وَشَاوِرْهُمْ فِي الْأَمْرِ﴾ ثمّ سأله عن أبيه، فأخبره أنّه قد مَضى، واسْتَغْفَر له.

Then he went on to ask him about his father, but he told him that that was now in the past, and he sought forgiveness for him.' [3:159]

164. In a report by Ṣafwān al-Jammāl, from Abū ʿAbd Allāh عليه السلام (and from Saʿd al-Iskāf, from Abū Jaʿfar عليه السلام), he narrated, 'A Bedouin once came to some people from the Banī ʿĀmir tribe and asked them about the whereabouts of the Prophet صلى الله عليه وآله as he could not find him, so they said, "He is in Quzaḥ."[62] So he went to look for him but did not find him.

Then they said, "He is in Mina." So he went to look for him there but did not find him.

So they said, "He is in ʿArafa." Again the man went there in search of the Prophet but could not find him.

Then they said, "He is in al-Mashʿar."[63] So he found him there at the station. He asked, "Describe the Prophet صلى الله عليه وآله for me."

So the people replied, "O Bedouin, even if he is in the middle of a throng of people there is no way you can miss him because they will be venerating him."

He replied, "Just describe him for me so that I do not have to ask anyone to point him out."

They said, "The Prophet of God is taller than average but shorter than a giant. He has a bright golden complexion, a fuller head of hair than anyone – neither straight nor curly – and a wider brow than anyone else. He has a forelock above the middle of his eyes, an aquiline nose and a wide brow. He has a thick beard, a gap between his teeth and a mole on his lower lip. His neck is like a silver vase, stretching away from his shoulder blades; his chest and stomach are flat. His fingers are straight and slender, making a strong fist. When he walks, he walks with a steadfast gait, and when he turns, he does so with his whole body, as if his limbs are as flexible as a rabbit's back. When he is standing with someone, he is never the first to part company unless his companion does so first; and when seated, he never stretches his legs out until after his companion has got up."

62 Quzaḥ is the name of a mountain in Muzdalifa near Mecca. See Ḥamawī, *Muʿjam al-buldān*, 4:341.

63 Al-Mashʿar is the place where all the people throng together during the pilgrimage.

١٦٤. في رواية صَفوان الجمّال، عن أبي عبد الله عليه السلام، وعن سعد الإسكاف، عن أبي جعفر عليه السلام، قال: جاء أعرابيّ – أحد بني عامر – فسأل عن النبيّ عليه السلام، فلم يَجِدْه، فقالوا: هو بقُزَح، فطلبه فلم يَجِده، قالوا: هو بمِنى، قال: فَطلبه فلم يجده، فقالوا: هو بعرَفة، فطلبه فلم يجده، فقالوا: هو بالمشْعَر قال: فوَجَده في الموْقِف، قال: حلُّوا لي النبيّ صلى الله عليه وآله. فقال الناس: يا أعرابيّ، ما أنكرَكَ! إذا وجدت النبيّ وسط القوم وَجَدْته مُفَخّمًا. قال: بل حلُّوه لي حتّى لا أسأل عنه أحدًا.

قالوا: فإنّ نبيَّ الله أطول من الرَّبْعَة، وأقْصَر من الطويل الفاحش، كأنَّ لونَهُ فِضّة وذَهَب، أرْجَل الناس جُمَّةً، وأوسع الناس جبهةً، بين عينيه غُرّة، أقنى الأنف واسع الجبين، كثّ اللّحية، مُفلَّج الأسنان، على شَفَته السُّفلى خَالٌ، كأنّ رقبته إبريق فِضّة، بعيد ما بين مُشَاشَة المَنْكِبين، كأنَّ بَطْنَه وصَدْره سواء، سَبْط البِنان، عظيم البَرَاثن، إذا مشى مشى مُتَكَفّيًا، وإذا التفت التفت بأجمعه، كأنّ يده من لِينها مَتْنُ أرنب، إذا قام مع إنسان لم يَنْفَتِل حتّى ينفتل صاحبه، وإذا جلس لم يَحُلل حَبْوَتَه حتّى يَقُوم جليسه.

فجاء الأعرابي، فلمّا نَظَر إلى النبيّ صلى الله عليه وآله وعرفه، قال بمِحْجَنِه على رأس ناقة رسول الله صلى الله عليه وآله عند ذنَب ناقَتِه، فأقبلت الناس تقول: ما أجرأك يا أعرابيّ! قال النبيّ صلى الله عليه وآله: دَعُوه، فإنّه أديب. ثمّ قال: ما حاجَتُك؟

قال: جاءتنا رُسُلُك أن تُقيموا الصلاة، وتؤتوا الزكاة، وتَحُجُّوا البيت، وتغتسلوا من الجنابة، وبعثني قومي إليك رائدًا أبغي أن استَحْلِفَك وأخشى أن تغْضَب.

So the Bedouin approached, and when he set eyes on the Prophet ﷺ he recognized him. He motioned to him, with his staff on the head of the Messenger of God's camel and with the tail of his own camel facing it. So the people rushed upon him, exclaiming: "O Bedouin, how dare you?"

The Prophet ﷺ said, "Leave him alone for he is here for a purpose."

Then he asked, "What do you require?"

He replied, "Your emissaries have come to us telling us to establish the prayer, give alms, come for pilgrimage to the House, and to purify ourselves by bathing after intimate relations. My people have sent me to you as their ambassador to extract an oath from you [of the truth of your mission], but I fear you will get angry."

He replied, "I will not get angry. Indeed, I am the one whom God has described in the Torah and the Gospel as Muḥammad, the Messenger of God, the chosen one, the specially selected one. He is neither rude nor brash in the markets. He never repays bad behaviour towards him with its like, but rather with a good turn. So ask me whatever you wish, for I am the one whom God has described in the Qur'an saying: ﴾*had you been harsh, or hard-hearted, they would have dispersed and left you*﴿ – so do ask whatever you wish."

He said, "Is it indeed God, the One who has raised up the heavens without any pillars, who has sent you?"

He replied, "Yes, it is He who has sent me."

He then said, "[Swear] By God, the One by whose command the heavens stay above, that He is the One who has sent down to you the Book, and who has dispatched you with the message to perform the daily prayer and give the prescribed alms?"

He replied, "Yes."

He asked, "Did He command you to purify yourself of intimate relations by bathing with all its conditions?"

He replied, "Yes."

So he said, "Then indeed we believe in God, His messengers, His Book, the Last Day, the Resurrection, the Balance of deeds, the standing [before God], and the permissible and prohibited, big and small."'

He continued, 'Then the Prophet ﷺ sought forgiveness for him and prayed for him.' [3:159]

قال ﷺ: لا أغضب، إنّي أنا الذي سمّاني الله في التوراة والإنجيل محمّد رسول الله، المجتبى المصطفى، ليس بفاحش، ولا سخّاب في الأسواق ولا يتبع السَّيئة السِّيئة، ولكن يتبع السيِّئة الحسنة، فسلني عمّا شِئت، وأنا الذي سَمّاني الله في القرآن ﴿وَلَوْ كُنْتَ فَظًّا غَلِيظَ الْقَلْبِ لَانْفَضُّوا مِنْ حَوْلِكَ﴾ فسَل عمّا شئت.

قال: إنَّ الله الذي رفع السماوات بغير عَمَدٍ، هو أرسلك؟ قال: نعم هو أرسلني. قال: بالله الذي قامت السماوات بأمره، هو الَّذي أنزل عليك الكتاب، وأرسلك بالصلاة المفروضة، والزكاة المعقولة؟ قال: نعم. قال: وهو أمرك بالاغتسال من الجنابة، وبالحدود كُلّها؟ قال: نعم. قال: فإنّا آمنّا بالله ورسله وكتابه، واليوم الآخر، والبعث والميزان والموقف، والحلال والحرام، صغيرة وكبيرة، قال: فاستغفر له النبيّ ﷺ. ودعا له.

165. From Aḥmad b. Muḥammad, from ʿAlī b. Mahziyār who narrated, ʿAbū Jaʿfar عليه السلام wrote to me, saying, "Ask so and so to refer to me and then to choose [the best course of action] for himself, for he knows best what is permissible in his country and how to deal with the sultans; and consultation is indeed blessed, for God said to His Prophet in the decisive verses in His Book: ﴿ *so pardon them and ask forgiveness for them. Consult with them about matters, then, when you have decided on a course of action, put your trust in God: God loves those who put their trust in Him.* ﴾ So if what he says is according to what is allowed, then I will endorse his opinion, and if it is not, then I would hope to set him on the right course of action, if God wills." ﴿ *Consult with them about matters* ﴾ – he said, "This means to seek the best course of action (*istikhāra*)."' [3:159]

166. From Samāʿa [b. Mihrān] who narrated, ʿAbū ʿAbd Allāh عليه السلام said, "Fraud refers to anything that is taken away unlawfully from the Imam, unlawfully consuming the property of the orphan, and taking unlawful gains." [3:161]

167. From ʿAmmār b. Marwān who narrated, 'I asked Abū ʿAbd Allāh عليه السلام about God's statement: ﴿ *Can the man who pursues God's good pleasure be like the man who has brought God's wrath upon himself and whose home will be Hell – a foul destination?* ﴾ So he said, "They are the Imams. By God, ʿAmmār, the believers are ranked by God according to their support and their acknowledgement of us; so God multiplies the good deeds of the believers accordingly and raises them to the highest ranks. ʿAmmār, as for the phrase: ﴿ *like the man who has brought God's wrath upon himself and whose home will be Hell– a foul destination?* ﴾, by God, these are the people who denied ʿAlī b. Abī Ṭālib of his right and the Imams from among us, the Ahl al-Bayt, of their rights. For that reason they brought God's wrath upon themselves."' [3:162]

168. From Abū al-Ḥasan al-Riḍā عليه السلام that he mentioned God's verse: ﴿ *They are in different ranks in God's eyes* ﴾ and said, 'A rank is the distance between the earth and the sky.' [3:163]

١٦٥ . أحمد بن محمّد، عن عليّ بن مَهْزيار، قال: كتب إليّ أبو جعفر عليه السلام: أن سَل فلاناً أن يُشير عليَّ ويتخيّر لنفسه، فهو يعلم ما يَجُوز في بلده، وكيف يُعامل السّلاطين، فإنّ المشُورة مباركة، قال الله لنبيه صلى الله عليه وآله في محكم كتابه: ﴿فَاعْفُ عَنْهُمْ وَاسْتَغْفِرْ لَهُمْ وَشَاوِرْهُمْ فِي الأَمْرِ فَإِذَا عَزَمْتَ فَتَوَكَّلْ عَلَى اللهِ إِنَّ اللهَ يُحِبُّ الْمُتَوَكِّلِينَ﴾ فإن كان ما يقُول ممّا يَجُوز كتبت أُصوّب رأيه، وإن كان غير ذلك رَجوتُ أن أضعه على الطريق الواضح إن شاء الله ﴿وَشَاوِرْهُمْ فِي الأَمْرِ﴾ قال: يعني الاستخارة.

١٦٦ . عن سماعة، قال: قال أبو عبد الله عليه السلام: الغُلول: كلّ شيء غُلَّ عن الإمام، وأكل مال اليتيم شُبهة، والسُّحت شبهة.

١٦٧ . عن عمّار بن مروان، قال: سألتُ أبا عبد الله عليه السلام عن قول الله تعالى: ﴿أَفَمَنِ اتَّبَعَ رِضْوَانَ اللهِ كَمَنْ بَاءَ بِسَخَطٍ مِنَ اللهِ وَمَأْوَاهُ جَهَنَّمُ وَبِئْسَ الْمَصِيرُ﴾. فقال: ﴿هُمْ﴾ الأئمّة والله يا عمّار، ﴿دَرَجَاتٌ﴾ للمؤمنين ﴿عِنْدَ اللهِ﴾، وبموالاتهم وبمعرفتهم. إيّانا يضاعف الله للمؤمنين حسناتهم، ويرفع لهم الدرجات العُلى.

وأمّا قوله يا عمّار: ﴿كَمَنْ بَاءَ بِسَخَطٍ مِنَ اللهِ﴾ إلى قوله: ﴿الْمَصِيرُ﴾ فهم والله الذين جَحَدوا حقَّ عليّ بن أبي طالب عليه السلام وحقّ الأئمّة منّا أهل البيت، فباءوا لذلك بسَخطٍ من الله.

١٦٨ . عن أبي الحسن الرضا عليه السلام، أنه ذكر قول الله تعالى: ﴿هُمْ دَرَجَاتٌ عِنْدَ اللهِ﴾، قال: الدَّرَجة ما بين السماء إلى الأرض.

169. From Muḥammad b. Abī Ḥamza, from whoever mentioned it from Abū ʿAbd Allāh ﷺ regarding God's verse: ﴾*Why do you* [*believers*] *say, when a calamity befalls you, even after you have inflicted twice as much damage* [*on your enemy*], *'How did this happen?'*﴿ that he said, 'On the Day of Badr the Muslims took one hundred and forty men, killing seventy and capturing seventy; and on the Day of Uḥud it was seventy of the Muslims who fell.' He continued, 'So they were grieved because of this, so God, Blessed and most High, revealed: ﴾*Why do you* [*believers*] *say, when a calamity befalls you, even after you have inflicted twice as much damage* [*on your enemy*], *'How did this happen?'?* [*Prophet*], *say, 'You brought it upon yourselves.' God has power over everything.*﴿' [3:165]

170. From Jābir, from Abū Jaʿfar ﷺ who narrated, 'A man came to the Messenger of God ﷺ saying, "I desire to participate actively in *jihād*." He replied, "Then fight in the way of God, for if you are killed you will be alive with God and well provided for; and if you die then your reward is upon God; and if you come back alive, then you will have been emancipated from sins committed against God. This is the interpretation of: ﴾[*Prophet*], *do not think of those who have been killed in God's way as dead.*﴿"' [3:169]

171. From Sālim b. Abī Maryam[64] who narrated, 'Abū ʿAbd Allāh ﷺ said to me, "The Messenger of God ﷺ dispatched ʿAlī on ten occasions. [The verse]: ﴾*Those who responded to God and the Messenger after suffering defeat, who do good and remain conscious of God, will have a great reward*﴿ was indeed revealed about the Commander of the Faithful ﷺ."' [3:172]

172. From Jābir, from Muḥammad b. ʿAlī ﷺ who narrated, 'When the Prophet ﷺ dispatched the Commander of the Faithful and ʿAmmār b. Yāsir to the people of Mecca, they [i.e. his critics] said, "He is sending this young man, when he should have sent someone else to the people of Mecca with their notables and strong men! By God, pre-Islamic times were better than the situation we are in now." So they went and spoke to these two, trying to

64 We could not find any individual by this name in either Ḥillī's *Khulāṣat al-aqwāl* or Khūʾī's *Muʿjam*.

١٦٩. عن محمّد بن أبي حمزة، عمَّن ذكره، عن أبي عبدالله عليه السلام، في قول الله تعالى: ﴿أَوَلَمَّا أَصَابَتْكُم مُّصِيبَةٌ قَدْ أَصَبْتُم مِّثْلَيْهَا﴾. قال: كان المسلمون قد أصابوا ببدر مائة وأربعين رجلاً، قتلوا سبعين رجلاً، وأسروا سبعين، فلمّا كان يوم أُحد أُصيب من المسلمين سبعون رجلاً، قال: فاغتمّوا بذلك، فأنزل الله تبارك وتعالى: ﴿أَوَلَمَّا أَصَابَتْكُم مُّصِيبَةٌ قَدْ أَصَبْتُم مِّثْلَيْهَا﴾.

١٧٠. عن جابر، عن أبي جعفر عليه السلام، قال: أتى رجلٌ رسول الله صلى الله عليه وآله فقال: إنّي راغبٌ نشيطٌ في الجِهاد، قال: فَجَاهِدْ في سَبيل الله، فإنّك إن تُقْتَل كُنت حيّاً عند الله تُرْزَق، وإن مُتَّ فقد وَقَعَ أجْرُك على الله، وإن رَجَعْتَ خَرَجْتَ من الذُّنوب إلى الله، هذا تفسير ﴿وَلَا تَحْسَبَنَّ الَّذِينَ قُتِلُوا فِي سَبِيلِ اللَّهِ أَمْوَاتًا﴾ الآية.

١٧١. عن سالم بن أبي مريم، قال: قال لي أبو عبدالله عليه السلام: إنَّ رسول الله عليه السلام بعث عليّاً عليه السلام في عشرة ﴿اسْتَجَابُوا لِلَّهِ وَالرَّسُولِ مِن بَعْدِ مَا أَصَابَهُمُ الْقَرْحُ﴾ إلى ﴿أَجْرٌ عَظِيمٌ﴾ إنّما نَزَلت في أمير المؤمنين عليه السلام.

١٧٢. عن جابر، عن محمّد بن علي عليه السلام، قال: لمّا وجّه النبي صلى الله عليه وآله أمير المؤمنين عليه السلام وعمّار بن ياسر إلى أهل مكّة، قالوا: بَعَث هذا الصبيّ، ولو بَعَث غيره إلى أهل مكّة، وفي مكّة صَناديد قُرَيش ورجالها! والله الكُفر أولى بنا ممّا نحن فيه. فساروا وقالوا لهما، وخوّفوهما بأهل مكّة، وغَلّظوا عليهما الأمر.

scare them away from going to the people of Mecca and painting the mission as distressful.

So ʿAlī ﴾ said, ﴾ *God is enough for us: He is the best protector* ﴿ and they left. When they arrived in Mecca, God informed His Prophet ﷺ of what they had been saying to ʿAlī, and what ʿAlī had replied to them. So God revealed this verse about them, mentioning them by name: ﴾ *Those whose faith only increased when people said, 'Fear your enemy: they have amassed a great army against you,' and who replied, 'God is enough for us: He is the best protector.' So they returned with grace and bounty from God; no harm befell them. They pursued God's good pleasure. God's favour is great indeed.* ﴿ The way it was actually revealed was: ﴾ ***Have you not seen how the two of them met ʿAlī and ʿAmmār, saying, 'Verily Abū Sufyān, ʿAbd Allāh b. ʿĀmir and the people of Mecca have amassed a great army against you, so fear them.' This only increased their faith and they said, 'God is enough for us: He is the best protector.*** ﴿' [3:173*]

173. From Muḥammad b. Muslim, from Abū Jaʿfar ؏; he narrated, 'I said to him, "Tell me about the disbeliever – is death better for him or life?" He replied, "Death is better for both the believer and the disbeliever."

I asked, "And why is that?" He replied, "Because God says: ﴾ *That which is with God is best for those who are truly good* ﴿(3:198) and He says: ﴾ *The disbelievers should not think that it is better for them that We give them more time: when We give them more time they become more sinful – a shameful torment awaits them.* ﴿"' [3:178]

174. From Yūnus who, without mentioning his source, cited him [i.e. an infallible] as having said - 'I said to him, "Did the Messenger of God ﷺ marry his daughter to so and so?" He replied, "Yes." I asked, "How could he get the other one married [like that]?" He replied, "He did it; and God has revealed: ﴾ *The disbelievers should not think that it is better for them that We give them more time: when We give them more time they become more sinful – a shameful torment awaits them.* ﴿"' [3:178]

فقال عليّ عليه السلام: حَسْبُنا الله ونِعم الوكيل. ومضيا، فلمّا دخلا مكّة، أخبر الله نبيّه صلى الله عليه وآله بقوله تعالى: ألم تر إلى ﴿الَّذِينَ قَالَ لَهُمُ النَّاسُ إِنَّ النَّاسَ قَدْ جَمَعُوا لَكُمْ فَاخْشَوْهُمْ فَزَادَهُمْ إِيمَانًا وَقَالُوا حَسْبُنَا اللَّهُ وَنِعْمَ الْوَكِيلُ ۞ فَانْقَلَبُوا بِنِعْمَةٍ مِنَ اللَّهِ وَفَضْلٍ لَمْ يَمْسَسْهُمْ سُوءٌ وَاتَّبَعُوا رِضْوَانَ اللَّهِ وَاللَّهُ ذُو فَضْلٍ عَظِيمٍ﴾.

وإنّما نَزَلت: ألم تَرَ إلى فلان وفلان، لَقُوا عليًّا وعمّارًا، فقالا: إنّ أبا سفيان وعبدالله بن عامر وأهل مكّة، قد جَمَعُوا لكم فاخشوهم، فزادهم إيمانًا، وقالوا: حَسْبُنا الله ونِعم الوكيل.

١٧٣. عن محمّد بن مسلم، عن أبي جعفر عليه السلام، قال: قلتُ له: أخبرني عن الكافر، الموت خيرٌ له أم الحياة؟ فقال: الموتُ خيرٌ للمؤمن والكافر.

قلت: ولِمَ؟ قال: لأنّ الله يقول: ﴿وَمَا عِنْدَ اللَّهِ خَيْرٌ لِلْأَبْرَارِ﴾ ويقول: ﴿وَلَا يَحْسَبَنَّ الَّذِينَ كَفَرُوا أَنَّمَا نُمْلِي لَهُمْ خَيْرٌ لِأَنْفُسِهِمْ إِنَّمَا نُمْلِي لَهُمْ لِيَزْدَادُوا إِثْمًا وَلَهُمْ عَذَابٌ مُهِينٌ﴾.

١٧٤. عن يونس، رفعه، قال: قلتُ له: زَوّج رسول الله صلى الله عليه وآله ابنته فلانًا؟ قال: نعم. قلت: كيف زوّجه الأُخرى؟ قال: قد فعل، فأنزل الله ﴿وَلَا يَحْسَبَنَّ الَّذِينَ كَفَرُوا أَنَّمَا نُمْلِي لَهُمْ خَيْرٌ لِأَنْفُسِهِمْ﴾ إلى ﴿عَذَابٌ مُهِينٌ﴾.

175. From ʿAjalān Abū Ṣāliḥ[65] who narrated, 'I heard Abū ʿAbd Allāh ﷺ say, "Every few days and nights a voice calls out from the sky: 'O people of truth, detach yourselves; O people of falsehood, detach yourselves.' So this lot separates from those and that lot from these."' He continued, 'I said to him, "May God make you prosper – can they carry on intermingling with each other after this call?" He replied, "Never. He says in His Book: ﴾*Nor was it God's aim to leave you, believers, as you were, with no separation between the bad and the good.*﴿"' [3:179]

176. From Muḥammad b. Muslim who narrated, 'I asked Abū Jaʿfar ﷺ about God's verse: ﴾*Whatever they meanly withhold will be hung around their necks on the Day of Resurrection. It is God who will inherit the heavens and earth.*﴿

He replied, "Any servant who refuses to give alms (*zakāt*) out of his wealth, on the Day of Resurrection God will make this into a fiery snake coiled around his neck, who will mangle his flesh until the account has been settled. This is as per God's verse: ﴾*Whatever they meanly withhold will be hung around their necks on the Day of Resurrection.*﴿" He continued, "The alms that they stingily withhold."' [3:180]

177. From Ibn Sinān, from Abū ʿAbd Allāh ﷺ, on his father's authority, from his forefathers, peace be upon them, who said, 'The Messenger of God ﷺ said, "Anyone who owes alms due out of his camels, cows or sheep, and refuses to pay them will be resurrected on the Day of Judgement at the bottom of a desolate pit, and he will be head-butted by every horned creature, mangled by every fanged creature, and trampled by every hoofed animal, until God has finished settling the accounts of His servants. Anyone on whom alms is due from his palm plantations, farmland or vineyards, and he refuses to pay the alms thereof, will have his land added onto seven more and hung around his neck on the Day of Judgement."' [3:180]

---

65 Abū Ṣāliḥ ʿAjalān, a reliable narrator and companion of Imam Jaʿfar al-Ṣādiq. See Ḥillī, *Khulāṣat al-aqwāl*, 225 (nr. 749).

١٧٥ . عن عجلان أبي صالح، قال: سَمِعتُ أبا عبد الله عليه السلام يقول: لا تمضي الأيام والليالي حتّى ينادي منادٍ من السماء: يا أهل الحق اعتزلوا، يا أهل الباطل اعتزلوا، فيُعزَل هؤلاء من هؤلاء؛ ويُعزَل هؤلاء من هؤلاء.

قال: قلتُ: أصلحك الله، يُخالط هؤلاء هؤلاء بعد ذلك النِداء؟ قال: كلاّ، إنّه يقول في الكتاب: ﴿مَا كَانَ اللَّهُ لِيَذَرَ الْمُؤْمِنِينَ عَلَىٰ مَا أَنْتُمْ عَلَيْهِ حَتَّىٰ يَمِيزَ الْخَبِيثَ مِنَ الطَّيِّبِ﴾.

١٧٦ . عن محمّد بن مسلم، قال: سألتُ أبا جعفر عليه السلام عن قول الله: ﴿سَيُطَوَّقُونَ مَا بَخِلُوا بِهِ يَوْمَ الْقِيَامَةِ وَلِلَّهِ مِيرَاثُ السَّمَاوَاتِ وَالْأَرْضِ﴾.

قال: ما مِن عبدٍ منَعَ زكاة ماله، إلاّ جعل الله ذلك يوم القيامة ثُعبانًا من نار مُطوّقًا في عُنُقه، ينهَش من لَحمِهِ حتّى يفرغ من الحساب، وهو قول الله ﴿سَيُطَوَّقُونَ مَا بَخِلُوا بِهِ يَوْمَ الْقِيَامَةِ﴾، قال: ما بَخِلُوا من الزكاة.

١٧٧ . عن ابن سنان، عن أبي عبد الله، عن أبيه، عن آبائه عليهم السلام، قال: قال رسول الله صلى الله عليه وآله: ما مِن ذي زكاة مالٍ: إبل، ولا بَقَر، ولا غنَم، يمنع زكاة ماله، إلاّ أُقيم يوم القيامة بقاعٍ قَفرٍ يَنْطَحه كلُّ ذات قرنٍ بقَرْنها، ويَنْهَشه كلُّ ذاتِ ناب بأنيابها، ويَطأه كلُّ ذات ظِلْفٍ بظِلْفها حتّى يَفْرَغ الله من حساب خَلْقه، وما من ذي زكاة مالٍ: نخل، ولا زرع، ولا كرم، يمنع زكاة ماله، إلاّ قُلِّدَت أرضه في سبعة أرضين، يُطَوّق بها إلى يوم القيامة.

178. From Yūsuf al-Ṭāṭarī[66] who heard Abū Ja'far عليه السلام say mentioning the alms (*zakāt*), 'The one who refuses to pay the alms, on the Day of Resurrection God will transform his wealth into a large fiery cobra with two flaps, coiled around him, which will be told: "Hold him tightly just as he used to hold you tightly in the world;" and this is God's verse: ﴿ *Whatever they meanly withhold will be hung around their necks on the Day of Resurrection. It is God who will inherit the heavens and earth.* ﴾' [3:180]

179. It has been said on their authority, peace be upon them, 'The one who refuses to pay the alms will be coiled by a venomous cobra who will mangle his flesh, and this is as per His verse: ﴿ *Whatever they meanly withhold will be hung around their necks on the Day of Resurrection. It is God who will inherit the heavens and earth.* ﴾' [3:180]

180. From Samā'a [b. Mihrān] who narrated, 'I heard Abū 'Abd Allāh عليه السلام say regarding God's words: ﴿ *say [Prophet], 'Messengers before me have come to you with clear signs, including the one you mention. If you are sincere, why did you kill them?'* ﴾: "He knew, of course, that these were not the same ones who killed them, but that they had an innate penchant towards those who killed; so God terms them killers for their leanings to their penchant and their acceptance of that act."' [3:183]

181. From 'Umar b. Ma'mar[67] who said, 'Abū 'Abd Allāh عليه السلام said, "May God curse the Qadarīs; may God curse the Ḥarūrīs; may God curse the Murji'a, may God curse the Murji'a."'

I said to him, "May I be your ransom – why did you curse these people once, and those twice?" So he replied, "These people [i.e. the Murji'a] claim that those who killed us are still believers, so their hands [lit. clothes] are stained with our blood until the Day of Resurrection. Have you not heard God's words: ﴿ *To those who say, 'God has commanded us not to believe in any messenger unless he brings us an offering that fire [from heaven] consumes,' say*

---

66 Abū Dāwūd Yūsuf b. Ibrāhīm al-Ṭāṭarī, about whom there is scant information. According to Shaykh al-Mufīd he is one of the unknown (*majhūl*) companions of Imam Ja'far al-Ṣādiq. See Khū'ī, *Mu'jam*, 21: 171–2 (nr. 13802 and 13803).

67 'Umar b. Ma'mar, about whom there is scant information, was reportedly a companion of Imam Ja'far al-Ṣādiq. See Khū'ī, *Mu'jam*, 14: 64 (nr. 8819).

١٧٨. عن يوسف الطاطري، أنّه سَمِع أبا جعفر عليه السلام يقول وذكر الزكاة، فقال: الذي يمنع الزكاة يُحوِّل الله ماله يوم القيامة شُجاعًا من نارٍ له ريمتان، فيطوّقه إيّاه، ثمّ يقال له: الزَمْه كما لزِمَكَ في الدنيا، وهو قول الله تعالى: ﴿سَيُطَوَّقُونَ مَا بَخِلُوا بِهِ﴾ الآية.

١٧٩. وعنهم (صلى الله عليه وآله)، قال: مانع الزكاة يُطوّق بشجاع أقْرَعَ يأْكُلُ من لحمه، وهو قوله تعالى: ﴿سَيُطَوَّقُونَ مَا بَخِلُوا بِهِ﴾ الآية.

١٨٠. عن سَماعة، قال: سَمِعتُ أبا عبدالله عليه السلام يقول في قول الله تعالى: ﴿قُلْ قَدْ جَاءَكُمْ رُسُلٌ مِنْ قَبْلِي بِالْبَيِّنَاتِ وَبِالَّذِي قُلْتُمْ فَلِمَ قَتَلْتُمُوهُمْ إِنْ كُنْتُمْ صَادِقِينَ﴾ وقد علِمَ أنّ هؤلاء لم يَقْتُلُوا، ولكن قد كان هواهم مع الذين قتلوا، فسمّاهم الله قاتلين لمتابعة هواهم ورِضاهم لذلك الفعل.

١٨١. عن عمر بن مَعْمَر، قال: قال أبو عبدالله عليه السلام: لَعَنَ الله القَدَرِيّة، لعن الله الحَرُوريّة، لعن الله المُرجئة، لعن الله المُرجئة.

قلتُ له: جُعِلت فداك، كيف لعنت هؤلاءِ مرّةً، ولعنت هؤلاءِ مرّتين؟ فقال: إنَّ هؤلاء زَعَمُوا أنّ الذين قَتَلُونا مؤمنين، فثيابهم ملطّخة بدمائنا إلى يوم القيامة، أما تسمع لقول الله: ﴿الَّذِينَ قَالُوا إِنَّ اللَّهَ عَهِدَ إِلَيْنَا أَلَّا نُؤْمِنَ لِرَسُولٍ حَتَّىٰ يَأْتِيَنَا بِقُرْبَانٍ تَأْكُلُهُ النَّارُ قُلْ قَدْ جَاءَكُمْ رُسُلٌ مِنْ قَبْلِي بِالْبَيِّنَاتِ﴾ إلى قوله: ﴿صَادِقِينَ﴾؟ قال: فكان بين الذين خُوطِبُوا بهذا القول وبين القاتلين خمسمائة عام، فسمّاهم الله قاتلين برضاهم بما صَنَع أُولئك.

[*Prophet*], *'Messengers before me have come to you with clear signs, including the one you mention. If you are sincere, why did you kill them?* ﴿" He continued, "Five hundred years separated the addressees of this verse and the actual killers [of the prophets], but God termed them killers because of their acceptance of what those people had done."' [3:183]

182. From Muḥammad b. Hāshim[68], from whoever narrated it from Abū 'Abd Allāh عليه السلام who said, 'When this verse was revealed: ﴾*say* [*Prophet*], *'Messengers before me have come to you with clear signs, including the one you mention. If you are sincere, why did you kill them?* ﴿ – of course, he knew that they would say, "By God, neither have we committed any such act nor witnessed it."' He continued, 'However, they had been told to disassociate from their killers, and yet they refused.' [3:183]

183. From Muḥammad b. al-Arqaṭ[69], from Abū 'Abd Allāh عليه السلام. 'He asked me, "Do you live in Kufa?"

I replied, "Yes."

He said, "So you all see the murderers of Ḥusayn عليه السلام in your midst?"

I replied, "May I be your ransom – I have not seen any of them."

He said, "Then that is because you only consider the murderer to be the one who killed or the one who gave the orders to kill. Have you not heard God's words: ﴾*say* [*Prophet*], *'Messengers before me have come to you with clear signs, including the one you mention. If you are sincere, why did you kill them?* ﴿? Which messenger was there before Muḥammad ﷺ who lived amongst them, when there was no messenger between him and 'Īsā? Rather, they accepted the killing of those [prophets] so they were called killers too."' [3:183]

184. From Jābir, from Abū Ja'far عليه السلام who said, 'When the Messenger of God ﷺ passed away, 'Alī عليه السلام said, "Indeed we belong to God and to Him we shall return. What a great calamity this is that has affected the close ones and

68 Muḥammad b. Hāshim, Muḥammad b. Hāshim al-Ṭā'ī and Muḥammad b. Hāshim al-Qarshī are three separate individuals. See Khū'ī, *Mu'jam*, 18: 337 (nr. 11975, 11976 and 11977).

69 We could not find any individual by this name in either Ḥillī's *Khulāṣat al-aqwāl* or Khū'ī's *Mu'jam*.

١٨٢ . عن محمّد بن هاشم، عمّن حدّثه، عن أبي عبدالله عليه السلام، قال: لمّا نزلت هذه الآية: ﴿قُلْ قَدْ جَاءَكُمْ رُسُلٌ مِنْ قَبْلِي بِالْبَيِّنَاتِ وَبِالَّذِي قُلْتُمْ فَلِمَ قَتَلْتُمُوهُمْ إِنْ كُنْتُمْ صَادِقِينَ﴾ وقد علِمَ أن قالوا: والله ما قَتَلنَا ولا شَهِدنا، قال: وإنّما قيل لهم ابرءُوا من قَتَلتِهم فأبوا.

١٨٣ . عن محمّد بن الأرقط، عن أبي عبدالله عليه السلام، قال لي: تنْزِل الكوفة؟

قلت: نعم.

قال: فتَرَون قَتَلة الحسين عليه السلام بين أظهركم؟

قال: قلت: جُعلت فِداك ما بقي منهم أحد.

قال: فإذن أنت لا ترى القاتل إلاّ من قَتَل أو من وَلِيَ القتل، ألم تَسمع إلى قول الله: ﴿قُلْ قَدْ جَاءَكُمْ رُسُلٌ مِنْ قَبْلِي بِالْبَيِّنَاتِ وَبِالَّذِي قُلْتُمْ فَلِمَ قَتَلْتُمُوهُمْ إِنْ كُنْتُمْ صَادِقِينَ﴾ فأي رسول قَتَلَ الذين كان محمّد صلى الله عليه وآله بين أظهرهم؟ ولم يكن بينه وبين عيسى رسول، إنّما رَضُوا قَتْلَ أولئك فسُمّوا قاتلين.

١٨٤ . عن جابر، عن أبي جعفر عليه السلام، قالا: إنّ عليًا عليه السلام، لمّا غمّض رسول الله صلى الله عليه وآله، قال: إنّا لله وإنّا إليه راجعون، يا لها من مُصيبةٍ خَصّت الأقربين، وعَمّت المؤمنين، لم يُصابوا بمثلها قطُّ، ولا عاينوا مِثلها. فلمّا قبر رسول الله صلى الله عليه وآله سَمِعُوا مناديًا ينادي من سقف البيت: ﴿إِنَّمَا يُرِيدُ اللهُ لِيُذْهِبَ عَنْكُمُ الرِّجْسَ أَهْلَ الْبَيْتِ وَيُطَهِّرَكُمْ تَطْهِيرًا﴾ والسلام عليكم أهل البيت ورحمة الله وبركاته ﴿كُلُّ نَفْسٍ ذَائِقَةُ الْمَوْتِ وَإِنَّمَا تُوَفَّوْنَ

encompassed all believers, never having been afflicted in this way before, nor seen anything like it." So when the Messenger of God ﷺ was being buried, they heard a voice calling out from the roof of the house: ﴾*Indeed God wishes to keep uncleanness away from you, people of the* [*Prophet's*] *House, and to purify you thoroughly*﴿(33:33) and peace, God's mercy, and His blessings be upon you, O People of the House. ﴾*Every soul will taste death and you will be paid in full only on the Day of Resurrection. Whoever is kept away from the Fire and admitted to the Garden will have triumphed. The present world is only an illusory pleasure.*﴿ Indeed, God has a substitute in place of every departed, a consolation for every grief, and a gain for every loss incurred – so trust in God, rely on Him, and place your hope in Him alone, for the truly grief-stricken is indeed the one who is deprived of divine reward."' [3:185]

185. From al-Ḥusayn, from Abū ʿAbd Allāh عليه السلام who said, 'When the Messenger of God ﷺ passed away, Jibrīl came to them while the Prophet ﷺ was shrouded. In the house were ʿAlī, Fāṭima, al-Ḥasan and al-Ḥusayn, so he said, "Peace be upon you, O Household of mercy. ﴾*Every soul will taste death and you will be paid in full only on the Day of Resurrection. Whoever is kept away from the Fire and admitted to the Garden will have triumphed. The present world is only an illusory pleasure.*﴿ Indeed, God has a consolation for every grief, a gain for every loss incurred, and a substitute in place of every departed – so trust in God and place your hope in Him, for indeed the truly grief-stricken is the one who is deprived of Divine reward. This is the last foothold of this worldly life."' He continued, 'They said, "We heard a voice but did not see anyone."' [3:185]

186. From Hishām b. Sālim, from Abū ʿAbd Allāh عليه السلام who said, 'When the Messenger of God ﷺ passed away they heard a voice from the side of the house, but did not see anyone there. It said: ﴾*Every soul will taste death and you will be paid in full only on the Day of Resurrection. Whoever is kept away from the Fire and admitted to the Garden will have triumphed.*﴿ Then it continued, "Indeed, God has a substitute and a consolation for every grief and a gain from any loss incurred – so trust in God and place your hope in Him alone. Indeed, the truly deprived one is the one who is deprived of Divine reward. Maintain your Prophet's modesty." So when he had placed him on the bed,

أُجُورَكُمْ يَوْمَ الْقِيَامَةِ فَمَن زُحْزِحَ عَنِ النَّارِ وَأُدْخِلَ الْجَنَّةَ فَقَدْ فَازَ وَمَا الْحَيَاةُ الدُّنْيَا إِلاَّ مَتَاعُ الْغُرُورِ ﴾ إنّ في الله خلفًا من كلّ ذاهب، وعَزاءً من كلّ مُصيبة، ودَركًا من كلّ ما فات، فبالله فَثِقُوا، وعليه فتوكّلوا، وإيّاه فارْجُوا، إنّما المُصاب من حُرِم الثّواب.

١٨٥. عن الحسين، عن أبي عبدالله ﵇، قال: لمّا قُبِض رسول الله ﷺ جاءهم جبْرَئيل والنبيّ ﷺ مُسَجّىً، وفي البيت عليّ وفاطمة والحسن والحسين، فقال: السلام عليكم يا أهل بيت الرحمة ﴿ كُلُّ نَفْسٍ ذَائِقَةُ الْمَوْتِ ﴾ إلى ﴿ مَتَاعُ الْغُرُورِ ﴾ إنّ في الله عزاءً من كُلّ مُصيبةٍ، ودَركًا من كُلّ ما فات، وخَلَفًا من كُلّ هالك، فبالله فَثِقُوا، وإيّاه فارْجُوا، إنّما المُصاب من حُرِم الثّواب، هذا آخر وطئي من الدنيا، قال: قالوا: فَسَمِعنا صوتًا، فلم نَرَ شَخْصًا.

١٨٦. عن هِشام بن سالم، عن أبي عبدالله ﵇، قال: لمّا قُبِض رسول الله ﷺ سَمِعوا صوتًا من جانب البيت، ولم يَرَوا شخصًا، يقول: ﴿ كُلُّ نَفْسٍ ذَائِقَةُ الْمَوْتِ ﴾ إلى قوله ﴿ فَقَدْ فَازَ ﴾. ثمّ قال: إنّ في الله خَلفًا وعزاءً من كلّ مصيبةٍ، ودركًا لِما فات، فبالله فَثِقُوا وإيّاه فارجوا، وإنّما المحْرُوم من حُرِم الثّواب، واسْتُروا عَوْرَة نبيّكم. فلمّا وَضَعه على السَّرير نُودي: يا عليّ، لا تَخْلَع القَميص، قال: فَغَسَّله عليّ ﵇ في قميصه.

he was instructed: "O 'Alī, do not remove his shirt." So 'Alī washed him with his shirt on, peace be upon them both.' [3:185]

187. From Muḥammad b. Yūnus[70], from one of our associates who said, 'Abū Ja'far عليه السلام told me, ﴾***Every soul will either taste death or be resurrected***﴿ – this is how it was revealed to Muḥammad صلى الله عليه وآله; in that there is no one from this community who will not be resurrected. The believers will be resurrected in a pleasant form, while those who sinned will be resurrected in a state [befitting] of God's contempt for them.' [3:185*]

188. From Zurāra who narrated, 'Abū Ja'far عليه السلام said, ﴾*Every soul will taste death*﴿ – except the one who is killed, he does not taste death.' He continued, 'He must return [to life] to taste death.' [3:185]

189. From Abū Khālid al-Kābulī[71] who said, "Alī b. al-Ḥusayn عليه السلام said: "If I had permission to, I felt like speaking to the people on three occasions. So God did for me exactly what I love."' He continued, 'With his hand on his chest, he said: "It is God's order, however, that we remain patient. Then he recited the verse: ﴾*you are sure to hear much that is hurtful from those who were given the Scripture before you and from those who associate others with God. If you are steadfast and mindful of God, that is the best course.*﴿ Then he again lifted his hand and placed it on his chest.' [3:186]

190. From Abū Ḥamza al-Thumālī, from Abū Ja'far عليه السلام who said, 'The believer is continuously in the state of prayer as long as he is engaged in the remembrance of God whether he is standing, sitting or lying down, because God says: ﴾*Those who remember God standing, sitting, and lying down*﴿.'

There is a similar narration in another report from Abū Ḥamza, from Abū Ja'far عليه السلام. [3:191]

---

70 There are several companions of the fifth and sixth Imam with the name Muḥammad b. Yūnus. See Khū'ī, *Mu'jam*, 19: 73–4.

71 Abū Khālid Wardān Kankar al-Kābulī, a close disciple of the fourth Imam. See Ḥillī, *Khulāṣat*, 287 (nr. 1059); Khū'ī, *Mu'jam*, 15: 133–7 (nr. 9779).

١٨٧ . عن محمّد بن يونس، عن بعض أصحابنا، قال: قال لي أبو جعفر عليه السلام: (كُلُّ نَفْسٍ ذَائِقَةُ الموتِ أو منشورة) [كذا] نُزِل بها على محمّد صلى الله عليه وآله، إنّه ليس أحدٌ من هذه الأمّة إلاّ سَيُنْشَرُون، فأمّا المؤمنون فيُنْشَرُون إلى قُرّة عين، وأمّا الفُجّار فيُنشرون إلى خِزي الله إيّاهم.

١٨٨ . عن زُرارة، قال: قال أبو جعفر عليه السلام: ﴿كُلُّ نَفْسٍ ذَائِقَةُ الْمَوْتِ﴾ لم يَذُق الموت مَن قُتِل، وقال عليه السلام: لابُدّ من أن يرجع حتّى يَذُوق الموت.

١٨٩ . عن أبي خالد الكابُلي، قال: قال عليّ بن الحسين عليه السلام: لَوَدَدْتُ أنّه أُذن لي فكلّمت الناس ثلاثًا، ثمّ صَنَع الله بي ما أُحِبّ، قال بيده على صدره، ثمّ قال: ولكنّها عَزْمَةٌ من الله أن نَصْبِر، ثمّ تلا هذه الآية: ﴿وَلَتَسْمَعُنَّ مِنَ الَّذِينَ أُوتُوا الْكِتَابَ مِنْ قَبْلِكُمْ وَمِنَ الَّذِينَ أَشْرَكُوا أَذًى كَثِيرًا وَإِنْ تَصْبِرُوا وَتَتَّقُوا فَإِنَّ ذَلِكَ مِنْ عَزْمِ الْأُمُورِ﴾ وأقبل يَرْفَعُ يده ويَضَعها على صدره.

١٩٠ . عن أبي حمزة الثُّمالي، عن أبي جعفر عليه السلام، قال: لا يزال المؤمن في صلاةٍ ما كان في ذِكر الله، إن كان قائمًا أو جالسًا أو مُضْطَجعًا، لأنّ الله يقول: ﴿الَّذِينَ يَذْكُرُونَ اللَّهَ قِيَامًا وَقُعُودًا وَعَلَى جُنُوبِهِمْ﴾ الآية.

وفي رواية أُخرى، عن أبي حمزة، عن أبي جعفر عليه السلام، مثله.

191. In a narration from Abū Ḥamza, from Abū Jaʿfar; he said, 'I heard him say about God's verse: ﴾*Those who remember God standing*﴿, "The able-bodied ones; ﴾*sitting*﴿ meaning those who are ill, and ﴾*lying down*﴿ are those who are frailer and in greater pain than those who can pray while seated."' [3:191]

192. In another narration from Abū Ḥamza, from Abū Jaʿfar عليه السلام who said: '﴾*Those who remember God standing, sitting, and lying down*﴿ – The able-bodied one prays standing and sitting, the one who is ill prays sitting down, and the one who prays lying down is even weaker than the ill person who is able to pray whilst seated.' [3:191]

193. From Yūnus b. Ẓibyān who narrated, 'I asked Abū Jaʿfar عليه السلام about God's words: ﴾*The evildoers have no one to help them.*﴿ He replied, "They have no imams [lit. leaders] that they can call by name."' [3:192]

194. From ʿAbd al-Raḥmān b. Kathīr, from Abū ʿAbd Allāh عليه السلام who said regarding the verse: ﴾*Our Lord! We have heard someone calling us to faith – "Believe in your Lord" – and we have believed*﴿, 'It is the Commander of the Faithful who was addressed from the sky to believe in the Messenger, so he believed in him.' [3:193]

195. From al-Aṣbagh b. Nubāta, from ʿAlī عليه السلام regarding His verse: ﴾*a reward from God. What God has is best for those who are truly good.*﴿ He said, 'The Messenger of God said, "You are the reward and your helpers [or your companions] are the ones who are truly good."' [3:198]

196. From Muḥammad b. Muslim, from Abū Jaʿfar عليه السلام who said, 'Death is good for the believers, for God says: ﴾*What God has is best for those who are truly good.*﴿' He said, 'The Messenger of God said, "You are the reward and your helpers [or your companions] are the ones who are truly good."' [3:198]

١٩١. وفي رواية عن أبي حمزة، عن أبي جعفر عليه السلام، قال: سَمِعتُه يقول في قول الله: ﴿الَّذِينَ يَذْكُرُونَ اللَّهَ قِيَامًا﴾ الأصِحّاء ﴿وَقُعُودًا﴾ يعني المرضى ﴿وَعَلَىٰ جُنُوبِهِمْ﴾ قال: أعَلُّ ممَّن يُصلّي جالسًا وأوجع.

١٩٢. وفي رواية أُخرى، عن أبي حمزة، عن أبي جعفر عليه السلام ﴿الَّذِينَ يَذْكُرُونَ اللَّهَ قِيَامًا وَقُعُودًا وَعَلَىٰ جُنُوبِهِمْ﴾، قال: الصَّحيح يُصلّي قائمًا وقعودًا، والمريض يُصلّي جالسًا، وعلى جُنُوبِهم: أضعف من المريض الَّذي يُصلّي جالسًا.

١٩٣. عن يُونس بن ظِبيان، قال: سألتُ أبا جعفر عليه السلام عن قول الله تعالى: ﴿وَمَا لِلظَّالِمِينَ مِنْ أَنصَارٍ﴾، قال: ما لهم من أئمّةٍ يُسمُّونهم بأسمائهم.

١٩٤. عن عبد الرّحمن بن كَثير، عن أبي عبدالله عليه السلام، في قوله تعالى: ﴿رَبَّنَا إِنَّنَا سَمِعْنَا مُنَادِيًا يُنَادِي لِلْإِيمَانِ أَنْ آمِنُوا بِرَبِّكُمْ فَآمَنَّا﴾، قال: هوأمير المؤمنين عليه السلام، نُودي من السماء: أن آمِن بالرسول، فآمَن به.

١٩٥. عن الأصبغ بن نُباتة، عن عليّ عليه السلام، قال: قال رسول الله صلى الله عليه وآله، في قوله: ﴿ثَوَابًا مِنْ عِندِ اللَّهِ ۗ وَمَا عِندَ اللَّهِ خَيْرٌ لِلْأَبْرَارِ﴾ قال: أنت الثواب، وأنصارُك الأبرار.

١٩٦. عن محمّد بن مسلم، عن أبي جعفر عليه السلام، قال: الموتُ خيرٌ للمؤمن، لأنّ الله يقول: ﴿وَمَا عِندَ اللَّهِ خَيْرٌ لِلْأَبْرَارِ﴾، قال: قال رسول الله صلى الله عليه وآله، لعليّ عليه السلام: أنت الثواب، وأصحابك الأبرار.

197. From Masʿada b. Ṣadaqa, from Abū ʿAbd Allāh عليه السلام who said regarding the words of God, Blessed and most High: '﴾*be steadfast*﴿ in the face of sins, ﴾*and persevere*﴿ with obligatory acts, ﴾*and always be mindful of God*﴿ means: command the good and prohibit wrongdoing.' Then he said, 'And which wrongdoing is worse than the community's injustice towards us and their killing us. ﴾*Be ready*﴿ implies on the path of God – and we are the path between God and His creation. We are the rank at the forefront, so whoever defends us has defended the Prophet ﷺ and that which he brought from God. ﴾[*S*]*o that you may prosper*﴿ means: so that Paradise may be granted to you if you do that, and similar to that is the verse: ﴾*Who speaks better than someone who calls people to God, does what is right, and says, 'I am one of those devoted to God'?*﴿(41:33) – If this verse had indeed been revealed about the muezzins (callers to prayer) as the exegetes interpret it, then the Qadarīs would have been victorious, and the innovators along with them.' [3:200]

198. From Ibn Abī Yaʿfūr, from Abū ʿAbd Allāh عليه السلام who said about God's verse: ﴾*You who believe, be steadfast, and persevere; be ready*﴿, 'Be steadfast upon the obligatory acts, persevere in the face of calamities, and be ready to fight for the *a'imma* (Imams).' [3:200]

199. From Yaʿqūb al-Sarrāj[72] who narrated, 'I asked Abū ʿAbd Allāh عليه السلام, "Will the earth ever be devoid of a scholar from among you that people may resort to?"

He narrated: So he said to me, "If that were the case, Abū Yūsuf, then God would not be worshipped. The earth will never be devoid of a scholar from among us, available for people to resort to with regards to the permissible and the prohibited; and that is clearly evident in God's Book. God says: ﴾*You who believe, be steadfast*﴿ upon your religion, ﴾*and persevere*﴿ against your enemy who opposes you, ﴾*and be ready*﴿ to defend your Imam, ﴾*and always be mindful of God*﴿ in all that He has commanded you and made incumbent upon you."' [3:200]

---

72 Abū Yūsuf Yaʿqūb al-Sarrāj al-Kūfī, a reliable narrator according to Najāshī, but weak according to Ibn al-Ghaḍā'irī. See Ḥillī, *Khulāṣat al-aqwāl*, 299 (nr. 1113); Modarressi, *Tradition and Survival*, 397 (nr. 223).

١٩٧. عن مَسْعَدة بن صدقة، عن أبي عبدالله عليه السلام، في قول الله تبارك وتعالى: ﴿اصْبِرُوا﴾ يقول: عن المعاصي ﴿وَصَابِرُوا﴾ على الفرائض، ﴿وَاتَّقُوا اللَّهَ﴾ يقول: آمُروا بالمعروف وانْهَوا عن المنكَر.

ثمّ قال: وأيّ مُنكرٍ من ظُلم الأُمَّة لنا، وقتلهم إيّانا! ﴿وَرَابِطُوا﴾ يقول: في سبيل الله، ونحن السبيل فيما بين الله وخَلْقه، ونحن الرِّباط الأدنى، فمن جاهَدَ عنّا فقد جاهَدَ عن النبيّ صلى الله عليه وآله وما جاء به من عند الله ﴿لَعَلَّكُمْ تُفْلِحُونَ﴾ لعلَّ الجنَّة تُوجب لكم إن فَعلْتُم ذلك، ونظيرها من قول الله: ﴿وَمَنْ أَحْسَنُ قَوْلًا مِمَّنْ دَعَا إِلَى اللَّهِ وَعَمِلَ صَالِحًا وَقَالَ إِنَّنِي مِنَ الْمُسْلِمِينَ﴾ ولوكانت هذه الآية في المؤذّنين — كما فسّرها المفسّرون — لفاز القَدَريّة وأهل البِدَع معهم.

١٩٨. عن ابن أبي يَعْفُور، عن أبي عبدالله عليه السلام، في قول الله تعالى: ﴿يَا أَيُّهَا الَّذِينَ آمَنُوا اصْبِرُوا وَصَابِرُوا وَرَابِطُوا﴾. قال: اصبِروا على الفرائض، وصابِروا على المصائب، ورابِطوا على الأئمة.

١٩٩. عن يعقوب السّراج، قال: قلتُ لأبي عبدالله عليه السلام: تبقى الأرض يومًا بغير عالمٍ منكم، يَفْزَع الناس إليه؟

قال: فقال لي: إذًا لا يُعْبَد الله. يا أبا يوسف، لا تَخْلُو الأرض من عالِمٍ منّا ظاهر يَفْزَع الناس إليه في حلالهم وحرامهم، وإنَّ ذلك لمبيَّن في كتاب الله، قال الله تعالى: ﴿يا

200. In another narration on his authority: '﴾*Be steadfast*﴿ against those who harm us.' I asked, 'What about: ﴾*and persevere*﴿?' He replied, 'With your [Divinely appointed] protector (*walī*) against your enemy.' I asked, 'What about: ﴾*and be ready*﴿?' He said, 'It is to be stationed with your Imam, and: ﴾*always be mindful of God, so that you may prosper*﴿' I asked, 'Revelation?' He replied, 'Yes.' [3:200]

201. From Abū al-Ṭufayl, from Abū Jaʿfar عليه السلام who said regarding this verse, 'It was revealed about us; and the fight that He has commanded us to be ready for has not yet happened. The fighter will be from our lineage, and a descendant of Ibn al-Nāthil will be the opponent.' [3:200]

202. From Burayd, from Abū Jaʿfar عليه السلام who said regarding His verse: 'By ﴾*Be steadfast*﴿ it means in the face of sins; ﴾*and persevere*﴿ means dissimulation (*taqiyya*), ﴾*and be ready*﴿ means [to defend] the Imams.'

Then he said, 'Do you know that it means they stay put as long as we stay put, and when we make a move, they mobilize – ﴾***and always be mindful of God, your Lord, when we stay put, so that you may prosper.***﴿'

He continued, 'I asked, "May I be your ransom – but they read it: ﴾*always be mindful of God, so that you may prosper.*﴿" He replied, "That is how you all read it, and this is how we read it."' [3:200*]

203. From Abū Ḥamza, from Abū Jaʿfar عليه السلام who said, 'The believer remains in a state of prayer as long as he is engaged in the remembrance of God, be it standing, sitting or lying down, because God says: ﴾*Those who remember God standing, sitting, and lying down.*﴿' [3:191]

أَيُّهَا الَّذِينَ آمَنُوا اصْبِرُوا﴾ على دينكم ﴿وَصَابِرُوا﴾ عدوّكم ممّن يُخالفكم ﴿وَرَابِطُوا﴾ أمامكم ﴿وَاتَّقُوا اللَّهَ﴾ فيما أمرَكم به وافترض عليكم.

٢٠٠. وفي رواية أُخرى عنه: ﴿اصْبِرُوا﴾ على الأذى فينا. قلت: ﴿وَصَابِرُوا﴾؟ قال: على عدوّكم مع وليّكم. قلت: ﴿وَرَابِطُوا﴾؟ قال: المقام مع إمامكم. ﴿وَاتَّقُوا اللَّهَ لَعَلَّكُمْ تُفْلِحُونَ﴾ قلت: تنزيل؟ قال: نعم.

٢٠١. عن أبي الطّفيل، عن أبي جعفر عليه السلام، في هذه الآية، قال: نزلت فينا، ولم يكن الرّباط الذي أمرنا به بعد، وسيكون ذلك، يكون من نَسْلنا المرابط، ومن نَسْل ابن ناثِل المرابط.

٢٠٢. عن بُريد، عن أبي جعفر عليه السلام، في قوله: ﴿اصْبِرُوا﴾ يعني بذلك عن المعاصي ﴿وَصَابِرُوا﴾ يعني التقيّة ﴿وَرَابِطُوا﴾ يعني الأئمّة.

ثمّ قال: تدري ما يعني البُدوا ما لَبَدْنا، فاذا تحرّكنا فتحرّكوا ﴿وَاتَّقُوا اللَّهَ﴾ ما لَبَدْنا ﴿ربّكم لَعَلَّكُمْ تُفْلِحُونَ﴾.

قال: قلت: جُعِلتُ فداك، إنّما نقرأها ﴿وَاتَّقُوا اللَّهَ﴾ قال: أنتم تقرؤونها كذا، ونحن نقرأها كذا.

٢٠٣. عن أبي حمزة، عن أبي جعفر عليه السلام، قال: لا يزال المؤمن في صلاة ما كان في ذكر الله، إن كان قائمًا أو جالسًا أو مضطجعًا، لأنّ الله تعالى يقول: ﴿الَّذِينَ يَذْكُرُونَ اللَّهَ قِيَامًا وَقُعُودًا وَعَلَى جُنُوبِهِمْ﴾.

Women

4. Women

1. From Zirr b. Ḥubaysh[1] from the Commander of the Faithful ʿAlī b. Abī Ṭālib عليه السلام who said, 'Whoever recites the Chapter of Women (*sūrat al-nisā'*) every Friday will be safe from the squeezing of the grave.'

2. From Muḥammad b. ʿĪsā from ʿĪsā b. ʿAbd Allāh al-ʿAlawī[2], on his father's authority, on his grandfather's authority, from the Commander of the Faithful عليه السلام who said, 'Ḥawwā' was created from a fragment from Ādam's side, and the word "fragment" refers to the smallest rib. God replaced it with flesh.' [4:1]

3. With the same chain of transmission on his father's authority, from his forefathers, he said, 'Ḥawwā' was created from Ādam's side while he was sleeping.' [4:1]

4. From Abū ʿAlī al-Wāsiṭī[3] who said, 'Abū ʿAbd Allāh عليه السلام said, "God, most High, created Ādam from water and earth, so man's interest lies in water and earth; and God created Ḥawwā' from Ādam, so women's interests lie with men, so keep them locked up indoors."' [4:1]

---

1 Zirr b. Ḥubaysh, a notable and trustworthy companion of ʿAlī b. Abī Ṭālib and a person on whom ʿĀṣim relied for his recitation (*qirāʿa*) of the Qur'an. See Ḥillī, *Khulāṣat*, 152 (nr. 440); Khū'ī, *Muʿjam*, 8: 225 (nr. 4670).

2 ʿĪsā b. ʿAbd Allāh b. Muḥammad b. ʿUmar b. ʿAlī b. Abī Ṭālib al-ʿAlawī, who is known as Mubārak, was a great-grandson of ʿAlī b. Abī Ṭālib and an expert historian and genealogist. See Khū'ī, *Muʿjam*, 14:216 (nr. 9217); Modarressi, *Tradition and Survival*, 294–8 (nr. 109).

3 Abū ʿAlī al-Wāsiṭī, about whom there is no reliable information. See Khū'ī, *Muʿjam*, 22: 277 (nr. 14618).

بسم الله الرحمن الرحيم

من سورة النساء

١. عن زِرّ بن حُبيش، عن أمير المؤمنين عليّ بن أبي طالب عليه السلام، قال: من قرأ سورة النساء في كُلّ جمعة أُومِن من ضَغْطَةَ القَبْر.

٢. عن محمّد بن عيسى، عن عيسى بن عبدالله العلوي، عن أبيه، عن جدّه، عن أمير المؤمنين عليه السلام، قال: خُلِقَت حَوّاء من قُصَيْرَى جَنْب آدم عليه السلام — والقُصَيْرَى: هو الضِّلع الأصغر — وأبدل الله مكانه لحمًا.

٣. وبإسناده عن أبيه، عن آبائه عليهم السلام، قال: خُلِقت حوّاء من جنب آدم وهو راقد.

٤. عن أبي علي الواسطي، قال: قال أبو عبدالله عليه السلام: إنّ الله تعالى خلق آدم من الماء والطين، فهمّة ابن آدم في الماء والطين، وإنّ الله خَلَق حوّاء من آدم عليه السلام، فهمّة النساء الرجال، فحصّنوهنّ في البيوت.

5. From Abū Bakr al-Ḥaḍramī from Abū Ja'far who said, 'Ādam had four sons, so God made four beautiful maidens descend to them, marrying each one of the four; then they begot children. Then God raised them back up and married the four to four *jinns*, and they too had offspring. So the gentleness that there is [in the offspring] is from Ādam, whereas the beauty is from the maidens and bad-nature or ugliness from the *jinn*.' [4:1]

6. From Abū Bakr al-Ḥaḍramī from Abū Ja'far عليه السلام. He narrated, 'He asked me, "What do people say about Ādam getting his children married?" I replied, "They say: In each pregnancy, Ḥawwā' gave birth to a boy and a girl. So the boy from one birth married the girl from another birth, and the girl from one birth married the boy from another until they procreated."

So Abū Ja'far عليه السلام said, "That is not how it was – the Magians have influenced you. Rather, Ādam had a son called Hibatullāh (gift from God), and when he grew up he asked God to get him married. So God sent a beautiful maiden down from the Garden, and he got her married to him. She gave birth to four sons. Then Ādam had another son who, when he grew up, he was commanded to get him married to a *jinn*, who bore him four daughters. So the sons of this one married the daughters of that one. So whatever beauty you find is from the side of the maiden, whatever gentleness is from Ādam, and any rancour is from the *jinn*. After they had procreated the maiden went back up to the heavens."' [4:1]

7. From 'Amr b. Abī al-Miqdām, on his father's authority who said, 'I asked Abū Ja'far عليه السلام about the material substance from which Ḥawwā' had been created?

So he replied, "What is it that these people say?"

So I said, "They say God created her from one of Ādam's ribs."

So he said, "They lie. Was God not capable of creating her from something other than his rib?"

So I said, "May I be your ransom, O son of the Messenger of God ﷺ – what did He create her from then?"

He replied, "My father told me, from his forefathers who said, 'The Messenger of God ﷺ said, "God, Blessed and most High, took a handful of clay and kneaded it with His Right Hand – and both His Hands are right – and

٥. عن أبي بكر الحضرمي، عن أبي جعفر ﴿عليه السلام﴾، قال: إنّ آدم ولد أربعة ذكور، فأهبط الله إليهم أربعة من الحُور العِين، فزَوّج كُلّ واحدٍ منهم واحدةً فتوالدوا، ثمّ إنّ الله رَفَعَهنّ، وزوّج هؤلاء الأربعة أربعةً من الجنّ، فصار النَّسل فيهم، فماكان من حِلمٍ فمن آدم، وما كان من جمالٍ من قِبل الحُور العين، ماكان من قُبحٍ أو سُوء خُلقٍ فمن الجِنّ.

٦. عن أبي بكر الحضرمي، عن أبي جعفر ﴿عليه السلام﴾، قال: قال لي: ما يقول الناس في تزويج آدم ولده؟ قلت: يقولون: إنّ حَوّاء كانت تَلِد لآدم في كلّ بطن غُلاماً وجاريةً، فتزوّج الغُلام الجارية التي من البطن الآخر الثاني، وتزوّج الجارية الغُلام الذي من البطن الآخر الثاني حتّى توالدوا.

فقال: أبو جعفر ﴿عليه السلام﴾: ليس هذا كذلك، يُحجّكم المَجُوس، ولكنّه لما ولد آدم هِبَة الله وكبُر، سأل الله أن يُزوِّجه، فأنزل الله له حوراء من الجنّة فزوَّجها إيّاه، فولدت له أربعة بنين، ثمّ لود آدم ابناً آخر، فلمّا كبر أمره فتزوّج إلى الجانّ، فولد له أربع بنات، فَتَزَوَّج بنو هذا بنات هذا، فما كان من جمالٍ فمن قبل الحور العين، وماكان من حِلم فمن قِبَل آدم، وما كان من حِقْدٍ فمن قِبَل الجانّ، فلمّا تَوَالَدُوا صَعِدت الحوراء إلى السماء.

٧. عن عمرو بن أبي المِقدام، عن أبيه، قال: سألتُ أبا جعفر ﴿عليه السلام﴾: من أيّ شيء خَلَق الله حَوّاء؟ فقال: أيّ شيءٍ يقول هذا الخلق؟ قلت: يقولون: إنّ الله خَلَقَها من ضلع من أضلاع آدم. فقال: كَذَبوا، أكان يعجزه أن يَخْلُقها من غير ضِلعه؟

he created Ādam from it; then there was some clay left over, from which He created Ḥawwā'."' [4:1]

8. From al-Aṣbagh b. al-Nubāta who said, 'I heard the Commander of the Faithful عليه السلام say, "Some of you get angry and are not appeased such that it takes you into the Fire as a result. So whenever any of you are angered by one of your kin, you should go closer to him, for kinship [lit. the womb] is such that when touched by fellow kin, it calms down. It is attached to the Throne and demolishes it like iron [i.e. when ties of kinship are severed], and a voice calls out: 'O God, maintain ties with whoever maintains ties with me, and cut off whoever cuts me off' – and this is the purport of God's words in His Book: ﴾*be mindful of God, in whose name you make requests of one another. Beware of severing the ties of kinship: God is always watching over you.*﴿ Anyone who is angered while standing should immediately ground himself to the earth, for it removes Shayṭān's filth."' [4:1]

9. From 'Umar b. Ḥanẓala, on his authority regarding God's verse: ﴾*be mindful of God, in whose name you make requests of one another. Beware of severing the ties of kinship*﴿ – he said, 'They are the ties of kinship between people. God has commanded for them to be maintained and has given them great emphasis – do you not see that he has juxtaposed them to His Own Self?' [4:1]

10. From Jamīl b. Darrāj from Abū 'Abd Allāh عليه السلام. He narrated, 'I asked him about God's verse: ﴾*be mindful of God, in whose name you make requests of one another. Beware of severing the ties of kinship.*﴿ He replied, "They are the ties of kinship between people. God, Blessed and most High, has commanded for them to be maintained and has given them great emphasis – do you not see that he has juxtaposed them to His Own Self?"' [4:1]

فقلت: جُعِلت فِداك، يا بن رسول الله: من أيّ شيءٍ خَلَقها؟ فقال أخبرني أبي عن آبائه، قال: قال رسول الله ﷺ: إنّ الله تبارك وتعالى قَبَض قَبْضةً من طِين، فخلطها بيمينه - كِلتا يديه يمين — فَخَلَقَ منها آدم، وفضلت فَضْلةٌ من الطّين، فَخَلق منها حوّاء.

٨. عن الأصبغ بن نُباتة، قال: سَمِعتُ أمير المؤمنين عليه السلام يقول: إنّ أحدكم ليَغْضَب فما يرضى حتّى يَدْخُل به النّار، فأيّما رجل منكم غَضِب على ذي رَحِمه فليدنُ منه، فإنّ الرّحِم إذا مسّتها الرّحِم استقرّت، وإنّها مُتَعَلّقة بالعَرْش تنتقضه انتقاض الحديد، فينادي: اللّهم صِلْ مَن وَصَلَني، واقْطَع مَن قَطَعني، وذلك قول الله في كتابه: ﴿وَاتَّقُوا اللَّهَ الَّذِي تَسَاءَلُونَ بِهِ وَالأَرْحَامَ إِنَّ اللَّهَ كَانَ عَلَيْكُمْ رَقِيباً﴾ وأيّما رجل غَضِب وهو قائم فليَلْزَم الأرض من فَوره، فإنّه يُذْهِب رِجزَ الشيطان.

٩. عن عمر بن حَنْظَلة، عنه، عن قول الله تعالى: ﴿وَاتَّقُوا اللَّهَ الَّذِي تَسَاءَلُونَ بِهِ وَالأَرْحَامَ﴾، قال: هي أرحام النّاس، إنّ الله أمَرَ بِصِلَتِها وعَظّمها، ألا ترى أنّه جعلها معه.

١٠. عن جميل بن دَرّاج، عن أبي عبدالله عليه السلام، قال: سألتُهُ عن قول الله تعالى: ﴿وَاتَّقُوا اللَّهَ الَّذِي تَسَاءَلُونَ بِهِ وَالأَرْحَامَ﴾، قال: هي أرحام الناس، أمر الله تبارك وتعالى بصِلتها وعظّمها، ألا ترى أنّه جَعَلها معه؟

11. From Samāʿa b. Mihrān from Abū ʿAbd Allāh عليه السلام and Abū al-Ḥasan عليه السلام that he said: '﴾ *a great sin* ﴿ – this is on account of which the earth will throw out its burdens.'[4] [4:2]

12. From Samāʿa from Abū ʿAbd Allāh عليه السلام. He said, 'I asked him about a man who consumes the property of the orphan – can he be pardoned? So he replied, "That is up to his [i.e. the orphan's] family, because God says: ﴾ *Those who consume the property of orphans unjustly are actually swallowing fire into their own bellies: they will burn in the blazing Flame* ﴿(4:10) [and He says: ﴾ *it is a great sin.* ﴿]"' [4:2]

13. From Yūnus b. ʿAbd al-Raḥmān from whoever told him from Abū ʿAbd Allāh عليه السلام who said, 'There is a measure of extravagance in everything except women. God says: ﴾ *then you may marry whichever* [*other*] *women seem good to you, two, three, or four* ﴿ and: ﴾ *your slaves are lawful for you.* ﴿(4:24)' [4:3]

14. From Manṣūr b. Ḥāzim, from Abū ʿAbd Allāh عليه السلام who said, 'It is not permissible for a man's fluid to flow in the wombs of more than four free women.' [4:3]

15. From ʿAbd Allāh b. al-Qaddāḥ from Abū ʿAbd Allāh عليه السلام, on his father's authority who said, 'A man came to the Commander of the Faithful عليه السلام and said, "O Commander of the Faithful, I have pain in my stomach."

So the Commander of the Faithful عليه السلام asked him, "Do you have a wife?"

He replied, "Yes."

He said, "Ask her to gift you a little of her wealth gladly and willingly, then buy some honey with that. Pour some rainwater onto it and drink it, for indeed, I have heard God say in His Book: ﴾ *and how We send blessed water down from the sky,* ﴿(50:9) and: ﴾ *From their bellies comes a drink of different colours in which there is healing for people,* ﴿(16:69) and: ﴾ *though if they are happy to give up some of it for you, you may enjoy it with a clear conscience* ﴿ – you will be cured, if God wills."'

He continued, 'So he did that and was cured.' [4:4]

---

4 I.e. A terrible earthquake; c.f. Qur'an 99: The Earthquake.

١١. عن سَماعة بن مِهران، عن أبي عبدالله عليه السلام، أو أبي الحسن عليه السلام، أنّه قال: ﴿حُوبًا كَبِيرًا﴾، قال: هو مِمّا تُخرج الأرض من أثقالها.

١٢. عن سَماعة، عن أبي عبدالله عليه السلام، قال: سألتُهُ عن رجلٍ أكل مال اليتيم، هل له توبة؟ فقال: يُؤدّى إلى أهله، لأنّ الله تعالى: يقول: ﴿إِنَّ الَّذِينَ يَأْكُلُونَ أَمْوَالَ الْيَتَامَىٰ ظُلْمًا إِنَّمَا يَأْكُلُونَ فِي بُطُونِهِمْ نَارًا وَسَيَصْلَوْنَ سَعِيرًا﴾، وقال: ﴿إِنَّهُ كَانَ حُوبًا كَبِيرًا﴾.

١٣. عن يونس بن عبد الرّحمن، عمّن أخبره، عن أبي عبدالله عليه السلام، قال: في كلّ شيء إسراف إلاّ في النساء، قال الله تعالى: ﴿فَانكِحُوا مَا طَابَ لَكُم مِّنَ النِّسَاءِ مَثْنَىٰ وَثُلَاثَ وَرُبَاعَ﴾، وقال: وَأُحِلّ لَكُم ﴿مَا مَلَكَتْ أَيْمَانُكُمْ﴾.

١٤. عن منصور بن حازم، عن أبي عبدالله عليه السلام، قال: لا يحِلّ لماء الرّجل أن يجري في أكثر من أربعة أرحام من الحرائر.

١٥. عن عبدالله بن القدّاح، عن أبي عبدالله، عن أبيه عليهما السلام، قال: جاء رجُلٌ إلى أمير المؤُمنين عليه السلام، فقال: يا أمير المؤُمنين، بي وَجَعٌ في بطني. فقال له أمير المؤمنين عليه السلام، ألك زوجة؟ قال: نعم. قال: استوهب منها شيئًا طيّبة به نفسها من مالها، ثمّ اشْترِ به عَسلاً، ثمّ اسكُب عليه من ماء السماء، ثمّ اشْرَبْهُ، فإنّي أسمع الله يقول في كتابه: ﴿وَنَزَّلْنَا مِنَ السَّمَاءِ مَاءً مُّبَارَكًا﴾، وقال: ﴿يَخْرُجُ مِن بُطُونِهَا شَرَابٌ مُّخْتَلِفٌ أَلْوَانُهُ فِيهِ شِفَاءٌ

16. From Samāʿa b. Mihrān, from Abū ʿAbd Allāh عليه السلام or Abū al-Ḥasan عليه السلام. He said, ʻI asked him about God's verse: ﴾*though if they are happy to give up some of it for you, you may enjoy it with a clear conscience.*﴿ He replied, "By that He means their wealth which they own and which is in their possession."ʼ [4:4]

17. From Saʿīd b. Yasār[5] who said, ʻI asked Abū ʿAbd Allāh عليه السلام, "May I be your ransom – a woman entrusted her wealth to her husband for him to invest, saying to him when she gave it to him: ʻSpend out of it, and if something happens to me [i.e. before you can return it] then whatever you have spent of it is lawfully and agreeably yours.ʼ"

He replied, "Repeat the matter [for me], Saʿīd." So just as I was about to repeat the matter for him, the man in question himself set about explaining it, having been with me at the time. So he repeated the same thing to him. When he had finished, he pointed to the man with his finger and said, "If you know for certain that she had entrusted it to you between you, her and God, then it is lawfully and agreeably yours" three times. Then he said, "God says: ﴾*though if they are happy to give up some of it for you, you may enjoy it with a clear conscience.*﴿"ʼ [4:4]

18. From Ḥumrān from Abū ʿAbd Allāh عليه السلام who said, ʻA man complained to the Commander of the Faithful عليه السلام of an ailment, so he said to him, "Ask your wife for a dirham from her bridal gift and buy some honey with it, then drink it with rainwater." So he did as he was told and was cured. So he asked the Commander of the Faithful عليه السلام about that: "Is it something you heard from the Prophet صلى الله عليه وآله?" He replied, "No, but I have heard God say in His Book: ﴾*though if they are happy to give up some of it for you, you may enjoy it with a clear conscience*﴿ and ﴾*From their bellies comes a drink of different colours in which there is healing for people*﴿(16:69) and ﴾*and how We send blessed water down from the sky*﴿(50:9); so combine the enjoyment with the blessing and the healing, and then expect a full recovery as a result of it."ʼ [4:4]

---

5 Saʿīd b. Yasār al-Ḍabīʿī, originally of Kufa, was a reliable companion of the sixth and seventh Imams. See Ḥillī, *Khulāṣat al-aqwāl*, 158 (nr. 459); Modarressi, *Tradition and Survival*, 366–7 (nr. 184).

للنّــاسِ﴾، وقال: ﴿فَــإِنْ طِــبْنَ لَكُمْ عَنْ شَيْءٍ مِنْهُ نَفْسًــا فَكُلُوهُ هَنِيئًــا مَرِيئًــا﴾ . فإذا اجْتمعت البركة والشِّفاء والهنيء والمرِيء شُفيتَ إن شاء الله، قال: ففعل ذلك فشُفي .

١٦ . عن سماعة بن مِهران، عن أبي عبدالله عليه السلام، أو أبي الحسن عليه السلام، قال: سألتُهُ عن قول الله تعالى: ﴿فَــإِنْ طِــبْنَ لَكُمْ عَنْ شَيْءٍ مِنْــهُ نَفْسًــا فَكُلُوهُ هَنِيئًــا مَرِيئًــا﴾، قال: يعني بذلك أموالهُنّ الّتي في أيديهِنّ ممّا ملَكْنَ .

١٧ . عن سعيد بن يَسار، قال: قُلْتُ لأبي عبدالله عليه السلام: جُعِلتُ فِداك، امرأة دفعت إلى زوجها مالاً ليعمل به، وقالت له حين دفعتْهُ إليه: أنْفِق منه، فإنْ حَدَثَ بي حَدثٌ فما أنفقتَ منه فلَكَ حلالٌ طيِّبٌ، وإن حدث بِك حدثٌ فما أنْفقتَ منه فلك حلالٌ طيِّبٌ؟

قال: أعِدْ يا سعيد المسألة. فلمّا ذهبت أعرض عليه المسألة، عرض فيها صاحبها، وكان معي، فأعاد عليه مثل ذلك، فلمّا فرغ أشار بإصبعه إلى صاحب المسألة، فقال: يا هذا، إن كُنتَ تعلم أنّها قد أفْضَت بذلك إليك فيما بينك وبينها وبين الله، فحلالٌ طيّبٌ، ثلاث مرّات، ثمّ قال: يقول الله تبارك وتعالى: ﴿فَــإِنْ طِــبْنَ لَكُمْ عَنْ شَيْءٍ مِنْــهُ نَفْسًــا فَكُلُوهُ هَنِيئًــا مَرِيئًــا﴾ .

١٨ . عن حُمران، عن أبي عبدالله عليه السلام، قال: اشتكى رجلٌ إلى أمير المؤمنين عليه السلام، فقال له: سَلْ من امرأتك دِرْهمًا من صَداقِها، فاشْتَرِ به عَسلاً، فاشْرَبْهُ بماء السّماء؛ ففَعل ما أمر به فبرِئ. فسُئِلَ أمير المؤمنين عليه السلام عن ذلك، أشيء سمِعتَهُ من النبيّ صلى الله عليه وآله؟ قال: لا، ولكِنّي سمِعْتُ الله عزّ وجلّ يقول في كتابه: ﴿فَــإِنْ طِــبْنَ لَكُمْ عَنْ شَيْءٍ مِنْــهُ نَفْسًــا فَكُلُوهُ

19. From ʿAlī b. Riʾāb[6] from Zurāra who said, ʿA woman cannot retract that which she has gifted to her husband, whether the marriage has been consummated or not. Does God not say: ﴾*though if they are happy to give up some of it for you, you may enjoy it with a clear conscience*﴿?' [4:4]

20. From Yūnus b. Yaʿqūb who said, 'I asked Abū ʿAbd Allāh عليه السلام about God's words: ﴾*Do not entrust your property to the feeble-minded.*﴿ He said, "Someone you do not trust."' [4:5]

21. From Ḥammād from Abū ʿAbd Allāh عليه السلام who said regarding someone who continues to drink alcohol even after God prohibited it through His Messenger صلى الله عليه وآله: 'He is not worthy of marriage if he proposes, nor is he to be believed if he narrates a *ḥadīth*, nor can he mediate on someone's behalf if summoned, nor is he to be trusted to safeguard a deposit left in his care; and any such person who entrusts something in his care and he damages it or loses it, he cannot expect God to compensate him for it or replace it for him.'

Abū ʿAbd Allāh continued, 'I wanted to give so-and-so some merchandise to take to Yemen to trade [on my behalf], so I went to Abū Jaʿfar عليه السلام and asked, "I want to send some merchandise for trade with so-and-so."

So he replied, "Do you not know that he drinks alcohol?"

So I replied, "I had heard from believers that they say that [about him.]"

So he said, "You should believe them for God says: ﴾*he believes in God and trusts the believers.*﴿(9:61)"

Then he said, "If you entrust him with merchandise and it becomes damaged or lost, then it is not up to God to compensate you or replace it for you."

So I asked, "And why not?"

He replied, "Because God, most High, says: ﴾*Do not entrust your property to the feeble-minded. God has made it a means of support for you*﴿ – and is there anyone more feeble-minded than the drunkard? A servant still retains some margin for error as long as he does not drink alcohol, but when he does that God strips him of that cloak, and his offspring, his brother, his

6 ʿAlī b. Riʾāb, about whom there is scant information, was the author of a major *aṣl* and is regarded in high esteem. See Ḥillī, *Khulāṣat al-aqwāl*, 176 (nr. 524); Modarressi, *Tradition and Survival*, 189–91 (nr. 35).

هَنِيٓـًٔا مَّرِيٓـًٔا﴾، وقال: ﴿يَخْرُجُ مِنۢ بُطُونِهَا شَرَابٌ مُّخْتَلِفٌ أَلْوَانُهُۥ فِيهِ شِفَآءٌ لِّلنَّاسِ﴾، وقال: ﴿وَنَزَّلْنَا مِنَ ٱلسَّمَآءِ مَآءً مُّبَٰرَكًا﴾ فاجتمع الهَنيء وَالمَرِيء والبركة والشِّفاء، فرجوتَ بذلك البُرء.

١٩. عن عليّ بن رِئاب، عن زُرارة، قال: لا تَرْجِع المرأة فيما تَهَب لزوجها، حيزَت أو لم تُحَز، أليس الله يقول: ﴿فَإِن طِبْنَ لَكُمْ عَن شَىْءٍ مِّنْهُ نَفْسًا فَكُلُوهُ هَنِيٓـًٔا مَّرِيٓـًٔا﴾.

٢٠. عن يُونس بن يعقوب، قال: سألتُ أبا عبدالله عليه السلام في قول الله: ﴿وَلَا تُؤْتُوا۟ ٱلسُّفَهَآءَ أَمْوَٰلَكُمُ﴾، قال: من لا تَثِق به.

٢١. عن حمّاد، عن أبي عبدالله عليه السلام، فيمن شَرِبَ الخَمر بعد أن حرّمها الله على لسان نبيّه عليه السلام. قال: ليس بأهل أن يُزَوّج إذا خطب، وأن يُصدَّق إذا حدّث، ولا يُشفّع إذا شَفَع، ولا يُؤتَمن على أمانةٍ، فمن ائتمنه على أمانةٍ فأهلكها أو ضيّعها، فليس للّذي ائتمنه أن يأجُرهُ الله ولا يُخْلِف عليه.

قال أبو عبدالله عليه السلام: إنّي أردتُ أن أَستبضِع بِضاعةً إلى اليمن، فأتيتُ أبا جعفر عليه السلام فقلت: إنّي أردتُ أن أستبضِعَ فلانًا، فقال لي: أما عَلِمتَ أنّه يشرب الخمر؟ فقلتُ: قد بَلغَني عن المؤمنين أنّهم يقولون ذلك. فقال: صدِّقْهم لأنّ الله يقول: ﴿يُؤْمِنُ بِٱللَّهِ وَيُؤْمِنُ لِلْمُؤْمِنِينَ﴾.

ثمّ قال: إنّك إن استَبْضَعتَهُ فهلَكَت أو ضاعَت، فليس على الله أن يأجُرك ولا يُخْلِف عليك. فقُلتُ: ولِمَ؟ قال: لأنّ الله تعالى يقول: ﴿وَلَا تُؤْتُوا۟ ٱلسُّفَهَآءَ أَمْوَٰلَكُمُ ٱلَّتِى جَعَلَ

sight, his hands and his feet are all [means for] Iblīs, who drives him to every evil deed and turns him away from every good."' [4:5]

22. From Ibrāhīm b. 'Abd al-Ḥamīd who narrated, 'I asked Abū Ja'far عليه السلام about this verse: ﴾*Do not entrust your property to the feeble-minded.*﴿ He said, "Anyone who drinks an intoxicant is feeble-minded."' [4:5]

23. From 'Alī b. Abī Ḥamza [al-Thumālī][7], from Abū 'Abd Allāh عليه السلام. He said, 'I asked him about God's words: ﴾*Do not entrust your property to the feeble-minded.*﴿ He replied, "They are the orphans – do not give them their wealth until you know that they have attained maturity." I asked, "But how is it that their property is termed as our property?" He replied, "Since you are the one to manage their inheritance for them."' [4:5]

24. In 'Abd Allāh b. Sinān's report on his authority he said, 'Do not entrust it to the drunkards and the women.' [4:5]

25. From 'Abd Allāh b. Asbāṭ, from Abū 'Abd Allāh عليه السلام. He said, 'I heard him say, "Najda, the Ḥarūrī,[8] once wrote to Ibn 'Abbās asking him about the orphan and when his status as an orphan terminates. So he wrote back to him: 'As for the orphan, the termination of his orphanhood is his coming of age, and this is marked by the nocturnal emission, except if sound judgement is not perceived in him even thereafter, in which case he is either feeble-minded or weak, and then he is to be restrained.'"' [4:5]

26. From Yūnus b. Ya'qūb who narrated, 'I asked Abū 'Abd Allāh عليه السلام about God's words: ﴾*if you find they have sound judgement, hand over their property to them*﴿ – what is this sound judgement that should be perceived in them? He replied, "[The ability] to look after their own property."' [4:6]

---

7 'Alī b. Abī Ḥamza al-Thumālī, not to be confused with his namesake 'Alī b. Abī Ḥamza al-Baṭā'inī, was a reliable narrator of the Imams' traditions. See Ḥillī, *Khulāṣat al-aqwāl*, 181 (nr. 540).

8 Najda b. 'Āmir al-Ḥarūrī al-Ḥanafī (d. 69/689) was the head of the Najdiyya sect named after him, also known as al-Ḥarūriyya or al-Najadāt. See Khayr al-Dīn al-Ziriklī, *Kitāb al-a'lām* (Beirut: Dār al-'ilm li l-malāyīn, 1986), 8:10 and Sharīf Yaḥyā al-Amīn, *Mu'jam al-firaq al-islāmiyya*, 246.

اللهُ لَكُمْ قِيَامًا﴾ فهل سفيهٌ أسفه من شارِب الخمر؟ إنّ العبد لا يزال في فُسحةٍ من ربّه ما لم يشرب الخمر، فإذا شرِبها خرق الله عليه سِرْباله، فكان ولده وأخوه وسمعه وبصره ويده ورجله إبليس، يسوقه إلى كُلّ شرّ، وَيصرِفه عن كُلّ خير.

٢٢. عن إبراهيم بن عبد الحميد، قال: سأَلْتُ أبا جعفرٍ عليه السلام عن هذه الآية ﴿وَلَا تُؤْتُوا السُّفَهَاءَ أَمْوَالَكُمُ﴾، قال: كُلُّ من يَشْرَب الْمُسْكِر فهو سفيهٌ.

٢٣. عن عليّ بن أبي حمزة، عن أبي عبد الله عليه السلام، قال: سألْتُهُ عن قول الله: ﴿وَلَا تُؤْتُوا السُّفَهَاءَ أَمْوَالَكُمُ﴾، قال: هم اليتامى، لا تُعطوهم أموالهم حتّى تَعرِفوا منهم الرُّشد.

قُلتُ: فكيف يكون أموالهم أموالنا؟ فقال: إذا كُنْت أنت الوارث لهم.

٢٤. وفي رواية عبد الله بن سِنان، عنه، قال: لا تُؤتُوها شُرّابَ الخمر والنّساء.

٢٥. عن عبد الله بن أسباط، عن أبي عبد الله عليه السلام، قال: سَمِعتُهُ يقول: إنّ نجدة الحروري كتب إلى ابن عبّاس يسأله عن اليتيم متى ينقضي يُتْمُهُ؟ فكتب إليه: أمّا اليتيم فانقطاع يُتمِهِ أشُدُّهُ ــ وهو الاحتلام ــ إلاّ أن لا يُؤنَس منه رُشدٌ بعد ذلك، فيكون سفيهًا، أو ضعيفًا، فليسند عليه.

٢٦. عن يونس بن يعقوب، قال: قُلتُ لأبي عبد الله عليه السلام: قول الله تعالى: ﴿فَإِنْ آنَسْتُمْ مِنْهُمْ رُشْدًا فَادْفَعُوا إِلَيْهِمْ أَمْوَالَهُمْ﴾ أيّ شَيءٍ الرُّشد الّذي يُؤنَس منهم؟ قال: حِفظ ماله.

27. From ʿAbd Allāh b. al-Mughīra from Jaʿfar b. Muḥammad عليه السلام regarding God's words: ﴾ *if you find they have sound judgement, hand over their property to them.* ﴿ He narrated, 'So he said, "When you see that they love the family of Muḥammad, then promote them [for responsibility]."' [4:6]

28. From Muḥammad b. Muslim who narrated, 'I asked him about a man who has cattle that belongs to his orphaned nephew in his care. Can he combine them with his own livestock? He replied, "If he is the one refilling their watering troughs, tarring their hooves and rounding up their strays, then he can drink from their milk, being careful not to over-milk them nor cause any harm to their young." Then he recited the verse: ﴾ *if the guardian is well-off he should abstain from the orphan's property, and if he is poor he should use only what is fair.* ﴿' [4:6]

29. From Abū Usāma [Zayd al-Shahhām] from Abū ʿAbd Allāh عليه السلام regarding His verse: ﴾ *he should use only what is fair.* ﴿ He said, 'That is the man who has devoted himself to the custody of orphans' property, so he stands up for what belongs to them and protects it, which leaves him too busy to go out and earn a living for himself, so there is no problem if he uses what is fair from that if there is abundance in their wealth. However, if their wealth is little then he must not use any of it.' [4:6]

30. From Samāʿa, from Abū ʿAbd Allāh عليه السلام or Abū al-Ḥasan عليه السلام. He said, 'I asked him about His verse: ﴾ *if the guardian is well-off he should abstain from the orphan's property, and if he is poor he should use only what is fair.* ﴿ He replied, "Of course, one who manages something [i.e. wealth] for orphans while he is himself needy and does not own anything while litigating for their property and maintaining land belonging to them, he can use as much as he needs but not squander. However, if [the upkeep of] their land does not preoccupy him from applying himself to earn for himself, then he must ensure not to induce any loss in their wealth."' [4:6]

31. From Isḥāq b. ʿAmmār from Abū Baṣīr from Abū ʿAbd Allāh عليه السلام with respect to God's verse: ﴾ *if the guardian is well-off he should abstain from the orphan's property, and if he is poor he should use only what is fair* ﴿ he said, 'This is regarding the man who devotes himself to the land and the livestock

٢٧. عن عبد الله بن المُغيرة، عن جعفر بن محمّد عليه السلام، في قول الله: ﴿فَإِنْ آنَسْتُمْ مِنْهُمْ رُشْدًا فَادْفَعُوا إِلَيْهِمْ أَمْوَالَهُمْ﴾، قال: فقال: إذا رأيتموهم يُحِبّون آل محمّد، فارْفعوهم درجةً.

٢٨. عن محمّد بن مسلم، قال: سألتُهُ عن رجل بيده ماشيةٌ لابنِ أخٍ يتيم في حِجره، أيَخْلُط أمرها بأمر ماشيته؟ فقال: إن كان يُليط حِياضها، ويقوم على هنائها، ويرُدّ شاردها، فليَشْرب من ألبانها غير مُجتهدٍ للحِلاب، ولا مُضرّ بالولد، ثمّ قال: ﴿وَمَنْ كَانَ غَنِيًّا فَلْيَسْتَعْفِفْ وَمَنْ كَانَ فَقِيرًا فَلْيَأْكُلْ بِالْمَعْرُوفِ﴾.

٢٩. أبو أُسامة، عن أبي عبد الله عليه السلام، في قوله: ﴿فَلْيَأْكُلْ بِالْمَعْرُوفِ﴾. فقال: ذلك رجلٌ يحبِس نفسه على أموال اليتامى، فيقوم لهُمْ فيها، ويقوم لهم عليها، فقد شغل نفسه عن طلب المعيشة، فلا بأس أن يأْكُل بالمعروف، إذا كان يُصْلِح أموالهم، وإن كان المال قليلاً، فلا يأْكُل منه شيئًا.

٣٠. عن سماعة، عن أبي عبد الله عليه السلام، أو أبي الحسن عليه السلام، قال: سألتُهُ عن قوله تعالى: ﴿وَمَنْ كَانَ غَنِيًّا فَلْيَسْتَعْفِفْ وَمَنْ كَانَ فَقِيرًا فَلْيَأْكُلْ بِالْمَعْرُوفِ﴾. قال: بلى، من كان يلي شيئًا لليتامى، وهو مُحتاج، وليس له شيءٌ، وهو يتقاضى أموالهم، ويقوم في ضيعتهم، فليأْكُل بقدرٍ ولا يُسْرِف، وإن كان ضَيعتهم لا تَشغَلُه عمّا يُعالج لِنفسه، فلا يرزأنّ من أموالهم شيئًا.

٣١. عن إسحاق بن عمّار، عن أبي بصير، عن أبي عبد الله عليه السلام، في قول الله تعالى: ﴿وَمَنْ كَانَ غَنِيًّا فَلْيَسْتَعْفِفْ وَمَنْ كَانَ فَقِيرًا فَلْيَأْكُلْ بِالْمَعْرُوفِ﴾. فقال: هذا رجلٌ يحبِس

belonging to the orphan, applying himself therein; so he can consume what is fair from that, but that does not permit him to their dinars and dirhams [i.e. the monetary wealth] that are deposited in his care.' [4:6]

32. From Zurāra from Abū Ja'far عليه السلام who said, 'I asked him about God's words: ﴾*and if he is poor he should use only what is fair.*﴿ He replied, "That is if he has devoted himself exclusively to their property, not being able to earn for himself, so he can consume what is fair from their property."' [4:6]

33. From Rifā'a from Abū 'Abd Allāh عليه السلام who said regarding His verse: ﴾*he should use only what is fair*﴿, 'My father used to say that this has been abrogated.' [4:6]

34. From Abū Baṣīr from Abū 'Abd Allāh عليه السلام who said about God's verse: ﴾*If other relatives, orphans, or needy people are present at the distribution, give them something too*﴿: 'The verse of laws (*āyat al-farā'iḍ*) has abrogated it.'[9] [4:8]

35. In another narration from Abū Baṣīr, from Abū Ja'far عليه السلام: ﴾*If other relatives, orphans, or needy people are present at the distribution, give them something too*﴿ – I asked, 'Has it been abrogated?' He replied, 'No, if they are present you should give them.' [4:8]

36. In another narration from Abū Baṣīr, from Abū Ja'far عليه السلام. He said, 'I asked him about God's words: ﴾*If other relatives, orphans, or needy people are present at the distribution.*﴿ He replied, "The verse of laws has abrogated it."' [4:8]

---

9 *Āyat al-farā'iḍ* or the verse of laws is the name given to verse 11 of Women (*sūrat al-nisā'*) because of the laws of inheritance expounded within it.

نفسه لليتيم على حرثٍ أو ماشيةٍ، ويَشغَل فيها نفسه، فليأكُل منه بالمعروف، وليس ذلك في الدّنانير والدراهم الّتي عنده موضوعة.

٣٢. عن زُرارة، عن أبي جعفر عليه السلام، قال: سألتُهُ عن قول الله تعالى: ﴿وَمَن كَانَ فَقِيرًا فَلْيَأْكُلْ بِالْمَعْرُوفِ﴾. قال: ذلك إذا حبس نفسه في أموالهم، فلا يَحترِف لنفسه، فليأكُل بالمعروف من مالهم.

٣٣. عن رِفاعة، عن أبي عبد الله عليه السلام، في قوله: ﴿فَلْيَأْكُلْ بِالْمَعْرُوفِ﴾. قال: كان أبي عليه السلام يقول: إنّها منسوخة.

٣٤. عن أبي بصير، عن أبي عبد الله عليه السلام، عن قول الله عزّ وجلّ: ﴿وَإِذَا حَضَرَ الْقِسْمَةَ أُولُوا الْقُرْبَىٰ وَالْيَتَامَىٰ وَالْمَسَاكِينُ فَارْزُقُوهُم مِّنْهُ﴾. قال: نسختها آية الفرائِض.

٣٥. في رواية أُخرى، عن أبي بصير، عن أبي جعفر عليه السلام ﴿وَإِذَا حَضَرَ الْقِسْمَةَ أُولُوا الْقُرْبَىٰ وَالْيَتَامَىٰ وَالْمَسَاكِينُ فَارْزُقُوهُم مِّنْهُ وَقُولُوا لَهُمْ قَوْلًا مَّعْرُوفًا﴾، قلتُ: أمَنسوخة هي؟ قال: لا، إذا حضرك فأعطِهم.

٣٦. وفي رواية أُخرى، عن أبي بصير، عن أبي جعفر عليه السلام، قال: سألتُهُ عن قول الله: ﴿وَإِذَا حَضَرَ الْقِسْمَةَ أُولُوا الْقُرْبَىٰ﴾، قال: نَسَخَتها آية الفرائض.

37. From 'Abd al-A'lā, the client of the Sām clan, who said, 'Abū 'Abd Allāh عليه السلام remarked, "Whoever wrongs an orphan, God will subjugate him under someone who will either oppress him or his offspring or his descendants after them."' He continued, 'So I thought to myself: he is the one wronging, and his offspring and descendants will be the ones subjugated? So he said to me before I uttered anything, "Indeed God says: ﴾*Let those who would fear for the future of their own helpless children, if they were to die, show the same concern [for orphans]; let them be mindful of God and speak out for justice.*﴿"' [4:9]

38. From Samā'a, from Abū 'Abd Allāh عليه السلام or Abū al-Ḥasan عليه السلام that God has threatened two chastisements for the consumption of the property of orphans. The first one is the chastisement of the Fire in the Hereafter. The other is the chastisement in this world where He says: ﴾*Let those who would fear for the future of their own helpless children, if they were to die, show the same concern [for orphans]; let them be mindful of God and speak out for justice.*﴿ He said, 'By that, He means: let them fear for the mistreatment of their own children just as they mistreated these orphans.' [4:9]

39. From al-Ḥalabī from Abū 'Abd Allāh عليه السلام that [it is written] in the book of 'Alī b. Abī Ṭālib عليه السلام that the one who wrongfully consumes the property of the orphan will face the terrible consequences of that in his descendants after him, and he followed this by saying, 'This is [the chastisement] in this world, for God says: ﴾*Let those who would fear for the future of their own helpless children, if they were to die, show the same concern [for orphans]; let them be mindful of God and speak out for justice.*﴿ As for the Hereafter, God says: ﴾*Those who consume the property of orphans unjustly are actually swallowing fire into their own bellies: they will burn in the blazing Flame.*﴿' [4:9–10]

40. From Muḥammad b. Muslim, from one of the two [Imams al-Bāqir or al-Ṣādiq عليه السلام] – he said, 'What proportion of the consumption of the property of orphans is it that merits the Fire?' He replied, 'Two dirhams.' [4:10]

٣٧. عن عبد الأعلى مولى آل سام، قال: قال أبو عبد الله عليه السلام مُبتدِئًا: من ظلم سلّط الله عليه من يَظْلمه أو على عقِبه، أو عقِب عقِبه، قال: فذكرتُ في نفسي فقلتُ: يَظلِم هو فيسلط على عقِبه، أو عقِب عقِبه؟ فقال لي قبل أن أتكلّم: إنّ الله يقول: ﴿وَلْيَخْشَ الَّذِينَ لَوْ تَرَكُوا مِنْ خَلْفِهِمْ ذُرِّيَّةً ضِعَافًا خَافُوا عَلَيْهِمْ فَلْيَتَّقُوا اللَّهَ وَلْيَقُولُوا قَوْلًا سَدِيدًا﴾.

٣٨. عن سماعة، عن أبي عبد الله عليه السلام، أو أبي الحسن عليه السلام: أنّ الله أوعد في مال اليتيم عُقُوبتين اثنتين: أمّا إحداهما فعقوبة الآخرة النّار، وأمّا الأُخرى فعُقوبة الدنيا، قوله: ﴿وَلْيَخْشَ الَّذِينَ لَوْ تَرَكُوا مِنْ خَلْفِهِمْ ذُرِّيَّةً ضِعَافًا خَافُوا عَلَيْهِمْ فَلْيَتَّقُوا اللَّهَ وَلْيَقُولُوا قَوْلًا سَدِيدًا﴾، قال: يعني بذلك لِيَخشَ أن أُخلفه في ذُرّيّته كما صنع هو بهؤلاء اليتامى.

٣٩. عن الحلبي، عن أبي عبد الله عليه السلام، أنّ في كِتاب عليّ بن أبي طالب عليه السلام: أنّ آكِل مال اليتيم ظُلمًا سيُدرِكه وبالَ ذلك في عَقبه من بعده، ويلحقه وبال ذلك [في الآخرة]. أمّا في الدنيا فإنّ الله تعالى قال: ﴿وَلْيَخْشَ الَّذِينَ لَوْ تَرَكُوا مِنْ خَلْفِهِمْ ذُرِّيَّةً ضِعَافًا خَافُوا عَلَيْهِمْ﴾ الآية، وأمّا في الآخرة فإنّ الله تعالى يقول: ﴿إِنَّ الَّذِينَ يَأْكُلُونَ أَمْوَالَ الْيَتَامَىٰ ظُلْمًا إِنَّمَا يَأْكُلُونَ فِي بُطُونِهِمْ نَارًا وَسَيَصْلَوْنَ سَعِيرًا﴾.

٤٠. عن محمّد بن مسلم، عن أحدهما عليهما السلام، قال: قلتُ: في كم يجب لآكل مال اليتيم النّار؟ قال: في درهمَين.

41. From Samāʿa, from Abū ʿAbd Allāh عليه السلام or Abū al-Ḥasan عليه السلام. He said, 'I asked him about a man who consumed the property of the orphan – can he be pardoned? He replied, "He is rendered to his family [to decide]." He continued, "That is because God says: ﴾ *Those who consume the property of orphans unjustly are actually swallowing fire into their own bellies: they will burn in the blazing Flame.* ﴿' [4:10]

42. From Aḥmad b. Muḥammad who said, 'I asked Abū al-Ḥasan عليه السلام about the man who has some property belonging to an orphan in his possession and he is needy, so he uses some of it to spend on himself and his dependants intending to repay it back to him. Is he included among those about whom God says: ﴾ *Those who consume the property of orphans unjustly are actually swallowing fire into their own bellies: they will burn in the blazing Flame* ﴿? He replied, "No, but he must not consume anything without that intention, and he must not squander it."

I asked him, "What is the smallest amount of an orphan's property that entails one as having swallowed fire into his belly if he consumes it without intending to repay it?" He replied, "The small and the large amount are both equal if the intention to return it to them was absent."' [4:10]

43. From Zurāra and Muḥammad b. Muslim, from Abū ʿAbd Allāh عليه السلام that he said, 'If the guarantor of the orphan's property invests what is deposited in his care, then the profit belongs to the orphan.' He said, 'We asked him about His verse: ﴾ *and if he is poor he should use only what is fair.* ﴿ He replied, "That is only if he has devoted himself exclusively to them and their property and cannot earn for himself [as a result], then he may use what is fair from their wealth."' [4:6]

44. From al-ʿAjalān who narrated, 'I asked Abū ʿAbd Allāh عليه السلام, "What about the one who consumes the property of the orphan?" So he said, "It is as God has said: ﴾ *They are actually swallowing fire into their own bellies: they will burn in the blazing Flame.* ﴿"

He said without me even asking him, "Whoever looks after an orphan until his orphanhood expires or until he is self-sufficient, God makes the Garden obligatory for him just as He has made the Fire obligatory for one who consumes the property of the orphan."' [4:10]

٤١. عن سماعة، عن أبي عبد الله عليه السلام، أو أبي الحسن عليه السلام، قال: سألتُهُ عن رجلٍ أكل مال اليتيم، هل له توبة؟ قال: بردّه إل أهله، قال: ذلك بأنّ الله يقول: ﴿إِنَّ الَّذِينَ يَأْكُلُونَ أَمْوَالَ الْيَتَامَى ظُلْمًا إِنَّمَا يَأْكُلُونَ فِي بُطُونِهِمْ نَارًا وَسَيَصْلَوْنَ سَعِيرًا﴾.

٤٢. عن أحمد بن محمّد، قال: سألتُ أبا الحسن عليه السلام عن الرجُل يكون في يده مال الأيتام، فيحتاج فيمدّ يده، فيُنْفِق منه عليه وعلى عياله، وهو ينوي أن يَرُدّه إليهم، أهوممّن قال الله: ﴿إِنَّ الَّذِينَ يَأْكُلُونَ أَمْوَالَ الْيَتَامَى ظُلْمًا﴾ الآية؟ قال: لا، ولكن ينبغي له ألاّ يأكُل إلاّ بِقصدٍ ولا يُسْرِف.

قلتُ له: كم أدنى ما يكون من مال اليتيم إذا هو أكله وهو لا ينوي ردّه حتّى يكون يأكل في بطنه نارًا؟ قال: قليله وكثيره واحد. إذا كان من نفسه ونيّته أن لا يَرُدّه إليهم.

٤٣. عن زُرارة ومحمّد بن مُسلم، عن أبي عبد الله عليه السلام، أنّه قال: مال اليتيم إن عَمِلَ به من وُضِع على يديه ضَمِنَه، ولليتيم رِبحه.

قال: قلنا له: قوله: ﴿وَمَن كَانَ فَقِيرًا فَلْيَأْكُلْ بِالْمَعْرُوفِ﴾؟ قال: إنّما ذلك إذا حَبَسَ نفسه عَلَيْهِم في أموالهم، فلم يتّخِذ لنفسه، فليأكُل بالمعروف من مالهم.

٤٤. عن عجلان، قال: قلتُ لأبي عبد الله عليه السلام: من أكل مال اليتيم؟ فقال: هو كما قال الله تعالى: ﴿إِنَّمَا يَأْكُلُونَ فِي بُطُونِهِمْ نَارًا وَسَيَصْلَوْنَ سَعِيرًا﴾.

[ثمّ] قال هو من غير أن أسأله: من عال يتيمًا حتّى ينقضي يُتمُهُ، أو يستغني بنفسه، أوجب الله له الجنّة، كما أوجب لآكل مال اليتيم النّار.

45. From Abū Ibrāhīm who said, 'I asked him about a man who has some wealth in his possession that belongs to another man, either through trade or a loan, and he [i.e. the latter] dies before he could return it to him, and he leaves behind young orphans. So this belongs to them, but he has not remitted it to them. Does he count as one who consumes the property of the orphan unjustly? He replied, "If he intends to remit it to them, then no."

So al-Aḥwal said, "I asked Abū al-Ḥasan Mūsā ﵇, 'And if he does consume it without the intention to remit it, then is he included among those who unjustly consume the property of orphans?' He replied, 'Yes.'"' [4:10]

46. From 'Ubayd b. Zurāra[10], from Abū 'Abd Allāh ﵇. He said, 'I asked him about the grave sins, so he said, "One of them is the unjust consumption of the orphan's property, and there is no discrepancy in this matter among our associates, praise be to God."' [4:10]

47. From Abū al-Jārūd, from Abū Ja'far ﵇ who narrated, 'The Messenger of God ﷺ said, "Some people will be raised up from their graves on the Day of Resurrection with fire blowing out of their mouths." So he was asked, "O Messenger of God, who are these people?" He replied: ﴾ *Those who consume the property of orphans unjustly are actually swallowing fire into their own bellies: they will burn in the blazing Flame.* ﴿' [4:10]

48. From Abū Baṣīr who narrated, 'I asked Abū Ja'far ﵇, "May God make you prosper – what is the smallest thing that will warrant the servant entry into the Fire?" He replied, "One who consumes even a dirham from the property of the orphan; and *we* are the orphans."' [4:10]

49. From Abū Jamīla al-Mufaḍḍal b. Ṣāliḥ, from one of his associates, from one of the two [Imams] who said, 'Fāṭima – may God's blessings be upon her – went to Abū Bakr and asked for her inheritance from the Prophet of God ﷺ, so he said, "The Messenger of God does not leave inheritors." So she said, "Do you reject God and belie His Book? God says: ﴾ *Concerning your*

10 'Ubayd b. Zurāra b. A'yan al-Shaybānī, a reliable and trustworthy narrator of Imam Ja'far al-Ṣādiq's traditions. See Ḥillī, *Khulāṣat al-aqwāl*, 222 (nr. 735); Modarressi, *Tradition and Survival*, 383–4 (nr. 206).

٤٥. عن أبي إبراهيم، قال: سألتُهُ عن الرجُل يكون للرّجل عنده المال، إمّا بِبَيع أو بِقرض، فيموت ولَم يَقضِه إيّاه، فيترُك أيْتامًا صِغارًا، فيبقى لهم عليه فلا يقضيهم، أيكون ممّن يأْكل مال اليتيم ظُلمًا؟ قال: إذا كان يَنوي أن يُؤدّي إليهم فلا.

قال الأحول: سألتُ أبا الحسن موسى عليه السلام: إنّما هو يأْكله ولا يُريدُ أداءه، من الّذين يأكلون أموال اليتامى؟ قال: نعم.

٤٦. عن عبيد بن زُرارة، عن أبي عبد الله عليه السلام، قال: سألتُهُ عن الكبائر، فقال: منها أكلُ مال اليتيم ظُلمًا، وليس في هذا بين أصحابنا اختلاف والحمد لله.

٤٧. عن أبي الجارود، عن أبي جعفر عليه السلام، قال: قال رسول الله صلى الله عليه وآله: يُبعث أُناس من قبُورهم يوم القيامة، تُؤجّج أفواههم نارًا، فقيل له: يا رسول الله، من هؤلاء؟ قال: ﴿إنّ الّذِينَ يَأْكُلُونَ أَمْوَالَ الْيَتَامَى ظُلْمًا إِنَّمَا يَأْكُلُونَ فِي بُطُونِهِمْ نَارًا وَسَيَصْلَوْنَ سَعِيرًا﴾.

٤٨. عن أبي بصير، قال: قلتُ لأبي جعفر عليه السلام: أصلحك الله، ما أيسر ما يدخُل به العبد النّار؟ قال: من أكل من مال اليتيم دِرْهمًا، ونحن اليتيم.

٤٩. عن أبي جميلة المُفضّل بن صالح، عن بعض أصحابه، عن أحدهما عليهما السلام، قال: إنّ فاطمة صلوات الله عليها انطلقت إلى أبي بكر فطلبت ميراثها من نبيّ الله صلى الله عليه وآله، فقال: إنّ نبيّ الله لا يُورَث، فقالت: أكفرت بالله، وكذّبت بكتابه، قال الله تعالى: ﴿يُوصِيكُمُ اللهُ فِي أَوْلَادِكُمْ لِلذَّكَرِ مِثْلُ حَظِّ الأُنْثَيَيْنِ﴾.

children, God commands you that a son should have the equivalent share of two daughters. ﴿"' [4:11]

50. From Sālim al-Ashall[11] who said, 'I heard Abū Jaʿfar عليه السلام say, "God, Blessed and most High, has included parents among all people due inheritance, and they each receive at least a sixth."' [4:11]

51. From Bukayr b. Aʿyan[12] from Abū ʿAbd Allāh عليه السلام who said, 'Children and siblings are the ones who either get more or less [inheritance].' [4:11]

52. From Abū al-ʿAbbās who said, 'I heard Abū ʿAbd Allāh عليه السلام say, "The brother and sister receive no less than a third, even if it is two brothers, or a brother and two sisters, for God says: ﴾*his mother has a third, unless he has brothers, in which case she has a sixth.*﴿"' [4:11]

53. From al-Faḍl b. ʿAbd al-Malik[13] who said, 'I asked Abū ʿAbd Allāh عليه السلام about a mother and two sisters. He replied, "[The mother gets] a third because God says: ﴾*his mother has a third, unless he has brothers*﴿. He did not say: unless he has sisters."' [4:11]

54. From Zurāra from Abū Jaʿfar عليه السلام who said regarding God's verse: ﴾*his mother has a third, unless he has brothers, in which case she has a sixth*﴿, 'It can mean either the brothers from one father and mother, or the brothers from his father [alone].' [4:11]

55. From Muḥammad b. Qays who said, 'I heard Abū Jaʿfar عليه السلام say regarding debts and bequests, "[Repayment of] debts precedes bequests, then

---

11 Sālim b. ʿAbd al-Raḥmān al-Ashall, who is counted among the companions of Imam al-Bāqir, is unknown (*majhūl*) according to al-ʿAllāma al-Ḥillī. See Ḥillī, *Khulāṣat al-aqwāl*, 354 (nr. 1403); Khūʾī, *Muʿjam*, 9: 13 (nr. 4940).

12 Abū ʿAbd Allāh Bukayr b. Aʿyan al-Shaybānī al-Kūfī, a prominent companion of Imam Jaʿfar al-Ṣādiq and member of the notable Aʿyan family. See Ḥillī, *Khulāṣat al-aqwāl*, 83 (nr. 170); Khūʾī, *Muʿjam*, 4: 265–8 (nr. 1882).

13 Abū al-ʿAbbās al-Faḍl b. ʿAbd al-Malik al-Baqbāq, about whom there is scant information, was a narrator of Imam Jaʿfar al-Ṣādiq's traditions. See Ḥillī, *Khulāṣat al-aqwāl*, 229 (nr. 773); Modarressi, *Tradition and Survival*, 220–1 (nr. 58).

٥٠. عن سالِمِ الأشلّ، قال: سَمِعتُ أبا جعفر عليه السلام يقول: إنّ الله تبارك وتعالى أدخل الوالدين على جميع أهل المواريث، فلم يُنْقِصهما من السُّدُس.

٥١. عن بُكير بن أعين، عن أبي عبدالله عليه السلام، قال: الولدُ والإخوة هُم الّذين يُزادون ويُنْقَصون.

٥٢. عن أبي العبّاس، قال: سَمِعتُ أبا عبدالله عليه السلام يقول: لا يحجُب عن الثُّلث الأخ والأُخت حتّى يكونا أخوَين أو أخًا وأُختَين، فإنّ الله تعالى يقول: ﴿فَإِن كَانَ لَهُۥٓ إِخۡوَةٞ فَلِأُمِّهِ ٱلسُّدُسُ﴾.

٥٣. عن الفضل بن عبد الملك، قال: سألتُ أبا عبدالله عليه السلام عن أُمّ وأُختَين، قال: للأُمّ الثُّلُث، لأنّ الله يقول: ﴿فَإِن كَانَ لَهُۥٓ إِخۡوَةٞ﴾ ولم يقُلْ: فإن كان له أخوات.

٥٤. عن زُرارة، عن أبي جعفر عليه السلام، في قول الله تعالى: ﴿فَإِن كَانَ لَهُۥٓ إِخۡوَةٞ فَلِأُمِّهِ ٱلسُّدُسُ﴾ يعنِي إخوةً لأبٍ وأُمٍّ وإخوةً لأب.

٥٥. عن محمّد بن قيس، قال: سمِعتُ أبا جعفر عليه السلام يقول في الدَّين والوصيّة، فقال عليه السلام: إنّ الدَّين قبل الوصيّة، فقال عليه السلام: إنّ الدَّين قبل الوصيّة، ثمّ الوصيّة على أثر الدَّيْن، ثمّ الميراث ولا وَصيّة لِوارِث.

bequests come from the balance after [repayment of] debts, then inheritance. And there is no bequest for one who inherits [automatically].”’ [4:12]

56. From Sālim al-Ashall who said, ‘I heard Abū Ja‘far عليه السلام say, “God has included the husband and wife among all people due inheritance, and they each receive at least a quarter and an eighth.”’ [4:12]

57. From Bukayr [b. A‘yan] from Abū ‘Abd Allāh عليه السلام who said, ‘If a woman dies leaving her husband, parents, and sons and daughters, the husband receives a quarter according to God’s Book, the parents a sixth each, and whatever is left is divided whereby a son gets the equivalent of the share of two daughters.’ [4:12]

58. From Bukayr b. A‘yan from Abū ‘Abd Allāh عليه السلام who said, ‘What God means in His statement: ﴾*If a man or a woman dies leaving no children or parents, but a single brother or sister, he or she should take one-sixth of the inheritance; if there are more siblings, they share one-third between them,*﴿ is specifically the brothers and sisters from the same mother.’ [4:12]

59. From Muḥammad b. Muslim, from Abū Ja‘far عليه السلام. He narrated, ‘I said to him, “What do you say about a woman who dies leaving her husband, her brothers from the same mother, and brothers and sisters from her father?”

He replied, “The husband gets a half, [then the remainder is divided into] three parts: her brothers from her mother each get a third, so two equal parts for brothers and sisters. That leaves one part for the brothers and sisters from the father: the male receiving the equivalent of the share of two females, because set ratios do not differ, and because the husband gets no less than a half, and the brothers from her mother no less than a third, all sharing equally from that third if there are more than one; and if there is only one, then he receives one-sixth. What God means by the verse: ﴾*If a man or a woman dies leaving no children or parents, but a single brother or sister, he or she should take one-sixth of the inheritance; if there are more siblings, they share one-third between them*﴿ is specifically the brothers and sisters from the same mother.”’ [4:12]

٥٦ . عن سالِمِ الأشلّ، قال: سَمِعتُ أبا جعفر عليه السلام يقول: إنّ الله أدخل الزوج والمرأة على جميع أهل المواريث، فلم يُنْقِصهما من الرُّبع والثُّمن.

٥٧ . عن بُكير بن أعين، عن أبي عبد الله عليه السلام، قال: الّذي عنَى الله في قوله: ﴿وَإِنْ كَانَ رَجُلٌ يُورَثُ كَلَالَةً أَوِ امْرَأَةٌ وَلَهُ أَخٌ أَوْ أُخْتٌ فَلِكُلِّ وَاحِدٍ مِنْهُمَا السُّدُسُ فَإِنْ كَانُوا أَكْثَرَ مِنْ ذَٰلِكَ فَهُمْ شُرَكَاءُ فِي الثُّلُثِ﴾ إنّما عنى بذلك الإخوة والأخوات من الأُمّ خاصّة.

٥٨ . عن بُكير بن أعين، عن أبي عبد الله عليه السلام، قال: الّذي عنى الله في قوله: ﴿وَإِنْ كَانَ رَجُلٌ يُورَثُ كَلَالَةً أَوِ امْرَأَةٌ وَلَهُ أَخٌ أَوْ أُخْتٌ فَلِكُلِّ وَاحِدٍ مِنْهُمَا السُّدُسُ فَإِنْ كَانُوا أَكْثَرَ مِنْ ذَٰلِكَ فَهُمْ شُرَكَاءُ فِي الثُّلُثِ﴾ إنّما عنى بذلك الإخوة والأخوات من الأُمّ خاصّة.

٥٩ . عن محمّد بن مسلم، عن أبي جعفر عليه السلام، قال: قلتُ له: ما تقول في امرأةٍ ماتت وتركت زوجها وإخوتها لأمّها، وإخوة وأخوات لأبيها؟

قال: للزّوج النصف ثلاثة أسهُم، ولإخوتها من الأُمّ الثُّلُث سَهمان، الذكر والأُنثى فيه سواء، وبقي سهمٌ للإخوة والأخوات من الأب، للذكر مثل حظّ الأُنثيين، لأنّ السّهام لا تعول، ولأنّ الزّوج لا ينقُص من النّصف، ولا الإخوة من الأمّ من ثُلُثهم، فإن كانوا أكثر من ذلك، فهم شُركاء في الثُّلُث، وإن كان واحِدًا فله السُّدُس، وأمّا الّذي عنى الله تعالى في قوله: ﴿وَإِنْ كَانَ رَجُلٌ يُورَثُ كَلَالَةً أَوِ امْرَأَةٌ وَلَهُ أَخٌ أَوْ أُخْتٌ فَلِكُلِّ

60. From Jābir from Abū Jaʿfar عليه السلام who said regarding the verse ﴾*If any of your women commit a lewd act, call four witnesses from among you, then, if they testify to their guilt, keep the women at home until death comes to them or until God shows them another way*﴿: 'It has been abrogated; and "another way" refers to the prescribed punishments.' [4:15]

61. From Abū Baṣīr, from Abū ʿAbd Allāh عليه السلام. He said, 'I asked him about this verse ﴾*If any of your women commit a lewd act, call four witnesses from among you, then, if they testify to their guilt, keep the women at home until death comes to them or until God shows them another way.*﴿

He said, "It has been abrogated."'

He said, 'I asked, "How was it before?"

He replied, "If a woman committed a lewd act and four witnesses testified against her, she was kept at home without contact, conversation or company; and her food and drink were brought to her until she died."

I asked, "What about His statement ﴾*or until God shows them another way*﴿?"

He replied, "He made the [alternative] way lashing, stoning and solitary confinement in their houses."'

He said, "What about His verse: ﴾*Should two among you commit a lewd act*﴿?"

He replied, "This refers to the virgin who commits the same lewd act as the married woman, ﴾*so punish them both*﴿" – he said, "She is to be confined, ﴾*but if they repent and mend their ways, leave them alone – God is always ready to accept repentance, He is full of mercy.*﴿" [4:15–16]

62. From Abū ʿAmr al-Zubayrī from Abū ʿAbd Allāh عليه السلام with regard to the verse ﴾*Yet I am most forgiving towards those who repent, believe, do righteous deeds, and stay on the right path;*﴿(20:82) he said, 'This verse has an interpretation, and that interpretation indicates that God does not accept a single good deed from a servant unless accompanied by a commitment to it [i.e. the repentance] and to what he has stipulated upon the believers therein, according to that interpretation. And He said: ﴾*But God only undertakes to accept repentance from those who do evil out of ignorance,*﴿ which means every sin that the servant commits, even if he did it knowingly, because he was ignorant while risking his soul to disobey his Lord; and He, Blessed and most

وَاحِدٍ مِنهُمَا السُّدُسُ فَإِن كَانُوا أَكثَرَ مِن ذَلِكَ فَهُم شُرَكَاءُ فِي الثُّلُثِ﴾ إنّما عنى بذلك الإخوة والأخوات من الأمّ خاصّة.

٦٠. عن جابر، عن أبي جعفر ﷺ، في قول الله: ﴿وَاللَّاتِي يَأْتِينَ الْفَاحِشَةَ مِن نِسَائِكُمْ﴾ إلى: ﴿سَبِيلًا﴾ قال: منسوخة، والسبيل هو الحدود.

٦١. عن أبي بصير، عن أبي عبدالله ﷺ، قال: سألتُهُ عن هذه الآية: ﴿وَاللَّاتِي يَأْتِينَ الْفَاحِشَةَ مِن نِسَائِكُمْ﴾ إلى ﴿سَبِيلًا﴾

قال: هذه منسوخة.

قال: قلت: كيف كانت؟

قال: كانت المرأة إذا فجرت فقام عليها أربعة شهود أُدخِلَت بيتًا، ولم تُحدَّث، ولم تُكلَّم، ولم تُجالَس، وأُتِيَت فيه بطعامها وشرابها حتّى تموت.

قلت: فقوله: ﴿أَوْ يَجْعَلَ اللَّهُ لَهُنَّ سَبِيلًا﴾؟ قال: جعَلَ السبيل الجَلد والرّجم والإمساك في البيوت.

قال: قلتُ قوله: ﴿وَاللَّذَانِ يَأْتِيَانِهَا مِنكُمْ﴾؟

قال: يعني البِكْر إذا أتت الفاحشة الّتي أتتها هذه الثيب ﴿فَآذُوهُمَا﴾ قال: تُحبَس ﴿فَإِن تَابَا وَأَصْلَحَا فَأَعْرِضُوا عَنْهُمَا إِنَّ اللَّهَ كَانَ تَوَّابًا رَحِيمًا﴾.

٦٢. عن أبي عمرو الزُّبيري، عن أبي عبدالله ﷺ، في قول الله تعالى: ﴿وَإِنِّي لَغَفَّارٌ لِمَن تَابَ وَآمَنَ وَعَمِلَ صَالِحًا ثُمَّ اهْتَدَى﴾. قال: لِهذه الآية تفسيرٌ، يدُلُّ ذلك التفسير

High, has also said when narrating the story of Yūsuf and his brothers: ﴾*Do you now realize what you did to Joseph and his brother when you were ignorant?*﴿(12:89), so he attributed them [i.e. their misdeed] to ignorance for risking their souls to disobey God.' [4:17]

63. From al-Ḥalabī from Abū 'Abd Allāh عليه السلام regarding God's verse ﴾*It is not true repentance when people continue to do evil until death confronts them and then say, 'Now I repent,'*﴿: He said, 'That is escaping, he is repenting at a time when repentance will neither avail him nor will it be accepted from him.' [4:18]

64. From Zurāra from Abū Ja'far عليه السلام who said, 'Once the soul has reached here – and he lifted his hand to his throat – there will be no repentance for the knowledgeable man, but there will be for the ignorant one.' [4:18]

65. From Ibrāhīm b. Maymūn[14] from Abū 'Abd Allāh عليه السلام. He said, 'I asked him about God's verse: ﴾*It is not lawful for you to inherit women against their will, nor should you treat your wives harshly, hoping to take back some of the bride-gift you gave them.*﴿

He said, "[It refers to] The man who has an orphan girl in his care, preventing her from getting married so that he may inherit from her as she is related to him."

I asked, "[What about]: ﴾*nor should you treat your wives harshly, hoping to take back some of the bride-gift you gave them*﴿?"

He replied, "The man who mistreats his wife so much that she seeks to be ransomed from him; and God has forbidden that."' [4:19]

14 Ibrāhīm b. Maymūn, about whom there is scant information. See Khū'ī, *Mu'jam*, 1: 282 (nr. 320).

على أنّ الله لا يقبَل من عمل عملاً إلاّ ممّن لقيه بالوفاء منه بذلك التفسير، وما اشترط فيه على المؤمنين، وقال: ﴿إِنَّمَا التَّوْبَةُ عَلَى اللهِ لِلَّذِينَ يَعْمَلُونَ السُّوءَ بِجَهَالَةٍ﴾ يعني كلّ ذنبٍ عَمِله العبد، وإن كان به عالِمًا، فهو جاهل حين خاطر بنفسه في معصية ربّه، وقد قال في ذلك تبارك وتعالى يحكي قول يوسف لإخوته: ﴿هَلْ عَلِمْتُم مَا فَعَلْتُم بِيُوسُفَ وَأَخِيهِ إِذْ أَنتُمْ جَاهِلُونَ﴾ فنسبهم إلى الجهل لِمُخاطرتهم بأنفسهم في معصية الله.

٦٣. عن الحلبي، عن أبي عبد الله عليه السلام، في قول الله تعالى: ﴿وَلَيْسَتِ التَّوْبَةُ لِلَّذِينَ يَعْمَلُونَ السَّيِّئَاتِ حَتَّى إِذَا حَضَرَ أَحَدَهُمُ الْمَوْتُ قَالَ إِنِّي تُبْتُ الآنَ﴾، قال: هُوَ الفرّار تابَ حين لم ينفعه التّوبة ولم تُقبَل منه.

٦٤. عن زُرارة، عن أبي جعفر عليه السلام، قال: إذا بلغت النفس هذه — وأهوى بيده إلى حنجرته — لم يكُن للعالِم توبة، وكانت للجاهل توبة.

٦٥. عن إبراهيم بن ميمون، عن أبي عبد الله عليه السلام، قال سألتُهُ عن قول الله عزّ وجلّ: ﴿لاَ يَحِلُّ لَكُمْ أَن تَرِثُوا النِّسَاءَ كَرْهًا وَلاَ تَعْضُلُوهُنَّ لِتَذْهَبُوا بِبَعْضِ مَا آتَيْتُمُوهُنَّ﴾.

قال: الرجُل تكون في حِجره اليتيمة، فيمنعها من التزويج، ليرثها بما تكون قريبةً له.

قلتُ: ﴿وَلاَ تَعْضُلُوهُنَّ لِتَذْهَبُوا بِبَعْضِ مَا آتَيْتُمُوهُنَّ﴾؟ قال: الرجُل تكون له المرأة، فيضُرّ بها حتّى تفتدي منه، فنهى الله عن ذلك.

66. From Hāshim b. 'Abd Allāh b. al-Sarī al-Jabalī[15] who said, 'I asked him about the verse ﴾*nor should you treat your wives harshly, hoping to take back some of the bride-gift you gave them.*﴿' He continued, 'So he spoke a few words then said, "It is as the Nabateans believed that when one threw a garment over a woman, it meant she could not marry anyone else apart from him, and this was in pre-Islamic times."' [4:19]

67. From 'Umar b. Yazīd who said, 'I asked Abū 'Abd Allāh عليه السلام, "Tell me about someone who gets married with more than the customary (*sunna*) bride-gift – is that allowed?"

He replied, "If it exceeds the customary bride-gift, then this part is not counted as the bride-gift but as a present, because God says ﴾*do not take any of her bride-gift back, even if you have given her a great amount of gold*﴿ – here it [the gold] means as an [additional] present and does not refer to the bride-gift itself. Have you not considered that when he presents her with a bride-gift, then she seeks to dissolve the marriage, she has to give back her entire bride-gift, and whatever exceeds the customary bride-gift is counted as a present to her, as I told you. So after that, for whatever reason [she seeks a divorce], she has to give back the same bride-gift as the women of her time."

I asked, "How is it given and how much is the bride-gift of her contemporaries?"

He said, "The bride-gift of believing women is five hundred [dirhams], and this is the customary bride-gift. It can be less than five hundred but not more than that. If her bride-gift and the bride-gift of her contemporaries was less than five hundred, then she gives back whatever that was. Whoever proudly flaunts his large bride-gift [to his wife], exceeding five hundred, then for whatever reason [she seeks a divorce] she only has to pay back the bride-gift of her contemporaries, which should not exceed the customary bride-gift of five hundred dirhams."' [4:19]

68. From Yūsuf al-'Ijlī who said, 'I asked Abū Ja'far عليه السلام about God's verse ﴾*and they have taken a solemn pledge from you?*﴿ He replied, "The pledge is his

15 We could not find mention of this individual in either Ḥillī's *Khulāṣat al-aqwāl* or Khū'ī's *Mu'jam*.

٦٦. عن هاشم بن عبد الله بن السّري البجلي، قال: سألتُهُ عن قوله تعالى: ﴿وَلَا تَعْضُلُوهُنَّ لِتَذْهَبُوا بِبَعْضِ مَا آتَيْتُمُوهُنَّ﴾، قال: فحكى كلامًا، ثمّ قال: كما يقولون بالنّبطيّة، إذا طرح عليها الثوب عضلها، فلا تستطيع تزويج غيره، وكان هذا في الجاهليّة.

٦٧. عن عمر بن يزيد، قال: قلت لأبي عبد الله عليه السلام: أخبرني عمّن تزوّج على أكثر من مَهْر السُّنّة، أيجوز له ذلك؟

قال: إذا جاز مَهْر السُّنّة فليس هذا مهرًا، إنّما هو نحل، لأنّ الله يقول: ﴿فَإِنْ آتَيْتُمْ إِحْدَاهُنَّ قِنطَارًا فَلَا تَأْخُذُوا مِنْهُ شَيْئًا﴾ إنّما عنى النّحل ولم يعنِ المَهْر، ألا ترى أنّها إذا أمرها مَهْرًا ثمّ اختلعت كان لها أن تأخذ المَهْر كملاً؟ فما زاد على مَهْر السُّنّة فإنّما هو نحل كما أخبرتك، فمِن ثمّ وجب لها مَهر نسائها لِعلّة من العلل.

قلتُ: كيف يُعطى وكَم مهر نسائها؟

قال: إنّ مَهْر المؤمنات خمسمائة، وهو مَهْر السُّنّة، وقد يكون أقلّ من خمسمائة، ولا يكون أكثر من ذلك، ومن كان مهرها ومهر نسائها أقلّ من خمسمائة أُعْطي ذلك الشيء، ومن فخر وَبَذخ بالمَهْر، فازْداد على خمسمائة، ثمّ وجب لها مَهْر نسائها في علّة من العلل، لم يَزِد على مَهْر السُّنّة خمسمائة دِرهَم.

٦٨. عن يوسف العِجْلي، قال: سألتُ أبا جعفر عليه السلام عن قول الله عزّ وجلّ: ﴿وَأَخَذْنَ مِنكُم مِّيثَاقًا غَلِيظًا﴾، قال: المِيثاق الكَلِمة الّتي عُقِد بها النّكاح، وأمّا قوله: ﴿غَلِيظًا﴾ فهو ماء الرجل الذي يُفضيه إلى المرأة.

word by which he contracted the marriage, and the word ﴾*solemn*﴿ refers to the man's fluid that he releases in her."' [4:21]

69. From Muḥammad b. Muslim from Abū Ja'far عليه السلام that he stated: 'God says: ﴾*Do not marry women that your fathers married*﴿, so a man is not allowed to marry his grandfather's wife.' [4:22]

70. From al-Ḥusayn b. Zayd who said, 'I heard Abū 'Abd Allāh عليه السلام say, "God has forbidden for us to marry the Prophet's wives. God says: ﴾*Do not marry women that your fathers married.*﴿"' [4:22]

71. From Muḥammad b. Muslim, from one of the two [Imam al-Bāqir or al-Ṣādiq]. He said, 'I asked him, "What do you say about God's verse: ﴾*You [Prophet] are not permitted to take any further wives, nor to exchange the wives you have for others*﴿(33:52)?" He replied, "What He means by it is those that God has forbidden for him to marry in the verse: ﴾*You are forbidden to take as wives your mothers*﴿"' [4:23]

72. From Muḥammad b. Muslim, from one of the two [Imams al-Bāqir or al-Ṣādiq] about a man who had a servant girl with whom he consummated marriage, then he sold her to someone else who set her free. She subsequently married and had a child. Is her original owner allowed to marry her daughter? He replied, 'No, she is forbidden to him as she is his stepdaughter, and this is regardless of whether she is a free woman or a slave.' Then he read the verse: ﴾*and the stepdaughters in your care – those born of women with whom you have consummated marriage.*﴿ [4:23]

73. From Abū al-'Abbās about a man who has a slave-girl with whom he consummates marriage, then sells her – is he allowed to marry her daughter? He replied, 'No, she is included in God's statement: ﴾*and the stepdaughters in your care – those born of women with whom you have consummated marriage.*﴿' [4:23]

74. From Abū Ḥamza who said, 'I asked Abū Ja'far عليه السلام about a man who marries a woman then divorces her before consummating the marriage – is he allowed to marry her daughter?

٦٩. عن محمّد بن مسلم، عن أبي جعفر عليه السلام: يقول الله تعالى: ﴿وَلَا تَنكِحُوا مَا نَكَحَ آبَاؤُكُم مِّنَ النِّسَاءِ﴾ فلا يَصْلُح للرجل أن يَنْكِح امرأة جدّه.

٧٠. عن الحسين بن زيد، قال: سَمِعتُ أبا عبدالله عليه السلام يقول: إنّ الله حرّم علينا نساء النبيّ صلى الله عليه وآله يقول الله: ﴿وَلَا تَنكِحُوا مَا نَكَحَ آبَاؤُكُم مِّنَ النِّسَاءِ﴾.

٧١. عن محمّد بن مسلم، عن أحدهما عليهما السلام، قال قلت له: أرأيت قول الله: ﴿لَا يَحِلُّ لَكَ النِّسَاءُ مِن بَعْدُ وَلَا أَن تَبَدَّلَ بِهِنَّ مِنْ أَزْوَاجٍ﴾؟

قال: إنّما عنى به الّتي حرّم عليه في هذه الآية ﴿حُرِّمَتْ عَلَيْكُمْ أُمَّهَاتُكُمْ﴾.

٧٢. عن محمّد بن مسلم، عن أحدهما عليهما السلام، عن رجل كانت له جارية يطؤها، قد باعها من رجلٍ، فأعتقها فتزوّجت فولدت، يَصْلُح لمولاها الأوّل أن يتزوّج ابنتها؟

قال: لا، هي عليه حرام، وهي ربيبته، والحُرّة والمملوكة في هذا سَواء، ثمّ قرأ هذه الآية ﴿وَرَبَائِبُكُمُ اللَّاتِي فِي حُجُورِكُم مِّن نِّسَائِكُمُ﴾.

٧٣. عن أبي العباس: في الرجل تكون له الجارية، يُصيب منها ثمّ يبيعها، هل له أن يَنْكِح ابنتها؟ قال: لا، هي كما قال الله تعالى: ﴿وَرَبَائِبُكُمُ اللَّاتِي فِي حُجُورِكُم﴾.

٧٤. عن أبي حمزة، قال سألتُ أبا جعفر عليه السلام عن رجلٍ تزوّج امرأةً وطلّقها قبل أن يدخل بها، أتحِلّ له ابنتها؟

So he replied, "The Commander of the Faithful عليه السلام judged such a case and said that there was no objection. God says: ﴾*and the stepdaughters in your care – those born of women with whom you have consummated marriage, if you have not consummated the marriage, then you will not be blamed.*﴿ However, if he married the daughter then divorced her before consummating the marriage, he is not allowed to marry her mother."'

He continued, 'I asked, "Are they not the same?"

He replied, "No, this one is not like that one. God says: ﴾*You are forbidden* [...] *your wives' mothers*﴿ without any exception in this case, unlike the stipulation [of the absence of consummation] in that case. Here it is undefined and without condition, whereas, in that case, there is a condition."' [4:23]

75. From Manṣūr b. Ḥāzim who said, 'I asked Abū ʿAbd Allāh عليه السلام: "A man who marries a woman without having consummated the marriage, is he allowed to marry her mother?"'

He said, 'So he replied, "A man from among us had done this and saw no problem with it."'

He said, 'So I said to him, "By God, the Shīʿa pride themselves over people through this. Ibn Masʿūd issued a ruling regarding this controversy that there was no problem with it, so ʿAlī عليه السلام asked him, 'Where did you get that from?' He replied, 'God's verse: ﴾*and the stepdaughters in your care – those born of women with whom you have consummated marriage, if you have not consummated the marriage, then you will not be blamed.*﴿'

So he said, ʿAlī (as) said: 'This is an exceptional clause, whereas that is as it has been revealed.'"[16]

He said, "So I kept quiet and regretted what I had said." Then I asked him, "May God make you prosper – what do you say about it?"

He replied, "O Shaykh, you tell me of how ʿAlī judged the matter and then ask me what I would say about it!"' [4:23]

---

16 This is in reference to the prohibition of a man taking his wives' mothers in the preceding phrase.

قال: فقال: قد قضى في هذا أمير المؤمنين عليه السلام، لا بأس به، إنّ الله يقول: ﴿وَرَبَائِبُكُمُ اللاَّتِي فِي حُجُورِكُم مِّن نِّسَائِكُمُ اللاَّتِي دَخَلْتُم بِهِنَّ فَإِن لَّمْ تَكُونُوا دَخَلْتُم بِهِنَّ فَلاَ جُنَاحَ عَلَيْكُمْ﴾ ولو تزوّج الابنة ثمّ طلّقها قبل أن يدخل بها لم تَحِلّ له أُمُّها.

قال: قلت: أليس هما سَواء؟

قال: فقال: لا، ليس هذه مثل هذه، إنّ الله يقول: ﴿وَأُمَّهَاتُ نِسَائِكُمْ﴾ لم يستثنِ في هذه كما اشترط في تلك، هذه هنا مبهمةٌ ليس فيها شَرطٌ، وتلك فيها شَرط.

٧٥. عن منصور بن حازم، قال: قلتُ لأبي عبد الله عليه السلام: رجل تزوّج امرأةً ولم يدخل بها، تَحِلّ له أُمّها؟

قال: فقال: قد فعل ذلك رجلٌ منّا فلم يَرَ به بأسًا.

قال: فقلتُ له: واللهِ ما تفخر الشيعة على الناس إلاّ بهذا، إنّ ابن مسعود أفتى في هذه الشخينة، أنّه لا بأس بذلك. فقال له عليّ عليه السلام: ومن أين أخذتها؟ قال: من قول الله تعالى: ﴿وَرَبَائِبُكُمُ اللاَّتِي فِي حُجُورِكُم مِّن نِّسَائِكُمُ اللاَّتِي دَخَلْتُم بِهِنَّ فَإِن لَّمْ تَكُونُوا دَخَلْتُم بِهِنَّ فَلاَ جُنَاحَ عَلَيْكُمْ﴾ قال: فقال عليّ عليه السلام: إنّ هذه مُستثناة، وتلك مرسلةٌ.

قال: فسكتُّ، فندمتُ على قولي، فقلت: أصلحك الله، فما تقول فيها؟

قال: فقال: يا شيخ، تُخبرني أنّ عليًّا عليه السلام قد قضى فيها، وتقول لي: ما تقول فيها؟!

76. From 'Ubayd from Abū 'Abd Allāh عليه السلام about a man who has a slave-girl with whom he consummates marriage, then sells her – Is he allowed to marry her daughter? He replied, 'No, she is, according to God's verse: ﴾ *the stepdaughters in your care– those born of women with whom you have consummated marriage.* ﴿' [4:23]

77. From Isḥāq b. 'Ammār from Ja'far b. Muḥammad عليه السلام on his father's authority that 'Alī عليه السلام used to say, 'The stepdaughters are forbidden for you to marry, as well as their mothers with whom you had consummated a marriage, whether they were under your roof or not. As for [the permissibility of] the mothers of your wives, whether or not you have consummated the marriage, is undefined. So forbid that which God has forbidden, and define not what God has kept undefined.' [4:23]

78. From 'Īsā b. 'Abd Allāh who narrated, 'Abū 'Abd Allāh عليه السلام was asked about two sisters who are slave-girls and one of whom is taken into marriage, is the other permissible for him? So he replied, "He cannot marry the other one unless it is [a marriage] devoid of intercourse, but it would be better for him if he does not do so, for she would be as the wife whose husband cannot have intercourse with her while she is menstruating, as per God's command: ﴾ *Do not approach them until they are cleansed* ﴿(2:222) and: ﴾ *You are forbidden* [...] *two sisters simultaneously – with the exception of what is past* ﴿, meaning in marriage; for it would be acceptable for a man to have intimate contact with his wife while she is menstruating without intercourse." [4:23]

79. From Abū 'Awn who said, 'I heard Abū Ṣāliḥ al-Ḥanafī say, "Alī عليه السلام said one day: 'Ask me anything,' so Ibn al-Kawwā said, 'Tell me about [the permissibility of marrying] the daughter of your milk-brother and two sisters simultaneously?'

So he said, 'You are venturing into a minefield. Ask about that which concerns you or that which will be of benefit to you.'

So Ibn al-Kawwā said, 'I am only asking you about what we do not know. We would not ask you about what we already know.'

Then he said, 'As for two sisters who are slave-girls, one verse allows it whilst one forbids it, and I neither allow it nor forbid it; and neither would I do it, nor anyone from the People of my Household.'"' [4:23]

٧٦. عن عبيد، عن أبي عبدالله عليه السلام، في الرجل يكون له الجارية، فيصيب منها ثمّ يبيعها، هل له أن يَنْكِح ابنتها؟ قال: لا، هي مثل قول الله: ﴿وَرَبَائِبُكُمُ اللاَّتِي فِي حُجُورِكُمْ مِنْ نِسَائِكُمُ اللاَّتِي دَخَلْتُمْ بِهِنَّ﴾.

٧٧. عن إسحاق بن عمّار، عن جعفر بن محمّد، عن أبيه عليهما السلام، أنّ عليّاً عليه السلام كان يقول: الربائبُ عليكم حرامٌ مع الأُمّهات الآّتي دَخَلتم بهنّ في الحُجُور أو غير الحُجُور. والأُمّهات مبهماتٌ دُخِل بالبنات أو لم يُدْخَل بهنّ، فحَرِّموا وأبْهِمُوا ما أبهم الله.

٧٨. عن عيسى بن عبدالله، قال: سُئِل أبو عبدالله عليه السلام عن أُختين مملوكتين ينكِح إحداهما أتحلُّ له الأخرى؟ فقال: ليس ينكِح الأخرى إلاّ دون الفَرج، وإن لم يفعل فهو خيرٌ له، نظير تلك المرأة تحيض فتَحْرُم على زوجها أن يأتيها في فَرجها، لقول الله: ﴿وَلاَ تَقْرَبُوهُنَّ حَتَّى يَطْهُرْنَ﴾، قال: ﴿وَأَنْ تَجْمَعُوا بَيْنَ الأُخْتَيْنِ إِلاَّ مَا قَدْ سَلَفَ﴾ يعني في النِكاح، فيستقيم للرجل أن يأتي امرأته وهي حائض فيما دون الفَرج.

٧٩. عن أبي عَون، قال: سَمِعتُ أبا صالح الحنفي، قال: قال عليّ عليه السلام ذات يوم: سَلُوني، فقال ابن الكوّاء: أخبرني عن بنت الأخ من الرَّضاعة، وعن المملوكتين الأُختين؟

فقال: إنّك لذاهبٌ في التِيه، سَل ما يَعينك أو ما ينفع.

فقال ابن الكوّاء: إنّما نسألك عمّا لا نعلم، فأمّا ما نعلم فلا نسألك عنه.

ثمّ قال: أمّا الأُختان المملوكتان أحلّتهما آية وحرّمتهما آية، ولا أُحلّه ولا أُحرّمه، ولا أفعله أنا ولا واحدٌ من أهل بيتي.

80. From Muḥammad b. Muslim who said, 'I asked Abū Jaʿfar عليه السلام about God's verse: ﴾*women already married, other than your slaves.*﴿ He said, "This is when a man orders his male slave away from his slave-girl that he is sleeping with, saying, 'Move away from her and do not approach her.' Then he keeps her away from him until she menstruates, and then he sleeps with her thereafter. When she menstruates [again] after he has touched her, he should send her back to him without [further] intercourse."' [4:24]

81. From Abū Baṣīr from Abū ʿAbd Allāh عليه السلام regarding the verse: ﴾*women already married, other than your slaves.*﴿ He said, 'They are ones who have husbands.' [4:24]

82. From ʿAbd Allāh b. Sinān from Abū ʿAbd Allāh عليه السلام regarding the verse ﴾*women already married, other than your slaves.*﴿ He said, 'I heard him say, "[It is when] you command your male slave who is sleeping with your female slave to stay away from her until she menstruates, after which you can enjoy her."' [4:24]

83. From Ibn Muskān from Abū Baṣīr from one of the two [Imam al-Bāqir or al-Ṣādiq] regarding God's verse ﴾*women already married, other than your slaves.*﴿ He said, 'They are ones who have husbands. ﴾*[O]ther than your slaves*﴿ – if you have got your slave-girl married to your slave-boy, you can take her away from him if you wish.' So I asked, 'What if it is the wife of someone else's slave-boy?' He replied, 'He cannot take her away from him unless she is sold [to him], so when he sells her, part of her belongs to someone other than him [her husband]. So the buyer can either separate them if he so wishes, or acquiesce.' [4:24]

84. From Ibn Khurrazād from whoever narrated it to him from Abū ʿAbd Allāh regarding the verse ﴾*women already married.*﴿ He said, 'All married women.' [4:24]

٨٠. عن محمّد بن مسلم، قال: سألتُ أبا جعفر عليه السلام عن قول الله عزّ وجلّ: ﴿وَالْمُحْصَنَاتُ مِنَ النِّسَاءِ إِلَّا مَا مَلَكَتْ أَيْمَانُكُمْ﴾. قال: هو أن يأمرُ الرجل عبده وتحته أمته فيقول له: اعْتَزِلها فلا تَقْرَبها، ثمّ يَحْبِسها عنه حتّى تحيض، ثمّ يَمَسَّها، فإذا حاضت بعد مسّه إيّاها ردَّها عليه بغير نِكاح.

٨١. عن أبي بصير، عن أبي عبدالله عليه السلام، في ﴿وَالْمُحْصَنَاتُ مِنَ النِّسَاءِ إِلَّا مَا مَلَكَتْ أَيْمَانُكُمْ﴾، قال: هُنّ ذوات الأزواج.

٨٢. عن عبدالله بن سِنان، عن أبي عبدالله عليه السلام، في ﴿وَالْمُحْصَنَاتُ مِنَ النِّسَاءِ إِلَّا مَا مَلَكَتْ أَيْمَانُكُمْ﴾، قال: سَمِعته يقول: تأمُر عبدك وتحته أَمَتُك، فيعتزلها حتّى تحيض، فتُصيب منها.

٨٣. عن ابن مُسكان، عن أبي بصير، عن أحدهما عليه السلام، في قول الله تعالى: ﴿وَالْمُحْصَنَاتُ مِنَ النِّسَاءِ إِلَّا مَا مَلَكَتْ أَيْمَانُكُمْ﴾، قال: هُنّ ذوات الأزواج ﴿إِلَّا مَا مَلَكَتْ أَيْمَانُكُمْ﴾ إن كُنتَ زوّجتَ أمَتك غُلامَك، نَزَعْتَها منه إذا شئت.

فقلتُ: أرأيت إن زَوّج غير غُلامه؟ قال: ليس له أن ينزِع حتّى تُباع، فإن باعها صار بُضْعُها في يد غيره، وإن شاء المشتري فرّق، وإن شاء أقرّ.

٨٤. عن ابن خُرّزاد، عمّن رواه عن أبي عبدالله عليه السلام، في قوله تعالى: ﴿وَالْمُحْصَنَاتُ مِنَ النِّسَاءِ﴾، قال: كُلّ ذوات الأزواج.

85. From Muḥammad b. Muslim from Abū Jaʿfar عليه السلام who said, 'Jābir b. ʿAbd Allāh related from the Messenger of God ﷺ that they went out to fight with him, so he made temporary marriage (*mutʿa*) permissible for them and did not prohibit it. And ʿAlī عليه السلام would say, "Were it not for the ruling of Ibn al-Khaṭṭāb's, meaning ʿUmar, which preceded me, only very few people would ever have fornicated. As Ibn ʿAbbās used to say, ﴾***If you wish to enjoy women through marriage for a stipulated period, give them their bride-gift – this is obligatory – though if you should choose mutually, after fulfilling this obligation***﴿ – and these people reject it while the Messenger of God ﷺ had permitted it and never forbade it."' [4:24*]

86. From Abū Baṣīr from Abū Jaʿfar عليه السلام who said about temporary marriage, 'This verse was revealed: ﴾*If you wish to enjoy women through marriage, give them their bride-gift – this is obligatory – though if you should choose mutually, after fulfilling this obligation, to do otherwise* [*with the bride-gift*], *you will not be blamed.*﴿' He continued, 'There is no objection for you to extend the period or for her to do so when the stipulated term between them runs out. He should say, "I seek to make you permissible for myself for another term" with her consent. She is not allowed to marry anyone other than you until after her waiting period which is two menstrual cycles.' [4:24]

87. From Abū Baṣīr, from Abū Jaʿfar عليه السلام. He said, 'He used to read it as: ﴾***If you wish to enjoy women through marriage for a stipulated term, give them their bride-gift – this is obligatory – though if you should choose mutually, after fulfilling this obligation***﴿. So he said, "This is when he marries her for the stipulated term, then renews it for some time after that term."' [4:24*]

88. From ʿAbd al-Salām[17], from Abū ʿAbd Allāh عليه السلام. He said, 'I asked him, "What do you say about temporary marriage?" He said, "The verse of God: ﴾*If you wish to enjoy women through marriage, give them their bride-gift – this is obligatory – though if you should choose mutually, after fulfilling this obligation, to do otherwise* [*with the bride-gift*], *you will not be blamed.*﴿"'

He said, 'I asked him, "May I be your ransom – is she [i.e. the temporary wife] included among the four [wives]?"

17 This name is too vague to identify exactly which ʿAbd al-Salām this is referring to.

٨٥. عن محمّد بن مسلم، عن أبي جعفر عليه السلام، قال: قال جابر بن عبد الله، عن رسول الله صلى الله عليه وآله: أنَّهم غزَوا معه، فأحَلَّ لهم المتُعة ولم يُحَرِّمْها، وكان عليّ عليه السلام، يقول: لولا ما سبقني به ابن الخطّاب – يعني عمر – ما زنى إلاّ شقيّ.

وكان ابن عباس يقول: ﴿فَمَا اسْتَمْتَعْتُم بِهِ مِنْهُنَّ﴾ إلى أجل مسمّى ﴿فَآتُوهُنَّ أُجُورَهُنَّ فَرِيضَةً﴾ وهؤلاءِ يكفُرون بها، ورسول الله صلى الله عليه وآله أحلّها ولم يُحرِّمْها.

٨٦. عن أبي بصير، عن أبي جعفر عليه السلام، في المتُعة، قال: نزلت هذه الآية: ﴿فَمَا اسْتَمْتَعْتُم بِهِ مِنْهُنَّ فَآتُوهُنَّ أُجُورَهُنَّ فَرِيضَةً وَلاَ جُنَاحَ عَلَيْكُمْ فِيمَا تَرَاضَيْتُم بِهِ مِن بَعْدِ الْفَرِيضَةِ﴾، قال: لا بأس بأن تَزيدها وتَزيدك، إذا انقطع الأجل فيما بينكما، يقول: اسْتَحْلَلْتُك بأجل آخر، بِرِضىً منها، ولا تَحِلّ لغيرك حتّى تنقضي عِدَّتها، وعِدَّتها حَيضَتان.

٨٧. عن أبي بصير، عن أبي جعفر عليه السلام، قال: كان يقرأ ﴿فَمَا اسْتَمْتَعْتُم بِهِ مِنْهُنَّ﴾ إلى أجلٍ مُسمّى ﴿فَآتُوهُنَّ أُجُورَهُنَّ فَرِيضَةً وَلاَ جُنَاحَ عَلَيْكُمْ فِيمَا تَرَاضَيْتُم بِهِ مِن بَعْدِ الْفَرِيضَةِ﴾، فقال: هوأن يَتزَوّجها إلى أجلٍ مُسمّىً، ثمَّ يُحْدِث شيئًا بعد الأجل.

٨٨. عن عبد السلام، عن أبي عبد الله عليه السلام، قال: قلتُ له: ما تقول في المتُعة؟ قال: قول الله: ﴿فَمَا اسْتَمْتَعْتُم بِهِ مِنْهُنَّ فَآتُوهُنَّ أُجُورَهُنَّ فَرِيضَةً﴾ إلى أجل مسمّى ﴿وَلاَ جُنَاحَ عَلَيْكُمْ فِيمَا تَرَاضَيْتُم بِهِ مِن بَعْدِ الْفَرِيضَةِ﴾.

قال: قلتُ جعلتُ فِداك، أهي من الأربع: قال: ليست من الأربع، إنّما هي إجارة.

He replied, "She is not included among the four, rather she is hired."

So I asked, "What if he or she wants to extend it before the stipulated term expires?"

He replied, "There is no problem as long as it is consented by both of them, both the term and the time." He added, "He can extend it after the time has expired."' [4:24]

89. From Aḥmad b. Muḥammad b. Abī Naṣr who said, 'I asked al-Riḍā ﷺ, "Does a girl need the consent of her family for temporary marriage?" He replied, "Yes. God says: ﴾*so marry them with their people's consent.*﴿"' [4:25]

90. Muḥammad b. Ṣadaqa al-Baṣrī said, 'I asked him about temporary marriage: does this not constitute the same thing as marrying slave-girls? He said, "Yes. Have you not read God's verse: ﴾*If any of you does not have the means to marry a believing free woman, then marry a believing slave - God knows best* [*the depth of*] *your faith: you are* [*all*] *part of the same family – so marry them with their people's consent and their proper bride-gifts.* [*Make them*] *married women, not adulteresses or lovers*﴿? So just as a man should not marry a slave-girl when he has the means to marry a free woman, neither should he contract a temporary marriage with a slave whilst having the means to marry a free woman."' [4:25]

91. From Abū al-'Abbās who said, 'I asked Abū 'Abd Allāh ﷺ, "What if a man marries a girl without the consent of her family?" He replied, "It is fornication. God says: ﴾*so marry them with their people's consent.*﴿"' [4:25]

92. From 'Abd Allāh b. Sinān, from Abū 'Abd Allāh ﷺ. He said, 'I asked him about the 'believing slave-girls,' so he replied, "They are Muslim [women]."' [4:25]

93. From Muḥammad b. Muslim, from one of the two [Imam al-Bāqir or al-Ṣādiq]. He said, 'I asked him about God's statement about slave-girls: ﴾*when they are married*﴿ – what constitutes 'marriage' with them? He replied, "He must consummate the marriage with her." I asked, "But if he does not consummate it then she is not punishable [if she commits adultery thereafter]?" He replied, "Yes."' [4:25]

فقلتُ: إن أراد أن يزداد وتزداد قبل انقضاء الأجل الذي أُجِّل؟

قال: لا بأس أن يكون ذلك برضىً منه ومنها، بالأجل والوقت، وقال: يزيدها بعدما يمضي الأجل.

٨٩. عن أحمد بن محمّد بن أبي نصر، قال: سألتُ الرضا ﵇: يُتَمَتَّعُ بالأمة بإذن أهلها؟ قال: نعم، إنَّ الله يقول: ﴿فَانكِحُوهُنَّ بِإِذْنِ أَهْلِهِنَّ﴾.

٩٠. وقال محمّد بن صَدَقة البصري: سألتُه عن المتُعة، أليس هي بمنزلة الإماء؟ قال: نعم، أما تقرأ قول الله: ﴿وَمَن لَّمْ يَسْتَطِعْ مِنكُمْ طَوْلاً أَن يَنكِحَ الْمُحْصَنَاتِ الْمُؤْمِنَاتِ﴾ إلى قوله: ﴿وَلاَ مُتَّخِذَاتِ أَخْدَانٍ﴾؟ فكما لا يَسَع الرجل أن يَتَزوّج الأَمَة وهو يستطيع أن يَتَزوّج بالحُرّة، فكذلك لا يَسَع الرجل أن يتمتّع بالأمة وهو يستطيع أن يَتَزوّج بالحُرّة.

٩١. عن أبي العباس، قال: قلتُ لأبي عبدالله ﵇: يَتَزَوّج الرجل بالأَمَة بغير إذن أهلها؟ قال: هو زنا، إنَّ الله يقول: ﴿فَانكِحُوهُنَّ بِإِذْنِ أَهْلِهِنَّ﴾.

٩٢. عن عبدالله بن سِنان، عن أبي عبدالله ﵇، قال سألتُه عن المُحْصَنات من الإماء، قال: هُنَّ المُسلمات.

٩٣. عن محمّد بن مسلم، عن أحدهما ﵉، قال: سألتُه عن قول الله تعالى في الإماء: ﴿إِذَا أُحْصِنَّ﴾ ما إحصانُهنّ؟ قال: يُدْخَل بِهنّ.

قلت: فإن لم يُدْخَل بِهنَّ، ما عليهنَّ حدّ؟ قال: بلى.

94. From ʿAbd Allāh b. Sinān from Abū ʿAbd Allāh عليه السلام regarding God's verse regarding slave-girls ﴾*when they are married*﴿, he said, 'Marriage to them means the consummation of it.' I asked, 'So if he does not sleep with them then they commit adultery, are they punishable?' He replied, 'Yes, half of the prescribed punishment. If she commits adultery as a married woman, however, then it is stoning.' [4:25]

95. From Ḥarīz who said, 'I asked him about the 'married' one, so he replied, "It is he who already has someone that fulfils his needs."' [4:25]

96. From al-Qāsim b. Sulaymān who said, 'I asked Abū ʿAbd Allāh عليه السلام about God's verse: ﴾*If they commit adultery when they are married, their punishment will be half that of free women.*﴿ He said, "It means if they commit adultery after having consummated the marriage."' [4:25]

97. From ʿAbbād b. Ṣuhayb[18] from Abū ʿAbd Allāh عليه السلام who said, 'A Muslim man must not marry slave-girls unless he fears that he will sin, and he is only allowed to marry one slave-girl.' [4:25]

98. From Asbāṭ b. Sālim who said, 'I was with Abū ʿAbd Allāh عليه السلام when a man came to him and said, "Tell me about God's verse ﴾*You who believe, do not wrongfully consume each other's wealth.*﴿" He replied, "By that, He meant gambling. As for His words: ﴾*Do not kill each other*﴿, by that He means for a man from among the Muslims, vehement against the polytheists, to come into their homes [by himself] and to kill them; so God has forbidden them from doing that."' [4:29]

99. And he said, 'In another narration from Abū ʿAlī which he cited – without a source – an infallible as having said, "A man would attack the polytheists by himself until he either killed or was himself killed, so God revealed this verse: ﴾*Do not kill each other, for God is merciful to you.*﴿"' [4:29]

18 Abū Bakr ʿAbbād b. Ṣuhayb al-Tamīmī al-Kulaybī al-Yarbūʿī (d. *ca.* 202/817), originally of Basra, was an adherent of the Batrī *madhhab* but is nevertheless regarded a reliable narrator of Imam Jaʿfar al-Ṣādiq's traditions. According to Modarressi, he was a prolific Sunnī narrator with 'pro-Muʿtazilite and Shīʿite sympathies.' See Ḥillī, *Khulāṣat al-aqwāl*, 380 (nr. 1527); Modarressi, *Tradition and Survival*, 131–3 (nr. 2).

٩٤. عن عبدالله بن سِنان، عن أبي عبدالله ﵇، في قول الله تعالى في الإماء ﴿إِذَا أُحْصِنَّ﴾، قال: إحصانُهنّ أن يُدْخَل بِهنّ.

قلت: فإن لم يُدْخَل بِهنّ، فأحْدثن حَدَثًا، هل عليهنّ حدّ؟ قال: نعم، نِصف الحُرّ، فإن زَنَت وهي مُحْصَنة فالرّجْم.

٩٥. عن حَريز، قال: سألتُهُ عن المُحْصَن، فقال: الذي عنده ما يُغنيه.

٩٦. عن القاسم بن سليمان، قال: سألتُ أبا عبدالله ﵇ عن قول الله: ﴿فَإِذَا أُحْصِنَّ فَإِنْ أَتَيْنَ بِفَاحِشَةٍ فَعَلَيْهِنَّ نِصْفُ مَا عَلَى الْمُحْصَنَاتِ مِنَ الْعَذَابِ﴾، قال: يعني نِكاحهنّ إذا أتَيْنَ بفاحِشةٍ.

٩٧. عن عبّاد بن صُهيب، عن أبي عبدالله ﵇، قال: لا ينبغي للرجل المسلم أن يَتزوّج من الإماء، إلاّ من خشي العَنَت، ولا يَحِلُّ له من الإماء إلاّ واحدة.

٩٨. عن أسباط بن سالم، قال: كنتُ عند أبي عبدالله ﵇ فجاءه رجلٌ، فقال له: أخبرني عن قول الله: ﴿يَا أَيُّهَا الَّذِينَ آمَنُوا لاَ تَأْكُلُوا أَمْوَالَكُمْ بَيْنَكُمْ بِالْبَاطِلِ﴾. قال: عنى بذلك القِمار، وأمّا قوله: ﴿وَلاَ تَقْتُلُوا أَنفُسَكُمْ﴾ عنى بذلك الرجل من المسلمين يَشِدّ على المشركين في منازلهم فيُقْتَل، فَنَهاهم الله عن ذلك.

٩٩. وقال: في رواية أُخرى عن أبي عليّ، رفعه، قال: كان الرجل يحمل على المشركين وحده حتّى يَقْتُل أو يُقْتَل، فأنزل الله تعالى هذه الآية ﴿وَلاَ تَقْتُلُوا أَنفُسَكُمْ إِنَّ اللهَ كَانَ بِكُمْ رَحِيماً﴾.

100. From Asbāṭ who said, 'I asked Abū 'Abd Allāh عليه السلام about God's verse: ﴾ *You who believe, do not wrongfully consume each other's wealth* ﴿, so he replied, "This is gambling."' [4:29]

101. From Samā'a who said, 'I asked him about a man who has just enough money to subsist on whilst having a debt to pay. Should he continue maintaining his family with it until God, Blessed and most High, makes him affluent? Or should he repay the debt and then have to borrow again after that in such a corrupt climate of fervent profiteering? Or should he accept alms and use what he has at his disposal to repay the debt?

He replied, "He should use whatever he has to repay the debt and accept alms. He should not borrow money from people unless he can guarantee that he will be able to repay what he borrowed from them, or that they can lend it to him until he has the means to repay it, for God says: ﴾ *You who believe, do not wrongfully consume each other's wealth but trade by mutual consent.* ﴿ Nor should he borrow again on top of that unless he can guarantee it, even if it means he has to go door to door for a morsel or two, or a date or two unless he has a guarantor who will repay his debt after his death. Indeed, no sooner does one of us die than God appoints a guarantor for him to manage his affairs and repay his debt."' [4:29]

102. From Isḥāq b. 'Abd Allāh b. Muḥammad b. 'Alī b. al-Ḥusayn عليه السلام who said, 'Al-Ḥasan b. Zayd narrated to me on his father's authority, from 'Alī b. Abī Ṭālib عليه السلام who said, "I asked the Messenger of God ﷺ about splints that cover injuries – how would one perform the ablution (*wuḍū'*) and the bath obligatory after major ritual impurity (*ghusl*) with a splint on? He replied, 'It suffices him to wipe over it with water for both *wuḍū'* and *ghusl*.'

I asked, 'What if it was cold and by pouring water over his body, he feared for his life?' So the Messenger of God ﷺ read: ﴾ *Do not kill each other, for God is merciful to you.* ﴿"' [4:29]

١٠٠. عن أسباط، قال: سألتُ أبا عبدالله عليه السلام عن قول الله: ﴿يَا أَيُّهَا الَّذِينَ آمَنُوا لاَ تَأْكُلُوا أَمْوَالَكُمْ بَيْنَكُمْ بِالْبَاطِلِ﴾، قال: هو القِمار.

١٠١. عن سَمَاعة، قال: سألتُهُ عن الرجل يكون عنده شيء يتبلّغ به وعليه دَين، أيُطْعِمه عياله حتّى يأتيه الله تبارك وتعالى بمَيسرة، أو يقضي دَينه، أو يستقرض على ظهره في خُبث الزمان وشِدّة المكاسب، أو يَقْبَل الصّدَقة ويقضي بما كان عنده دَينه؟

قال: يقضي بما كان عنده دَينه ويَقْبَل الصَّدَقة، ولا يأخُذ أموال النّاس إلاّ وعنده وفاء بما يأخُذ منهم، أو يَقْرِضونه إلى مَيسرة، فإنّ الله يقول: ﴿يَا أَيُّهَا الَّذِينَ آمَنُوا لاَ تَأْكُلُوا أَمْوَالَكُمْ بَيْنَكُمْ بِالْبَاطِلِ إِلاَّ أَنْ تَكُونَ تِجَارَةً عَنْ تَرَاضٍ مِنْكُمْ﴾ فلا يستقرض على ظهره إلاّ وعنده وفاء، ولو طاف على أبواب الناس فزوّدوه باللُّقمة والُّقمتين والتَّمرة والتمرتين، إلاّ أن يكون له وليّ يقضي دَينه من بعده، إنّه ليس منّا من ميّت يمُوت إلاّ جعل الله له وليًّا يقوم في عِدَتِهِ ودَينه.

١٠٢. عن إسحاق بن عبدالله بن محمّد بن عليّ بن الحسين عليه السلام، قال: حدَّثني الحسن بن زيد، عن أبيه، عن عليّ بن أبي طالب عليه السلام، قال: سألتُ رسول الله صلى الله عليه وآله وسلم عن الجبائر تكون على الكسير، كيف يتوضّأ صاحبها، وكيف يغتسل إذا أجنب؟ قال: يُجزيه المسح بالماء عليها في الجَنَابة والوُضُوء.

قلت: فإن كانَ في بَرْدٍ يُخاف على نفسه إذا أفرغ الماء على جسده؟ فقرأ رسول الله صلى الله عليه وآله وسلم ﴿وَلاَ تَقْتُلُوا أَنْفُسَكُمْ إِنَّ اللهَ كَانَ بِكُمْ رَحِيمًا﴾.

103. From Muḥammad b. ʿAlī from Abū ʿAbd Allāh ؑ regarding the verse: ﴾*You who believe, do not wrongfully consume each other's wealth*﴿ he said, 'He has prohibited gambling. The Quraysh used to gamble putting a man's family and wealth at stake, so God forbade them from doing that.' Then he read: ﴾*Do not kill each other, for God is merciful to you*﴿ and said, 'The Muslims used to enter their enemies' houses during military invasions, which facilitated for the enemies to kill them however they wished. So God forbade them from entering their houses during invasions.' [4:29]

104. From Muyassar[19], from Abū Jaʿfar ؑ. He said, "Alqama al-Ḥaḍramī, Abū Ḥassān al-ʿIjlī, ʿAbd Allāh b. ʿAjalān and I were waiting for Abū Jaʿfar ؑ when he came out to meet us and said, "Greetings and welcome. By God, I love your scent and your spirits, and you are indeed on the path of God."

So ʿAlqama asked, "So would you bear witness that whoever is on the path of God is worthy of Paradise?"'

He continued, 'He paused for a moment and then said, "Enlighten your souls, for if you have not committed any grave sins then I bear witness to that."

We asked, "And what are the grave sins?"

He replied, "They are seven in God's Book."

So we said, "Then please list them for us – may we be your ransom."

He replied, "(1) Associating anything with God, the Great; (2) usurping the property of orphans; (3) consuming interest after knowledge [of its prohibition]; (4) insolence to one's parents; (5) fleeing from the battlefield; (6) murdering a believer, and (7) falsely accusing a chaste woman of fornication."

We said, "None of us have ever committed any of these."

So he said, "Then you are thus [people of paradise]."' [4:31]

19 This is most likely a reference to Muyassar b. ʿAbd al-ʿAzīz, a reliable companion of the fifth and sixth Imams and someone upon whom the biographical writers lavish much praise. See Ḥillī, *Khulāṣat al-aqwāl*, 278–9 (nr. 1022); Khūʾī, *Muʿjam*, 20:114–8 (nr. 12950).

١٠٣. عن محمّد بن علي، عن أبي عبدالله ﵇، في قول الله تعالى: ﴿يَا أَيُّهَا الَّذِينَ آمَنُوا لاَ تَأْكُلُوا أَمْوَالَكُمْ بَيْـنَكُمْ بِالْبَـاطِلِ﴾، قال: نهى عن القِمار، وكانت قريش تُقامر الرجل بأهله وماله، فنهاهم الله عن ذلك.

وقرأ قوله: ﴿وَلاَ تَقْتُـلُوا أَنْفُسَكُمْ إِنَّ اللهَ كَانَ بِكُمْ رَحِيمًا﴾، قال: كان المسلمون يَدْخُلون على عدوّهم في المَغارات.

١٠٤. عن مُيَسّر، عن أبي جعفر ﵇، قال: كنتُ أنا وعَلْقَمة الحَضْرمي، وأبو حسّان العِجلي، وعبدالله بن عَجْلان، ننتظر أبا جعفر ﵇، فخرج علينا، فقال: مرحبًا وأهلاً، والله إنّي لأُحبّ ريحكم وأرواحكم، وإنّكم لعلى دين الله.

فقال عَلْقَمة: فمن كان على دين الله تَشْهَد أنّه من أهل الجنّة؟

قال: فمكث هُنَيهةً، قال: نَوّروا أنفسكم، فإن لم تكونوا اقترفتم الكبائر فأنا أشهد.

قلنا: وما الكبائر؟

قال: هي في كتاب الله على سبع.

قلنا: فعُدّها علينا جعَلَنا الله فِداك. قال: الشّرك بالله العظيم، وأكل مال اليتيم، وأكل الربا بعد البيّنة، وعُقُوق الوالدين، والفِرار من الزّحف، وقتل المؤمن، وقذف المُحْصَنة.

قلنا: ما منّا أحدٌ أصاب من هذه شيئًا. قال: فأنتم إذن.

105. From Muʿādh b. Kathīr[20], from Abū ʿAbd Allāh عليه السلام who said, 'O Muʿādh, there are seven grave sins that have all been revealed about us, and yet been taken lightly as regards us. The gravest of all of them is association of anything with God, and murdering a soul that God has deemed sacrosanct, insolence to one's parents, falsely accusing a chaste woman, usurping the property of orphans, fleeing from the battlefield and denying our rights as the People of the Household (*ahl al-bayt*). As for association of anything with God, God is the One who has said what He has said about us, and the Messenger of God صلى الله عليه وآله has also said the same, but they belie God and His Messenger. As for the sin of killing a soul which is pure and sacrosanct in the eyes of God, then know that they killed al-Ḥusayn b. ʿAlī عليه السلام and his companions. As for insolence to one's parents, God has said in His Book: ﴿*The Prophet is more protective over the believers than they are themselves, while his wives are their mothers*﴾(33:6) – he is a father to them, and they have been insolent to the Messenger of God صلى الله عليه وآله with regard to his progeny and the People of his Household. Concerning the false accusation of chaste women, they vilified Fāṭima, peace be upon her, on their pulpits. As for usurping the property of orphans, they did away with any trace of us in God's Book; and fleeing from the battlefield – they begrudgingly gave their allegiance to the Commander of the Faithful عليه السلام then fled from him and betrayed him. As for denying our right, this is something that they still use to discriminate against us.'

106. Another narration mentions reneging to a state of disbelief [as one of the grave sins]. [4:31]

107. From Abū Khadīja[21], from Abū ʿAbd Allāh عليه السلام who said, 'Lying against God, His Messenger and His vicegerents, peace be upon them, is a grave sin.' [4:31]

108. From al-ʿAbbās b. Hilāl, from Abū al-Ḥasan al-Riḍā عليه السلام that he mentioned God's verse: ﴿*But if you avoid the great sins you have been forbidden*﴾ as

20 Muʿādh b. Kathīr Bayyāʿ al-Aksiyya al-Kisāʾī, concerning whom there is scant information. See Khūʾī, *Muʿjam*, 19:204–5 (nr. 12449).

21 The standalone agnomen Abū Khadīja in the chains of transmission of Shīʿī *ḥadīths* nearly always refers to Sālim b. Mukarram.

١٠٥. عن مُعاذ بن كَثير، عن أبي عبدالله عليه السلام، قال: يا مُعاذ، الكبائر سبع، فينا أُنزلت، ومنّا اسْتُخِفّت، وأكبر الكبائر: الشّرك بالله، وقتل النفس التي حَرّم الله، وعُقُوق الوالدين، وقَذْف المُحْصَنات، وأكل مال اليتيم، والفِرار من الزّحْف، وإنكار حقّنا أهل البيت.

فأمّا الشِرك بالله، فإنّ الله قال فينا ما قال، وقال رسول الله صلى الله عليه وآله ما قال، فكذّبوا الله وكذّبوا رسوله، وأمّا قتل النفس الّتي حرّم الله، فقد قتلوا الحسين بن علي عليهما السلام وأصحابه، وأمّا عُقُوق الوالدين، فإنّ الله قال في كتابه ﴿النَّبِيُّ أَوْلَى بِالْمُؤْمِنِينَ مِنْ أَنْفُسِهِمْ وَأَزْوَاجُهُ أُمَّهَاتُهُمْ﴾ وهو أب لهم، فقد عقّوا رسول الله صلى الله عليه وآله في ذُريّته وأهل بيته، وأمّا قَذْف المُحْصَنات، فقد قَذّفُوا فاطمة عليها السلام على مَنابِرِهم، وأمّا أكل مال اليتيم، فقد ذهبوا بفيئنا في كتاب الله، وأمّا الفِرار من الزّحف، فقد أعطوا أمير المؤمنين عليه السلام بيعتهم غير كارهين ثمّ فرّوا عنه وخَذَلوه، وأمّا إنكار حقّنا، فهذا ممّا لا يَتَعاجمون فيه.

١٠٦. وفي خبر آخر: والتَّعرُّب بعد الهِجْرة.

١٠٧. عن أبي عبدالله عليه السلام، قال: الكَذِب على الله وعلى رسوله وعلى الأوصياء عليهم السلام من الكبائر.

١٠٨. عن العباس بن هلال، عن أبي الحسن الرضا عليه السلام، أنه ذكر قول الله ﴿إِنْ تَجْتَنِبُوا كَبَائِرَ مَا تُنْهَوْنَ عَنْهُ﴾ عبادة الأوثان، وشرب الخمر، وقتل النَّفس، وعُقُوق الوالدين، وقَذْف المُحْصَنات، والفِرار من الزّحف، وأكل مال اليتيم.

being (1) idol-worship, (2) drinking wine, (3) murder, (4) insolence to one's parents, (5) falsely accusing chaste women, (6) fleeing from the battlefield and (7) consuming the property of orphans. [4:31]

109. In another narration on his authority, it is the wrongful consumption of an orphan's property and anything for which God has obligated chastisement in the Fire. [4:31]

110. From Abū ʿAbd Allāh عليه السلام in another narration on his authority: '[...] and denying what God has revealed: they have denied our right and rejected us, and this is something that no one can contest.' [4:31]

111. From Sulaymān al-Jaʿfarī who said, 'I asked Abū al-Ḥasan al-Riḍā, "What do you say about the ruler's policies?" So he replied, "Sulaymān, getting involved in their policies, aiding them and striving to fulfil their needs is tantamount to infidelity; and looking up to them supportively is one of the grave sins, punishable by Hellfire."' [4:31]

112. From al-Sakūnī, from Jaʿfar b. Muḥammad عليه السلام on his father's authority, from ʿAlī عليه السلام who said, 'Intoxication is a grave sin as is the fraudulent execution of a will.' [4:31]

113. From Muḥammad b. [al-]Fuḍayl, from Abū al-Ḥasan عليه السلام regarding God's verse: ﴾*But if you avoid the great sins you have been forbidden, We shall wipe out your minor misdeeds.*﴿ He said, 'Whoever, being a believer, refrains from the sins that are punishable by Hellfire, God will wipe away his misdeeds.' [4:31]

114. Abū ʿAbd Allāh said at the end of his exegesis of it: 'So be God-conscious and do not be audacious.' [4:31]

115. From Kathīr al-Nawwāʾ[22] who said, 'I asked Abū Jaʿfar عليه السلام about the grave sins. He replied, "It is every sin that God has threatened to chastise with the Hellfire."' [4:31]

---

22 Kathīr al-Nawwāʾ, though of the Batriyya school, is said to have been a reliable associate of Imam al-Bāqir and Imam al-Ṣādiq. See Khūʾī, *Muʿjam*, 15:112–4 (nr. 9736).

١٠٩. وفي رواية أُخرى عنه: أكل مال اليتيم ظُلماً، وكُلّ ما أوجب الله عليه النار.

١١٠. عن أبي عبدالله ، في رواية أُخرى عنه: وإنكار ما أنزل الله، أنكروا حقّنا وجَحَدُونا، وهذا لا يُتَعاجَمُ فيه أحد.

١١١. عن سُليمان الجعفري، قال: قلتُ لأبي الحسن الرضا : ما تقول في أعمال السلطان؟ فقال: يا سليمان، الدُّخول في أعمالهم، والعَوْن لهم، والسعي في حوائجهم عديل الكُفر، والنَّظر إليهم على العَمْد من الكبائر الّتي يُستَحقّ بها النار.

١١٢. عن السّكوني، عن جعفر بن محمّد، عن أبيه، عن عليّ ، قال: السُّكر من الكبائر، والحيف في الوصيّة من الكبائر.

١١٣. عن محمّد بن الفضيل، عن أبي الحسن ، في قول الله تعالى: ﴿إِن تَجۡتَنِبُواْ كَبَآئِرَ مَا تُنۡهَوۡنَ عَنۡهُ نُكَفِّرۡ عَنكُمۡ سَيِّـَٔاتِكُمۡ﴾، قال: من اجتنب ما وعد الله عليه النار، إذا كان مؤمناً، كفّر الله عنه سيّئاته.

١١٤. وقال أبو عبدالله في آخر ما فسّر: فاتّقوا الله ولا تجتَرُوا.

١١٥. عن كَثير النوّاء، قال: سألتُ أبا جعفر عن الكبائر؟ قال: كلُّ شيءٍ أوعد الله عليه النار.

116. From ʿAbd al-Raḥmān b. Abī Najrān[23] who said, 'I asked Abū ʿAbd Allāh عليه السلام about God's verse: ﴾*Do not covet what God has given to some of you more than others.*﴿ He said, "A man should not wish for another man's wife nor his daughter, but he can wish to have like them."' [4:32]

117. From Ismāʿīl b. Kathīr[24], who without mentioning his source cited the Prophet ﷺ as having said, 'When this verse was revealed: ﴾*you should rather ask God for some of His bounty,*﴿ the Prophet's companions asked amongst themselves, "What is this bounty? Which one of you will ask the Messenger of God ﷺ about it?"

So ʿAlī b. Abī Ṭālib عليه السلام said, "I will ask him about it." So he asked him about that bounty and what it was, so the Messenger of God ﷺ said, "God has created humans and apportioned their sustenance for them in that which is permissible and He has averted them from what is prohibited. So whoever indulges himself in the prohibited, God will reduce his share of the permissible in proportion to his consumption of the prohibited, and he will be accountable for it."' [4:32]

118. From Ibn al-Hudhayl, from Abū ʿAbd Allāh عليه السلام who said, 'God has indeed distributed sustenance between all His servants, and has distinguished great bounty that He has not [yet] distributed to anyone. God says: ﴾*you should rather ask God for some of His bounty.*﴿' [4:32]

119. From Ibrāhīm b. Abī al-Bilād[25], on his father's authority, from Abū Jaʿfar عليه السلام that he said, 'God has decreed and apportioned lawful sustenance that brings with it good health for every single person. And on the other hand, he has averted the prohibited away from it. So if he consumes anything of the prohibited, God deducts it from the lawful [sustenance] that He has decreed for him. And God possesses great bounty besides these two.' [4:32]

---

23 Abū al-Faḍl ʿAbd al-Raḥmān b. Abī Najrān (=ʿAmr b. Muslim) al-Tamīmī, an extremely reliable and trustworthy companion of Imam ʿAlī b. Mūsā al-Riḍā. See Ḥillī, *Khulāṣat al-aqwāl*, 205 (nr. 652).

24 There are multiple individuals with this name in the works of Shīʿī *ḥadīth* and *rijāl*.

25 Abū al-Ḥasan Ibrāhīm b. Abī al-Bilād (=Yaḥyā' b. Salīm), a reliable and trustworthy companion of the sixth, seventh and eighth Imams. See Ḥillī, *Khulāṣat al-aqwāl*, 47–8 (nr. 4).

١١٦. عن عبد الرّحمن بن أبي نجْران، قال: سألتُ أبا عبدالله عليه السلام عن قول الله تعالى: ﴿وَلَا تَتَمَنَّوْا مَا فَضَّلَ اللَّهُ بِهِ بَعْضَكُمْ عَلَى بَعْضٍ﴾، قال: لا يتمنّى الرجل امرأة الرجل ولا ابنته، ولكن يتمنّى مثلهما.

١١٧. عن إسماعيل بن كَثير، رفع الحديث إلى النبيّ صلى الله عليه وآله، قال: لمّا نزلت هذه الآية ﴿وَسْئَلُوا اللَّهَ مِن فَضْلِهِ﴾، قال: فقال أصحاب النبي صلى الله عليه وآله: ما هذا الفضل، أيُّكم يسأل رسول الله صلى الله عليه وآله عن ذلك؟

قال: فقال عليّ بن أبي طالب عليه السلام: أنا أسأله عنه، فسأله عن ذلك الفضل ما هو؟ فقال رسول الله صلى الله عليه وآله: إنَّ اللهَ خَلَق خَلْقَه وقَسَّم لهم أرزاقهم من حِلّها، وعَرَض لهم بالحرام، فمن انْتَهَكَ حرامًا، نَقَصَ له من الحلال بقدر ما انْتَهَك من الحرام، وحُوسِب به.

١١٨. عن ابن الهُذيل، عن أبي عبدالله عليه السلام، قال: إنَّ الله قسَّم الأرزاق بين عباده، وأفضل فضلاً كثيرًا لم يُقسّمه بين أحد، قال الله ﴿وَسْئَلُوا اللَّهَ مِن فَضْلِهِ﴾.

١١٩. عن إبراهيم بن أبي البلاد، عن أبيه، عن أبي جعفر عليه السلام، أنّه قال: ليس من نفسٍ إلاّ وقد فرض الله لها رزقها حلالاً يأتيها في عافيةٍ، وعرض لها بالحرام من وجهٍ آخر، فإن هي تناولت من الحرام شيئًا، قاصَّها به من الحلال الذي فَرَض الله لها، وعند الله سواهما فضل كثير.

120. From al-Ḥusayn b. Muslim[26], from Abū Ja'far [Muḥammad al-Jawād] عليه السلام. He said, 'I said to him, "May I be your ransom – they say that sleeping after dawn is abominable because [people's] sustenance is apportioned at that time." So he replied, "Sustenance has already been assigned and apportioned, but God has a bounty that He distributes from the break of dawn until sunrise, and this is His verse: ﴾*you should rather ask God for some of His bounty.*﴿" Then he said, "The remembrance of God after the break of dawn is more effective in the quest for livelihood than travelling through the land."' [4:32]

121. From al-Ḥasan b. Maḥbūb who said, 'I wrote to al-Riḍā عليه السلام and asked him about God's words: ﴾ *We have appointed heirs for everything that parents and close relatives leave behind, including those to whom you have pledged your hands* [*in marriage*], *so give them their share.*﴿ He said, "What he means by that is the Imams through whom God has taken your pledges."' [4:33]

122. From [al-Ḥusayn] Ibn Muslim, from Abū Ja'far عليه السلام who said, 'The Commander of the Faithful عليه السلام was judging the case of a woman whom a man had married, stipulating to her and to her family that if he married another wife neglecting her in the process or took a concubine, she could divorce him. So he said, "God's condition comes before your condition. If he wants he can honour his condition, and if not he can keep his wife and marry another alongside her and take a concubine beside her; and he can neglect her if she gives him cause to do that. God says in His Book: ﴾*then you may marry whichever* [*other*] *women seem good to you, two, three, or four,*﴿(4:2) and: ﴾*your slaves are lawful to you*﴿ and: ﴾*If you fear high-handedness from your wives, remind them* [*of the teachings of God*], *then ignore them when you go to bed, then hit them. If they obey you, you have no right to act against them: God is most High and Great.*﴿"' [4:34]

123. From Zurāra, from Abū Ja'far [Muḥammad al-Bāqir] عليه السلام who said, 'If the wife behaves high-handedly with the husband then it is divorce initiated by her, and he can take back from her what she received from him. And if

---

26 Al-Ḥusayn b. Muslim, about whom there is scant information, was a companion of the ninth Imam Muḥammad al-Jawād. See Khū'ī, *Mu'jam*, 7:99 (nr. 3659).

١٢٠. عن الحسين بن مسلم، عن أبي جعفر ﵇، قال: قلتُ له: جُعِلتُ فِداك، إنّهم يقولونَ إنَّ النوم بعد الفجر مكروهٌ، لأنَّ الأرزاق تقسَّم في ذلك الوقت؟

فقال: الأرزاق مَوْظُوفة مَقْسُومة، ولله فضل يُقسّمه ما بين طُلُوع الفجر إلى طُلُوع الشمس، وذلك قوله: ﴿وَسۡـَٔلُواْ ٱللَّهَ مِن فَضۡلِهِۦٓ﴾، ثمّ قال: وذِكر الله بعد طُلُوع الفجر، أبلغ في طَلَب الرزق من الضَّرب في الأرض.

١٢١. عن الحسن بن محبوب، قال: كتبتُ إلى الرضا ﵇، وسألته عن قول الله تعالى: ﴿وَلِكُلّٖ جَعَلۡنَا مَوَٰلِيَ مِمَّا تَرَكَ ٱلۡوَٰلِدَانِ وَٱلۡأَقۡرَبُونَۚ وَٱلَّذِينَ عَقَدَتۡ أَيۡمَٰنُكُمۡ﴾، قال: إنّما عنى بذلك الأئمّة ﵇، بهم عقد الله أيمانكم.

١٢٢. عن ابن مسلم، عن أبي جعفر ﵇، قال: قضى أمير المؤمنين ﵇ في امرأة تزوّجها رجلٌ، وشَرَط عليها وعلى أهلها إن تزوّج عليها امرأةً وهجرها، أو أتى عليها سُرِّيَّة، فإنّها طالق.

فقال: شَرطُ الله قبل شَرطكم، إن شاء وَفَى بشرطه، وإن شاء أمسك امرأته، ونكح عليها، وتسرّى عليها وهجرها، إن أتت سبيل ذلك، قال الله تعالى في كتابه: ﴿فَٱنكِحُواْ مَا طَابَ لَكُم مِّنَ ٱلنِّسَآءِ مَثۡنَىٰ وَثُلَٰثَ وَرُبَٰعَ﴾، وقال: أُحِلَّ لكم ﴿مِمَّا مَلَكَتۡ أَيۡمَٰنُكُمۡ﴾، وقال: ﴿وَٱلَّٰتِي تَخَافُونَ نُشُوزَهُنَّ فَعِظُوهُنَّ وَٱهۡجُرُوهُنَّ فِي ٱلۡمَضَاجِعِ وَٱضۡرِبُوهُنَّۖ فَإِنۡ أَطَعۡنَكُمۡ فَلَا تَبۡغُواْ عَلَيۡهِنَّ سَبِيلًاۗ إِنَّ ٱللَّهَ كَانَ عَلِيّٗا كَبِيرٗا﴾.

١٢٣. عن زُرارة، عن أبي جعفر ﵇، قال: إذا نَشَزت المرأة على الرجل فهي الخُلْعَة، فليأخُذ منها ما قدر عليه، وإذا نَشَز الرجل مع نُشُوز المرأة فهو الشِّقاق.

the man behaves high-handedly on top of her high-handedness then it is a break-up.' [4:34]

124. From Muḥammad b. Muslim, from Abū Jaʿfar عليه السلام. He said, 'I asked him about God's verse: ﴿ *appoint one arbiter from his family and one from hers.* ﴾ He said, "The two reconcilers cannot part ways without deliberation."' [4:35]

125. From Zayd al-Shaḥḥām, from Abū 'Abd Allāh عليه السلام about God's verse: ﴿ *appoint one arbiter from his family and one from hers.* ﴾ He said, 'The two arbiters cannot part ways until they have deliberated with the husband and the wife.' [4:35]

126. In another report from al-Ḥalabī, on his authority: 'It must be stipulated to both of them that they can get back together if they both wish, and separate if they both wish to do so. It is equally permissible for them to get back together or to separate.' [4:35]

127. In Faḍāla's narration: 'So if they both accept and are endorsed to separate, then they may separate for it is allowed.' [4:35]

128. From Muḥammad b. Sīrīn, from 'Ubayda who said, 'A man and wife came to 'Alī b. Abī Ṭālib عليه السلام, each one accompanied by a group of people. So he عليه السلام said, '﴿ *appoint one arbiter from his family and one from hers.* ﴾

Then he said to the arbiters, "Do you know what you have to do? If you see that they can get back together then you must reconcile them, and if you see that they should separate then you must let them separate."

So the woman said, "I accept God's Book both for and against my best interests." And the man said, "If that means separation, then no." So 'Alī عليه السلام said, "You cannot leave until you attest to what she has just attested."' [4:35]

129. From Abū Baṣīr, from Abū 'Abd Allāh عليه السلام who said, 'The Messenger of God صلى الله عليه وآله is one of the parents and 'Alī is the other.' So I asked, 'Where is that to be found in God's Book?' He replied, 'Read: ﴿ *Worship God; join nothing with Him. Be good to your parents.* ﴾' [4:36]

١٢٤. عن محمّد بن مسلم، عن أبي جعفر عليه السلام، قال: سألتُهُ عن قول الله تعالى: ﴿فَابْعَثُوا حَكَمًا مِنْ أَهْلِهِ وَحَكَمًا مِنْ أَهْلِهَا﴾، قال: ليس للمُصْلِحَين أن يُفَرّقا حتّى يَسْتأمِرا.

١٢٥. عن زيد الشحّام، عن أبي عبدالله عليه السلام، عن قول الله ﴿فَابْعَثُوا حَكَمًا مِنْ أَهْلِهِ وَحَكَمًا مِنْ أَهْلِهَا﴾، قال: ليس للحَكَمين أن يُفرّقا حتّى يستأمرا الرجل والمرأة.

١٢٦. وفي خبر آخر، عن الحلبي، عنه: ويشترط عليهما إن شاءا جَمَعا، وإن شاءا فَرّقا، فإن جمعا فجائز، وإن فرّقا فجائز.

١٢٧. وفي رواية فَضالة: فإن رَضِيا وقلّداهما الفُرقة ففرّقا، فهو جائز.

١٢٨. عن محمّد بن سِيرين، عن عبيدة، قال: أتى عليّ بن أبي طالب عليه السلام رجل وامرأة، مع كلّ واحدٍ منهما فِئام من الناس، فقال عليه السلام: ابعثوا حَكَمًا من أهله، وحَكَمًا من أهلها.

ثمّ قال للحَكَمين: هل تدريان ما عليكما؟ عليكما إن رأيتما أن تجمعا جمعتما، وإن رأيتما أن تفرّقا فرّقتما.

فقالت المرأة: رَضِيتُ بكتاب الله عليَّ ولي. فقال الرجل: أمّا في الفُرقة فلا. فقال علي عليه السلام: ما تبرح حتّى تُقرَّ بما أقرّت به.

١٢٩. عن أبي بصير، عن أبي عبدالله عليه السلام، قال: إنّ رسول الله صلى الله عليه وآله أحد الوالدين، وعليّ صلى الله عليه وآله الآخر: فقلت: أين موضع ذلك في كتاب الله؟ قال: اقرأ ﴿وَاعْبُدُوا اللهَ وَلَا تُشْرِكُوا بِهِ شَيْئًا وَبِالْوَالِدَيْنِ إِحْسَانًا﴾.

130. From Abū Baṣīr, from Abū Jaʿfar عليه السلام regarding God's verse: ﴾*Be good to your parents*﴿ he said: 'The Messenger of God ﷺ is one of the parents and 'Alī is the other.' And he mentioned that the verse was in [the Chapter of] Women. [4:36]

131. From Abū Ṣāliḥ, from Ibn 'Abbās regarding God's words: ﴾*to neighbours near*﴿ – he said: 'those related to you', and: ﴾and far﴿ – he said: 'those to whom you are not related,' and: ﴾*the companion at your side*﴿ – he said: 'your travelling companion.' [4:36]

132. From Abū Baṣīr who said, 'I asked Abū Jaʿfar عليه السلام about God's verse: ﴾***On the day** when We bring a witness from each community, with you* [*Muḥammad*] *as a witness against these people?*﴿ He replied, "The Prophet ﷺ will come on the Day of Judgement with a witness from each community with the vicegerent of the prophet sent to them. And you, 'Alī, will be brought as a witness over my community on the Day of Judgement."' [4:41*]

133. From Abū Maʿmar al-Saʿdī who said, "Alī b. Abī Ṭālib عليه السلام said, describing the Day of Judgement, "They will gather together in a place where all creatures will be able to speak, but none will speak without the permission of the all-Merciful, and he will only speak the truth. Then the messengers will be made to stand and will be asked, and that is the meaning of His statement to Muḥammad ﷺ: ﴾*What will they do when We bring a witness from each community, with you* [*Muhammad*] *as a witness against these people?*﴿ – and he is the witness over all witnesses; the witnesses being the messengers, peace be upon them."' [4:41]

134. From Masʿada b. Ṣadaqa, from Jaʿfar b. Muḥammad, on his grandfather's authority; he said, 'The Commander of the Faithful عليه السلام said in his sermon, describing the terror of the Day of Judgement, "The mouths will be sealed shut and will not be able to speak, but the hands will speak, the legs will bear witness, and the skins will assert what they had done, so they will not be able to hide a single thing from God."' [4:42]

١٣٠. عن أبي بصير، عن أبي جعفر عليه السلام، في قول الله: ﴿وَبِالْوَالِدَيْنِ إِحْسَانًا﴾، قال: إنّ رسول الله صلى الله عليه وآله أحد الوالدين، وعليّ عليه السلام الآخر، وذكر أنّها الآية التي في النساء.

١٣١. عن أبي صالح، عن ابن عباس، في قول الله تعالى: ﴿وَالْجَارِ ذِي الْقُرْبَى﴾، قال: ذو القربى ﴿وَالْجَارِ الْجُنُبِ﴾، قال: الذي ليس بينك وبينه قرابة ﴿وَالصَّاحِبِ بِالْجَنْبِ﴾، قال: الصّاحب في السّفر.

١٣٢. عن أبي بصير، قال: سألتُ أبا جعفر عليه السلام عن قول الله تعالى ﴿فَكَيْفَ إِذَا جِئْنَا مِنْ كُلِّ أُمَّةٍ بِشَهِيدٍ وَجِئْنَا بِكَ عَلَى هَؤُلَاءِ شَهِيدًا﴾، قال: يُؤتى النبي صلى الله عليه وآله يوم القيامة من كُلّ أمّةٍ بشهيد، بوصيّ نبيّها، وأوتي بك يا عليّ شهيدًا على أمّتي يوم القيامة.

١٣٣. عن أبي مَعْمَر السَّعدي، قال: عليّ بن أبي طالب عليه السلام في صفة يوم القيامة: يجتمعون في موطن يُسْتَنْطَقُ فيه جميع الخَلْق، فلا يتكلّمُ أحدٌ إلاّ من أذن له الرّحمن وقال صوابًا، فتُقام الرسل فتُسأل، فذلك قوله لمحمّد صلى الله عليه وآله: ﴿فَكَيْفَ إِذَا جِئْنَا مِنْ كُلِّ أُمَّةٍ بِشَهِيدٍ وَجِئْنَا بِكَ عَلَى هَؤُلَاءِ شَهِيدًا﴾ وهو الشهيد على الشُّهداء، والشُّهداء هم الرُّسل عليهم السلام.

١٣٤. عن مَسْعَدة بن صَدَقة، عن جعفر بن محمّد، عن جدّه عليهم السلام، قال: قال أمير المؤمنين عليه السلام في خطبته يَصِف هَول يوم القيامة: ختم اللهُ على الأفواه فلا تُكلّم، فتكلّمت الأيدي، وشَهِدت الأرْجُل، ونَطَقت الجلود لما عَمِلوا، فلا يَكْتُمون الله حديثًا.

135. From Zurāra, from Abū Jaʿfar ﵇ who said, 'Do not stand for prayer lazily, drowsily or lethargically, for they come from the vice of hypocrisy; and God has forbidden the believers from standing to pray while they are intoxicated, meaning by sleep.' [4:43]

136. From Muḥammad b. al-Faḍl[27], from Abū al-Ḥasan ['Alī b. Mūsā al-Riḍā] ﵇ who said about God's verse: ﴿*do not come anywhere near the prayer if you are intoxicated, not until you know what you are saying*﴾: 'This was before alcohol was banned.' [4:43]

137. And from al-Ḥalabī, on his authority ﵇. He ﵇ said, 'Intoxication means sleep.' [4:43]

138. From al-Ḥalabī who said, 'I asked him ﵇ about God's verse: ﴿*You who believe, do not come anywhere near the prayer if you are intoxicated, not until you know what you are saying.*﴾ He said, "Do not come anywhere near the prayer while you are intoxicated, meaning sleep – i.e. while you are overtaken with drowsiness that prevents you from knowing what you are saying in your bowing, your prostration and your aggrandising of God. It is not as many people describe it to be, claiming that the believers used to get intoxicated by alcohol. The believer neither drinks any intoxicant nor becomes intoxicated."' [4:43]

139. From Zurāra, from Abū Jaʿfar ﵇. He said, 'I asked him, "Is the menstruating woman and the one in a state of major ritual impurity [after sexual relations] allowed to enter the mosque or not?" So he replied, "They cannot enter the mosque unless it is just to pass through it. God says: ﴿*nor if you are in a state of major ritual impurity – though you may pass through the mosque – not until you have bathed.*﴾ They may take something from the mosque, but not place anything inside it."' [4:43]

140. From Abū Maryam who said, 'I asked Abū Jaʿfar ﵇, "What do you say about a man who performs the ablution then calls his servant-girl to take

27 Muḥammad b. al-Faḍl al-Kūfī, a reliable companion of Imam al-Riḍā. See Ḥillī, *Khulāṣat al-aqwāl*, 237 (nr. 812).

١٣٥ . عن زُرارة، عن أبي جعفر عليه السلام، قال: لا تَقُم إلى الصلاة متكاسلاً ولا متناعسًا ولا متثاقلاً، فإنّها من خلل النِّفاق، وإنَّ الله نهى المؤمنين أن يقوموا إلى الصلاة وهم سُكارى، يعني من النوم.

١٣٦ . عن محمّد بن الفضيل، عن أبي الحسن عليه السلام، في قول الله تعالى: ﴿لَا تَقْرَبُوا الصَّلَاةَ وَأَنتُمْ سُكَارَىٰ حَتَّىٰ تَعْلَمُوا مَا تَقُولُونَ﴾، قال: هذا قبل أن يُحرِّم الخمر.

١٣٧ . وعن الحلبي عنه عليه السلام، قال: يعني سُكر النوم.

١٣٨ . وعن الحلبي، قال: سألتُهُ عليه السلام عن قول الله تعالى: ﴿يَا أَيُّهَا الَّذِينَ آمَنُوا لَا تَقْرَبُوا الصَّلَاةَ وَأَنتُمْ سُكَارَىٰ حَتَّىٰ تَعْلَمُوا مَا تَقُولُونَ﴾. قال: لا تَقرَبُوا الصَّلَوٰةَ وأنتم سكارى، يعني سُكر النوم، يقول: وبكم نُعاس يمنعكم أن تعلموا ما تقولون في رُكوعكم وسُجودكم وتكبيركم، وليس كما يَصفِ كثيرٌ من الناس، يَزعُمون أنّ المؤمنين يَسكَرون من الشراب، والمؤمن لا يشرب مُسكرًا ولا يَسْكَر.

١٣٩ . عن زُرارة، عن أبي جعفر عليه السلام، قال: قلتُ له: الحائضُ والجُنبُ يَدخُلان المسجد إلاّ مُجتازين، إنَّ الله تعالى يقول: ﴿وَلَا جُنُبًا إِلَّا عَابِرِي سَبِيلٍ حَتَّىٰ تَغْتَسِلُوا﴾ ويأخُذان من المسجد الشيء، ولا يضعان فيه شيئًا.

١٤٠ . عن أبي مريم، قال: قلتُ لأبي جعفر عليه السلام: ما تقول في الرجل يتوضّأ ثمّ يدعو جاريته، فتأخُذ بيده حتّى ينتهي إلى المسجد، فإنّ مَن عندنا يزعُمون أنّها الملامَسَة؟ فقال: لا

him by the hand to the mosque, for there are some people amongst us who claim that that is 'the touching of women' [resulting in ritual impurity]?" So he replied, "No, by God. There is nothing wrong with that. And you may do that often, but that is not what 'touching a woman' refers to [in the verse] – that is specifically having sexual intercourse with a woman."' [4:43]

141. From Manṣūr b. Ḥāzim, from Abū ʿAbd Allāh عليه السلام who said, 'To touch (*al-lams*) refers to sexual intercourse.' [4:43]

142. From al-Ḥalabī, on his authority – he said, 'It is sexual intercourse, but God is discrete and loves discretion, so He did not express it in the same way that they do.' [4:43]

143. From al-Ḥalabī, from Abū ʿAbd Allāh عليه السلام. He said, 'Qays b. Zamāna asked him, "I perform the ablution then I call my servant-girl so she takes me by the hand so that I can stand and pray; so do I have to repeat the ablution?" So he replied, "No." He said, "But they claim that this is 'touching'?" He replied, "No, by God. 'Touching' here is only sexual intimacy or intercourse." Then he continued, "Abū Jaʿfar عليه السلام, in his old age, would perform the ablution, then call the servant-girl to take him by the hand, after which he would stand and pray."' [4:43]

144. From Abū Ayyūb, from Abū ʿAbd Allāh عليه السلام who said, 'Dry ablution (*tayammum*) on sand performed by one who cannot find water is the same as one who performs it in a pond of water. Does God not say: ﴿*then find some clean sand and wipe your faces and hands with it*﴾?'

He said, 'I asked, "What if he finds water right at the end of the time for prayer?"'

He said, 'So he replied, "His prayer [time] will expire." I asked him, "So would he pray another prayer with the [same] dry ablution?" He replied, "If he sees water and is able to use it, then his dry ablution is void."' [4:43]

145. From Zurāra, from Abū Jaʿfar عليه السلام who said, ''Ammār b. Yāsir came to the Messenger of God ﷺ and said, "O Messenger of God, I entered into the state of major impurity last night and did not have any water." So he asked, "So what did you do?" He replied, "I removed my clothes, then went on the

والله، ما بذاك بأس، وربما فعلته، وما يعني بهذا – أي ﴿لَامَسْتُمُ النِّسَاءَ﴾ – إلاّ المُواقعة دون الفَرْج.

١٤١. عن منصور بن حازم، عن أبي عبد الله عليه السلام، قال: اللّمس الجِماع.

١٤٢. عن الحلبي، عنه عليه السلام، قال: الجِماع، ولكنّ الله ستير يُحِبّ السّتر، فلم يُسمّ كما تُسمّون.

١٤٣. عن الحلبي، عن أبي عبد الله عليه السلام، قال: سأله قيس بن رُمّانة، قال: أتوضّأ ثمّ أدعو الجارية فتمسِك بيدي، فأقوم وأُصلّي، أعليّ وضوء؟ فقال: لا. قال: فإنّهم يزعُمون أنّهُ اللّمس؟ قال: لا والله، ما اللّمس إلاّ الوِقاع، يعني الجِماع. ثمّ قال: قد كان أبو جعفر عليه السلام بعد ما كَبِرَ يتوضّأ ثمّ يدعو الجارية، فتأخُذ بيده، فيقوم فيُصلّي.

١٤٤. عن أبي أيّوب، عن أبي عبد الله عليه السلام، قال: التيمّم بالصّعيد لمن لم يجد الماء، كمن توضّأ من غديرٍ من ماء، أليس الله تعالى يقول: ﴿فَتَيَمَّمُوا صَعِيدًا طَيِّبًا﴾؟

قال: قلتُ: فإن أصاب الماء وهو في آخر الوقت؟ قال: فقال: قد مضت صلاته.

قال: قلتُ له: فيُصلّي بالتيمّم صلاةً أُخرى؟ قال: إذا رأى الماء، وكان يقدِر عليه، انتقض التيمّم.

١٤٥. عن زُرارة، عن أبي جعفر عليه السلام، قال: أتى رسول الله صلى الله عليه وآله وسلم عمّار ابن ياسر، فقال: يا رسول الله، أجنبتُ اللّيلة، ولم يكُن معي ماءٌ، قال: كيف صنعتَ؟ قال: طرحت ثيابي، ثمّ قمت على الصّعيد فتمعّكت. فقال: هكذا يصنع الحمار، إنّما قال الله: ﴿فَتَيَمَّمُوا صَعِيدًا

sand and rolled around in it." So he said, "That is what donkeys do. What God has said is: ﴾*then find some clean sand and wipe your faces and hands with it.*﴿"' He continued, 'Then he struck his hand on the earth and wiped one over the other, then he wiped both his hands on his forehead, and then wiped both palms over each other.' [4:43]

146. And in another narration on his authority, he said, 'The Messenger of God ﷺ said, "You did what donkeys do! The Lord of the water is the Lord of the sand too. It suffices you to strike your palms on the earth, then shake them off, then wipe your face and your hands as God has commanded you."' [4:43]

147. From al-Ḥusayn b. Abī Ṭalḥa who said, 'I asked the righteous servant [i.e. Imam Mūsā al-Kāẓim] about God's verse: ﴾*or had intercourse, and cannot find any water, then find some clean sand and wipe your faces and hands with it*﴿ – to what extent is that? What if they cannot find any [water] for sale nor free of charge? And if he finds enough to perform ablution with, for a hundred thousand or even a thousand, then to what extent [should he expend]? He replied, "That is up to his own earnestness."' [4:43]

148. From Jābir al-Juʿfī who said, 'Abū Jaʿfar ؑ said to me in a long narration of his, "O Jābir, the first of the western lands to be destroyed will be Shām, where they will be divided between three banners: the banner of Aṣhab, the banner of Abqaʿ and the banner of Sufyānī. Sufyānī and Abqaʿ will clash and fight, and he will kill him and all those with him. The people under Aṣhab will then be left with no choice but to march towards Iraq while an army will march to Qirqīsa[28] where it will kill one hundred thousand of the tyrannical opponents. Sufyānī will dispatch a contingent of seventy thousand soldiers to Kufa where they will kill, crucify and capture the people of Kufa while other banners will approach from Khurasan, quickly descending upon the houses. They will be accompanied by a group of the Qā'im's companions. A man from among the protégés of the people of Kufa will go out to Ḍaʿfā' and will be killed by the commander of Sufyānī's army between Ḥīra and

28 According to Ḥamawī (*Muʿjam al-buldān*, 4:328) it should be Qarqīsiyā', a town on the bank of the river Khabur which feeds into the Euphrates.

طَيِّباً﴾، قال: فَضَرَب بيده الأرض، ثمّ مسح إحداهما على الأُخرى، ثمّ مسح يديه بجبينه، ثمّ مسح كفّيه كلّ واحدةٍ منهما على الأُخرى.

١٤٦. وفي رواية أُخرى، عنه، قال: قال رسول الله ﷺ: صنعتَ كما يَصْنَع الحِمار، إنّ ربَّ الماء هو ربُّ الصَّعيد، إنَّما يُجزيك أن تَضْرِب بكفّيك ثمّ تَنْفُضهما، ثمّ تمسح بوجهك ويديك كما أمرك الله.

١٤٧. عن الحسين بن أبي طلحة، قال: سألتُ عبدًا صالحًا في قوله ﴿أَوْ لَامَسْتُمُ النِّسَاءَ فَلَمْ تَجِدُوا مَاءً فَتَيَمَّمُوا صَعِيدًا طَيِّبًا﴾ ما حَدُّ ذلك؟ فإن لم تَجِدُوا بشِراء أو بغير شِراء، إن وجد قَدر وضوئه بمائة ألف، أو بألف وكم بلغ؟ قال: ذلك على قَدر جِدَته.

١٤٨. عن جابر الجُعفي، قال: قال لي أبو جعفر عليه السلام — في حديث له طويل -: يا جابر، أوّل أرض المغرب تَخْرَب أرض الشام، يختلفون عند ذلك على رايات ثلاث: راية الأصهب، وراية الأبقع، وراية السُّفياني، فيلقي السُّفياني الأبقع، فيَقْتُله ومَن معه، ويقتل الأصهب، ثمّ لا يكون له همٌّ إلاّ الإقبال نحو العراق، ومرّ جيش بقرقيسا، فيَقْتُلون بها مائة ألف من الجبّارين.

ويبعث السفياني جيشًا إلى الكوفة، وعِدّتهم سبعون ألفًا، فيُصيبون من أهل الكوفة قتلاً وصَلْبًا وسَبيًا، فبينا هم كذلك إذ أقبلت راياتٌ من ناحية خُراسان تطوي المنازل طيًّا حثيثًا، ومعهم نَفَرٌ من أصحاب القائم عليه السلام، [ثمّ] يخرُج رجلٌ من موالي أهل الكوفة في ضُعفاء، فيَقْتُله أمير جيش السُّفياني بين الحِيرة والكُوفة.

Kufa. Then Sufyānī will dispatch a contingent to Medina, whereupon the Mahdī عليه السلام will flee Medina and head towards Mecca. As soon as the commander of Sufyānī's army hears that the Mahdī has left Medina, he will send an army to track him, and they will not be able to catch up to him, until he enters Mecca fearfully vigilant, just like Mūsā b. ʿImrān."

He continued, "The army led by Sufyānī's commander will enter the wilderness [surrounding Mecca] and a caller will call out from the sky: 'O wilderness, annihilate these people.' So the land will swallow them up, and no one will be able to escape except three people from the tribe of Kalb, whose faces God will turn to the backs of their heads. And these are the people about whom the verse was revealed: ﴾*People of the Book, believe in what We have sent down* ***to Our servant***﴿ meaning the Qā'im ﴾*before We wipe out [your sense of] direction, turning faces back to front.*﴿"' [4:47]

149. From ʿUmar b. Shimr, from Jābir who said, 'Abū Jaʿfar عليه السلام said, "This verse was revealed to Muḥammad صلى الله عليه وآله in the following manner: ﴾*People of the Book, believe in what We have sent down* ***about ʿAlī*** *to confirm what you already have before We wipe out [your sense of] direction, turning their faces back to front, or reject them, as We rejected those who broke the Sabbath: God's will is always done.*﴿ As for His words: ﴾*to confirm what you already have*﴿ – it means 'to corroborate the Messenger of God صلى الله عليه وآله.'"' [4:47*]

150. From Jābir, from Abū Jaʿfar عليه السلام who said, 'As for His verse: ﴾*God does not forgive the joining of partners with Him*﴿, it means that He does not forgive the one who rejects the divinely appointed authority of ʿAlī; as for His verse: ﴾*anything less than that He forgives to whoever He will*﴿, it means to one who adheres to ʿAlī عليه السلام.' [4:48]

151. From Abū al-ʿAbbās who said, 'I asked Abū ʿAbd Allāh عليه السلام about the minimum [deed] stipulated for a person so that he may be considered as someone associating [with God]. He replied, "Whoever invents an opinion and is loved or hated on account of it."' [4:48]

ويبعث السُّفياني بعثًا إلى المدينة، فيَفِرُّ المهديّ عليه السلام منها إلى مكّة، فيَبْلُغ أمير جيش السُّفياني أنّ المهدي قد خرج من المدينة، فيبعث جيشًا على أثره، فلا يُدركه حتّى يَدْخُل مكّة خائفًا يترقّب على سُنّة موسى بن عِمران.

قال: وينزل جيش أمير السُّفياني البَيداء، فينادي منادٍ من السماء: يا بيداء أبيدي بالقوم؛ فيخسف بهم البيداء، فلا يَفْلِت منهم إلاّ ثلاثة نفرٍ يُحوّل الله وجوههم في أقفيتهم وهم من كلب، وفيهم أُنزِلت هذه الآية ﴿يَا أَيُّهَا الَّذِينَ أُوتُوا الْكِتَابَ آمِنُوا بِمَا نَزَّلْنَا مُصَدِّقًا لِمَا مَعَكُمْ﴾ يعني القائم عليه السلام ﴿مِنْ قَبْلِ أَنْ نَطْمِسَ وُجُوهًا فَنَرُدَّهَا عَلَى أَدْبَارِهَا﴾.

١٤٩. وروى عمرو بن شِمر، عن جابر، قال: قال أبو جعفر عليه السلام: نزلت هذه الآية على محمد صلى الله عليه وآله هكذا (يَا أَيُّهَا الَّذِينَ أُوتُوا الْكِتَابَ آمِنُوا بِمَا أَنْزَلْتُ فِي عَلِيّ مُصَدِّقًا لِمَا مَعَكُمْ مِنْ قَبْلِ أَنْ نَطْمِسَ وُجُوهًا فَنَرُدَّهَا عَلَى أَدْبَارِهَا أَوْ نَلْعَنَهُمْ) إلى قوله: ﴿مَفْعُولًا﴾.

وأمّا قوله ﴿مُصَدِّقًا لِمَا مَعَكُمْ﴾ يعني مُصدّقًا برسول الله صلى الله عليه وآله.

١٥٠. عن جابر، عن أبي جعفر عليه السلام، قال: أمّا قوله: ﴿إِنَّ اللَّهَ لَا يَغْفِرُ أَنْ يُشْرَكَ بِهِ﴾ يعني أنّه لا يَغْفِر لمن يكفُر بولاية عليّ عليه السلام. وأمّا قوله: ﴿وَيَغْفِرُ مَا دُونَ ذَٰلِكَ لِمَنْ يَشَاءُ﴾ يعني لمن والى عليًّا عليه السلام.

١٥١. عن أبي العباس، قال: سألتُ أبا عبد الله عليه السلام عن أدنى ما يكون به الإنسان مُشرِكًا؟ قال: مَن ابتدع رأيًا، فأحبَّ عليه، أو أبغض.

152. From Qutayba al-Aʿshā[29] who said, 'I asked al-Ṣādiq عليه السلام about His verse: ﴾ *God does not forgive the joining of partners with Him: anything less than that He forgives to whoever He will.* ﴿ He said, "Everything else is included in the exception."' [4:48]

153. In another narration on his authority: 'The grave sins are included in the exception.' [4:48]

154. From Burayd b. Muʿāwiya who said, 'I was with Abū Jaʿfar عليه السلام and asked him about God's verse: ﴾ *obey God and the Messenger, and those in authority among you.* ﴿' He said, 'So his reply was: ﴾ *Do you not see how those given a share of the Scripture, [evidently] now believe in idols and evil powers?* ﴿ They are so-and-so [Abū Bakr] and so-and-so [*ʿUmar*]. ﴾ *They say of the disbelievers, 'They are more rightly guided than the believers.'* ﴿ The leaders to misguidance and those who call towards the Fire say that these are more rightly guided than Muḥammad and his adherents. ﴾ *Those are the ones God has rejected: you [Prophet] will not find anyone to help those God has rejected. Or do they have any share of what He possesses?* ﴿ This refers to the Imamate and the Caliphate. ﴾ *If they did they would not give away so much as the groove of a date stone.* ﴿ We are the people to whom God is referring here, and the ﴾ *date stone* ﴿ is the small dot that you see in the middle of the date stone. ﴾ *Or do they envy [other] people for the bounty God has granted them?* ﴿ We are the ones envied for the Imamate that God has granted us over all of the rest of people. ﴾ *We gave the descendants of Ibrāhīm the Scripture and wisdom – and We gave them a great kingdom.* ﴿

He continued, "So we made messengers, prophets, and Imams from among them, so how can they attest it being given to the descendants of Ibrāhīm and yet deny it with respect to the descendants of Muḥammad صلى الله عليه وآله? ﴾ *But some of them believed in it and some turned away from it. Hell blazes fiercely enough. We shall send those who reject Our revelations to the Fire. When their skins have been burned away, We shall replace them with new ones so that they may continue to feel the pain: God is mighty and wise. As for those who believe and do good deeds, We shall admit them into Gardens graced with*

---

29 Abū Muḥammad Qutayba b. Muḥammad al-Aʿshā al-Muʾaddib, a reliable and trustworthy companion of Imam Jaʿfar al-Ṣādiq. See Ḥillī, *Khulāṣat al-aqwāl*, 232 (nr. 789).

١٥٢. عن قُتيبة الأعشى، قال: سألتُ الصادق عليه السلام عن قوله تعالى: ﴿إِنَّ اللَّهَ لَا يَغْفِرُ أَنْ يُشْرَكَ بِهِ وَيَغْفِرُ مَا دُونَ ذَٰلِكَ لِمَنْ يَشَاءُ﴾، قال: دخل في الاستثناء كلُّ شيء.

١٥٣. وفي رواية أُخرى، عنه: دخل الكبائر في الاستثناء.

١٥٤. عن بُريد بن مُعاوية، قال: كنتُ عند أبي جعفر عليه السلام فسألتُه عن قول الله تعالى: ﴿أَطِيعُوا اللَّهَ وَأَطِيعُوا الرَّسُولَ وَأُولِي الْأَمْرِ مِنْكُمْ﴾، قال: فكان جوابه أن قال: ﴿أَلَمْ تَرَ إِلَى الَّذِينَ أُوتُوا نَصِيبًا مِنَ الْكِتَابِ يُؤْمِنُونَ بِالْجِبْتِ وَالطَّاغُوتِ﴾ فلان وفلان ﴿وَيَقُولُونَ لِلَّذِينَ كَفَرُوا هَٰؤُلَاءِ أَهْدَىٰ مِنَ الَّذِينَ آمَنُوا سَبِيلًا﴾ الأئمّة الضالّة والدُّعاة إلى النار، هؤلاء أهدى من آل محمّد وأوليائهم سبيلاً ﴿أُولَٰئِكَ الَّذِينَ لَعَنَهُمُ اللَّهُ وَمَنْ يَلْعَنِ اللَّهُ فَلَنْ تَجِدَ لَهُ نَصِيرًا ۞ أَمْ لَهُمْ نَصِيبٌ مِنَ الْمُلْكِ﴾ يعني الإمامة والخلافة ﴿فَإِذًا لَا يُؤْتُونَ النَّاسَ نَقِيرًا﴾ نحن الناس الذين عنى الله، والنَّقير: النُّقطة التي رأيت في وسط النّواة ﴿أَمْ يَحْسُدُونَ النَّاسَ عَلَىٰ مَا آتَاهُمُ اللَّهُ مِنْ فَضْلِهِ﴾ فنحن المَحْسُودون على ما آتانا الله من الإمامة دون خلق الله جميعًا ﴿فَقَدْ آتَيْنَا آلَ إِبْرَاهِيمَ الْكِتَابَ وَالْحِكْمَةَ وَآتَيْنَاهُمْ مُلْكًا عَظِيمًا﴾

فجعلنا منهم الرسل والأنبياء والأئمّة، فكيف يُقرّون بذلك في آل إبراهيم وينكرونه في آل محمّد صلى الله عليه وآله وسلم ﴿فَمِنْهُمْ مَنْ آمَنَ بِهِ وَمِنْهُمْ مَنْ صَدَّ عَنْهُ وَكَفَىٰ بِجَهَنَّمَ سَعِيرًا﴾ إلى قوله: ﴿وَنُدْخِلُهُمْ ظِلًّا ظَلِيلًا﴾.

flowing streams and there they will remain forever. They will have pure spouses there, and We shall admit them into cool refreshing shade. ﴿"

He continued, 'I asked him, "What does the ﴾*great kingdom*﴿ refer to *vis-à-vis* the descendants of Ibrāhīm?"

He replied, "That he designated the Imams to be from them, and whoever obeys them obeys God, and whoever transgresses against them transgresses against God, so this is the great kingdom."

Then he continued, "﴾*God commands you [people] to return things entrusted to you to their rightful owners, and, if you judge between people, to do so with justice: God's instructions to you are excellent, for He hears and sees everything.*﴿"

He said, "It is us that He is referring to, that the first one from among us should relay the books, the knowledge, and the weapons to the Imam after him; ﴾*and, if you judge between people, to do so with justice*﴿ that you have in your keep. Then he addressed the people, saying: ﴾*You who believe*﴿ and this includes all believers until the Day of Resurrection ﴾*obey God and the Messenger, and those in authority among you.*﴿ It is us that He means, especially when you fear a contention for authority then refer the matter back to God, His Messenger and those in authority among you. This is how it was revealed. How can He command them to obey those in authority on the one hand, whilst making concessions for them in their conflicts? Rather, this has been addressed to those who have been placed in charge and who have been told to obey God, the Messenger and those in authority among you."' [4:51–59]

155. Exactly the same thing has been narrated from Burayd al-ʿIjlī, from Abū Jaʿfar عليه السلام with the addition of: ﴾*and, if you judge between people, to do so with justice*﴿ when your authority is manifest, for you to judge with justice if it comes into your jurisdiction [literally: into your hands].' [4:58]

156. From Abū al-Ṣabbāḥ al-Kinānī who said, 'Abū 'Abd Allāh عليه السلام said, "O Abū al-Ṣabbāḥ, we are the people whose obedience God has obligated; to us belong the spoils of war; to us belongs the cream of the crop. We are the ones well-grounded in knowledge and we are the ones who are envied, and it is with respect to us that God says in His Book: ﴾*Or do they envy [other] people for the bounty God has granted them?*﴿"' [4:54]

قال: قلت: قوله: في آل إبراهيم ﴿وَآتَيْنَاهُم مُّلْكًا عَظِيمًا﴾ ما المُلك العظيم؟ قال: أن جَعَل منهم أئمّةً، من أطاعهم أطاع الله، ومن عصاهم عصى الله، فهو المُلك العظيم.

قال: ثمّ قال: ﴿إِنَّ اللهَ يَأْمُرُكُمْ أَن تُؤَدُّوا الأَمَانَاتِ إِلَى أَهْلِهَا﴾ إلى: ﴿سَمِيعًا بَصِيرًا﴾

قال: إيّانا عنى أن يُؤدّي الأوّل منّا إلى الإمام الذي بعده الكُتب والعِلم والسّلاح ﴿وَإِذَا حَكَمْتُم بَيْنَ النَّاسِ أَن تَحْكُمُوا بِالْعَدْلِ﴾ الذي في أيديكم، ثمّ قال للناس: ﴿يَا أَيُّهَا الَّذِينَ آمَنُوا﴾ فجمع المؤمنين إلى يوم القيامة ﴿أَطِيعُوا اللهَ وَأَطِيعُوا الرَّسُولَ وَأُوْلِي الأَمْرِ مِنكُمْ﴾ إيّانا عنى خاصّة، فإن خِفتم تنازعًا في الأمر، فارجعوا إلى الله، وإلى الرسول، وأُولي الأمر منكم. هكذا نزلت، وكيف يأمُرهم بطاعة أُولي الأمر، ويرخّص لهم في منازعتهم، إنّما قيل ذلك للمأمورين الذين قيل لهم: ﴿أَطِيعُوا اللهَ وَأَطِيعُوا الرَّسُولَ وَأُوْلِي الأَمْرِ مِنكُمْ﴾.

١٥٥. بُريد العجلي، عن أبي جعفر عليه السلام -مثله سواء- وزاد فيه ﴿أَن تَحْكُمُوا بِالْعَدْلِ﴾ إذا ظهرتم ﴿أَن تَحْكُمُوا بِالْعَدْلِ﴾ إذا بَدَت في أيديكم.

١٥٦. عن أبي الصّباح الكِناني، قال: قال أبو عبد الله عليه السلام: يا أبا الصّباح، نحن قومٌ فَرَض الله طاعتنا، لنا الأنفال، ولنا صَفْو المال، ونحن الرّاسخون في العلم، ونحن المَحْسُودون الذين قال الله في كتابه: ﴿أَمْ يَحْسُدُونَ النَّاسَ عَلَى مَا آتَاهُمُ اللهُ مِن فَضْلِهِ﴾.

157. From Yūnus b. Ẓibyān who said, 'Abū 'Abd Allāh عليه السلام said, "While Mūsā b. 'Imrān عليه السلام was conversing with his Lord and speaking to Him, he noticed a man under the shade of God's Throne, so he asked, 'My Lord, who is this being shaded by Your Throne?' So He replied, 'O Mūsā, this is one of the people untouched by other people's envy for the bounty that God has granted them.'"' [4:54]

158. From Abū Sa'īd al-Mu'addib, from Ibn 'Abbās who said regarding the verse: ﴾*Or do they envy* [*other*] *people for the bounty God has granted them?*﴿ 'We are the people, and His bounty is prophethood.' [4:54]

159. From Abū Khālid al-Kābulī, from Abū Ja'far عليه السلام: ﴾*A great kingdom*﴿ is that He placed Imams in their midst, and whoever obeys them obeys God, and whoever transgresses against them transgresses against God, and this is a great kingdom – ﴾*and We gave them a great kingdom.*﴿' [4:54]

160. In another report on his authority, he said, 'The mandatory obedience.' [4:54]

161. Ḥumrān, on his authority: ﴾*We gave the descendants of Ibrāhīm the Scripture*﴿ – he said: 'Prophethood,' ﴾*and wisdom*﴿ – he said: comprehension and judgement, ﴾*and We gave them a great kingdom*﴿ – he said: obedience.' [4:54]

162. From Abū Ḥamza, from Abū Ja'far عليه السلام: '﴾*We gave the descendants of Ibrāhīm the Scripture*﴿ – this is prophethood, ﴾*and wisdom*﴿ – they are the wise men from among the choicest of prophets, and the ﴾*great kingdom*﴿ are the choicest Imams of guidance.' [4:54]

١٥٧. عن يونس بن ظِبيان، قال: قال أبو عبدالله عليه السلام: بينما موسى بن عمران عليه السلام يناجي ربَّه ويُكلّمه، إذ رأى رجلاً تحت ظِلّ العرش، فقال: يا ربّ، من هذا الذي قد أظلَّه عرشك، فقال: يا موسى، هذا مِمَّن لم يَحْسُد الناس على ما آتاهم الله من فضله.

١٥٨. عن أبي سعيد المؤدِّب، عن ابن عباس، في قوله ﴿أَمْ يَحْسُدُونَ النَّاسَ عَلَىٰ مَا آتَاهُمُ اللَّهُ مِن فَضْلِهِ﴾، قال: نحن الناس، وفضله النبوّة.

١٥٩. عن أبي خالد الكابُلي، عن أبي جعفر عليه السلام: ﴿مُلْكًا عَظِيمًا﴾ أن جعل فيهم أئمّةً، من أطاعهم أطاع الله، ومن عصاهم عصى الله، فهذا مُلكٌ عظيمٌ ﴿وَآتَيْنَاهُم مُّلْكًا عَظِيمًا﴾.

١٦٠. وعنه عليه السلام: في رواية أُخرى، قال: الطاعة المفروضة.

١٦١. حُمران، عنه عليه السلام ﴿فَقَدْ آتَيْنَا آلَ إِبْرَاهِيمَ الْكِتَابَ﴾، قال: النبوّة ﴿وَالْحِكْمَةَ﴾، قال: الفَهْم والقضاء، و﴿مُلْكًا عَظِيمًا﴾، قال: الطاعة.

١٦٢. عن أبي حمزة، عن أبي جعفر عليه السلام ﴿فَقَدْ آتَيْنَا آلَ إِبْرَاهِيمَ الْكِتَابَ﴾ فهو النبوّة ﴿وَالْحِكْمَةَ﴾ فهم الحكماء من الأنبياء من الصَّفوة، وأمّا المُلك العظيم فهم الأئمّة الهُداة من الصَّفوة.

163. From Dāwūd b. Farqad who said, 'I heard Abū 'Abd Allāh say while Ismā'īl, his son, was in his company and asked about: ﴾ *Or do they envy [other] people for the bounty God has granted them? We gave the descendants of Ibrāhīm the Scripture and wisdom – and We gave them a great kingdom.* ﴿

He replied, "The great kingdom is the obligation of obedience."

He asked: ﴾ *but some of them believed in it and some turned away from it.* ﴿

So I exclaimed, "I seek God's forgiveness."

So Ismā'īl asked me, "For what, Dāwūd?"

So I replied, "Because I have been reading it as: ﴾ *but some of them believe in it, and some turned away from it.* ﴿"

So Abū 'Abd Allāh عليه السلام said, "Actually it is: ﴾ *but some from among these* [i.e. the descendants of Ibrāhīm] *believed in this, and some turned away from it.* ﴿"' [4:55]

164. From Zurāra, Ḥumrān and Muḥammad b. Muslim, from Abū Ja'far and Abū 'Abd Allāh, peace be upon them both, who said, 'The Imam is recognized by three features: (1) he is the worthiest of all people to succeed the one who preceded him; (2) he has the weaponry of the Prophet ﷺ in his possession; (3) and he has the bequest, which is what God refers to when He says in His Book: ﴾ *God commands you [people] to return things entrusted to you to their rightful owners.* ﴿'

He continued, 'The weaponry in our midst holds the same position as the Ark of the Covenant for the Children of Israel; the kingdom revolves around wherever the weapons reside, just as it used to do with the Ark.' [4:58]

165. From al-Ḥalabī, from Zurāra: ﴾ *to return things entrusted to you to their rightful owners* ﴿ – he says, 'Return the authority to its rightful owner;' ﴾ *and, if you judge between people, to do so with justice* ﴿ – he said, 'They are the progeny and family of Muḥammad, peace be upon them.' [4:58]

١٦٣ . عن داود بن فرقد، قال: سَمِعتُ أبا عبدالله عليه السلام وعنده إسماعيل ابنه عليه السلام يقول: ﴿أَمْ يَحْسُدُونَ النَّاسَ عَلَىٰ مَا آتَاهُمُ اللهُ مِن فَضْلِهِ﴾ الآية.

قال: فقال: المُلك العظيم: افتراض الطاعة.

قال: ﴿فَمِنْهُم مَّنْ آمَنَ بِهِ وَمِنْهُم مَّن صَدَّ عَنْهُ﴾

قال: فقلت: أستغفرُ الله. فقال لي إسماعيل: لِمَ يا داود؟

قلتُ: لأنّي كثيرًا قرأتها ﴿وَمِنْهُم مَّنْ آمَنَ بِهِ وَمِنْهُم مَّن صَدَّ عَنْهُ﴾.

قال: فقال أبو عبدالله عليه السلام: إنّما هو، فمن هؤلاء — ولد إبراهيم — من آمن بهذا، ومنهم من صدّ عنه.

١٦٤ . عن زُرارة، وحُمران، ومحمّد بن مسلم، عن أبي جعفر، وأبي عبدالله عليهما السلام، قال: الإمام يُعرَف بثلاث خِصال: إنّه أولى الناس بالذي كان قبله، وإنّ عنده سِلاح النبيّ صلى الله عليه وآله وعنده الوصيّة، وهي التي قال الله في كتابه: ﴿إِنَّ اللهَ يَأْمُرُكُمْ أَن تُؤَدُّوا الأَمَانَاتِ إِلَىٰ أَهْلِهَا﴾.

وقال: إنّ السِّلاح فينا بمنزلة التابوت في بني إسرائيل، يَدُور المُلك حيث دار السِّلاح، كما كان يَدُور حيث دار التابوت.

١٦٥ . عن الحلبي، عن زُرارة ﴿أَن تُؤَدُّوا الأَمَانَاتِ إِلَىٰ أَهْلِهَا﴾ يقول: أدّوا الولاية إلى أهلها ﴿وَإِذَا حَكَمْتُم بَيْنَ النَّاسِ أَن تَحْكُمُوا بِالْعَدْلِ﴾، قال: هم آل محمّد عليه وآله السلام.

166. In a narration by Muḥammad b. [al-]Fuḍayl, from Abū al-Ḥasan عليه السلام, 'They are the Imams from the family of Muḥammad, and the Imam bequeaths the Imamate to an Imam after himself, and he cannot choose someone other than him nor take it away from him.' [4:58]

167. From Abū Jaʿfar عليه السلام who said regarding His verse: ﴿*God's instructions to you are excellent*﴾, 'It has been revealed about us, and God is the ultimate resort.' [4:58]

168. In a narration of Ibn Abī Yaʿfūr, from Abū ʿAbd Allāh عليه السلام: ﴿*God commands you [people] to return things entrusted to you to their rightful owners, and, if you judge between people, to do so with justice*﴾; he said, 'God commanded the Imam to bequeath whatever he has in his possession to the Imam that comes after him, and God commanded the Imams to judge between people with justice, and He commanded the people to obey them.' [4:58]

169. From Jābir al-Juʿfī who said, 'I asked Abū Jaʿfar عليه السلام about this verse: ﴿*obey God and the Messenger, and those in authority among you.*﴾ He replied, "[They are] the vicegerents."' [4:59]

170. In a narration of Abū Baṣīr's on his authority; he said, 'It was revealed about ʿAlī b. Abī Ṭālib عليه السلام.' I said to him, 'People ask us what prevented Him from specifying ʿAlī's and his household's name in the Book itself?'

So Abū Jaʿfar عليه السلام said, 'Tell them: God revealed about the prayer to His messenger, but did not specify three or four [units to be prayed], such that it was the Messenger of God صلى الله عليه وآله who was the one to expound that for them. And He sent down revelations about the Hajj but did not specify to circumambulate seven times until the Messenger of God صلى الله عليه وآله expounded that for them. He revealed: ﴿*obey God and the Messenger, and those in authority among you*﴾, and it was revealed about ʿAlī, al-Ḥasan and al-Ḥusayn, and he said regarding ʿAlī: "For whomsoever I am master, ʿAlī is his master."

And the Messenger of God صلى الله عليه وآله also said, "I leave behind me God's Book and my Household (*ahl al-bayt*), and I have asked God never to separate them until they come and meet me at the Fountain, and He granted me that." He also said, "Do not teach them for they are more knowledgeable than you.

١٦٦. في رواية محمّد بن الفُضيل، عن أبي الحسن عليه السلام: هم الأئمّة من آل محمّد، يؤدّي الإمام الإمامة إلى إمام بعده، ولا يَخُصُّ بها غيره، ولا يزْويها عنه.

١٦٧. أبو جعفر عليه السلام ﴿إِنَّ اللَّهَ نِعِمَّا يَعِظُكُم بِهِ﴾، قال: فينا نزلت، والله المستعان.

١٦٨. وفي رواية ابن أبي يعفور، عن أبي عبد الله عليه السلام، قال: ﴿إِنَّ اللَّهَ يَأْمُرُكُمْ أَن تُؤَدُّوا الْأَمَانَاتِ إِلَىٰ أَهْلِهَا وَإِذَا حَكَمْتُم بَيْنَ النَّاسِ أَن تَحْكُمُوا بِالْعَدْلِ﴾ قال: أمر الله الإمام أن يدفع ما عنده إلى الإمام الذي بعده، وأمر الأئمّة أن يحكموا بالعدل، وأمر الناس أن يُطيعوهم.

١٦٩. عن جابر الجُعفي، قال: سألتُ أبا جعفر عليه السلام عن هذه الآية ﴿أَطِيعُوا اللَّهَ وَأَطِيعُوا الرَّسُولَ وَأُولِي الْأَمْرِ مِنكُمْ﴾. قال: الأوصياء.

١٧٠. وفي رواية أبي بصير، عنه عليه السلام، قال: نزلت في عليّ بن أبي طالب عليه السلام. قلت له: إنّ الناس، يقولون لنا: فما منعه أن يُسمّي عليًّا وأهل بيته في كتابه؟

فقال أبو جعفر عليه السلام: قولوا لهم: إنّ الله أنزَل على رسوله الصلاة، ولم يُسمّ ثلاثًا ولا أربعًا حتّى كان رسول الله صلى الله عليه وآله هو الذي فسّر ذلك، وأنزل الحجّ فلم يُنزِل طُوفوا أُسبوعًا حتّى فسّر ذلك لهم رسول الله صلى الله عليه وآله، وأنزل ﴿أَطِيعُوا اللَّهَ وَأَطِيعُوا الرَّسُولَ وَأُولِي الْأَمْرِ مِنكُمْ﴾ فنزلت في عليّ والحسن والحسين. وقال صلى الله عليه وآله في عليّ: «من كنت مولاه، فعليّ مولاه».

They will never take you out from the gate of guidance and into the gate of misguidance."

If the Messenger of God ﷺ had remained quiet and not explicitly shown its rightful owner, the families of 'Abbās and 'Aqīl and so-and-so and so-and-so would all have claimed it for themselves, but God revealed in His Book: ﴾*God wishes to keep uncleanness away from you, people of the* [*Prophet's*] *House, and to purify you thoroughly,*﴿(33:33) and the inner meaning of this verse addresses 'Alī, al-Ḥasan, al-Ḥusayn and Fāṭima, peace be upon them. So the Messenger of God ﷺ took 'Alī, Fāṭima, al-Ḥasan and al-Ḥusayn by the hand and brought them under the blanket in Umm Salama's house saying, 'O God, every prophet has a certain anchorage and household, and these are my anchorage and my Household.'

So Umm Salama asked, 'Am I not one of your Household?' He replied, 'You are in a good place, but these are my anchorage and my Household.'

When the Messenger of God ﷺ passed away, 'Alī was the worthiest of all people of it [i.e. the Imamate] because of his seniority and because of his having announced and appointed him and held him up by the hand [previously]. And when he [i.e. 'Alī] was passing away, he could not and would not appoint Muḥammad b. 'Alī or 'Abbās b. 'Alī, the martyr, nor any of his other children, otherwise al-Ḥasan and al-Ḥusayn would say that God has revealed about us exactly the same as what He revealed about you, and He has commanded our obedience just as He did yours, and the Messenger of God ﷺ proclaimed about us just as he proclaimed regarding you, and He has kept all uncleanliness away from us just as He did with you.

So when 'Alī passed away, al-Ḥasan was the worthiest of it because of his seniority, and when al-Ḥasan b. 'Alī was the Imam he could not and would not say that ﴾*in God's Scripture, blood-relatives have a stronger claim than others*﴿(33:6) and designate his children for it, for then al-Ḥusayn (عليه السلام) could say that God has revealed about me exactly as He has revealed about you and your father, and he has commanded my obedience just as He did yours and your father's, and has kept uncleanliness away from me just as He did from you and your father.

So when it passed on to al-Ḥusayn (عليه السلام) no one else could lay claim to it the way that he could after his father and his brother, and that is where what God, Mighty and Exalted, says: ﴾*blood-relatives have a stronger claim than*

وقال رسول الله ﷺ: «أوصيكم بكتاب الله وأهل بيتي، إنّي سألتُ الله أن لا يُفرّق بينهما حتّى يُوردهما عليَّ الحوض، فأعطاني ذلك، فلا تعلّموهم فإنّي أعلم منكم، إنّهم لن يُخرجوكم من باب هُدىً، ولن يُدْخِلوكم في باب ضَلال».

ولو سَكَتَ رسول الله ﷺ، ولم يُبيّن أهلها، لادّعاها آل عباس وآل عقيل وآل فلان وآل فلان، ولكنّ أنزل الله في كتابه: ﴿إِنَّمَا يُرِيدُ اللَّهُ لِيُذْهِبَ عَنكُمُ الرِّجْسَ أَهْلَ الْبَيْتِ وَيُطَهِّرَكُمْ تَطْهِيرًا﴾ فكان عليّ والحسن والحسين وفاطمة عليهم السلام تأويل هذه الآية، فأخَذَ رسول الله ﷺ بيد عليّ وفاطمة والحسن والحسين، فأدخلهم تحت الكِساء في بيت أمّ سَلَمَة، وقال: اللّهمّ إنّ لكُلّ نبيّ ثَقَلاً وأهلاً، فهؤلاء ثَقَلي وأهلي».

فقالت أمّ سَلَمَة: ألستُ من أهلك؟ قال: «إنّكِ على خير، ولكن هؤلاء ثَقَلي وأهلي».

فلمّا قُبِض رسول الله ﷺ كان عليّ أولى الناس بها لكِبَره، ولمّا بلّغ رسول الله ﷺ فأقامه وأخذ بيده، فلمّا حُضِر عليّ لم يستطع ولم يكُن ليفعل أن يُدْخِل محمّد بن عليّ ولا العباس بن علي ولا أحدًا من ولده، إذًا لقال الحسن والحسين عليهما السلام: أنزل الله فينا كما أنزل فيك، وأمر بطاعتنا كما أمر بطاعتك، وبلّغ رسول الله ﷺ فينا كما أنزل فيك، وأذهب عنّا الرجس، كما أذهبه عنك.

فلمّا مضى عليّ عليه السلام كان الحسن عليه السلام أولى بها لكِبَره، فلمّا حُضِر الحسن بن علي عليهما السلام لم يستطع ولم يكن ليفعل أن يقول: ﴿وَأُولُوا الْأَرْحَامِ بَعْضُهُمْ أَوْلَىٰ بِبَعْضٍ﴾ فيجعلها لولده، إذًا لقال الحسين عليه السلام: أنزل الله فيّ كما أنزل فيك وفي أبيك، وأمر بطاعتي كما أمر بطاعتك وطاعة أبيك، وأذهب الرجس عنّي كما أذهب عنك وعن أبيك.

others﴿ was applied, so it [i.e. the Imamate] passed on from al-Ḥusayn to ʿAlī b. al-Ḥusayn, then after ʿAlī b. al-Ḥusayn to Muḥammad b. ʿAlī.'"

Then Abū Jaʿfar عليه السلام said, "Uncleanliness is doubt, and by God we do not ever doubt in our religion."' [4:59]

171. From Abū Baṣīr, from Abū ʿAbd Allāh عليه السلام who spoke similarly with regard to God's verses and added the following, 'And alms-giving was revealed to him but God did not specify that it was a dirham from every forty dirhams, but it was the Messenger of God ﷺ who expounded that for them.' At the end of it he mentioned that when it passed on to al-Ḥusayn, no one from his family could lay claim to it as he did after his brother and his father عليه السلام should they have wished to take it away from him, which they would never have done. Then after it had been passed on to al-Ḥusayn b. ʿAlī, the inner meaning of this verse came to be applied: ﴾*blood-relatives have a stronger claim than others*﴿, and after al-Ḥusayn b. ʿAlī it passed on to ʿAlī b. al-Ḥusayn, after ʿAlī b. al-Ḥusayn, it passed on to Muḥammad b. ʿAlī عليه السلام. [4:59]

172. From Abān that he went to Abū al-Ḥasan al-Riḍā عليه السلام. He said, 'I asked him about God's verse: ﴾*You who believe, obey God and the Messenger, and those in authority among you.*﴿ So he replied, "That is ʿAlī b. Abī Ṭālib," then he fell silent. After he had been silent for a while, I asked, "Then who?" So he replied, "Then al-Ḥasan." Then again he fell silent, and when a while had passed, I asked, "Then who?" He replied, "al-Ḥusayn." I asked, "Then who?" He replied, "Then ʿAlī b. al-Ḥusayn," and fell silent again. He continued to remain quiet after each one until I repeated the question and he replied until he had named all of them until the last one, peace be upon them all.' [4:59]

فلمّا أن صارت إلى الحسين عليه السلام لم يَبْقَ أحد يستطيع أن يَدّعى كم يدّعي هو على أبيه وعلى أخيه، فلمّا أن صارت إلى الحسين عليه السلام جرى [تأويل قوله تعالى]: ﴿أُولُوا الأَرْحَامِ بَعْضُهُمْ أَوْلَى بِبَعْضٍ فِي كِتَابِ اللهِ﴾ ثمّ صارت من بعد الحسين عليه السلام إلى عليّ بن الحسين، ثمّ من بعد عليّ بن الحسين إلى محمّد بن علي عليهم الصلاة والسلام.

ثمّ قال أبو جعفر عليه السلام: الرِّجس هو الشكّ، والله لا نَشُكُّ في ديننا أبدًا.

١٧١. عن أبي بصير، عن أبي عبد الله عليه السلام، عن قول الله تعالى، فذكر نحو هذا الحديث، وقال فيه زيادة: فنزلت عليه الزكاة فلم يُسَمِّ الله من كلّ أربعين دِرْهَمًا دِرْهَمًا حتّى كان رسول الله صلى الله عليه وآله هو الذي فَسّر ذلك لهم. وذكر في آخره: فلمّا أن صارت إلى الحسين عليه السلام، لم يكُن أحدٌ من أهله يستطيع أن يَدّعي عليه كما كان هو يدّعي على أخيه وعلى أبيه عليهما السلام، لو أرادا أن يَصْرِفا الأمر عنه، ولم يكونا ليفعلا، ثمّ صارت حين أفضت إلى الحسين بن عليّ عليهما السلام فجرى تأويل هذه الآية ﴿وَأُولُوا الأَرْحَامِ بَعْضُهُمْ أَوْلَى بِبَعْضٍ فِي كِتَابِ اللهِ﴾ ثمّ صارت من بعد الحسين لعليّ بن الحسين، ثمّ صارت من بعد عليّ بن الحسين إلى محمّد بن عليّ عليهم السلام.

١٧٢. عن أبان: أنّه دخل على أبي الحسن الرضا عليه السلام، قال: فسألته عن قول الله: ﴿يَا أَيُّهَا الَّذِينَ آمَنُوا أَطِيعُوا اللهَ وَأَطِيعُوا الرَّسُولَ وَأُولِي الأَمْرِ مِنْكُمْ﴾.

فقال: ذلك عليّ بن أبي طالب عليه السلام ثمّ سكت، قال: فلمّا طال سُكُوته، قلت: ثمّ من؟ قال: ثمّ الحسن. ثمّ سكت. فلمّا طال سكوته قلتُ: ثم مَن؟ قال: الحسين. قلتُ: ثمّ

173. From ʿImrān al-Ḥalabī who said, 'I heard Abū ʿAbd Allāh ﷺ say, "Indeed you have received this matter directly, meaning from its source, about God's statement: ﴾*obey God and the Messenger, and those in authority among you*﴿, and from God's Messenger's statement: '[...] that which if you hold fast to, you will never be led astray, neither by him nor by the other [i.e. Abū Bakr and ʿUmar].'"' [4:59]

174. From ʿAbd Allāh b. ʿAjalān[30], from Abū Jaʿfar ﷺ who regarding God's verse: ﴾*Obey God and the Messenger, and those in authority among you*﴿ said: 'It is about ʿAlī and the Imams, whom God has designated in place of the prophets, except that they do not legislate the permissibility or prohibition of anything.' [4:59]

175. From Ḥakīm who said, 'I said to Abū ʿAbd Allāh ﷺ, "May I be your ransom – please tell me who ﴾*those is authority*﴿ are, and whose obedience God has commanded." So he said to me, "They are ʿAlī b. Abī Ṭālib, al-Ḥasan, al-Ḥusayn, ʿAlī b. al-Ḥusayn, Muḥammad b. ʿAlī and I, Jaʿfar. So praise God, who has enabled you to recognise your Imams and leaders while the rest of the people have rejected them."' [4:59]

176. From Yaḥyā b. al-Sarī who said, 'I said to Abū ʿAbd Allāh ﷺ, "Tell me about the pillars of Islam upon which the religion is founded, where it is not acceptable for anyone to fall short of them at all, such that if anyone were to fall short in his knowledge of them it would corrupt his practice and his actions would not be accepted; and the one who knows them and acts in accordance with them, his practice is correct, his actions are accepted and even if he is ignorant of any other matter besides these, it does not affect him negatively as long as he knows these [pillars]."

So he replied, "Yes. The testimony that there is no god but God, faith in His Messenger ﷺ, the acceptance of all that he brought from God, the right due from your wealth as alms, and the authority that God has commanded to be adhered to – the authority of Muḥammad's Household."

30 ʿAbd Allāh b. ʿAjalān, a praiseworthy narrator of the Imams' traditions. See Ḥillī, *Khulāṣat al-aqwāl*, 197 (nr. 613).

مَن؟ قال: ثمّ عليّ بن الحسين وسكت؛ فلم يَزَل يَسْكُت عند كلّ واحدٍ حتّى أُعيد المسألة، فيقول، حتّى سمّاهم إلى آخرهم عليهم السلام.

١٧٣. عن عِمران الحلبي، قال: سَمِعتُ أبا عبدالله عليه السلام يقول: إنّكم أخذتُم هذا الأمر من جَذْوه – يعني من أصله – عن قول الله تعالى: ﴿أَطِيعُوا اللَّهَ وَأَطِيعُوا الرَّسُولَ وَأُولِي الْأَمْرِ مِنْكُمْ﴾ ومن قول رسول الله صلى الله عليه وآله: «ما إن تمسّكتم به لن تَضِلّوا» لا من قول فلان، ولا من قول فلان.

١٧٤. عن عبدالله بن عَجلان، عن أبي جعفر عليه السلام، في قوله تعالى: ﴿أَطِيعُوا اللَّهَ وَأَطِيعُوا الرَّسُولَ وَأُولِي الْأَمْرِ مِنْكُمْ﴾، قال: هي في عليّ وفي الأئمة عليهم السلام، جعلهم الله مواضع الأنبياء، غير أنّهم لا يُحِلّون شيئًا، ولا يحرّمونه.

١٧٥. عن حكيم، قال: قلتُ لأبي عبدالله عليه السلام: جُعِلت فداك، أخبِرني مَن أُولي الأمر الذين أمر الله بطاعتهم؟

فقال لي: أُولئك عليّ بن أبي طالب والحسن، والحسين، وعليّ بن الحسين، ومحمّد بن علي وجعفر أنا، فاحْمَدُوا الله الّذي عرّفكم أئمّتكم وقادتكم حين جَحَدَهُم الناس.

١٧٦. عن يحيى بن السَّري، قال: قلت لأبي عبدالله عليه السلام: أخبرني بدعائم الإسلام التي بُني عليها الدين، لا يَسَع أحدًا التقصير في شيءٍ منها، التي من قَصّر عن معرفة شيءٍ منها

He continued, "The Messenger of God ﷺ has said, 'Whoever dies without knowing his Imam dies a death of pre-Islamic ignorance.' So the Imam was ʿAlī, then al-Ḥasan b. ʿAlī, then al-Ḥusayn b. ʿAlī, then ʿAlī b. al-Ḥusayn, then Muḥammad b. ʿAlī, i.e. Abū Jaʿfar. Before Abū Jaʿfar the Shīʿa did not know the practices which ought to be performed in the Hajj, nor the permissible and the prohibited until his time. So he performed the Hajj with them and explained its practices, as well as what was permissible and prohibited until they became needless of other people, and in fact, the same people that they had previously learned from now began learning from them, and this is exactly how it is. The earth cannot be devoid of an Imam."' [4:59]

177. From ʿAmr b. Saʿīd[31] who said, 'I asked Abū al-Ḥasan ؑ about His verse: ﴾*Obey God and the Messenger, and those in authority among you.*﴿ He replied, "ʿAlī b. Abī Ṭālib and the vicegerents after him."' [4:59]

178. From Sulaym b. Qays al-Hilālī who said, 'I heard ʿAlī ؑ say, "Never was there a case about the revelation of any of the verses of the Qurʾān which the Prophet ﷺ did not recite and dictate to me, and which I did not write down with my own hand. Furthermore, he informed me of their inner meanings, with complete elucidations, indicating the verses that were abrogating and the verses that had been abrogated, the decisive verses and the ambiguous ones. Then the Prophet supplicated God to bestow upon me its understanding and its unfailing memory. Ever since the Prophet prayed for me I have never forgotten a single verse from the Book of God, nor did I forget the knowledge which the Prophet imparted to me and that I had taken down in my own hand. Nothing of what was revealed to the Prophet, the lawful and the unlawful, nothing of the Divine imperatives and the prohibitions, nothing of what has been and what would be regarding obedience and disobedience did the Prophet neglect to teach me. I grasped it fully and forgot not a word from it. Then the Prophet put his hand over my chest and supplicated God to fill my heart with knowledge and understanding, wisdom and enlightenment, and for me to neither forget anything nor to fail to recall anything that I had not written down.

31 ʿAmr b. Saʿīd al-Madāʾinī, a reliable companion and narrator of Imam al-Riḍā's traditions. See Ḥillī, *Khulāṣat al-aqwāl*, 213 (nr. 697).

فَسَد عليه دينُه، ولم يُقْبَل منه عَمَلُه، ومن عَرَفها وعَمِل بها صَلَح له دينه، وقُبِل منه عَمَلُه، ولم يضُرّه ما هو فيه بجهل شيءٍ من الأُمور إن جَهِله؟

فقال: نعم، شهادة أن لا إله إلاّ الله، والإيمان برسوله ﷺ، والإقرار بما جاء من عند الله، وحقّ من الأموال الزكاة، والولاية التي أمر الله بها ولاية آل محمّد.

قال: وقال رسول الله ﷺ: «مَن مات ولا يعرِف إمامه مات مِيتةً جاهلية»، فكان الإمام عليّ بن أبي طالب، ثمّ كان الحسن بن عليّ، ثمّ كان الحسين بن عليّ، ثمّ كان عليّ بن الحسين، ثمّ كان محمّد بن علي أبو جعفر. وكانت الشيعة قبل أن يكون أبو جعفر، وهم لا يعرفون مناسِك حجّهم، ولا حلالهم، ولا حرامهم، حتّى كان أبو جعفر، فنَهَج لهم وبيّن مناسك حجّهم، وحلالهم وحرامهم، حتّى استغنوا عن الناس، وصار النّاس يتعلّمون منهم بعد ما كانوا يتعلّمون من الناس، وهكذا يكون الأمر، والأرض لا تكون إلاّ بإمام.

١٧٧. عن عمرو بن سعيد، قال: سألتُ أبا الحسن عليه السلام عن قوله تعالى: ﴿أَطِيعُوا اللهَ وَأَطِيعُوا الرَّسُولَ وَأُولِي الأَمْرِ مِنكُمْ﴾، قال: قال: عليّ بن أبي طالب عليه السلام والأوصياء من بعده.

١٧٨. عن سُليم بن قيس الهِلالي، قال: سَمِعتُ علياً عليه السلام يقول: ما نزلت على رسول الله ﷺ آيةٌ من القرآن إلاّ أقرأنيها، وأملاها عليّ، فأكْتُبها بخطّي، وعلّمني تأويلها وتفسيرها، وناسخها ومنسوخها، ومحكمها ومتشابهها، ودعا الله لي أن يعلّمني فَهْمها وحِفظها، فما نسيتُ آيةً من كتاب الله، ولا عِلماً أملاه عليّ فكتبتُه منذ دعا لي بما دعا، وما نزل شيء علّمه من حلالٍ

I then inquired, 'O Messenger of God, are you still afraid of my being forgetful after this?'

So he replied, 'No, I am never afraid of your being either forgetful or ignorant, for my Lord has informed me that He has answered my supplication for you and for your associates who will come after you.'

So I asked, 'O Messenger of God, who are my associates after me?'

He replied, 'Those whom God has linked to Himself and to me, saying: ﴾*obey God and the Messenger, and those in authority among you*﴿ – the Imams.'

So I asked, 'O Messenger of God, who are they?'

So he replied, 'The vicegerents are from my lineage until they meet me at the Fountain. Each one of them is a rightly-guided guide unharmed by those who will forsake them. They are with the Qur'an and the Qur'an is with them, and they will never separate from each other. It is through them that my community will be helped, through them that they will have prosperity, through them that they will be protected, and through them that their supplications will be answered.'

So I asked, 'O Messenger of God, name them for me.'

So he said to me, 'This son of mine, placing his hand on al-Ḥasan's head, then this son of mine, placing his hand on al-Ḥusayn's head, then his son named ʿAlī who will be born in your lifetime so pass on my greetings to him. Then they will continue after him until there are twelve in total from the lineage of Muḥammad.'

So I asked him, 'May my parents be ransomed for you – name them please.'

So he named them, one by one, and by God, my brother, O son of Hilāl, the Mahdī of this community is one of them, the one who will fill the earth with equity and justice just as it will have been filled with injustice and tyranny. By God, I know those who will pay allegiance to him between the *rukn* and the *maqām* and I know the names of their fathers and their tribes."' [4:59]

ولا حرامٍ، أمرٍ ولا نهيٍ، كان أو يكون، من طاعةٍ أو معصيةٍ، إلاّ علّمنيه وحَفِظته، فلم أنسَ منه حرفًا واحدًا، ثمّ وضع يده على صدري ودعا الله لي أن يملأ قلبي عِلمًا وفَهْمًا وحِكمة ونُورًا، لم أنسَ شيئًا، ولم يَفُتْني شيء لم أكْتُبه.

فقلت: يا رسول الله، وتَخَوّفتَ عليّ النسيان فيما بعد؟

فقال: لستُ أتخوّف عليك نسيانًا ولا جهلاً، وقد أخبرني ربّي أنّه قد استجاب لي فيك وفي شُركائك الذين يكونون من بعدك.

فقلت: يا رسول الله، ومن شُركائي من بعدي؟

قال: الذين قَرَنهم الله بنفسه وبي. فقال: ﴿أَطِيعُوا اللَّهَ وَأَطِيعُوا الرَّسُولَ وَأُولِي الْأَمْرِ مِنكُمْ﴾ الأئمّة.

فقلت: يا رسول الله، ومن هم؟

فقال: الأوصياء منّي إلى أن يَرِدُوا عليّ الحوض، كلّهم هادٍ مُهتدٍ، لا يضرُّهم من خَذَلهم، هم مع القرآن، والقرآن معهم، لا يُفارقهم ولا يُفارقونه، بهم تُنْصَر أُمّتي، وبهم يُمْطَرون، وبهم يُدْفَع عنهم، وبهم يُسْتَجاب دُعاؤهم.

فقلت: يا رسول الله، سَمِّهم لي.

فقال: ابْني هذا ووضع يدَه على رأس الحسن، ثمّ ابني هذا ووضع يدَه على رأس الحسين، ثمّ ابنٍ له يقال له عليّ، وسيُولَد في حياتك، فاقْرَأْه منّي السلام، ثمّ تكمّله إلى اثني عشر من وُلد محمّد ﷺ.

فقلتُ له: بأبي أنت وأمّي سَمِّهم.

179. From Muḥammad b. Muslim who said, 'Abū Ja'far ﷺ said: ﴾*If you are in dispute over any matter, refer it to God and the Messenger,* ***and those in authority among you.***﴿' [4:59*]

180. In another narration from 'Āmir b. Sa'īd al-Juhnī, from Jābir, on his authority: '[...] and those vested with authority are from the family of Muḥammad ﷺ.' [4:59]

181. From Yūnus, the protégé of 'Alī, from Abū 'Abd Allāh ﷺ who said, 'When someone is engaged in a dispute with a fellow brother then invites him to go to one of his associates to judge between them, if the latter refuses, insistent upon taking the case to the ruler, then he is like one who turns to unjust tyrants for judgement, and God has said: ﴾*yet still want to turn to unjust tyrants for judgement, although they have been ordered to reject them? Satan wants to lead them far astray.*﴿' [4:60]

182. From Abū Baṣīr, from Abū 'Abd Allāh ﷺ regarding the verse of God most High: ﴾*Do you [Prophet] not see those who claim to believe in what has been sent down to you, and in what was sent down before you, yet still want to turn to unjust tyrants for judgement.*﴿ He said, 'Abū Muḥammad, if you had a right upon someone and you invited him to refer the matter to equitable judges and he refused, insistent upon taking the case to oppressive judges for them to rule in his favour, then he is among those who turn to unjust tyrants for judgement.' [4:60]

فسمّاهم لي رجلاً رجلاً، فيهم والله – يا أخا بني هلال – مهديّ أمة محمّد، الذي يملأ الأرض قِسطًا وعَدلاً كما مُلئت جَورًا وظُلمًا، واللهِ إنّي لأعرِف من يُبايعه بين الركُن والمقام، وأعرِف أسماء آبائهم وقبائلهم.

١٧٩. عن محمّد بن مسلم، قال: قال أبو جعفر عليه السلام: ﴿فَإِن تَنَازَعْتُمْ فِي شَيْءٍ فَارْجِعُوهُ إِلَى اللَّهِ وَإِلَى الرَّسُولِ وَإِلَى أُولِي الْأَمْرِ مِنكُمْ﴾.

١٨٠. وفي رواية عامر بن سعيد الجُهني، عن جابر، عنه عليه السلام ﴿وَأُولِي الْأَمْرِ﴾ من آل محمّد صلى الله عليه وآله وسلم.

١٨١. عن يونس مولى عليّ، عن أبي عبدالله عليه السلام، قال: من كانت بينه وبين أخيه منازعةٌ، فدعاه إلى رجل من أصحابه يحكم بينهما، فأبى إلاّ أن يرافعه إلى السلطان، فهوكمن حاكم إلى الجِبت والطّاغوت، وقد قال الله تعالى: ﴿يُرِيدُونَ أَن يَتَحَاكَمُوا إِلَى الطَّاغُوتِ﴾ إلى قوله ﴿بَعِيدًا﴾.

١٨٢. عن أبي بصير، عن أبي عبدالله عليه السلام، في قوله تعالى: ﴿أَلَمْ تَرَ إِلَى الَّذِينَ يَزْعُمُونَ أَنَّهُمْ آمَنُوا بِمَا أُنزِلَ إِلَيْكَ وَمَا أُنزِلَ مِن قَبْلِكَ يُرِيدُونَ أَن يَتَحَاكَمُوا إِلَى الطَّاغُوتِ﴾. فقال: يا أبا محمّد، إنّه لوكان لك على رجلٍ حقّ، فدعوته إلى حُكّام أهل العدل، فأبى عليك إلاّ أن يرافعك إلى حُكّام أهل الجَور ليقضوا له، كان ممّن حاكَمَ إلى الطاغوت.

183. From Manṣūr b. [Yūnus] Buzurj[32], from whoever narrated it to him from Abū Jaʿfar عليه السلام regarding the verse: ﴾*If disaster strikes them because of what they themselves have done* [...]﴿ He said, 'By God, the corrupt people will cause even the land by the basin to collapse.' There is a similar report from Jābir from Abū Jaʿfar عليه السلام. [4:62]

184. From ʿAbd Allāh [b.] al-Najāshī[33] who said, 'I heard Abū ʿAbd Allāh عليه السلام say: ﴾*God knows well what is in the hearts of these people, so ignore what they say, instruct them, and speak to them about themselves using penetrating words.*﴿ (4:63) By God, this refers to those two [i.e. Abū Bakr and ʿUmar]; ﴾*All the messengers We sent were meant to be obeyed, by God's leave. If only [the hypocrites] had come to you [Prophet] when they wronged themselves, and begged God's forgiveness, and the Messenger had asked forgiveness for them, they would have found that God accepts repentance and is most merciful*﴿ (4:65) By God, this refers to the Prophet and ʿAlī, for what they had done, i.e. had they come to you with it, O ʿAlī, and asked forgiveness for what they had done, ﴾*and the Messenger had asked forgiveness for them, they would have found that God accepts repentance and is most merciful. But no! By your Lord, they will not be true believers until they let you decide between them in all matters of dispute.*﴿ (4:65)'

Then Abū ʿAbd Allāh said, 'By God, this is exactly ʿAlī, ﴾*and find no resistance in their souls to your decisions*﴿ (4:65) – said by your very mouth, O Messenger of God, by which he meant the divinely appointed authority of ʿAlī, ﴾*accepting*﴿ ʿAlī b. Abī Ṭālib عليه السلام ﴾*totally* [...]﴿' [4:63–65]

185. From Muḥammad b. ʿAlī, from Abū Junāda al-Ḥuṣayn b. al-Mukhāriq b. ʿAbd al-Raḥmān, from Warqāʾ b. Ḥubshī b. Junāda al-Salūlī from the first Abū al-Ḥasan on his father's authority: ﴾*God knows well what is in the hearts of these*

---

32 Abū Yaḥyā Manṣūr b. Yūnus Buzurj, though Wāqifī, was a narrator of the sixth and seventh Imams. His reliability is disputed among the scholars of *rijāl*. Al-ʿAllāmah al-Ḥillī prefers to suspend judgement on him. See Ḥillī, *Khulāṣat al-aqwāl*, 408 (nr. 1650); Modarressi, *Tradition and Survival*, 318–9 (nr. 136).

33 Abū Bujayr ʿAbd Allāh b. al-Najāshī, originally of Zaydī persuasion, later converted his allegiance to Imam Jaʿfar al-Ṣādiq with whom he had an exchange of correspondences. His reliability as a trustworthy narrator is unestablished among *rijāl* scholars. See Ḥillī, *Khulāṣat al-aqwāl*, 197–8 (nr. 615).

١٨٣ . عن منصور بن بُزُرْج، عمّن حدّثه، عن أبي جعفر عليه السلام، في قوله تعالى: ﴿فَكَيْفَ إِذَا أَصَابَتْهُم مُّصِيبَةٌ بِمَا قَدَّمَتْ أَيْدِيهِمْ﴾، قال: الخَسْفُ والله عند الحوض بالفاسقين.

عن جابر، عن أبي جعفر عليه السلام مثله.

١٨٤ . عن عبدالله النجاشي، قال: سَمِعتُ أبا عبدالله عليه السلام يقول: ﴿أُولَٰئِكَ الَّذِينَ يَعْلَمُ اللَّهُ مَا فِي قُلُوبِهِمْ فَأَعْرِضْ عَنْهُمْ وَعِظْهُمْ وَقُل لَّهُمْ فِي أَنفُسِهِمْ قَوْلًا بَلِيغًا﴾ يعني والله فلانًا وفلانًا ﴿وَمَا أَرْسَلْنَا مِن رَّسُولٍ إِلَّا لِيُطَاعَ بِإِذْنِ اللَّهِ﴾ إلى قوله: ﴿تَوَّابًا رَّحِيمًا﴾ يعني والله النبي صلى الله عليه وآله وعليًّا بما صنعوا، أي لو جاءوك بها يا عليّ فاستغفروا ممّا صنعوا ﴿وَاسْتَغْفَرَ لَهُمُ الرَّسُولُ لَوَجَدُوا اللَّهَ تَوَّابًا رَّحِيمًا ۝ فَلَا وَرَبِّكَ لَا يُؤْمِنُونَ حَتَّىٰ يُحَكِّمُوكَ فِيمَا شَجَرَ بَيْنَهُمْ﴾.

ثمّ قال أبو عبدالله عليه السلام: هو والله عليّ عليه السلام بعينه ﴿ثُمَّ لَا يَجِدُوا فِي أَنفُسِهِمْ حَرَجًا مِّمَّا قَضَيْتَ﴾ على لسانك يا رسول الله، يعني به ولاية عليّ عليه السلام ﴿وَيُسَلِّمُوا تَسْلِيمًا﴾ لعليّ بن أبي طالب عليه السلام.

١٨٥ . عن محمّد بن عليّ، عن أبي جُنادة الحُصين بن المُخارق بن عبد الرحمن بن ورقاء بن حُبشي بن جُنادة السَّلُولي، عن أبي الحسن الأوّل، عن أبيه عليه السلام ﴿أُولَٰئِكَ الَّذِينَ يَعْلَمُ اللَّهُ مَا فِي قُلُوبِهِمْ فَأَعْرِضْ عَنْهُمْ﴾ فقد سبقت عليم كلمة الشقاوة، وسبق لهم العذاب ﴿وَقُل لَّهُمْ فِي أَنفُسِهِمْ قَوْلًا بَلِيغًا﴾.

people, so ignore what they say ﴿ – for they have already been told about their wretchedness and the chastisement, ﴾ *and speak to them about themselves using penetrating words.* ﴿' [4:63]

186. From 'Abd Allāh b. Yaḥyā al-Kāhilī[34], from Abū 'Abd Allāh عليه السلام. He said, 'I heard him say, "By God, if people were to worship God alone without any partners, establish the prayer, pay the alms, go for Hajj to the House, fast in the month of Ramadan but were not accepting of us, they would in fact be polytheists (*mushrikīn*) as a result of that; so it is incumbent upon them to accept.

And if people were to worship God, establish the prayer, pay the alms, go for Hajj, fast in Ramadan, and then say of something that the Messenger of God had done: 'If only he had done it this way instead of how he went about it,' they too would be polytheists as a result of that.

And if people were to worship God alone, then say of something that the Messenger of God ﷺ had done: 'Why has he done it this way?' and rejected it inside themselves, they would be polytheists as a result of that. Then he recited: ﴾ *But no! By your Lord, they will not be true believers until they let you decide between them in all matters of dispute, and find no resistance in their souls to your decisions, accepting them totally.* ﴿' [4:65]

187. From Abū Baṣīr, from Abū 'Abd Allāh عليه السلام: ﴾ *and find no resistance in their souls to your decisions, accepting them totally.* ﴿'[35] [4:65]

188. From Jābir, from Abū Ja'far عليه السلام: ﴾ *But no! By your Lord, they will not be true believers until they let you decide between them in all matters of dispute, and*

34 Abū Muḥammad 'Abd Allāh b. Yaḥyā al-Kāhilī, a highly praised and reliable companion of the sixth and seventh Imams. He was a leading affiliate of Imam Mūsā al-Kāẓim and a close companion of 'Alī b. Yaqṭīn. See Ḥillī, *Khulāṣat al-aqwāl*, 198 (nr. 616); Modarressi, *Tradition and Survival*, 162–3 (nr. 18).

35 There is clearly something missing from this narration and the one following it, even though this is how the sources quote it. Majlisī in *Biḥār al-anwār* quotes it from Kulaynī's *al-Kāfī* with a chain of transmission from Abū Baṣīr, from Abū 'Abd Allāh saying, ﴾ *and find no resistance in their souls to your decisions* ﴿ regarding the issue of the divinely appointed authority, ﴾ *accepting them totally* ﴿ in obedience to God.' See Majlisī, *Biḥār al-anwār*, 23:302 (*Kitāb al-imāma, abwāb al-āyāt al-nāzila fīhim*, ch. 17, nr. 59).

١٨٦. عن عبدالله بن يحيى الكاهلي، عن أبي عبدالله عليه السلام، قال: سمِعتُه يقول: والله لو أنَّ قومًا عبدوا الله وحده لا شريك له، وأقاموا الصلاة، وآتوا الزكاة، وحجّوا البيت، وصاموا رمضان، ثمّ لم يسلمّوا إلينا، لكانوا بذلك مشركين، فعليهم بالتسليم.

ولو أنَّ قومًا عبدوا الله، وأقاموا الصلاة وآتوا الزكاة، وحجّوا البيت، وصاموا رمضان، ثمّ قالوا لشيءٍ صنعه رسول الله صلى الله عليه وآله وسلم: لو صنع كذا وكذا، خلاف الذي صنع، لكانوا بذلك مشركين.

ولو أنَّ قومًا عبدوا الله ووَحَّدوه، ثمّ قالوا لشيءٍ صنعه رسول الله صلى الله عليه وآله وسلم: لِمَ صنع كذا وكذا، ووجدوا ذلك في أنفسهم، لكانوا بذلك مشركين، ثمّ قرأ ﴿فَلَا وَرَبِّكَ لَا يُؤْمِنُونَ حَتَّىٰ يُحَكِّمُوكَ فِيمَا شَجَرَ بَيْنَهُمْ﴾ إلى قوله: ﴿يُسَلِّمُوا تَسْلِيمًا﴾..

١٨٧. عن أبي بصير، عن أبي عبدالله عليه السلام ﴿ثُمَّ لَا يَجِدُوا فِي أَنفُسِهِمْ حَرَجًا مِّمَّا قَضَيْتَ وَيُسَلِّمُوا تَسْلِيمًا﴾.

١٨٨. عن جابر، عن أبي جعفر عليه السلام ﴿فَلَا وَرَبِّكَ لَا يُؤْمِنُونَ حَتَّىٰ يُحَكِّمُوكَ فِيمَا شَجَرَ بَيْنَهُمْ ولا يَجِدُوا فِي أَنفُسِهِمْ حَرَجًا مِّمَّا قضى محمّد وآل محمّد عليهم السلام وَيُسَلِّمُوا تَسْلِيمًا﴾.

find no resistance in their souls to the decisions of Muḥammad and his household, accepting them totally. ﴾' [4:65]

189. From Ayyūb b. al-Ḥurr who said, 'I heard Abū 'Abd Allāh state regarding His verse: ﴿*But no! By your Lord, they will not be true believers until they let you decide between them in all matters of dispute, and find no resistance in their souls to your decisions, accepting them totally*﴾, swearing three consecutive oaths – "They cannot be thus [i.e. true believers] as long as that black dot remains in the heart, even if one fasted and prayed."' [4:65]

190. From Abū Baṣīr, from Abū 'Abd Allāh ﷺ: '﴿*If We had ordered, 'Lay down your lives'*﴾ for the Imam willingly, ﴿*or 'Leave your homes'*﴾ with pleasure for his sake, ﴿*they would not have done so, except for a few.*﴾ ﴿*If they*﴾ – the opponents – ﴿*had done as they were told,*﴾ i.e. with respect to 'Alī, ﴿*it would have been far better for them.*﴾' [4:66]

191. From 'Abd Allāh b. Jundab[36], from al-Riḍā ﷺ who said, 'God must rightfully make our guardian (*walī*) a companion of the messengers, the truthful ones, those who bear witness to the truth and the righteous ones, and what excellent companions these are.' [4:69]

192. From Abū Baṣīr who said, 'Abū 'Abd Allāh ﷺ said, "O Muḥammad, God has mentioned you all in His Book saying: ﴿*They will be among those He has blessed: the messengers, the truthful, those who bear witness to the truth, and the righteous – what excellent companions these are!*﴾ So the Messenger of God ﷺ in this context is the prophet, we are the truthful ones who bear witness to the truth, and you are the righteous ones, characterized by righteousness as God has termed you."' [4:69]

193. From Sulaymān b. Khālid, from Abū 'Abd Allāh ﷺ: '﴿*You who believe*﴾ – He called them believers, without any merit (and they were not really believers). He said: ﴿*You who believe, be on your guard. March* [*to battle*] *in small groups or as one body. Among you there is the sort of person who is sure to*

36 'Abd Allāh b. Jundab al-Bajalī, a reliable companion of the seventh and eighth Imams. See Ḥillī, *Khulāṣat al-aqwāl*, 193 (nr. 601).

١٨٩. عن أيّوب بن الحرّ، قال: سَمِعتُ أبا عبدالله عليه السلام يقول: في قوله تعالى: ﴿فَلَا وَرَبِّكَ لَا يُؤْمِنُونَ حَتَّىٰ يُحَكِّمُوكَ فِيمَا شَجَرَ بَيْنَهُمْ﴾ إلى ﴿يُسَلِّمُوا تَسْلِيمًا﴾ فحلف ثلاثة أيمان متتابعًا، لا يكون ذلك حتّى تكون تلك النُّكتة السوداء في القلب، وإن صام وصلّى.

١٩٠. عن أبي بصير، عن أبي عبدالله عليه السلام ﴿وَلَوْ أَنَّا كَتَبْنَا عَلَيْهِمْ أَنِ اقْتُلُوا أَنفُسَكُمْ﴾ وسلّموا للإمام تسليمًا ﴿أَوِ اخْرُجُوا مِن دِيَارِكُم﴾ رضًا له ﴿مَّا فَعَلُوهُ إِلَّا قَلِيلٌ مِّنْهُمْ وَلَوْ﴾ أنّ أهل الخلاف ﴿فَعَلُوا مَا يُوعَظُونَ بِهِ لَكَانَ خَيْرًا لَّهُمْ﴾ يعني في عليّ.

١٩١. عن عبدالله بن جُندب، عن الرضا عليه السلام، قال: حقّ على الله أن يجعل وليّنا رفيقًا للنبيّين والصدّيقين والشُّهداء والصالحين وحسن أولئك رفيقًا.

١٩٢. عن أبي بصير، قال: قال أبو عبدالله عليه السلام: يا أبا محمّد، لقد ذكركم الله في كتابه فقال: ﴿فَأُولَٰئِكَ مَعَ الَّذِينَ أَنْعَمَ اللَّهُ عَلَيْهِم مِّنَ النَّبِيِّينَ وَالصِّدِّيقِينَ وَالشُّهَدَاءِ وَالصَّالِحِينَ﴾ الآية، فرسول الله صلى الله عليه وآله في هذا الموضوع النبيّ، ونحن الصدّيقون والشُّهداء، وأنتم الصالحون، فتسمّوا بالصّلاح كما سمّاكم الله.

١٩٣. عن سليمان بن خالد، عن أبي عبدالله عليه السلام ﴿يَا أَيُّهَا الَّذِينَ آمَنُوا﴾ فسمّاهم مُؤمنين وليسوا هم بمؤمنين ولا كرامة، قال: ﴿يَا أَيُّهَا الَّذِينَ آمَنُوا خُذُوا حِذْرَكُمْ فَانفِرُوا ثُبَاتٍ أَوِ انفِرُوا جَمِيعًا﴾ إلى قوله: ﴿فَأَفُوزَ فَوْزًا عَظِيمًا﴾ ولو أنّ أهل السماء والأرض قالوا: قد أنعم

lag behind: if a calamity befalls you, he says, 'God has been gracious to me that I was not there with them,' yet he is sure to say, if you are favoured by God, 'If only I had been with them, I could have made great gains'﴿, and if anyone from the inhabitants of the heavens and the earth were ever to say "God has been gracious to me that I was not with the Messenger of God," they would indeed be polytheists as a result; and when they are favoured by God, he says, "If only I had been with them, I would have fought in the way of God."' [4:71–73]

194. From Sa'īd b. al-Musayyab[37], from 'Alī b. al-Ḥusayn عليه السلام who said, 'Khadīja died a year before the migration (*hijra*) and Abū Ṭālib died a year after Khadīja's passing; so when the Messenger of God ﷺ had lost them both residing in Mecca became unbearable for him, and he was overcome by severe grief, fearing for himself at the hands of the disbelievers of the Quraysh. So he complained to Jibra'īl about that, and God revealed to him: "O Muḥammad, leave this town whose people are oppressors and migrate to Medina, for you no longer have any supporter left in Mecca, and declare war on the polytheists." Thereupon the Messenger of God ﷺ made his way to Medina.' [4:75]

195. From Ḥumrān, from Abū Ja'far عليه السلام who said regarding the verse: ﴾*the oppressed men, women, and children who cry out, 'Lord, rescue us from this town whose people are oppressors! By Your grace, give us a protector and give us a helper!'*﴿ 'That is us.' [4:75]

196. From Samā'a who said, 'I asked Abū 'Abd Allāh عليه السلام about the ﴾*oppressed ones.*﴿ He said, "They are the people under the care of guardianship." I asked, "Which guardianship do you mean?" He replied, "Not the [Divine] guardianship, but in marital relations, inheritance, and societal interactions. They are neither believers nor disbelievers, and among them are those who are left to God's discretion. As for His verse: ﴾*the oppressed men, women, and children who cry out, 'Lord, rescue us from this town whose people are oppressors! By Your grace, give us a protector and give us a helper!'*﴿ – that is us."' [4:75]

---

37 Sa'īd b. al-Musayyab, about whom there is no seeming consensus regarding his reliability as a narrator of the Imams' traditions, is said to have been a close disciple of Imam 'Alī b. al-Ḥusayn. See Ḥillī, *Khulāṣat al-aqwāl*, 156–7 (nr. 453).

اللهِ عليَّ إذ لم أكُن مع رسول الله ﷺ، لكانوا بذلك مشركين، وإذا أصابَهُم فَضْلٌ مِنَ اللهِ، قال: يا ليتني كنتُ معهم فأُقاتل في سبيل الله.

١٩٤. عن سعيد بن المسيّب، عن عليّ بن الحسين عليهما السلام، قال: كانت خديجة ماتت قبل الهجرة بسنة، ومات أبو طالب بعد موت خديجة بسنة، فلمّا فقدهما رسول الله ﷺ شنأ المقام بمكّة، ودخله حزنٌ شديدٌ، وأشفق على نفسه من كُفّار قريش، فشكا إلى جَبْرَئيل ذلك، فأوحى الله إليه: يا محمّد، اخرُج من القرية الظالم أهلها، وهاجر إلى المدينة، فليس لك اليوم بمكّة ناصر، وانصب للمشركين حربًا؛ فعند ذلك توجّه رسول الله ﷺ إلى المدينة.

١٩٥. عن حُمران، عن أبي جعفر عليه السلام، قال: ﴿الْمُسْتَضْعَفِينَ مِنَ الرِّجَالِ وَالنِّسَاءِ وَالْوِلْدَانِ الَّذِينَ يَقُولُونَ رَبَّنَا أَخْرِجْنَا مِنْ هَٰذِهِ الْقَرْيَةِ الظَّالِمِ أَهْلُهَا﴾ إلى: ﴿نَصِيرًا﴾ قال: نحن أولئك.

١٩٦. عن سَماعة، قال: سألتُ أبا عبدالله عليه السلام عن المستضعفين؟ قال: هم أهل الولاية. قلت: أيّ ولاية تعني؟ قال: ليست ولاية، ولكنّها في المناكحة والمواريث والمخالطة، وهم ليسوا بالمؤمنين ولا الكفّار، ومنهم المُرْجَون لأمر الله، فأمّا قوله: ﴿وَالْمُسْتَضْعَفِينَ .. الَّذِينَ يَقُولُونَ رَبَّنَا أَخْرِجْنَا﴾ إلى ﴿نَصِيرًا﴾ فأولئك نحن.

197. From Idrīs, a protégé of ʿAbd Allāh b. Jaʿfar, from Abū ʿAbd Allāh عليه السلام who said, interpreting this verse: '﴾ *[Prophet], do you not see those who were told, 'Restrain yourselves from fighting'* ﴿ with al-Ḥasan, ﴾ *and perform the prayer? So when fighting was ordained for them* ﴿ with al-Ḥusayn, they said: ﴾ *'Lord, why have You ordained fighting for us? If only You would give us just a little more time',* ﴿ until the reappearance of the Qā'im عليه السلام, for surely victory and triumph will come with him. God said: ﴾ *'Little is the enjoyment in this world, the Hereafter is far better for those who are mindful of God: you will not be wronged by as much as the fibre in a date stone.'* ﴿' [4:77]

198. From Muḥammad b. Muslim, from Abū Jaʿfar عليه السلام who said, 'By God, what al-Ḥasan b. ʿAlī عليه السلام did was better for this community than everything that the sun shines on. By God, it is about him that this verse was revealed: ﴾ *[Prophet], do you not see those who were told, 'Restrain yourselves from fighting, perform the prayer, and pay the prescribed alms.'* ﴿ They are supposed to obey the Imam, when instead they sought to fight, ﴾ *and when fighting was ordained for them* ﴿ alongside al-Ḥusayn ﴾ *they said, 'Lord, why have You ordained fighting for us? If only You would give us just a little more time'* ﴿, and His verse: ﴾ *Our Lord, give us a little more time: we shall answer Your call and follow the messengers* ﴿(14:44) – they wanted to delay it until the time of the Qā'im عليه السلام.' [4:77]

199. Al-Ḥalabī narrated on his authority: he عليه السلام said, '﴾ *Restrain yourselves* ﴿ means [restrain] your tongues.' [4:77]

200. In a narration by al-Ḥasan b. Ziyād al-ʿAṭṭār, from Abū ʿAbd Allāh عليه السلام who said regarding His statement: ﴾ *Restrain yourselves from fighting, perform the prayer* ﴿, 'This was revealed about al-Ḥasan b. ʿAlī عليه السلام whom God commanded to desist from fighting.' ﴾ *And when fighting was ordained for them* ﴿ – he said, 'This was revealed about al-Ḥusayn b. ʿAlī, for whom God ordained fighting and for all the people of the earth to fight alongside him.' [4:77]

١٩٧. عن إدريس مولى لعبدالله بن جعفر، عن أبي عبدالله عليه السلام، في تفسير هذه الآية ﴿أَلَمْ تَرَ إِلَى الَّذِينَ قِيلَ لَهُمْ كُفُّوا أَيْدِيَكُمْ﴾ مع الحسن عليه السلام ﴿وَأَقِيمُوا الصَّلَاةَ ... فَلَمَّا كُتِبَ عَلَيْهِمُ الْقِتَالُ﴾ مع الحسين عليه السلام ﴿قَالُوا رَبَّنَا لِمَ كَتَبْتَ عَلَيْنَا الْقِتَالَ لَوْلَا أَخَّرْتَنَا إِلَى أَجَلٍ قَرِيبٍ﴾ إلى خروج القائم عليه السلام، فإنّ معه النّصر والظّفر، قال الله تعالى: ﴿قُلْ مَتَاعُ الدُّنْيَا قَلِيلٌ وَالْآخِرَةُ خَيْرٌ لِمَنِ اتَّقَى﴾ الآية.

١٩٨. عن محمّد بن مسلم، عن أبي جعفر عليه السلام، قال: والله الذي صَنَعه الحسن بن علي عليهما السلام كان خيرًا لهذه الأُمة ممّا طلعت عليه الشمس، والله لفيه نزلت هذه الآية ﴿أَلَمْ تَرَ إِلَى الَّذِينَ قِيلَ لَهُمْ كُفُّوا أَيْدِيَكُمْ وَأَقِيمُوا الصَّلَاةَ وَآتُوا الزَّكَاةَ﴾ إنّما هي طاعة الإمام، فطلبوا القتال ﴿فَلَمَّا كُتِبَ عَلَيْهِمُ الْقِتَالُ﴾ مع الحسين عليه السلام ﴿قَالُوا رَبَّنَا لِمَ كَتَبْتَ عَلَيْنَا الْقِتَالَ لَوْلَا أَخَّرْتَنَا إِلَى أَجَلٍ قَرِيبٍ﴾ وقوله: ﴿رَبَّنَا أَخِّرْنَا إِلَى أَجَلٍ قَرِيبٍ نُجِبْ دَعْوَتَكَ وَنَتَّبِعِ الرُّسُلَ﴾ أرادوا تأخير ذلك إلى القائم عليه السلام.

١٩٩. الحَلَبي، عنه عليه السلام ﴿كُفُّوا أَيْدِيَكُمْ﴾ قال: يعني ألسنتكم.

٢٠٠. وفي رواية الحسن بن زياد العطّار، عن أبي عبدالله عليه السلام، في قوله تعالى: ﴿كُفُّوا أَيْدِيَكُمْ وَأَقِيمُوا الصَّلَاةَ﴾، قال: نزلت في الحسن بن عليّ عليه السلام، أمره الله بالكفّ ﴿فَلَمَّا كُتِبَ عَلَيْهِمُ الْقِتَالُ﴾ قال: نزلت في الحسين بن عليّ، كتب الله عليه وعلى أهل الأرض أن يُقاتِلوا معه.

201. From ʿAlī b. Asbāṭ who, without mentioning his source, cited Abū Jaʿfar saying, 'Were the people of the earth to have all fought alongside him, they would have killed all of them.' [4:77]

202. From Ṣafwān b. Yaḥyā, from Abū al-Ḥasan عليه السلام who said, 'God, Blessed and most High, said: "O son of Ādam, it is only by My will that you are able to will anything and to speak, and it is only by My strength that you are able to perform your duty to Me, and it is only by My bounty that you feel strong enough to transgress against Me. ﴾*Anything good that happens to you is from God; anything bad is* [*ultimately*] *from yourself*﴿, and that is because I have a greater right over your good deeds than you, whilst you have greater ownership of your sins than Me, and because I cannot be taken to task for what I do, but they will surely be taken to task."' [4:79]

203. In a narration by al-Ḥasan b. ʿAlī al-Washshāʾ, from al-Riḍā عليه السلام: 'Whilst you have greater ownership of your sins than Me, having committed wrongdoings with the strength that I bestowed upon you.' [4:79]

204. From Zurāra, from Abū Jaʿfar عليه السلام who said, 'The crux, essence, and key to the matter, the doorway to the prophets, the pleasure of the all-Merciful is obedience to the Imam after having acknowledged him.' Then he said, 'God says: ﴾*Whoever obeys the Messenger obeys God. If some pay no heed, We have not sent you to be their keeper.*﴿ Indeed, if a man were to pray the whole night, fast during the day, give away all his wealth in charity and go for Hajj his whole life without acknowledging the authority of God's vicegerent, then God would not be obliged to reward him, and nor is he considered to be from among the people of faith.' Then he said, 'It is only by His grace and mercy that God will give the good-doer from among such people admission into Paradise.' [4:80]

٢٠١. عن علي بن أسباط، يرفعه عن أبي جعفر ﷺ، قال: لو قاتل معه أهل الأرض، لقُتِلوا كُلّهم.

٢٠٢. عن صَفوان بن يحيى، عن أبي الحسن ﷺ، قال: قال الله تبارك وتعالى: يا ابن آدم، بمشيّتي كنتَ أنت الذي تشاء وتقول، وبقوّتي أدّيتَ إليّ فريضتي، وبنعمتي قَوِيتَ على معصيتي ﴿مَا أَصَابَكَ مِنْ حَسَنَةٍ فَمِنَ اللَّهِ وَمَا أَصَابَكَ مِن سَيِّئَةٍ فَمِن نَّفْسِكَ﴾ وذاك أنّي أولى بحسناتك منك، وأنت أولى بسيّئاتك منّي، وذاك أنّي لا أسأل عمّا أفعل وهم يُسألون.

٢٠٣. وفي رواية الحسن بن علي الوشّاء، عن الرضا ﷺ: وأنت أولى بسيّئاتك منّي، عَمِلتَ المعاصي بقوّتي التي جعلت فيك.

٢٠٤. عن زُرارة، عن أبي جعفر ﷺ، قال: ذَروة الأمر وسَنامه ومِفتاحه، وباب الأنبياء، ورضا الرحمن، الطاعة للإمام بعد معرفته.

ثمّ قال: إنّ الله تعالى يقول: ﴿مَن يُطِعِ الرَّسُولَ فَقَدْ أَطَاعَ اللَّهَ﴾ إلى ﴿حَفِيظًا﴾ أما لو أنّ رجلاً قام ليله، وصام نهاره، وتصدّق بجميع ماله، وحجّ جميع دهره، ولم يعرِف ولايةَ وليّ الله فيواليه، ويكون جميع أعماله بولاية منه إليه، ما كان الله حقّ في ثوابه، ولا كان من أهل الإيمان.

ثمّ قال: أُولئك، المُحسِن منهم يُدْخِله الله بفضله ورحمته.

205. From Abū Isḥāq al-Naḥwī[38] who said, 'I heard Abū 'Abd Allāh عليه السلام say, "God nurtured His Prophet on His love, and said: ﴾ *Truly you have a strong character;* ﴿ then He accorded him the power to command saying: ﴾ *so accept whatever the Messenger gives you, and abstain from whatever he forbids you,* ﴿ (59:7) and He said: ﴾ *Whoever obeys the Messenger obeys God.* ﴿ (4:80) And the Messenger of God, peace be upon him and his family, accorded to 'Alī عليه السلام the power to command, trusting him fully. Now you have accepted whilst other people reject, so by God, we like for you to speak out when we speak out, and to remain quiet when we remain quiet. By God, when it comes to matters between you and God, He has not ordained any goodness for one who opposes our command therein."' [4:80]

206. From Muḥammad b. 'Ajalān who said, 'I heard him say, "God reproached the people for spreading things about, saying: ﴾ *Whenever news of any matter comes to them, whether concerning peace or war, they spread it about* ﴿, so beware of spreading things."' [4:83]

207. From 'Abd Allāh b. 'Ajalān, from Abū Ja'far عليه السلام who said regarding the verse: ﴾ *if they referred it to the Messenger and those in authority among them* ﴿, 'They are the Imams.' [4:83]

208. From 'Abd Allāh b. Jundab who said, 'Abū al-Ḥasan al-Riḍā عليه السلام wrote to me saying: "You mentioned – may God bless you – these people whom you describe as having been brothers to you yesterday, and the dispute that has now resulted in their opposition and enmity towards you, as well as their disassociation from you; and those who twisted the truth from the time of my father, God's peace and blessings be upon him."

Then at the end of the letter he mentioned that Shayṭān had insinuated ideas into these people, beguiled them with controversy and obscured matters of their religion. And that was when their calumny became manifest, their doctrines happened to clash, and they lied about their own teacher,

38 Abū Isḥāq Tha'laba b. Maymūn al-Naḥwī, protégé of the Banū Asad and later Banū Salāma, was a prominent figure of the Shī'ī community in his time. A respected and renowned reciter of the Qur'an, *faqīh* and linguist known for his asceticism and devotion, he was one of the leading companions of Imam Ja'far al-Ṣādiq and Imam Mūsā al-Kāẓim. See Ḥillī, *Khulāṣat al-aqwāl*, 86–7 (nr. 181); Modarressi, *Tradition and Survival*, 380 (nr. 203).

٢٠٥. عن أبي إسحاق النحوي، قال: سَمِعتُ أبا عبد الله عليه السلام يقول: إنّ الله أدّب نبيّه صلى الله عليه وآله على محبّته فقال: ﴿إِنَّكَ لَعَلَىٰ خُلُقٍ عَظِيمٍ﴾. قال: ثمّ فوّض إليه الأمر فقال: ﴿مَا آتَاكُمُ الرَّسُولُ فَخُذُوهُ وَمَا نَهَاكُمْ عَنْهُ فَانْتَهُوا﴾ وقال: ﴿مَنْ يُطِعِ الرَّسُولَ فَقَدْ أَطَاعَ اللَّهَ﴾. وإنّ رسول الله عليه وآله السلام فوّض إلى عليّ عليه السلام وائتمنه، فسلّمتم وجحد الناس، فوالله لنُحبّكم أن تقولوا إذا قلنا، وأن تَصْمُتوا إذا صَمَتنا، ونحن فيما بينكم وبين الله، والله ما جعل لأحدٍ من خيرٍ في خلاف أمره.

٢٠٦. عن محمّد بن عجلان، قال: سَمِعتُه يقول: إنّ الله عيّر قومًا بالإذاعة، فقال: ﴿وَإِذَا جَاءَهُمْ أَمْرٌ مِنَ الْأَمْنِ أَوِ الْخَوْفِ أَذَاعُوا بِهِ﴾ فإيّاكم والإذاعة.

٢٠٧. عن عبد الله بن عجلان، عن أبي جعفر عليه السلام، في قوله تعالى: ﴿وَلَوْ رَدُّوهُ إِلَى الرَّسُولِ وَإِلَىٰ أُولِي الْأَمْرِ مِنْهُمْ﴾، قال: هم الأئمّة عليهم السلام.

٢٠٨. عن عبد الله بن جُندب، قال: كتب إليّ أبو الحسن الرضا عليه السلام: ذكرت رحمك الله هؤلاء القوم الذين وصفت أنّهم كانوا بالأمس لكم إخوانًا، والّذي صاروا إليه من الخِلاف لكم، والعَداوة لكم، والبَراءة منكم، والذين تأفّكوا به من حياة أبي صلوات الله عليه ورحمته.

وذَكَر في آخر الكتاب: أنّ هؤلاء القوم سَنَح لهم شيطان، اغترّهم بالشُّبهة، ولَبّس عليهم أمر دينهم، وذلك لمّا ظهرت فِريتهم، واتّفقت كلمتهم، وكذبوا على عالمهم، وأرادوا الهُدى من تِلقاء أنفسهم، فقالوا لِمَ، ومن، وكيف، فأتاهم الهُلك من مأمن احتياطهم، وذلك بما كسبت أيديهم وما ربُّك بظلاّم للعبيد، ولم يَكُن ذلك لهم ولا عليهم، بل كان

now wanting to give guidance from their sentiments, and questioning: why and who and how? So ruin came to them from the very safety net of their cautious ways, brought upon themselves as a result of their deeds – and your Lord is never unjust to His servants. This was neither in their favour nor against them. Rather the duty incumbent and mandatory upon them was to halt in the face of confusion and to refer all that they were ignorant of back to their teacher and the one who could seek out its meaning, because God says in the decisive verses of His Book: ﴾*if they referred it to the Messenger and those in authority among them, those seeking its meaning would have found it out from them*﴿ – meaning the family of Muḥammad, for they are the ones who extrapolate the meanings of the Qur'an and know the permissible and the prohibited, and they are the proofs of God over His creation.' [4:83]

209. From Zurāra, from Abū Ja'far عليه السلام (and Ḥumrān, from Abū 'Abd Allāh عليه السلام) regarding the verse of God, most High: ﴾*were it not for God's bounty and mercy towards you*﴿, he said, 'God's bounty is His Messenger, and His mercy is the divinely mandated authority of the Imams, peace be upon them.' [4:83]

210. From Muḥammad b. al-Fuḍayl, from Abū al-Ḥasan عليه السلام regarding the verse: ﴾*were it not for God's bounty and mercy towards you*﴿ he said, 'The bounty is the Messenger of God, peace be upon him and his family, and His mercy is the Commander of the Faithful عليه السلام.' [4:83]

211. From Muḥammad b. al-Fuḍayl, from the righteous servant [i.e. Imam Mūsā al-Kāẓim] who said, 'The mercy is the Messenger of God, peace be upon him and his family, and the bounty is 'Alī b. Abī Ṭālib.' [4:83]

212. From Ibn Muskān, from whoever narrated it from Abū 'Abd Allāh عليه السلام with respect to God's verse: ﴾*were it not for God's bounty and mercy towards you, you would almost all have followed Satan*﴿, so Abū 'Abd Allāh عليه السلام said, 'You are indeed asking about the stance on pre-destination, and this is neither my doctrine nor that of my forefathers, nor have I found any of the Ahl al-Bayt opining thus.' [4:83]

الفرض عليهم، والواجب لهم من ذلك الوقوف عند التحيّر، وردّ ما جَهِلوه من ذلك إلى عالمه ومستنبطه، لأنّ الله يقول في محكم كتابه: ﴿وَلَوْ رَدُّوهُ إِلَى الرَّسُولِ وَإِلَى أُوْلِي الأَمْرِ مِنْهُمْ لَعَلِمَهُ الَّذِينَ يَسْتَنْبِطُونَهُ مِنْهُمْ﴾ يعني آل محمّد، وهم الذين يستنبطون من القرآن، ويَعْرِفون الحلال والحرام، وهم الحجّة لله على خلقه.

٢٠٩. عن زُرارة، عن أبي جعفر عليه السلام وحُمران، عن أبي عبدالله عليه السلام، في قوله تعالى: ﴿لَوْلا فَضْلُ اللهِ عَلَيْكُمْ وَرَحْمَتُهُ﴾، قال: فضل الله: رسوله، ورحمته: ولاية الأئمّة عليهم السلام.

٢١٠. عن محمّد بن الفضيل، عن أبي الحسن عليه السلام، في قوله: ﴿وَلَوْلا فَضْلُ اللهِ عَلَيْكُمْ وَرَحْمَتُهُ﴾، قال: الفضل: رسول الله عليه وآله السلام، ورحمته: أمير المؤمنين عليه السلام.

٢١١. ومحمّد بن الفضيل، عن العبد الصالح عليه السلام، قال: الرحمة: رسول الله عليه وآله السلام، والفضل: عليّ بن أبي طالب عليه السلام.

٢١٢. عن ابن مُسكان، عمَّن رواه، عن أبي عبدالله عليه السلام، في قول الله تعالى: ﴿وَلَوْلا فَضْلُ اللهِ عَلَيْكُمْ وَرَحْمَتُهُ لاتَّبَعْتُمُ الشَّيْطَانَ إِلاَّ قَلِيلاً﴾، فقال أبو عبدالله عليه السلام: إنّك لتسأل عن كلام القَدَر وما هو من ديني، ولا دين آبائي، ولا وجدتُ أحدًا من أهل بيتي يقول به.

213. From Sulaymān b. Khālid who said, 'I asked Abū 'Abd Allāh عليه السلام about people asking 'Alī that if the right was indeed his, what was preventing him from fighting for it?

He replied, "God does not task any one person to do thus apart from the Messenger of God ﷺ. He said: ﴾*So [Prophet] fight in God's way. You are accountable only for yourself. Urge the believers on.*﴿ This [command] is for none other than the Messenger; to people other than him, it is: ﴾*unless manoeuvring to fight or to join a fighting group*﴿(8:16) – and there was no such fighting group to help him achieve his cause on that day.﴿' [4:84]

214. From Zayd al-Shaḥḥām, from Ja'far b. Muḥammad عليه السلام who said, 'Never did the Messenger of God ﷺ say no when he was asked for something. If he had it, he would give it, and if he did not, he would say, "It will come, if God wills." And he never concurred with wrongdoing. Since the verse: ﴾*So [Prophet] fight in God's way. You are accountable only for yourself*﴿ was revealed, he never dispatched a troop out but rather preferred [to fight] himself.' [4:84]

215. From Abān, from Abū 'Abd Allāh عليه السلام regarding the revelation of: ﴾*You are accountable only for yourself*﴿ to the Messenger of God ﷺ, he said, 'It was only the most courageous of people who sought refuge in the Messenger of God ﷺ.' [4:84]

216. From al-Thumālī, from 'Īṣ, from Abū 'Abd Allāh عليه السلام, 'The Messenger of God ﷺ said, "He tasked me with that which no one has been tasked with previously – to fight in the way of God alone, and he said: ﴾*Urge the believers to fight*﴿, and he said, 'Indeed you have been given the easy task of remembering God.'" [4:84]

217. From Ibrāhīm b. Mihzam[39], on his father's authority from a man from Abū Ja'far عليه السلام who said, 'Each person has an internal greed avid for evil, so keep away from it and God will suffice you as a people, and keep others away

39 Ibrāhīm b. Mihzam al-Asadī, better known as Ibn Abī Burda, is regarded as having been a very reliable companion and narrator of the sixth and seventh Imams. See Ḥillī, *Khulāṣat al-aqwāl*, 51 (nr. 19); Modarressi, *Tradition and Survival*, 286 (nr. 103).

٢١٣. عن سُليمان بن خالد، قال: قلتُ لأبي عبد الله عليه السلام: قول الناس لعليّ عليه السلام: إن كان له حقّ فما منعه أن يقوم به؟

قال: فقال: إنّ الله لم يكلّف هذا إلاّ إنسانًا واحدًا رسول الله صلى الله عليه وآله، قال: ﴿فَقَاتِلْ فِي سَبِيلِ اللَّهِ لَا تُكَلَّفُ إِلَّا نَفْسَكَ وَحَرِّضِ الْمُؤْمِنِينَ﴾ فليس هذا إلاّ للرّسول، وقال لغيره: ﴿إِلَّا مُتَحَرِّفًا لِقِتَالٍ أَوْ مُتَحَيِّزًا إِلَىٰ فِئَةٍ﴾ فلم يكن يومئذٍ فئةٌ يُعينونه على أمره.

٢١٤. عن زيد الشحّام، عن جعفر بن محمّد عليهما السلام، قال: ما سُئِل رسول الله عليه وآله السلام شيئًا قَطّ فقال لا، إن كان عنده أعطاه، وإن لم يكُن عنده قال: يكون إن شاء الله، ولا كافأ بالسيئة قطُّ، وما لقي سَرِيّة مذ نزلت عليه ﴿فَقَاتِلْ فِي سَبِيلِ اللَّهِ لَا تُكَلَّفُ إِلَّا نَفْسَكَ﴾ إلاّ ولي بنفسه.

٢١٥. أبان، عن أبي عبد الله عليه السلام: لمّا نزلت على رسول الله عليه وآله السلام ﴿لَا تُكَلَّفُ إِلَّا نَفْسَكَ﴾، قال: كان أشجع الناس من لاذ برسول الله صلى الله عليه وآله.

٢١٦. عن الثُّمالي، عن عيص، عن أبي عبد الله عليه السلام، قال: رسول الله صلى الله عليه وآله – كُلِّف ما لم يُكَلَّف أحدٌ – أن يُقاتل في سبيل الله وحده، وقال: ﴿حَرِّضِ الْمُؤْمِنِينَ عَلَى الْقِتَالِ﴾ وقال: إنّما كُلِّفتم اليسير من الأمر، أن تذكُروا الله.

from it too; God says: ﴾*for God is stronger in might and more terrible in punishment*﴿ – do not teach evil.' [4:84]

218. From Sayf b.'Amīra[40] who said, 'I asked Abū 'Abd Allāh عليه السلام about the verse: ﴾*from fighting against you or against their own people, God could have given them power over you, and they would have fought you.*﴿ He said, "My father used to say that it had been revealed about the tribe of Banī Mudlij who stood aloof neither fighting against the Prophet ﷺ nor siding with their own people." I then asked, "So what did he do with them?" He replied, "The Prophet ﷺ did not fight them until he had finished with his enemy, then he spurned them in the same manner. He said: ﴾*their hearts shrink*﴿ – this is distress."' [4:90]

219. From Mas'ada b. Ṣadaqa who said, 'Ja'far b. Muḥammad عليه السلام was asked about God's verse: ﴾*Never should a believer kill another believer, except by mistake. If anyone kills a believer by mistake he must free one Muslim slave and pay compensation to the victim's relatives.*﴿ (4:92) He said, "Freeing one Muslim slave is in atonement for [the sin] that is between him and God. As for paying compensation to the victim's relatives, ﴾*if the victim belonged to a people at war with you.*﴿ He continued, "Then if the victim belonged to a polytheistic people with whom they have no treaty, but he was a believer, then a believing slave should be set free, as regards [the sin] that is between him and God, and no compensation is due. And if he belonged to people with whom you have a treaty, and he was a believer, then a believing slave must be set free, in atonement for the sin that is between him and God, and compensation paid to his family."' [4:92]

220. From Ḥafṣ b. al-Bakhtarī, from whoever said it from Abū 'Abd Allāh عليه السلام, regarding the verse: ﴾*Never should a believer kill another believer, except by mistake. If anyone kills a believer by mistake he must free one Muslim slave and pay compensation to the victim's relatives, unless they charitably forgo it; if the victim belonged to a people at war with you but is a believer* [...]﴿ He said, 'If he belonged to a polytheistic people then a believing slave must be freed in

40 Sayf b. 'Amīra al-Nakha'ī, a reliable companion of the sixth and seventh Imams. See Ḥillī, *Khulāṣat al-aqwāl*, 160 (nr. 468); Modarressi, *Tradition and Survival*, 371 (nr. 192).

٢١٧ . عن إبراهيم بن مِهْزَم، عن أبيه، عن رجلٍ، عن أبي جعفر عليه السلام، قال: إنّ لكلٍ كلبًا يبغي الشّر فاجتنبوه، يُكفكم الله بغيركم، إنّ الله يقول: ﴿وَاللّهُ أَشَدُّ بَأْسًا وَأَشَدُّ تَنكِيلاً﴾ لا تعلموا بالشرّ.

٢١٨ . عن سَيف بن عَميرة، قال: سألتُ أبا عبدالله عليه السلام ﴿أَن يُقَاتِلُوكُمْ أَوْ يُقَاتِلُوا قَوْمَهُمْ وَلَوْ شَاءَ اللّهُ لَسَلَّطَهُمْ عَلَيْكُمْ فَلَقَاتَلُوكُمْ﴾، قال: كان أبي يقول: نزلت في بني مُدلج، اعتزلوا فلم يقاتلوا النبيّ صلى الله عليه وآله، ولم يكُونوا مع قومهم.

قلت: فما صنع بهم؟ قال: لم يقاتلهم النبيّ عليه وآله السلام حتى فرَغ من عدوّه، ثمّ نبذ إليهم على سَواء. قال: ﴿حَصِرَتْ صُدُورُهُمْ﴾ هو الضيّق.

٢١٩ . عن مَسْعَدة بن صَدَقة، قال: سُئِل جعفر بن محمّد عليهما السلام عن قول الله عزّ وجلّ: ﴿وَمَا كَانَ لِمُؤْمِنٍ أَن يَقْتُلَ مُؤْمِنًا إِلاَّ خَطَأً وَمَن قَتَلَ مُؤْمِنًا خَطَأً فَتَحْرِيرُ رَقَبَةٍ مُّؤْمِنَةٍ وَدِيَةٌ مُّسَلَّمَةٌ إِلَى أَهْلِهِ﴾ . قال: أمّا تحرير رقبة مؤمنة ففيما بينه وبين الله، وأمّا الدِّيَة المُسَلَّمَة إلى أولياء المقتول ﴿فَإِن كَانَ مِن قَوْمٍ عَدُوٍّ لَّكُمْ﴾ قال: وإن كان من أهل الشِّرك الذين ليس لهم في الصُّلح ﴿وَهُوَ مُؤْمِنٌ فَتَحْرِيرُ رَقَبَةٍ مُّؤْمِنَةٍ﴾ فيما بينه وبين الله، وليس عليه الدِّيَة. ﴿وَإِن كَانَ مِن قَوْمٍ بَيْنَكُمْ وَبَيْنَهُمْ مِّيثَاقٌ﴾ وهو مؤمن، فتحرير رقبة مؤمنة فيما بينه وبين الله، ودِيَة مُسلَّمة إلى أهله.

٢٢٠ . عن حَفْص بن البَخْتَري، عمَّن ذكره، عن أبي عبدالله عليه السلام، في قوله تعالى: ﴿وَمَا كَانَ لِمُؤْمِنٍ أَن يَقْتُلَ مُؤْمِنًا إِلاَّ خَطَأً﴾ إلى قوله: ﴿فَإِن كَانَ مِن قَوْمٍ عَدُوٍّ لَّكُمْ

atonement for the sin between him and God, and no compensation is due. ﴾*If he belonged to a people with whom you have a treaty, then compensation should be handed over to his relatives, and a believing slave set free.*﴿' He continued, 'He said, "Freeing a believing slave in atonement to the sin that is between him and God, and compensation handed over to his family."' [4:92]

221. From Maʿmar b. Yaḥyā[41] who said, 'I asked Abū ʿAbd Allāh عليه السلام about a man who repudiates his wife (*ẓihār*)[42] – is it permissible for him to free a new-born slave as a penalty for that? So he replied, "The new-born slave is allowed to be freed in all circumstances except as the penalty for murder, for indeed God says: ﴾*a believing slave must be set free*﴿, meaning one who has attested to faith and has reached the age of culpability."' [4:92]

222. From Kurdawayh al-Hamadānī[43], from Abū al-Ḥasan عليه السلام regarding God's verse: ﴾*a believing slave must be set free*﴿ – how is 'believing' identified? He replied, 'According to their innate disposition.' [4:92]

223. From al-Sakūnī, from Jaʿfar, on his father's authority, from ʿAlī عليه السلام who said, 'The believing slave that God mentions is someone who is in their right mind, including the slave who knows nothing other than what you have told them since childhood.' [4:92]

224. From ʿĀmir b. al-Aḥwaṣ who said, 'I asked Abū Jaʿfar عليه السلام about the emancipated slave, so he replied, "Look in the Qur'an and what there is in there about freeing a slave. This, ʿĀmir, is the emancipated slave who does not fall under the guardianship of any person save God. And whoever has God's guardianship also has the Prophet's, and whoever was under the

41 Maʿmar b. Yaḥyā b. Musāfir al-ʿIjlī, a reliable narrator of the fifth and sixth Imam's traditions. See Ḥillī, *Khulāṣat al-aqwāl*, 277 (nr. 1011); Modarressi, *Tradition and Survival*, 317 (nr. 134).

42 The pre-Islamic Arabian custom of divorce whereby a man would repudiate his wife by likening her to his mother's back, which deprived the wife of her marital rights yet prevented her from marrying again.

43 Though mentioned in several chains of narration, he is described as being unknown (*majhūl*).

وَهُوَ مُؤْمِنٌ﴾ . قال: إذا كان من أهل الشّرك ﴿فَتَحْرِيرُ رَقَبَةٍ مُؤْمِنَةٍ﴾ فيما بينه وبين الله، وليس عليه دِيَة ﴿وَإِنْ كَانَ مِنْ قَوْمٍ بَيْنَكُمْ وَبَيْنَهُمْ مِيثَاقٌ فَدِيَةٌ مُسَلَّمَةٌ إِلَى أَهْلِهِ وَتَحْرِيرُ رَقَبَةٍ مُؤْمِنَةٍ﴾ قال: قال: تحرير رقبةٍ مؤمنةٍ فيما بينه وبين الله، ودِيَة مُسَلَّمة إلى أوليائه.

٢٢١ . عن مَعْمَر بن يحيى، قال: سألتُ أبا عبدالله عليه السلام عن الرجل يُظاهر امرأته، يجوز عتق المولود في الكفّارة؟ فقال: كلّ العتق يجُوز فيه المولود إلاّ في كفّارة القتل، فإنّ الله يقول: ﴿فَتَحْرِيرُ رَقَبَةٍ مُؤْمِنَةٍ﴾ يعني مُقِرّة، وقد بَلَغَتِ الحِنْث.

٢٢٢ . عن كُرْدَوَيه الهمداني، عن أبي الحسن عليه السلام، في قول الله: ﴿فَتَحْرِيرُ رَقَبَةٍ مُؤْمِنَةٍ﴾ وكيف تُعْرَف المؤمنة؟ قال: على الفِطْرة.

٢٢٣ . عن السّكوني، عن جعفر، عن أبيه، عن علي عليهم السلام، قال: الرَّقَبة المُؤمنة الّتي ذكرها الله إذا عَقَلت، والنَّسَمة الّتي لا تعلم إلاّ ما قلته، وهي صغيرة.

٢٢٤ . عن عامر بن [أبي] الأحوص، قال: سألتُ أبا جعفر عليه السلام عن السائبة. فقال: انظُر في القرآن، فما كان فيه ﴿فَتَحْرِيرُ رَقَبَةٍ﴾ فذلك ـ يا عامر ـ السائبة الّتي لا ولاء لأحدٍ من الناس عليها إلاّ الله، فما كان ولاءه لله فلله، وما كان ولاءه لرسول الله صلى الله عليه وآله فإنّ ولاءه للإمام، وجنايته على الإمام، وميراثه له.

guardianship of the Messenger of God ﷺ is now under the Imam's, and retribution and inheritance matters will be under his jurisdiction."' [4:92]

225. From Ibn Abī 'Umayr, from one of his associates, from one of the two [Imam al-Bāqir or al-Ṣādiq] that he said, 'Retaliation is due for any crime whose objective is intentional, and the accidental crime is one that strikes other than the originally intended target.' [4:92]

226. From Zurāra, from Abū 'Abd Allāh عليه السلام who said, 'The accident is one where the victim is targeted but never intended to be killed as a result of something that would not normally cause death. And the obvious accident is one where another is mistakenly struck instead of the original target.' [4:92]

227. From 'Abd al-Raḥmān b. al-Ḥajjāj who said, 'Abū 'Abd Allāh عليه السلام asked me about Yaḥyā b. Sa'īd[44] – "Does he clash with your legal decrees?" So I replied, "Yes, two young men were fighting with each other in the public square when one of them bit the other's hand. He, in turn, took a rock and smashed the biter's hand, which became infected and frostbitten in the cold, and he died as a result. The matter was taken to Yaḥyā b. Sa'īd, who ruled against the man who killed with a rock with retaliation.

Ibn Shubrama and Ibn Abī Laylā said to 'Īsā b. Mūsā, 'This is something that would never be dealt with like this by us. He cannot be sentenced to retaliation for killing with a rock or a whip.' They maintained their stance until 'Īsā b. Mūsā charged him with compensation to pay instead." So he said, "Some of us would charge him to pay a penalty in charity."

I said, "They allege that it was an accident and that it is only considered an intentional act if he was struck with an iron object [or knife]." So he عليه السلام said, "Rather that [i.e. the accident] is when a particular target is intended, and another is struck instead. Any target, however, that you have had a motive to strike and manage to do so is intentional."' [4:92]

44 Abū Zakariyya Yaḥyā b. Sa'īd al-Qaṭṭān (d. 198/813), regarded a reliable narrator even though he was Sunnī. See Ḥillī, *Khulāṣat al-aqwāl*, 417 (nr. 1690); Modarressi, *Tradition and Survival*, 396 (nr. 221).

٢٢٥. عن ابن أبي عُمير، عن أصحابه، عن أحدهما عليهما السلام، قال: كلّ ما أُريد به ففيه القَوَد، وإنّما الخطأ أن يُريد الشيء فيُصيب غيره.

٢٢٦. عن زُرارة، عن أبي عبدالله عليه السلام، قال: الخطأ أن تَعمِده ولا تُريد قتله بما لا يقتل مثله، والخطأ الذي ليس فيه شكٌّ أن تعمِد آخر فتُصيبه.

٢٢٧. عن عبد الرّحمن بن الحجّاج، قال: سألني أبو عبدالله عليه السلام عن يحيى بن سعيد: هل يخالف قضاياكم؟ قلت: نعم، اقتتل غلامان بالرَّحبة، فعضَّ أحدهما على يد الآخر، فرفع المعضوض حجراً فشَجَّ يد العاضِّ، فكَزَّ من البرد فمات، ورُفع إلى يحيى بن سعيد فأقاد من الضارب بحَجَر.

فقال ابن شُبرمة وابن أبي ليلى لعيسى بن موسى: إنَّ هذا أمرٌ لم يكن عندنا، لا يُقاد عنه بالحَجَر ولا بالسَّوط، فلم يزالوا حتّى وَداه عيسى بن موسى. فقال: إنَّ مَن عندنا يُقيدون بالوَكزَة.

قلت: يَزعُمون أنّه خطأ، وأنَّ العَمْد لا يكون إلّا بالحديد؟ فقال: إنّما الخطأ أن يُريد شيئاً فيُصيب غيره، فأمّا ما كلّ شيءٍ قَصَدتَ إليه فأصبتَه فهو العَمْد.

228. From Ibn Sinān, from Abū ʿAbd Allāh ﵇ who said, 'The Commander of the Faithful ﵇, in cases warranting compensation, ruled for the accidental killing with motive if it was committed with a stick, a whip or a rock, to be compensated with a heavy fine of one hundred camels: forty young camels between six and nine years of age, thirty she-camels three years of age, and thirty suckling she-camels not more than two years old.

For the unintentional, accidental killing, it was thirty she-camels aged three, thirty suckling she-camels, thirty camels of six years of age, and twenty suckling male camels. The cash value of each camel was one hundred dirhams and ten dinars. If one could not pay the value of camels, then sheep could be substituted for camels – twenty ewes for every camel.' [4:92]

229. From ʿAbd al-Raḥmān, from Abū ʿAbd Allāh ﵇ who said, "ʿAlī used to say, "[The compensation due] for an accidental killing is twenty-five suckling she-camels, twenty-five she-camels three years of age, twenty-five six-year-old camels, and twenty-five camels aged five years."

For the accidental killing with motive, he ruled thirty-three young she-camels between two and nine years of age, and thirty-four three-year-old she-camels.' [4:92]

230. From ʿAlī b. Abī Ḥamza, from Abū ʿAbd Allāh ﵇ who said, 'The compensation due for an accidental killing – if the man was not the intended target – is one hundred camels or ten thousand in cash, or one thousand sheep.'

And he said, 'The compensation enforced for an accidental killing with motive is higher than the compensation for an accidental killing, which is valued according to the camels' ages: thirty-three she-camels aged three years, thirty-three five-year-old she-camels, and thirty-four six-year-old she-camels, each one of them fertile.' [4:92]

231. From al-Faḍl b. ʿAbd al-Malik, from Abū ʿAbd Allāh ﵇. He said, 'I asked him about the [indubitable] accidental killing – is it the one where compensation and penalty are due, and when a man strikes another without intending to kill him thereby? He replied, "Yes." I asked, "So if one was to throw something and it hit a man [and killed him]?" He replied, "That is the indubitable accident, for which compensation and penalty are due."' [4:92]

٢٢٨. عن ابن سِنان، عن أبي عبدالله ﵇، قال: قضى أمير المؤمنين ﵇ في أبواب الدِّيات في الخطأ شِبه العَمْد، إذا قتل بالعَصا، أو بالسَّوط، أو بالحجارة، يُغلّظ دِيَته، وهو مائة من الإبل: أربعون خَلِفة بين ثَنِيّةٍ إلى بازل عامها، وثلاثون حقّة، وثَلاثون بنت لَبُون.

وقال في الخطأ دون العَمْد: يكون فيه ثَلاثون حقّة، وثَلاثون بنت لَبُون، وعشرون بنت مَخَاض، وعشرون ابن لَبُون ذَكَر، وقيمة كلّ بعير من الوَرِق مائة دِرهَم وعشرة دنانير، ومن الغَنَم إذا لم يَكن بقيمة ناب الإبل لكُلّ بعيرٍ عشرون شاة.

٢٢٩. عن عبد الرّحمن، عن أبي عبدالله ﵇، قال: كان عليّ ﵇ يقول في الخطأ خمسة وعشرون بنت لَبُون، وخمس وعشرون بنت مَخَاض، وخمس وعشرون حِقّة، وخمس وعشرون جَذَعة. وقال في شِبه العَمْد: ثَلاثة وثَلاثون جَذَعة بين ثنيّة إلى بازِل عامها، كُلّها خَلِفة، وأربع وثَلاثون ثَنِيّة.

٢٣٠. عن عليّ بن أبي حمزة، عن أبي عبدالله ﵇، قال: دِيَة الخطأ إذا لم يُرِد الرجل، مائة من الإبل، أو عشرة آلاف من الوَرِق، أو ألف من الشاة.

وقال: دِيَة المُغلَّظة التي شِبه العَمْد وليس بعَمْد، أفضل من دِيَة الخطأ، بأسنان الإبل ثَلاث وثَلاثون حِقّة، وثلاث وثَلاثون جَذَعة، وأربع وثلاثون ثِنيّة، كُلّها طَرُوقة الفَحْل.

٢٣١. عن الفضل بن عبد الملك، عن أبي عبدالله ﵇، قال: سألتُهُ عن الخطأ الذي فيه الدِّيَة والكَفّارة، أهو الرجل يَضْرب الرجل، ولا يَتَعمّد قتله؟ قال: نعم.

232. From Ibn Abī ʿUmayr, from one of our associates, from Abū ʿAbd Allāh عليه السلام about a Muslim man living in a polytheistic place and who had been killed by Muslims, then the Imam comes to know about it afterwards. He said, 'A believing slave must be freed in his place, and that is as per God's words: ﴿*if the victim belonged to a people at war with you but is a believer, then the compensation is only to free a believing slave.*﴾' [4:92]

233. From al-Zuhrī, from ʿAlī b. al-Ḥusayn عليه السلام who said, 'Whoever kills someone by accident and does not have the means to free a slave, it is obligatory for him to fast for two months consecutively; God says: ﴿*If anyone kills a believer by mistake he must free one Muslim slave and pay compensation to the victim's relatives* [...] *Anyone who lacks the means to do this must fast for two consecutive months by way of repentance to God.*﴾' [4:92]

234. From al-Mufaḍḍal b. ʿUmar who said, 'I heard Abū ʿAbd Allāh عليه السلام say, "Fasting in the months of Shaʿbān and Ramadan consecutively is a means of repentance to God."' [4:92]

235. In a narration by Ismāʿīl b. ʿAbd al-Khāliq[45], on his authority: ﴿*repentance to God*﴾ – 'By God, it is from murder, *ẓihār*, and as a penalty.' [4:92]

236. In a narration by Abū al-Ṣabbāḥ al-Kinānī, on his authority, 'By God, fasting in Shaʿbān and in the month of Ramadan is a means of repentance to God.' [4:92]

45 Ismāʿīl b. ʿAbd al-Khāliq b. ʿAbd Rabbih b. Abī Maymūna b. Yasār, protégé of the Banū Asad, was a leading representative of the Imāmiyya in his day. He was a close disciple and reliable narrator of the sixth and seventh Imams. See Ḥillī, *Khulāṣat al-aqwāl*, 56 (nr. 39); Modarressi, *Tradition and Survival*, 303–4 (nr. 115).

قلت: فإذا رمى شيئًا فأصاب رجلاً؟ قال: ذاك الخطأ الذي لا شكّ فيه، وعليه الكفّارة والدِّيَة.

٢٣٢. عن ابن أبي عُمير، عن بعض أصحابنا، عن أبي عبد الله عليه السلام، في رجلٍ مسلمٍ كان في أرض الشِّرك، فقتله المسلمون، ثمّ عَلِم به الإمام بعد؟ قال: يُعتِق مكانه رقبةً مؤمنةً، وذلك في قول الله: ﴿فَإِن كَانَ مِن قَوۡمٍ عَدُوٍّ لَّكُمۡ وَهُوَ مُؤۡمِنٞ فَتَحۡرِيرُ رَقَبَةٖ مُّؤۡمِنَةٖ﴾.

٢٣٣. عن الزُّهريّ، عن علي بن الحسين عليهما السلام، قال: صيام شهرين متتابعين مَن قتل خطأً لمن لم يجد العِتق واجب، قال الله: ﴿وَمَن قَتَلَ مُؤۡمِنًا خَطَـٔٗا فَتَحۡرِيرُ رَقَبَةٖ مُّؤۡمِنَةٖ وَدِيَةٞ مُّسَلَّمَةٌ إِلَىٰٓ أَهۡلِهِۦٓ... فَمَن لَّمۡ يَجِدۡ فَصِيَامُ شَهۡرَيۡنِ مُتَتَابِعَيۡنِ﴾.

٢٣٤. عن المفضَّل بن عمر، قال: سَمِعتُ أبا عبد الله عليه السلام يقول: صوم شعبان وصوم شهر رمضان متتابعين ﴿تَوۡبَةٗ مِّنَ ٱللَّهِ﴾.

٢٣٥. وفي رواية إسماعيل بن عبد الخالق، عنه: ﴿تَوۡبَةٗ مِّنَ ٱللَّهِ﴾ والله من القتل، والظِّهار، والكَفّارة.

٢٣٦. وفي رواية أبي الصبّاح الكِناني، عنه عليه السلام: صوم شعبان، وشهر رَمَضان ﴿تَوۡبَةٗ﴾ والله ﴿مِّنَ ٱللَّهِ﴾.

237. From Samāʿa [b. Mihrān] who said, 'I asked him about the statement of God, Blessed and most High: ﴾*If anyone kills a believer deliberately, the punishment for him is Hell, and there he will remain: God is angry with him, and rejects him.*﴿ He replied, "The one who kills deliberately here is one who kills him over his faith, and this is the deliberation that God mentions here."

I asked, "So a man who draws his sword on another man and kills him out of anger, rather than having anything against his faith – he has indeed killed him so does the statement not apply to him?" He replied, "No, this is not what the Book mentions, even though retaliation and compensation are due in this case too if it is accepted." I asked, "Is he entitled to repentance?" He replied, "Yes. He can free a slave, fast for two months consecutively, feed sixty poor people and implore [God to forgive him], and I expect that he would be forgiven."' [4:93]

238. From Samāʿa b. Mihrān, from Abū ʿAbd Allāh عليه السلام or Abū al-Ḥasan عليه السلام. He said, 'I asked one of the two about one who kills a believer – is he entitled to repentance?

He replied, "Not until he pays compensation to his family, frees a believing slave, fasts for two months consecutively and seeks forgiveness from his Lord, imploring him humbly, then I expect he would be forgiven for having done that."

I asked, "What if he does not have the means to pay the compensation due?"

He replied, "He should ask from fellow Muslims until he can pay the compensation to his family."'

239. Samāʿa said, 'I asked him about His verse: ﴾*If anyone kills a believer deliberately.*﴿ He said, "Whoever kills a believer deliberately because of his faith – and that is the deliberation that God talks about in His Book – then ﴾*He has prepared a tremendous torment for him.*﴿

I asked, "What if two men are arguing about something and one draws his sword and strikes the other, killing him?"

He replied, "That is not the deliberation that God, Blessed and most High, is talking about."'

From Samāʿa who said, 'I asked him [...] (as quoted above).' [4:93]

٢٣٧. عن سَماعة، قال: قلتُ له: قول الله تبارك وتعالى: ﴿وَمَن يَقْتُلْ مُؤْمِنًا مُّتَعَمِّدًا فَجَزَآؤُهُ جَهَنَّمُ خَالِدًا فِيهَا وَغَضِبَ اللهُ عَلَيْهِ وَلَعَنَهُ﴾؟ قال: المتُعمّد الذي يقتله على دينه، فذاك التعمّد الذي ذكر الله.

قال: قلت فرجلٌ جاء إلى رجلٍ فضربه بسيفه حتّى قتله لغضب، لا لعيب على دينه، قتله وهو يقول بقوله؟ قال: ليس هذا الذي ذُكر في الكتاب، ولكن يُقاد به، والدِّية إن قبلت.

قلت: فله توبة؟ قال: نعم، يُعتِق رقبةً، ويصوم شهرين متتابعين، ويُطعِم ستّين مسكينًا، ويتوب ويتضرّع، فأرجو أن يتاب عليه.

٢٣٨. عن سَماعة بن مِهران، عن أبي عبد الله عليه السلام - أو أبي الحسن عليه السلام - قال: سألتُ أحدهما عليهما السلام عمَّن قَتَل مؤمنًا، هل له توبة؟ قال: لا حتّى يُؤدّي دِيَته إلى أهله، ويُعتِق رقبةً مؤمنةً، ويصوم شهرين متتابعين، ويستغفر ربّه ويتضرّع إليه، فأرجو أن يُتاب عليه إذا هو فعل ذلك.

قلت: إن لم يكن له ما يؤدّي دِيَته؟ قال: يسأل المسلمين حتّى يؤدّي دِيته إلى أهله.

٢٣٩. قال سَماعة: سألتُه عن قوله: ﴿وَمَن يَقْتُلْ مُؤْمِنًا مُّتَعَمِّدًا﴾، قال: من قَتَل مؤمنًا متعمّدًا على دِينه، فذلك التعمّد الذي قال الله في كتابه: ﴿وَأَعَدَّ لَهُ عَذَابًا عَظِيمًا﴾.

قلت: فالرجل يقع بينه وبين الرجل شيءُ، فيضرِبه بسيفه فيَقتُله؟ قال: ليس ذاك التعمّد الذي قال الله تبارك وتعالى.

عن سماعة، قال: سألته «الحديث».

240. From Hishām b. Sālim, from Abū 'Abd Allāh who said, 'The believer has ample margin [for error] in his religion as long as he does not spill blood unlawfully.' And he said, 'The one who deliberately kills a believer will not succeed in being granted repentance.' [4:93]

241. From Ibn Sinān, from Abū 'Abd Allāh عليه السلام; he said, 'I asked him about the believer who deliberately kills another believer – is he entitled to repentance? He replied, "If he killed him for his faith, then there is no repentance for him; but if he killed him in anger or for some other reason to do with worldly matters then his repentance is his [own life in] retribution. If no one knew about it, he must go to the family of the victim and confess to them of having killed their relative. If they pardon him and do not kill him, he must pay them compensation, free a slave, fast for two months consecutively and feed sixty poor people by way of repentance to God."' [4:93]

242. From Zurāra, from Abū 'Abd Allāh عليه السلام who said, 'Deliberate [murder] is to intentionally kill someone with something that would generally cause death.' [4:93]

243. From 'Alī b. Ja'far, from his brother Mūsā عليه السلام. He said, 'I asked him about a man who kills his slave. He replied, "He must free a slave, fast for two months consecutively and feed sixty poor people, then he can repent after that."' [4:93]

244. From Abū Baṣīr, from Abū 'Abd Allāh عليه السلام: ﴿ *do not say to someone who offers you a greeting of peace, 'You are not a believer'.* ﴾ [4:94]

245. From Zurāra, from Abū Ja'far عليه السلام about the verse: ﴿ *The truly helpless men, women, and children who have no means in their power nor any way to leave.* ﴾ He said, 'They are in no position to embrace the faith, and children or adult men and women with the mental capacity of children cannot be disbelievers.' [4:98]

246. From Abū Baṣīr, from Abū 'Abd Allāh عليه السلام who said, 'Whoever can recognise the diversity of people is not truly helpless.' [4:98]

٢٤٠. عن هِشام بن سالم، عن أبي عبدالله عليه السلام، قال: لا يزال المؤمن في فُسحةٍ من دينه ما لم يُصِب دمًا حرامًا، وقال: لا يُوفّق قاتل المؤمن مُتعمّدًا للتوبة.

٢٤١. عن ابن سِنان، عن أبي عبدالله عليه السلام، قال: سُئل عن المؤمن يقتل المؤمن متعمّدًا، له توبة؟ قال: إن كان قتله لإيمانه فلا توبة له، وإن كان قتله لغضبٍ أو بسبب شيءٍ من أمر الدنيا، فإنّ توبته أن يُقاد منه، وإن لم يَكُن عَلِم به أحدٌ، انطلق إلى أولياء المَقتول، فأقرّ عندهم بقتل صاحبهم، فإن عَفَوا عنه فلم يقتلوه أعطاهم الدِّيَة، وأعتق نَسَمةً، وصام شهرين متتابعين، وأطعم ستّين مسكينًا توبةً إلى الله.

٢٤٢. عن زُرارة، عن أبي عبدالله عليه السلام، قال: العَمْد أن تَعْمِده فتقتُله بما بمثله يُقْتَل.

٢٤٣. عن عليّ بن جعفر، عن أخيه موسى عليه السلام، قال: سألتُه عن رجلٍ قتل مملوكه. قال: عليه عِتقُ رقبةٍ، وصوم شهرين متتابعين، وإطعام ستّين مسكينًا، ثمّ تكون التوبة بعد ذلك.

٢٤٤. عن أبي بصير، عن أبي عبدالله عليه السلام ﴿وَلَا تَقُولُوا لِمَنْ أَلْقَىٰ إِلَيْكُمُ السَّلَامَ لَسْتَ مُؤْمِنًا﴾.

٢٤٥. عن زُرارة، عن أبي جعفر عليه السلام في ﴿الْمُسْتَضْعَفِينَ... لَا يَسْتَطِيعُونَ حِيلَةً وَلَا يَهْتَدُونَ سَبِيلًا﴾، وقال ﴿لَا يَسْتَطِيعُونَ حِيلَةً﴾ [إلى] الإيمان، ولا يكفرون الصبيان وأشباه عُقُول الصبيان من النساء والرجال.

٢٤٦. عن أبي بصير، عن أبي عبدالله عليه السلام، قال: من عَرَف اختلاف الناس فليس بمستضعف.

247. From Abū Khadīja, from Abū ʿAbd Allāh عليه السلام about the verse: ﴾ *The truly helpless men, women, and children who have no means in their power nor any way to leave.* ﴿ He said, 'They are not able to leave in order to join the path of the people of truth, nor do they have the means at their disposal to oppose the enemies.' He continued, 'These people will enter Paradise due to their good deeds and their refraining from prohibited acts that God has forbidden, but they will not attain the ranks of the devoted ones.' [4:98]

248. From Zurāra who said: 'Abū Jaʿfar عليه السلام said while I was talking to him about the truly helpless people, "Where are the people of the heights,[(7:46–48)] where are the ones waiting for God's decision about them,[(9:106)] where are the people who have done some righteous deeds mixed with some wrong,[(9:102)] where are those whose hearts were brought together,[(8:63)] where are the people whom God uses as proofs, where are the truly helpless men, women and children who neither have any means at their disposal nor any way to leave to be guided aright? – Those are the ones whom God may well pardon, for He is most pardoning and most forgiving."' [4:98]

249. From Zurāra who said, 'I asked Abū ʿAbd Allāh عليه السلام, "Can we marry the Murjiʾa, Ḥarūrī or Qadarī women?" He replied, "No, you should marry pure women,"'[46] Zurāra said, 'I asked, "Are there exclusively only either believing or disbelieving women?" So Abū ʿAbd Allāh عليه السلام said, "Then what about God's exclusion – surely God's word is truer than yours: ﴾ *except the truly helpless men, women, and children who have no means in their power nor any way to leave.* ﴿"' [4:98]

250. From Zurāra, from Abū Jaʿfar عليه السلام who said, 'I asked him about God's verse: ﴾ *except the truly helpless men, women* ﴿, so he replied, "This is someone who is neither able to disbelieve that he may do so, nor does he have the means to be guided on the path of faith, nor is he able to believe. Children cannot

46 Ṭurayḥī quotes a narration to further elucidate this: 'Take on the simple woman (*al-balhāʾ*)', I asked: "Who are simple women?" He replied, "Those who stay indoors and are chaste."' See Fakhr al-Dīn al-Ṭurayḥī, *Majmaʿ al-baḥrayn wa-maṭlaʿ al-nayyirayn* (Tehran: al-Maktaba al-Murtaḍawiyya, 1996), 6:343.

٢٤٧. عن أبي خديجة، عن أبي عبد الله عليه السلام، قال: ﴿الْمُسْتَضْعَفِينَ مِنَ الرِّجَالِ وَالنِّسَاءِ ... لا يَسْتَطِيعُونَ حِيلَةً وَلا يَهْتَدُونَ سَبِيلاً﴾. قال: ﴿لا يَسْتَطِيعُونَ حِيلَةً﴾ [إلى] سبيل أهل الحق فيَدْخلون فيه، ولا يستطيعون حيلة أهل النَّصب فيَنْصِبون.

قال: هؤلاء يَدْخُلون الجنّة بأعمالٍ حسنةٍ، وباجتناب المحارم الّتي نهى الله عنها، ولا ينالون منازل الأبرار.

٢٤٨. عن زُرارة، قال: قال أبو جعفر عليه السلام وأنا أُكلّمه في المستضعفين: أين أصحاب الأعراف؟ أين المرْجَون لأمر الله؟ أين الذين خَلَطوا عملاً صالحًا وآخر سيِّئًا؟ أين المؤلَّفة قلوبهم؟ أين أهل تبيان الله؟ أين ﴿الْمُسْتَضْعَفِينَ مِنَ الرِّجَالِ وَالنِّسَاءِ وَالْوِلْدَانِ لا يَسْتَطِيعُونَ حِيلَةً وَلا يَهْتَدُونَ سَبِيلاً ۞ فَأُولَئِكَ عَسَى اللَّهُ أَنْ يَعْفُوَ عَنْهُمْ وَكَانَ اللَّهُ عَفُوًّا غَفُورًا﴾.

٢٤٩. عن زُرارة، قال: قلت لأبي عبد الله عليه السلام: أتزوّج المرُجئة، أو الحَرُورية، أو القَدَرية؟ قال: لا، عليك بالبُلْه من النساء. قال زُرارة: فقلتُ ما هو إلاّ مؤمنة أو كافرة؟ فقال أبو عبد الله عليه السلام: فأين أهل استثناء الله؟ قول الله من قولك: ﴿إِلاَّ الْمُسْتَضْعَفِينَ مِنَ الرِّجَالِ وَالنِّسَاءِ وَالْوِلْدَانِ﴾ إلى قوله: ﴿سَبِيلاً﴾.

٢٥٠. عن زُرارة، عن أبي جعفر عليه السلام، قال: سألتُهُ عن قول الله: ﴿إِلاَّ الْمُسْتَضْعَفِينَ مِنَ الرِّجَالِ وَالنِّسَاءِ﴾. فقال: هو الذي لا يستطيع الكُفر فيكفُر، ولا يهتدي سبيل

be disbelievers, and adult men and women who have the mental capacity of children are not held responsible for their deeds."' [4:98]

251. From Ḥumrān who said, 'I asked Abū 'Abd Allāh عليه السلام about God's verse: ﴾ *except the truly helpless men, women.* ﴿ (4:98) He said, "They are the people under care of guardianship."

So I asked, "Which guardianship?" So he replied, "Not the divine guardianship in religion, but the care of a guardian to be able to marry, to inherit and to interact in society. They are neither classed as believers nor disbelievers, but they await God's decision about them."' [4:98]

252. From Sulaymān b. Khālid who said, 'I asked Abū 'Abd Allāh عليه السلام about God's verse: ﴾ *except the truly helpless men, women, and children who have no means in their power nor any way to leave.* ﴿ (4:98) He said, "Sulaymān, some of these truly helpless people are even more strong-willed than you. The truly helpless ones are a group of people who fast, pray, restrain their appetites and guard their private parts, and they cannot see that the right [to guide] is being held by other than us, and they take instead from the branches of the tree." He continued: "﴾ *God may well pardon these* ﴿, for having taken from the branches of the tree, unaware of those people. And if He pardons them, then it is because God has mercy on them; and if He chastises them then it is because of their own deviation from that which He had made known to them."' [4:98]

253. From Sulaymān b. Khālid, from Abū Ja'far عليه السلام who said, 'I asked him about the truly helpless people, so he replied, "It is the simple woman who only stays indoors and the servant who, if you were to tell them to pray, they will pray – they only know what they are told; and the foreign slave who only knows what you tell him, the senile old man and the young child. These are the truly helpless ones. As for the obstinate, argumentative and quarrelsome man who is able to carry out financial transactions by himself, and refuses to be helped in anything – can you say that he is a truly helpless one? No, not in the least."' [4:98]

الإيمان، لا يستطيع أن يُؤمِن، ولا يستطيع أن يَكْفُر، الصبيان ومن كان من الرجال والنساء على مثل عُقُول الصِّبيان مرفوعٌ عنهم القلم.

٢٥١. عن حُمران، قال: سألتُ أبا عبدالله عليه السلام عن قول الله تعالى ﴿إِلَّا ٱلْمُسْتَضْعَفِينَ﴾، قال: هم أهل الولاية.

فقلتُ: أيّ ولاية؟ فقال: أما إنّها ليست بولايةٍ في الدين، ولكنّها الولاية في المناكحة والموارثة والمخالطة، وهم ليسوا بالمؤمنين، ولا بالكفّار، وهم المُرْجون لأمر الله.

٢٥٢. عن سُليمان بن خالد، قال: سألتُ أبا عبدالله عليه السلام عن قوله تعالى: ﴿إِلَّا ٱلْمُسْتَضْعَفِينَ مِنَ ٱلرِّجَالِ وَٱلنِّسَاءِ ... وَلَا يَهْتَدُونَ سَبِيلًا﴾. قال: يا سليمان، مِن هؤلاء المستضعفين مَن هوأثخن رقبةً منك، المستضعفون قوم يَصُومون ويُصلّون تعِفّ بُطُونهم وفُرُوجهم، لا يرون أنّ الحقّ في غيرنا، آخذين بأغصان الشجرة، فقال: ﴿فَأُوْلَٰٓئِكَ عَسَى ٱللَّهُ أَن يَعْفُوَ عَنْهُمْ﴾ [إذا] كانوا آخذين بالأغصان، و [إن] لم يعرِفوا أُولئك، فإن عفا عنهم فيرحَمهم الله، وإن عذّبهم فبضلالتهم عمّا عرّفهم.

٢٥٣. عن سُليمان بن خالد، عن أبي جعفر عليه السلام، قال: سألتُه عن المستضعفين. فقال: البَلْهاء في خِدرها، والخادم تقول لها: صلّي، فتصلّي، لا تدري إلاّ ما قلت لها، والجليب الذي لا يدري إلاّ ما قلتَ له، والكبير الفاني، والصبيّ، والصغير، هؤلاء المستضعفون، فأمّا رجل شديدُ العُنُق، جَدِل، خَصِم، يتولّى الشِّراء والبيع، لا تستطيع أن تغبِنه في شيءٍ، تقول هذا المستضعف؟ لا، ولا كرامة.

254. From Abū al-Ṣabbāḥ who said, 'I asked Abū 'Abd Allāh ﵇, "What is your opinion about a man who is invited to [embrace] this authority [i.e. the divinely mandated authority of the Ahl al-Bayt] and he acknowledges it whilst being in a remote place. Suddenly he hears news of the death of the Imam, and while he is waiting [to come] death overtakes him too." So he replied, "By God, he holds the same position as one who died while migrating towards God and His Messenger ﷺ, and his reward from God is certain."' [4:100]

255. From Ibn Abī 'Umayr who said, 'Zurāra sent his son 'Ubayd to Medina to find out any news about Abū al-Ḥasan and 'Abd Allāh[47] for him, but his son 'Ubayd died before he could return to him.' Muḥammad b. Abī 'Umayr continued, 'Muḥammad b. Ḥakīm narrated to me saying, "I told the first Abū al-Ḥasan [i.e. Imam al-Kāẓim ﵇] about this and mentioned to him about Zurāra sending his son 'Ubayd over to Medina. So Abū al-Ḥasan ﵇ said, "Indeed, I expect Zurāra to be among those about whom God says: ﴾ *and if anyone leaves home as a migrant towards God and His Messenger and is then overtaken by death, his reward from God is sure.* ﴿"' [4:100]

256. From al-Ḥarīz who said, 'Zurāra and Muḥammad b. Muslim narrated, "We asked Abū Ja'far ﵇: 'What do you say about the prayer while travelling – how is it [to be performed] and how many?' He replied, 'God says: ﴾ *When you [believers] are travelling in the land, you will not be blamed for shortening your prayers* ﴿, so shortening the prayers during travel has become obligatory just like the obligation of performing the complete prayer whilst settled in one place.'

We asked, 'But He has said: ﴾ *you will not be blamed for shortening your prayers* ﴿, and He has not actually commanded us to do so, so how can God have obligated this the same way as He has obligated the complete prayer while settled [in one place]?'

He replied, 'Has God not said regarding Ṣafā and Marwa: ﴾ *so for those who make major or minor pilgrimage to the House, it is no offence to circulate*

---

47 Referring to 'Abd Allāh al-Afṭaḥ who, in the view of Twelver Shī'as, wrongfully claimed the Imamate after his father Imam Ja'far al-Ṣādiq. He is the eponymous founder of the Faṭḥiyya *madhhab*.

٢٥٤. عن أبي الصبّاح، قال: قلتُ لأبي عبدالله عليه السلام: ما تقول في رجلٍ دُعي إلى هذا الأمر فعرفه، وهو في أرضٍ منقطعةٍ، إذ جاءه موت الإمام، فبينا هو ينتظر إذ جاءه الموت؟ فقال: هو والله بمنزلة من هاجر إلى الله ورسوله فمات، فقد وقع أجره على الله.

٢٥٥. عن ابن أبي عمير، قال: وجّه زُرارة ابنه عبيدًا إلى المدينة يستخبر له خبر أبي الحسن عليه السلام وعبدالله، فمات قبل أن يَرْجِع إليه ابنه. قال محمّد بن أبي عُمير: حدَّثني محمّد بن حكيم، قال: قلتُ لأبي الحسن الأوّل، فذكرت له زُرارة وتوجيهه ابنه عبيدًا إلى المدينة؟ فقال أبو الحسن عليه السلام: إنّي لأرجو أن يكون زُرارة ممّن قال الله تعالى: ﴿وَمَن يَخْرُجْ مِن بَيْتِهِ مُهَاجِرًا إِلَى اللهِ وَرَسُولِهِ ثُمَّ يُدْرِكْهُ الْمَوْتُ فَقَدْ وَقَعَ أَجْرُهُ عَلَى اللهِ﴾.

٢٥٦. عن حَرِيز، قال: قال زُرارة ومحمّد بن مسلم: قلنا لأبي جعفر عليه السلام: ما تقول في الصلاة في السفر؟ كيف هي، وكم هي؟ قال: إنّ الله يقول: ﴿وَإِذَا ضَرَبْتُمْ فِي الْأَرْضِ فَلَيْسَ عَلَيْكُمْ جُنَاحٌ أَن تَقْصُرُوا مِنَ الصَّلَاةِ﴾ فصار التقصير في السفر واجبًا، كوجوب التمام في الحضر.

قالا: قلنا: إنّما قال: ﴿فَلَيْسَ عَلَيْكُمْ جُنَاحٌ﴾ ولم يقل: افعلوا، فكيف أوجب ذلك كما أوجب التمام في الحضر؟

قال: أو ليس قد قال الله في الصفا والمَرْوَة: ﴿فَمَنْ حَجَّ الْبَيْتَ أَوِ اعْتَمَرَ فَلَا جُنَاحَ عَلَيْهِ أَن يَطَّوَّفَ بِهِمَا﴾ ألا ترى أنّ الطواف بهما واجبٌ مفروضٌ، لأنّ

between the two﴾? Can you not see that circulating between the two is an obligatory act because God has mentioned them both in His Book and His Prophet ﷺ performed both acts? Similarly, shortening the prayer during travel is something that His Prophet ﷺ did, so God has mentioned it in the Book.'

We asked, 'So if someone performs four units of prayer whilst travelling, does he have to re-do them or not?'

He replied, 'If you had previously read to him the verse about shortening the prayer and it has been explained to him, and he still prayed four, then he must re-do them. But if you had not read it to him and he did not know about it, then he does not have to re-do it. The prayer during travel is performed as the obligatory two-units for every prayer except for the dusk prayer (*maghrib*), for that is three units and cannot be shortened. The Messenger of God ﷺ left it as three units both during travel as well as settlement.'"' [4:101]

257. From Ibrāhīm, from 'Umar, from Abū 'Abd Allāh عليه السلام who said, 'God has made five prayers [a day] obligatory on the one residing in a place, and He has obligated the traveller to perform two units of prayer on the whole, and He has obligated a single unit for one who is fearful [of attack], and this is as per God's statement: ﴿*you will not be blamed for shortening your prayers, if you fear the disbelievers may harm you*﴾ – He is talking about the two units of prayer becoming a single unit.' [4:101]

258. From Abān b. Taghlib, from Ja'far b. Muḥammad عليه السلام who said, 'The *maghrib* prayer during fear is performed by making two groups: one facing the enemy and one behind him [i.e. the imam]. So he leads them in prayer [for the first unit], then he remains standing while they perform the other two units by themselves, and finish off with the *taslīm* to each other. Then the second group comes, and joins [the imam] who leads them in the rest of the two units, and they pray one unit by themselves so that there is a *qirā'a* [compulsory recitation in the standing position] for the first group of people, and a *qirā'a* for the second group.' [4:102]

259. From Zurāra and Muḥammad b. Muslim, from Abū Ja'far عليه السلام who said, 'If the time for prayer sets in during fear, the imam divides them into two

الله ذكره في كتابه، وصنعه نبيّه صلى الله عليه وآله؟ وكذلك التقصير في السفرشيءٌ صنعه النبي صلى الله عليه وآله، فذكره الله في الكتاب.

قالا: قلنا: فمن صلّى في السفر أربعًا، أيُعيد أم لا؟ قال: إن كان [قد] قرئت عليه آية التقصير وفُسّرت له فصلّى أربعًا أعاد، وإن لم يكُن قرئت عليه ولم يعلمها فلا إعادة عليه، والصلاة في السفركلّها الفريضة ركعتان كُلّ صلاة إلاّ المغرب، فإنّها ثلاث ليس فيها تقصير، تركها رسول الله صلى الله عليه وآله في السّفر والحَضر ثلاث ركعاتٍ.

٢٥٧. عن إبراهيم بن عمر، عن أبي عبدالله عليه السلام، قال: فرض الله على المقيم خمس صلوات، وفرض على المسافر ركعتين تمام، وفرض على الخائف ركعة، وهو قول الله: ﴿لاَ جُنَاحَ عَلَيْكُمْ أَنْ تَقْصُرُوا مِنَ الصَّلاَةِ إِنْ خِفْتُمْ أَنْ يَفْتِنَكُمُ الَّذِينَ كَفَرُوا﴾ يقول: من الركّعتين فتصير ركعة.

٢٥٨. عن أبان بن تغلِب، عن جعفر بن محمّد عليهما السلام، قال: صلاة المغرب في الخوف أن يجعل أصحابه طائفتين: بإزاء العدوّ واحدة، والأُخرى خلفه، فيُصلّي بهم، ثمّ ينصِب قائمًا، ويصلّون هم تمام ركعتين، ثمّ يُسلِّم بعضهم على بعضٍ، ثمّ تأتي الطائفة الأُخرىٰ فيصلّي بهم ركعتين، فيصلّون هم ركعة، فيكون للأوّلين قراءة، وللآخرين قراءة.

٢٥٩. عن زُرارة ومحمّد بن مسلم، عن أبي جعفر عليه السلام، قال: إذا حضرت الصلاة في الخوف، فَرّقهم الإمام فرقتين، فِرقةٌ مقبِلة على عدوّهم، وفِرقة خلفه؛ كما قال الله تبارك وتعالى،

groups, one facing the enemy and one behind him, as God, Blessed and most High has outlined. So he starts them off with the *takbīr* then leads them in one unit of prayer, then he stands up again after lifting his head from the prostration and remains standing while the people who were praying behind him complete another unit, each person praying it by himself. Then they finish off with the *taslīm* to each other, and go and exchange places with their companions, who then come and stand behind the imam who is still standing.

They start with the *takbīr* themselves and join the imam in the prayer. So he leads them in one unit, and completes it with the *taslīm*, so that the first group got to begin the prayer with the *takbīr* and the second group get the *taslīm* with the imam. So when the imam recites the *taslīm*, each person from the second group stands up and prays the second unit by himself, so in effect the imam has prayed two units and each person from the whole party has prayed two units each, one in congregation and one by himself.

If the fear of attack is so intense, such as in the midst of a battle or an armed skirmish or close combat where people are fighting each other, then know that the Commander of the Faithful ﷺ on the eve of the Battle of Ṣiffīn, which was the night of *al-Harīr*, had not led them in prayer for the *dhuhr, ʿasr, maghrib* or *ʿishā'* prayers when the times for each one had set in. Instead, they recited *la ilāha illa Llāh, subḥān Allāh, al-ḥamdu li-Llāh* and supplicated God, and that was their prayer; and he did not command them to re-do their prayer [afterwards].

If the *maghrib* prayer is to be performed during fear [of attack], he [i.e. the imam] should divide them into two groups. He should lead one group in two units of prayer, then sit down [for *tashahhud*], then motion to them with his hand and each person should stand up and perform the remaining unit and finish it off with the *taslīm*, and then exchange places with their companions. The second group then comes, recites the *takbīr* [themselves] and joins the prayer. Then the imam stands up and leads them in one unit of prayer, then finishes off his with *taslīm*, after which each person stands up again to perform another unit, joining it up with the one they had just prayed with the imam, and then stands up to pray the last unit without any *qirā'a*. So the imam will have prayed three units in total; the first group will have prayed three units: two in congregation and one by themselves; and the second group will have prayed three units: one in congregation and two

فيُكبّر بهم، ثمّ يصلّي بهم رَكْعَة، ثمّ يقوم بعدما يرفع رأسه من السُّجود، فيمثل قائمًا، ويقوم الذين صلّوا خلفه ركْعة، فيصلّي كلّ إنسانٍ منهم لنفسه ركْعة، ثمّ يسلّم بعضهم على بعض.

ثمّ يذهبون إلى أصحابهم فيقومون مقامهم، ويجيء الآخرون، والإمام قائم، فيكبّرون ويَدْخُلون في الصلاة خلفه، فيصلّي بهم رَكْعَةً، ثمّ يسلّم، فيكون للأوّلين استفتاح الصلاة بالتكبير، وللآخرين التسليم من الإمام، فإذا سَلّم الإمام قام كُلّ إنسانٍ من الطائفة الأخيرة، فيصلّي لنفسه رَكْعَةً واحدةً، فتمّت للإمام رَكْعتان، ولكلّ إنسانٍ من القوم رَكْعتَان: واحدة في جماعة، والأُخرى وَحْدانًا.

وإذا كان الخوف أشدّ من ذلك مثل المضاربة والمناوشة والمعانقة وتَلاَحُم القتال، فإنّ أمير المؤمنين عليه السلام ليلة صفّين — وهي ليلة الهَرِير - لم يَكُن صلّى بهم الظهر والعصر والمغرب والعشاء عند وقت كلّ صلاة إلاّ بالتهليل والتسبيح والتحميد والدُّعاء، فكانت تلك صلاتهم، لم يأمُرهم بإعادة الصلاة.

وإذا كانت المغرب في الخوف، فرّقهم فِرقتين، فصلّى بفِرقة رَكْعتين ثمّ جلس، ثمّ أشار إليهم بيده، فقام كُلّ إنسانٍ منهم فصلّى رَكْعة، ثمّ سلّموا، وقاموا مقام أصحابهم، وجاءت الطائفة الأُخرى، فكبّروا ودخلوا في الصلاة، وقام الإمام فصلّى بهم رَكْعةً، ثمّ سلّم، ثمّ قام كلّ إنسانٍ منهم فصلّى رَكْعَةً فشفَّعها بالتي صلّى مع الإمام، ثمّ قام فصلّى ركعةً ليس فيها قراءة، فتمّت للإمام ثَلاث رَكَعاتٍ وللأوّلين ثلاث رَكَعات: رَكْعتين في جماعةٍ، ورَكْعة وَحْدانًا، وللآخرين ثَلاث رَكَعات: رَكْعة جماعة، ورَكْعَتين وَحْدانًا، فصار للأوّلين افتتاح التكبير وافتتاح الصلاة، وللآخرين التسليم.

by themselves. The first group got the start of the prayer and the *takbīr*, and the second group the *taslīm*.' [4:102]

260. From Muḥammad b. Muslim, from one of the two [Imams] who said about the *maghrib* prayer during travel, 'There is no harm to you if you delay it by an hour, then pray it with the final *'ishā'* prayer if you like, and if you prefer you can walk for an hour until twilight has fallen. Indeed, the Messenger of God ﷺ performed the midday prayer and the *'asr* (afternoon) prayer together, and the *maghrib* and *'ishā'* prayer together at the end of the day, and he used to delay as well as pray on time. God, most High, says: ﴿*prayer is obligatory for the believers at prescribed times*﴾ – by this He meant specifically the obligation of it on the believers and nothing else. If it were as they claim, then the Messenger of God ﷺ would not have prayed like that, being more knowledgeable and more aware than them. And were it have been better to do so, then surely Muḥammad ﷺ, the Messenger of God, would have commanded thus. On the day of the Battle of Ṣiffīn, the people with the Commander of the Faithful عليه السلام missed their *dhuhr, 'asr, maghrib* and *'ishā'* prayers; so 'Alī the Commander of the Faithful عليه السلام commanded them to recite *Allāhu akbar, lā ilāha illa Llāh,* and *subḥān Allāh*, riding and on foot, as per God's statement: ﴿*If you are in danger, pray when you are out walking or riding,*﴾(2:239) so 'Alī عليه السلام commanded them to do this, and that is what they did.' [4:103]

261. From Zurāra who said, 'I asked Abū Ja'far عليه السلام about God's verse: ﴿*prayer is obligatory for the believers at prescribed times*﴾, so he replied, "It means a prescribed obligation, and not set times that he has stipulated where if that exact time passes, and one prays after it then his prayer is not counted. If it were indeed thus, then Sulaymān, son of Dāwūd, would have perished as a result of performing his prayer outside the time of it. However, one should pray when He has stipulated to do so."' [4:103]

262. From Manṣūr b. Khālid who said, 'I heard Abū 'Abd Allāh عليه السلام say whilst reciting the verse: ﴿*prayer is obligatory for the believers at prescribed times*﴾, "If it were at specifically set times as they claim then people would perish, for the matter would be too constricted for them. However, it is a prescribed obligation for them."' [4:103]

٢٦٠. عن محمّد بن مسلم، عن أحدهما عليهما السلام، قال في صلاة المغرب في السفر: لا يَضُرّك أن تؤخّر ساعة ثمّ تصلّيها، إن أحببت أن تُصلّي العِشاء الآخرة، وإن شئت مشيت ساعة إلى أن يغيب الشّفق، إنّ رسول الله ﷺ صلّى صلاة الهاجرة والعصر جميعًا، والمغرب والعشاء الآخرة جميعًا، وكان يُؤخّر ويقدّم، إنّ الله تعالى قال: ﴿إِنَّ الصَّلَاةَ كَانَتْ عَلَى الْمُؤْمِنِينَ كِتَابًا مَوْقُوتًا﴾ إنّما عنى وجوبها على المؤمنين لم يعنِ غيره، إنّه لو كان كما يقولون، لم يصلّ رسول الله ﷺ هكذا، وكان أعلم وأخبر، ولو كان خيرًا لأَمر به محمّد رسول الله ﷺ، وقد فات الناس مع أمير المؤمنين عليه السلام يوم صفّين صلاة الظهر والعصر والمغرب والعشاء الآخرة، فأمرهم عليّ أمير المؤمنين فكبّروا وهلّلوا وسبّحوا رجالاً وركبانًا، لقول الله: ﴿فَإِنْ خِفْتُمْ فَرِجَالًا أَوْ رُكْبَانًا﴾ فأمرهم عليّ عليه السلام فصَنَعوا ذلك.

٢٦١. عن زُرارة، قال: قلتُ لأبي جعفر عليه السلام: قول الله: ﴿إِنَّ الصَّلَاةَ كَانَتْ عَلَى الْمُؤْمِنِينَ كِتَابًا مَوْقُوتًا﴾؟ قال: يعني كتابًا مفروضًا، وليس يعني وقتًا وقتها، إن جاز ذلك الوقت ثمّ صلاّها لم تكن صلاته مُؤدّاة، لو كان ذلك كذلك لهلك سليمان بن داود حين صلاّها بغير وقتها، ولكنّه متى ما ذكرها صلاّها.

٢٦٢. عن منصور بن خالد، قال: سَمِعتُ أبا عبد الله عليه السلام وهو يقول: ﴿إِنَّ الصَّلَاةَ كَانَتْ عَلَى الْمُؤْمِنِينَ كِتَابًا مَوْقُوتًا﴾. قال: لو كانت مَوقُوتًا كما يقولون لهلك الناس، ولكان الأمر ضيّقًا، ولكنّها كانت على المؤمنين كتابًا موجوبًا.

263. From Zurāra who said, 'I asked Abū Jaʿfar عليه السلام about this verse: ﴾*prayer is obligatory for the believers at prescribed times*﴿, so he said, "Prayer does have a set time, but there is ample time in its performance, where one may pray it early sometimes and late at other times, except for the Friday prayer, for that is at a specific time. What God means here rather by 'prescribed times' is that it is mandatory; He means that it is an obligatory act."' [4:103]

264. From Zurāra, from Abū Jaʿfar عليه السلام. [About] ﴾*prayer is obligatory for the believers at prescribed times*﴿, he said, 'If it were such that it has to be performed exactly at that time, otherwise it is not accepted, then it would be a catastrophe. However, whenever you are able to perform it, then do so.' [4:103]

265. In another narration, from Zurāra, from Abū Jaʿfar عليه السلام; he said, 'I heard him say regarding God's verse: ﴾*prayer is obligatory for the believers at prescribed times*﴿, "He actually refers to its obligation for the believers. And if it were as they claim, then Sulaymān son of Dāwūd عليه السلام would have perished when he said: ﴾*until* [*the sun*] *had disappeared behind the* [*night's*] *veil*﴿, for it would have only been on time if he had prayed it before then, whilst there is no prayer with a longer time-span than the *ʿaṣr* prayer."' [4:103]

266. In another narration from Zurāra, from Abū Jaʿfar عليه السلام regarding God's verse: ﴾*prayer is obligatory for the believers at prescribed times*﴿, he said, 'What He means by that is its obligation upon the believers, and not that they have a specific time, and that whoever has neglected that has failed the prayer. However, there is a loss [of time] thereby.' [4:103]

267. From ʿAbd al-Ḥamīd b. ʿAwwāḍ, from Abū ʿAbd Allāh عليه السلام who said, 'God has said: ﴾*prayer is obligatory for the believers at prescribed times.*﴿ He said, 'What He actually means is its obligation upon the believers, and nothing more.' [4:103]

268. From ʿUbayd, from Abū Jaʿfar عليه السلام or Abū ʿAbd Allāh عليه السلام. He said, 'I asked him about God's verse: ﴾*prayer is obligatory for the believers at prescribed times.*﴿ He said, "It is a prescribed obligation, but not how there is a specific

٢٦٣ . عن زُرارة، قال: سألتُ أبا جعفر عليه السلام عن هذه الآية ﴿إِنَّ الصَّلَاةَ كَانَتْ عَلَى الْمُؤْمِنِينَ كِتَابًا مَوْقُوتًا﴾ . فقال: إنّ للصلاة وقتًا، والأمر فيه واسع، يُقدّم مرّة ويُؤخّر مرّة إلاّ الجمعة، فإنّما هو وقتٌ واحدٌ، وإنّما عنى الله كتابًا موقوتًا أي واجبًا، يعني بها أنّها الفريضة .

٢٦٤ . عن زُرارة، عن أبي جعفر عليه السلام ﴿إِنَّ الصَّلَاةَ كَانَتْ عَلَى الْمُؤْمِنِينَ كِتَابًا مَوْقُوتًا﴾، قال: لو عنى أنّها في وقت لا تُقبَل إلاّ فيه، كانت مُصيبةً، ولكن متى أدّيتها فقد أدّيتها .

٢٦٥ . وفي رواية أُخرى عن زُرارة، عن أبي جعفر عليه السلام، قال: سَمِعتُه يقول في قول الله: ﴿إِنَّ الصَّلَاةَ كَانَتْ عَلَى الْمُؤْمِنِينَ كِتَابًا مَوْقُوتًا﴾ . قال: إنّما يعني وجوبها على المؤمنين، ولو كان كما يقولون إذًا لهلك سليمان ابن داود عليهما السلام حين قال: ﴿حَتَّىٰ تَوَارَتْ بِالْحِجَابِ﴾ لأنّه لو صلاّها قبل ذلك كانت في وقت، وليس صلاةٌ أطول وقتًا من صلاة العصر .

٢٦٦ . وفي رواية أُخرى عن زُرارة، عن أبي جعفر عليه السلام، في قول الله: ﴿إِنَّ الصَّلَاةَ كَانَتْ عَلَى الْمُؤْمِنِينَ كِتَابًا مَوْقُوتًا﴾ . فقال: يعني بذلك وُجوبَها على المؤمنين، وليس لها وقت مَن تَركه أفرط الصلاة، ولكن لها تضييع .

٢٦٧ . عن عبد الحميد بن عَوّاض، عن أبي عبد الله عليه السلام، قال: إنّ الله قال: ﴿إِنَّ الصَّلَاةَ كَانَتْ عَلَى الْمُؤْمِنِينَ كِتَابًا مَوْقُوتًا﴾، قال: إنّما عنى وجوبها على المؤمنين، ولم يعنِ غيره .

٢٦٨ . عن عُبيد، عن أبي جعفر عليه السلام - أو أبي عبد الله عليه السلام - قال: سألتُهُ عن قول الله عزّ وجلّ: ﴿إِنَّ الصَّلَاةَ كَانَتْ عَلَى الْمُؤْمِنِينَ كِتَابًا مَوْقُوتًا﴾ . قال: كتابٌ واجبٌ،

time for Hajj or Ramadan, where if you miss it, you miss it. Prayer is such that whenever you perform it, [you are counted as] having prayed."' [4:103]

269. From 'Āmir b. Kathīr al-Sarrāj, who was one of Ḥusayn b. 'Alī's propagandists, from 'Aṭā' al-Hamadānī, from Abū Ja'far عليه السلام, regarding His verse: ﴿*when they plot at night, saying things that do not please Him*﴾, he said, 'It is *x*, *y* and *z* [i.e. Abū Bakr, 'Umar and 'Uthmān] and 'Ubayda b. al-Jarrāḥ.' [4:108]

270. In a narration by 'Umar b. Sa'īd, from Abū al-Ḥasan عليه السلام who said, '[They are] those two and 'Ubayda b. al-Jarrāḥ.' [4:108]

271. In a narration by 'Umar b. Ṣāliḥ, he said, 'The first, the second, and 'Ubayda b. al-Jarrāḥ.' [4:108]

272. From 'Abd Allāh b. Ḥammād al-Anṣārī, from 'Abd Allāh b. Sinān who said, 'Abū 'Abd Allāh said that backbiting (*ghība*) is where you talk about your brother regarding something that God has kept concealed. But when you say something about him that is not true, then that is what God's statement refers to: ﴿*then he has burdened himself with deceit as well as flagrant sin.*﴾' [4:112]

273. From Ibrāhīm b. 'Abd al-Ḥamīd, from some people from Qum, from Abū 'Abd Allāh عليه السلام regarding His verse: ﴿*There is no good in most of their secret talk, only in commanding charity, or good, or reconciliation between people*﴾, he said, 'By "good" he refers to loans.' [4:114]

274. From Ḥarīz, from one of our associates, from one of the two [Imams] who said, 'When the Commander of the Faithful was in Kufa, the people came to him saying, "Delegate an imam for us who can lead the prayer for us in the month of Ramadan." So he replied, "No," and prohibited them from gathering together in it. So in the evening they began to say, "Lament over Ramadan! What a sad Ramadan it will be." So Ḥārith al-A'war came to him with a group of people saying, "O Commander of the Faithful, the people are upset and averse to your words." So upon hearing this he said, "Leave them, they do not want to be led in prayer by anyone other than whom they choose themselves." Then he said: ﴿*and whoever follows a path other than*

أما إنّه ليس مثل الوقت للحجّ ولا رمضان، إذا فاتك فقد فاتك، وإنّ الصلاة إذا صلّيت فقد صلّيت.

٢٦٩. عن عامر بن كثير السّرّاج، وكان داعية الحسين بن عليّ، عن عطاء الهمداني، عن أبي جعفر ﵇، في قوله تعالى ﴿إِذْ يُبَيِّتُونَ مَا لَا يَرْضَىٰ مِنَ الْقَوْلِ﴾ قال: فلان وفلان وفلان وأبو عبيدة بن الجرّاح.

٢٧٠. وفي رواية عمر بن سعيد، عن أبي الحسن ﵇، قال: هما وأبو عبيدة بن الجرّاح.

٢٧١. وفي رواية عمر بن صالح، قال: الأوّل والثاني وأبو عبيدة بن الجرّاح.

٢٧٢. عن عبدالله بن حمّاد الأنصاري، عن عبدالله بن سِنان، قال: قال أبو عبدالله ﵇: الغِيبة أن تقول في أخيك ما هو فيه ممّا قد سَتَره الله عليه، فأمّا إذا قلتَ ما ليس فيه، فذلك قول الله: ﴿فَقَدِ احْتَمَلَ بُهْتَانًا وَإِثْمًا مُبِينًا﴾.

٢٧٣. عن إبراهيم بن عبد الحميد، عن بعض القُمّيّين، عن أبي عبدالله ﵇، في قوله تعالى: ﴿لَا خَيْرَ فِي كَثِيرٍ مِنْ نَجْوَاهُمْ إِلَّا مَنْ أَمَرَ بِصَدَقَةٍ أَوْ مَعْرُوفٍ أَوْ إِصْلَاحٍ بَيْنَ النَّاسِ﴾ يعني بالمعروف القَرْض.

٢٧٤. عن حَرِيز، عن بعض أصحابنا، عن أحدهما عليهما السلام، قال: لـمّا كان أمير المؤمنين ﵇ في الكوفة أتاه الناس، فقالوا: اجعل لنا إمامًا يَؤُمّنا في شهر رمضان. فقال: لا،

that of the believers, We shall leave him on his chosen path – We shall burn him in Hell, an evil destination. ﴾' [4:115]

275. From ʿAmr b. Abī al-Miqdām, on his father's authority, from a man from among the Anṣār who said, 'Al-Ashʿath al-Kindī, Jarīr al-Bajalī, and I went out to the outskirts of Kufa to al-Firas[48] when a lizard passed by us, so al-Ashʿath and Jarīr exclaimed: "Peace be upon you, O Commander of the Faithful," in contradiction of ʿAlī b. Abī Ṭālib ﵇. So when the Anṣārī parted from them, he related this to ʿAlī ﵇, and ʿAlī said, "Leave them, for he[49] will be their imam on the Day of Resurrection. Have you not heard God's statement: ﴿ *We shall leave him on his chosen path.* ﴾"' [4:115]

276. From Muḥammad b. Ismāʿīl al-Rāzī, from a man whose name he mentioned, from Abū ʿAbd Allāh ﵇. He said, 'A man entered into the presence of Abū ʿAbd Allāh and said, "Peace be upon you, O Commander of the Faithful," so he got up immediately and said, "That is not a title fit for anyone except for the Commander of the Faithful [i.e. ʿAlī b. Abī Ṭālib] ﵇ himself. God has named him thus, and no one else can be called that apart from him, and he took it on, except that it was coined [for others]. And even if it were not specifically for him, it suits him the best. This is as per God's verse in His Book: ﴿ *In His place the idolaters invoke only females, and Satan, the rebel.* ﴾"' He said, 'So I asked, "What will your Qāʾim be addressed with then?" He replied, "He will be addressed with: 'Peace be upon you, O remnant of God (*baqiyyat Allāh*), Peace be upon you, O son of God's Messenger.'"' [4:117]

48 Qaṣr al-Firas was one of four palaces in the ancient city of al-Ḥīra. See ʿAbd al-Muʾmin al-Baghdādī, *Marāṣid al-iṭlāʿ ʿalā asmāʾ al-amkina wa-l-buqāʿ* (Beirut: Dār al-maʿrifa, 1953), 3:1027.

49 In reference to Muʿāwiya, whom the two men were referring to when they invoked him by the title 'Commander of the Faithful' (*amīr al-muʾminīn*), which according to Shīʿī tradition is exclusively reserved for ʿAlī b. Abī Ṭālib.

ونهاهم أن يجتمعوا فيه، فلمّا أمسوا جعلوا يقولون: ابكوا في رمضان، وارمضاناه، فأتاه الحارث الأعور في أُناس، فقال: يا أمير المؤمنين، ضجّ الناس وكَرِهوا قولك، فقال عند ذلك: دَعُوهم وما يُريدون، ليصلّي بهم مَن شاءوا، ثمّ قال: ﴿وَمَنْ ... وَيَتَّبِعْ غَيْرَ سَبِيلِ الْمُؤْمِنِينَ نُوَلِّهِ مَا تَوَلَّى وَنُصْلِهِ جَهَنَّمَ وَسَاءَتْ مَصِيرًا﴾.

٢٧٥. عن عمرو بن أبي المِقدام، عن أبيه، عن رجلٍ من الأنصار، قال: خرجتُ أنا والأشعث الكندي وجَرير البَجَلي حتّى إذا كنّا بظهر الكوفة بالفِرس، مرَّ بنا ضَبٌّ فقال الأشعث وجرير: السلام عليك يا أمير المؤمنين! خِلافًا على عليّ ابن أبي طالب عليه السلام، فلمّا خرج الأنصاري قال لعليّ عليه السلام، فقال عليّ عليه السلام: دَعْهُما فهو إمامهما يوم القيامة، أما تسمع إلى الله وهو يقول: ﴿نُوَلِّهِ مَا تَوَلَّى﴾.

٢٧٦. عن محمّد بن إسماعيل الرازي، عن رجلٍ سمّاه، عن أبي عبد الله عليه السلام، قال: دخل رجلٌ على أبي عبد الله عليه السلام فقال: السلام عليك يا أمير المؤمنين، فقام على قدميه فقال: مه، هذا اسم لا يَصْلُح إلّا لأمير المؤمنين عليه السلام، الله سمّاه به، ولم يُسمّ به أحد غيره فرضي به إلّا كان منكوحًا، وإن لم يكُن به ابتُلي به، وهو قول الله في كتابه: ﴿إِنْ يَدْعُونَ مِنْ دُونِهِ إِلَّا إِنَاثًا وَإِنْ يَدْعُونَ إِلَّا شَيْطَانًا مَرِيدًا﴾.

قال: قلتُ: فماذا يُدعى به قائمكم، قال: يقال له: السلام عليك يا بقيّة الله، السلام عليك يا بن رسول الله.

277. From Muḥammad b. Yūnus, from one of his associates, from Abū ʿAbd Allāh عليه السلام who said about God's verse: ﴾*I will command them to tamper with God's creation*﴿, '[It is] God's authoritative command that He has ordered to be [followed].' [4:119]

278. From Jābir, from Abū Jaʿfar عليه السلام who said regarding God's verse: ﴾*I will command them to tamper with God's creation*﴿, '[It is] God's authoritative command that He has ordered to be [followed].' [4:119]

279. From Jābir, from Abū Jaʿfar عليه السلام, who said regarding God's verse: ﴾*I will command them to tamper with God's creation*﴿, '[It is] God's religion.' [4:119]

280. From Jābir, from the Prophet صلى الله عليه وآله who said, 'Iblīs was the first one to ever sing, the first one to lament, and the first one to dance. He sang when Ādam ate from the tree; he danced when he was demoted to earth and when he himself was made to settle on earth, he lamented, remembering what he had had in Paradise. So Ādam said, "My Lord, this is the one that You have made my enemy, but I was not able to resist him in the garden, so how will I be able to resist him now unless You assist me?"

So God said, "Each sin will be counted as one, whereas each good deed will count as ten or even seventy good deeds."

Ādam asked, "What else, my Lord?"

He replied, "Every time a child is born from your progeny, I will make an angel or two accompany it and protect it."

"What else, my Lord?" asked Ādam.

He replied, "I will accept your repentance as long as there is still life in the body."

He asked again, "What else, my Lord?"

He replied, "I will forgive sins indisputably."

Then Ādam said, "That suffices me."

So Iblīs spoke up, "My Lord, you have been kind to me, but you have favoured him over me, and if you do not give me more I will not be able to overpower him."

So God said, "For every child born in his progeny, you will beget two."

He asked, "What else, my Lord?"

So He said, "You will be able to course in him as the blood in his veins."

٢٧٧. عن محمّد بن يونس، عن بعض أصحابه، عن أبي عبدالله عليه السلام، في قول الله تعالى: ﴿وَلَآمُرَنَّهُمۡ فَلَيُغَيِّرُنَّ خَلۡقَ ٱللَّهِ﴾، قال: أمر الله بما أمر به.

٢٧٨. عن جابر، عن أبي جعفر عليه السلام، في قول الله ﴿وَلَآمُرَنَّهُمۡ فَلَيُغَيِّرُنَّ خَلۡقَ ٱللَّهِ﴾، قال: أمر الله بما أمر به.

٢٧٩. عن جابر، عن أبي جعفر عليه السلام، في قول الله تعالى: ﴿وَلَآمُرَنَّهُمۡ فَلَيُغَيِّرُنَّ خَلۡقَ ٱللَّهِ﴾، قال: دين الله.

٢٨٠. عن جابر، عن النبي صلى الله عليه وآله، قال: كان إبليس أوّل من ناح، وأوّل من تغنّى، وأوّل من حدا، قال: لـمّا أكل آدم من الشجرة تغنّى، فلمّا أُهْبِط حدا به، فلمّا استقرّ على الأرض ناح، فأذكره ما في الجنّة.

فقال آدم عليه السلام: ربّ هذا الذي جعلت بيني وبينه العداوة، لم أقوَ عليه وأنا في الجنّة، وإن لم تعنّي عليه لم أقوَ عليه. فقال الله: السيّئة بالسيّئة، والحسنة بعشر أمثالها إلى سبعمائة.

قال: ربّ زدني، قال: لا يُولَد لك ولد إلاّ جعلت معه مَلَكين يحفظانه. قال: ربّ زدني. قال: التوبةُ معروضةٌ في الجسد ما دام فيه الروح. قال: ربّ زدني. قال: أغفر الذنوب ولا أُبالي. قال: حسبي.

قال: فقال إبليس: ربّ هذا الّذي كرّمت عليّ وفضّلته، وإن لم تُفضّل عليّ لم أقوَ عليه. قال: لا يُولَد له ولدٌ إلاّ ولد لك ولدان. قال: ربّ زدني. قال: تجري منه مجرى الدم

He asked, "What else, my Lord?"

He replied, "You and your offspring will be able to set up home in their hearts."

"What else, my Lord?" Iblīs asked again.

He replied, "You will be able to make promises to them and raise false hopes in them, ﴾ *but Satan's promises are nothing but delusion.* ﴿"' [4:120]

281. From Muḥammad b. Muslim, from Abū Jaʿfar عليه السلام who said, 'When this verse was revealed: ﴾ *anyone who does wrong will be requited for it* ﴿, some of the companions of God's Messenger ﷺ exclaimed, "What a harsh verse this is!" So the Messenger of God ﷺ said to them, "Are you not afflicted in your possessions, your own selves, and your offspring?" They replied, "Yes," so he said, "This is the means through which God records good deeds for you and wipes away wrongdoings."' [4:123]

282. From Ibn Sinān, from Jaʿfar b. Muḥammad عليه السلام who said, 'When anyone from among you travels and returns home from his journey, he should bring something small for his family even if it be a stone; for Ibrāhīm – God's blessings be upon him and his family – when he was going through financial hardship, went to his people, but his people were facing a drought, so he came back as he had left. When he approached the house he got down from his donkey and filled his sack full of sand so as to appease his wife Sāra with it. So when he entered the house, he took the sack down from the donkey, then started to perform his prayer. Sāra came, opened the sack and found it filled with flour. So she kneaded it into a dough and made some bread from it, then called to Ibrāhīm: "Finish your prayer, then come and eat." So he asked her, "Where did you get this?" She said, "From the flour that was in the sack." So he raised his head to the sky and said, "I bear witness that You are indeed the true friend."' [4:125]

283. From Sulaymān b. al-Farrāʾ, from whoever mentioned it from Abū ʿAbd Allāh عليه السلام; and from Muḥammad b. Hārūn, from whoever narrated it from Abū Jaʿfar عليه السلام who said, 'When God took Ibrāhīm as a friend, the news of the friendship was brought to him by the Angel of Death in the form of a luminous young man dressed in two white garments, with water and oil dripping from his head. As Ibrāhīm عليه السلام entered his house coming back home

في العُرُوق. قال: ربّ زدني. قال: تتّخذ أنت وذُريّتك في صدورهم مساكن. قال: ربّ زدني. قال: تَعِدهم وتُمنّيهم ﴿وَمَا يَعِدُهُمُ الشَّيْطَانُ إِلاَّ غُرُورًا﴾.

٢٨١. عن محمد بن مسلم، عن أبي جعفر عليه السلام، قال: لـمّا نزلت هذه الآية ﴿مَنْ يَعْمَلْ سُوءًا يُجْزَ بِهِ﴾ قال بعض أصحاب رسول الله صلى الله عليه وآله: ما أشدُّها من آية! فقال لهم رسول الله صلى الله عليه وآله: أما تبتلون في أموالكم وأنفسكم وذراريكم؟ قالوا: بلى. قال: هذا ممّا يَكْتُب الله لكم به الحسنات، ويمحو به السيّئات.

٢٨٢. عن ابن سِنان، عن جعفر بن محمد عليهما السلام، قال: إذا سافر أحدكم، فقدم من سفره، فليأتِ أهله بما تيسّر ولو بحَجَرٍ، فإنّ إبراهيم صلوات الله عليه كان إذا ضاق أتى قومه، وإنه ضاق ضيقة فأتى قومه، فوافق منهم أزمةً، فرجع كما ذهب، فلـمّا قَرُب من منزله نزل عن حماره، فملأ خُرْجَه رَملاً، إرادة أن يُسكّن به من روح سارة، فلـمّا دخل منزله حطّ الخُرْج عن الحمار، وافتتح الصلاة، فجاءت سارة، ففتحت الخُرْج، فوجدته مملوًّا دقيقًا، فاعتجنت منه واختبزت، ثمّ قالت لإبراهيم عليه السلام: انفتل من صلاتك فكُل. فقال لها: أنّى لكِ هذا؟ قالت: من الدقيق الذي في الخُرْج، فرفع رأسه إلى السماء، فقال: أشهد أنّك الخليل.

٢٨٣. عن سُليمان الفرّاء، عمّن ذكره، عن أبي عبدالله عليه السلام، وعن محمد بن هارون، عمّن رواه، عن أبي جعفر عليه السلام، قال: لـمّا اتّخذ الله إبراهيم خليلاً أتاه ببشارة الخُلّة مَلَك الموت في صورة شابّ أبيض، عليه ثوبان أبيضان، يقطُر رأسه ماءً ودهنًا، فدخل إبراهيم عليه السلام الدار،

from outside – now Ibrāhīm was a protective man, and whenever he left the house for something he would lock his door and take the key with him – so one day, he left the house for some work, locked his door and went. When he came back and opened the door, he found a man standing inside – the most handsome man that there could ever be. So he grabbed him and asked, "O servant of God, how did you enter my house?"

So he replied, "Its Lord gave me entrance therein."

So Ibrāhīm said, "Its Lord does indeed have greater right over it than me – so who are you?"

He replied, "I am the Angel of Death."

So Ibrāhīm عليه السلام was alarmed and asked, "Have you come to take away my soul?"

So he said, "No, but God has adopted a certain servant of His as a friend, so I have come to give him the glad tidings of it."

So Ibrāhīm asked, "So who is this servant that I may be at his service until I die?"

The angel replied, "It is you."

So he went to Sāra and told her, "Indeed, God has adopted me as a friend."' [4:125]

284. From Aḥmad b. Muḥammad, from Abū al-Ḥasan al-Riḍā عليه السلام who said about God's verse: ﴿*If a wife fears high-handedness or alienation from her husband*﴾, 'The high-handedness of a husband is for him to intend to divorce his wife, so she can say to him: "You can forego some of your responsibilities towards me, and I will give you such and such, and absolve you from having to spend my day and night with me," according to the terms of their settlement, and this is allowed.' [4:128]

285. From 'Alī b. Abī Ḥamza, from Abū 'Abd Allāh عليه السلام. He said, 'I asked him about God's verse: ﴿*If a wife fears high-handedness or alienation from her husband.*﴾ He said, "If this is the case and he intends to divorce her, she can say to him, 'Keep me, and I will let you off some of your responsibilities and absolve you from having to spend my day and night with me.' She can do all this for him, so there is no blame on either of them."' [4:128]

فاستقبله خارجًا من الدار، وكان إبراهيم عليه السلام رجلاً غيورًا، وكان إذا خرج في حاجة أغلق بابه، وأخذ مفتاحه معه.

فخرج ذات يوم في حاجةٍ، وأغلق بابه، ثمّ رجع ففتح بابه، فإذا هو برجلٍ قائمٍ كأحسن ما يكون من الرجال، فأخذه، وقال: يا عبدالله، ما أدخلك داري؟

فقال: ربُّها أدخلنيها.

فقال إبراهيم عليه السلام: ربُّها أحقّ بها منّي، فمن أنت؟

قال: أنا مَلَك الموت.

قال: ففَزِع إبراهيم عليه السلام، فقال: جئتني لتَسْلُبني رُوحي؟ فقال: لا، ولكنّ الله اتّخذ عبدًا خليلاً فجئته ببِشارة. فقال إبراهيم: فمن هذا النّبي لعلّي أخدِمه حتّى أموت؟ فقال: أنت هو. قال: فدخل على سارة، فقال: إنّ الله اتّخذني خليلاً.

٢٨٤. عن أحمد بن محمد، عن أبي الحسن الرضا عليه السلام في قول الله: ﴿وَإِنِ امْرَأَةٌ خَافَتْ مِنْ بَعْلِهَا نُشُوزًا أَوْ إِعْرَاضًا﴾. قال: النشوز الرجل يَهُمّ بطلاق امرأته، فتقول له: ادَع ما على ظهرك وأعطيك كذا وكذا، وأُحلّلك من يومي وليلتي، على ما اصطلحا، فهو جائز.

٢٨٥. عن عليّ بن أبي حمزة، عن أبي عبدالله عليه السلام، قال: سألتُه عن قول الله: ﴿وَإِنِ امْرَأَةٌ خَافَتْ مِنْ بَعْلِهَا نُشُوزًا أَوْ إِعْرَاضًا﴾. قال: إذا كان كذلك فهمّ بطلاقها، قالت له: أمْسِكني وأدَع لك بعض ما عليك، وأُحلّلك من يومي وليلتي، كلّ ذلك له، فلا جُناح عليهما.

286. From Zurāra who said, 'Abū Ja'far ﷺ was asked about the daytime-wife – should it be stipulated at the time of the marriage contract whether he is to come to her whenever he wishes during the day, or every Friday, or once a month for example? And that she is entitled to a certain amount of living allowance? He replied, "That kind of condition means nothing – whoever marries a woman must provide for her and give her whatever allowance a wife is entitled to. But if he marries a woman and she fears ill-treatment on his part, or that he will marry another wife alongside her, then she can settle by foregoing her right to her share of the living allowance or part of it thereof, and that is allowed without any problem."' [4:128]

287. From al-Ḥalabī, from Abū 'Abd Allāh ﷺ who said regarding the verse: ﴿*If a wife fears high-handedness or alienation from her husband*﴾, 'This refers to the woman who lives with a husband who hates her, saying, "I want to divorce you," so she can say to him, "Do not do that for I would hate to be stigmatized, but you can be excused from spending the night with me and do what you like instead, and it is up to you what you want to do apart from that, so leave me to be." And this is the purport of His verse: ﴿*neither of them will be blamed if they come to a peaceful settlement, for peace is best*﴾ – this is the peace-making.' [4:128]

288. From Hishām b. Sālim, from Abū 'Abd Allāh ﷺ who said regarding God's verse: ﴿*You will never be able to treat your wives with equal fairness, however much you may desire to do so*﴾, 'In love.' [4:129]

289. From Jābir who said, 'I asked Muḥammad b. 'Alī ﷺ about God's verse in His Book: ﴿*As for those who believe, then reject the faith.*﴾ He said, "[They are] the first two, the third, the fourth, 'Abd al-Raḥmān, and Ṭalḥa, and there were seventeen men in total." He continued, "When the Prophet ﷺ dispatched 'Alī b. Abī Ṭālib ﷺ and 'Ammār b. Yāsir – may God have mercy on him – to the people of Mecca, they said: 'He is sending this young boy. Would it not have been better to send someone else, O Ḥudhayfa, to the people of Mecca, with their notables and strong men?' They used to call 'Alī 'the young boy' because he was called 'young boy' in God's Book when God says: ﴿*Who speaks better than someone who calls people to God, does what is right* ***from when he was a young boy****, and says, 'I am one of those devoted to*

٢٨٦ . عن زُرارة، قال: سُئِل أبو جعفر عليه السلام عن النهاريّة يشترط عليها عند عقد النكاح أن يأتيها ما شاء نهارًا، أو من كلّ جُمعةٍ أو شهرٍ يومًا، ومن النفقة كذا وكذا. قال: فليس ذلك الشرط بشيءٍ، مَن تزوّج امرأةً فلها ما للمرأة من النَّفَقة والقِسمة، ولكنّه إن تَزَوَّج امرأةً خافت منه نُشُوزًا، أو خافت أن يَتزوّج عليها، فصالحت من حقّها على شيءٍ من قسمتها أو بعضها، فإنّ ذلك جائزٌ لا بأس به.

٢٨٧ . عن الحلبي، عن أبي عبدالله عليه السلام، في قوله: ﴿وَإِنِ امْرَأَةٌ خَافَتْ مِنۢ بَعْلِهَا نُشُوزًا أَوْ إِعْرَاضًا﴾. قال: هي المرأة تكون عند الرجل فيكْرَهها، فيقول: إنّي أُريد أن أُطلّقك، فتقول: لا تفعل فإنّي أكره أن يُشْمتَ بي، ولكن انظُر ليلتي فاصْنَع ما شئت، وما كان من سوى ذلك فهو لك، فدَعني على حالي، فهو قوله ﴿فَلَا جُنَاحَ عَلَيْهِمَآ أَن يُصْلِحَا بَيْنَهُمَا صُلْحًا وَالصُّلْحُ خَيْرٌ﴾ فهو هذا الصُّلح.

٢٨٨ . عن هِشام بن سالم، عن أبي عبدالله عليه السلام، في قول الله تعالى: ﴿وَلَن تَسْتَطِيعُوٓا أَن تَعْدِلُوا بَيْنَ النِّسَآءِ وَلَوْ حَرَصْتُمْ فَلَا تَمِيلُوا كُلَّ الْمَيْلِ فَتَذَرُوهَا كَالْمُعَلَّقَةِ وَإِن تُصْلِحُوا وَتَتَّقُوا فَإِنَّ اللَّهَ كَانَ غَفُورًا رَّحِيمًا﴾، قال عليه السلام: في المودّة.

٢٨٩ . عن جابر، قال: قلت لمحمد بن عليّ عليهما السلام: قول الله تعالى في كتابه ﴿الَّذِينَ آمَنُوا ثُمَّ كَفَرُوا﴾؟، قال: هما والثالث والرابع وعبد الرّحمن وطلحة، وكانوا سبعة عشر رجلاً. قال: لـمّا وجّه النبي صلى الله عليه وآله عليّ بن أبي طالب عليه السلام وعمّار بن ياسر رحمه الله إلى أهل مكّة، قالوا: بعث هذا الصبيّ، ولو بعث غيره يا حذيفة إلى أهل مكّة، وفي صناديدها

God'?﴿(41:33) So they said, 'By God, the state of disbelief was better than the situation we are in now.' So they went and spoke to these two, trying to scare them away from going to the people of Mecca and making the mission seem distressful. So 'Alī عليه السلام said, ﴾*God is enough for us: He is the best protector,*﴿ and they left.

When they arrived in Mecca, God informed His Prophet ﷺ of what they had been saying to 'Alī, and what 'Alī had replied to them. So God revealed this verse about them in His Book, mentioning them by name: ﴾*Those whose faith only increased when people said, 'Fear your enemy: they have amassed a great army against you,' and who replied, 'God is enough for us: He is the best protector.' So they returned with grace and bounty from God; no harm befell them. They pursued God's good pleasure. God's favour is great indeed.*﴿ The way it was actually revealed was: ﴾***Have you not seen how so-and-so and so-and-so met Alī and Ammār, saying, 'Verily Abū Sufyān, 'Abd Allāh b. 'Āmir and the people of Mecca have amassed a great army against you, so fear them.' This only increased their faith and they said, 'God is enough for us: He is the best protector.'***﴿ So they are the two people about whom God says: ﴾*As for those who believe, then reject the faith then believe again, then reject the faith again and become increasingly defiant, God will not forgive them, nor will He guide them on any path.*﴿ This is the first instance of their disbelief.

The second instance was at the statement of the Prophet, peace be upon him and his family: 'A man from among these people will rise over you with a shining face; the example of his position with God is like the position of 'Īsā, where not a single person remained who did not wish to be a part of his family.' Just then, 'Alī came out, his face shining, so he exclaimed: 'There he is.' So they left enraged, saying, 'What is left now other than to make him a prophet! By God, going back to our gods is better than what we hear him say about his cousin, and we must surely block 'Alī if this continues.' So God revealed: ﴾*When the son of Maryam is cited as an example, your people [Prophet] laugh and jeer, saying, 'Are our gods better or him?' They cite him only to challenge you: they are a contentious people.*﴿(43:57–58) So this is the second instance of disbelief.

Their disbelief increased even more when God said: ﴾*Those who believe and do good deeds are the best of creation.*﴿(98:7) So the Prophet ﷺ said, 'O 'Alī, you begin and end your day as the best of creation.' So the people asked

– وكانوا يُسمّون علياً عليه السلام الصبيّ، لأنّه كان اسمه في كتاب الله الصبيّ لقول الله تعالى: ﴿وَمَنْ أَحْسَنُ قَوْلاً مِمَّنْ دَعَا إِلَى اللهِ وَعَمِلَ صَالِحًا﴾ وهو صبيّ ﴿وَقَالَ إِنَّنِي مِنَ الْمُسْلِمِينَ﴾ - والله الكفر بنا أولى ممّا نحن فيه، فساروا فقالوا لهما، وخوّفوهما بأهل مكّة، فعرضوا لهما، وغلّظوا عليهما الأمر . فقال عليّ صلوات الله عليه: حسبنا الله ونعم الوكيل، ومضى .

فلمّا دخلا مكّة، أخبر الله نبيّه صلى الله عليه وآله بقولهم لعليّ، وبقول عليّ عليه السلام لهم، فأنزل الله بأسمائهم في كتابه، وذلك قول الله: ألم تر إلى ﴿الَّذِينَ قَالَ لَهُمُ النَّاسُ إِنَّ النَّاسَ قَدْ جَمَعُوا لَكُمْ فَاخْشَوْهُمْ فَزَادَهُمْ إِيمَانًا وَقَالُوا حَسْبُنَا اللهُ وَنِعْمَ الْوَكِيلُ﴾ إلى قوله: ﴿وَاللهُ ذُو فَضْلٍ عَظِيمٍ﴾ .

وإنّما نزلت (ألم تَرَ إلى فلان وفلان لَقيا علياً وعماراً فقالا: إنّ أبا سفيان وعبدالله بن عامر وأهل مكة قد جمعوا لكم فاخشوهم، فقالوا: حسبنا الله ونعم الوكيل) وهما اللّذان قال الله: ﴿إِنَّ الَّذِينَ آمَنُوا ثُمَّ كَفَرُوا﴾ إلى آخر الآية، فهذا أوّل كفرهم .

والكفر الثاني قول النبيّ عليه وآله السلام: «يَطّلُع عليكم من هذا الشّعب رجلٌ، فيَطّلُع عليكم بوجهه، فمثله عند الله كمثل عيسى» . لم يبق منهم أحدٌ إلاّ تمنّى أن يكون بعض أهله، فإذا بعليّ عليه السلام قد خرج، وطلع بوجهه، قال: هو هذا، فخرجوا غضاباً وقالوا: ما بقي إلاّ أن يجعله نبيّاً، والله الرجوع إلى آلهتنا خيرٌ ممّا نسمع منه في ابن عمّه، وليَصُدّنا عليّ إن دام هذا، فأنزل الله ﴿وَلَمَّا ضُرِبَ ابْنُ مَرْيَمَ مَثَلاً إِذَا قَوْمُكَ مِنْهُ يَصِدُّونَ﴾ إلى آخر الآية، فهذا الكفر الثاني .

him, 'Is he even better than Ādam, Nūḥ, Ibrāhīm and the other prophets?' So God revealed: ﴿*God chose Ādam, Nūḥ, Ibrāhīm's family, and the family of ʿImrān, over all other people, in one line of descent - God hears and knows all.*﴾ (3:33) So they asked: 'Is he even better than you, O Muḥammad?' He said, 'God says: ﴿*Say [Muhammad], 'People, I am the Messenger of God to you all'*﴾(7:158) – but he is better than you all, and his offspring are better than yours, and whoever follows him is better than whoever follows you.' So they stood up enraged and said, 'Returning to disbelief is increasingly easier for us to bear than what he says about his cousin,' and that is God's statement: ﴿*and become increasingly defiant.*﴾'"' [4:137]

290. From Zurāra, Ḥumrān and Muḥammad b. Muslim, from Abū Jaʿfar عليه السلام and Abū 'Abd Allāh عليه السلام who said regarding God's verse: ﴿*As for those who believe, then reject the faith then believe again, then reject the faith again and become increasingly defiant*﴾, 'It was revealed about 'Abd Allāh b. Abī Sarḥ, whom 'Uthmān dispatched to Egypt. He said: ﴿*and become increasingly defiant*﴾ when there was not an iota of faith left in him.' [4:137]

291. From Abū Baṣīr who said, 'I heard him say: ﴿*As for those who believe, then reject the faith then believe again, then reject the faith again and become increasingly defiant*﴾ – whoever asserts that wine is prohibited then drinks it, whoever asserts that adultery is prohibited then goes and commits it, and whoever asserts that the alms is a duty but does not pay it.' [4:137]

292. From 'Abd al-Raḥmān b. Kathīr al-Hāshimī, from Abū 'Abd Allāh عليه السلام who said about God's verse: ﴿*As for those who believe, then reject the faith then believe again, then reject the faith again and become increasingly defiant*﴾, 'This was revealed about *x* and *y*, who believed in the Messenger of God صلى الله عليه وآله to begin with but then disbelieved when the divinely mandated authority [of 'Alī] was put forth to them, when he said: "For whomsoever I am master, 'Alī is his master." At that time, they professed belief by pledging allegiance to the Commander of the Faithful عليه السلام, where they stated to him their acceptance of God's and His Messenger's command, pledging allegiance to him thereby, but then they disbelieved when the Messenger of God صلى الله عليه وآله passed away. They did not keep their pledge of allegiance and became increasingly defiant

وزاد الكفر حين قال الله تعالى: ﴿إِنَّ الَّذِينَ آمَنُوا وَعَمِلُوا الصَّالِحَاتِ أُولَٰئِكَ هُمْ خَيْرُ الْبَرِيَّةِ﴾، فقال النبي ﷺ: «يا عليُّ، أصبحت وأمسيت خير البريّة» . فقال له النّاس: هو خيرٌ من آدم ونُوح، ومن إبراهيم، ومن الأنبياء! فأنزل الله ﴿إِنَّ اللَّهَ اصْطَفَىٰ آدَمَ وَنُوحًا وَآلَ إِبْرَاهِيمَ﴾ إلى ﴿سَمِيعٌ عَلِيمٌ﴾ .

قالوا: فهو خير منك يا محمّد؟ قال الله: ﴿قُلْ ... إِنِّي رَسُولُ اللَّهِ إِلَيْكُمْ جَمِيعًا﴾ ولكنّه خيرٌ منكم، وذُريّته خيرٌ من ذريّتكم، ومن اتّبعه خيرٌ ممّن اتّبعكم. فقاموا غضابًا وقالوا زيادة: الرجوع إلى الكفر أهون علينا ممّا يقول في ابن عمّه، وذلك قول الله ﴿ثُمَّ ازْدَادُوا كُفْرًا﴾ .

٢٩٠ . عن زُرارة وحُمران ومحمّد بن مسلم، عن أبي جعفر وأبي عبدالله عليهما السلام، في قول الله: ﴿إِنَّ الَّذِينَ آمَنُوا ثُمَّ كَفَرُوا ثُمَّ آمَنُوا ثُمَّ كَفَرُوا ثُمَّ ازْدَادُوا كُفْرًا﴾ . قال: نزلت في عبدالله بن أبي سَرْح، الذي بعثه عثمان إلى مِصر، قال: وازدادوا كُفرًا حين لم يبقَ فيه من الإيمان شيء .

٢٩١ . عن أبي بصير، قال: سَمِعتُه يقول: ﴿إِنَّ الَّذِينَ آمَنُوا ثُمَّ كَفَرُوا... ثُمَّ ازْدَادُوا كُفْرًا﴾ من زَعَم أنّ الخمر حرام ثمّ شَرِبها، ومن زَعَم أنّ الزنا حرام ثمّ زنى، ومن زَعَم أن الزكاة حقّ ولم يُؤدّها .

٢٩٢ . عن عبد الرّحمن بن كَثير الهاشمي، عن أبي عبدالله عليه السلام، في قول الله تعالى: ﴿إِنَّ الَّذِينَ آمَنُوا ثُمَّ كَفَرُوا ثُمَّ آمَنُوا ثُمَّ كَفَرُوا ثُمَّ ازْدَادُوا كُفْرًا﴾ . قال: نزلت في فلان وفلان، آمنوا برسول الله ﷺ في أوّل الأمر، ثمّ كفروا حين عُرضت عليهم الولاية، حيث قال ﷺ: «من كنتُ مولاه فعليّ مولاه» ثمّ آمنوا بالبيعة لأمير المؤمنين عليه السلام حيث قالوا

by making those who had pledged allegiance to him now pledge the same to them, and these people have no iota of faith left in them.' [4:137]

293. From Muḥammad b. al-Fuḍayl, from Abū al-Ḥasan al-Riḍā عليه السلام who said regarding God's verse: ﴾*As He has already revealed to you [believers] in the Scripture, if you hear people denying and ridiculing God's revelation, do not sit with them unless they start to talk of other things, or else you yourselves will become like them*﴿, 'If you hear someone repudiating the truth and belying it, ridiculing its adherents, then get up from there and do not sit in his company.' [4:140]

294. From Shuʿayb al-ʿAqarqūfī[50] who said, 'I asked Abū ʿAbd Allāh عليه السلام about God's verse: ﴾*As He has already revealed to you [believers] in the Scripture, if you hear people denying and ridiculing God's revelation, do not sit with them unless they start to talk of other things, or else you yourselves will become like them*﴿, so he replied, "By this He means when you hear someone repudiating the truth and belying it, and slandering the Imams, then get up from there and do not sit in his company, whoever he may be."' [4:140]

295. From Abū ʿAmr al-Zubayrī, from Abū ʿAbd Allāh عليه السلام who said, 'God, Blessed and most High, has made faith incumbent upon the limbs of people and has apportioned it between them so that not a single limb remains without having been assigned a certain part of faith different to that assigned to other limbs. Among these are the two ears with which man hears, so He has obligated the auditory faculty to steer clear of listening to anything that God has forbidden, and to refrain from anything that is not permissible for it of the things that God has prohibited, and from giving ear to all that displeases God, most High. About that He says: ﴾*As He has already revealed to you [believers] in the Scripture, if you hear people denying and ridiculing God's revelation, do not sit with them unless they start to talk of other things*﴿. Then He made an exception for instances of forgetfulness saying: ﴾*If Satan should make you forget, then, when you have remembered, do not sit with those who*

---

50 Abū Yaʿqūb Shuʿayb al-ʿAqarqūfī, a prominent and reliable companion of Imam Jaʿfar al-Ṣādiq. He was the nephew of Abū Baṣīr Yaḥyā b. al-Qāsim. See Ḥillī, *Khulāṣat al-aqwāl*, 167 (nr. 688); Modarressi, *Tradition and Survival*, 371 (nr. 193).

له: بأمر الله وأمر رسوله، فبايعوه، ثمّ كفروا حين مضى رسول الله ﷺ، فلم يُقرّوا بالبيعة، ثمّ ازدادوا كُفراً بأخذهم من بايعوه بالبيعة لهم، فهؤلاء لم يبقَ فيهم من الإيمان شيء.

٢٩٣. عن محمّد بن الفضيل، عن أبي الحسن الرضا عليه السلام، في قول الله تعالى: ﴿وَقَدْ نَزَّلَ عَلَيْكُمْ فِي الْكِتَابِ أَنْ إِذَا سَمِعْتُمْ آيَاتِ اللَّهِ﴾ إلى قوله: ﴿إِنَّكُمْ إِذًا مِثْلُهُمْ﴾، قال: إذا سَمِعت الرجل يَجحَد الحقّ ويكذّب به ويقع في أهله، فقُم من عنده ولا تُقاعِده.

٢٩٤. عن شُعيب العقَرقُوفي، قال: سألتُ أبا عبد الله عليه السلام عن قول الله: ﴿وَقَدْ نَزَّلَ عَلَيْكُمْ فِي الْكِتَابِ﴾ إلى قوله: ﴿إِنَّكُمْ إِذًا مِثْلُهُمْ﴾. فقال: إنّما عنى الله بهذا إذا سَمِعت الرجل يَجحَد الحقّ ويكذّب به ويَقَع في الأئمّة، فقُم من عنده ولا تقاعده، كائناً من كان.

٢٩٥. عن أبي عمرو الزُبيري، عن أبي عبد الله عليه السلام، قال: إنّ الله تبارك وتعالى فرض الإيمان على جَوارح بني آدم، وقسّمه عليها، فليس من جوارحه جارحةٌ إلاّ وقد وكّلت من الإيمان بغير ما وكّلت أُختها، فمنها أُذناه اللّتان يسمع بهما، ففرض على السمع أن يَتنَزّه عن الاستماع إلى ما حرّم الله، وأن يُعرِض عمّا لا يَحِلُّ له فيما نهى الله عنه، والإصغاء إلى ما أسخط الله تعالى، فقال في ذلك: ﴿وَقَدْ نَزَّلَ عَلَيْكُمْ فِي الْكِتَابِ﴾ إلى قوله: ﴿حَتَّىٰ يَخُوضُوا فِي حَدِيثٍ غَيْرِهِ﴾، ثمّ استثنى موضع النسيان فقال: ﴿وَإِمَّا يُنسِيَنَّكَ الشَّيْطَانُ فَلَا تَقْعُدْ بَعْدَ الذِّكْرَىٰ مَعَ الْقَوْمِ الظَّالِمِينَ﴾.

وقال: ﴿فَبَشِّرْ عِبَادِ الَّذِينَ يَسْتَمِعُونَ الْقَوْلَ فَيَتَّبِعُونَ أَحْسَنَهُ﴾ إلى قوله: ﴿أُولُوا الْأَلْبَابِ﴾، وقال: ﴿قَدْ أَفْلَحَ الْمُؤْمِنُونَ الَّذِينَ هُمْ فِي صَلَاتِهِمْ خَاشِعُونَ ۝ وَالَّذِينَ

are doing wrong. ﴾(6:68) He also says: ﴿ *those who listen to what is said and follow what is best. These are the ones that God has guided; these are the people of understanding.* ﴾(39:18)

And He says: ﴿ [*How*] *prosperous indeed are the believers! Those who pray humbly, who shun idle talk,* ﴾(23:1–3) and: ﴿ *and those who turn away whenever they hear frivolous talk* [...] ﴾(28:55) He also says: ﴿ *and who, when they see some frivolity, pass by with dignity.* ﴾(25:72) This is the faith that God has made incumbent upon the hearing, and for it to not listen to anything that God has not made permissible. This is its job and a part of faith.' [4:140]

296. From Zurāra, from Abū Jaʿfar عليه السلام who said, 'Do not stand for prayer lazily, drowsily or lethargically, for they result from the vice of hypocrisy. God says of the hypocrites: ﴿ *When they stand up to pray, they do so sluggishly, showing off in front of people, and remember God only a little.* ﴾' [4:142]

297. From Muḥammad b. al-Fuḍayl, from Abū al-Ḥasan al-Riḍā عليه السلام. He said, 'I wrote to him to ask him about a certain issue, so he wrote back to me saying: "God says: ﴿ *The hypocrites try to deceive God, but it is He who causes them to be deceived. When they stand up to pray, they do so sluggishly, showing off in front of people, and remember God only a little, wavering all the time between this and that, belonging neither to one side nor the other. If God leaves someone to stray, you* [*Prophet*] *will never find a way for him* ﴾ – they are neither from among the family [of the Prophet] nor from the believers nor from the Muslims. They display faith but conceal disbelief and denial inside themselves – God rejects them."' [4:142–143]

298. From Masʿada b. Ziyād[51], from Jaʿfar b. Muḥammad عليه السلام on his father's authority that the Messenger of God صلى الله عليه وآله was asked where salvation for the future lies. So he replied, 'Salvation lies in not trying to deceive God, lest He causes you to be deceived instead; for whoever tries to deceive God, He causes him to be deceived and wrests faith away from him – if only he was aware that he himself is being deceived.'

---

51 Masʿada b. Ziyād al-Ribʿī, a reliable companion and narrator of Imam Jaʿfar al-Ṣādiq's traditions. See Ḥillī, *Khulāṣat al-aqwāl*, 281 (nr. 1029); Modarressi, *Tradition and Survival*, 323–5 (nr. 140).

هُمْ عَنِ اللَّغْوِ مُعْرِضُونَ﴾، وقال: ﴿وَإِذَا سَمِعُوا اللَّغْوَ أَعْرَضُوا عَنْهُ﴾، وقال: ﴿وَإِذَا مَرُّوا بِاللَّغْوِ مَرُّوا كِرَامًا﴾ فهذا ما فرض الله على السمع من الإيمان، ولا يُصغي إلى مالا يحِلُّ، وهو عمله، وهو من الإيمان.

٢٩٦. عن زُرارة، عن أبي جعفر عليه السلام، قال: لا تَقُم إلى الصلاة مُتَكاسلاً، ولا مُتَناعسًا ولا مُتَثاقلاً، فإنّها من خِلال النِّفاق، قال للمنافقين: ﴿وَإِذَا قَامُوا إِلَى الصَّلَاةِ قَامُوا كُسَالَى يُرَاءُونَ النَّاسَ وَلَا يَذْكُرُونَ اللَّهَ إِلَّا قَلِيلًا﴾.

٢٩٧. عن محمّد بن الفضيل، عن أبي الحسن الرضا عليه السلام، قال: كَتبتُ إليه أسأله عن مسألة، فكتب إليّ: أنَّ الله يقول: ﴿إِنَّ الْمُنَافِقِينَ يُخَادِعُونَ اللَّهَ وَهُوَ خَادِعُهُمْ وَإِذَا قَامُوا إِلَى الصَّلَاةِ﴾ إلى قوله: ﴿سَبِيلًا﴾ ليسوا من عترة [رسول الله]، وليسوا من المؤمنين، وليسوا من المسلمين، يُظْهِرون الإيمان ويُسِرّون الكفر والتكذيب، لعنهم الله.

٢٩٨. عن مَسْعَدة بن زياد، عن جعفر بن محمّد، عن أبيه عليهما السلام: أنَّ رسول الله صلى الله عليه وآله سُئِل فيما النجاة غدًا؟ فقال صلى الله عليه وآله: النجاة أن لا تخادعوا الله فيَخْدعكم، فإنّه من يُخادع الله يَخْدَعه، ويَخْلَع منه الإيمان، ونفسه يَخْدَع لو يَشْعُر.

فقيل: فكيف يُخادع الله؟ قال: يعمل بما أمره الله، ثمّ يُريد به غيره، فاتّقوا الرياء، فإنّه شِرك بالله، إن المُرائي يُدعى يوم القيامة بأربعة أسماء: يا كافر، يا فاجر، يا غادر، يا خاسر، حَبِطَ عَمَلُك، وبَطَل أجْرُك، ولا خَلاق لك اليوم، فالتمِس أجْرَك ممّن كُنتَ تعمل له.

So he was asked, 'So how does one try to deceive God?' He replied, 'He does what God has commanded him to do, but it is intended for someone else [to see], so be God-conscious and refrain from showing off for that is associating others with God. The one who shows off will be called forward on the Day of Resurrection by four names: O disbeliever, O corrupt one, O treacherous one, O loser – your deeds have been wasted and your reward lost. There is no share for you today, so go and get your reward from the one that you used to act for.' [4:142]

299. From al-Faḍl b. Abī Qurra[52], from Abū 'Abd Allāh عليه السلام who said regarding God's verse: ﴾*God does not like bad words to be made public unless someone has been wronged*﴿, 'Whoever hosts someone as a guest and then criticises their guest is as one who has wronged them, and then you cannot blame people for what they say about him.' [4:148]

300. And Abū al-Jārūd on his authority; he said, 'Bad words made public means to talk about someone's personal matters.' [4:148]

301. From Abū al-'Abbās, from Abū 'Abd Allāh عليه السلام. He narrated, 'He said to recite the verse: ﴾*for saying 'Our minds are closed'*﴿ – He will write it on their backs.' [4:155]

302. From al-Ḥārith b. al-Mughīra[53], from Abū 'Abd Allāh عليه السلام who said regarding God's verse: ﴾*There is not one of the People of the Book who will not believe in him* ['Īsā] *before his death, and on the Day of Resurrection he will be a witness against them*﴿, 'He is the Messenger of God صلى الله عليه وآله.' [4:159]

303. From al-Mufaḍḍal b. Muḥammad who said, 'I asked Abū 'Abd Allāh عليه السلام about God's verse: ﴾*There is not one of the People of the Book who will not believe in* ['Īsā] *before his death*﴿, so he replied, "This has been revealed

52 Al-Faḍl b. Abī Qurra al-Tamīmī al-Sahandī, a weak and unreliable narrator of Imam Ja'far al-Ṣādiq's traditions. See Ḥillī, *Khulāṣat al-aqwāl*, 386 (nr. 1551); Modarressi, *Tradition and Survival*, 221–2 (nr. 59).

53 Al-Ḥārith b. al-Mughīra al-Naṣrī, a praiseworthy and reliable companion of Muḥammad al-Bāqir, Ja'far al-Ṣādiq and Mūsā al-Kāẓim. See Ḥillī, *Khulāṣat al-aqwāl*, 123 (nr. 318); Modarressi, *Tradition and Survival*, 242–3 (nr. 75).

٢٩٩. عن الفضيل بن أبي قُرّة، عن أبي عبدالله عليه السلام، في قول الله تعالى: ﴿لَا يُحِبُّ اللَّهُ الْجَهْرَ بِالسُّوءِ مِنَ الْقَوْلِ إِلَّا مَنْ ظُلِمَ﴾. قال: من أضاف قومًا فأساء ضيافتهم، فهو ممّن ظلم، فلا جُناح عليهم فيما قالوا فيه.

٣٠٠. وأبو الجارُود، عنه عليه السلام، قال: الجَهْر بالسُّوء من القول أن يذكر الرجل بما فيه.

٣٠١. عن أبي العباس، عن أبي عبدالله عليه السلام، قال: قال: إن تقرأ هذه الآية ﴿وَقَالُوا قُلُوبُنَا غُلْفٌ﴾ يكتبها إلى أدبارها.

٣٠٢. عن الحارث بن المُغيرة، عن أبي عبدالله عليه السلام، وفي قول الله تعالى: ﴿وَإِنْ مِنْ أَهْلِ الْكِتَابِ إِلَّا لَيُؤْمِنَنَّ بِهِ قَبْلَ مَوْتِهِ وَيَوْمَ الْقِيَامَةِ يَكُونُ عَلَيْهِمْ شَهِيدًا﴾، قال: هو رسول الله صلى الله عليه وآله وسلم.

٣٠٣. عن المُفضّل بن محمّد، قال: سألتُ أبا عبدالله عليه السلام عن قول الله: ﴿وَإِنْ مِنْ أَهْلِ الْكِتَابِ إِلَّا لَيُؤْمِنَنَّ بِهِ قَبْلَ مَوْتِهِ﴾. فقال: هذه نزلت فينا خاصّة، إنّه ليس رجلٌ من ولد فاطمة عليها السلام يموت ولا يَخْرُج من الدنيا حتى يُقِرّ للإمام بإمامته، كما أقرّ ولد يعقوب ليوسف عليهما السلام حين قالوا: ﴿تَاللَّهِ لَقَدْ آثَرَكَ اللَّهُ عَلَيْنَا﴾.

specifically about us, that no man born from the lineage of Fāṭima leaves this world without attesting to the Imamate of the Imam [of his time], just as the sons of Yaʿqūb attested to Yūsuf when they acceded: ﴾*By God! God really did favour you over all of us and we were in the wrong!*﴿(12:91)"' [4:159]

304. From Ibn Sinān, from Abū ʿAbd Allāh عليه السلام, regarding God's words about ʿĪsā عليه السلام: ﴾*There is not one of the People of the Book who will not believe in* [ʿĪsā] *before his death, and on the Day of Resurrection he will be a witness against them*﴿, so he said, 'The belief of the People of the Book is actually in Muḥammad ﷺ.' [4:159]

305. From al-Mishraqī, from someone else regarding the verse: ﴾*There is not one of the People of the Book who will not believe in* [ʿĪsā] *before his death*﴿ – by that He means Muḥammad ﷺ: That no Christian or Jew will die without realising that he was indeed the Messenger of God, and that they had been disbelieving in him. [4:159]

306. From Jābir, from Abū Jaʿfar عليه السلام who said regarding His verse: ﴾*There is not one of the People of the Book who will not believe in* [ʿĪsā] *before his death, and on the Day of Resurrection he will be a witness against them*﴿, 'Not a single person, from every single religion, from the first people to the last, will die without seeing the Messenger of God ﷺ and the Commander of the Faithful عليه السلام in truth.' [4:159]

307. From ʿAbd Allāh b. Abī Yaʿfūr who said, 'I heard Abū ʿAbd Allāh عليه السلام say, "Whoever plants wheat in the ground and his crop does not flourish, or it turns out to be full of chaff, then it is as a result of wrongdoing in his upkeep and maintenance of the land, or as a result of wrongdoing towards his farmers and ploughmen, because God says: ﴾*For the wrongdoings done by the Jews, We forbade them certain good things that had been permitted to them before*﴿, meaning the meats of camels, cows, and sheep." He also said, "Whenever Isrāʾīl [i.e. Yaʿqūb] used to eat beef, he would be gripped by pain in his side, so he made beef unlawful for himself. This was before the revelation of the Torah. And when the Torah was revealed, he neither prohibited it nor ate it."' [4:160]

٣٠٤. عن ابن سِنان، عن أبي عبد الله عليه السلام، في قول الله في عيسى عليه السلام: ﴿وَإِن مِّنْ أَهْلِ الْكِتَابِ إِلَّا لَيُؤْمِنَنَّ بِهِ قَبْلَ مَوْتِهِ وَيَوْمَ الْقِيَامَةِ يَكُونُ عَلَيْهِمْ شَهِيدًا﴾، فقال: إيمان أَهْلِ الكتاب، إنّما هو بمحمّد صلى الله عليه وآله وسلم.

٣٠٥. عن المِشْرَقي، عن غير واحدٍ، في قوله: ﴿وَإِن مِّنْ أَهْلِ الْكِتَابِ إِلَّا لَيُؤْمِنَنَّ بِهِ قَبْلَ مَوْتِهِ﴾ يعني بذلك محمّدًا صلى الله عليه وآله وسلم، إنّه لا يموت يهوديّ ولا نصرانيّ أبدًا حتّى يعرف أنّه رسول الله صلى الله عليه وآله وسلم، وأنّه قد كان به كافرًا.

٣٠٦. عن جابر، عن أبي جعفر عليه السلام، في قوله: ﴿وَإِن مِّنْ أَهْلِ الْكِتَابِ إِلَّا لَيُؤْمِنَنَّ بِهِ قَبْلَ مَوْتِهِ وَيَوْمَ الْقِيَامَةِ يَكُونُ عَلَيْهِمْ شَهِيدًا﴾. قال: ليس من أحدٍ من جميع الأديان يموت إلاّ رأى رسول الله صلى الله عليه وآله وسلم وأمير المؤمنين عليه السلام حقًّا من الأوّلين والآخرين.

٣٠٧. عن عبد الله بن أبي يَعْفور، قال: سَمِعتُ أبا عبد الله عليه السلام يقول: من زَرَع حِنطة في أرض فلم يَزْكُ زَرْعَه، أو خرج زَرْعُه كثير الشعير، فبظُلم عمله في مِلك رقَبَة الأرض، أو بظُلم لمزارعيه وأكَرَته، لأنَّ الله تعالى يقول: ﴿فَبِظُلْمٍ مِّنَ الَّذِينَ هَادُوا حَرَّمْنَا عَلَيْهِمْ طَيِّبَاتٍ أُحِلَّتْ لَهُمْ﴾ يعني لحوم الإبل والبقر والغنم. وقال: إنَّ إسرائيل كان إذا أكل من لحم الإبل هيَّج عليه وَجَع الخاصرة، فحرّم على نفسه لحم الإبل، وذلك من قبل أن تنزّل التوراة، فلمّا أُنزلت التوراة لم يحرّمه ولم يأكله.

308. From Zurāra and Ḥumrān, from Abū Jaʿfar عليه السلام and Abū ʿAbd Allāh عليه السلام; he said: '﴾*I have sent revelation to you* [*Prophet*] *as I did to Nūḥ*﴿ so he combined all of the revelation unto him.' [4:163]

309. From al-Thumālī, from Abū Jaʿfar عليه السلام who said, 'Between Ādam and Nūḥ there were prophets with private missions and those with public missions, and that is why their mention in the Qur'an is also covert and the reason why they have not been named in the same way as the prophets with public missions have, and this is the purport of God's words: ﴾*and messengers we have not mentioned to you*﴿, meaning the names of those with private missions, unlike the mention by name of the prophets with public missions.' [4:164]

310. From Abū Ḥamza al-Thumālī who said, 'I heard Abū Jaʿfar عليه السلام say: ﴾*But God Himself bears witness to what He has sent down to you* ***regarding* ʿ*Alī*** *– He sent it down with His full knowledge – the angels too bear witness, though God is sufficient witness.*﴿' He continued, 'I heard him say: "Jibra'īl brought down this verse in the following manner: ﴾*God will not forgive those who have disbelieved and wronged the family of Muḥammad with respect to their rights, nor will He guide them to any path except that of Hell, where they will remain forever – this is easy for God.*﴿ Then he said: ﴾*The Messenger has come to you* [*people*] *with the truth from your Lord with respect to the guardianship of ʿAlī, so believe – that is best for you – for even if you disbelieve in his guardianship, all that is in the heavens and the earth still belongs to God, and He is all knowing and all wise.*﴿"' [4:166–170*]

311. From ʿAbd Allāh b. Sulaymān[54] who said, 'I asked Abū ʿAbd Allāh عليه السلام about His verse: ﴾*People, convincing proof has come to you from your Lord and We have sent a clear light down to you.*﴿ He replied, "The convincing proof is Muḥammad, peace be upon him and his family, and the light is ʿAlī عليه السلام."' He said, 'I asked him about ﴾*a straight path.*﴿ He replied, "The straight path is ʿAlī عليه السلام."' [4:174]

---

54 There are several companions with this name in Shīʿī works of *rijāl*.

٣٠٨. عن زُرارة وحُمران، عن أبي جعفر عليه السلام وأبي عبدالله عليه السلام، قال الله: ﴿إِنِّي أَوْحَيْتُ إِلَيْكَ كَمَا أَوْحَيْتُ إِلَى نُوحٍ وَالنَّبِيِّينَ مِنْ بَعْدِهِ﴾ فجمع له كلّ وحي.

٣٠٩. عن الثّمالي، عن أبي جعفر عليه السلام، قال: كان ما بين آدم وبين نوح من الأنبياء مُسْتَخْفِين، ولذلك خفي ذِكرهم في القرآن، فلم يُسمّوا كما سُمّي من استعلن من الأنبياء، وهو قول الله: ﴿وَرُسُلًا لَمْ نَقْصُصْهُمْ عَلَيْكَ﴾ يعني: لم أُسَمِّ المُسْتَخفين كما سَمّيت المُسْتَعلنين من الأنبياء.

٣١٠. عن أبي حمزة الثّمالي، قال: سَمِعتُ أبا جعفر عليه السلام يقول: ﴿لَكِنِ اللَّهُ يَشْهَدُ بِمَا أَنْزَلَ إِلَيْكَ﴾ في عليّ ﴿أَنْزَلَهُ بِعِلْمِهِ وَالْمَلَائِكَةُ يَشْهَدُونَ وَكَفَى بِاللَّهِ شَهِيدًا﴾. قال: وسَمِعتُه يقول: نَزَل جبْرَئيل عليه السلام بهذه الآية هكذا ﴿إِنَّ الَّذِينَ كَفَرُوا وَظَلَمُوا﴾ آل محمّد حقّهم ﴿لَمْ يَكُنِ اللَّهُ لِيَغْفِرَ لَهُمْ وَلَا لِيَهْدِيَهُمْ طَرِيقًا﴾ إلى قوله: ﴿يَسِيرًا﴾.

ثم قال: ﴿يَا أَيُّهَا النَّاسُ قَدْ جَاءَكُمُ الرَّسُولُ بِالْحَقِّ مِنْ رَبِّكُمْ﴾ في ولاية عليّ ﴿فَآمِنُوا خَيْرًا لَكُمْ وَإِنْ تَكْفُرُوا﴾ بولايته ﴿فَإِنَّ لِلَّهِ مَا فِي السَّمَوَاتِ وَالْأَرْضِ وَكَانَ اللَّهُ عَلِيمًا حَكِيمًا﴾.

٣١١. عن عبدالله بن سُليمان، قال: قلتُ لأبي عبدالله عليه السلام: قوله ﴿قَدْ جَاءَكُمْ بُرْهَانٌ مِنْ رَبِّكُمْ وَأَنْزَلْنَا إِلَيْكُمْ نُورًا مُبِينًا﴾؟ قال: البرهان محمّد عليه وآله السلام، والنُّور عليّ عليه السلام.

قال: قلتُ له: ﴿صِرَاطًا مُسْتَقِيمًا﴾؟، قال: الصراط المستقيم عليّ عليه السلام.

312. From Bukayr b. Aʿyan who said, 'I was with Abū Jaʿfar عليه السلام when a man entered and asked him, "What do you say regarding [the inheritance due to] two sisters and a husband?"'

He said, 'Abū Jaʿfar said, "The husband receives half [of the estate] and the two sisters the remainder."

So the man said, "That is not what the people say."

He asked, "What do they say?"

He replied, "They say: The two sisters receive two-thirds and the husband receives half, and they divide it into seven parts."

So Abū Jaʿfar عليه السلام said, "And why do they say that?"

He replied, "Because God designated two-thirds for two sisters and a half for the husband."

He asked, "So what would they say if it were a brother instead of two sisters?"

He replied, "The husband would get a half, and the remainder would go to the brother."

So he said to him, "So they would give a half to the one that God commanded be given a whole part and four-sevenths to one that God commanded be given two-thirds?"

He replied, "Where has God mentioned that?"'

He said, 'So Abū Jaʿfar عليه السلام replied, "Read the verse that comes at the end of the chapter: ﴿ *They ask you [Prophet] for a ruling. Say, 'God gives you a ruling about inheritance from someone who dies childless with no surviving parents. If a man leaves a sister, she is entitled to half of the inheritance; if she has no child her brother is her sole heir.* ﴾"'

He continued, 'So Abū Jaʿfar عليه السلام said, "Rather, they should have designated half of the wealth for the husband, then divided the rest into nine parts."'

He said, 'So the man said, "That is what they say."

So Abū Jaʿfar عليه السلام said, "Oh so that is what they say?" Then he approached me and said, "Bukayr, have you looked into the verse of laws?"

I replied, "And what should I do with a ruling that I consider void?"

He replied, "Look into it, for if this [case] is brought, it will strengthen you against it."' [4:176]

٣١٢. عن بُكير بن أعيَن، قال: كنتُ عند أبي جعفر عليه السلام، فدخل عليه رجلٌ، فقال: ما تقول في أُختين وزوج؟

قال: فقال أبو جعفر عليه السلام: للزوج النصف، وللأُختين ما بقي.

قال: فقال الرجل: ليس هكذا يقول الناس.

قال: فما يقولون؟

قال: يقولون: للأُختين الثُّلثان، وللزوج النصف، ويقسّمون على سبعة.

قال: فقال أبو جعفر عليه السلام: ولِمَ قالوا ذلك؟ قال: لأنَّ الله سمّى للأُختين الثُّلثين، وللزَّوج النصف.

قال: فما يقولون لو كان مكان الأُختين أخ؟ قال: يقولون للزوج النصف، وما بقي فللأخ.

فقال له: فيُعطون من أمر الله له بالكُلّ النصف، ومن أمر الله بالثُّلثين أربعة من سبعة.

قال: وأين سمّى الله له ذلك؟ قال: فقال أبو جعفر عليه السلام: اقرأ الآية الّتي في آخر السورة ﴿يَسْتَفْتُونَكَ قُلِ اللَّهُ يُفْتِيكُمْ فِي الْكَلَالَةِ إِنِ امْرُؤٌ هَلَكَ لَيْسَ لَهُ وَلَدٌ وَلَهُ أُخْتٌ فَلَهَا نِصْفُ مَا تَرَكَ وَهُوَ يَرِثُهَا إِنْ لَمْ يَكُنْ لَهَا وَلَد﴾.

قال: فقال أبو جعفر عليه السلام: فإنّما كان ينبغي لهم أن يجعلوا لهذا المال للزوج النصف، ثمّ يقسّموا على تسعة.

قال: فقال الرجل: هكذا يقولون. قال: فقال أبو جعفر عليه السلام: فهكذا يقولون. ثمّ أقبل عليّ فقال: يا بُكير، نظرتَ في الفرائض؟ قال: قلتُ وما أصنع بشيءٍ هو عندي باطل؟ قال: فقال: انظُر فيها، فإنّه إذا جاءت تلك كان أقوى لك عليها.

313. From Ḥamza b. Ḥumrān[55] who said, 'I asked Abū 'Abd Allāh عليه السلام about the meaning of the word *kalāla* [in the verse]. He replied, "It is someone who is childless with no surviving parents."' [4:176]

314. From Muḥammad b. Muslim, from Abū Ja'far عليه السلام who said, 'If a man dies and leaves behind his mother, his father, and his daughter or his son, or any one of those four, then the verse does not apply to him: ﴾ *Say, 'God gives you a ruling about inheritance from someone who dies childless with no surviving parents.* ﴿ Such a person leaves behind neither mother nor father nor son nor daughter as an heir – only a husband or a wife. The husband receives no less than half if there is no child, and the wife no less than a quarter in the absence of a child.' [4:176]

315. From Muḥammad b. Muslim, from Abū Ja'far عليه السلام who said regarding the verse: ﴾ *Say, 'God gives you a ruling about inheritance from someone who dies childless with no surviving parents. If a man leaves a sister...'* ﴿, 'God meant specifically a sister from the same mother and father or a paternal sister, and she receives a half from his estate, and he is her sole heir if she was childless. And if there are several siblings, male and female, then the male receives twice the share of the female, for they are the ones who are affected by loss and gain, and similarly their children.' [4:176]

316. From Zurāra who said, 'I will tell you something, not leaving anything out thereof, and what I am about to tell you is the clear truth, by God. He said, "If one dies leaving behind his mother or his father, or his son or his daughter, then leaving behind any one of these four means that God's verse in His Book: ﴾ *Say, 'God gives you a ruling about inheritance from someone who dies childless with no surviving parents* ﴿ does not apply to him. And with the existence of a mother, father, son, or daughter, the only other person in the world who can inherit is the husband or the wife. He would be her sole heir if she was childless, meaning that he inherits all her wealth."' [4:176]

55 Ḥamza b. Ḥumrān b. A'yan al-Shaybānī, a reliable companion of Imam Ja'far al-Ṣādiq. See Khū'ī, *Mu'jam*, 7:279–81 (nr. 4037); Modarressi, *Tradition and Survival*, 239–40 (nr. 73).

٣١٣. عن حمزة بن حُمران، قال: سألتُ أبا عبدالله عليه السلام عن الكَلالة، قال: ما لم يكن له والد ولا ولد.

٣١٤. عن محمّد بن مسلم: عن أبي جعفر عليه السلام، قال: إذا ترك الرجل أُمّه وأباه وابنته أو ابنه، فإذا ترك واحدًا من هؤلاء الأربعة، فليس هو من الذي عنى الله تعالى في قوله: ﴿قُلِ اللَّهُ يُفْتِيكُمْ فِي الْكَلَالَةِ﴾ ليس يَرِث مع الأمّ ولا مع الأب ولا مع الابن ولا مع البنتُ إلاّ زوج أو زوجة، فإنّ الزوج لا ينقص من النصف شيئًا، إذا لم يكن معه ولد، ولا تنقص الزوجة من الربع شيئًا إذا لم يكن معها ولد.

٣١٥. عن محمّد بن مسلم، عن أبي جعفر عليه السلام، في قوله ﴿يَسْتَفْتُونَكَ قُلِ اللَّهُ يُفْتِيكُمْ فِي الْكَلَالَةِ إِنِ امْرُؤٌ هَلَكَ لَيْسَ لَهُ وَلَدٌ وَلَهُ أُخْتٌ﴾ إنّما عنى الله الأخت من الأب والأمّ، أو أخت لأب، فلها النصف ممّا ترك، وهو يرثها إن لم يكن لها ولد، وإن كانوا إخوة رجالاً ونساءً، فللذّكر مثل حظّ الأنثيين، فهم الذين يزدادون وينقصون، وكذلك أولادهم يزدادون وينقصون.

٣١٦. عن زُرارة، قال: سأخبرك ولا أزوي لك شيئًا، والذي أقول لك هو والله الحقّ.

قال: فإذا ترك أمّه أو أباه أو ابنه أو ابنته، فإذا ترك واحدًا من هذه الأربعة، فليس الذي عنى الله في كتابه ﴿يَسْتَفْتُونَكَ قُلِ اللَّهُ يُفْتِيكُمْ فِي الْكَلَالَةِ﴾ ولا يَرث مع الأب ولا مع الأمّ ولا مع الابنة أحدٌ من الخَلق غير الزوج والزوجة، وهو يرثها إن لم يكن لها ولدٌ، يعني جميع مالها.

317. From Bukayr who said, 'A man went to Abū Ja'far ﷺ and asked him about a woman who dies leaving her husband, maternal brothers and a paternal sister.

He said, "The husband gets a half, and [the remainder is divided into thirds] – the maternal brothers get two-thirds between them, and the paternal sister gets one-third."

So the man said to him, "The laws of Zayd, Ibn Mas'ūd, the [Sunnī] majority and the judges contradict that, O Abū Ja'far. They say that the paternal sister and the maternal sibling each get one-third, as a sixth out of eight parts."

So Abū Ja'far said, "And why do they say that?"

He replied, "Because God says: ﴾*If a man leaves a sister, she is entitled to half of the inheritance.*﴿"

So Abū Ja'far said, "If you use God's commands as proof indeed, then why do you reduce the brother's share when God has designated a half for her [i.e. the sister], and God has designated a whole for the brother, and a whole is greater than a half. For the sister he has said: ﴾*she is entitled to half*﴿ and for the brother: ﴾*her brother is her sole heir*﴿ meaning all the inheritance if she had no child. So to one for whom God designated everything, you give nothing according to some of your laws, and you give a whole share to the one for whom God has designated a half."' [4:176]

٣١٧. عن بُكير، قال: دَخَل رجلٌ على أبي جعفر ﷺ، فسأله عن امرأةٍ تركت زوجها، وإخوتها لأمّها، وأختًا لأب. قال: للزّوج النصف ثلاثة أسْهُم، وللإخوة من الأمّ الثُلث سَهْمان، وللأخت للأب سَهْم.

فقال له الرجل: فإنّ فرائض زيد وابن مسعود وفرائض العامة والقُضاة على غير ذا، يا أبا جعفر، يقولون: للأُخت للأب والأمّ ثلاثة أسْهُم، نصيب من ستّة، تعول إلى ثمانية؟

فقال أبو جعفر ﷺ: ولِمَ قالوا ذلك؟ قال: لأنّ الله تعالى قال: ﴿وَلَهُۥٓ أُخۡتٞ فَلَهَا نِصۡفُ مَا تَرَكَۚ﴾.

فقال أبو جعفر ﷺ: فما لكم نقصتم الأخ إن كنتم تحتجّون بأمر الله؟ فإنّ الله سمّى لها النصف، وإنّ الله سمّى للأخ الكلّ، فالكلُّ أكثر من النصف، فإنّه قال: ﴿فَلَهَا نِصۡفُ مَا تَرَكَۚ﴾ وقال للأخ: ﴿وَهُوَ يَرِثُهَآ﴾ يعني جميع المال، إن لم يَكُن لها ولدٌ، فلا تُعطون الذي جعل الله له الجميع في بعض فرائضكم شيئًا، وتُعطون الذي جعل الله له النصف تامًّا؟

www.ingramcontent.com/pod-product-compliance
Lightning Source LLC
Chambersburg PA
CBHW070105120526
44588CB00032B/872
9781838032074